Project Management Professional (PMP) Certification Exam Prep

3rd Edition – Updated

Aligned with PMBOK® Guide, Fifth Edition and the PMP® Exam Content Outline dated June 2015

For exams after January 11, 2016

Sohel Akhter, MSc, PMP, CCNA, ISMS

Please feel free to contact the author for all your project management and PMP certification training needs. All inquiries should be addressed to: Info@pmaofna.com.

First Edition: December, 2013
Second Edition: December, 2014
Third Edition: July, 2015
Third Edition – Updated: Oct, 2015
Editor: AJ Mercier, MS, MBA, PMP

ISBN-13:978-1492310549 (CreateSpace-Assigned)
ISBN-10:1492310549
Library of Congress Control Number: 2013920050
CreateSpace Independent Publishing Platform, North Charleston, SC

To the love of my life, Aoni – my beautiful, lovely wife.
Thank you for giving me the best three gifts of my life – Mayisha, Eric, and Aurora.

PMP Quick Reference Guide (Pamphlet) and PMP Flash Cards – 340 Cards

Also By Sohel Akhter, MSc, PMP, CCNA, ISMS

Available on amazon.com - http://amazon.com/author/sohel

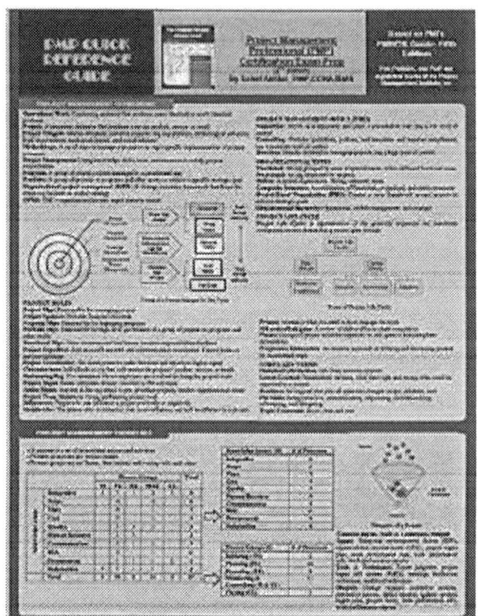

Quick Reference Guide (Pamphlet)

The quick reference guide is an 8 page summary for "Project Management Professional (PMP) Certification Exam Prep". Based on the newest edition of the PMBOK®, the 5th edition, this last chance review guide will help any student studying for the PMP exam gain more knowledge and self-assurance before their exam. This handy, easy to carry guide includes hundreds of topics, processes, glossary items, general project management terms, test taking tips, and graphics to help jog the memory of students preparing for the big exam. Exhibiting all 47 processes along with the key inputs, tools, and outputs, this guide also illustrates techniques, tables, and graphs to emphasize the essential information at a glance. Included are over 250 individual PMP prep glossary items, grouped within the knowledge area where they are most frequently used. Important formulas and values are methodically structured for prompt look-up, bringing pertinent information together in one resource. This reference guide is printed on heavy duty UV coated stock. Note that all this useful PMP Exam Prep information is on one 8.5 x 11" roll-fold (4 panels) brochure (opens to 34" x 11").

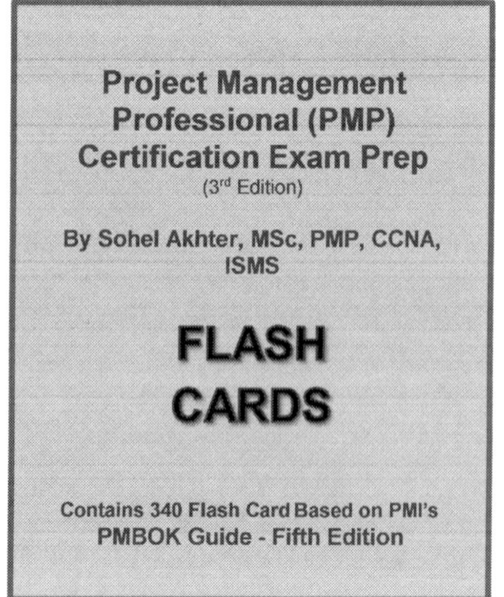

Flash Cards

If you are looking for a way to prepare for the PMP® or CAPM® exam that fits into your hectic schedule, now you have the solution. Studies have shown that spaced repetition is the most effectual form of learning, and nothing outperforms flashcards when it comes to making repetitive learning entertaining and speedy.

These flashcards cut through to the crucial core facts and components of the PMP® /CAPM® exam. Perfectly aligned with the "Project Management Professional (PMP) Certification Exam Prep", this companion product will help students memorize the most important information instantly and efficiently. Over 600 of the most critical and challenging to recall exam-related terms and concepts are now available for study as you drive, fly, travel, or take your lunch break.

This flashcard study system uses repetitive methods of study to break apart and quickly solve incomprehensible test questions. These flashcards empower you to study small, digestible bits of information that are easy to learn and give you exposure to the distinctive question types and concepts.

TABLE OF CONTENTS

TABELE OF CONTENTS

TABELE OF CONTENTS

ABOUT THE AUTHOR

Sohel Akhter is a program management consultant, trainer, and an adjunct professor for the City University of New York's MBA program. He is a top-level management professional with a distinguished management history of over fifteen years in information technology, networking, and software engineering within multiple industry settings.

Sohel's specialties include: PMO setup, WI MAX deployment, SAP implementation, strategic planning, business automation, and enterprise solution. Additionally, he has led many companies in various industries to success with his excellent project management skills, including Bank, Multinational, SMB, IT service providers, and ISPs. As a top-level executive in large organizations, he has managed teams of several hundred employees.

Sohel has been providing project management training, PMP certification exam prep boot camp, and PM consultancy globally for several years. He has conducted PM training and consultancy at all sizes of organizations for senior management, implementation team members, and end users for national and other foreign companies. Sohel has helped hundreds of participants pass their PMP exam.

Email: info@pmaofna.com
Web: http://amazon.com/author/sohel
Linkedin Profile: www.linkedin.com/in/sohelakhterpmp/

I would like to take this opportunity to thank the hundreds of people who have attended my PMP boot camps and project management courses at the City University of New York (CUNY) over the past years. Your questions, suggestions, and feedback have helped me create this book and will help thousands of others earn their PMP certifications.

If you are looking to become a certified project management professional, this book will certainly boost your confidence and ensure success on the PMP exam.

These days, job competition is fierce; you need an extra edge in everything you do. The Project Management Professional (PMP) credential is critical to remaining current, marketable, and at the top of the list in the project management business.

This easy-to-follow *Project Management Professional (PMP) Certification Exam Prep* covers everything you need to know to pass your exam. This study guide is informative, covering exactly what you need to know, and organized in a logical format for certification exam prep. I kept this book free of unnecessary bloviations that only clutter the studying process. Whether you're considering a career in project management, or looking to boost your current career, this guide will help you pass your certification exam in one try.

This easy-to-read, practical, to-the-point book covers all essential procedures and concepts of project management with the appropriate amount of detail, case studies, and examples. The reader should be able to easily understand all difficult concepts and connect them to their real life experience. This book is specially designed to assist the project managers prepare and pass the PMP® exam on their first try. Additionally, with over 580 questions and answers, this guide will make the actual exam a breeze.

Please feel free to contact me for all your project management and PMP® certification training needs.

I wish you all the best.

Sohel Akhter, MSc, PMP, CCNA, ISMS
Email: info@pmaofna.com

Introduction

Project Management Institute (PMI), established in 1969, is the leading global professional association for project managers. It administers a globally accepted and recognized, examination-based professional certification program.

PMI's Project Management Professional (PMP®) credential is one of the most important, prestigious, well-reputed, industry-recognized certifications for project managers.
Join the growing community of over 650,000 PMPs and 25,000 CAPMs.

Benefits of the PMP® Certification

Individual:

- PMPs are globally recognized and demanded.
- Demonstrates the experience, education, and competency to successfully lead and direct projects.
- Increases marketability to employers and gains higher salary; according to the PMI Salary Survey – Sixth Edition, a PMP certification increases salary by up to 15 to 20 percent more than that of non-credentialed colleagues and peers.
- Increases employee value to an organization.
- Provides professional/personal recognition.
- Creates job growth opportunities within an organization.
- Expedites professional advancement.
- Increases PM knowledge.

Organization:

- Reduces time spent completing projects deliverables.
- Decreases costs by saving time and effort to build deliverables.
- Minimizes changes, risks, and issues by defining projects before they start.
- Assures quality of deliverables, increasing likelihood of meeting customers' requirements.
- Monitors and controls the project more efficiently, especially during the execution phase.
- Manages suppliers more effectively with comprehensive supplier contracts.
- Improves staff performance by clarifying roles, responsibilities, and delivery expectations.
- Increases the likelihood of overall project success.
- Saves substantial amount of money, time, and frustration.
- Drastically improves project development process and procedures.
- Increases productivity and gives the company an edge over the competition.

Qualification

PMP Eligibility Criteria

Candidates applying for certification as a project management professional must satisfy educational and other requirements (Categories 1 or 2) and agree to abide by the project management professional code of conduct.

PMP Certification Requirements

- Approved Application (Demonstrated experience based on level of formal education, PM education, and an agreement to abide by the code of professional conduct)
- Successful completion of PMP Exam
- Maintenance of the post-certification requirements

Category	College/University Education	PM Training	Hours Leading and Directing Projects	Methods of PM Experience
Category 1	Baccalaureate or equivalent university degree	35 hours	4,500 hours Equivalent to three years	At least thirty-six (36) unique (nonoverlapping) months within last 8 years.
Category 2	High school diploma or equivalent secondary school credential	35 hours	7,500 hours Equivalent to five years	At least sixty (60) unique (nonoverlapping) months of project management experience.

Certification Fees:

PMI Member: $405 USD (Savings of $21 USD), **Nonmember:** $555 USD
PMI Membership Fee: $129. Registration is good for one year.
Submit online:www.pmi.org/en/Certification/Project-Management-Professional-PMP.aspx or
PMI® Certification Department, Four Campus Boulevard, Newtown Square, PA 19073 – 3299.

The Road to Become a PMP

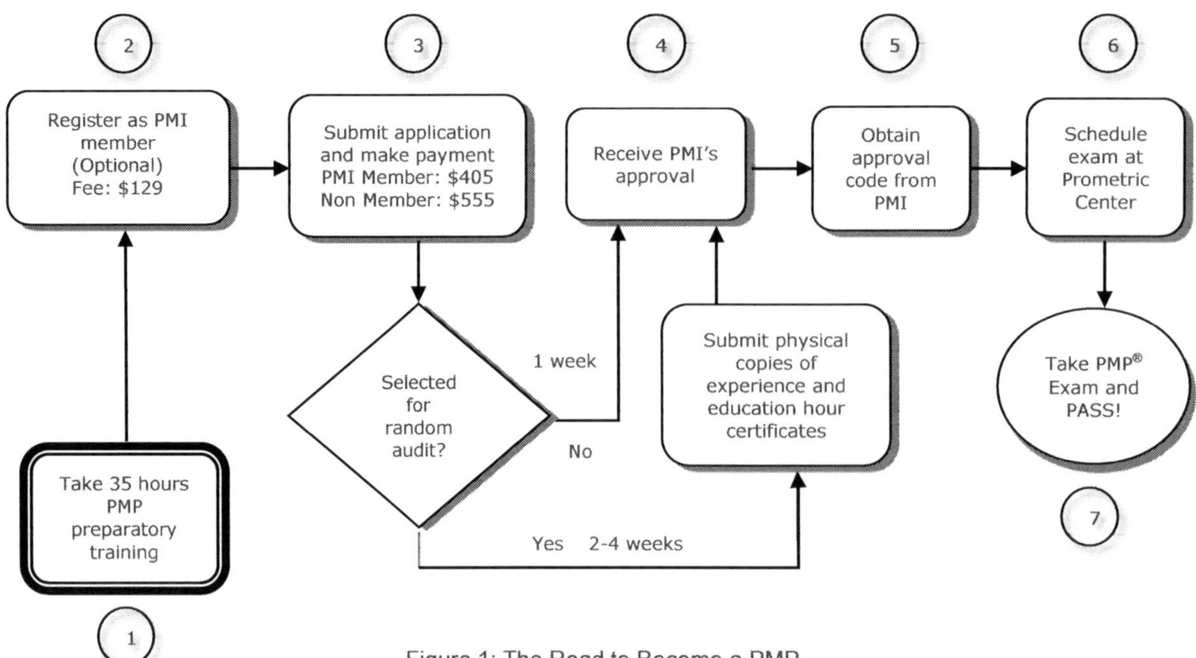

Figure 1: The Road to Become a PMP

The PMP Exam: An Overview

- It is a "standardized test" that measures the application of knowledge, skills, tools, and techniques that are utilized in the practice of project management.
- The exam is based primarily on a Guide to the Project Management Body of Knowledge (*PMBOK®*), but the exam is not solely based on the PMBOK®. Exam questions can be from any contemporary project management resource.
- It will test your knowledge of PMI's processes, your understanding of the terms used to describe the processes, and your ability to apply the processes to situations.
- It will test your ability to apply key formulas to scheduling, budgeting, estimating, and other areas. You can expect to have as many as ten to fifteen formula-related and ten to fifteen earned-value questions on the exam.
- Most of the questions on the exam will be situational (e.g., What will be the best course of action? What will you do next? What have you done wrong? Etc.).
- It will test your understanding of professional responsibility as it applies to project management.
- The exam will not test your intelligence, common sense, knowledge of industry practices, knowledge on how to use software applications in project management, or any other location-/project-specific knowledge.
- It is offered only by Prometric (www.prometric.com) at various locations.
- The exam is a four-hour computer-based test with two hundred multiple-choice questions.
- In order to pass, candidates must correctly answer a minimum of 114 to 121 (65 percent to 69 percent) of the 175 scored questions. Twenty-five pretest questions randomly placed throughout the new examination will not be included in the pass/fail determination.
- All the questions have four choices and only one correct answer.
- There is no negative marking for wrong answers.
- The questions may jump from topic to topic, and a single question may integrate multiple concepts.
- The nature of the questions do not change based on the answers to the previous questions.
- The testing system will allow to mark questions for review, and you can go back to them prior to finishing the exam.
- Volunteers are trained to write questions that are vetted by a group and then refined and approved. The questions are generated randomly from a database containing hundreds of stored questions.
- If you do not pass, you may take the exam up to three times in a calendar year.

PMP Exam Syllabus

Five Process Groups	Ten Knowledge Areas	Percentage of Items/Domains
– Initiating – Planning – Executing – Monitoring & Controlling – Closing	– Integration Management – Scope Management – Time Management – Cost Management – Quality Management – Human Resource Management – Communications Management – Risk Management – Procurement Management – Stakeholder Management	– Initiating: 13% – Planning: 24% – Executing: 31% – Monitoring & Controlling: 25% – Closing: 7% – Total Number of Scored Questions: 175 – Total Number of Unscored (Pretest) Questions: 25 – Total Number of Questions: 200

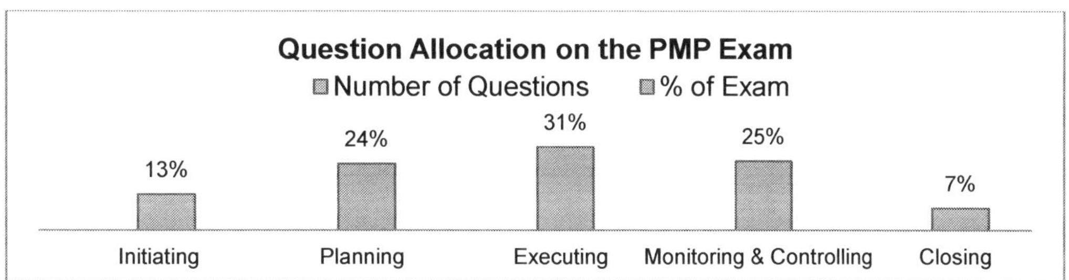

Figure 2: Question Allocation on the PMP Exam

Recent Changes in PMP Exam

A recently completed Role Delineation Study (RDS) provided an updated description of the project management professional role. It serves as the foundation for the PMP exam and ensures its validity and relevance. The RDS captures perspectives of project management practitioners from all industries, work settings, and regions. Research included a large-scale survey of global Project Management Professional (PMP)® certification holders to validate updates to domains, tasks, knowledge, and skills.

Modifications Made as a Result of the RDS

The following modifications were made as a result of the RDS:

- Modification to existing tasks
- 8 new tasks
- A few tasks removed
- Weighting of PMP exam

Key changes include:

- Emphasis on business strategy and benefits realization
- Value of lessons learned
- Project charter responsibilities
- Enhancing stakeholder relationships

Modification	Domain 1: Initiating	Domain 2: Planning	Domain 3: Executing	Domain 4: Monitoring & Controlling	Domain 5: Closing
Task Added	Task 2, 7,and 8	Task 13	Task 6 and 7	Task 6 and 7	N/A
Weighting	N/A	NA	Increased to 31% from 30%	N/A	Reduced to 7% from 8%

Note: In addition to domain-specific knowledge and skills, these specifications include a set of cross-cutting knowledge and skills used in multiple domains as listed below:

Domain	Tasks	Knowledge and Skills
Initiating: 13 %	**Task1:** Perform project assessment **Task2:** Identify key deliverables - new **Task3:** Perform stakeholder analysis **Task 4:** Identify high level risks, assumptions, and constraints **Task 5:** Participated in the development of the project charter **Task 6:** Obtain project charter approval **Task 7:** Conduct benefit analysis - new **Task 8:** Inform stakeholders of the approved project charter - new	– Analytical skills – Benefit analysis techniques – Elements of a project charter – Estimation tools and techniques – Strategic management
Planning: 24%	**Task 1:** Review and assess detailed project requirements, constraints, and assumptions with stakeholders **Task2**: Develop a scope management plan **Task3:** Develop the cost management plan **Task4:** Develop the project schedule **Task 5:** Develop a human resource management plan **Task 6:** Develop the communications management plan **Task 7:** Develop the procurement management plan **Task 8:** Develop the quality management plan **Task 9:** Develop the change management plan **Task 10:** Develop the risk management plan **Task 11:** Present the project management plan to the relevant stakeholders **Task 12:** Conduct kick-off meeting **Task 13:** Develop the stakeholder management plan - new	– Estimations tools and techniques – Requirements gathering techniques – Scope deconstruction (e.g., WBS, Scope backlog) tools and techniques – Scope management planning – Time management planning – Cost management planning – Workflow diagramming techniques – Human resource planning – Communications planning – Lean and efficiency principles – Quality management planning – Regulatory and environmental impacts assessment planning – Risk management planning – Contract types and selection criteria – Procurement planning – Stakeholder management planning – Change management planning
Executing:31 %	**Task 1:** Acquire and manage project resources **Task 2:** Manage task execution **Task 3:** Implement the quality management plan **Task 4:** Implement approved changes and corrective actions **Task 5:** Implement approved actions **Task 6:** Manage the flow of information - new **Task 7:** Maintain stakeholder relationships - new	– Continuous improvement processes – Contract management techniques – Elements of a statement of work – Interdependencies among project elements – Project budgeting tools and techniques – Quality standard tools – Vendor management techniques – Interaction of work breakdown structure elements – Project monitoring tools and techniques
Monitoring & Controlling: 25%	**Task 1:** Measure project performance **Task 2:** Manage changes to the project **Task 3:** Verify that project deliverables conform to the quality standards **Task 4:** Monitor and assess risks **Task 5:** Review the issue log **Task 6:** Capture, analyze, and manage lessons learned - new **Task 7:** Monitor procurement activities - new	– Performance measurement and tracking techniques (e.g., EV, CPM, PERT, Trend Analysis) – Process analysis techniques (e.g., LEAN, Six Sigma, Kanban) – Project control limits (e.g., thresholds, tolerance) – Project finance principles – Project monitoring tools and techniques – Project quality best practices and standards (e.g., ISO, BS, CMMI, IEEE) – Quality measurement tools – Risk identification and analysis techniques – Risk response techniques – Quality validation and verification techniques
Closing: 7%	**Task 1:** Obtain final acceptance of the project deliverables **Task 2:** Transfer the ownership of deliverables to the assigned stakeholders **Task 3:** Obtain financial, legal, and administrative closure **Task 4:** Prepare and share the final project report	– Archiving practices and statutes – Compliance (statute/ organization) – Contract closure requirements – Close-out procedures – Feedback techniques – Performance measurement techniques – Project review techniques

	Task 5: Create lessons learned **Task 6:** Archive project documents and materials **Task 7:** Obtain feedback from relevant stakeholders	– Transition planning technique
Cross-Cutting Knowledge and Skills	– Active listening – Applicable laws and regulations – Benefits realization – Brainstorming techniques – Business acumen – Change management techniques – Coaching, mentoring, training, and motivational techniques – Communication channels, tools, techniques, and methods – Configuration management – Conflict resolution – Customer satisfaction metrics – Data gathering techniques – Decision making – Delegation techniques – Diversity and cultural sensitivity – Emotional intelligence – Expert judgment technique – Facilitation – Generational sensitivity and diversity	– Information management tools, techniques, and methods – Interpersonal skills – Knowledge management – Leadership tools, techniques, and skills – Lessons learned management techniques – Meeting management techniques – Negotiating and influencing techniques and skills – Organizational and operational awareness – Peer-review processes – Presentation tools and techniques – Prioritization time management – Problem-solving tools and techniques – Project finance principles – Quality assurance and control techniques – Relationship management – Risk assessment techniques – Situational awareness – Stakeholder management techniques – Team-building techniques – Virtual/remote team management

PMP Exam Preparation Strategy

Resources

- *A Guide to the Project Management Body of Knowledge* (*PMBOK® Guide*) – Fifth Edition, Paperback, Publisher: Project Management Institute, Author: Project Management Institute, ISBN: 9781933890517
- Training material from PMP preparatory training
- Tools
  - Sohel's PMP Quick Reference Guide, PMP Exercise Book, and PMP Flash Cards – available at: http://amazon.com/author/sohel
  - Practice exams
  - Your own mind maps and notes
- Formal Education
  - PMP exam prep courses
- Study Groups
  - Check out your local PMI chapter and websites

Planning	Execution
– Determine your qualifications and project management education. – Select the type of training and supplier based on your needs. – Set target date to take the exam, and complete the application process. – Make your test appointment once you get approval from PMI. – Plan three to four weeks of intensive self-study, and allocate daily study time. – Take an exam prep course. – Obtain information about study groups. – Obtain sample exam questions. – Create and follow a study plan.	– Study all domains. – Memorize the glossary and chapter overviews (inputs, tools & techniques, outputs). – Understand the PMBOK® Five Process Groups and the ten Knowledge Areas. – Understand all examples and charts. – Become familiar with all the definitions at the end of the PMBOK®, and refer to our study material. – Use quizzes and practice exams to measure progress. – Discuss materials with other PMP candidates. – Go through this PMP book at least twice. – Finally, take as many practice exams as possible; this will eliminate any uncertainty or doubts.

Day Before Exam Day	On the Exam Day
– Check out the exam location prior to the exam date so that you do not get lost on the exam day. – Plan to arrive twenty to thirty minutes early. – Exercise and get a good night's sleep.	– Bring two forms of ID & eligibility letter. – Be prepared to sit for a long time. – Write down everything on the scratch paper that is provided once you begin the exam. o Formulas o All processes o Challenging terms o Any mnemonics or memory joggers

What is on the PMP Exam?

- Around twenty-six questions from initiating, forty-eight from planning, sixty from executing, fifty from monitoring & controlling, and sixteen from closing.
- The exam can be thought of as divided into three categories:

Easier Questions	Medium Questions	Harder Questions
Sixty easier questions = 30 percent of the exam – Ethical questions – Supporting PMI – Following process – Obvious inputs, tools, and outputs	Eighty medium questions = 40 percent of the exam – More detailed inputs, tools, and outputs – Ranking the order in which procedures should be performed – Specific terms and vocabulary from the PMBOK® – Why a particular process is performed – Questions related to the delineation of project roles and responsibilities	Sixty harder questions = 30 percent of the exam – Trick questions (may be long or wordy) – Highly situational questions that have answers that are not obvious – Questions with more than one correct answer from which you need to select the best answer – Mathematical or logical questions

Post Certification

- Celebrate your success.
- Update your résumé.
- Maintain your PMP Certification.
- PMPs must complete and submit a minimum of sixty Professional Development Units (PDUs) during each continuing certification cycle.
    - PDU is the measuring unit used to quantify approved learning and professional service activities related to project management. Typically, one PDU is earned for one hour of learning.
    - A PMP's continuing certification cycle can be identified by the dates on his/her PMP certificate.
    - Options to earn PDUs:
      Category A: PMI Registered Education Providers (REPs) courses
      Category B: Continuing education
      Category C: Self-directed learning
      Category D: Creating PM knowledge
      Category E: Service to professional/community organization
      Category F: Professional PM experience
    - Track, record, and submit PDUs regularly.
    - For more detail please visit www.pmi.org or call 610–356–4600.

* * Note: Refer to the topic "How to pass PMP on your first try" on page 531 for more detail. * *

CHAPTER 2

PROJECT MANAGEMENT FRAMEWORK

CHAPTER TWO

Definition of a Project

A project is a temporary endeavor that produces a unique product, service, or result. It is temporary in nature and has a definite beginning and ending. A project is completed when its goals and objectives have been met and signed off by the stakeholders. A successful project is one that meets or exceeds the expectations of the stakeholders.

Projects make up almost half of the work that most organizations do. The following are ways that projects help organizations meet their strategic goals and objectives:

Market Demands: Developing fuel-efficient cars in response to high gasoline prices and pollution

Customer Requests: Developing a new website for customers to automate their billing process

Organization Requirements: Shifting an office to another location

Technological Advances: Implementing new products or services based on new inventions in genetics, nanotechnology, and robotics

Legal Requirements: Implementing guidelines for handling of a new toxic material

Ecological Impact: Reducing greenhouse gasses or other ecological impact

Social Need: Resolving a social problem or fulfilling a social need in an impoverished region

Project work is different from *operational work*, which is any continuing endeavor that produces many identical or nearly identical products or provides repetitive services (e.g., frying burgers, manufacturing cars, teaching algebra).

Subprojects: Projects divided into more manageable components.

Project Management

The project manager is the individual ultimately responsible for managing the project.

Project management is the application of knowledge, skills, tools, and techniques to satisfy project requirements. Project management is performed by applying and integrating the forty-seven project management processes, which are logically grouped into five process groups: initiating, planning, executing, monitoring & controlling, and closing. Managing a project typically requires:

- Establishing project objectives
- Identifying project requirements
- Specifying quality of the deliverables
- Estimating resources and timescales
- Preparing a business case to justify the investment
- Securing corporate agreement and funding
- Developing and implementing a management plan for the project
- Leading and motivating the project delivery team
- Managing the risks, issues and changes on the project
- Monitoring progress against plan
- Managing the project budget
- Maintaining communications with everyone involved in the project
- Managing stakeholders
- Balancing project constraints (i.e., cost, time, quality, resources, scope, risk, etc.)
- Closing the project in a controlled fashion when appropriate

Investment in effective project management will have a number of benefits to both the host organization and the people involved in delivering the project. It will:

- Provide a greater likelihood of achieving the desired result
- Ensure efficient and best value use of resources
- Satisfy the differing needs of the project's stakeholders

Methodology: A methodology is a set of steps to manage a project or an organization's specific implementation of project processes.

Operations Management

Operations Management deals with the design and management of ongoing products, services, and supply chains. It considers the acquisition, development, and utilization of resources that firms need to deliver the goods and services their clients want.

Operations Management ranges from strategic to tactical and operational levels. Representative strategic issues include determining the size and location of manufacturing plants, deciding the structure of service or telecommunications networks, and designing technology supply chains.

Tactical issues include plant layout and structure, project management methods, and equipment selection and replacement. Operational issues include production scheduling and control, inventory management, quality control and inspection, traffic and materials handling, and equipment maintenance policies.

Program Management

A program is a group of related projects managed in a coordinated way to capitalize on benefits and control what is not achievable by managing those projects individually.

Program management is the centralized and coordinated management of a program to obtain the strategic objectives and benefits sought through the inception of the program.

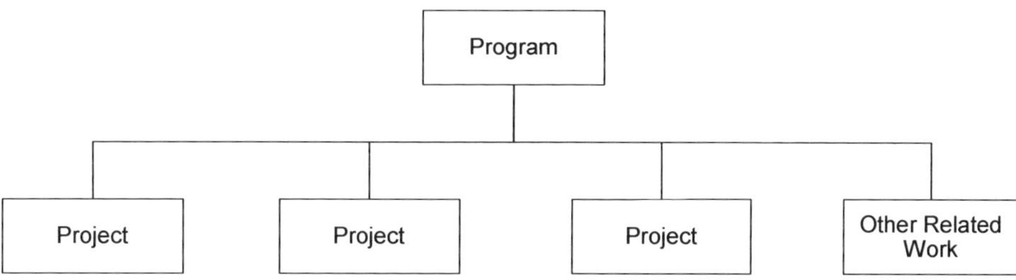

Figure 2-1: Program

Program management focuses on the projects' interdependencies and helps to determine the optimal approach for managing them. For example, building a new shopping mall can be a program with many related projects such as excavation, interior design, construction, store placement, sales, marketing, and facilities management.

For a group of projects to be classified as a program, there must be some value-add in managing them together as a program. If there is no value-add, they should not be classified as a program. A project may or may not be part of a program, but a program will always have projects.

There are many advantages to using program management to manage related projects, although it can be challenging to pull off well. Issues like governance and risk can be managed more successfully if a single umbrella team is coordinating efforts, since the program team has an overall view of processes and progress that individual project leaders lack.

Portfolio Management

A portfolio can be described as a group of projects, programs, and other works to achieve a specific strategic business goal. The programs may not be related other than the fact that they are helping to achieve the common strategic goal.

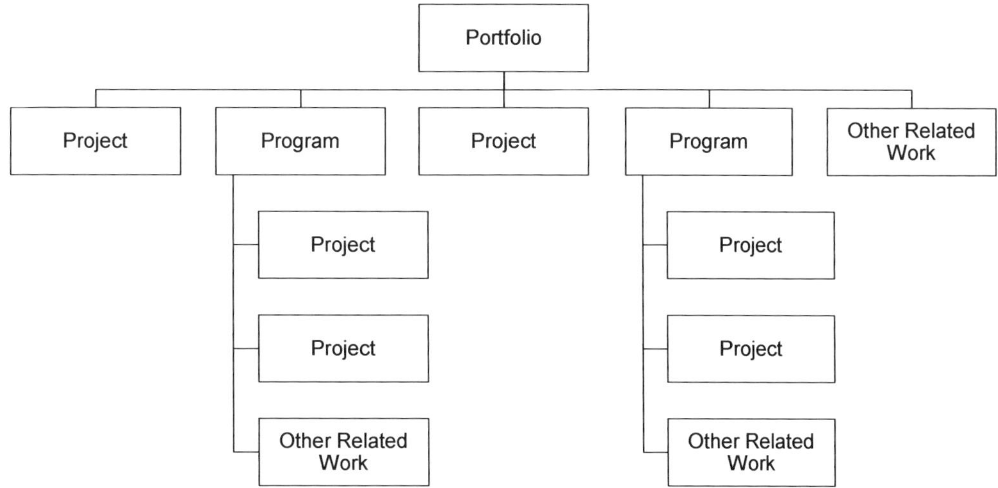

Figure 2-2: Portfolio Management

Portfolio management encompasses identifying, prioritizing, authorizing, managing, and controlling the collection of projects, programs, other work, and sometimes other portfolios to achieve strategic business objectives. For example, a construction business has several business units such as retail and single and multifamily residential. All programs, projects, and work within all of these business units collectively make up the portfolio for this construction business.

Interrelationships among Project Management, Program Management, Portfolio Management, and Organizational Project Management (OPM)

Organizational Project Management (OPM) is a strategy execution framework that keeps the entire organization focused on the overall strategy. It provides guidance on how to prioritize, manage, execute, and measure projects, programs, portfolios, and other organizational work and practices to achieve better results, improved performance, and a substantial advantage over competitors.

Projects are a means of achieving organizational goals and objectives in the context of a strategic plan. A group of projects within a program contributes to benefits of the program, objectives of the portfolio, and the strategic plan of the organization. For instance, by managing four related technology projects as a program, an IT organization may be able to save a substantial amount of money and valuable time by developing several common components only once and leveraging them across all of the projects that use these components.

In a mature organization, project management exists in a broader context governed by program management and portfolio management. Organizations set strategic goals for the entire organization, and these strategies and priorities are linked and have relationships between portfolios and programs and between programs and individual projects.

Organizational planning can establish the funding and support for the component projects on the basis of specific lines of business, risk categories, and other factors. An organization's strategic goals and objectives are the primary factor guiding investments. Projects, programs, or other related works that contribute the least to the portfolio's strategic objectives may be excluded.

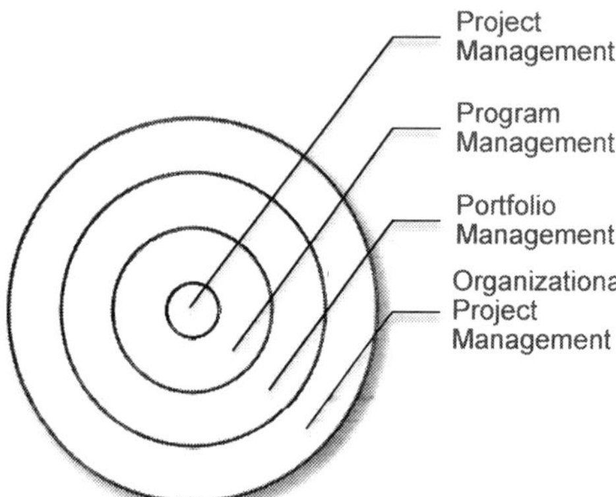

Figure 2-3: Relationships among Project Management, Program Management, Portfolio Management, and Organizational Project Management

Interrelationships among Project Management, Operations Management, and Organizational Strategy

Operations Management is an ongoing organizational function that performs activities to produce products or supply services. For instance, production operations, manufacturing, IT service management, and accounting operations. Furthermore, operations are permanent endeavors that produce repetitive outputs. Resources are assigned to do the same tasks according to operating procedures and policies.

In contrast, projects are temporary and help the business to meet organizational goals and to respond quickly and easily to the external environment. Organizations use projects to change operations, products, and services to meet business need, gain competitive advantage, and respond to new markets.

Different Objectives

Projects require project management whereas operations requires business process management or operations management. However, projects and operations do meet at various points during the life-cycle of a product or service. For example, when:

- Re-engineering business processes
- Developing or changing products and services
- Improving operations or product development

The goal of process management is to improve processes continually. Improving operational processes may increase effectiveness, cut costs, and gain competitive advantage.

Projects are about driving change in the organization. For instance, using business process re-engineering to align business need with customer expectation.

Different Skills

Moreover, the skills needed by the project managers are different to those needed by operational managers.

Project Manager	Operational Manager
Role ends with project	Routine
Temporary team	Stable organization
Many different skills	Specialist skills
Work not done before	Work repeatable
Time, cost, and scope constraints	Annual planning cycle
Difficult to estimate time and budget	Budgets set and fixed events

Table 2-1: Skills Needed by Project Manager and Operational Managers

Interrelationships among Project Management, Organizational Strategies, and Organizational Governance

Strategy literature deals heavily with models, tools, and techniques for formulating organizational strategy – determining what business the organization wishes to be in.

Governance literature mostly discusses the topic from the Board perspective, outlining roles and responsibilities of boards, policy frameworks, ethical and responsible decision making. The focus is usually on financial responsibility and value creation, governance charters, and structures.

Project management literature focuses predominantly on the functions of managing projects and project lifecycles.

These are three very important topics which individually receive a lot of attention. Without a properly executed and governed business strategy, an organization will simply not deliver the desired benefits for its shareholders.

So the fundamental proposition is this:

The desired benefits of organizational strategy will be achieved faster and more efficiently when strategic objectives are implemented using a project management approach, and that effective governance is enabled by an organizational approach to project management.

Business Value

Business value is a highly subjective measure because it involves estimating the value of intangible assets like trade secrets, trademarks, public benefit, and brand recognition. In management, business value is an informal term that includes all forms of value that determine the health and well-being of the firm in the long run.

Business value expands concept of value of the firm beyond economic value (also known as economic profit, economic value added, and shareholder value) to include other forms of value such as employee value, customer value, supplier value, channel partner value, alliance partner value, managerial value, and societal value. Many of these forms of value are not directly measured in monetary terms.

Business value often embraces intangible assets not necessarily attributable to any stakeholder group. Examples include intellectual capital and a firm's business model. Examples of tangible elements include fixtures, monetary assets, stockholder equity, and utility. The balanced scorecard methodology is one of the most popular methods for measuring and managing business value.

An organization may determine processes to meet strategic goals and achieve greater business value from their investment through the efficient use of operations, project, program, and portfolio management. Organizations can further facilitate the association of these project, program, and portfolio management activities by reinforcing organizational enablers such as structural, cultural, technological, and human resource practices.

Project Management Office (PMO)

A Project Management Office (PMO) is a centralized organizational unit that oversees and coordinates the management of projects and programs under its domain throughout the organization.

The primary role of a PMO is to support the project managers in a variety of ways as well as to direct management of a project if necessary. The following are the three types of PMO that can exist in an organization:

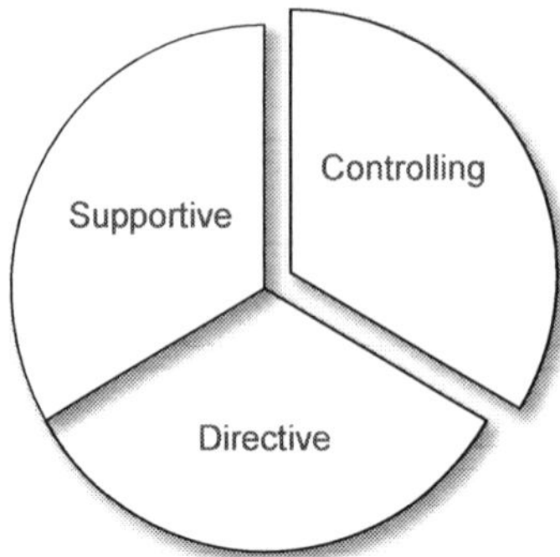

Figure 2- 4: PMO Structure

Supportive: Mostly serves as a project repository and plays a consultative role. This type of PMO usually has a low level of control over projects and programs.

Controlling: Provides guidelines, policies, and templates and requires compliances. This type of PMO usually has a moderate level of control over projects and programs.

Directive: This type of PMO is directly involved in managing programs and projects and has a high level of control over projects and programs.

Other key responsibilities may include the following:

- Establish and maintain templates, policies, procedures, best practices, and standards for project management methodologies
- Help gather lessons learned and make them available to other projects
- Maintain and archive project documentation for future reference
- Help provide resources
- Be part of change control board
- Monitor compliance with organizational processes, policies, procedures, etc.
- Provide centralized communication about the projects
- Be heavily involved during project initiation as a key decision maker and integral stakeholder to make recommendations, prioritize projects, terminate projects, or take other actions as required
- Manage the interdependencies between projects

Differences between the roles of project managers and the PMO are illustrated below:

PMO	Project Manager
The PMO optimizes the shared organizational resources across all programs and projects.	The project manager controls the assigned resources in the project.
The PMO manages methodologies, standards, overall risk, opportunities, and interdependencies among projects at the enterprise level.	The project manager manages the constraints such as scope, time, cost, quality, and risk.
The PMO is focused on the overall strategic goals and objectives of the entire organization.	The project manager is concerned about specific project objectives.

Table 2-2: Differences between the Roles of the PMO and Project Managers

Constraints

The concept of triple constraints is central to successful project management. It provides a framework for understanding trade-offs in managing competing project requirements. Originally, project constraints were referred to as the "triple constraints" and included cost, time, and scope. When one of the components of the triple constraints is changed, the other two are affected.

For example, if the duration of the project is reduced, the budget needs to be increased for additional resources for the completion of the same amount of work in less time. If budget cannot be increased, you may need to explore the option of reducing the scope or targeted quality to deliver the project's end result within the same budget in less time. Stakeholders may also complicate the situation since they have different priorities and considerations as to which factors are the most important. Furthermore, additional risks are created whenever project requirements or objectives are changed.

The classic approach to the triple constraints and new project constraints are represented in the following diagrams:

Figure 2-5: The Triple Constraints and New Project Constraints

New project constraints may include, but are not limited to the following:

- Scope
- Quality
- Cost
- Time
- Resources
- Risk
- Communication
- Customer Satisfaction

Senior management in an organization gets involved in setting priority among these constraints directly or indirectly. The primary job of the project manager is to manage these different project constraints by assessing the situations, prioritizing competing demands, and analyzing the impact of changes on all the constraints.

Exercise 1: What questions will you ask in determining whether there is a need for a formal project management process in your organization?

Stakeholder Management

A stakeholder is a person or an organization that is actively involved with the work of the project or whose vested interests may be positively or negatively impacted by the execution or completion of the project. Examples of stakeholders include project managers, customers, sponsors, the PMO, functional managers, the project team, board of directors, vendors, suppliers, department managers, and operations management.

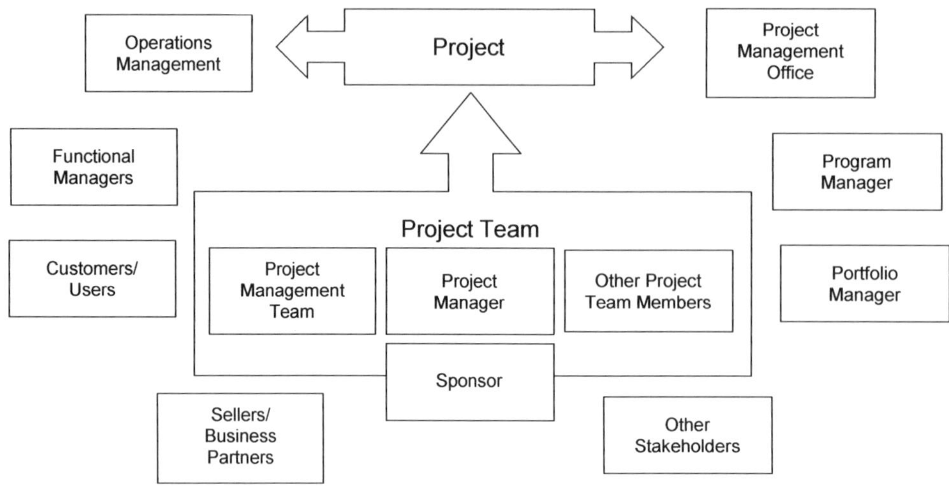

Figure 2-6: The Relationship Between the Project and Stakeholders

Depending on the complexity, size, and type, most projects have a diverse number of internal and external stakeholders at different levels of the organization with different authority levels.
Stakeholder identification is a continuous and sometimes difficult process, and the influence of a stakeholder may not become evident until later stages of the project. It is essential to identify stakeholders and classify them according to their level of interest, influence, importance, and expectation at the early stage of the project as much as possible. Stakeholders who were omitted during the identification process could possibly cause the project significant delay and additional cost by requesting changes to implement their requirements.

It is essential to focus on meeting and exceeding the stakeholders' expectations by continuously communicating with them, clarifying and resolving their issues, addressing their concerns, and improving the project performance by implementing their change requests.

Stakeholder management requires the following:

- Identifying both internal and external stakeholders
- Determining stakeholder requirements
- Determining stakeholder expectations
- Determining stakeholder influence and interest levels
- Determining stakeholder information needed from the project
- Communicating with stakeholders
- Identifying stakeholder influence-controlling strategies

Stakeholder Name	Org	Contact Info	Influence Level (1–5)	Interest Level (1–5)	Classification	Expectation	Information Need	Role
Mr. Seth Daniel	Statistic	347-222-1111	4	5	Internal	All the key features of the project.	– Status Update – Issue logs – Biweekly Reports	User acceptance tester

Table 2-3: A Stakeholder Register

Operational Stakeholders in Project Management

Stakeholders who perform and conduct business operations are called operational stakeholders. The following are examples of operational stakeholders:

- Line managers
- System support analysts
- Customer service representatives
- Manufacturing line supervisors
- Plant operators
- Help desk agents
- Maintenance workers
- Call center personnel

In order to gain insight and evade unnecessary issues, project managers should always consider and appropriately include operational stakeholders in all phases of project and capture their inputs. Like other stakeholders, operational stakeholders should be fully engaged and their expectations must be identified in the stakeholder register. Also, their positive and negative influence should be addressed while planning for risks in the project.

Organizational Influence on Project Management

Four primary areas within the organization can have a significant influence on how projects are structured, scheduled, budgeted, and controlled, and they have to do with the organization's leadership, cultures & styles, communications, and structures.

Organizational Leadership

There is a consistent rule within most organizations that everything starts from the top and rolls down. This rule also is true in the area of managing projects. If the executive staff does not understand the importance and benefits of projects, they will not always be supportive of what managers are trying to accomplish and the approach they are taking in using projects to manage activities within the organization. This can come across in several forms, behaviors, attitudes, and actions such as:

- Poor selection of key managers in critical roles
- Approval or nonapproval of certain projects and activities
- Unnecessary timelines or budget constraints creating undue stress on projects and activities
- Misunderstanding or ignorance of critical activity update information
- Personality conflicts with project managers
- Hidden agendas that drive inconsistent or confusing decisions

Executive management must understand the impact their leadership can have on the organization if it is not performed at the highest level of integrity, professionalism, and cooperation among themselves and with those reporting to them.

Organizational Cultures and Styles

Most organizations have developed unique and describable cultures. These cultures are reflected in numerous factors, including, but not limited to:

- Shared values, norms, beliefs, and expectations
- Policies and procedures
- Motivation and award systems
- View of authority relationships
- Work ethic and work hours

Organizational cultures often have a direct influence on the project. For example:

- A team proposing an unusual or high-risk approach is more likely to secure approval in an aggressive or entrepreneurial organization.
- A project manager with a highly participative style is apt to encounter problems in a rigidly hierarchical organization, while a project manager with an authoritarian style will be equally challenged in a participative organization.

Organizational Communications

Organizational structure can greatly impact communication necessary to complete projects successfully. In a company with structure that fosters interdepartmental communication and frequent dialogue between management and subordinates, projects have a great chance for success. In a company where departments exist in vacuums and one does not know what the other is doing, projects may not succeed. Good communication allows support for projects and less duplication of efforts. If all departments and personnel work together to a common goal and agree on the mission and outcome on the onset, projects will thrive.

Organizational Structures

An organization is a unique entity and every organization has its own style and culture that affect the availability of resources and how projects are conducted. There are six types of organizational structures, broken into the following three categories:

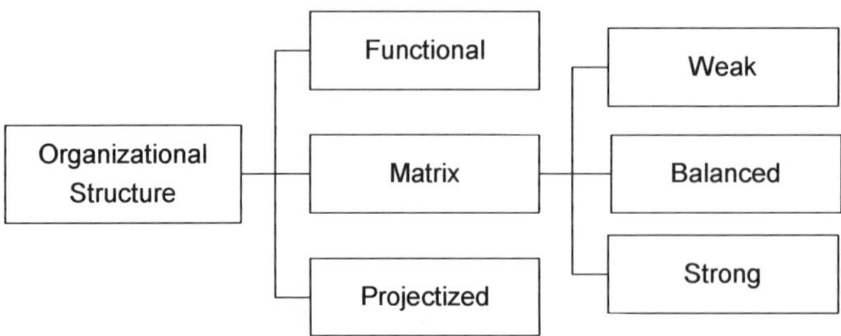

Figure 2-7: Organizational Structures

Functional Organization

Characteristics	Details
Description	The organization is grouped by areas of specialization within different functional areas (e.g., accounting, marketing, engineering, etc.)
Person in Charge	Functional (Department) manager
Advantages	– Employees have one supervisor with a clear chain of command – Similar resources are grouped by specialty – Team members have clearly defined career path in their areas of specialization – Easier management of specialists and their job assignments
Disadvantages	– No defined career path in project management – Project manager has little or no authority and could even be part-time – Multiple projects compete for limited resources and priority – Team members give more importance to their functional responsibility to the detriment of the project
Project Manager Authority	Little to none
Resources Availability for Project Work	Little to none
Who Controls Project Spending	Functional manager
Project Manager's Role	Part-time
Project Management Support Staff	Part-time

Table 2-4: Characteristics of a Functional Organization

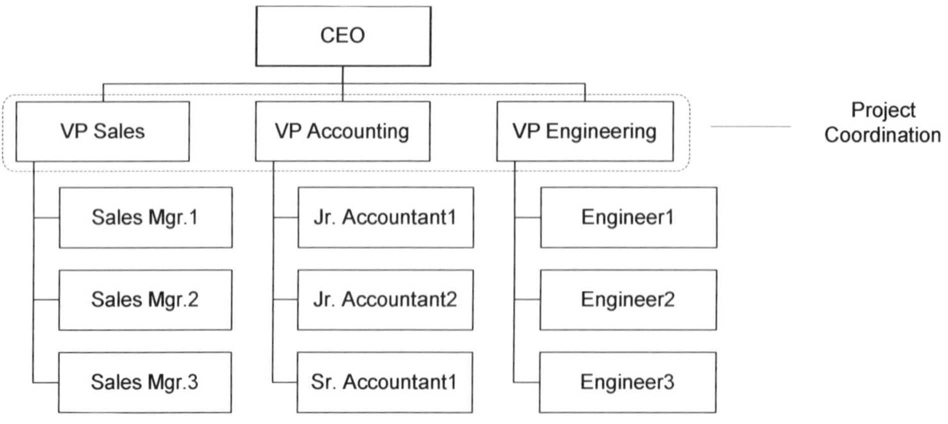

Figure 2-8: A Functional Organization

Projectized Organization

Characteristics	Details
Description	Most commonly found in consulting environment, the organization is structured by projects. Project managers run projects and have official authority over the project team.
Person in Charge	Project managers
Advantages	– Project manager has full authority and control – Efficient and convenient project organization – Strong loyalty to the project – More effective communication than in functional organization
Disadvantages	– Less efficient use of resources – Professional growth and development can be challenging – No home when project is completed
Project Manager Authority	High to almost total
Resources Availability for Project Work	High to almost total
Who Controls Project Spending	Project manager
Project Manager's Role	Full-time
Project Management Support Staff	Full-time

Table 2-5: Characteristics of a Projectized Organization

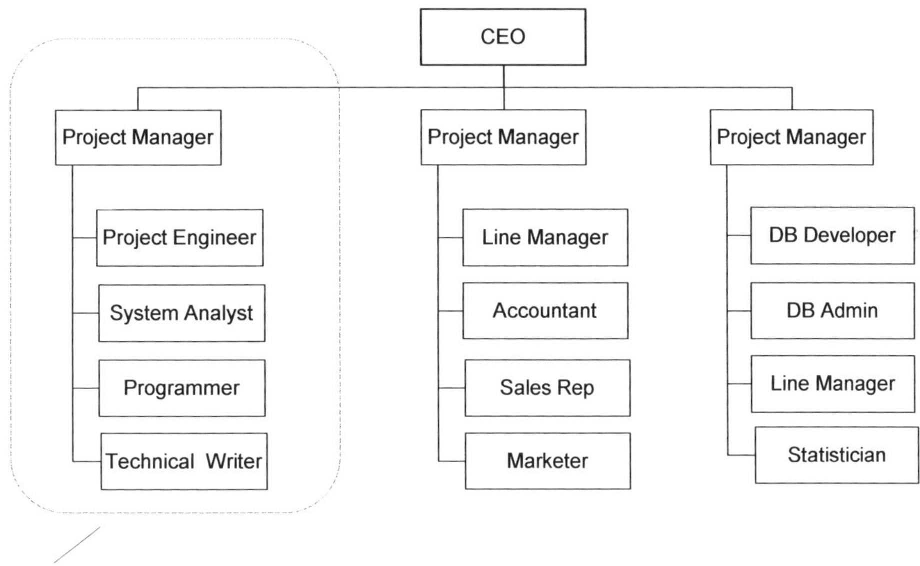

Figure 2-9: A Projectized Organization

Matrix Organization

Characteristics	Details		
Description	This hybrid organization is a blend of both a functional organization and a projectized organization. The three matrix forms are strong matrix – project manager has more authority, weak matrix – functional manager has more authority, and balanced matrix – power is shared evenly between the project manager and functional manager.		
Person in Charge	Authority and power are shared between project manager and functional manager.		
Advantages	– Best of both worlds – Better coordination – Maximum utilization of resources		
Disadvantages	– Higher potential for conflicts and confusion as resources report to a functional manager and also to a project manager for project-related activities – Usually extra administration and management time are required – Allocation of resources is more complicated		
	Weak	**Balanced**	**Strong**
Project Manager Authority	Low	Low to moderate	Moderate to high
Resources Availability for Project Work	Low	Low to moderate	Moderate to high
Who Controls Project Spending	Functional manager	Shared	Project manager
Project Manager's Role	Part-time	Full-time	Full-time
Project Management Support Staff	Part-time	Part-time	Full-time

Table 2-6: Characteristics of a Matrix Organization

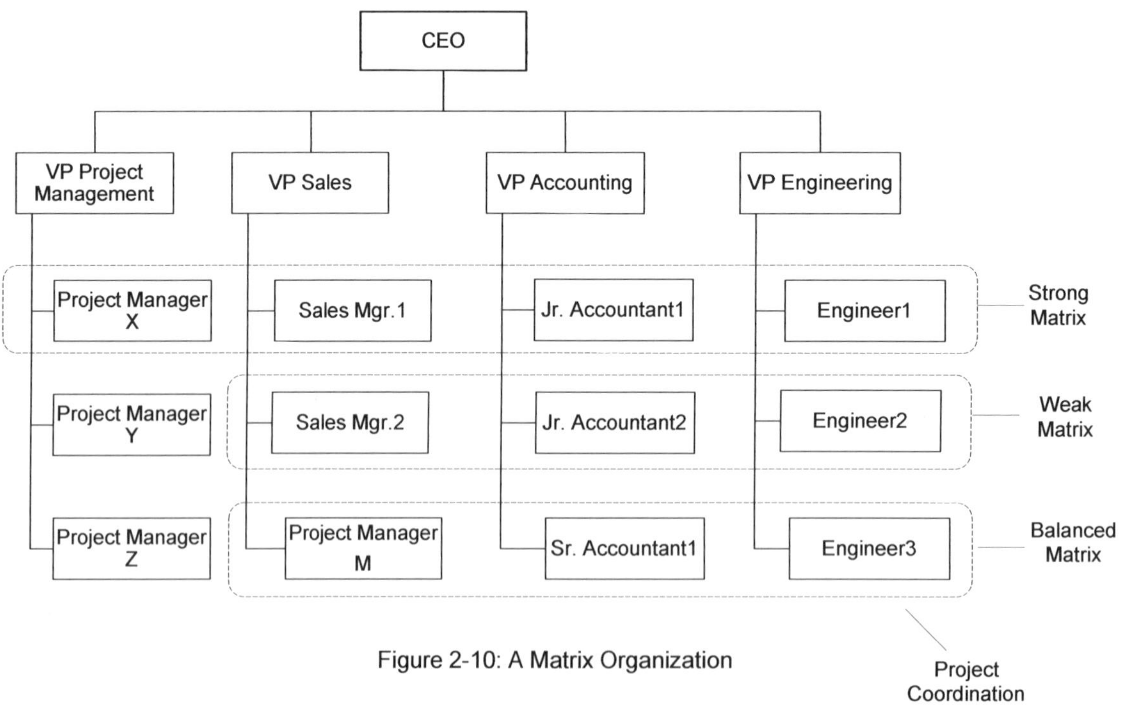

Figure 2-10: A Matrix Organization

In addition to the functional, projectized, and matrix organizations, you also need to be familiar with the following concepts:

Composite Structure: Composite structure is a combination of functional, projectized, and matrix organizational structures. For example, a functional organization may create a special project team or task force to handle a critical project and may have many characteristics of a projectized organizational structure and may include full-time staff from different functional departments with their own set of operating procedures, standards, and reporting structures.

Project-Based Organization (PBO): A project-based organization creates a temporary framework around their projects to achieve strategic goals and to minimize the impact, constraints, and obstacles of the established organizational structure.

Organizational Hierarchy: There are mainly three types of organizational hierarchy—operational, middle management, and strategic. The project manager's interaction with people at these different hierarchies depends on the priority and importance of the project as well as the size, culture, existing systems, and processes in the organization.

Exercise 2: Identify what type of organization you are working for in the following situations:

1. You are reporting only to your manager and mostly work on operational activities.
2. You are working on a data center project and report to the project manager only.
3. You are reporting to both the project manager and your manager.
4. You are working in a task force on a critical project.

Exercise 3: Match the following characteristics to the appropriate organizational structures.

1. Similar resources are grouped by specialty.
2. The project manager has moderate to high level of authority.
3. The authority is shared between the functional manager and the project manager.
4. The project manager role is like a coordinator or expeditor (communication coordinator or staff assistant).
5. The project manager has full control over the budget.
6. Employees have one supervisor with a clear chain of command.
7. Team members are often co-located.
8. The project manager has full authority and control.
9. The project manager has little or no authority and could even be part-time.
10. Resources report directly to the project manager.

Exercise 4: Why would a projectized organization provide the most effective platform for building an effective team?

Power of Project Managers in Different Organizational Structures

- The authority of the project manager varies greatly depending on the organizational structure.
- In a projectized organization, the project manager has almost total authority.
- A strong matrix maintains many characteristics of a projectized organization where much of the authority rests with the project manager.
- In a balanced matrix, the authority is shared between the functional manager and the project manager and the project manager does not have full authority over the project and its funding.
- A weak matrix maintains many characteristics of functional organization; the project manager role is like a coordinator or expeditor (communication coordinator or staff assistant) than that of a true project manager.
- In a functional organization, the project manager has no real authority and power.

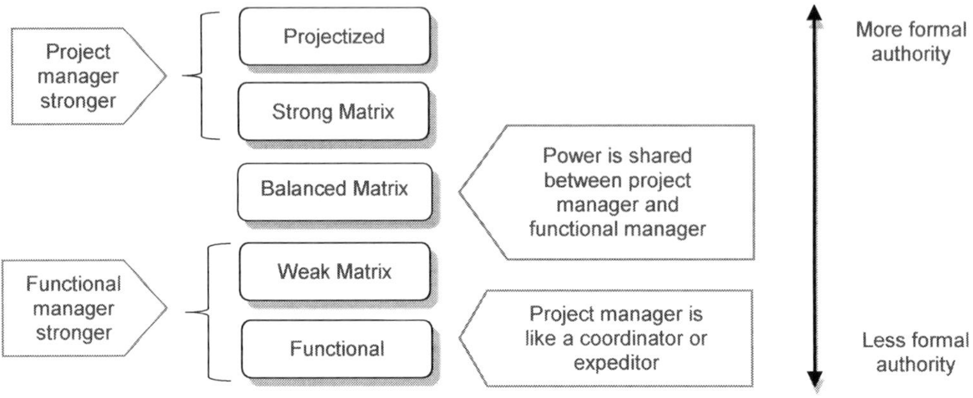

Figure 2-11:Power of a Project Manger in Different Organizational Structures

Project Roles

There are several roles in a project that are described briefly in the following table. Detailed explanations of these roles and their corresponding responsibilities are further discussed in the Human Resource Management chapter.

Roles	Description
Project Manager	The one responsible for managing the project
Project Sponsor	Provides financial resources for the project
Program Manager	Responsible for managing programs that may consist of several related projects
Portfolio Manager	Responsible for high-level governance of a group of projects or programs and other works to achieve strategic business goals
Functional Manager	Usually owns the resources that are loaned to the projects and has human resource responsibilities for these resources
Project Expeditor	Acts primarily as a staff assistant and communication coordinator. The project expeditor cannot personally make or enforce decisions
Project Coordinator	Similar to expeditor, except the project coordinator has some power to make decisions and reports to senior management
Customer/User	Individuals or organization that will receive the projects' product, service, or result
Performing Organization	The enterprise whose employees are involved in doing the project work
Project Management Team	Members directly involved in project management activities
Senior Management	Anyone in the organization senior to the project manager who may be responsible for prioritizing projects, defining strategic goals and objectives, and making sure projects are aligned with the organization's objectives
Project Team Members	Group performing the work of the project
Influencers	People or groups not related to the product or use of the product but who, due to position, can influence the course of a project positively or negatively
Stakeholder	The person has indirect or direct responsibility for the outcome of the project, he or she may exert influence over the project and its results, and will be affected by the outcome of the project
Steering Committee	A committee that consists of high level managers and executives who are involved in project prioritization and decision making processes

Table 2-7: Project Roles

Project Governance

Project governance is the management framework within which project decisions are made. The role of project governance is to provide a decision making framework that is logical, robust, and repeatable to govern an organization's capital investments. This framework provides the structure, processes, decision-making models, and tools to the project manager and team for managing the project. It also provides the team a comprehensive, coherent method of controlling the project and helps safeguarding project success by defining, documenting, and communicating reliable, repeatable project practices.

Project governance will:

- Outline the relationships between all internal and external groups involved in the project
- Describe the proper flow of information regarding the project to all stakeholders
- Ensure the appropriate review of issues encountered within each project
- Ensure that required approvals and direction for the project is obtained at each appropriate stage of the project

Important specific elements of good project governance include:

- A compelling business case, stating the objectives of the project, and specifying the in-scope and out-of-scope aspects
- A defined method of communication to each stakeholder
- A set of business-level requirements as agreed by all stakeholders
- An agreed specification for the project deliverables
- Clear assignment of project roles and responsibilities
- A current, published project plan that spans all project stages from project initiation through development to the transition to operations.
- A system of accurate upward status- and progress-reporting including time records.
- A central document repository for the project
- A process for the management and resolution of issues that arise during the project
- A process for the recording and communication of risks identified during the project
- A process for making decisions
- A process for phase exit or stage gate
- A standard for quality review of the key governance documents and of the project deliverables.

Core project governance principles

Project governance frameworks should be based around a number of core principles in order to ensure their effectiveness.

Principle 1: Ensure a single point of accountability for the success of the project
Principle 2: Ensure project ownership independent of asset ownership, service ownership or other stakeholder group
Principle 3: Ensure separation of stakeholder management and project decision making activities
Principle 4: Ensure separation of project governance and organizational governance structures

Roles

A key role in project governance is that of the project sponsor. The project sponsor has three main areas of responsibility which are to the board, the project manager, and the project stakeholders.

The board

For the board, the sponsor provides leadership on culture and values, owns the business case, keeps the project aligned with the organization's strategy and portfolio direction, governs project risk, works with other sponsors, focuses on realization of benefits, recommends opportunities to optimize cost/benefits, ensures continuity of sponsorship, and provides assurance, feedback, and lessons learned.

The project manager

For the project manager, the sponsor provides timely decisions, clarifies decision making framework, clarifies business priorities and strategy, communicates business issues, provides resources, engenders trust, manages relationships, supports the project manager's role and promotes ethical working.

Project stakeholders

For other project stakeholders, the project sponsor engages stakeholders, governs stakeholder communications, directs client relationship, directs governance of users, directs governance of suppliers and arbitrates between stakeholders.

Exercise 5:

Roles	Description
1. Project Manager	A. Provides financial resources for the project.
2. Project Sponsor	B. Anyone in the organization senior to the project manager who may be responsible for prioritizing projects, defining strategic goals and objectives, and making sure projects are aligned with the objectives.
3. Program Manager	C. The enterprise whose employees are involved in doing the project work.
4. Portfolio Manager	D. Acts primarily as a staff assistant and communication coordinator. This individual cannot personally make or enforce decisions.
5. Functional Manager	E. Acts primarily as a staff assistant and communication coordinator. This individual has some power to make decisions and reports to senior management.
6. Project Expeditor	F. The one responsible for managing the project.
7. Project Coordinator	G. Group performing the work of the project.
8. Customer/User	H. People or groups not related to the product or use of the product but who, due to position, can influence the course of a project positively or negatively.
9. Performing Organization	I. The person has indirect or direct responsibility for the outcome of the project, he or she may exert influence over the project and its results, and will be affected by the outcome of the project.
10. Management Team	J. Individuals or organization that will receive the projects' product, service, or result.
11. Senior Management	K. Responsible for managing programs that may consist of several related projects.
12. Team Members	L. A committee that consists of high level managers and executives who are involved in project prioritization and decision making processes.
13. Influencers	M. Responsible for high-level governance of a group of projects or programs and other works to achieve strategic business goals.
14. Stakeholder	N. Members directly involved in project management activities.
15. Steering Committee	O. Usually owns the resources that are loaned to the projects and has human resource responsibilities for these resources.

Exercise 6: Fill out the boxes with the information provided below.

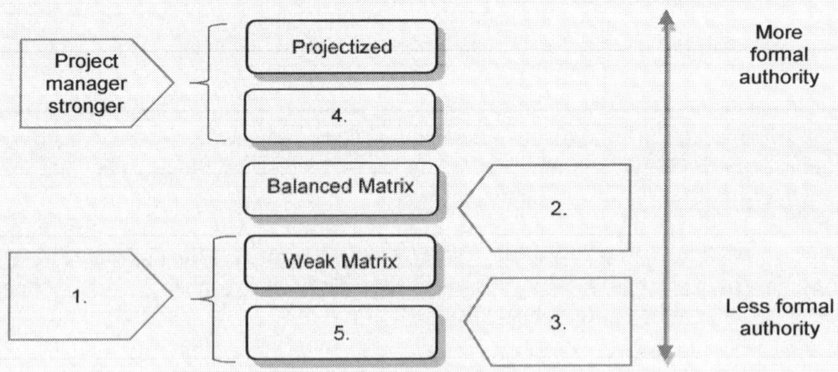

A. Functional manager stronger
B. Project manager is like a coordinator or expeditor
C. Functional
D. Strong Matrix
E. Power is shared between project manager and functional manager

Project Life Cycle

The project life cycle is simply a representation of the generally sequential and sometimes overlapping project phases that a project typically goes through. It is the logical breakdown of what needs to be done to produce the project deliverables, and sometimes it is referred to as the performing organization's methodology for projects.

The phases of a project life cycle can differ due to many factors (e.g., type of project, industry, size, and complexity, etc.). Regardless of the size and complexity, all projects can be mapped to the following life cycle structure:

- Initiating the project
- Planning and organizing the work of the project
- Performing the work of the project
- Closing out the project

Most projects are divided into phases, and all projects, regardless of the size, have a similar project life cycle structure. Some projects may have only one phase and others may consist of many phases. The work and the deliverables produced during the phase are typically unique to that phase. The number of the phases depends on the industry type and size and the complexity of the project. For instance, information technology projects may progress through phases, such as select, initiate, plan, requirements, design, program, test, implement, close, and maintain.

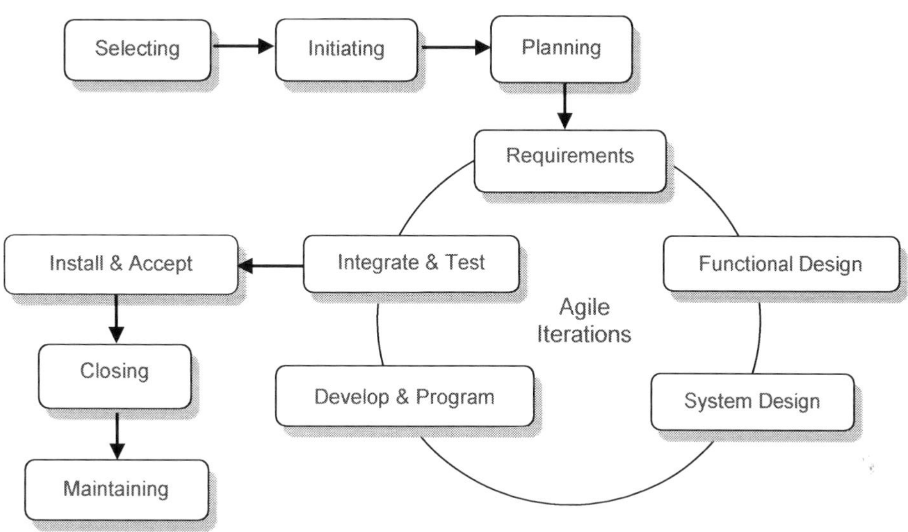

Figure 2-12: Project Life Cycle of a Software Development Project

Phase-to-Phase Relationships

Projects may consist of one or more phases and there are mainly three basic types of phase-to-phase relationships:

Sequential Relationship: In this kind of relationship, the successor phase can only start once the predecessor phase is completed.

This step-by-step approach eliminates the options to reduce the project duration, but it reduces uncertainties.

Overlapping Relationship: In this kind of relationship, the successor phase can start prior to the completion of the predecessor phase.

This approach can be applied as a schedule compression technique called "fast-tracking." This kind of relationship may increase project risk and potential for conflicts as a subsequent phase progresses before the accurate information is available from the previous phase.

Iterative Relationship: In this kind of relationship, a phase is planned at a given time and planning for subsequent phases is carried out as work progresses on the current phase or deliverables.

This type of relationship can reduce the ability to develop a long-term plan, but it is very suitable in an undefined, uncertain, and rapidly changing environment.

Project Life Cycle Types

There are different types of the project life cycle listed below:

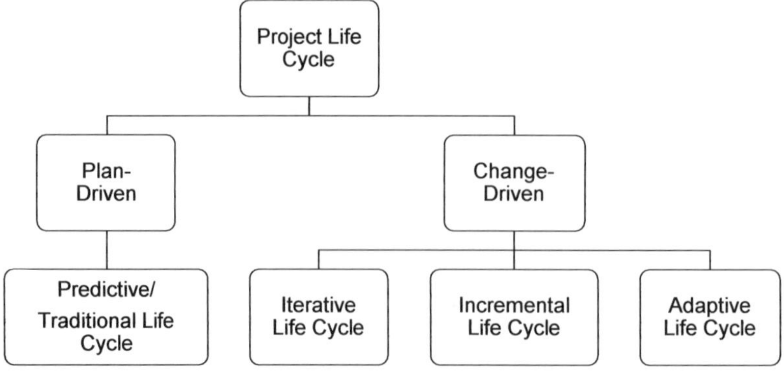

Figure 2-13: Project Life Cycle Types

Plan-Driven Project Life Cycle: Plan-driven projects have a predictive life cycle in which scope, schedule, and cost are determined in the early stage of the project prior to starting the project work to produce the deliverables. This predictive life cycle is also referred to as waterfall or traditional life cycle.

In this life cycle, when a project is initiated, the team will define the overall scope of the product and project, create a plan to develop the product, and then proceed through the phases to execute the plan within that defined scope. Any change to the scope will be carefully managed, and it may require re-planning and formal acceptance. For example, most construction projects are typically managed using this sort of predictive approach where projects usually go through feasibility, plan, design, build, and inspection and turnover phases.

Change-Driven Project Life Cycle: The change-driven project life cycle usually has a varying level of initial planning for scope, schedule, and cost.

Both iterative and incremental life cycles initially plan high-level scope that will be sufficient enough to estimate preliminary cost and schedule, and scope is developed a little more with each iteration.

Iterative Life Cycle: An iterative life cycle builds the concept in successive levels of detail to create the end result.

Incremental Life Cycle: An incremental life cycle delivers a complete, usable portion of the product in each iteration.

For instance, in an incremental life cycle to create a web-based application, requirements are prioritized into iterations that will deliver a fully functioning portion or modules of the application at the end of each iteration. On the other hand, a prototype will be created, the basic structure of the application will be developed, and more detail and resonance will be added until there is a fully functional application in case of an iterative life cycle.

A project may use a combination of iterative and incremental life cycles throughout the project or for phases of the project.

Adaptive Life Cycle: An adaptive life cycle is also referred to as an agile life cycle. An adaptive life cycle, as the name suggests, broadly defines the fixed scope, schedule, and cost with the clear understanding that it will be refined and adjusted as the project progresses. In this life cycle, requirements from customers are documented and prioritized in a backlog and work is planned in brief, quick increments so that the customers may modify and reprioritize requirements within time and cost constraints.

For instance, the adaptive approach is typically used in software development projects where the team conducts high-level feasibility study, design, and planning, followed by rapid, iterative periods of detailed design, coding, testing, and release.

Common Characteristics of Project Phases: All project phases result in one or more deliverables. They include a set of related work, the nature of which is described by the name of the phase (e.g., planning, testing, etc.).

All phases conclude with a review of the deliverable and related work:
- To determine if the project should continue and the next phase should be initiated.
- To detect and correct errors.
- These reviews are often called "phase exits" or "stage gates" or "kill points."

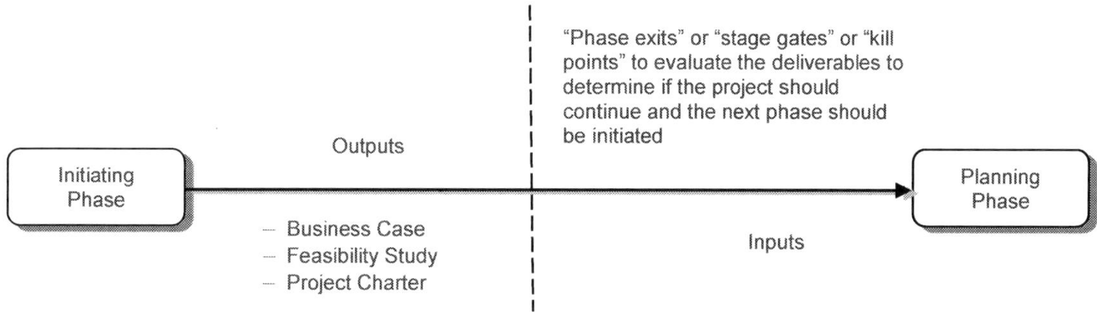

Figure 2-14: Phase Exits, Stage Gates, or Kill Points

- To take advantage of *progressive elaboration* (the product is defined and developed by incremental steps). It indicates that everything is not known upfront and that processes, assumptions, requirements, and decisions are continually reviewed and adjusted throughout the project life cycle as more comprehensive and specific information and more precise estimates become available.
- Cost and staffing start low, increase toward the end, and drop rapidly near closing.
- Project risk is highest at the beginning of the project and reduces as the project approaches its end.
- Stakeholder influence is highest at the start and diminishes as the project proceeds.
- Cost of changes is low in the beginning but extremely high later in the project.

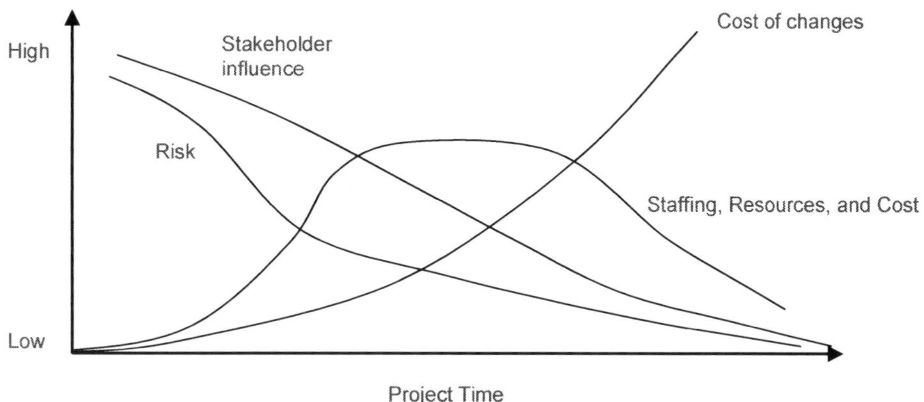

Figure 2-15: Common Characteristic of Project Phases

Exercise 7: Under what circumstances a project can be canceled?

Processes of a Project

Another way to view a project is as a series of processes. A process is a set of interrelated actions and activities that are performed to manage the work in order to achieve a pre-specified set of products, results, or services. The project management process incorporates the management efforts of initiating, planning, executing, monitoring & controlling, and closing of the project.

PMI has described the discipline of project management by defining forty-seven processes. These processes are characterized by three elements:

- **Inputs**: Any item, whether internal or external to the project that is required by a process before that process can proceed. It may be an output from a predecessor process.
- **Tools & Techniques**: Mechanisms applied to inputs to produce a product or result.
- **Outputs**: Documents or items that are produced by a process. Outputs may become an input to successor processes.

PMI groups processes into five areas, which collectively are defined as the project management process groups:

Process Group	Definition
Initiating Process Group	– Defines and authorizes a new project or a new phase of an existing project
Planning Process Group	– Defines and refines objectives – Plans the course of action to achieve objectives and scope
Executing Process Group	– Carries out the project management plan
Monitoring & Controlling Process Group	– Measures and monitors progress – Identifies variances from the project management plan – Recommends corrective actions
Closing Process Group	– Formally accepts the product, service, or result – Brings a project to an orderly close

Table 2-8: Process Groups of a Project

The following diagram illustrates how the process groups interact:

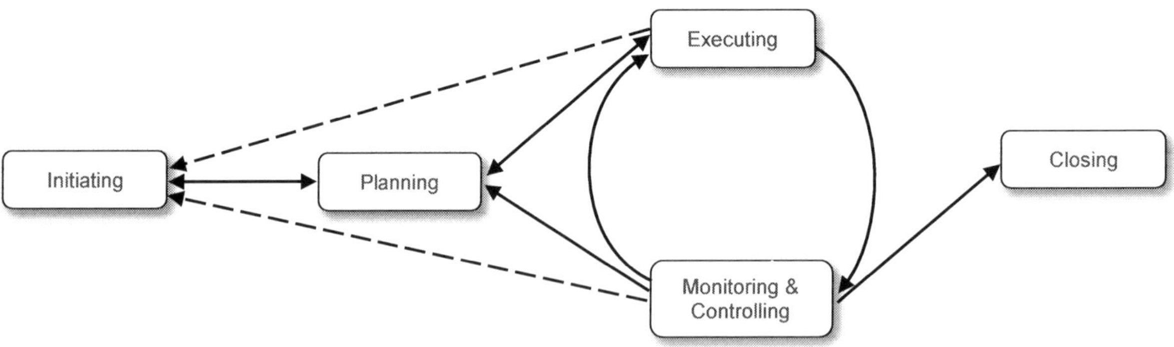

Figure 2-16: Project Management Process Groups

All the previously listed process groups have individual processes that collectively make up the group. For instance, the closing process group has two processes: Close Project and Close Procurements. All these process groups and their individual processes collectively make up the project management processes. The project manager and project team are responsible for determining which processes within each of these process groups are appropriate for the project considering the size, complexity, scope, available budget, inputs, tools & techniques, and outputs of each of these processes.

Note that there is a misconception that these process groups are the same as the project phases discussed in the previous chapter. It is critical to understand the difference between the project management process and the project life cycle and how overall project management process interacts with the project life cycle.

The project life cycle differs based on the industry, the organization, and the type of product, service, or result to be developed. Note that there is only one project management process, irrespective of the life cycle used. The process groups of initiating, planning, executing, monitoring & controlling, and closing do not change, even though we may consider variations in level of consideration and formality given to each of the process groups.

For small projects following a plan-driven or predictive life cycle, we may go through the overall project management process once, although portions of the process may be repeated or iterated throughout the project life cycle. On the other hand, these process groups are generally performed for each phase of a large project. For example, in a construction project, the effort of feasibility, plan, design, build, inspection, and turnover phases are each extensive enough to demand their own project management process groups. There would be a separate initiating process for each phase, followed by a planning effort for the work that will be carried out in the phase, the execution and control of the work, and a close-out of the phase, which typically involves a hand-off of deliverables (e.g., result of feasibility study). The project would then move on to the next phase and progress through the project management process groups again for the phase.

Large projects following a change-driven life cycle may be broken into phases, and then into smaller releases and iterations within those phases. The process groups are performed for each phase as well as generally within each release and iteration.

Exercise 8: You may have noticed that agile project management has been growing in popularity especially in the software development industry. List the major differences between agile project management and what is referred to as traditional project management.

Exercise 9: Match the following relationships with the proper description.

Relationship	Description
1. Sequential Relationship	A. In this kind of relationship, the successor phase can start prior to the completion of the predecessor phase.
2. Overlapping Relationship	B. In this kind of relationship, a phase is planned at a given time and planning for subsequent phases is carried out as work progresses on the current phase or deliverables.
3. Iterative Relationship	C. In this kind of relationship, the successor phase can only start once the predecessor phase is completed.

Exercise 10: List the necessity of stage gates / kill points / phase exits.

Common Inputs, Tools & Techniques, and Outputs

Out of the approximately 520 inputs, tools & techniques, and outputs for the forty-seven processes, there are a few common ones that are referred to repeatedly. Knowing them will greatly help you understand the entire project life cycle.

Project Information: A substantial amount of data and information is generated, collected, analyzed, transferred, and distributed in various formats to the team members, the sponsor, and other stakeholders throughout the project life cycle. Data is collected in the executing process group and then analyzed in context, aggregated, and transformed to become information during the monitoring & controlling process group. This information is stored, communicated, and distributed as reports in various formats.

Work Performance Data: The work performance data is the initial raw measurements and observations collected during the executing process when activities are performed to carry out the project work. For example, this can include the number of change requests, the number of defects, actual cost, actual durations, percent of work completed, actual start and finish dates of scheduled activities, quality, and technical performance measures, among other things.

Work Performance Information: The work performance data collected in the executing process is analyzed in context, aggregated, and transformed, becoming information used during the monitoring & controlling process. This can include, for example, the status of deliverables, the implementation status of change requests, and forecasted estimates to completion, among other things.

Work Performance Reports: The work performance information is compiled, stored, communicated, and distributed as reports in various formats to generate decisions or raise issues, awareness, or actions. This can include, for example, status reports, memos, information notes, electronic dashboard, recommendations, justifications, and updates.

Example: Suppose you are managing a project and receive the progress data from the team members. One of the activities took five days and was completed on May 7. You can define this as work performance data. The next step will be to analyze this data to make sure it conforms to the project management plan and assess what it means for the project as a whole. In our case the activity was supposed to be completed in three days and by May 5. Now, for the purpose of analysis, we need to ask some questions such as: Why did this activity take more time than planned? What will be the impact on the rest of the project? Is the performance of the project deteriorating? And were the resources on successor activities notified about the delay? You can define the result of this analysis as the work performance information. This work performance information can then be compiled, organized, stored, communicated, and distributed as the appropriate work performance reports.

The following diagram illustrates the flow of project information across various processes used to manage a project in different process groups:

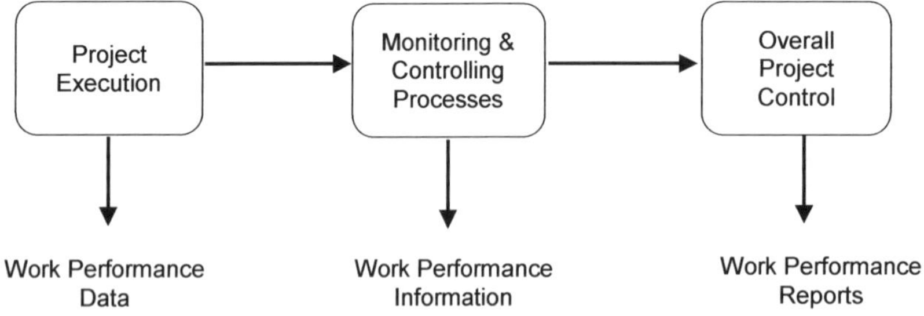

Figure 2-17: Flow of Project Information across Various Processes

Below is the list of common inputs, tools & techniques, and outputs:

Common Inputs	Enterprise Environmental Factors (EEF), Organizational Process Assets (OPA), project management plan, work performance data, work performance information, and work performance reports.
Common Tools & Techniques	Expert judgment, Project Management Information System (PMIS), meetings, facilitation techniques, and analytical techniques.
Common Outputs	Change requests, updates (project management plan, project documents, and OPA), work performance information, and work performance reports.

Table 2-9: Common Inputs, Tools & Techniques, and Outputs

Common Inputs

Enterprise Environmental Factors (EEFs): Enterprise Environmental Factors are things that impact the project but are not part of the project itself.

It is essential to consider these internal and external factors while planning the project to determine their influence on the project, as they can enhance or constrain project management options and may have negative or positive influences on the outcomes. Below are examples of some of the Enterprise Environmental Factors:

- Company's organizational structure
- Organizational values and work ethics
- Overall state of the marketplace
- Organization's and stakeholder's appetite for risk
- Political climate
- Government or industry standards
- Commercial database
- Project management information system in use such as an online automated system, scheduling software, information collection and distribution system, configuration management system, etc.
- Organizational culture and existing systems such as work authorization system
- Organization's established communication channels

Organizational Process Assets (OPAs): Organizational Process Assets are any and all process-related assets such as information, tools, documents, or knowledge that an organization possesses to help plan for the project.
These elements affect several aspects of the project, such as project management policies, performance measurement criteria, safety policies, templates, communication requirements, issue and defect management procedures, financial controls, risk control procedures, change control procedures, and the procedures used for authorizing work.
Project team members update and add to the Organizational Process Assets throughout the project as necessary. These assets can be grouped into two categories:

a. Processes and Procedures:

- Organizational policies, procedures, and guidelines for any area such as safety, ethics, risk, financial, change control, reporting, etc.
- Templates for common project documents such as WBS, network diagram, SOW, contract, etc.

b. Corporate Knowledgebase:

- Project information database
- Configuration management knowledgebase
- Historical information and past lessons learned
- Examples from previous projects
- Issue and defect management database
- Financial database

Exercise 11: Identify which of the following are Enterprise Environmental Factors (EEFs) and which are Organizational Process Assets (OPAs).

Items	EEF	OPA
1. Historical data of past projects		
2. Configuration management knowledgebase		
3. Local regulatory requirements		
4. Organization's process documents		
5. Commercial database		
6. Political scenario of the country		
7. Organization's culture		
8. Standard organization templates		
9. Economic scenario of project location		
10. Government or industry standards		

Project Management Plan: The project management plan is a single-approved document that defines how the project is executed, monitored and controlled, and closed. The project management plan can be documented at the summary level or at a very detailed level depending on the need of the project. It should include the following elements:

- Processes that will be used to perform each phase of the project
- The life cycle that will be used
- Methods for executing the work
- Change management plan for monitoring and controlling changes
- A configuration management plan
- Methods for configuration management
- Methods for identifying and maintaining the validity of performance baseline
- Communication needs and techniques to fulfill the needs of stakeholders

According to the PMBOK® guide, in addition to all these elements, the following subsidiary plans will be documented in the project management plan:

Components	Created in Process
Requirement management plan	Plan Scope Management
Scope management plan	Plan Scope Management
Scope baseline	Create WBS
Schedule management plan	Plan Time Management
Schedule baseline	Develop Schedule
Cost management plan	Plan Cost Management
Cost baseline	Determine Budget
Quality management plan	Plan Quality Management
Process improvement plan	Plan Quality Management
Human resource plan	Plan Human Resource Management
Communications management plan	Plan Communications Management
Risk management plan	Plan Risk Management
Procurement management plan	Plan Procurement Management
Stakeholder management plan	Plan Stakeholder Management
Change management plan	Develop Project Management Plan
Configuration management plan	Develop Project Management Plan

Table 2-10: Subsidiary Plans of a Project Management Plan

Common Tools & Techniques

Expert Judgment: Expert judgment means to rely upon or consult with an individual or group of people who have specialized skills, knowledge, and training in a particular area. Stakeholders, consultants, subject matter experts, PMO, industry experts, other experts in the organization, or other technical or professional organizations can be the experts in a project.

The tool of expert judgment is highly favored by the PMBOK® guide and is commonly found in planning processes. It can be used whenever the project manager and team do not have sufficient expertise.

Project Management Information System (PMIS): Project Management Information System (PMIS) is incorporated as part of the Enterprise Environmental Factors to several processes since it is part of the environment in which the project is performed. It consists of the data sources and tools & techniques used to gather, integrate, analyze, and disseminate the results of the combined outputs of the project management processes. It is an automated system that can serve as a repository for information and a tool to assist with communication and with tracking documents and deliverables. PMIS also supports the project from beginning to end by optimizing the schedule and helping collect and distribute information.

An important element of PMIS is the configuration management system, which also contains a change control system.

Configuration Management System: It is the subset of the Project Management Information System (PMIS) that describes the different versions and characteristics of the product, service, or result of the project and ensures accuracy and completeness of the description. Having a configuration management system is all about managing different configurations of a product. At some point in time, a product will be base lined, and different configurations, versions, and branches are managed from that point.

For instance, a software company may create a base package that must be implemented for each customer. The configuration management system is used to ensure that new custom functionalities don't break existing base features and that changes are evaluated across all relevant versions of the product.

Meetings: While planning, directing and managing project work, a project manager can use meetings to discuss various project-related topics and address concerns with the project team members and other stakeholders.

Facilitation Techniques: The project manager plays the role of a facilitator throughout the project life cycle. Facilitation techniques such as conflict resolution, brainstorming, problem solving, and meeting management are used by project manager to assist teams and individuals settle issues, reach consensus, and accomplish project activities.

Analytical Techniques: Various structured or unstructured techniques used to assess, analyze, and understand root causes, or forecast potential scenarios based on project or environmental variables.

Common Outputs

Change Requests: Through change requests, any changes impacting the project are communicated and appropriate actions are put into place to realign the objectives. These change requests, which may be direct or indirect, externally or internally initiated, and can be optional or contractually mandated, may modify the project's policies and procedures, scope, cost, schedule, or quality. Other change requests may cover required corrective and preventive actions to reduce the probability of negative impact in the future.

Change requests are frequent for scope, budget, and schedule as project work is executed, monitored, and controlled. These change requests must be processed through what is called a Perform Integrated Change Control process to be evaluated for impact on the entire project and ultimately approved or rejected. Change requests are typically related to the following:

- **Corrective Actions:** Any change to bring the expected future results in line with the project management plan.
- **Preventive Actions:** Any change to reduce the probability of the occurrence of a problem.
- **Defect Repairs:** Any recommendation to either repair the defect or completely replace a defective component.
- **Updates:** Any change to reflect updated or additional ideas or content to formally controlled documents, plans, and policies.

Exercise 12: Identify whether the following scenarios describe corrective or preventive actions:

1. You bring an extra set of training materials to your session, in case a new student shows up.
2. Your project is behind schedule, so you start working on activities in parallel.
3. You assign an extra resource to your project to deal with possible attrition.
4. An old machine was shutting down frequently, so you replaced it with a new one.

____

____

____

Updates (All Categories):

Updates of all kinds come out of planning, executing, and monitoring & controlling processes.

- Organizational Process Assets updates
- Project management plan updates
- Project documents updates

Work performance information and work performance reports described earlier are also common outputs.

Project Management Body of Knowledge

A Guide to the Project Management Body of Knowledge (PMBOK Guide) is a book which presents a set of standard terminology and guidelines (a body of knowledge) for project management.

The PMBOK Guide identifies that subset of the project management body of knowledge that is generally recognized as a good practice. "Generally recognized" means the knowledge and practices described are applicable to most projects most of the time and there is a consensus about their value and usefulness. "Good practice" means there is a general agreement that the application of the knowledge, skills, tools, and techniques can enhance the chance of success over many projects.

Other standards may be consulted for additional information, such as:

- The standard for Program Management addresses the management of programs.
- The standards for Portfolio Management addresses the management of portfolios.
- OPM3 is the PMI's organizational project management maturity model. This model helps to determine the level of ability of an organization to deliver the desired strategic outcomes in a reliable, controllable, and predictable manner.

Exercise 13: Crossword

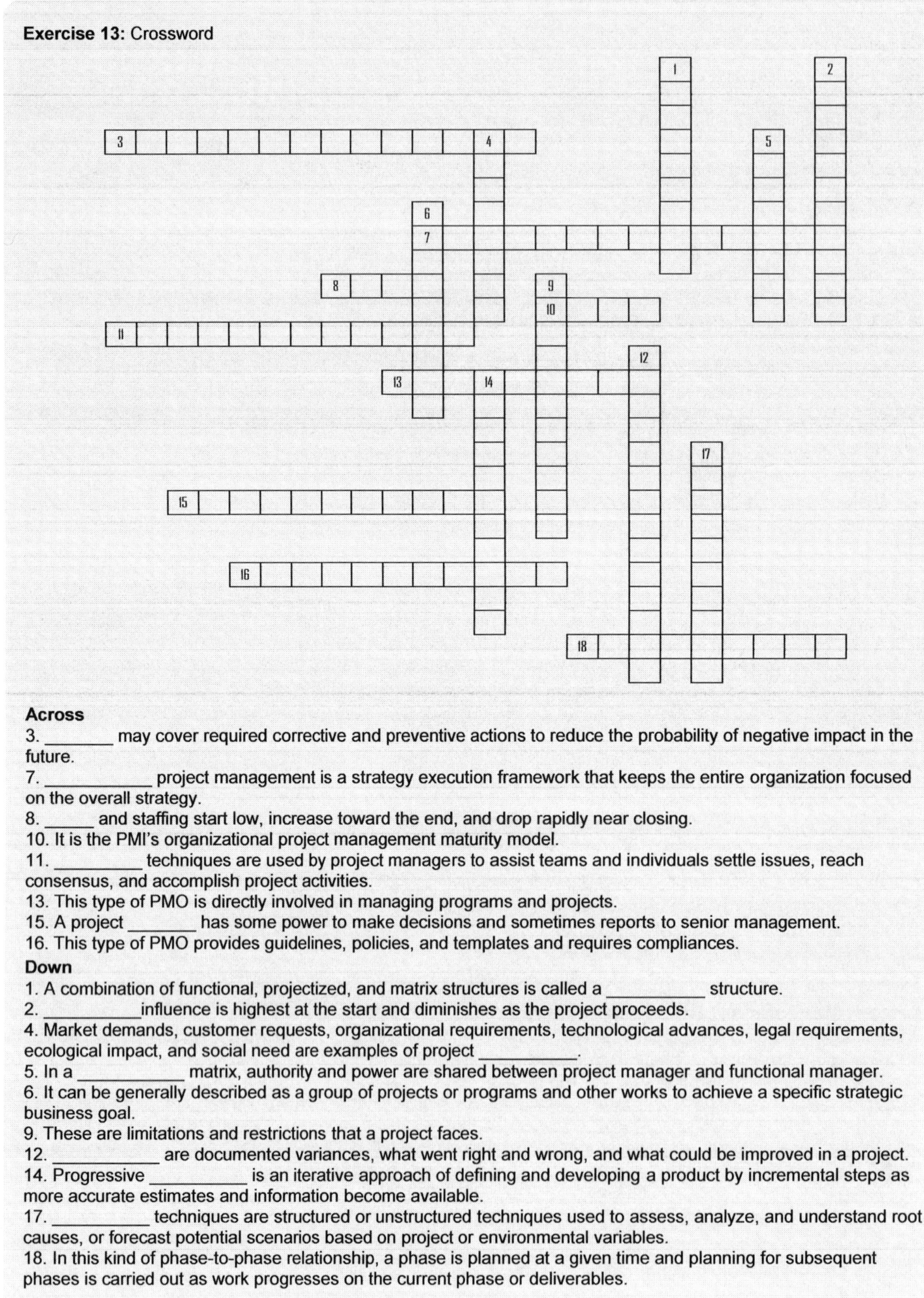

Across

3. _______ may cover required corrective and preventive actions to reduce the probability of negative impact in the future.
7. ___________ project management is a strategy execution framework that keeps the entire organization focused on the overall strategy.
8. _____ and staffing start low, increase toward the end, and drop rapidly near closing.
10. It is the PMI's organizational project management maturity model.
11. _________ techniques are used by project managers to assist teams and individuals settle issues, reach consensus, and accomplish project activities.
13. This type of PMO is directly involved in managing programs and projects.
15. A project _______ has some power to make decisions and sometimes reports to senior management.
16. This type of PMO provides guidelines, policies, and templates and requires compliances.

Down

1. A combination of functional, projectized, and matrix structures is called a __________ structure.
2. __________influence is highest at the start and diminishes as the project proceeds.
4. Market demands, customer requests, organizational requirements, technological advances, legal requirements, ecological impact, and social need are examples of project ___________.
5. In a ___________ matrix, authority and power are shared between project manager and functional manager.
6. It can be generally described as a group of projects or programs and other works to achieve a specific strategic business goal.
9. These are limitations and restrictions that a project faces.
12. ___________ are documented variances, what went right and wrong, and what could be improved in a project.
14. Progressive __________ is an iterative approach of defining and developing a product by incremental steps as more accurate estimates and information become available.
17. __________ techniques are structured or unstructured techniques used to assess, analyze, and understand root causes, or forecast potential scenarios based on project or environmental variables.
18. In this kind of phase-to-phase relationship, a phase is planned at a given time and planning for subsequent phases is carried out as work progresses on the current phase or deliverables.

Exercise 14: Answer the following:

1. Various structured or unstructured techniques used to assess, analyze, and understand root causes, or forecast potential scenarios based on project or environmental variables.
2. You assign an extra resource to your project to deal with possible attrition is an example of a ________ action.
3. In this kind of phase-to-phase relationship, a phase is planned at a given time and planning for subsequent phases is carried out as work progresses on the current phase or deliverables.
4. This staff assistant or communication coordinator has some power to make decisions and reports to senior management.
5. This type of PMO provides guidelines, policies, and templates and requires compliances.
6. In this organizational structure, authority and power are shared between project manager and functional manager.
7. An old machine was shutting down frequently, so you replaced it with a new one is an example of a ______ action.
8. It is the PMI's organizational project management maturity model.
9. It can be generally described as a group of projects or programs and other works to achieve a specific strategic business goal.
10. Techniques used by project managers to assist teams and individuals settle issues, reach consensus, and accomplish project activities.
11. Any continuing endeavor that produces many identical or nearly identical products or provides repetitive services.
12. __________influence is highest at the start and diminishes as the project proceeds.
13. This individual acts primarily as a staff assistant and communication coordinator but does not have any decision making power.
14. This type of PMO is directly involved in managing programs and projects.
15. In this organizational structure, employees have one supervisor with a clear chain of command and similar resources are grouped by specialty.
16. _____ and staffing start low, increase toward the end, and drop rapidly near closing.
17. It is the subset of the Project Management Information System (PMIS) that describes the different versions and characteristics of the product, service, or result of the project and ensures accuracy and completeness of the description.
18. An adaptive life cycle is also referred to as an ________ life cycle.
19. A predictive life cycle in which scope, schedule, and cost are determined in the early stage of the project prior to starting the project work to produce the deliverables.
20. It is a strategy execution framework that keeps the entire organization focused on the overall strategy.
21. This type of PMO mostly serves as a project repository and plays a consultative role.
22. A special project team or task force to handle a critical project and may have many characteristics of a projectized organizational structure and may include full-time staff from different functional departments with their own set of operating procedures, standards, and reporting structures.
23. In this type of phase-to-phase relationship, the successor phase can only start once the predecessor phase is completed.
24. Three defining characteristics of a project are _________.
25. Name some of the strategic considerations that play role in authorizing projects.
26. _______ may cover required corrective and preventive actions to reduce the probability of negative impact in the future.
27. These are limitations and restrictions such as limitations on time, budget, scope, quality, schedule, resource, and technology that a project faces.

Project Management Framework Summary

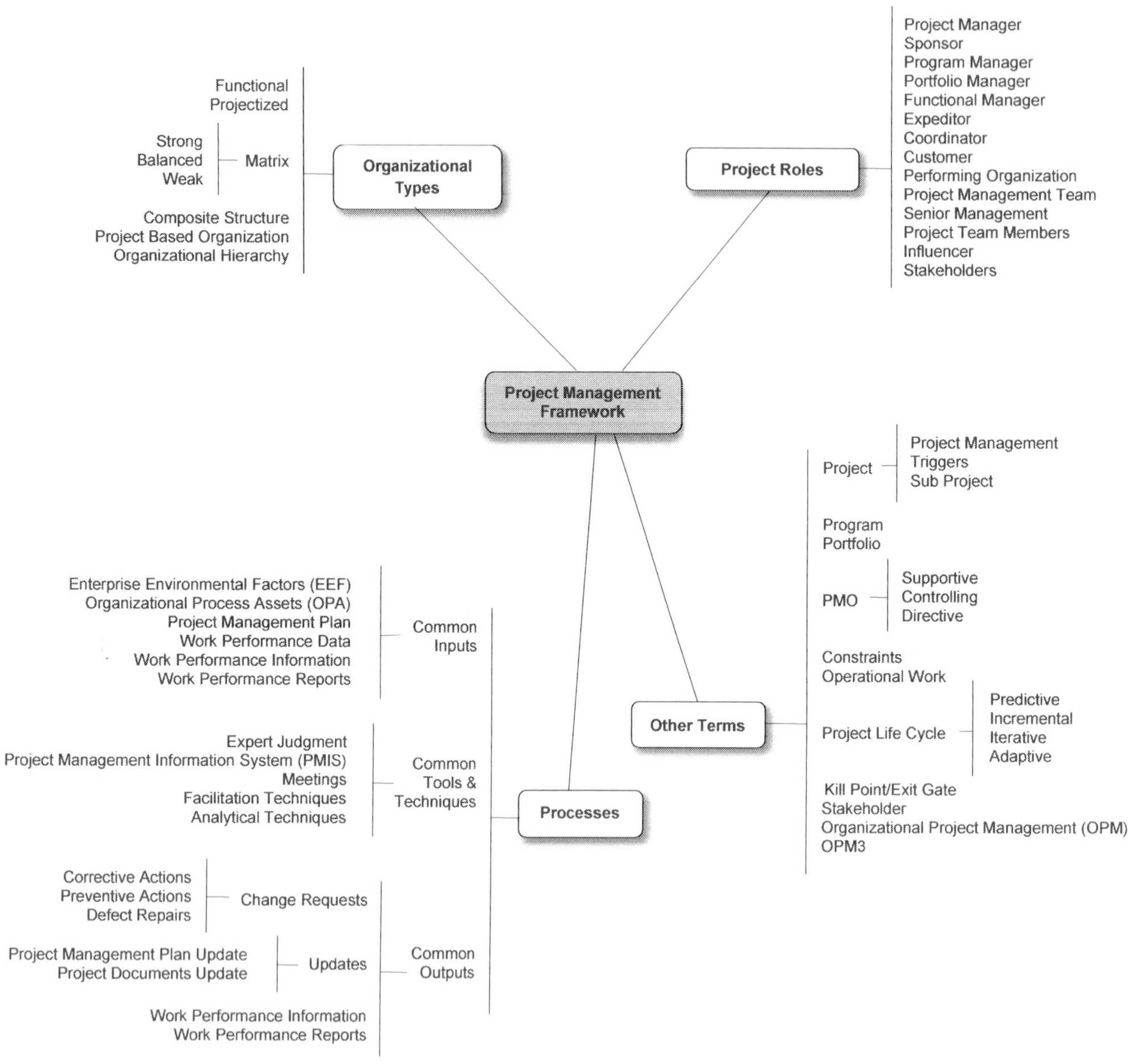

Figure 2-18: Project Management Framework Summary

Project Management Framework Key Terms

Operational Work: Continuing endeavor that produces many identical or nearly identical products
Project: A temporary endeavor that produces a unique product, service, or result
Project Triggers: Market demands, customer requests, organization requirements, technological advances, legal requirements, ecological impact, and social need.
Methodology: A set of steps to manage a project or an organization's specific implementation of project processes
Project Management: Application of knowledge, skills, tools & techniques, and resources to project activities to satisfy project requirements
Program: A group of related projects managed in a coordinated way
Portfolio: A group of projects or programs and other works to achieve a specific strategic goal
Organizational Project Management (OPM): A strategy execution framework that keeps the entire organization focused on overall strategy
OPM3: PMI's organizational project management maturity model

Project Roles

Project Manager: Responsible for leading the team and achieving the project objectives
Project Sponsor: Provides financial resources & accountable for enabling success
Program Manager: Responsible for managing programs
Portfolio Manager: Responsible for high-level governance of a group of projects or programs and other works
Functional Manager: Owns resources and has human resource responsibilities for them
Project Expeditor: Acts as a staff assistant and communication coordinator. Cannot make or enforce decisions
Project Coordinator: Has some power to make decisions and reports to higher management.
Customer/User: Individuals or organization that will receive the project's product, service, or result
Performing Organization: The enterprise whose employees are involved in doing the project work
Project Management Team: Members directly involved in PM activities
Senior Management: Anyone in the organization senior to project manager; prioritize projects, resolve organizational issues
Project Team Members: Group performing project work
Influencers: People who can influence a project positively or negatively
Stakeholder: A person who is interested, may exert influence, and will be affected by a project

Project Management Office (PMO)

Supportive: Serves as a repository and plays a consultative role; has a low level of control
Controlling: Provides guidelines, policies, and templates and requires compliances; has a moderate level of control
Directive: Directly involved in managing projects; has a high level of control

Organizational Types

Functional: An organization grouped by areas of specialization within different functional areas
Projectized: An organization structured by projects
Matrix: A hybrid organization. Types: Strong, balanced, weak
Composite Structure: A combination of functional, projectized, and matrix structures
Project-Based Organization (PBO): Creates a temporary framework around projects to achieve strategic goals
Organizational Hierarchy: Operational, middle management, and strategic

Project Life Cycle

Project Life Cycle: A representation of the generally sequential and sometimes overlapping project phases that a project goes through
Process: A set of interrelated actions and activities directed toward end results (ITTO)
Kill points/Exit gates/Stage gates: A review of deliverables at phase completion
Phases: Groups of project activities separated by exit gates to evaluate phase deliverables
Progressive Elaboration: An iterative approach of defining and developing a product by incremental steps as more accurate estimates and information become available

Other Terms

Historical Information: Information from previous projects
Lesson Learned: Documented variances, what went right and wrong, and what could be improved in a project
Baselines: An original plan plus all approved changes (scope, schedule, cost)
Project Manager's Skills: Being proactive, communicating, negotiating, problem-solving, influencing, and delegating.
Triple Constraints: Scope, time, and cost
Other Constraints: Quality, risk, resources, customer satisfaction, and communication

Project Management Framework Exercise Answers

Exercise 1:
- How are projects prioritized and selected?
- How are resources assigned to the project?
- How can resource management be improved?
- What are the key factors for project failures in the organization?
- How often projects are completed on time, within budget, and with the quality.
- How can project management be used to improve overall performance and efficiency?
- What is the level of customer satisfaction with the completed projects?
- Is the communication between different functional units effective?

Exercise 2:
1. Functional
2. Projectized
3. Matrix
4. Composite Structure

Exercise 3:
Projectized: 5, 7, 8, 10
Weak Matrix: 4
Balance Matrix: 3
Strong Matrix: 2
Functional: 1, 6, 9

Exercise 4:
- The project manager has full authority and control over the team.
- Efficient and convenient project organization.
- Strong loyalty to the project with no other priorities.
- The project team performance evaluation is linked to project success.

Exercise 5: 1. F, 2. A, 3. K, 4. M, 5. O, 6. D, 7. E, 8. J, 9. C, 10. N, 11.B, 12.G, 13.H, 14. I, 15. L

Exercise 6: 1. A, 2. E, 3. B, 4. D, 5. C

Exercise 7:
- The project doesn't make sense any more
- Changes in organizational strategic goals and objectives
- Changes in technology
- Market shifts
- Additional risks have been identified
- Lack of resources
- Lack of organizational capability

Exercise 8: Traditional or plan-driven projects have a predictive life cycle in which scope, schedule, and cost are determined in the early stage of the project prior to starting the project work to produce the deliverables.
In this life cycle, when a project is initiated, the team will define the overall scope of the product and project, create a plan to develop the product, and then proceed through the phases to execute the plan within that defined scope.
On the other hand, an agile life cycle broadly defines the fixed scope, schedule, and cost with the clear understanding that it will be refined and adjusted as the project progresses. Here, the focus is on shorter term results and deliverables.

Exercise 9:
1. C
2. A
3. B

Exercise 10:
- To determine if the project should continue and the next phase should be initiated.
- To detect and correct errors.

Exercise 11:
Enterprise Environmental Factors: 3, 5, 6, 7, 9, 10
Organizational Process Assets: 1, 2, 4, 8

Exercise 12:
1. Preventive action
2. Corrective action
3. Preventive action
4. Corrective action

Exercise 13:

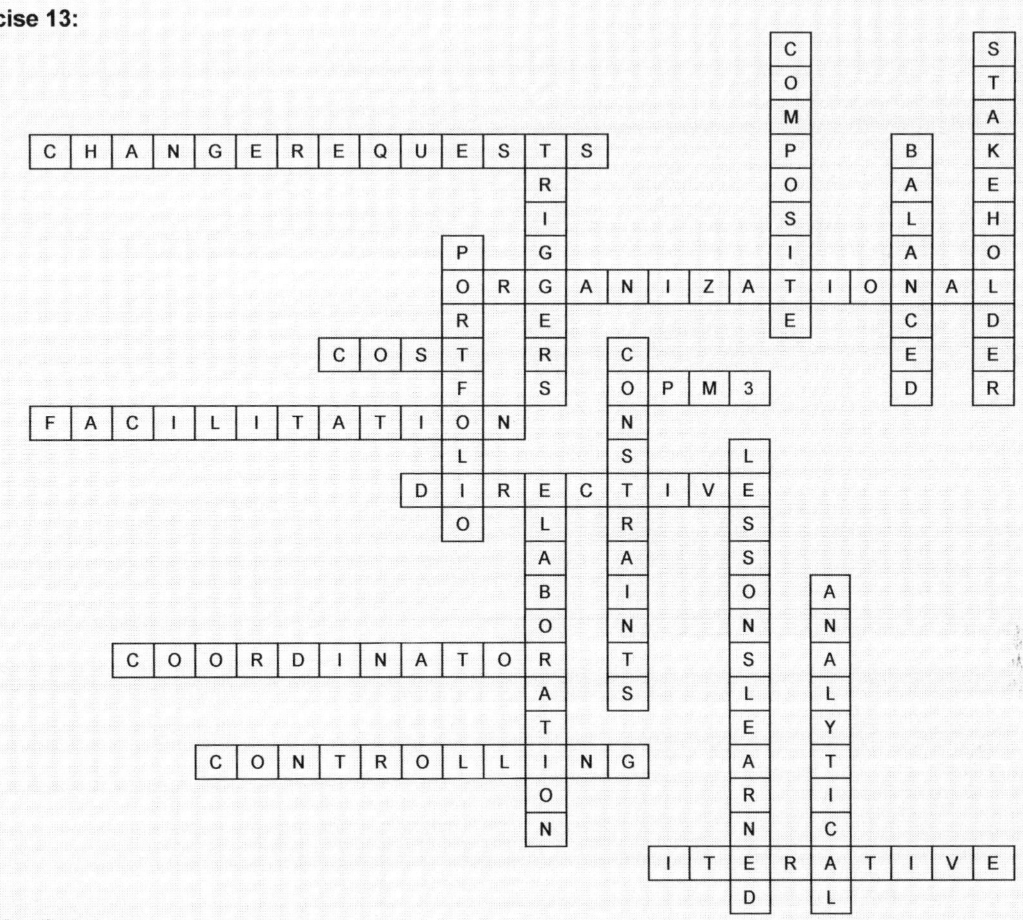

Exercise 14:

1. Analytical techniques
2. Preventive
3. Iterative relationship
4. Project coordinator
5. Controlling
6. Balanced matrix organization
7. Corrective
8. OPM3
9. Portfolio
10. Facilitation techniques
11. Operational work
12. Stakeholder
13. Project expeditor
14. Directive
15. Functional organization
16. Cost
17. Configuration management system
18. Agile
19. Plan-driven project life cycle
20. Organizational project management (OPM)
21. Supportive
22. Composite structure
23. Sequential relationship
24. Temporary, unique, and progressively elaborated
25. Market demands, customer requests, organizational requirements, technological advances, legal requirements, ecological impact, and social need
26. Change requests
27. Constraints

Project Management Framework Exam Tips

- Be able to differentiate among projects, programs, operational work, and portfolio.
- Be able to identify the key features of all five process groups.
- Be able to differentiate among the different organizational structures and authority of the project manager.
- Be able to differentiate among different types of PMOs and their roles.
- Be able to name common inputs, tools & techniques, and outputs.
- Be able to differentiate among different types of project life cycles.
- Be familiar with the concepts and terms in the project management framework summary table, Figure 2-18: Project Management Framework Summary.

Project Management Framework Questions

1. You have been assigned as project manager to implement a new and innovative smartphone application in a balanced matrix organizational structure. You experience difficulties in obtaining and assigning project resources in your project due to which one of the following factors?
   A. The power and authority are shared between you and the functional manager, and you do not have full authority over the project and its funding.
   B. Your role is like a coordinator or expeditor (communication coordinator or staff assistant).
   C. You have no real authority and power.
   D. The project budget is fully controlled by the functional manager.

2. Project Management Office (PMO), which is a centralized organizational unit to oversee and coordinate the management of projects and programs under its domain throughout the organization, has all of the following functions EXCEPT:
   A. Identify and develop the organization's methodology, administrative practices, guidelines, policies, procedures, and rules.
   B. Establish and maintain templates, policies, procedures, best practices, and standards for project management methodologies.
   C. Monitor compliance with organizational project management processes, policies, procedures, and other items.
   D. Be involved heavily during project initiation as a key decision maker and integral stakeholder to make recommendations, prioritize projects, terminate projects, or take other actions as required.

3. What is the name of PMI's organization maturity model for project management that helps to determine the level of ability of an organization to deliver the desired strategic outcomes in a reliable, controllable, and predictable manner?
   A. ISO 9000
   B. OPM3
   C. Project Management Maturity Model (PMMM)
   D. Six Sigma

4. Which one of the following PMO structures mostly provides guidelines, policies, and templates and requires compliances and usually has a moderate level of control over projects and programs?
   A. Supportive
   B. Controlling
   C. Directive
   D. Constructive

5. You are a project manager overseeing a web-based automation project in a weak matrix organization. You are playing the role of a communication coordinator with little power to make decisions and sometimes report to a high-level manager. Your role can be defined as a:
   A. Team lead
   B. Project coordinator
   C. Lead coordinator
   D. Project expeditor

6. Success in portfolio management, which can be generally described as a group of projects or programs and other works to achieve a specific strategic business goal, is generally defined as:
   A. Aggregate performance of all components.
   B. Control of changes to specific products and services.
   C. Compliance with schedule, budget, and specifications requirements.
   D. Realization of the business benefits and financial objectives.

7. Which one of the following PMO structures mostly serves as a project repository, plays a consultative role, and usually has a low level of control over projects and programs?
   A. Supportive
   B. Controlling
   C. Directive
   D. Constructive

8. You are overseeing the implementation of the internal website of your organization to view the company's event calendar. Your role is to coordinate activities, resources, equipment, and information on the project, but you have limited authority in making project decisions and have to negotiate with the functional manager to get required resources for your project. Which of the following kind of organization are you working in?
   A. Balanced matrix
   B. Composite structure
   C. Weak matrix
   D. Strong matrix

9. You are overseeing a complex project to implement a new wireless media streaming device. Due to the complex nature of the project, you need several highly skilled technical resources with very specialized expertise and domain knowledge. You obtain these resources from the organization resource pool and different departments, specifying the duration and bandwidth for which they will be required. You also commit to release these resources to respective departments once your needs are fulfilled. You are working in which kind of organizational structure?
   A. Composite structure
   B. Functional
   C. Projectized
   D. Matrix

10. Which one of the following is a strategy execution framework that keeps the entire organization focused on the overall strategy and provides guidance on how to prioritize, manage, execute, and measure projects, programs, portfolios, and other organizational work and practices to achieve a better result, improved performance, and a substantial advantage over the competitors?
   A. Organizational Project Management (OPM)
   B. Portfolio management
   C. Program management
   D. Process management

11. A software firm is in the process of implementing a critical accounting application for a dentist's office. In order to implement the project, full-time staff from several departments are selected to create a special project team or task force. It was decided that the task force members would not report to their functional managers or work on their functional activities while working on this critical project. This type of organizational structure is called:
   A. Functional organization
   B. Composite structure
   C. Projectized organization
   D. Balanced matrix organization

12. Which one of the following is NOT true about functional organizational structure?
   A. Project work is considered to be priority work in all functional groups.
   B. Similar resources are grouped by specialists.
   C. The project manager has little or no authority and could even be part time.
   D. Multiple projects compete for limited resources and priority.

13. Which one of the following is the logical breakdown of what needs to be done to produce the project deliverables and is sometimes referred to as the performing organization's methodology for projects?
   A. Product life cycle
   B. Project life cycle
   C. Feedback loop
   D. Product development

14. The application of knowledge, skills, tools, and techniques to satisfy the project needs by establishing project objectives, identifying project requirements, managing stakeholders, and balancing project constraints (i.e., cost, time, quality, scope, risk, and others) is referred to as:
   A. Project management
   B. Project administration
   C. Project initiation
   D. Project coordination

15. All of the following are examples of Organizational Process Assets EXCEPT:
   A. Organizational policies, procedures, and guidelines for any area such as safety, ethics, risk, financial, change control, reporting, and others.
   B. Existing facilities and infrastructure.
   C. Templates for common project documents such as WBS, network diagram, SOW, and contract.
   D. Historical information and past lessons learned.

16. You are a team member working on a software application project. You realize that the project manager is choosing a project life cycle that has a predictive life cycle in which scope, schedule, and cost are determined in the early stage of the project prior to starting project work to produce the deliverables. This type of project life cycle is also known as:
   A. Change-driven project life cycle
   B. Adaptive project life cycle
   C. Preferred project life cycle
   D. Plan-driven project life cycle

17. All project phases conclude with a review of the deliverables and related work (phase exits or stage gates or kill points) for the purpose of:
   A. Determining if the project should continue and the next phase should be initiated.
   B. Detecting defects and correcting errors.
   C. Assessing project risks.
   D. Enforcing formal control procedure of the project.

18. A project life cycle is a representation of the generally sequential and sometimes overlapping project phases that a project typically goes through. All of the following statements about the project life cycle are true EXCEPT:
   A. Cost and staffing start low, increase toward the end, and drop rapidly near closing.
   B. Project risk is highest at the beginning of the project and reduces as the project approaches its end.
   C. Stakeholder influence is lowest at the start and increases as the project proceeds.
   D. Cost of changes is low in the beginning but extremely high later in the project.

19. The level of power and authority of a project manager may fluctuate due to various factors. Typically, how much power and authority a project manager will have depends on which of the following?
   A. The organizational structure
   B. The negotiation skills of the project manager
   C. Project management knowledge and technical competency of the project manager
   D. The relationship of the project manager with senior management, especially with the sponsor

20. Which one of the following creates a temporary framework around their projects to achieve strategic goals and to minimize the impact, constraints, and obstacles of the established organizational structure?
   A. Project-Based Organization (PBO)
   B. Organizational hierarchy
   C. Composite structure
   D. Functional organization

21. In what kind of phase-to-phase relationship is a phase planned at a given time and planning for a subsequent phase is carried out as work progresses on the current phase or deliverables?
   A. Multi-phase relationship
   B. Iterative relationship
   C. Overlapping relationship
   D. Sequential relationship

22. Which one of the following is generally considered to be the characteristic of operational works?
   A. It is a continuing endeavor that produces many identical or nearly identical products or provides repetition.
   B. It is temporary in nature and has a definite beginning and ending.
   C. It is completed when its goals and objectives have been met and signed off by the stakeholders.
   D. It is a unique undertaking.

23. You are overseeing a project to implement a new video game console. Since everything is not known upfront, you take the approach of defining and developing the product by incremental steps and continually reviewing and adjusting processes, assumptions, requirements, and decisions throughout the project life cycle as the project progresses. You are engaged in which of the following?
   A. Project selection
   B. Monitoring & Controlling
   C. Progressive elaboration
   D. Decomposition

24. Which one of the following is TRUE about power of the project managers in different organizational structures?
    A. In a projectized organization, the project manager has no real authority and power.
    B. A strong matrix maintains many characteristics of projectized organization, where much of the authority rests with the project manager.
    C. In a weak matrix, the authority is shared between the functional manager and the project manager; the project manager does not have full authority over the project and its funding.
    D. A balanced matrix maintains many characteristics of a functional matrix; the project manager role is like that of a coordinator or expeditor (communication coordinator or staff assistant) than that of a true project manager.

25. You are managing a group of related or unrelated projects or programs and other works to achieve specific strategic business objectives and goals. You are a:
    A. Program owner
    B. Project manager
    C. Program manager
    D. Portfolio manager

26. As a project manager in a balanced matrix organization, what type of authority you have?
    A. Low to moderate
    B. Little to none
    C. High to almost total
    D. Moderate to high

27. You took over a software development project from another project manager who just left the company. You realize that the project is in a mess as there is a lack of management control and the previous project manager managed the project without much project organization. You decided to develop specific work plans for each of the 30 work packages and soon realize that the plan would help each phase, but would not control the integration of those phases into a cohesive whole. To your surprise, you also find out that there is no clearly defined project deliverables. You are in a desperate need to organize the project as soon as you can. What will be the BEST course of action?
    A. Capture lessons learned as you progress and update organizational process assets.
    B. Report the poor condition of the project to management.
    C. Adapt a life cycle approach to the project.
    D. Develop a detailed description of project deliverables.

28. You just completed a critical data center project for your organization. Currently the support team is conducting ongoing operations and maintenance to ensure that all routers, switches, firewalls, PCs, servers, and digital storages are operating as planned. A large portion of your project budget is allocated to maintenance and operations to run the data center smoothly. You will be sending out daily status updates and resolving issues but there is no need for planning or providing documentation. This ongoing operations and maintenance is extremely important to the products of your data center project and should be consider as:
    A. Not a part of your project
    B. An entirely separate project
    C. A separate phase in your project life cycle
    D. Activities in the closing process group

29. Steve is very concerned about all major constraints on his project as these constraints provide a framework for understanding trade-offs in managing competing project requirements. He identified scope, time, cost, quality, risk, resources, communications, and customer satisfaction to be the major constraints. Which one of the following is the prioritized order of all these constraints?
    A. Scope, time, cost, quality, risk, resources, communications, and customer satisfaction
    B. Time, scope, cost, quality, risk, resources, communications, and customer satisfaction
    C. Cost, scope, time, quality, risk, resources, communications, and customer satisfaction
    D. The all are of equal importance unless stated otherwise

30. The management framework within which project decisions are made is called:
    A. Project Management Information System (PMIS)
    B. Configuration management system
    C. Project management plan
    D. Project governance

Project Management Framework Answers

1. A: In a balanced matrix organization, the project manager is assigned full time, and the authority of the project manager is usually at an equal level with the functional manager. This can result in conflict regarding resource assignments and priorities and in the general management of the project. The control of the budget is shared between the project manager and the functional manager.

2. A: The PMO identifies and develops the project management methodology, best practices, policies, procedures, and standards but not the organizational methodology, administrative practices, guidelines, policies, procedures, and rules.

3. B: OPM3 is the PMI's organizational project management maturity model. This model helps to determine the level of ability of an organization to deliver the desired strategic outcomes in a reliable, controllable, and predictable manner.

4. B: The controlling PMO provides guidelines, policies, and templates and requires compliances. This type of PMO usually has a moderate level of control over projects and programs.

5. B: Both the project coordinator and the project expeditor play a supportive role to the project manager. A project coordinator role is similar to a project expeditor role as they both act primarily as staff assistants and communication coordinators. However, unlike a project expeditor, a project coordinator has some power to make decisions and reports to a high-level manager.

6. A: Portfolio management encompasses identifying, prioritizing, authorizing, managing, and controlling the collection of projects, programs, other work, and sometimes other portfolios to achieve strategic business objectives. It is generally associated with the relationships between components in the portfolio, effective resource management to protect priority components, and the aggregate results of the portfolio as they relate to strategic performance. The components may not be related other than the fact that they are helping to achieve the common strategic goal.

7. A: A Supportive PMO mostly serves as a project repository and plays a consultative role. This type of PMO usually has a low level of control over projects and programs.

8. C: You are working in a weak matrix organization. Your role is of a project expeditor or project coordinator where you mostly act as a staff assistant and communication coordinator with limited authority and no control over the project's budget. You have to negotiate with the functional manager to get needed resources for the project.

9. D: In the matrix structure, the personnel and other resources that a project manager requires are not permanently assigned to the project but are obtained from a pool and are controlled and monitored by a functional manager. Personnel required to perform specific functions in a particular project are assigned for the period necessary and are then returned to the control of the functional manager for reassignment.

10. A: Organizational Project Management (OPM) is a strategy execution framework that keeps the entire organization focused on the overall strategy. It provides guidance on how to prioritize, manage, execute, and measure projects, programs, portfolios, and other organizational work and practices to achieve a better result, improved performance, and a substantial advantage over the competitors. A portfolio can be generally described as a group of projects or programs and other works to achieve a specific strategic business goal. The programs may not be related other than the fact that they are helping to achieve the common strategic goal. A program is a group of related projects managed in a coordinated way to capitalize benefits and control what is not achievable by managing those projects individually. Program management is the centralized and coordinated management of a program to obtain the strategic objectives and benefits sought through the inception of the program. Project management is the application of knowledge, skills, tools, and techniques to satisfy project requirements.

11. B: Composite structure is a combination of functional, projectized, and matrix organizational structures. For example, a functional organization may create a special project team or task force to handle a critical project and may have many characteristics of projectized organization; it may include full-time staff from different functional departments with their own set of operating procedures, standards, and reporting structure.

12. A: In a functional structure, similar resources are grouped by technical expertise and are assigned to one supervisor. Team members give more importance to their functional responsibility to the detriment of the project.

13. B: The project life cycle is the logical breakdown of what needs to be done to produce the project deliverables, and sometimes it is referred to as the performing organization's methodology for projects. On the other hand, a product life cycle consists of generally sequential, nonoverlapping product phases determined by the manufacturing and control needs of the organization. For instance, as predicted by Moore's law, each year a microprocessor company introduces new models of processors that are faster and more powerful than their predecessors. Microprocessors that are obsolete or do not sell well are quickly retired from production. This product life cycle begins in R and D, extends to manufacturing, and finally ends with phase out.

14. A: Project management is the application of knowledge, skills, tools, and techniques to satisfy project requirements.

15. B: Enterprise Environmental Factors are things that impact the project but are not part of the project itself. Existing facilities and infrastructure are Enterprise Environmental Factors.

16. D: Plan-driven projects have a predictive life cycle in which scope, schedule, and cost are determined in the early stage of the project prior to starting project work to produce the deliverables. This predictive life cycle is also referred to as waterfall or traditional life cycle. For example, most construction projects are typically managed using this sort of predictive approach. A change-driven project life cycle usually has a varying level of initial planning for scope, schedule, and cost. An adaptive life cycle is a change-driven life cycle, and it is also referred to as an agile life cycle. An adaptive life cycle, as the name suggests, broadly defines the fixed scope, schedule, and cost with the clear understanding that they will be refined and adjusted as the project progresses. Preferred project life cycle is a made-up term.

17. A: At the conclusion of a project phase, the project manager and team should assess the performance of the project and determine if acceptable conditions exist to support a decision to continue or terminate the project. If the decision is to move forward with the project, then the decision is also made about whether the next phase should be initiated or not. Risk levels will vary as the project progresses, and the end of a phase is generally considered to be a good point to reassess risk. Project control procedures should be enforced throughout the project life cycle.

18. C: Stakeholder influence is highest at the start and diminishes as the project proceeds.

19. A: The authority of the project manager varies greatly depending on the organizational structure. In a projectized organization, the project manager has almost total authority. A strong matrix maintains many characteristics of projectized organization where much of the authority rests with the project manager. In a balanced matrix, the authority is shared between the functional manager and the project manager, and the project manager does not have full authority over the project and its funding. A weak matrix maintains many characteristics of a functional organization; the project manager's role is like that of a coordinator or expeditor (communication coordinator or staff assistant) than that of a true project manager. In a functional organization, the project manager has no real authority and power. Relationship, negotiation skills, and technical ability may affect the level of authority in some organizations, but managerial structure is generally the major factor.

20. A: A Project-Based Organization (PBO) creates a temporary framework around its projects to achieve strategic goals and to minimize the impact, constraints, and obstacles of the established organizational structure.

21. B: In an iterative relationship, a phase is planned at a given time; planning for a subsequent phase is carried out as work progresses on the current phase or deliverables. This type of relationship can reduce the ability to develop long-term planning, but it is very suitable in an undefined, uncertain, and rapidly changing environment. In a sequential relationship, the successor phase can only start once the predecessor phase is completed. This step-by-step approach eliminates the options to reduce the project duration, but it reduces uncertainties.

In an overlapping relationship, the successor phase can start prior to the completion of the predecessor phase. This technique can be applied as a schedule compression technique called "fast-tracking." This kind of relationship may increase project risk and potential for conflicts as a subsequent phase progresses before the accurate information is available from the previous phase.

22. A: Operational works are ongoing and support the day-to-day functions of an organization. Operational work differs from project work as operational work is any continuing endeavor that produces many identical or nearly identical products or provides repetitive services (e.g., frying burgers, manufacturing cars, and teaching algebra).

23. C: Progressive elaboration is defined as moving forward in increments and adding more detail as the project progresses.

24. B: The authority of the project manager varies greatly depending on the organizational structure. In a projectized organization, the project manager has almost total authority. A strong matrix maintains many characteristics of projectized organization where much of the authority rests with the project manager. In a balanced matrix, the authority is shared between the functional manager and the project manager; the project manager does not have full authority over the project and its funding. A weak matrix maintains many characteristics of a functional organization; the project manager role is like that of a coordinator or expeditor (communication coordinator or staff assistant) than that of a true project manager. In a functional organization, the project manager has no real authority and power.

25. D: A portfolio can be generally described as a group of projects or programs and other works to achieve a specific strategic business goal. The programs may not be related other than the fact that they are helping to achieve the common strategic goal. A portfolio manager is usually assigned to manage these groups of projects, programs, and other works. Portfolio management encompasses identifying, prioritizing, authorizing, managing, and controlling the collection of projects, programs, other work, and sometimes other portfolios to achieve strategic business objectives. For example, a construction business has several business units such as retail, single and multifamily residential, and others. Collectively, all the programs, projects, and work within all of these business units make up the portfolio for this construction business.

26. A: A project manager has a low to moderate authority in a balanced matrix organization.

27. C: Adapting a life cycle approach to effectively run the project will ensure overall control and successful completion of the deliverables. You may want to report the situation to management but it will not really solve the issue. Capturing lessons learned will certainly assist with the subsequent phases, but would not really help with controlling the project. Developing a detailed description of the project deliverables would not improve control.

28. A: Operations and maintenance are not considered to be temporary as they are ongoing. A project is always unique and temporary in nature. Thus, these activities should not be considered as a project or eve part of a project.

29. D: All major constraints are of equal importance unless stated otherwise. Senior management in an organization gets involved in setting priorities among these constraints directly or indirectly. The primary job of the project manager is to manage these different project constraints by assessing the situations, prioritizing competing demands, and analyzing the impact of changes on all the constraints.

30. D: Project governance is the management framework within which project decisions are made. The role of project governance is to provide a decision making framework that is logical, robust, and repeatable to govern an organization's capital investments.

This framework provides the structure, processes, decision-making models, and tools to the project manager and team for managing the project. It also provides the team a comprehensive, coherent method of controlling the project and helps safeguarding project success by defining, documenting, and communicating reliable, repeatable project practices.

The PMIS consists of the data sources and tools & techniques used to gather, integrate, analyze, and disseminate the results of the combined outputs of the project management processes. It is an automated system that can serve as a repository for information and a tool to assist with communication and with tracking documents and deliverables. The PMIS also supports the project from beginning to end by optimizing the schedule and helping collect and distribute information.

The configuration management system is the subset of the Project Management Information System (PMIS) that describes the different versions and characteristics of the product, service, or result of the project and ensures accuracy and completeness of the description.

The project management plan is a single-approved document that defines how the project is executed, monitored and controlled, and closed.

CHAPTER 3

PROJECT MANAGEMENT PROCESSES

Processes of a Project

Another way to view a project is as a series of processes. A process is a set of interrelated actions and activities that are performed to manage the work in order to achieve a pre-specified set of products, results, or services. The project management processes include the management efforts of initiating, planning, executing, monitoring & controlling, and closing.

PMI has described the discipline of project management by defining forty-seven processes. These processes are characterized by three elements:

- **Inputs:** Any item, whether internal or external to the project that is required by a process before that process can proceed. It may be an output from a predecessor process.
- **Tools & Techniques:** Mechanisms applied to inputs to produce a product or result.
- **Outputs:** Documents or items that are produced by a process. They may become inputs to a successor process.

For instance, a process called "Cook Noodles" may have the following inputs, tools & techniques, and outputs:

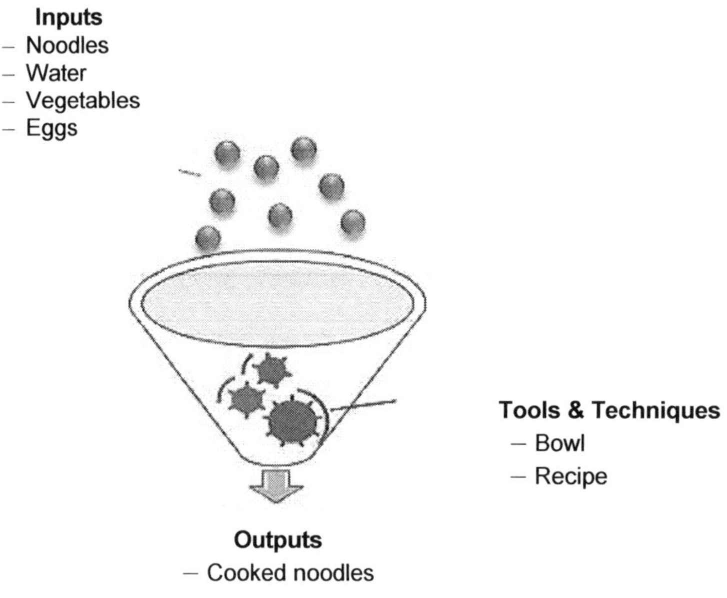

Figure 3-1: Elements of a Process

The start-plan-do-check and act-end cycle is an underlying concept that shows the integrative nature of the process groups. At a high-level, there are five project management process groups:

- Initiating the project (Start)
- Planning the project (Plan)
- Executing the project (Do)
- Monitoring & controlling the project (Check and act)
- Closing the project (End)

Project management processes are divided into five groups:

Process Group	Definition	Example – Vacation to Hawaii
Initiating Process Group	– Defines and authorizes a new project or a new phase of an existing project.	Determine the benefits of taking a vacation, approximate cost, available funds, and potential vacation spots. Select Hawaii.
Planning Process Group	– Defines and refines project goals and objectives. – Determines the scope of the project. – Plans the courses of action to achieve objectives and scope.	Put together an online itinerary with the flight and hotel information.
Executing Process Group	– Carries out the project management plan. – Performs the work to satisfy the project need.	Fly to Hawaii, stay in the luxury hotel and have a lot of fun exploring exotic places.
Monitoring & Controlling Process Group	– Measures and monitors progress. – Identifies variances from the project management plan. – Recommends corrective actions.	While taking your flight, make sure you got the window seat as requested, hotel has a scenic view as promised, and the tour guide is as good as claimed. File your complaints if needed and make sure you get the best service.
Closing Process Group	– Formally accepts the product, service, or result. – Brings project to an orderly end. – Gathers and stores all the project information for future reference.	Return home once the vacation is over, post all your fabulous photos online and share your experience with friends. Also post your comments and feedback about the hotel and travel agency.

Table 3-1: Project Management Process Groups

The above-listed process groups have individual processes that collectively make up the group. For instance, the closing process group has two processes, which are Close Project and Close Procurements. All these process groups, including all their individual processes, collectively make up the project management processes. The project manager and project team are responsible for determining which processes within each of these process groups are appropriate for the project based on the size, complexity, scope, available budget, inputs, tools & techniques, and outputs of each of these processes.

Note that there is a misconception that these process groups are the same as the project phases discussed in the previous chapter. It is vital to understand that project phases describe how the work that is required to produce the product of the project will be completed, and these forty-seven processes could be performed one or more times in each project phase.

The following diagram shows how the project management process groups fit together:

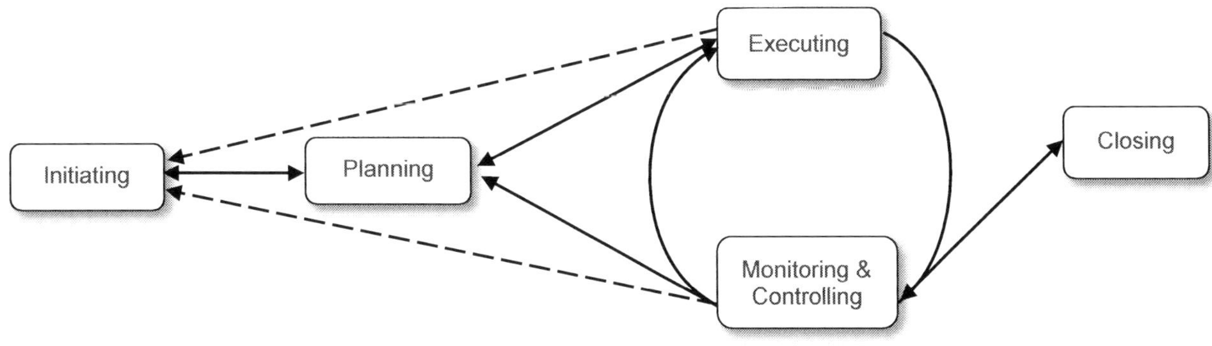

Figure 3-2: Project Management Process Groups

Common Project Management Processes Interactions

The five process groups are not one-time processes that are performed as discrete elements, neither are they completely linear. Instead, they interact and overlap with each other. As a project is refined, these iterative processes might be revisited and revised several times throughout the project life cycle as more information becomes available. Some planning must take place, then some executing, then some monitoring & controlling processes, followed by further planning, further executing, and so on.

The PMBOK® describes the underlying concept that the process groups are iterative as a Plan–Do–Check–Act cycle where each element in the cycle is result-oriented. The results from the plan cycle become inputs for the do cycle, and so on, just like the way project mangement process groups interact. For instance, the planning process group provides the executing process group with the project management plan and project documents, and as the project progresses, it often updates the project management plan and project documents as necessary per the findings.

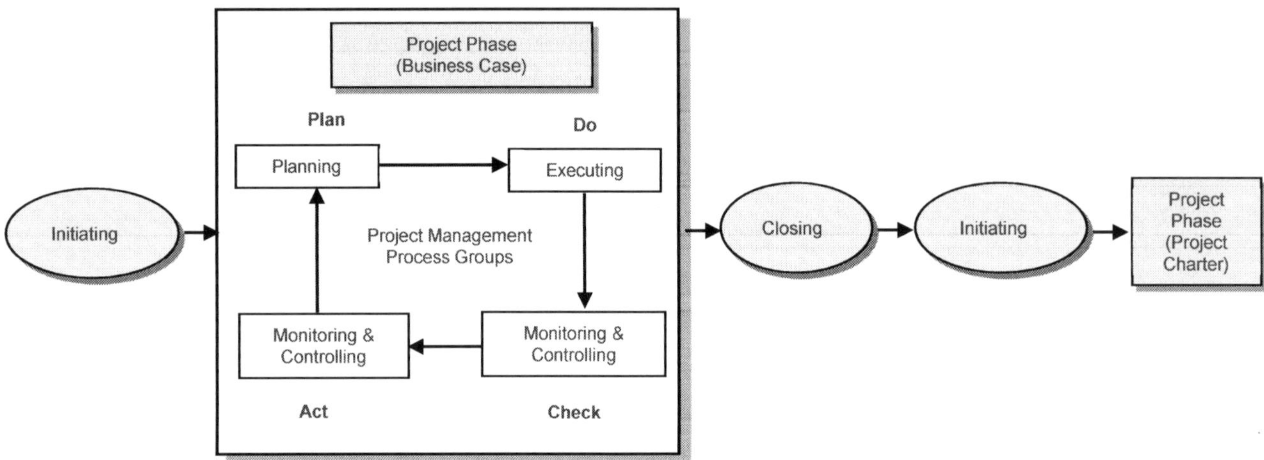

Figure 3-3: Project Management Process Groups Mapped to the Plan-Do-Check-Act Cycle

These process groups are not discrete or one-time events; they are overlapping activities that occur throughout the project life cycle. The project management process groups are linked by the outputs that are produced. The output of one process usually becomes an input to another process or is a deliverable of the project, subproject, or project phase. The following figure illustrates how the process groups interact and also displays the level of overlap at various times during the project life cycle.

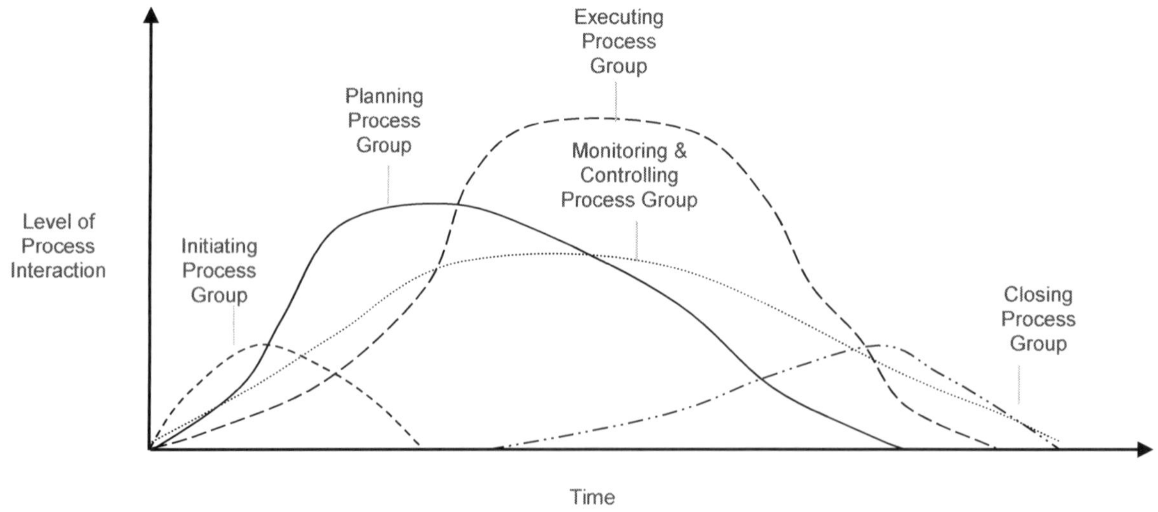

Figure 3-4: Process Groups Interact in a Phase or Project

Project Management Knowledge Areas

In addition to the general management knowledge described earlier, a project manager must master the areas of knowledge specifically developed for project management. The PMBOK® organizes the project processes according to ten knowledge areas. A knowledge area represents a complete set of activities, concepts, and terms that make up an area of specialization, a project management field, or a professional field. Each of the forty-seven project management processes defined earlier fits into one these knowledge areas below:

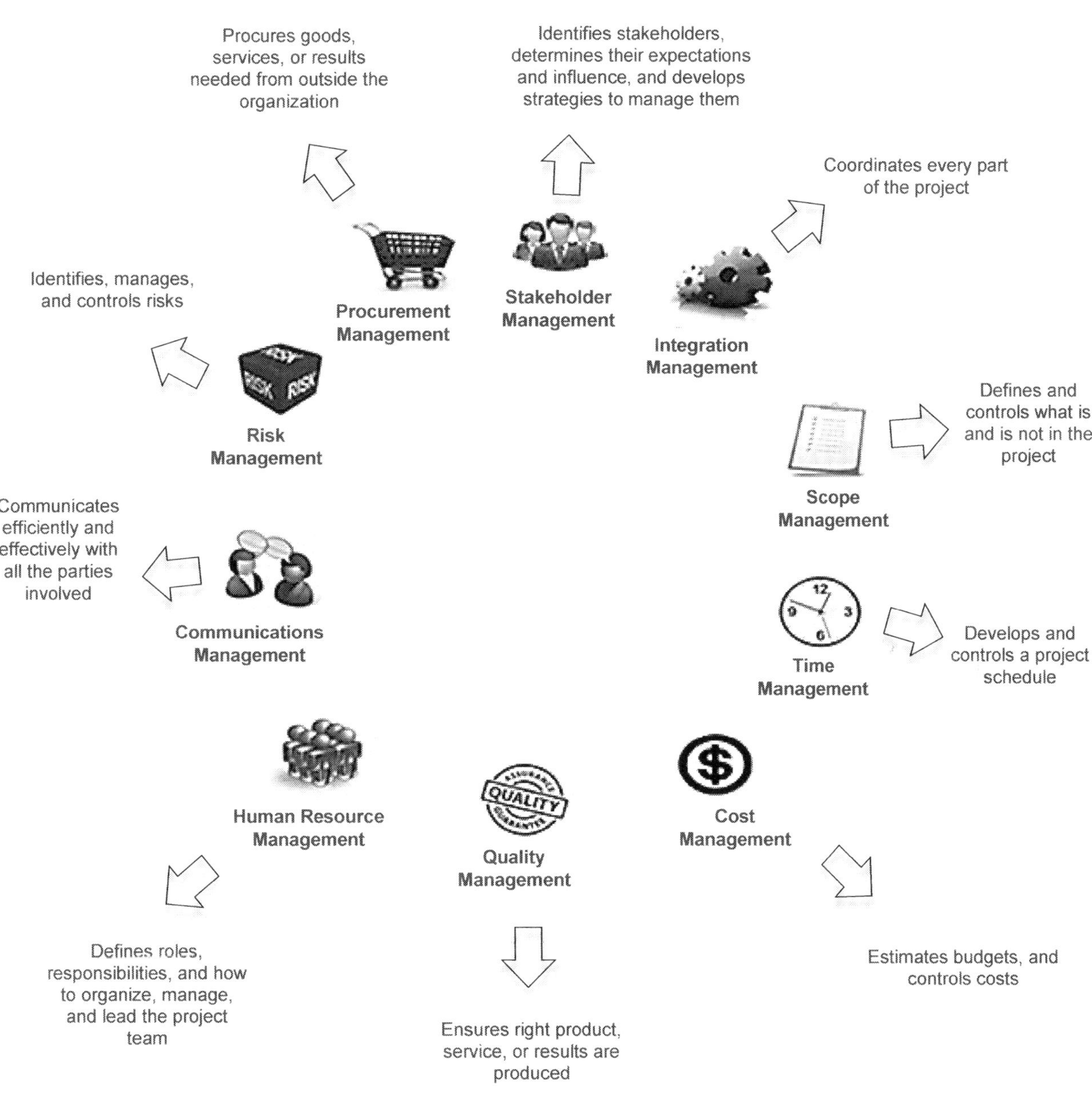

Figure 3-5: Project Management Ten Knowledge Areas

Process Groups and Knowledge Areas Mapping

The process groups and knowledge areas mapping according to the PMBOK® guide is displayed in the following table:

Knowledge Areas	Project Management Process Groups				
	Initiating	**Planning**	**Executing**	**Monitoring & Controlling**	**Closing**
Project Integration Management	– Develop Project Charter	– Develop Project Management Plan	– Direct and Manage Project Work	– Monitor and Control Project Work – Perform Integrated Change Control	– Close Project or Phase
Project Scope Management		– Plan Scope Management – Collect Requirements – Define Scope – Create WBS		– Validate Scope – Control Scope	
Project Time Management		– Plan Schedule Management – Define Activities – Sequence Activities – Estimate Activity Resources – Estimate Activity Durations – Develop Schedule		– Control Schedule	
Project Cost Management		– Plan Cost Management – Estimate Costs – Determine Budget		– Control Costs	
Project Quality Management		– Plan Quality Management	– Perform Quality Assurance	– Control Quality	
Project Human Resource Management		– Plan Human Resource Management	– Acquire Project Team – Develop Project Team – Manage Project Team		
Project Communications Management		– Plan Communications Management	– Manage Communications	– Control Communications	
Project Risk Management		– Plan Risk Management – Identify Risks – Perform Qualitative Risk Analysis – Perform Quantitative Risk Analysis – Plan Risk Responses		– Control Risks	
Project Procurement Management		– Plan Procurement Management	– Conduct Procurements	– Control Procurements	– Close Procurements
Project Stakeholder Management	– Identify Stakeholders	– Plan Stakeholder Management	– Manage Stakeholder Engagement	– Control Stakeholder Engagement	

Table 3-2: Process Groups and Knowledge Areas Mapping

Note: Only integration management and stakeholder management have processes in initiating. All knowledge areas have processes in planning. Scope, time, cost, and quality management have no processes in executing. Human resource management has no processes in monitoring and controlling. Only integration management and procurement management have processes in closing.

Initiating Process Group

The initiating process group defines a new project or phase, and is made up of only two processes: Develop Project Charter in integration management and Identify Stakeholders in stakeholder management. The project charter, identified stakeholders, and the stakeholder register are the key outputs of this process group.

When the project charter, which consists of measurable project objectives, a milestone schedule, an initial budget, etc., is approved in this process group, the project is officially authorized, and a project manager is assigned to the project.

The success of subsequent processes and activities greatly depends on the way a project is initiated. If a project is initiated properly, it will have the business need and feasibility clearly defined. It will also have a clear goal, objective reasons for selecting this project over other possibilities, a clear direction for the scope, a project manager assigned, and a list of stakeholders for the project. On the other hand, if a project is not initiated properly, it could result in limited or a total lack of authority for the project manager as well as ambiguous goals or uncertainties as to why the project was initiated.

High-level planning such as creating a high-level Work Breakdown Structure (WBS), order of magnitude estimates, and high-level risk identification can be performed in this process.

Initiating is performed if there is a business need, if there is a new project phase need, or as a result of numerous problems found in a later phase of the project that need to be reevaluated.

As per the following figure, initiation can be performed several times in a project depending on the organizational methodologies, funding, and other influencing factors. If a project is being performed in phases, each phase could have its own separate initiation to ensure that the project maintains its focus and that the business objectives and goals behind the project are still valid.

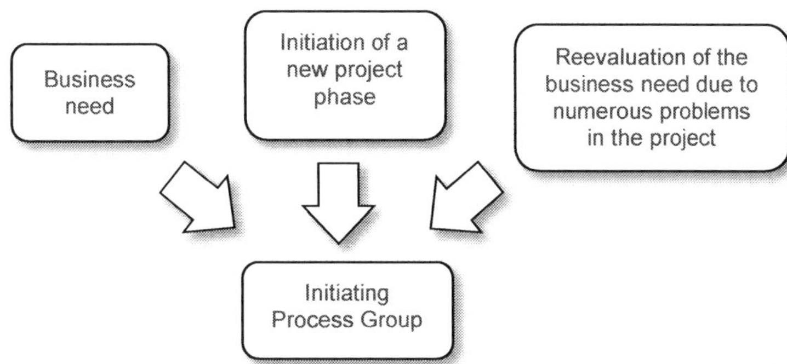

Figure 3-6: The Initiating Process Group

The initiating process group includes the following processes in the specified knowledge areas:

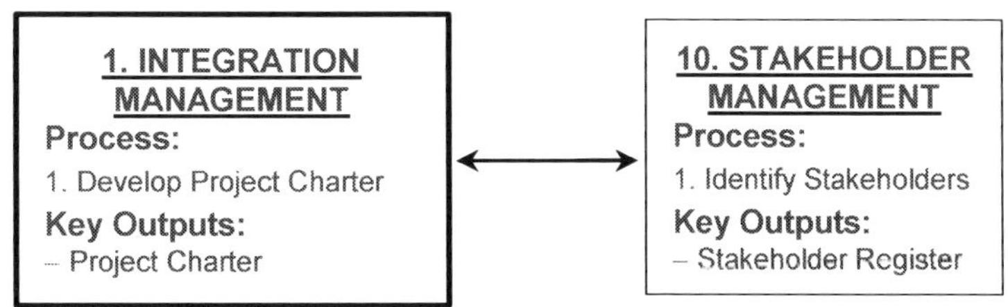

Figure 3-7: Initiating Process Group Processes and Key Outputs

Exercise 1: What do you need to initiate a project?

As per PMI, the initiating process group has the following tasks:

Tasks	Why?	How?
Task1: Perform project assessment.	To support the evaluation of the feasibility of new products or services within the given assumptions and constraints.	Based upon available information, lessons learned from previous projects, and meeting with relevant stakeholders
Task2: Identify key deliverables.	To manage customer expectations and direct the achievement of project goals.	Based on the business requirements.
Task3: Perform stakeholder analysis.	To align expectations and gain support for the project.	By using appropriate tools & techniques.
Task 4: Identify high level risks, assumptions, and constraints.	To propose an implementation strategy.	Based on the current environment, organizational factors, historical data, and expert judgment.
Task 5: Participate in the development of the project charter.	To ensure project stakeholders are in agreement on its elements.	By compiling and analyzing gathered information.
Task 6: Obtain project charter approval.	To formalize the authority assigned to the project manager and gain commitment and acceptance for the project.	By reviewing with the sponsor and others.
Task 7: Conduct benefit analysis.	To validate project alignment with organizational strategy and expected business value.	By discussing with relevant stakeholders.
Task 8: Inform stakeholders of the approved project charter.	To ensure common understanding of the key deliverables, milestones, and their roles and responsibilities.	By discussing with relevant stakeholders.

Table 3-3: Tasks in Initiating Process Group

Exercise 2: Identify the knowledge areas for the following scenarios.

Description	Knowledge Area
1. Estimating resources and duration to develop a realistic project schedule and controlling changes to that schedule.	
2. Defining the roles of all the team members and the responsibilities of each role as well as defining how to organize, manage, and lead the project team.	
3. Communicating efficiently and effectively with all the parties involved to keep everybody in the loop about the project.	
4. Coordinating every part of the project, balancing all the processes in the knowledge areas, and dealing with changes.	
5. Defining and controlling what is and is not in the project. Also making sure that all the work is being completed.	
6. Purchasing goods, services, or results needed from outside the organization, defining contracts, and selecting a contractor to do work for the project.	
7. Estimating, budgeting, and controlling costs so that the project can be completed within the approved budget.	
8. Identifying the internal and external stakeholders to determine their expectations and influence over the project and developing strategies to manage them.	
9. Ensuring that right product, service, or results are produced as efficiently and effectively as possible.	
10. Planning for positive or negative events that could happen in the project and dealing with them to increase the probability and impact of positive events and to decrease the probability and impact of adverse events.	

Planning Process Group

The planning process group consists of iterative and ongoing processes to establish the total scope of effort, define the objectives, and identify the course of action required to attain those objectives. The project management plan and project documents, as key outputs in the process group, cover all aspects of the scope, time, cost, quality, human resources, communication, risk, and procurements as listed below.

While planning the project and developing the project management plan and other project documents, the project team should seek valuable inputs and encourage involvement from all stakeholders. Required updates from approved changes reported during monitoring & controlling processes and especially during executing processes may have substantial impact on parts of the project management plan and other project documents. Modifications to these documents provide greater accuracy with respect to schedule, costs, and resource requirements to satisfy the defined project scope. Note that feedback and refinement process should not continue indefinitely and organizational procedures must dictate when the initial planning efforts should end. The nature of the project, established project boundaries, applicable monitoring & controlling activities, and the project environment in which project will be performed may influence these organizational procedures.

As per PMI, the planning process group has the following tasks:

Task	Why?	How?
Task 1: Review and assess detailed project requirements, constraints, and assumptions with stakeholders.	To establish detailed project deliverables.	Based on the project charter, lessons learned, and by using requirement gathering techniques.
Task2: Develop a scope management plan.	To define, maintain, and manage the scope of the project.	Based on the approved project scope and using scope management techniques.
Task3: Develop the cost management plan.	To manage project costs.	Based on the project scope, schedule, resources, approved project charter, and other information.
Task4: Develop the project schedule.	To manage timely completion of the project.	Based on the approved project deliverables and milestones, scope, and resource management plan.
Task 5: Develop a human resource management plan.	To create a project organizational structure and provide guidance regarding how resources will be assigned and managed.	By defining the roles and responsibilities of the project team members.
Task 6: Develop the communications management plan.	To define and manage the flow of the project information.	Based on the project organizational structure and stakeholder requirements.
Task 7: Develop the procurement management plan.	To ensure that required project resources will be available.	Based on the project scope, budget, and schedule.
Task 8: Develop the quality management plan and define the quality standards.	To prevent the occurrence of defects and control the cost of quality.	Based on the project scope, risks, and requirements.
Task 9: Develop the change management plan.	To track and manage changes.	By defining how changes will be addressed and controlled.
Task 10: Develop the risk management plan.	To manage uncertainties and opportunities throughout the project life cycle.	By identifying, analyzing, and prioritizing project risks; creating the risk register; and defining risk response strategies.
Task 11: Present the project management plan to the relevant stakeholders.	To obtain approval to proceed with the project execution.	According to applicable policies and procedures.
Task 12: Conduct kick-off meeting.	To inform and engage stakeholders and gain commitment.	By communicating the start of the project, key milestones, and other relevant information.
Task 13: Develop the stakeholder management plan.	To effectively manage stakeholders' expectations and engage them in project decisions.	By analyzing needs, interests, and potential impacts.

Table 3-4: Tasks in Planning Process Group

A project will enter the planning process group mostly when the initiating process group is completed or there is a need for replanning due to the finding of several defect repairs and/or corrective and preventive actions in a later phase of the project.

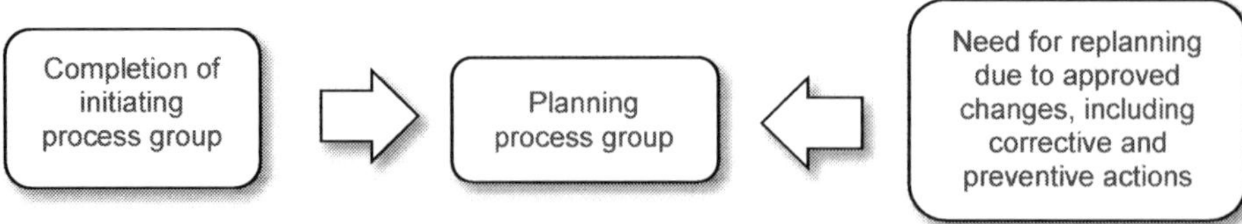

Figure 3-8: The Planning Process Group

The planning process group includes the following processes in the specified knowledge areas:

2. SCOPE MANAGEMENT

Processes:

1. Plan Scope Management
2. Collect Requirements
3. Define Scope
4. Create WBS

Key Outputs:

- Scope Management Plan
- Requirements Management Plan
- Requirements Documentation
- Requirements Traceability Matrix
- Project Scope Statement
- Scope Baseline

10. STAKEHOLDER MANAGEMENT

Process:

1. Plan Stakeholder Management

Key Outputs:

- Stakeholder Management Plan

9. PROCUREMENT MANAGEMENT

Process:

1. Plan Procurement Management

Key Outputs:

- Procurement Management Plan
- Procurement Statement of Work (SOW)
- Procurement Documents
- Source Selection Criteria
- Make-or-Buy Decisions

3. TIME MANAGEMENT

Processes:

1. Plan Schedule Management
2. Define Activities
3. Sequence Activities
4. Estimate Activity Resources
5. Estimate Activity Durations
6. Develop Schedule

Key Outputs:

- Schedule Management Plan
- Activity List
- Activity Attributes
- Milestone List
- Project Schedule Network Diagrams
- Activity Resource Requirements
- Resource Breakdown Structure
- Activity Duration Estimates
- Schedule Baseline
- Schedule Data
- Project Calendars

1. INTEGRATION MANAGEMENT

Process:

1. Develop Project Management Plan

Key Outputs:

- Project Management Plan

8. RISK MANAGEMENT

Process:

1. Plan Risk Management
2. Identify Risks
3. Perform Qualitative Risk Analysis
4. Perform Quantitative Risk Analysis
5. Plan Risk Responses

Key Outputs:

- Risk Management Plan
- Risk Register

7. COMMUNICATIONS MANAGEMENT

Process:

1. Plan Communications Management

Key Outputs:

- Communications Management Plan

4. COST MANAGEMENT

Processes:

1. Plan Cost Management
2. Estimate Costs
3. Determine Budget

Key Outputs:

- Cost Management Plan
- Activity Cost Estimates
- Basis of Estimates
- Project Funding Requirements
- Cost Baseline

5. QUALITY MANAGEMENT

Process:

1. Plan Quality Management

Key Outputs:

- Quality Management Plan
- Process Improvement Plan
- Quality Metrics
- Quality Checklists

6. HUMAN RESOUCE MANAGEMENT

Process:

1. Plan Human Resource Management

Key Outputs:

- Human Resource Management Plan

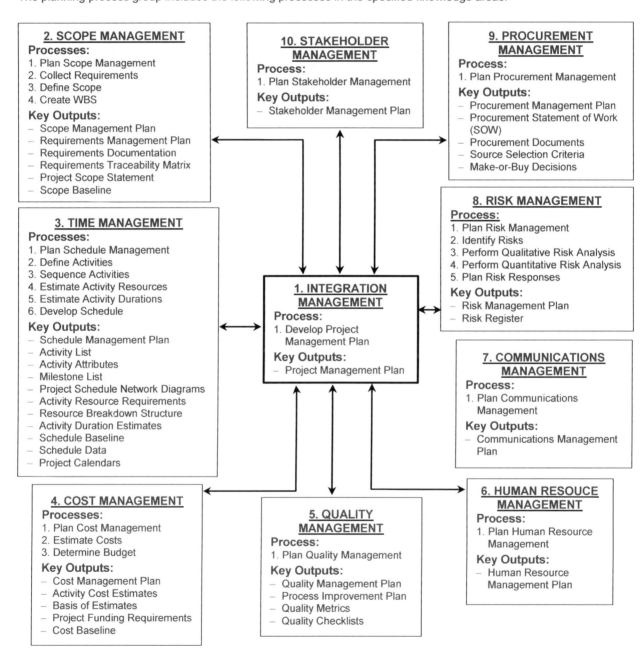

Figure 3-9: Planning Process Group Processes and Key Outputs

Executing Process Group

The executing process group consists of the processes to complete the work defined in the project management plan and ultimately satisfies the project specifications and objectives. Processes in this process group are utilized to organize people and resources, manage stakeholders' expectations, and integrate and perform project activities in accordance with the project management plan. In this process group, work is actually carried out: code is written, parts are assembled, information is distributed, houses are constructed, the team is developed and managed, roads are repaired, etc.

Findings in the executing process group may require replanning and rebaselining the project management plan and project documents, including changes to activity durations, resource availability, and unanticipated risks. Usually the project will enter the executing process group when the planning is completed or the project management plan has been updated due to change requests, including defect repairs and corrective and preventive actions. The approved change requests, which consist of corrective actions, preventive actions, and defect repairs are typically implemented in this process group.

Corrective actions: Actions that are taken to bring expected future performance of the project work in line with the project management plan.
Preventive actions: Actions that are taken to prevent similar mistakes from happening in the future. These actions reduce the probability of risk items in the project.
Defect repairs: Actions that are taken to repair defects or entirely replace components that are faulty or dysfunctional.

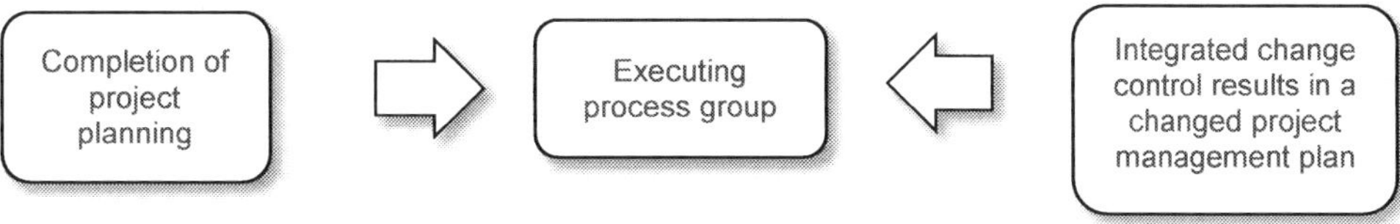

Figure 3-10: The Executing Process Group

Costs are usually high in this process group as it will utilize most of the project time and resources. Project managers typically face significant conflicts and challenges over schedules during executing.

As per PMI, the executing process groups has the following tasks:

Tasks	Why?	How?
Task 1: Acquire and manage project resources.	To meet project requirements.	By following the human resource and procurement management plans.
Task 2: Manage task execution.	To achieve project deliverables.	Based on the project management plan.
Task 3: Implement the quality management plan.	To ensure that work is performed in accordance with required quality standards.	By using the appropriate tools and techniques.
Task 4: Implement approved changes and corrective actions.	To meet project requirements.	By following the change management plan.
Task 5: Implement approved actions.	To minimize the impact of risks and take advantage of opportunities.	By following the risk management plan.
Task 6: Manage the flow of information.	To keep stakeholders informed and engaged.	By following the communications management plan.
Task 7: Maintain stakeholder relationships.	To receive continued support and manage expectations.	By following the stakeholder management plan.

Table 3-5: Tasks in Executing Process Group

The executing process group includes the following processes in the specified knowledge areas:

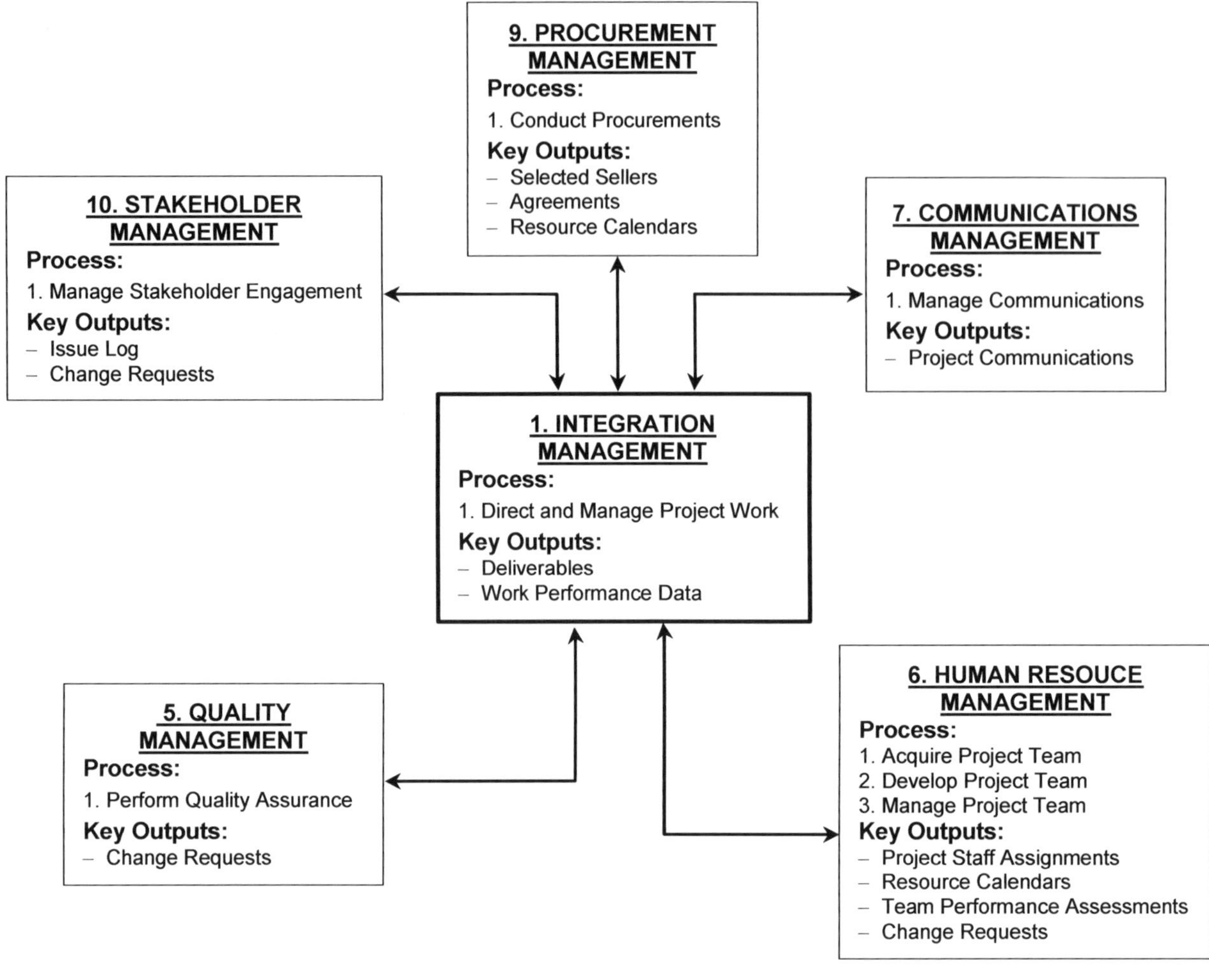

Figure 3-11: Executing Process Group Processes and Key Outputs

Exercise 3: Fill in the "?" with number of processes in each process group for all knowledge areas.

		Process Groups					Total # of Processes
		Initiating	Planning	Executing	Monitoring & Controlling	Closing	
Knowledge Areas	Integration	1	1	?	?	1	?
	Scope		?		2		6
	Time		?		1		?
	Cost		3		?		?
	Quality		?	?	1		?
	Human Resource		?	?			4
	Communications		1	?	1		?
	Risk		5		?		?
	Procurement		1	?	1	?	?
	Stakeholder	1	?	1	?		4
	# of Processes	2	?	8	11	2	?

Monitoring & Controlling Process Group

The processes in the monitoring & controlling process group track, measure, inspect, monitor, verify, review, compare, and regulate the progress and performance of the project, ensure that the plan is working, identify any areas in which changes to the plan are required, and initiate corresponding changes. This process group includes the following processes in the specified knowledge areas:

The monitoring & controlling process group is mostly focused on influencing future results by taking corrective and preventive actions. A project may transition to the monitoring & controlling process group when some of the deliverables, work performance information, or requested changes, including recommended corrective and preventive actions, and defect repair from all sources are available. As per findings in this process group, it may be required to revisit the initiating process group to review the project charter, the planning process group to replan parts of the project, the executing process group to repair defects, and the closing process group if the project is completed.

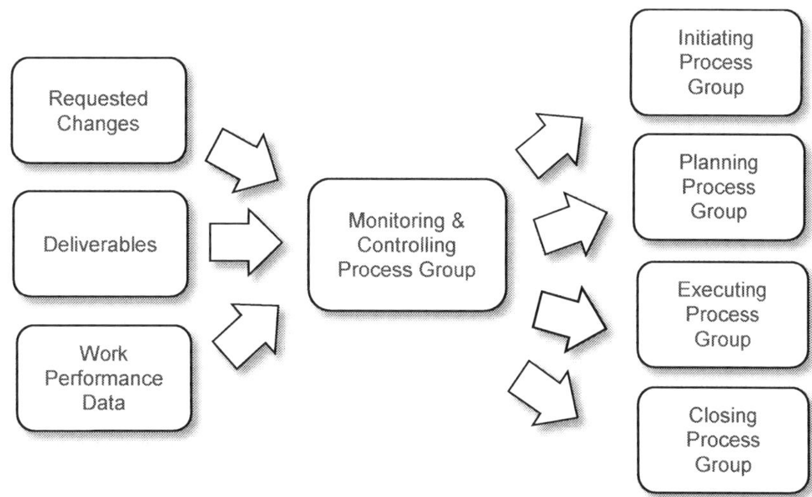

Figure 3-12: The Monitoring & Controlling Process Group

As per PMI, the monitoring & controlling process group has the following tasks:

Tasks	Why?	How?
Task 1: Measure project performance.	To identify and quantify any variances and corrective actions.	By using appropriate tools and techniques.
Task 2: Manage changes to the project.	To ensure that project goals remain aligned with business needs.	By following the change management plan.
Task 3: Verify that project deliverables conform to the quality standards.	To meet project requirements and business needs.	By using appropriate tools and techniques.
Task 4: Monitor and assess risks.	To manage the impact of risks and opportunities within the project.	By determining whether exposure has changed and evaluating the effectiveness of response strategies.
Task 5: Review the issue log.	To minimize impacts of issues.	By using appropriate tools and techniques.
Task 6: Capture, analyze, and manage lessons learned.	To enable continuous improvement.	By using lessons learned management techniques.
Task 7: Monitor procurement activities.	To verify compliance with project objectives.	By referring to the procurement management plan.

Table 3-6: Tasks in Monitoring & Controlling Process Group

The monitoring & controlling process group includes the following processes in the specified knowledge areas:

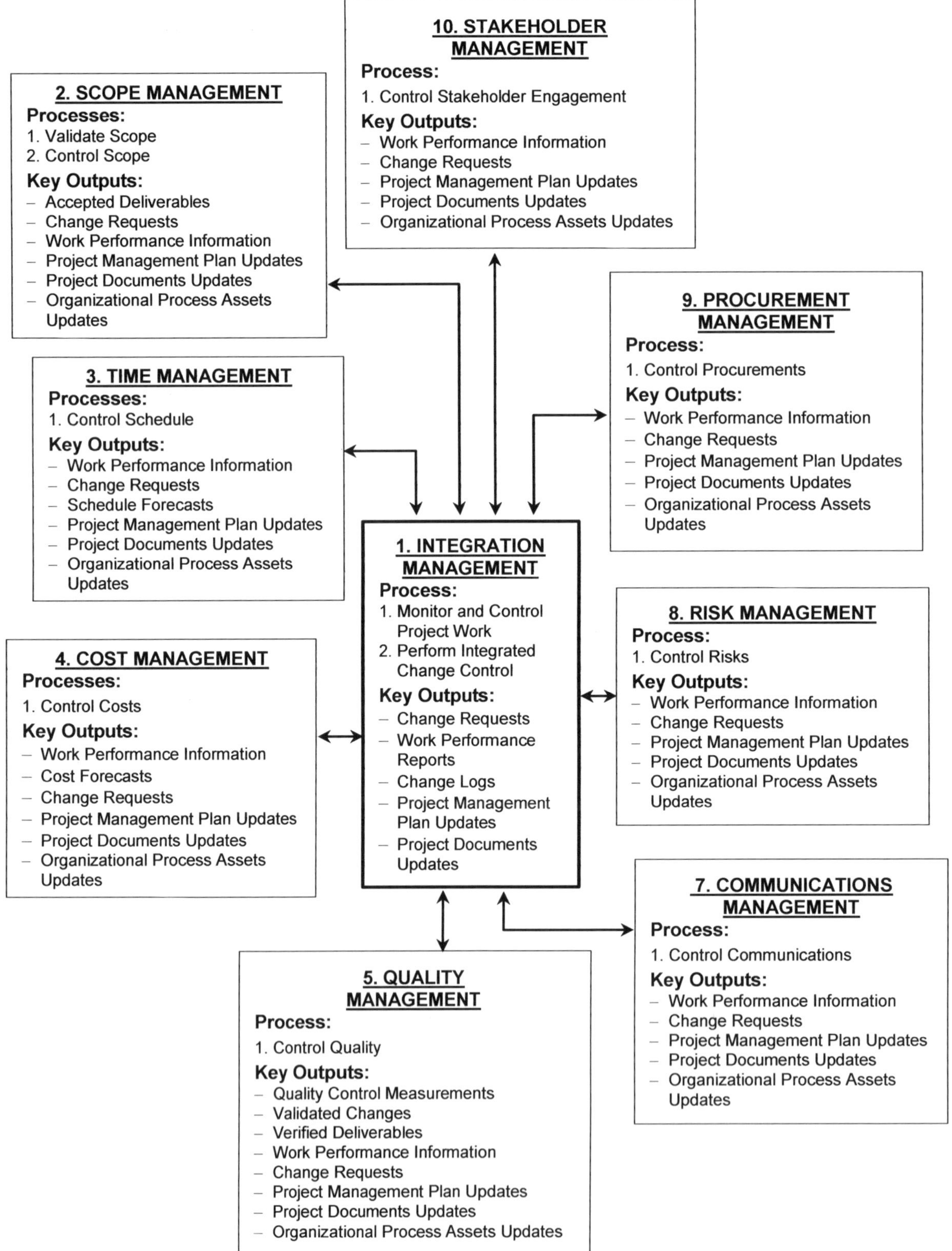

Figure 3-13: Monitoring & Controlling Process Group Processes and Key Outputs

Closing Process Group

The closing process group finalizes all activities across all project management process groups to formally complete the project, phase, or contractual obligations.

During project closing, the product is verified against scope, formal sign-off and formal acceptance are received from the customers, customer satisfaction is measured, final versions of the lessons learned are compiled and made available for future projects, appropriate organizational process assets are updated, the contract is closed, completed project deliverables are handed off to operations and maintenance, and resources are released.

A project will enter the closing process group when the project phase is completed, the entire project is completed, or the project is otherwise terminated.

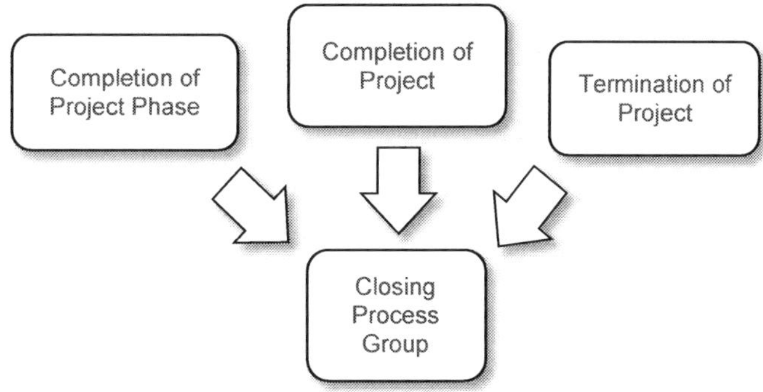

Figure 3-14: The Closing Process Group

As per PMI, the closing process group has the following tasks:

Tasks	Why?	How?
Task 1: Obtain final acceptance of the project deliverables.	To confirm that project scope and deliverables were achieved.	By discussing with relevant stakeholders.
Task 2: Transfer the ownership of deliverables to the assigned stakeholders.	To facilitate project closure.	By referring to the project management plan.
Task 3: Obtain financial, legal, and administrative closure.	To communicate formal project closure and ensure transfer of liability.	By using generally accepted practices and policies.
Task 4: Prepare and share the final project report.	To document and convey project performance and assist in project evaluation.	By referring to the communications management plan.
Task 5: Create lessons learned.	To update the organization's knowledge base.	By documenting throughout the project and conducting a comprehensive project review.
Task 6: Archive project documents and materials.	For potential use in future projects and audits.	Using generally accepted practices.
Task 7: Obtain feedback from relevant stakeholders.	To evaluate their satisfaction.	By using the appropriate tools and techniques.

Table 3-7: Tasks in Closing Process Group

The closing process group includes the following processes in the specified knowledge areas:

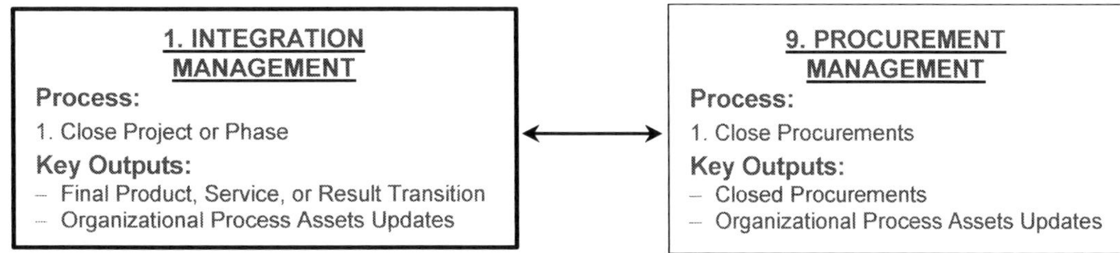

Figure 3-15: Closing Process Group Processes and Key Outputs

Process Groups Key Inputs and Outputs

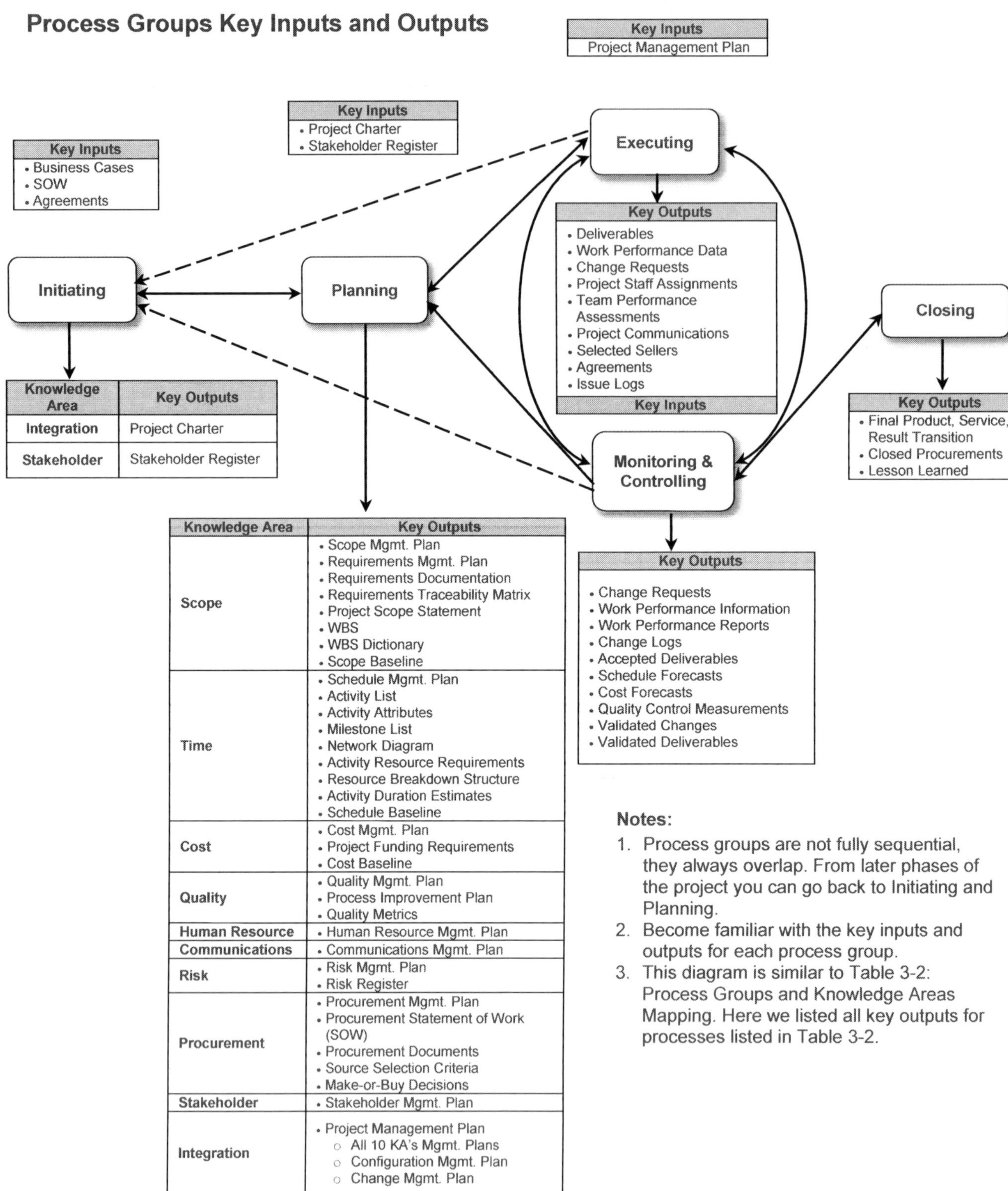

Notes:

1. Process groups are not fully sequential, they always overlap. From later phases of the project you can go back to Initiating and Planning.
2. Become familiar with the key inputs and outputs for each process group.
3. This diagram is similar to Table 3-2: Process Groups and Knowledge Areas Mapping. Here we listed all key outputs for processes listed in Table 3-2.

Figure 3-16: Process Groups Key Inputs and Outputs

Exercise 4: List items a project manager should be aware of within the monitoring & controlling process group.

____

____

____

____

Exercise 5: Identify whether the items below are Initiating, Planning, Executing, Monitoring & Controlling, or Closing work.

Actions	Process Group
1. Select a project from a list of possible projects based on an established selection method.	
2. Measure against the performance measurement baseline established in the project.	
3. Implement approved changes, which may contain corrective actions, preventive actions, and defect repairs.	
4. Hold team-building activities to build the team.	
5. Spend time and effort to improve quality in the project.	
6. Meet with functional managers to gain resource commitment.	
7. Determine the team and their roles.	
8. Evaluate customer's overall satisfaction with the project.	
9. Recalculate project cost and duration.	
10. Obtain seller's proposal to procurement document.	
11. Gather final lessons learned from team members, sponsors, customers, and other stakeholders.	
12. Analyze, track, and monitor project risks.	
13. Calculate Estimate to Complete (ETC) or from this point on how much more money you need to complete the project.	
14. Hand off the completed project deliverables to operations and maintenance.	
15. Monitor implementation of approved changes.	
16. Understand how project will meet the strategic goals and objectives of the organization.	
17. Determine how you will improve the processes in use on the project.	
18. Perform procurement inspection and audit.	
19. Determine high-level requirements, expectations, and risks.	
20. Gain approval from the stakeholders on final scope, using the project scope statement, prior to further planning.	
21. Assess performance to determine whether any corrective or preventive actions are required.	
22. Archive all relevant project records.	
23. Determine process on how changes will be handled in the project.	
24. Identify the communication needs and techniques to fulfill the needs of stakeholders.	
25. Obtain formal approval of the project charter.	
26. Decompose the deliverables into more manageable, smaller components (WBS).	
27. Manage stakeholders' engagement and expectation.	
28. Perform high-level estimating for the project schedule and budget.	
29. Perform quality audit to ensure the defined practices and procedures are being followed.	
30. Identify existing processes, standards, policies, and compliance requirements that affect the project.	
31. Assess individual team member's performance.	
32. Identify the work required to complete project deliverables.	
33. Implement the recognition and reward system to encourage team members.	
34. Identify newly arising risks.	
35. Decide what level of accuracy is needed for cost estimating.	
36. Select sellers and negotiate contract terms and conditions.	
37. Hold kick-off meeting.	

Exercise 6: Put all the processes in the right knowledge areas in the order they are typically performed.

Knowledge Areas	Processes	Knowledge Areas	Processes
Integration	1. 2. 3. 4. 5. 6.	**Human Resource**	1. 2. 3. 4.
Scope	1. 2. 3. 4. 5. 6.	**Communications**	1. 2. 3.
Time	1. 2. 3. 4. 5. 6. 7.	**Risk**	1. 2. 3. 4. 5. 6.
Cost	1. 2. 3. 4.	**Procurement**	1. 2. 3. 4.
Quality	1. 2. 3.	**Stakeholder**	1. 2. 3. 4.

1. Perform Integrated Change Control
2. Perform Qualitative Risk Analysis
3. Validate Scope
4. Control Scope
5. Plan Procurement Management
6. Plan Scope Management
7. Control Procurements
8. Plan Cost Management
9. Perform Quality Assurance
10. Acquire Project Team
11. Define Scope
12. Control Risks
13. Monitor and Control Project Work
14. Estimate Costs
15. Identify Stakeholders
16. Estimate Activity Durations
17. Control Costs
18. Close Project or Phase
19. Define Activities
20. Determine Budget
21. Develop Project Team
22. Control Communications
23. Perform Quantitative Risk Analysis
24. Collect Requirements
25. Conduct Procurements
26. Plan Quality Management
27. Identify Risks
28. Develop Project Management Plan
29. Plan Risk Responses
30. Create WBS
31. Plan Schedule Management
32. Sequence Activities
33. Develop Schedule
34. Plan Communications Management
35. Close Procurements
36. Plan Stakeholder Management
37. Manage Project Team
38. Estimate Activity Resources
39. Control Schedule
40. Control Quality
41. Direct and Manage Project Work
42. Plan Risk Management
43. Manage Communications
44. Develop Project Charter
45. Plan Human Resource Management
46. Manage Stakeholder Engagement
47. Control Stakeholder Engagement

Exercise 7: List items a project manager should be aware of within the closing process group.

Exercise 8: Crossword

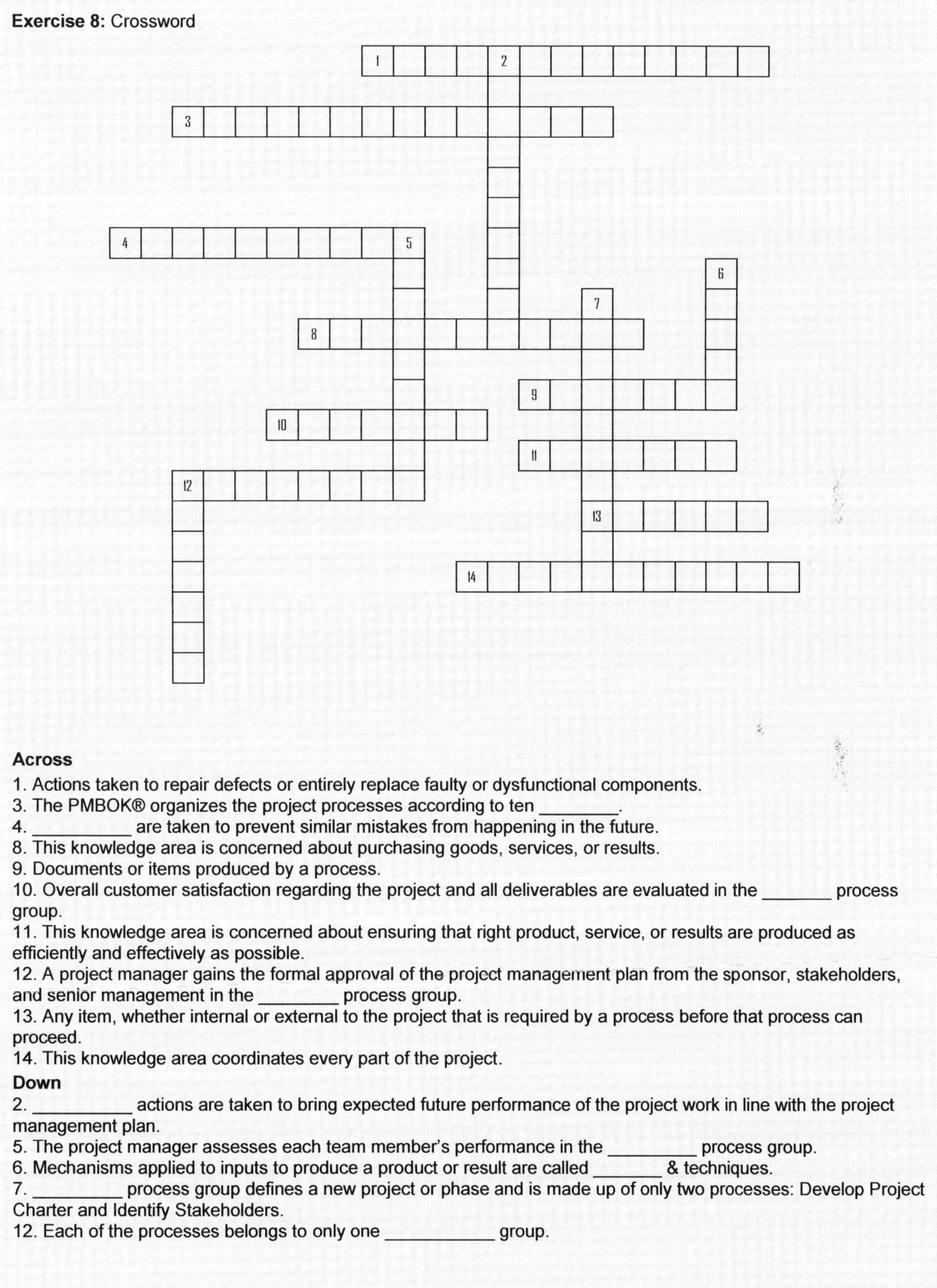

Across

1. Actions taken to repair defects or entirely replace faulty or dysfunctional components.
3. The PMBOK® organizes the project processes according to ten ________.
4. __________ are taken to prevent similar mistakes from happening in the future.
8. This knowledge area is concerned about purchasing goods, services, or results.
9. Documents or items produced by a process.
10. Overall customer satisfaction regarding the project and all deliverables are evaluated in the _______ process group.
11. This knowledge area is concerned about ensuring that right product, service, or results are produced as efficiently and effectively as possible.
12. A project manager gains the formal approval of the project management plan from the sponsor, stakeholders, and senior management in the ________ process group.
13. Any item, whether internal or external to the project that is required by a process before that process can proceed.
14. This knowledge area coordinates every part of the project.

Down

2. __________ actions are taken to bring expected future performance of the project work in line with the project management plan.
5. The project manager assesses each team member's performance in the ________ process group.
6. Mechanisms applied to inputs to produce a product or result are called _______ & techniques.
7. _________ process group defines a new project or phase and is made up of only two processes: Develop Project Charter and Identify Stakeholders.
12. Each of the processes belongs to only one ___________ group.

Exercise 9: Answer the following:

1. Documents or items produced by a process.
2. This process group defines and refines project goals and objectives and plans the courses of action to achieve objectives and scope.
3. The project manager assesses each team member's performance in the _________ process group.
4. It is a set of interrelated actions and activities that are performed to manage the work in order to achieve a pre-specified set of products, results, or services.
5. Your project is behind the schedule, so you started working on activities in parallel is an example of a _________ action.
6. Mechanisms applied to inputs to produce a product or result.
7. Actions taken to repair defects or entirely replace faulty or dysfunctional components.
8. Each of the processes belongs to only one _________ group.
9. This process group measures and monitors progress, identifies variances from the project management plan, and recommends corrective actions.
10. Any item, whether internal or external to the project that is required by a process before that process can proceed.
11. Overall customer satisfaction regarding the project and all deliverables are evaluated in _________ process group.
12. This knowledge area is concerned about purchasing goods, services, or results needed from outside the organization, defining contracts, and selecting a contractor to do work for the project.
13. In this process group, work is actually carried out: code is written, parts are assembled, information is distributed, houses are constructed, the team is developed and managed, roads are repaired, etc.
14. You bring an extra set of training materials to your session in case a new student shows up is an example of a _________ action.
15. A project manager gains the formal approval of the project management plan from the sponsor, stakeholders, and senior management in the _________ process group.
16. This knowledge area is concerned about ensuring that right product, service, or results are produced as efficiently and effectively as possible.
17. The way project management process groups may resemble to the elements of the Plan–Do–Check – Act cycle.
18. This knowledge area coordinates every part of the project.
19. A group of processes associated with planning or creating a project plan.
20. A systematic series of activities directed toward producing an end result.
21. A process group that defines a new project or phase and is made up of only two processes: Develop Project Charter in integration management and Identify Stakeholders in stakeholder management.
22. The PMBOK® organizes the project processes according to ten _________.
23. This knowledge area is concerned with identifying stakeholders, determining their expectations and influence, and developing strategies to manage them.
24. Work Performance data is an output of _________ processes and work performance information is output of _________ processes.
25. No _______ and _______ processes have change requests as an output.

Project Management Processes Summary

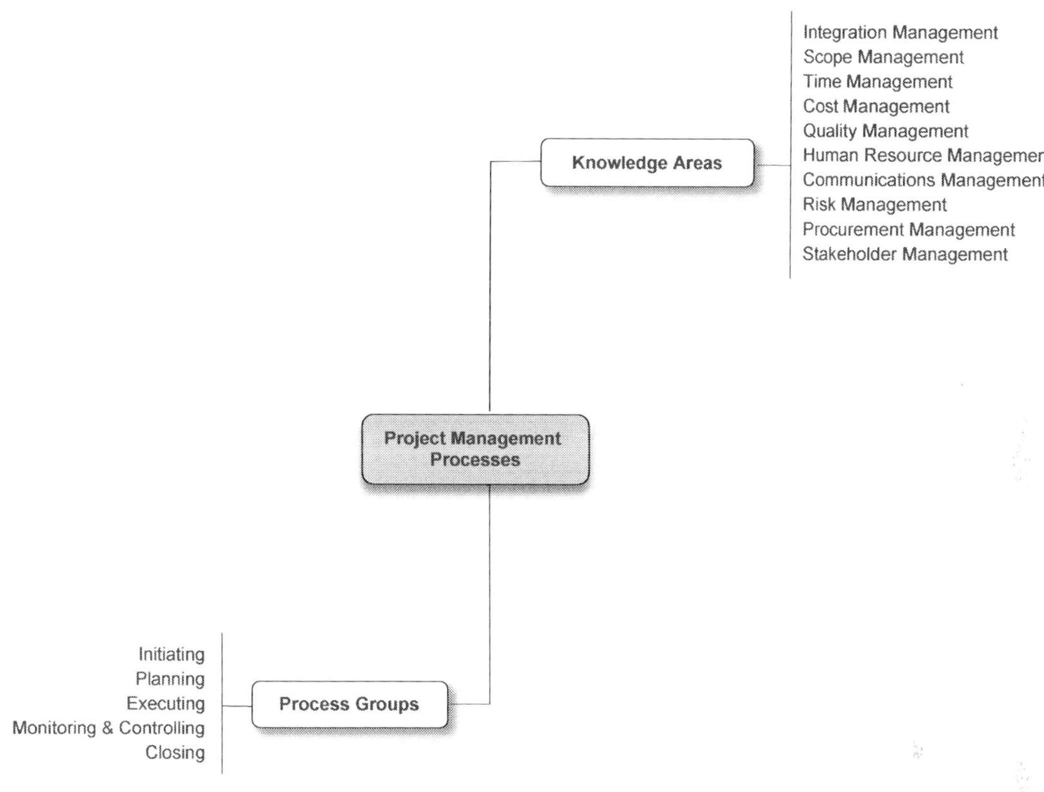

Figure 3-17: Project Management Processes Summary

Project Management Processes Key Terms

- A process is a set of interrelated actions and activities directed toward end results.
- Process groups are not project phases.
- Process groups are not linear; they interact and overlap with each other.

Knowledge Areas (10)	# of Processes
Integration	6
Scope	6
Time	7
Cost	4
Quality	3
Human Resource	4
Communications	3
Risk	6
Procurement	4
Stakeholder	4

Process Groups (5)	# of Processes
Initiating (IN)	2
Planning (PL)	24
Executing (EX)	8
Monitoring & Controlling (M & C)	11
Closing (CL)	2

		Process Groups					Total
		IN	PL	EX	M&C	CL	
Knowledge Areas	Integration	1	1	1	2	1	6
	Scope		4		2		6
	Time		6		1		7
	Cost		3		1		4
	Quality		1	1	1		3
	Human Resource		1	3			4
	Communications		1	1	1		3
	Risk		5		1		6
	Procurement		1	1	1	1	4
	Stakeholder	1	1	1	1		4
	Total	2	24	8	11	2	47

- Only integration management and stakeholder management have processes in initiating.
- All knowledge areas have processes in planning.
- Scope, time, cost, and quality management have no processes in executing.
- Human resource management has no processes in monitoring and controlling.
- Only integration management and procurement management have processes in closing.

Common Inputs, Tools & Techniques, Outputs

Inputs: Enterprise Environmental Factors (EEFs), Organizational Process Assets (OPAs), project management plan, work performance data, work performance information, work performance reports
Tools & Techniques: Expert judgment, Project Management Information System (PMIS), meetings, facilitation techniques, analytical techniques
Outputs: Change requests (corrective actions, preventive actions, defect repairs), updates (project management plan, project documents), work performance information, work performance reports

Sequence of Key Documents:

Business Case / Statement of Work (SOW) → Project Charter → Stakeholder Register → Requirements Documentation → Requirements Traceability Matrix → Project Scope Statement → WBS → Scope Baseline → Activity List → Network Diagram → Schedule Baseline → Cost Baseline → Quality Metrics → Risk Register

Project Management Processes Exercise Answers

Exercise 1: In order to initiate a project, a project manager should know or have the following:

- The purpose and objective of the project
- A list of potential stakeholders and team members
- A clear understanding of the company's strategic goals, objectives, and culture
- How the project will meet strategic goals and objectives of the organization
- Any industry standards and marketplace trends
- Historical records, including WBS, estimates, templates, and lessons learned
- Any existing relevant agreements or contracts
- Existing procedures, processes, and other major projects in the organization

Exercise 2:

1. Time
2. Human Resource
3. Communications
4. Integration
5. Scope
6. Procurement
7. Cost
8. Stakeholder
9. Quality
10. Risk

Exercise 3:

	Process Groups					Total # of Processes
	Initiating	Planning	Executing	Monitoring & Controlling	Closing	
Knowledge Areas						
Integration	1	1	1	2	1	**6**
Scope		4		2		**6**
Time		6		1		**7**
Cost		3		1		**4**
Quality		1	1	1		**3**
Human Resource		1	3			**4**
Communications		1	1	1		**3**
Risk		5		1		**6**
Procurement		1	1	1	1	**4**
Stakeholder	1	1	1	1		**4**
# of Processes	**2**	**24**	**8**	**11**	**2**	**47**

Exercise 4: A project manager should be aware of the following action items within the monitoring and controlling process group:

- Have a realistic and formal project management plan that is complete to the level suitable for the project.
- Have a plan ready for measuring project performance against the performance measurement baseline.
- Be responsible for meeting the expected performance measurement baseline.
- Analyze and evaluate work performance, data, information, and reports.
- Identify root causes of problems using techniques like process analysis (e.g., Lean, Six Sigma Kanban).
- Influence factors that cause changes to prevent them.
- Utilize time and cost reserves as appropriate.
- Take actions, including corrective and preventive as appropriate to correct any variances that warrant actions.
- Evaluate the effectiveness of implemented corrective and preventive actions.
- Create and implement workarounds if needed.
- Measure against other metrics included in the project management plan to track project performance.
- Ensure that deliverables are meeting expected standards.
- Obtain formal acceptance of the completed interim deliverables from customers and other stakeholders.
- Perform procurement inspections and audits to verify contract deliverables.
- Communicate project information to the appropriate people in a timely manner.
- Find out any risk triggers and identify new risks.
- Reevaluate identified risks, planned preventive plans, contingent plans, and fallback plans.
- Evaluate the effectiveness of implemented risk response plans and look for any secondary risks.
- Create performance reports, including status, progress, variance, earned value, trend, and forecasting reports.
- Submit change requests as a last resort if there are no other alternatives to make up the deviation.

- Consider organizational strategic goals and objectives when analyzing change requests.
- Analyze and evaluate sellers' work performance, data, information, and reports.
- Audit sellers' invoices and make payments.
- Review and resolve any claims.
- Keep stakeholders satisfied by addressing their concerns and implementing approved change requests.
- Make sure that stakeholders are fully engaged in the project.
- Resolve conflicts and problems.
- Update the project management plan and other documents as needed.
- Document lessons learned.

Exercise 5:

1. I	7. P	13. M & C	19. I	25. I	31. E	37. P
2. M & C	8. C	14. C	20. P	26. P	32. P	
3. E	9. M & C	15. M & C	21. M & C	27. E	33. E	
4. E	10. E	16. I	22. C	28. I	34. M & C	
5. M & C	11. C	17. P	23. P	29. E	35. P	
6. P	12. M & C	18. M & C	24. P	30. I	36. E	

Exercise 6:

Knowledge Areas	Processes	Knowledge Areas	Processes
Integration	1. Develop Project Charter 2. Develop Project Management Plan 3. Direct and Manage Project Work 4. Monitor and Control Project Work 5. Perform Integrated Change Control 6. Close Project or Phase	**Human Resource**	1. Plan Human Resource Management 2. Acquire Project Team 3. Develop Project Team 4. Manage Project Team
Scope	1. Plan Scope Management 2. Collect Requirements 3. Define Scope 4. Create WBS 5. Validate Scope 6. Control Scope	**Communications**	1. Plan Communications Management 2. Manage Communications 3. Control Communications
Time	1. Plan Schedule Management 2. Define Activities 3. Sequence Activities 4. Estimate Activity Resources 5. Estimate Activity Durations 6. Develop Schedule 7. Control Schedule	**Risk**	1. Plan Risk Management 2. Identify Risks 3. Perform Qualitative Risk Analysis 4. Perform Quantitative Risk Analysis 5. Plan Risk Responses 6. Control Risks
Cost	1. Plan Cost Management 2. Estimate Costs 3. Determine Budget 4. Control Costs	**Procurement**	1. Plan Procurement Management 2. Conduct Procurements 3. Control Procurements 4. Close Procurements
Quality	1. Plan Quality Management 2. Perform Quality Assurance 3. Control Quality	**Stakeholder**	1. Identify Stakeholders 2. Plan Stakeholder Management 3. Manage Stakeholder Engagement 4. Control Stakeholder Engagement.

Exercise 7: A project manager should be aware of the following action items within the closing process group:

- Confirm work completion to requirements.
- Verify project or phase meets the completion or exit criteria.
- Close procurements.
- Make final payments.
- Gain formal acceptance of the product.
- Complete final performance reporting.
- Index and archive project records.
- Update lessons learned knowledge base.
- Update organizational process assets.
- Handoff completed product.
- Evaluate customer satisfaction on the overall project and deliverables.
- Release resources.
- Close contract.

Exercise 8:

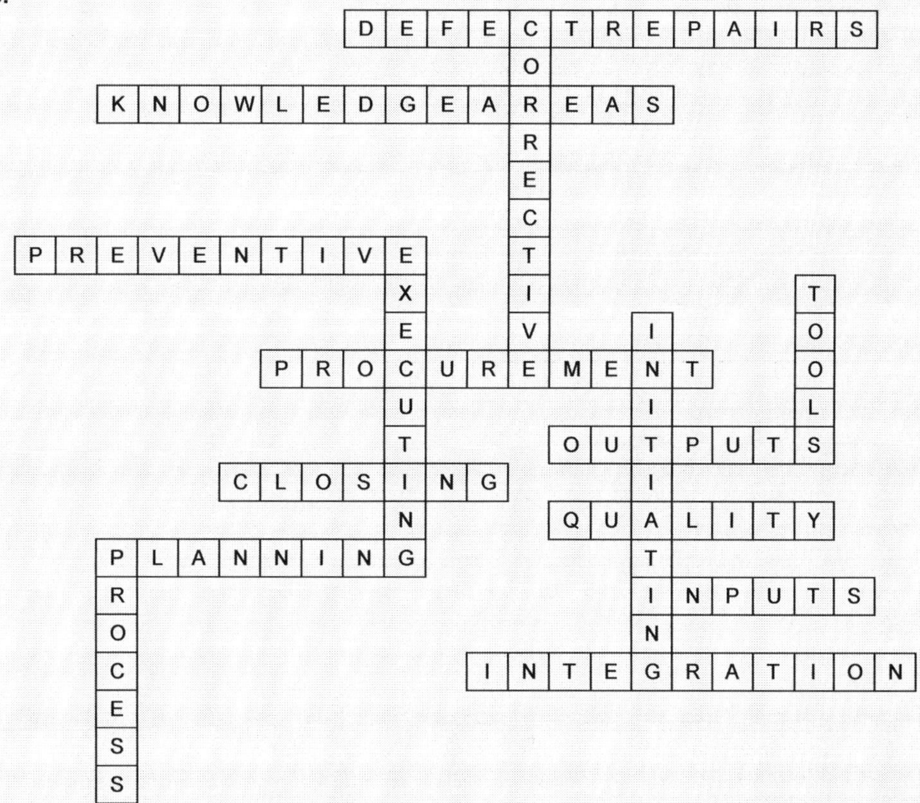

Exercise 9:

1. Outputs
2. Planning Process Group
3. Executing
4. Process
5. Corrective
6. Tools & techniques
7. Defect repairs
8. Process
9. Monitoring & controlling process group
10. Inputs
11. Closing
12. Project procurement management
13. Executing process group
14. Preventive action
15. Planning
16. Project quality management
17. Planning – Plan
    Executing – Do
    Monitoring & Controlling – Check and Act
18. Integration management
19. Planning processes
20. Processes
21. Initiating process group
22. Knowledge areas
23. Project stakeholder management
24. Executing, monitoring & controlling
25. Initiating, closing

Project Management Processes Exam Tips

- Be able to differentiate among the five process groups.
- Be able to identify the key features of all five process groups.
- Be able to name all ten knowledge areas.
- Be able to answer questions where you will need to analyze a specific situation and determine what you should do next.
- Be familiar with the concepts and terms in "Figure 3-16: Process Groups Key Inputs and Outputs" and "Figure 3-17: Project Management Processes Summary".

Project Management Processes Questions

1. Which statement is FALSE regarding the initiating process group?
   A. Cost and staffing start low, increase toward the end, and drop rapidly near closing.
   B. Project risk is highest at the beginning of the project and reduces as the project approaches its end.
   C. Stakeholder influence is highest at the start and diminishes as the project proceeds.
   D. The project manager and team are always identified as part of the initiating process group.

2. All of the following will occur during project initiating EXCEPT:
   A. Creation of a project scope statement.
   B. Identification of internal and external stakeholders.
   C. Development and review of the business case and a feasibility study.
   D. Assignment of the project manager to lead a project.

3. Which of the following will occur only during the planning process group?
   A. Identify stakeholders
   B. Develop schedule
   C. Acquire project team
   D. Validate scope

4. Which of the following process groups consists of the processes to complete the work defined in the project management plan and ultimately satisfies the project specifications and objectives?
   A. Planning process group
   B. Executing process group
   C. Initiating process group
   D. Closing process group

5. A knowledge area represents a complete set of activities, concepts, and terms that make up an area of specialization, project management field, or professional field. Each project management knowledge area is subdivided into which of the following?
   A. Best practices
   B. Policies
   C. Processes
   D. Guidelines

6. All of the following should be done during the closing process group EXCEPT:
   A. Formal sign-off and formal acceptance are received from the customers.
   B. Customer acceptance criteria are determined.
   C. Final versions of the lessons learned are compiled and made available for future projects.
   D. Completed project deliverables are handed off to operations and maintenance.

7. In which process group does the team track, measure, inspect, monitor, verify, review, compare, and regulate the progress and performance of the project; ensure that the plan is working; identify any areas in which changes to the plan are required; and initiate the corresponding changes?
   A. Monitoring & Controlling
   B. Closing
   C. Initiating
   D. Executing

8. You are overseeing a project for your organization to implement a web-based application for accessing pay and tax information online. Currently, you are in the process of implementing approved changes, corrective actions, preventive actions, and defect repairs in the project. You are in which of the following process groups?
   A. Executing
   B. Monitoring & Controlling
   C. Planning
   D. Closing

9. Which one of the following statements is FALSE about the executing process group?
   A. This process group usually takes the most time and resources.
   B. The processes in this process group measure and analyze the progress and performance of the project, ensure that the plan is working, identify any areas in which changes to the plan are required, and initiate the corresponding changes.
   C. Corrective actions, preventive actions, and defect repairs are implemented in this process group.
   D. This process group consists of processes to complete the work defined in the project management plan and ultimately satisfies the project specifications and objectives.

10. The sponsor has just signed the project charter and assigned you as a project manager to oversee a project to implement a simulator for a local golf club. What should you do FIRST as the project manager?
   A. Focus on identifying and classifying the stakeholders in the project.
   B. Start working on the project management plan.
   C. Develop the project schedule.
   D. Create the WBS.

11. You have been assigned to manage a project to design a new type of vinyl-based resilient floor material. You came up with a few orders of magnitude estimates, high-level risks, constraints, and assumptions for the project. What project management process group are you in?
   A. Monitoring & Controlling
   B. Closing
   C. Initiating
   D. Planning

12. Which one of the following process groups consists of iterative and ongoing processes to establish the total scope of effort, to define the objectives, and to identify the course of action required to attain those objectives?
   A. Planning
   B. Executing
   C. Initiating
   D. Monitoring & Controlling

13. Which of the following process groups serve as inputs to each other?
   A. Initiating, Planning
   B. Initiating, Executing
   C. Executing, Monitoring & Controlling
   D. Monitoring & Controlling, Closing

14. You are overseeing a construction project to construct a new fitness center at a local university. Currently, the team is working on collecting requirements and establishing estimates for the project. Which process group are you in?
   A. Initiating
   B. Executing
   C. Monitoring & Controlling
   D. Planning

15. Which one of the following is not an outcome when a project is initiated properly in the initiating process group?
   A. Authorizing the project manager to manage the project
   B. Defining the scope of the project
   C. Identifying the key stakeholders
   D. Understanding the goal, objective, and business need of the project

16. Which one of the following is NOT a planning process?
   A. Create WBS
   B. Perform Qualitative Risk Analysis
   C. Estimate Costs
   D. Develop Project Team

17. Steve has been overseeing a project to implement a new wireless media streaming device for a local networking company. The team has completed all the technical work in the project. The senior management asked Steve to report on the remaining activities in the project. Which one of the following will Steve report as the remaining work?
   A. Completion of the lessons learned
   B. Validation of the project scope
   C. Completion of the quality management plan
   D. Completion of risk response planning

18. You just finished creating your project charter. Which of the following will NOT be included in the charter?
   A. Detailed work package descriptions
   B. High-level roadmap and milestones
   C. Assumptions and constraints
   D. Authority level of the project manager

19. While working in the initiating process group, you are mainly focusing on creating a project charter and a stakeholder register. You will use all of the following as inputs EXCEPT:
   A. Organizational values and work ethics
   B. Project scope statement
   C. Configuration management knowledgebase
   D. Historical information and past lessons learned

20. Which one of the following is NOT a component of a change request?
   A. Corrective actions
   B. Preventive actions
   C. Defect repairs
   D. Issue Log

21. Your company, ITPro Consultancy, has assigned you as the project manager to upgrade the call center in your organization. The number of calls the customer support agents have to answer each month has increased drastically in the last five months, and the phone system is approaching the maximum load limit. While exploring the project status, you realize that the team just completed the Work Breakdown Structure (WBS) and WBS dictionary. The project team also started identifying risk items and developing a Risk Breakdown Structure (RBS). You are expecting to complete the project within the budget of $200,000 and in 7 months. What is the NEXT item the team should be working on?
   A. Complete identifying all risk items and the Risk Breakdown Structure (RBS).
   B. Participate in the development of the project scope statement.
   C. Focus on identifying and classifying the stakeholders in the project.
   D. Create an activity list and identify activity attributes.

22. Which one of the following is the BEST approach you can take while planning for your project?
   A. Develop the quality management plan prior to determining the process improvement plan and developing a quality checklist.
   B. Create a requirement traceability matrix before creating the Work Breakdown Structure (WBS).
   C. Develop a risk register before you document the high level risks, assumptions, and constraints.
   D. Inform stakeholders of the approved project charter and then start working on the networking diagram.

23. While managing a complex project, you realize that the processes of a certain process group occur simultaneously as the processes of all remaining 4 process groups. You are referring to:
   A. Monitoring and controlling
   B. Closing
   C. Executing
   D. Planning

24. Recently your stakeholder approved some of the deliverables that your team members just completed. These accepted deliverables will be used as inputs to which process group?
   A. Initiating
   B. Planning
   C. Executing
   D. Closing

25. Last week you submitted 5 new change requests to the Change Control Board (CCB). After exploring different options, the board approved 3 of the change requests. Approved change requests will be inputs to which process group?
   A. Initiating
   B. Planning
   C. Executing
   D. Closing

Project Management Processes Answers

1. D: The project manager is assigned during project initiating, but some of the team members will be acquired during executing process group.

2. A: The project scope statement is an output of the Define Scope process and is part of the planning process group.

3. B: Only develop schedule will occur during the planning process group. Identify stakeholders occurs during initiating, acquire project team occurs during executing, and validate scope occurs during monitoring & controlling.

4. B: The executing process group is intended to ensure that the work defined in the project plan is performed.

5. C: Each project management knowledge area is subdivided into specific processes, each of which is characterized by its inputs, tools & techniques, and outputs.

6. B: Customer acceptance criteria are determined during initiating process group.

7. A: During the monitoring & controlling process group, project performance is measured and analyzed, and needed changes are identified and approved.

8. A: Usually a project will enter the executing process group when the planning is completed or the project management plan has been updated due to change requests, including defect repairs and corrective and preventive actions. The executing process group involves coordinating people and resources as well as integrating and performing the activities of the project in accordance with the project management plan. These approved change requests for corrective actions, preventive actions, and defect repairs are implemented in the executing process group.

9. B: The processes in the monitoring & controlling process group track, measure, inspect, monitor, verify, review, compare, and regulate the progress and performance of the project; ensure that the plan is working; identify any areas in which changes to the plan are required; and initiate the corresponding changes.

10. A: The project charter is created and the project manager is assigned during the initiating process group. Stakeholder identification is also started during initiating and carried on throughout the project life cycle. It is essential to classify stakeholders according to their level of interest, influence, importance, and expectation at the early stage of the project as much as possible. Prior to jumping on planning, creating the WBS, and developing the project schedule, the project manager should focus on identifying and classifying the internal and external stakeholders in the project.

11. C: High-level risks, constraints, and assumptions are identified in the project charter, which is created during project initiating. Usually, orders of magnitude estimates are done during the initiating process group when not much information is available about the project.

12. A: The planning process group consists of iterative and ongoing processes to establish the total scope of effort to define the objectives and to identify the course of action required to attain those objectives.

13. C: The executing process group and the monitoring & controlling process group serve as inputs to each other. The planning process group and the executing process group also feed each other.

14. D: Requirements are collected from the customers and other stakeholders, and estimates on time, cost, resources, and other things are made during the planning process group.

15. B: Detailed project scope will be defined during the planning process group. The success of subsequent processes and activities greatly depends on the way a project is initiated. If a project is initiated properly, it would have a clear business need and feasibility, a clear goal, objective reasons for selecting this project over other possibilities, a clear direction for the scope, a project manager assigned, and a list of stakeholders for the project. On the other hand, if a project is not initiated properly, it could result in limited or a total lack of authority for the project manager as well as ambiguous goals or uncertainties as to why the project was initiated.

16. D: Develop project team is a process in the executing process group. All three remaining processes belong to the planning process group.

17. A: The lessons learned are usually done once the work is completed in the project. The quality management plan and the risk response plan are created during the planning process group. The validate scope process is done, not during closing, but in the monitoring & controlling process group.

18. A: High-level roadmap and milestones, assumptions and constraints, and authority level of the project manager should be included in the project charter. A project charter is created during initiating process group, but a project scope statement is created during planning process group. The scope baseline will have the scope statement, WBS, and details on WBS work packages.

19. B: Organizational process assets such as configuration management knowledgebase, historical information, and past lessons learned as well as enterprise environmental factors such as organizational values and work ethics are inputs in initiating process group. Project scope statement is an output of the planning process group.

20. D: A change request consists of corrective actions, preventive actions, and defect repairs. Corrective actions are taken to bring expected future performance of the project work in line with the project management plan. Preventive actions are taken to reduce the probability of risk items in the project. Defect repairs are taken to repair defects or entirely replace components that are faulty or dysfunctional. An issue is an obstacle that threatens project progress and can block the team from achieving its goals. An issue log is a written log to record issues that require solutions. It helps monitor who is responsible for resolving specific issues by a target date.

21. D: Refer to the "Figure 3-16: Process Groups Key Inputs and Outputs" and you should realize that during planning creating an activity list and identifying activity attributes come next after creating the WBS and WBS dictionary. Identifying and classifying the stakeholders in the project is part of stakeholder analysis which is usually done during initiating. Project scope must be defined and a project scope statement should be created prior to the creation of the WBS and WBS dictionary. The team must complete an activity list, network diagram, and participate in the development of the schedule and budget before risk identification can effectively be completed.

22. B: Refer to the "Figure 3-16: Process Groups Key Inputs and Outputs" and you should realize that you need to develop a requirement traceability matrix before the scope is define and a WBS is created for the project, so this is the best option. The process improvement plan and quality checklist are created as part of the quality management plan, not after it. A risk register is created in the planning process group, whereas the high level risks, assumptions, and constraints are identified during initiating. Starting the network diagram immediately after informing the stakeholders of the approved project charter skips several important steps, such as defining the requirements, scope, and activities.

23. A: Monitoring and controlling is something we are continuously doing in a project. Monitoring and controlling is not a phase of the project. Don't get confused thinking that we monitor and control only after executing.

24. D: Refer to the "Figure 3-13: Monitoring & Controlling Process Group Processes and Key Outputs" and "Figure 3-16: Process Groups Key Inputs and Outputs" and you should realize that accepted deliverables are outputs of the Validate Scope process in the monitoring and controlling process group. These accepted deliverables becomes inputs to the closing process group. The output of the closing process group is final product, service, or result transition.

25. C: You will be coming up with change requests both in the executing and monitoring and controlling process groups. These change requests will be an input to the Perform Integrated Change Control process in the monitoring and controlling process group. Approved change requests from the Perform Integrated Change Control process are fed back into the Direct and Manage Project Work process for implementation in the executing process group.

CHAPTER 4

PROJECT INTEGRATION MANAGEMENT

Project Integration Management

Project integration management maintains the "big picture" of the project throughout the life of the project by:

- Coordinating every part of the project
- Balancing all the processes in the knowledge areas
- Balancing project priorities

When the project is initiated, a project plan is assembled by the project manager. That plan is executed, the results of the work are verified, the changes to the project are controlled, and the project is closed.

The key roles of the project manager, project team, and project sponsor are as follows:

- Project manager: To perform integration
- Project team: To concentrate on completing the project activities
- Project sponsor: To protect the project team from unnecessary changes and loss of resources

Integration management is the only knowledge area that has processes occurring in all process groups, throughout the entire project life cycle.

		Process Groups					Total # of Processes
		Initiating	Planning	Executing	Monitoring & Controlling	Closing	
Knowledge Areas	Integration	1	1	1	2	1	6
	Scope		4		2		6
	Time		6		1		7
	Cost		3		1		4
	Quality		1	1	1		3
	Human Resource		1	3			4
	Communications		1	1	1		3
	Risk		5		1		6
	Procurement		1	1	1	1	4
	Stakeholder	1	1	1	1		4
	Total # of Processes	2	24	8	11	2	**47**

Table 4-1: Knowledge Areas and Process Groups Mapping

Project Integration Management Processes

Project Integration Management maintains the "big picture" throughout the life of the project and it coordinates every part of the project. In order to understand and remember the processes in Integration Management, refer back to the "Figure 3-16: Process Groups Key Inputs and Outputs". Understanding the key deliverables of each process group will help you to figure out the processes that create those deliverables throughout integration management.

The first process is Develop Project Charter from initiating process group since in the very beginning a project manager is assigned to the project and a project charter is developed. The second process is Develop Project Management Plan in planning process group as the project manager plans out all the work that needs to get accomplished. The project manager then makes sure the work is done properly by the Direct and Manage Project Work process in the execution process group and deals with changes along the way by the Monitor and Control Project Work and the Perform Integrated Change Control in the monitoring & controlling process group. At the end, once the project is finished, the project manager closes out the project by the Close Project or Phase process in closing process group.

As per PMI, project integration management has six key processes in the initiating, planning, executing, monitoring & controlling, and closing process groups.

Processes	Process Groups	Detail	Key Outputs
1. Develop Project Charter	Initiating	The process of developing a document that formally authorizes a project or a phase and documenting initial requirements that satisfy the stakeholders' needs and expectations.	– Project Charter
2. Develop Project Management Plan	Planning	The process of documenting the actions necessary to define, prepare, integrate, and coordinate all subsidiary plans.	– Project Management Plan
3. Direct and Manage Project Work	Executing	The process of performing the work defined in the project management plan to achieve the project's objectives.	– Deliverables
4. Monitor and Control Project Work	Monitoring & Controlling	The process of tracking, reviewing, and regulating the progress to meet the performance objectives defined in the project management plan.	– Change Requests – Work Performance Reports
5. Perform Integrated Change Control	Monitoring & Controlling	The process of reviewing all change requests and approving and managing all changes, including changes to the deliverables, organizational process assets, project documents, and the project management plan.	– Approved Change Requests – Change Log
6. Close Project or Phase	Closing	The process of finalizing all activities across all of the project management process groups to formally complete the project or phase.	– Final Product, Service, or Result Transition

Table 4-2: Six Project Integration Management Processes and Key Outputs

Project Integration Management Processes, Inputs, Tools & Techniques, and Outputs

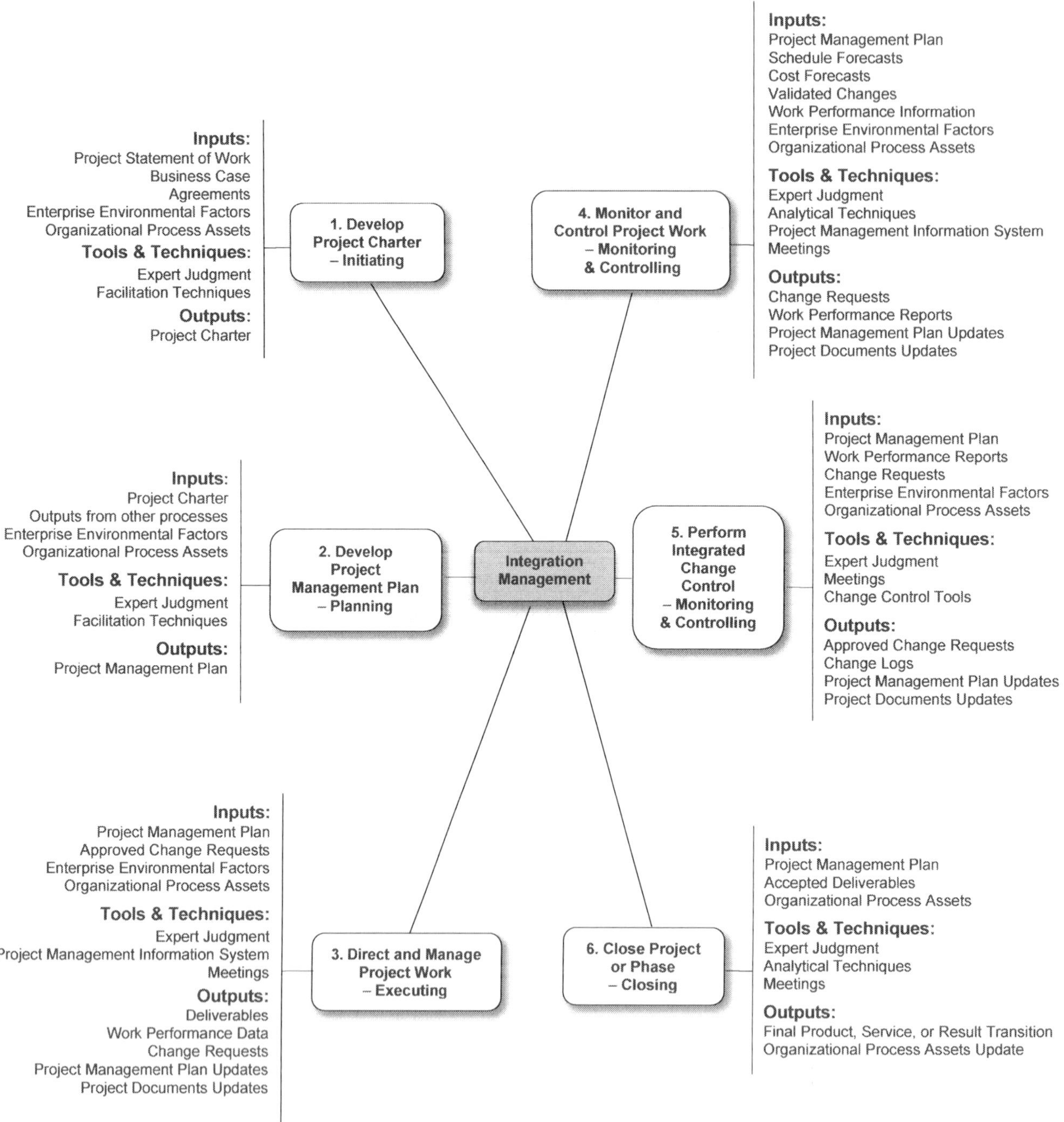

Figure 4-1: Project Integration Management Processes, Inputs, Tools & Techniques, and Outputs

Develop Project Charter

Develop Project Charter is the process of developing a document to formally authorize a project or a phase. It identifies the business objectives and needs, the current understanding of the stakeholders' expectations, and the new product, service, or result that it is intended to satisfy.

The approved project charter formally initiates the project. As per the PMBOK®, the Develop Project Charter process has the following inputs, tools & techniques, and outputs:

Figure 4-2: Develop Project Charter: Inputs, Tools & Techniques, and Outputs

Develop Project Charter: Inputs

- Project Statement of Work
- Business Case
- Agreements
- Enterprise Environmental Factors
- Organizational Process Assets

Project Statement of Work: The Project Statement of Work (PSOW) is a narrative description of products, results, or services to be supplied by the project. If supplied by the external customer, the SOW will usually be attached with the contract and the procurement document. The SOW describes the following:

- Business needs
- Product scope description or characteristic of the product, service, or result
- How the project supports the strategic plan

Business Case: A business case provides the required information from a business standpoint to determine whether or not the project is worth the required investment. Typically this includes the business need, the problem the project will solve, and the cost-benefit analysis. A project can be selected for one of several reasons, all of which should be explained in the business case.

Feasibility Study: Some organizations conduct a feasibility study prior to making a final decision about initiating a project in order to determine if the project is viable and also to figure out the probability of the project's success. This kind of study is conducted as the first phase of the project or in a separate project or subproject.

Project Selection Methods: There may be several potential projects in an organization. However, most organizations do not have the luxury to execute all of the proposed projects due to limited resources, cash flows, and different strategic objectives and priorities. Senior management selects projects from a set of potential projects based on the following:

- Project triggers
- Benefit measurement methods

Project Triggers: Factors that can prompt a project to begin. The following are examples of project triggers:

Market Demands: Developing fuel-efficient cars in response to high gasoline prices and pollution

Customer Requests: Developing a new website for customers to automate their billing process

Organization Requirements: Shifting an office to another location

Technological Advances: Implementing new products or services based on new inventions in genetics, nanotechnology, and robotics

Legal Requirements: Implementing guidelines for handling of a new toxic material

Ecological Impact: Reducing greenhouse gasses or other ecological impacts

Social Need: Resolving a social problem or fulfilling a social need in an impoverished region

Benefit Measurement Methods: Several methods are used for establishing value in order to analyze and prioritize projects. Below are the terms and techniques used to select projects:

Bigger is better for these measures:
A. Present Value (PV)
B. Net Present Value (NPV)
C. Discounted Cash Flow (DCF)
D. Internal Rate of Return (IRR)
E. Benefit Cost Ratio (BCR)
F. Economic Value Added (EVA)
G. Return on Investment (ROI)
H. Return on Invested Capital (ROIC)

Smaller is better for these measures:
I. Payback period
J. Opportunity cost

A. Present Value: Due to the time value of money, money received in the future is worth less than money received today. Present value is the value "today" of future cash flow due to a project or acquisition.

$$PV = \frac{FV}{(1+r)^n}$$

FV = Future value
r = Interest rate (Annual)
n = Number of years in time period

Exercise 1: What is the present value of $400,000 received three years from now if we expect the interest rate to be 10 percent? Is it more or less than $400,000?

B. Net Present Value: The Present Value of the benefits (income or revenue) minus the costs over many time periods. NPV is useful as it allows for a comparison of many projects to select the best one to initiate.

NPV = PV – Cost

- If NPV is positive, we can consider the investment a good choice unless a better one exists.
- A project with a higher NPV is generally selected.
- The number of years and cost are not relevant as they are accounted for in the calculation of NPV.

Exercise 2: You have two projects to choose from. Project A will take four years to complete and has an NPV of $50,000. Project B will take six years to complete and has an NPV of $90,000. Which one should you select?

Exercise 3: The following table indicates the yearly revenues of a five-year project. The cost of capital is 10 percent and the initial investment is $9,000. What is the net present value of your project?

Years	Revenue	Present Value
0	0	– 9,000
1	1000	
2	2000	
3	2000	
4	5000	
5	2000	

C. Discounted Cash Flow: A valuation method used to estimate the attractiveness of an investment opportunity. Discounted Cash Flow (DCF) analysis uses future free cash flow projections and discounts them (most often using the weighted average cost of capital) to arrive at a present value, which is used to evaluate the potential for investment. If the value arrived through DCF analysis is higher than the current cost of the investment, the opportunity may be a good one.

Calculated as:

$$DCF = \frac{CF1}{(1+r)^1} + \frac{CF2}{(1+r)^2} + \dots + \frac{CFn}{(1+r)^n}$$

CF = Cash Flow
r = Discount Rate

D. Rate of Return (or Internal Rate of Return – IRR): Calculates the percentage of the project cost returned as interest over the years following project completion.

- Computation of IRR is usually automated.
- IRR is commonly used to prioritize competing projects.

Exercise 4: Project A has an IRR of 15 percent, and Project B has an IRR of 9 percent. Which one would you prefer?

E. Benefit Cost Ratio: The ratio of benefits (in the form of savings or revenue generation) to production costs for the product, service, or result. It divides the expected revenue of a project by its cost. It is typically used in comparing projects.

- The higher the BCR, the more revenue potential.
- A BCR > 1 means benefit is greater than the cost,
  < 1 means cost is greater than benefit,
  = 1 means it is a break-even project.

Exercise 5: An innovative software application project will cost you $150,000, and you are expecting to sell it for $300,000 to a very potential market. What is the benefit cost ratio here?

Exercise 6: A project has a benefit of $90,000, and it will cost the organization $10,000. The benefit cost ratio is 90,000/10,000 or 9 to 1. What does a benefit cost ratio of 9 to 1 mean?

A. Cost is nine times the profit
B. The cost is greater than the benefit
C. Payback is nine times the cost
D. Profit is nine times the cost

F. Economic Value Added (EVA): This concept is concerned with whether the project returns to the company more value than it costs.
Example: Company ABC invested $200,000 in a project, and that project returned a net profit of $13,000 in the first year of operation. The organization could have invested that same $200,000 and earned a 7 percent return.

EVA = After Tax Profit – (Capital expenditures * Cost of Capital)
= 13,000 – (200,000 * .07) = – $1,000
ABC actually lost $1,000 as far as EVA is concerned.

G. Return on Investment (ROI): A percentage that shows what return a company can make by investing in a project or some other endeavor.

ROI = (Benefit – Cost) / Cost

Example: Company ABC invested in a project that costs them $175,000, and the project saved the company $240,000 in the first year alone.
In this case ROI is ($240,000 – $175,000) / $175,000 = $65,000 / $175,000 = 37 percent.

H. Return on Invested Capital (ROIC): The return that can be expected for every dollar of cash an organization invests in a project.

ROIC = Net Income (after tax) from project / Total Capital invested in the project

Example: Company ABC invested $190,000 in a project that generated $30,000 top line revenue in the first year, with $7,000 in operational costs and a tax liability of $3,350. To calculate the ROIC, first calculate the after-tax profit, $30,000 – $7,000 – $3,350 = $19,650, then divide that number by the total initial investment to determine the ROIC.
Thus, ROIC = $19,650/$190,000 = 10.3 percent

I. Payback Period: The number of time periods it will take a company to recoup its initial costs of producing the product, service, or result of the project. This method compares the initial investment with the expected cash inflows over the life of the product, service, or result of the project.

Exercise 7: Project A has a payback period of eight months, and Project B has a payback period of twelve months. Which one will you select?

Exercise 8: Company ABC invested $400,000 in a project with expected cash inflows of $40,000 per quarter for the first two years and $80,000 per quarter from year three. What is the payback period?

J. Opportunity Cost: The value of a project that is not undertaken so that another project can be executed. It is the cost of a lost opportunity, missing the benefit of the project not selected. In other words: If Company A decides to do Project 1 instead of Project 2, then Project 1 has an opportunity cost equal to the value of Project 2.

While selecting a project, the smaller the opportunity cost the better, since it is not desirable to miss out on a great opportunity.

Exercise 9: You have two projects to choose from: Project A with an NPV of $53,000 or Project B with an NPV of $79,000. What is the opportunity cost of selecting Project B?

A Few Other Important Terms

A. Depreciation: The systematic "writing-off" of the cost of assets over their usable life-spans.
There are two basic forms of depreciation:

Straight Line Depreciation subtracts the same amount of value during every year of the asset's usable life.
Example: A $500 item with a five-year useful life and no salvage value (value of the item at the end of its life) would be depreciated at $100/year.

Accelerated Depreciation reduces the value of an asset more quickly in the earlier part of its usable life. There are two forms of accelerated depreciation:

- Double Declining Balance
- Sum of the Years Digits

Accelerated depreciation depreciates faster than straight line.
Example: A $500 item with a five-year life and no salvage value would be depreciated at $140 the first year, $120 the second, $100 the next, etc.

B. Law of Diminishing Returns: This means that the more you put into something, the less you get out of it or the greater the likelihood that the return will not be as expected.

Adding twice as many resources to an activity may not get the activity done in half the time, since the communication will be much more complicated after adding additional resources, and these resources may have more conflicts and issues that will delay the activity even more.

C. Working Capital: The amount of money the company has available to invest, including investment in projects.
Working Capital = Current assets – Current liabilities

D. Sunk Cost: The amount already paid for a project and often used to describe what is written off as unrecoverable from a canceled project.

Exercise 10 You are halfway through a project with an initial budget of $50,000 and have spent $80,000. Do you consider the $50,000 over budget when determining whether to continue with the project?

____

____

____

____

Agreements: Agreements define initial intentions for a project and may be in the form of service-level agreements (SLA), letters of intent, contracts, or Memorandums of Understanding (MOU). Agreements can be verbal or written. A contract is not always relevant, since not all projects will be executed under a contract. A contract will be an input if the work is done for an external customer and will be signed prior to the project initiation.

Enterprise Environmental Factors: Company culture, industry standards, human resources, risk tolerances, governmental or industry standards, organizational infrastructure, marketplace conditions, etc., may influence the Develop Project Charter process.

Organizational Process Assets: Policies, procedures and guidelines, historical information, and the knowledge base of key learning from previous projects, etc., may influence the Develop Project Charter process.

Develop Project Charter: Tools & Techniques

- Expert Judgment
- Facilitation Techniques

Expert Judgment: Consultants, other units within the organization, industry groups, subject matter experts, professional and technical associations, stakeholders, Project Management Office (PMO), customers, the sponsor, etc., who have relevant specialized knowledge, training, and expertise can provide expert judgment to Develop Project Charter.

Facilitation Techniques: Several facilitation techniques such as brainstorming, problem solving, conflict resolution, and meeting management, etc., play a major role in the development of the project charter.

Develop Project Charter: Outputs

- Project Charter

Project Charter: Once a project is selected or a contract is signed to perform a project, a project charter is created to formally authorize a project or a phase. This charter documents the business objectives and needs, current understanding of the stakeholders' expectations, and the new product, service, or result that the project is intended to satisfy.

Following are the key factors of a project charter:

- Project title and high-level description
- Project manager assignment and authority level
- Business case
- Key stakeholders list
- Stakeholders' high-level requirements
- High-level product description/deliverables
- Measurable project objectives
- Project approval requirement
- Summary milestone schedule
- Summary budget
- High-level project risks
- Assumptions
- Constraints
- Project sponsor authorizing the project

Exercise 11: Why is a project charter so important for the project?

Project Charter Example for a Centralized Customer Support Help Desk System

Project Manager: John Smith, PMP

Executive Summary: ITPro Consultancy has always been committed to providing customers with a superior level of service, which is second to none in the telecommunications industry. However, recent increases in the number of customer complaints about its service levels have compromised its ability to achieve this vision. If the number of complaints continues to increase and its market brand of superior customer service weakens, the company will begin to lose critical market share to its competitors. To address the problem immediately, the board of directors has decided to centralize the help desk function and install a new, fully integrated help desk system. The entire project was outsourced to Netcom Direct for implementation within a short period of time.

Project Definition
Vision: The vision of this project is to centralize the help desk function and install a new, fully integrated help desk system to provide customers with a level of service that is second to none in the telecommunications industry.

Objectives: The key objective of this project is to establish a centralized, fully integrated help desk system and new telecommunications infrastructure.

Deliverables: The following items are considered to be within the scope of this project:
- Establish a central help desk premise and new telecommunications infrastructure.
- Relocate exiting help desk staffs to the new central location.
- Create new customer service guidelines, processes, and procedures.
- Implement a new help desk computer system to manage customer files.
- Integrate this new system with other ITPro Consultancy systems (e.g., the technicians' job allocation system).
- Market the new centralized help desk to reestablish its brand in the market.
- Communicate new customer service procedures to staffs and customers.
- Set departmental performance standards and key performance indicators.
- Measure and report actual performance against those standards.

Benefits: By centralizing the customer support function, ITPro Consultancy will gain the following business benefits:
- The centralized help desk will serve as a single source for customer information.
- Customer account information will readily be available.
- The company will gain a robust set of standards, processes, and systems for the delivery of customer service.
- Customer queues will be reduced.
- Help desk staff will be able to resolve queries more quickly.
- Customers will be more satisfied, as service problems are identified and resolved proactively through real-time monitoring of query status and automatic alerts on unresolved problems.
- ITPro Consultancy will be able to investigate the cause of each customer complaint and take action to ensure that service is improved.

Project Organization

Project Manager Assigned: John Smith, PMP

Customer Group	Customer Representative
ITPro Consultancy	The primary customer of this project is ITPro Consultancy customer support team. Mr. R is the project's key representative for ITPro Consultancy.
Stakeholder group	**Stakeholder Interest**
Entire Customer Support Team	All team members are responsible for and have a key interest in the successful completion of this project.
Senior Management Team	This project is a major undertaking for ITPro Consultancy. As such, the entire senior management team has asked to be kept fully informed of its progress.
President	As sponsor, the president of ITPro Consultancy has a vested interest in the success of this project.
Customer Support Team Lead	The customer support team lead has a vested interest in the success of the project, as the team success is dependent on the centralized customer support application.

Roles: The following key roles have been defined for this project:

Role	Resource Name	Organization	Responsibilities
Project Sponsor	Mr. N	ITPro Consultancy	– Leading the project board as chairman – Defining the vision, purpose, and objectives of the project – Approving the requirements, timetable, and resources – Approving the provision of funds and resources – Authorizing acceptance of the final solution delivered by the project
Project Board	Mr. X Mr. Y Mr. Z Mr. L Ms. M	ITPro Consultancy ITPro Consultancy ITPro Consultancy NetCom Direct NetCom Direct	– Overseeing the progress of the project – Resolving all high-level risks, issues, and change requests – Ensuring that the project team has everything it needs to deliver successfully
Project Manager	Mr. J	NetCom Direct	– Delivering the project on time, within budget, and to specification – Managing project staff, suppliers, customers, and all other project stakeholders – Undertaking the activities required to initiate, plan, execute, and close the project successfully
Project Leaders	Mr. F Ms. D Ms. K	NetCom Direct NetCom Direct NetCom Direct	– Undertaking all tasks allocated by the project manager per the project plan – Reporting progress of the execution of tasks to the project manager on a regular basis – Escalating risks and issues to be addressed by the project manager

Structure: The following organizational structure will be put in place to ensure the successful delivery of this project:

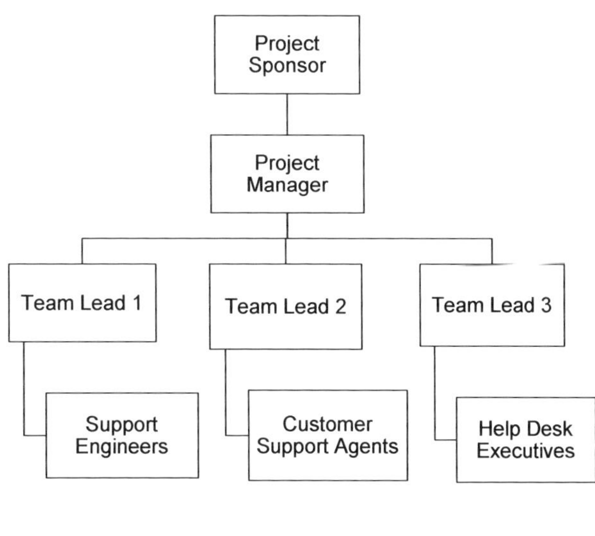

Schedule: The following schedule describes the key activities and timescales involved in implementing this project:

ID	Task List	Start Date	Duration
1	Planning	15-Mar-13	15 days
2	Collect Requirements	25-Mar-13	20 days
3	Explore Off-The-Shelf Help Desk Solution	25-Mar-13	15 days
4	System Design	1-Apr-13	8 days
5	Simulations & Prototype	8-Apr-13	15 days
6	Help Desk Implementation	20-Apr-13	10 days
7	Integration & Unit Testing	20-Apr-13	20 days
8	Data Migration to Centralized Database	20-Apr-13	15 days
9	Data Validation	30-Apr-13	10 days
10	Group Review	5-May-13	6 days
11	User Acceptance Testing	5-May-13	4 days
12	Release	12-May-13	2 days

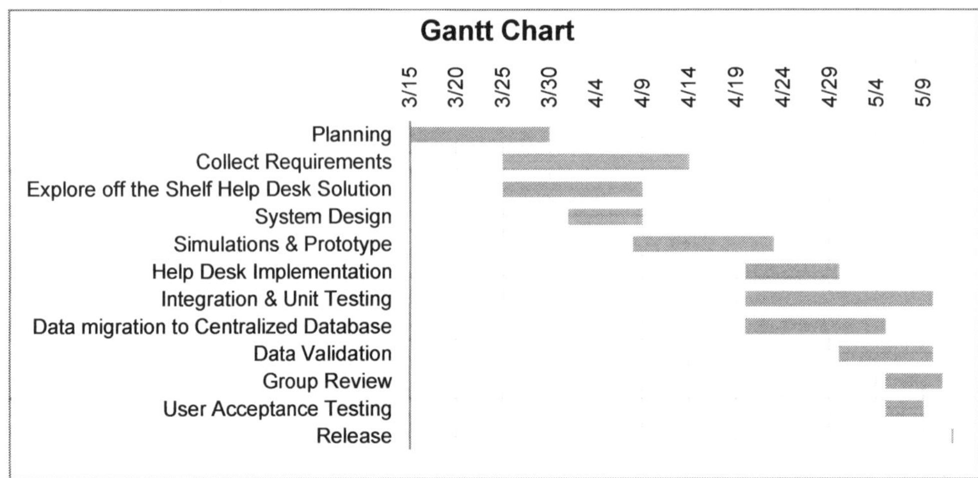

Resource Plan: To ensure that the project is fully resourced, the following general source list has been specified. A detailed resource plan will be created later in the project planning phase.

Role	Start Date	End Date	% Effort
Project Board - 3	1/1/13	6/30/13	10%
Project Sponsor - 1	1/1/13	6/30/13	30%
Project Manager - 1	1/1/13	6/30/13	100%
Team Leaders - 3	2/1/13	6/30/13	100%
Permissions and Planning Team - 1	1/1/13	6/30/13	50%
Quality Assurance and Control Team - 2	3/1/13	6/30/13	80%

Completion Criteria: The following table lists the criteria that must be met for closure of the project to be approved:

Process	Description
Vision	The project vision as stated within this document must have been achieved.
Scope	The project must have operated within the deliverables specified by this document.
Business Benefits	The project must have produced the business benefits specified in this document.
Deliverables	The project must have produced the deliverables specified by this document.
Acceptance	The customer must have signed off on all project deliverables as complete.
General	Where possible, the project must have produced the deliverables on schedule, under budget, and to the required level of specification.

Financial Plan: The following table lists the general financial expenditure required to complete this project successfully. A detailed financial plan will be created later in the project planning phase.

Business Category	Expense Description	Amount
Personal	Staff relocation.	$120,000
	Training and recruitment.	$70,000
Operations	Creation of new guidelines, processes, and standards.	$50,000
	Deployment of new help desk system.	$100,000
	Integration of new system with existing ITPro Consultancy systems.	$70,000
Premise	Purchase of new help desk system and telecommunications infrastructure.	$300,000
	Allocation of new office space in existing ITPro Consultancy premise.	$80,000
	Installation of new telecommunications equipment.	$50,000
	New office furniture and office equipment.	$25,000
	Closure of old help desk premises.	$10,000
Marketing	Advertising to existing client base.	$150,000
	Total Expense	**$1,025,000**

High-Level Risks: The following table lists the risks identified for this project to date:

Risk Description	Risk Likelihood	Risk Impact	Risk Mitigating Action
Client records are inaccurate or invalid.	Medium	Medium	Explain the benefits of the new system and the fact that some records will not be carried across.
Technology falls short of expected performance.	Medium	High	Test four off-the-shelf products to ensure that they will provide the required functionality and performance.
The central desk is unable to process the volume of calls or visits.	Low	High	Forecast the number of calls and visits and build a solution that is capable of handling the forecasted volume.

Issues: The following table lists the issues identified for this project to date:

Issue Description	Issue Priority	Action Required to Resolve Issue
The time for developing a customized help desk is limited.	High	Examine off-the-shelf help desk systems as a way to reduce system procurement and implementation time.
The current workload for staff is creating delays in the internal work activities that will be required to route customer calls to the new call center.	High	Schedule the telecommunications changeover on a date when staff work activities are minimal.
There are insufficient funds allocated within the current budget to allow this project to take place.	Medium	Approve the un-budgeted expenditure required to undertake this project.

Assumptions: Within this project, it is assumed that:

- There will be no legislative, business strategy, or policy changes during the lifetime of the project.
- The help desk system currently on the market will be available during the planning and execution phases of this project.
- Staff will be willing to change over to the new system and will offer their full support.

Constraints: The following constraints have been identified:

- The contingency available in the project budget is 10 percent.

Develop Project Management Plan

Develop Project Management Plan is an iterative and ongoing process to establish the total scope of effort, define the objectives, and identify the course of action required to attain those objectives.

The project management plan is developed through a series of integrated processes that take place until project closure. This plan defines how the project is executed, monitored & controlled, and closed. This process results in a project management plan that is progressively elaborated by updates and controlled and approved through the Perform Integrated Change Control process.

As per the PMBOK®, the Develop Project Management Plan process has the following inputs, tools & techniques, and outputs:

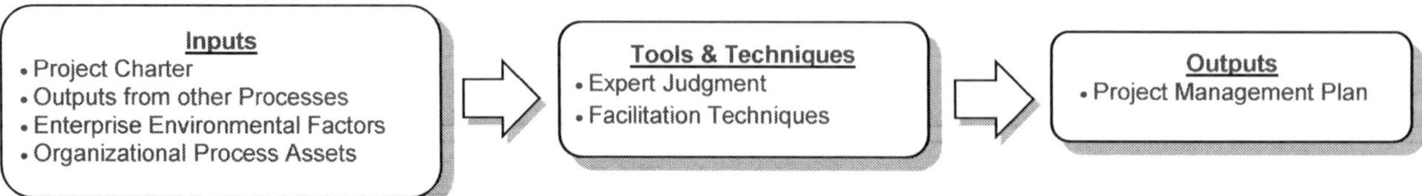

Figure 4-3: Develop Project Management Plan: Inputs, Tools & Techniques, and Outputs

Develop Project Management Plan: Inputs

- Project Charter
- Outputs from Other Processes
- Enterprise Environmental Factors
- Organizational Process Assets

Project Charter: The project charter documents the business objectives and needs, the current understanding of the stakeholders' needs, and the new product, service, or result that it is intended to satisfy.

Outputs from Other Processes: Outputs such as baselines and subsidiary management plans from the scope, time, cost, quality, risk, human resource, communication, procurement, and stakeholder planning processes are consolidated to create the project management plan.

Enterprise Environmental Factors: The factors that should be considered are company culture, industry or governmental standards, organizational infrastructure, marketplace conditions, and personnel administration. For instance, guidelines for employee hiring and firing, training records, and performance reviews, and Project Management Information System (PMIS) such as an information collection and distribution system, a configuration management system, a scheduling software tool, or other automated systems.

Organizational Process Assets: Policies, procedures and guidelines, historical information, knowledge base of key lessons from previous projects, project management plan templates, and change control procedures should be considered.

Develop Project Management Plan: Tools & Techniques

- Expert Judgment
- Facilitation Techniques

Expert Judgment: Specialists can provide expert judgment to tailor processes to meet the project needs, identify needs for resources and skill level, define the level of configuration management to apply, and identify technical and management detail while developing the project management plan.

Facilitation Techniques: Various facilitation techniques such as brainstorming, problem solving, conflict resolution, and meeting management, play a major role in the development of the project management plan.

Develop Project Management Plan: Outputs

- Project Management Plan

Project Management Plan: The project management plan is a single-approved document that defines how the project is executed, how it is monitored & controlled, and how it is closed. The project management plan can be documented at the summary level or at a very detailed level depending on the needs of the project. It should include the following elements:

- Processes that will be used to perform each phase of the project
- The life cycle that will be used
- Methods for executing the work
- A change management plan for monitoring & controlling changes
- A configuration management plan
- Methods for identifying and maintaining the validity of performance baseline
- Communication needs and techniques to fulfill the needs of stakeholders

In addition to all these elements, the following subsidiary plans will also be documented in the project management plan:

- **Knowledge Area Management Plans:** These plans define how all different knowledge areas will be developed, managed, executed, and controlled.
  - Scope management plan
  - Requirement management plan
  - Schedule management plan
  - Cost management plan
  - Quality management plan
  - Human resource management plan
  - Communications management plan
  - Risk management plan
  - Procurement management plan
  - Stakeholder management plan
- **Performance Measurement Baseline:** These are a record of what the project had planned, scheduled, and budgeted in terms of scope, schedule, and cost performance. These baselines are used to compare the project's actual performance against its planned performance.
  - **Scope baseline:** A combination of the project scope statement, Work Breakdown Structure (WBS), and WBS dictionary.
  - **Schedule baseline:** The approved schedule with duration, start and end dates, resources, and dependencies for each activity.
  - **Cost baseline:** The time-phased cost budget.
- **Other Plans**
  - **Process improvement plan:** This plan defines how processes that are used on the project will be evaluated and improved.
  - **Change management plan:** This plan defines how changes will be managed and controlled.
  - **Configuration management plan:** This plan defines how documentation changes concerning the project's deliverables and processes will be managed.

Exercise 12: List actions to create an approved, realistic, and formal project management plan.

Direct and Manage Project Work

The executing process group consists of the processes to complete the work defined in the project management plan to satisfy the project specifications and objectives. In this process, group work is actually carried out—code is written, parts are assembled, information is distributed, houses are constructed, the team is developed and managed, roads are repaired, etc. This process also involves managing people and keeping them engaged, improving the processes, requesting changes, and implementing approved changes.

The following approved changes are implemented in this process group:

Corrective actions: Actions that are taken to bring expected future performance of the project work in line with the project management plan.

Preventive actions: Actions that are taken to reduce the probability of risk items in the project.

Defect repairs: Actions that are taken to repair or replace any defective components.

As per the PMBOK®, the Direct and Manage Project Work process has the following inputs, tools & techniques, and outputs:

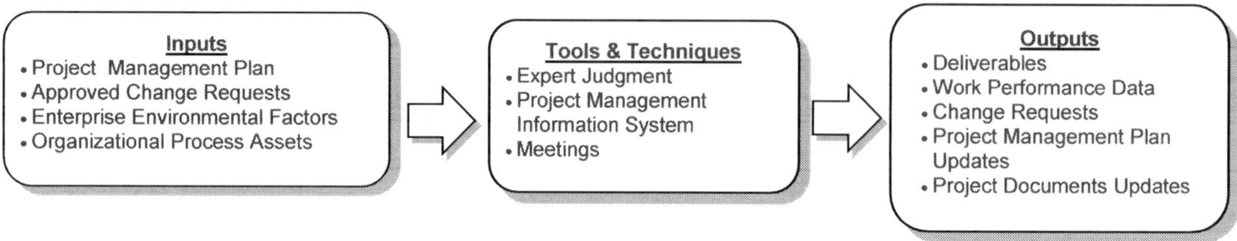

Figure 4-4: Direct and Manage Project Work: Inputs, Tools & Techniques, and Outputs

Direct and Manage Project Work: Inputs

- Project Management Plan
- Approved Change Requests
- Enterprise Environmental Factors
- Organizational Process Assets

Project Management Plan: This single-approved document defines how the project is executed, how it is monitored & controlled, and how it is closed.

Approved Change Requests: In the Perform Integrated Change Control process, some changes are approved and some are denied. Approved change requests may require implementation of preventive and corrective actions and may also modify policies, the project management plan, guidelines, procedures, costs, the schedule baseline, etc.

Enterprise Environmental Factors: Enterprise Environmental Factors such as company culture, organizational infrastructure, marketplace conditions, stakeholder risk tolerance, personnel, administrative policies, and Project Management Information System (PMIS) can influence the Direct and Manage Project Work process. Administrative policies include guidelines for employee hiring and firing, training records, and performance reviews. Project Management Information System includes information collection and distribution system, a configuration management system, a scheduling software tool, and other automated systems.

Organizational Process Assets: Organizational process assets such as policies, procedures and guidelines, historical information, the knowledge base of key learning from previous projects, issue and defect management procedures and database, communication requirements, process measurement database, change control procedures, etc., can influence the Direct and Manage Project Work process.

Direct and Manage Project Work: Tools & Techniques

- Expert Judgment
- Project Management Information System
- Meetings

Expert Judgment: Consultants, other units within the organization, industry groups, subject matter experts, professional and technical associations, stakeholders, the sponsor, etc., who have relevant specialized knowledge, training, and expertise can provide expert judgment to assess the inputs required to direct and manage the execution of the project management plan.

Project Management Information System: Project Management Information System (PMIS) such as a scheduling software tool, a configuration management system, an information collection and distribution system, or other online automated systems can be utilized during the Direct and Manage Project Work process.

Meetings: While directing and managing project work, a project manager can use meetings to discuss various project-related topics and address concerns with the project team members and other stakeholders.

A meeting agenda with well-defined agenda items, purpose, objectives, and a timetable should be sent out prior to the meeting, and meeting minutes and action items should be documented and sent out after the meeting.

A project manager can utilize the meeting to exchange information, brainstorm ideas, evaluate options, and make required decisions. Also, the project manager should make sure that each attendee has a specific role in the meeting and that there are proper ground rules to ensure the effectiveness of the meeting. Face-to-face meetings are more effective, but virtual meetings can also be effective through proper preparation and by utilizing the latest audio and video conferencing tools.

Direct and Manage Project Work: Outputs

- Deliverables
- Work Performance Data
- Change Requests
- Project Management Plan Updates
- Project Documents Updates

Deliverables: A deliverable is any unique and verifiable product, result, capability, or service that must be produced in order to complete a process, phase, or project.

Work Performance Data: Information on how far along a deliverable is and how it is progressing against the plan is routinely collected as the project progresses. There can be several work performance data of interest in the project, such as:

- Deliverable status
- Schedule progress
- Resource utilization
- Key performance indicators
- Costs incurred
- Number of defects
- Quality standards

Change Requests: Approved change requests may require implementation of preventive and corrective actions and may also modify policies, the project management plan, guidelines, procedures, costs, the schedule baseline, etc.

The following approved changes are included in the change requests:

Corrective actions: Actions that are taken to bring expected future performance of the project work in line with the project management plan.

Preventive actions: Actions that are taken to reduce the probability of risk items in the project.

Defect repairs: Actions that are taken to repair the defects or entirely replace the components.

Updates: Any changes to reflect updated or additional ideas or content to formally controlled documents, plans, etc.

Project Management Plan Updates: Most of the elements of the project management plan will be updated in this process.

Project Documents Updates: Documents such as requirements documents, the risk register, the stakeholder register, project logs (issues, assumptions, etc.) may be updated.

Monitor and Control Project Work

The Monitor and Control Project Work process tracks, measures, inspects, monitors, verifies, reviews, compares, and regulates the progress and performance of the project. This process ensures that the plan is working, identifies any areas in which changes to the plan are required, and initiates the corresponding changes.

The Monitor and Control Project Work process is concerned with:

- Comparing actual project performance against the project management plan
- Assessing performance to determine whether any corrective or preventive action is required
- Analysing, tracking, and monitoring project risks
- Maintaining an accurate base concerning the project's product
- Providing information to support status reporting
- Providing forecasts to update current costs and schedule information
- Monitoring implementation of approved changes

The following concept is important to the Monitor and Control Project Work process.

Work Authorization System: This is a formal, documented procedure to describe how to authorize and initiate work in the correct sequence at the appropriate time. It is a component of the enterprise environmental factors, which are inputs in this process.

Depending on the organizational structure, a work authorization system is usually implemented to make sure that work in a project is only started when a formal authorization is given either by the project manager or the functional manager.

For example, if you are managing a large construction project with hundreds of employees, you need to have a robust work authorization system. This will ensure that you are authorizing all kinds of foundational, electrical, painting, and plumbing work in the correct sequence at the right time.

As per the PMBOK®, the Monitor and Control Project Work process has the following inputs, tools & techniques, and outputs:

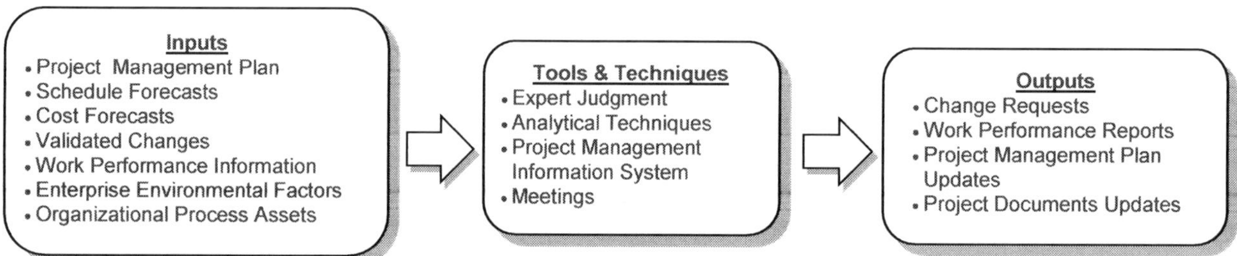

Figure 4-5: Monitor and Control Project Work: Inputs, Tools & Techniques, and Outputs

Monitor and Control Project Work: Inputs

- Project Management Plan
- Schedule Forecasts
- Cost Forecasts
- Validated Changes
- Work Performance Information
- Enterprise Environmental Factors
- Organizational Process Assets

Project Management Plan: The single-approved document that defines how the project is executed, how it is monitored and controlled, and how it is closed.

Schedule Forecasts: This kind of forecast, which is derived from the progress against the schedule baseline such as Schedule Variance (SV) and Schedule Performance Index (SPI), may be used to figure out if the project is ahead or behind schedule and if any change request is required or not.

Cost Forecasts: This kind of forecast, which is derived from the progress against the cost baseline such as Cost Variance (CV) and Cost Performance Index (CPI), may be used to figure out if the project is over or under budget and if any change request is required or not.

Validated Changes: A validated change will provide the required data to ensure that a change that is approved by the change control board is appropriately implemented.

Work Performance Information: Work performance information, once correlated and contextualized, provides essential key data so that necessary corrective and preventive actions can be taken. Examples of performance information can be:

- Current status
- Issues
- Scheduled activities
- Forecasts
- Significant achievements

Enterprise Environmental Factors: Enterprise environmental factors such as the company work authorization system, organizational infrastructure, governmental or industry standards, stakeholder risk tolerance, or a Project Management Information System (PMIS) such as an information collection and distribution system, a configuration management system, a scheduling software tool, or other automated system can influence the Monitor and Control Project Work process.

Organizational Process Assets: Organizational process assets such as policies, procedures and guidelines, historical information, a knowledge base of key learning from previous projects, the issue and defect management procedures and database, communication requirements, the process measurement database, issue and defect management procedures, etc., can influence the Monitor and Control Project Work process.

Monitor and Control Project Work: Tools & Techniques

- Expert Judgment
- Analytical Techniques
- Project Management Information System
- Meetings

Expert Judgment: The project manager, in collaboration with the team, determines the actions required to ensure that project performance matches expectations. Expert judgment is also used by the project management team to interpret and evaluate the information provided by the monitor and control processes.

Analytical Techniques: Several analytical techniques such as variance analysis, earned value management, trend analysis, root cause analysis, reserve analysis, regression analysis, grouping methods, and Failure Mode and Effect Analysis (FMEA), etc., are used to forecast potential outcomes in project.

Project Management Information System: The Project Management Information System (PMIS) is incorporated as part of the enterprise environmental factors to several processes since it is part of the environment in which the project is performed. It is an automated system that can serve as a repository for information and a tool to assist with communication and with tracking documents and deliverables. The PMIS also supports the project from beginning to end by optimizing the schedule and helping collect and distribute information.

Meetings: While monitoring & controlling project work, a project manager can use face-to-face, virtual, formal, informal, user group, and review meetings to discuss various project-related topics and to address concerns with the project team members and other stakeholders.

Monitor and Control Project Work: Outputs

- Change Requests
- Work Performance Reports
- Project Management Plan Updates
- Project Documents Updates

Change Requests: Approved change requests may require implementation of preventive and corrective actions and may also modify policies, the project management plan, guidelines, procedures, costs, the schedule baseline, etc. The following approved changes are included in the change requests:

Corrective actions: Actions that are taken to bring expected future performance of the project work in line with the project management plan.

Preventive actions: Actions that are taken to reduce the probability of risk items in the project.

Defect repairs: Actions that are taken to repair and/or entirely replace defective components.

Updates: Any changes to reflect updated or additional ideas or content to formally controlled documents, plans, etc.

Work Performance Reports: Work performance reports provide essential key data so that necessary corrective and preventive actions can be taken. Examples of performance reports can be:

- Current status
- Issues
- Memos
- Scheduled activities
- Recommendations
- Justification
- Forecasts
- Significant achievements

Project Management Plan Updates: Most of the elements of the project management plan will be updated in this process.

Project Documents Updates: Documents such as risk register, forecasts, performance reports, project logs (issues, assumptions, etc.) may be updated.

Exercise 13: When will you identify corrective actions, preventive actions, and defect repairs in your project?

Exercise 14: How will you approach a large project vs. a small project?

Exercise 15: Identify which process group each process belongs to.

Process Groups				
Initiating	Planning	Executing	Monitoring & Controlling	Closing

Process Names:

- Develop Project Management Plan
- Monitor and Control Project Work
- Close Project or Phase
- Perform Integrated Change Control
- Develop Project Charter
- Direct and Manage Project Work

Perform Integrated Change Control

Integrated Change Control is one of the two project management processes in the monitoring & controlling process group. This process is necessary for reviewing change requests and approving or disapproving and managing changes to the deliverables, project management plan and documents, and the organizational process assets.

Changes that may have positive or negative consequences arise on projects for a variety of reasons such as stakeholder requests, team member recommendations, vendor issues, project constraints, and many other reasons. The project manager does not have to implement all the changes since these changes will impact cost, schedule, scope, and quality, among other things. The project manager is responsible for managing these changes and making the following decisions:

- Should the change be implemented or not?
- If the change is implemented, what will the impact be on project constraints such as cost, time, scope, and quality?
- Will the benefit from the change reduce or increase the probability of project completion?

The following concepts are important to understand the Perform Integrated Change Control process:

Configuration Management System: A subset of the Project Management Information System (PMIS) that describes the different versions and characteristics of the product, service, or result of the project and ensures accuracy and completeness of the description.

Some of the configuration management activities in the Perform Integrated Change Control process are as follows:

- Configuration identification
- Configuration status accounting
- Configuration verification and audit

Change Control System: A change control system is usually a subset of the configuration management system. The system includes the documented procedures that describe how the deliverables of the project and associated project documentation are controlled, changed, and approved. A change control system also describes how to submit and manage change requests, including emergency changes, as well as how to track the status of change requests, including their approval status. Changes that are approved are also tracked and filed in the change control log for future reference.

Change Control Board: A Change Control Board (CCB) consists of members including stakeholders, managers, project team members, senior management, etc., and it is responsible for reviewing, approving, or denying change requests.

Some organizations have permanent CCB staffed by full-time employees who manage changes for the entire organization, in addition to the specific project. A project manager should consider establishing a CCB for the project if the organization does not already have one.

This process is performed throughout the project from project initiation to project closure.

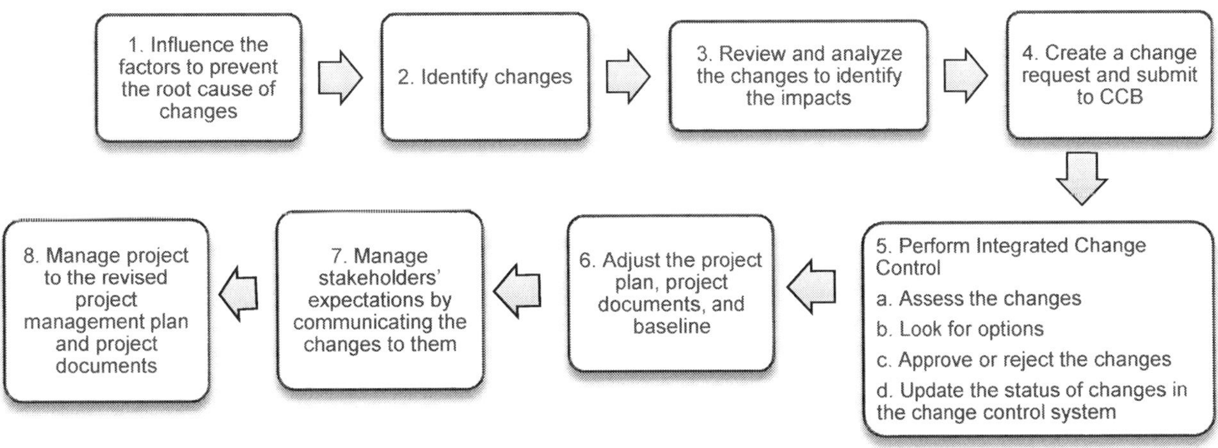

Figure 4-6: Perform Integrated Change Control Process

Change Form: The following form may be used to document requests for a change to the project.

Project Name: Help desk automation for NetPro	
Project Details: To centralize the help desk function and install a new, fully integrated help desk system to provide customers with a level of service that is second to none in the telecommunications industry.	
Project Manager: John Garcia	
Change Details: **ID:** 1.2 **Requester:** John Smith **Date requested:** 3/3/2013 **Urgency:** High **Description:** The client requested one more branch office to be added to the centralized help desk system. **Benefits:** Currently five branches are to be connected to the help desk system. Adding one more branch will help NetPro offer better customer support to five thousand additional customers.	
Impact Details: **Scope:** Project scope will be extended from five branch offices to six. **Schedule:** Project will be delayed by three weeks. **Cost:** It will cost an additional $7,000. **Resources:** Two resources from IT department need to be assigned for three weeks. **Risk:** Project schedule will be delayed, possibly impacting implementation of help desk for existing branches. **Quality:** The QA team needs to conduct one more round of regression testing. Customers will be asked to conduct the user acceptance testing for the new functionality.	
Approval Details:	
Submitted By: John Garcia Name: Signature: Date:	**Approved By** Name: Signature: Date:

Change Register

The purpose of the change register is to record the current status of all change requests for the project, thereby enabling the project manager to monitor and control the effects of the changes throughout the project life cycle.

Summary			Change Description		Approval		Implementation		
ID	Date Raised	Raised by	Desc.	Impact	Status	Date	Resource	Status	Date

As per the PMBOK®, the Perform Integrated Change Control process has the following inputs, tools & techniques, and outputs:

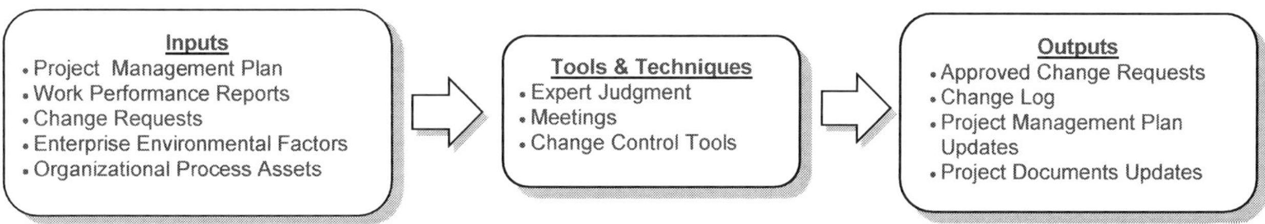

Figure 4-7: Perform Integrated Change Control: Inputs, Tools & Techniques, and Outputs

Perform Integrated Change Control: Inputs

- Project Management Plan
- Work Performance Reports
- Change Requests
- Enterprise Environmental Factors
- Organizational Process Assets

Project Management Plan: The single-approved document that defines how the project is executed, how it is monitored & controlled, how changes in the project will be handled, and how it is closed.

Work Performance Reports: Information on how far along a deliverable is and how it is progressing against the plan. These reports are routinely collected as the project progresses. There can be several work performance data of interest in the project such as:

- Deliverable status
- Schedule progress
- Costs incurred
- Quality standards

Change Requests: Approved change requests may require implementation of preventive and corrective actions and may also modify policies, the project management plan, guidelines, procedures, costs, the schedule baseline, etc.

Enterprise Environmental Factors: Factors that can influence the Integrated Change Control Process such as the Project Management Information System (PMIS) (including an information collection and distribution system, a configuration management system, a scheduling software tool, or other automated systems) and stakeholder risk tolerance, etc.

Organizational Process Assets: These are factors that can influence the Monitor and Control Project Work process and include policies, procedures and guidelines, historical information, the knowledge base of key learning from previous projects, issue and defect management procedures and database, communication requirements, the change control process, the configuration management knowledge base, the process measurement database, issue and defect management procedures, and more.

Perform Integrated Change Control: Tools & Techniques

- Expert Judgment
- Meetings
- Change Control Tools

Expert Judgment: Consultants, other units within the organization, industry groups, subject matter experts, professional and technical associations, stakeholders, the sponsor, etc., who have relevant specialized knowledge, training, and expertise and who can provide expert judgment to assess the changes as members of the change control board.

Meetings: In the change control meeting, the Change Control Board (CCB) members meet to review the benefits and impact of the change requests in order to approve or reject them.

Change Control Tools: Based on the needs of the project stakeholders, various manual or automated tools may be used to facilitate configuration and change management.

Perform Integrated Change Control: Outputs

- Approved Change Requests
- Change Log
- Project Management Plan Updates
- Project Documents Updates

Approved Change Requests: Change requests approved by the CCB will be implemented through the Direct and Manage Project Work process.

Change Log: Approved as well as rejected change requests are captured in the change log.

Change Request Status Updates: Once the change control board members approve a change request, it will be implemented in the Direct and Manage Project Work process. As part of the project documents updates, the status of all changes will be updated in the change request log.

Project Management Plan Updates: Some of the components of the project management plan will be updated.

Project Documents Updates: Change request log and other documents associated with the change control process will be updated.

Exercise 16: What should a project manager do to control changes in the project?

Close Project or Phase

During the Close Project or Phase process, the product is verified against scope, formal sign-off and formal acceptance are received from the customers, final performance reporting is completed, customer satisfaction is measured, a final version of the lessons learned is compiled and made available for future projects, appropriate organizational process assets are updated, completed project deliverables are handed off to operations and maintenance, resources are released, and the contract is closed.

The following financial, legal, and administrative activities are carried out during Close Project or Phase:

- Confirm work completion to requirements
- Close procurements
- Gain formal acceptance of the product
- Complete final performance reporting
- Index and archive project records
- Update lessons learned knowledge base
- Hand off completed product
- Release resources
- Close contract

Note that the Validate Scope process in scope management involves obtaining formal acceptance for many interim deliverables from the customers, whereas the Close Project or Phase process involves obtaining the final formal acceptance of the project or phase as a whole.

At a high-level, closing the contract precedes closing the project or phase.

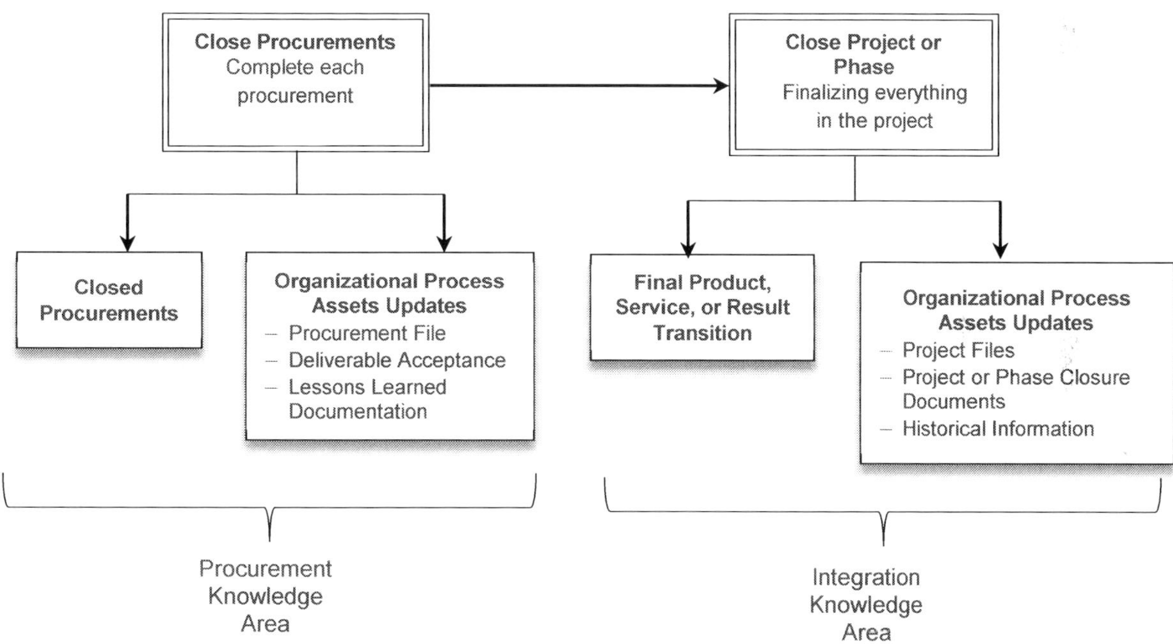

Figure 4-8: Close Procurements and Close Project or Phase Interaction

As per the PMBOK®, the Close Project or Phase process has the following inputs, tools & techniques, and outputs:

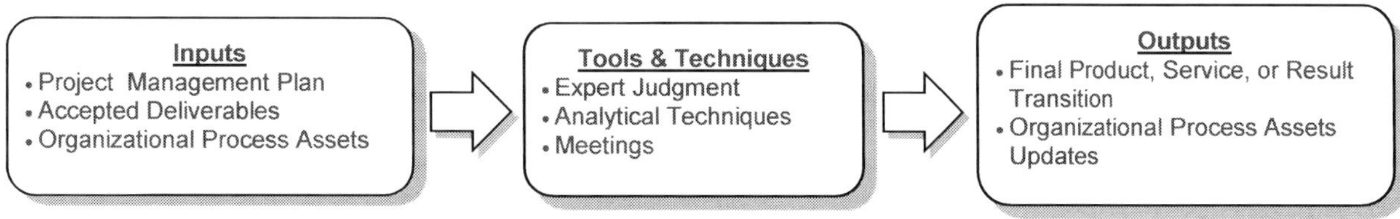

Figure 4-9: Close Project or Phase: Inputs, Tools & Techniques, and Outputs

Close Project or Phase: Inputs

- Project Management Plan
- Accepted Deliverables
- Organizational Process Assets

Project Management Plan: This single-approved document defines how the project is executed, how it is monitored and controlled, how changes in the project will be handled, and how it will be closed.

Accepted Deliverables: An accepted deliverable is any unique and verifiable product, result, capability, or service that was produced in order to complete a process, phase, or project.

Organizational Process Assets: Historical information and lessons learned knowledge base, along with the project or phase closure guidelines, can influence the Close Project or Phase process.

Close Project or Phase: Tools & Techniques

- Expert Judgment
- Analytical Techniques
- Meetings

Expert Judgment: Expert judgment is applied during the performance of administrative closure activities to ensure that the project or phase closure is performed as per the appropriate standards.

Analytical Techniques: Analytical techniques such as trend and regression analysis may be used in this process.

Meetings: Face-to-face, virtual, formal, informal, lessons learned user group, review, and closeout meetings are used in this process.

Close Project or Phase: Outputs

- Final Product, Service, or Result Transition
- Organizational Process Assets Updates

Final Product, Service, or Result Transition: Formal acceptance and handover of the final product, service, or result that the project was authorized to produce for project closure and the intermediate product, service, or result from the phase for phase closure.

Organizational Process Assets Updates: Organizational process assets such as formal acceptance documentation, project files, project closure documents, and historical information may be updated.

Lessons Learned Template Example

Project Name: Web-Based Accounting Automation Project Date: 3/3/2003			
Summary	Project Background		A web-based accounting application was developed for our client XYZ Corp. The purpose of the project was to automate all the accounting activities in order to make the processes faster and error free.
	Summary of Lessons Learned		The project was delivered on time, but it was over budget by $10,000. The team has utilized robust project schedule management processes, but failed to control the cost.
	Overall Recommendations		
Process Performance	Project Selection	Observations	
		Improvements	
	Initiating	Observations	
		Improvements	
	Planning	Observations	
		Improvements	
	Executing	Observations	
		Improvements	
	Controlling	Observations	
		Improvements	
	Closing	Observations	
		Improvements	
Tools Performance	Observations		
	Improvements		
Team Performance	Observations		
	Team Improvements		
Schedule Performance	Observations		
	Schedule Improvements		
Cost Performance	Observations		
	Cost Improvements		
Quality Performance	Observations		
	Quality Improvements		
Other Areas		Observations	
		Improvements	

Exercise 17: Crossword

Across

1. A subset of the Project Management Information System (PMIS) that describes the different versions and characteristics of the product, service, or result of the project and ensures accuracy and completeness of the description is called a ________ management system.
6. Working Capital = Current assets – Current ________.
10. A formal, documented procedure to describe how to authorize and initiate work in the correct sequence at the appropriate time is called a work ________ system.
11. The number of time periods to recoup initial costs of a project.
12. A board responsible for reviewing, approving, and communicating change requests is called change ______ board.
13. The process of performing the work defined in the project management plan to achieve the project's objectives is called _______ and Manage Project Work.
14. It contains the business needs and the cost-benefit analysis to justify and establish project boundaries.
15. Perform _______ Change Control is the process of reviewing, approving and managing all changes in the project.

Down

2. The value of a project that is not selected so that another project can be executed is called an _____ cost.
3. Project _______ management maintains the "big picture" of the project throughout the life of the project.
4. A problem in a deliverable that shows that it does not do what it supposed to do.
5. Methods for establishing value to analyze and prioritize projects are called ______ measurement methods.
7. Law of _______ returns suggest that the more you put into something, the less you get out of it or the return will not be as expected.
8. A study to determine if the project is viable and also to figure out the probability of the project's success.
9. Net Present Value (NPV) = Present Value (PV) – _______.
16. Project _________ names PM, defines project start and boundaries, creates a formal record, and helps senior management to formally accept and commit to the project.

Exercise 18: Answer the following:

1. It consists of members including stakeholders, managers, project team members, senior management, etc., and it is responsible for reviewing, approving, or denying change requests.
2. It is the subset of the Project Management Information System (PMIS) that describes the different versions and characteristics of the product, service, or result of the project and ensures accuracy and completeness of the description.
3. The process of performing the work defined in the project management plan to achieve the project's objectives.
4. It provides the required information from a business standpoint to determine whether or not the project is worth the required investment.
5. The number of time periods it will take a company to recoup its initial costs of producing the product, service, or result of the project.
6. The process of documenting the actions necessary to define, prepare, integrate, and coordinate all subsidiary plans.
7. The project management plan that defines how the project is executed, how it is monitored and controlled, and how it is closed, is a collection of ____.
8. It maintains the "big picture" of the project throughout the life of the project.
9. The key role of the ________ is to perform integration.
10. The value of a project that is not undertaken so that another project can be executed.
11. The process of reviewing all change requests and approving and managing all changes, including changes to the deliverables, organizational process assets, project documents, and the project management plan.
12. This is a formal, documented procedure to describe how to authorize and initiate work in the correct sequence at the appropriate time.
13. The key role of the _______ is to concentrate on completing the project activities.
14. The key role of the project ________ is to protect the project team from unnecessary changes and loss of resources.
15. A problem in a deliverable that shows that it does not do what it supposed to do.
16. This process tracks, measures, inspects, monitors, verifies, reviews, compares, and regulates the progress and performance of the project, ensures that the plan is working, identifies any areas in which changes to the plan are required, and initiates the corresponding changes.
17. In this process, group work is actually carried out.
18. The approved project _____ formally initiates the project.
19. The six processes of project integration management are __________.
20. The key outputs of project integration management processes are __________.
21. In integration management, change control tools are used as tools and techniques in _________ process.
22. Name some of the elements of the project charter.
23. Methods for establishing value to analyze and prioritize projects.
24. A study conducted by some organizations prior to making a final decision about initiating a project to determine if the project is viable and also to figure out the probability of the project's success.
25. A repository of historical information and lessons learned from previous projects.
26. A project management plan consists of ________.
27. The difference between "Monitor and Control Project Work" and "Monitoring and Controlling".
28. Change log is an output of the ________ process.

Project Integration Management Summary

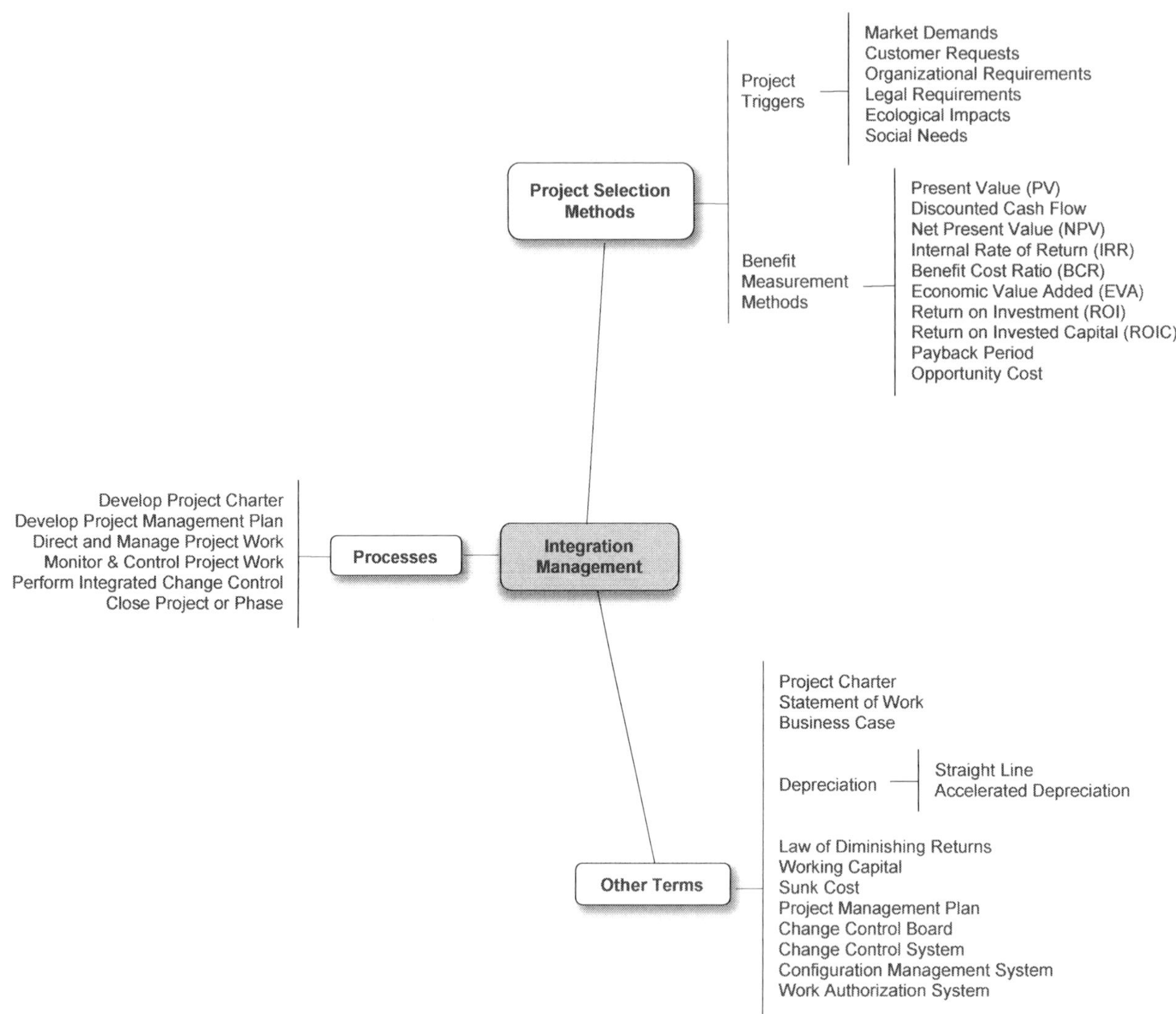

Figure 4-10: Project Integration Management Summary

Project Integration Management Key Terms

Project Charter: Names PM, defines project start and boundaries, creates a formal record, and helps senior management to formally accept and commit to the project.
Project Statement of Work (PSOW): A narrative description of products, results, or services to be supplied by the project.
Business Case: Contains the business needs and the cost-benefit analysis to justify and establish project boundaries. (Why us, why now?)
Feasibility Study: A study to determine if the project is viable and also to figure out the probability of the project's success.
Law of Diminishing Returns: Suggests that the more you put into something, the less you get out of it or the return will not be as expected.
Project Management Plan: A single-approved document that defines how a project is planned, executed, monitored, controlled, and closed. The sixteen components are listed in the table below.
Change Control Board: A board responsible for reviewing, approving, and communicating change requests.
Configuration Management System: A subset of the Project Management Information System (PMIS) that describes the different versions and characteristics of the product, service, or result of the project and ensures accuracy and completeness of the description.
Change Control System: A subset of the configuration management system that describes how the deliverables of the project and associated project documentation are controlled, changed, and approved.
Work Authorization System: A formal, documented procedure to describe how to authorize and initiate work in the correct sequence at the appropriate time.
Depreciation: Straight line, Accelerated (Double Declining, Sum of Years Digits)

Benefit Measurement Methods

(Bigger is better for the following)

Present Value (PV) $= FV/(1+r)^n$ and $FV = PV * (1+r)^n$

Net Present Value (NPV) = PV – Cost, Time is already factored in

Internal Rate of Return (IRR): No formula

Benefit Cost Ratio (BCR) = Benefit / Cost. A BCR > 1 means benefit is greater, < 1 means cost is greater, = 1 means it is a break-even project

Economic Value Add (EVA) = After tax profit – (Capital expenditures * Cost of capital)

Return on Investment (ROI) = (Benefit – Cost) / Cost
Return on Invested Capital (ROIC) = Net income (after tax) from project / Total capital invested in the project

(Smaller is better for the following)

Payback Period: The number of time periods to recoup initial costs of a project.

Opportunity Cost: The value of a project that is not undertaken so that another project can be executed.

Project Management Plan

Components	Created in Process
Requirements management plan	Plan Scope management
Scope management plan	Plan Scope management
Scope baseline	Create WBS
Schedule management plan	Plan Time management
Schedule baseline	Develop Schedule
Cost management plan	Plan Cost management
Cost baseline	Determine Budget
Quality management plan	Plan Quality management
Process improvement plan	Plan Quality management
Human resource plan	Plan Human Resource management
Communications management plan	Plan Communications management
Risk management plan	Plan Risk management
Procurement management plan	Plan Procurement management
Stakeholder management plan	Plan Stakeholder management
Change management plan	Develop Project management Plan
Configuration management plan	Develop Project management Plan

Project Integration Management Exercise Answers

Exercise 1: Less. We will not get the entire $400,000 till the end of the third year. But if we take $400,000 cash and put it in the bank right now, we will have more than $400,000 in three years.

$$PV = \frac{400{,}000}{(1+0.1)^3} = \$300{,}525$$

Exercise 2: Project B since it has the higher NPV. The number of years is not relevant here.

Exercise 3: Determine the present value for each year of the project using the following formula:

$$PV = \frac{FV}{(1+r)^n}$$

Years	Revenue	Present Value
0	0	– 9,000
1	1000	909
2	2000	1653
3	2000	1503
4	5000	3415
5	2000	1242

1. Sum up the present values and then subtract the initial investment ($9,000) from the sum of the present values.
2. Sum of present values = ($909 + $1653 + $1503 + $3415 + $1242) = $8722 and initial cost = $9,000
   Thus NPV is $8722 – $9,000 = – $278.
   The NPV is negative. Therefore, the project should not be selected.

Exercise 4: Project A since it has a higher IRR value.

Exercise 5: Benefit Cost Ratio = Benefits/Cost or 300,000/150,000 = 2 to 1.
For every dollar we are spending in this project, we will be getting $2 in benefits.

Exercise 6: C. Benefit cost ratio is related to revenue (payback), not just the smaller figure of profit.

Exercise 7: Project A since it will take the least amount of time to pay the investment back.

Exercise 8: Here the initial investment is $400,000. There are four quarters (three months each) in a year; thus,
Cash inflows for the first year is 4 * $40,000 = $160,000
So after two years the cash inflow will be $160,000 * 2 = $320,000

In the first quarter of the third year, the cash inflow will be $80,000; thus, total cash inflow by that time will be $320,000 + $80,000 = $400,000, which is equivalent to the initial investment.
The payback is two years and three months since it will take this quantity of time to get the initial investment back.

Exercise 9: $53,000, since it is the value of the Project A that was not selected, or the opportunity that was missed.

Exercise 10: No. Accounting standards say that sunk cost should not be considered when deciding whether to continue with a troubled project as this cost is unrecoverable and therefore irrelevant.

Exercise 11: The project charter is extremely important for the project because it:
- Formally authorizes a project.
- Gives the project manager authority to put resources together for the project.
- Documents the business objectives and high-level needs, current understanding of the stakeholders' expectations and success criteria for the project.
- Documents high-level risks items, assumptions, and constraints.
- Documents high-level budget and milestones.
- Links the project to the ongoing work of the organization.
- Establishes the project; thus, a project does not exist without a project charter.

Exercise 12:

- Identify a methodology to create the project management plan.
- Inform the sponsor about any constraints or requirements in the project charter that are not feasible.
- Evaluate impacts from other projects on your project.
- Determine methods for reporting, controlling, and incorporating changes.
- Identify improvements in the processes that are used on the project.
- Figure out the project requirements as completely and as accurately as possible.
- Identify stakeholders' skills and knowledge as well as their needs, expectations, interest and influence levels, roles, and responsibilities in the project.
- Negotiate for the best resources for the project if needed.
- Collect estimates from team members on their work assignments.
- Develop a project budget and a project schedule and perform schedule compression or optimization.
- Apply reserves on the project budget and schedule.
- Finalize the project schedule and obtain the team members' approval on activities and durations.
- Gain the resource managers' approval on the final schedule.

Exercise 13: Change requests such as corrective actions, preventive actions, and defect repairs can be identified in any of the monitor & control group processes.

- **Validate Scope process:** When meeting with customers and stakeholders to gain formal acceptance on completed interim deliverables
- **Control Scope, Control Costs, and Control Schedule processes:** When tracking project performance against the performance measurement baselines
- **Perform Quality Assurance:** When making sure the team is complying with the policies, procedures, and guidelines
- **Control Quality:** When making sure deliverables meet quality standards
- **Control Communications:** When making sure project communications are sent out to all stakeholders as per the communications management plan
- **Manage Project Team:** When working closely with team members, you discover that some of them are not performing
- **Control Risks:** When you identify unanticipated risk events
- **Control Procurements:** When working closely with sellers, you discover that they are not performing as per the contract
- **Manage Stakeholder Engagement:** When working closely with stakeholders to keep them happy and satisfied by addressing their concerns and issues
- **Control Stakeholder Engagement:** When making sure you are implementing stakeholder management strategies to keep them fully involved in your project

Exercise 14: Regardless of the size of the project, the following should be done for all projects:

- **Project Charter:** Defining project objective, high-level needs, roadmap, risk, assumptions, and constraints.
- **Stakeholder Register:** Identifying stakeholders and all their details. A large project will require more effort to manage expectations, relationships, and involvement as it will have numerous stakeholders.
- **Work Breakdown Structure (WBS):** Decomposing project work into smaller components. A large project will have hundreds of components.
- **Requirement Document:** Defining product scope. A large project will have substantial amount of requirements from stakeholders.
- **Project Scope Statement:** Defining work needed for the project. A large project will require more time to complete due to complexity and size.
- **Risk Register:** Identifying and developing risk response strategies. A large project will require spending considerable amount of time to identify risks and develop preventive, contingent, and fallback plans as it will have numerous risk items to address.
- **Project Management Plan:** Defining actions for completing the project. A large project will require a broader and more complex plan to deal with a large number of team members and stakeholders.
- **Project Schedule:** Defining major milestones with start and completion dates. A large project will have hundreds of activities to plan and track. A large project will also have a complex network diagram with various relationships and dependencies among activities.
- **Project Budget:** Defining cost estimates and a budget. A large project will have numerous cost items to track.
- **Change Control Process:** Identifying how to deal with changes in the project. A large project will require a more formal process to deal with numerous changes.

Overall, a large project will be more difficult to manage, obtain good estimates, and communicate due to the incorporation of different time zones, languages, cultures, and laws. It may require spending more time with multiple sellers due to numerous contracts and service level agreements. It will also require a rigorous tracking system to track all different project metrics.

Exercise 15:

Process Groups				
Initiating	**Planning**	**Executing**	**Monitoring & Controlling**	**Closing**
– Develop Project Charter	– Develop Project Management Plan	– Direct and Manage Project Work	– Monitor and Control Project Work – Perform Integrated Change Control	– Close Project or Phase

Exercise 16: A project manager should take the following actions to control changes in the project:

- Prevent root causes of changes whenever possible.
- Make sure to identify all key stakeholders and understand their expectations and requirements from the project.
- Make sure to have a robust requirements document with acceptance criterial as well as functional, nonfunctional, and quality requirements.
- Have a strict change control process.
- Spend quality time identifying all potential risk items and developing response strategies.
- Try to prevent issues from happening rather than dealing with them.
- Have a contingency plan and create time and cost reserves.
- Follow the change control process rigorously.
- Make sure to have a Change Control Board (CCB) to approve and reject changes in the project.
- Update project baselines only with approved changes.
- Have guidelines and templates in place for creating change requests for CCB's review.
- Have clear roles and responsibilities for the CCB members for approving and rejecting changes.
- Reevaluate the business case and project charter if there are excessive changes.
- Consider terminating the project and starting a new one with defined requirements if there are excessive changes.

Exercise 17:

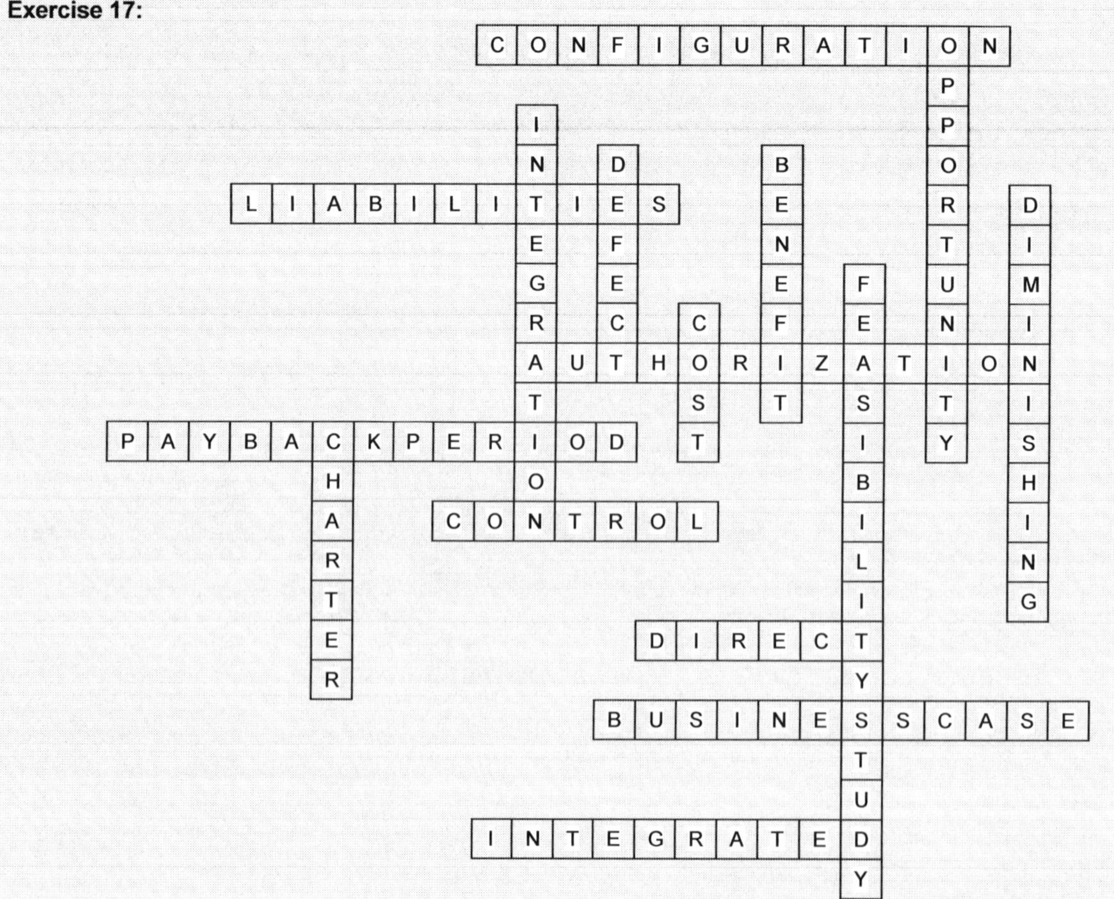

Exercise 18:

1. A Change Control Board (CCB)
2. Configuration management system
3. Direct and Manage Project Work
4. A business case
5. Payback period
6. Develop Project Management Plan
7. Subsidiary plans
8. Project integration management
9. Project manager
10. Opportunity cost
11. Perform Integrated Change Control
12. Work authorization system
13. Project team
14. Sponsor
15. Defect
16. Monitor and Control Project Work
17. Direct and Manage Project Work
18. Charter
19. Develop Project Charter, Develop Project Management Plan, Direct and Manage Project Work, Monitor and Control Project Work, Perform Integrated Change Control, and Close Project or Phase
20. Develop Project Charter – Project Charter
    Develop Project Management Plan – Project Management Plan
    Direct and Manage Project Work – Deliverables
    Monitor and Control Project Work – Change Requests, Work Performance Reports
    Perform Integrated Change Control – Approved Change Requests, Change Log
    Close Project or Phase – Final Product, Service, or Result Transition
21. Perform Integrated Change Control
22. Project purpose or justification, project objective, high-level requirements, high-level risks, high-level schedule, summary budget, key stakeholder list, project manager assigned, assumptions and constraints
23. Benefit measurement methods
24. Feasibility study
25. Lessons learned knowledge base
26. Scope management plan, requirements management plan, schedule management plan, cost management plan, quality management plan, human resource management plan, communications management plan, risk management plan, procurement management plan, stakeholder management plan, scope baseline, cost baseline, schedule baseline, change management plan, configuration management plan, and process improvement plan
27. "Monitor and Control Project Work" is a process and "Monitoring and Controlling" is a process group.
28. Perform Integrated Change Control

Project Integration Management Exam Tips

- Be able to name all knowledge areas.
- Be able to distinguish between the seven needs or triggers for project creation.
- Be able to perform the calculation for different project selection methods.
- Be able to identify key inputs, tools & techniques and outputs of all the six processes of project integration management.
- Be able to describe the purpose of the configuration management system, the change control system and the Change Control Board (CCB).
- Be able to name the primary activities of the six integration management processes.
- Be able to answer questions where you will need to analyze a specific situation and determine what you should do next.
- Be able to calculate the values for project benefits measurement methods such as PV, NPV, ROI, and EVA, etc.
- Be familiar with the concepts and terms in the project integration management summary table, Figure 4-10: Project Integration Management Summary.

Project Integration Management Questions

1. You recently took over a project in the middle of executing from another project manager who left the organization. You became extremely worried to find out that a substantial amount of new change requests are coming from your key stakeholders, customers, and even from your manager. You are anxious that the changes will drastically increase the cost and time of the project, and you are not sure about how to process these incoming change requests. What should you refer to for any kind of help in this situation?
   A. The previous project manager who can provide guidance and relevant information
   B. The project charter to find out the key success criteria from the stakeholders
   C. The project requirements document to know more about the project requirements
   D. The project management plan

2. John, the project manager, is in the process of Develop Project Charter to develop a document to formally authorize a project or a phase and identify the business objectives and needs, current understanding of the stakeholders' expectations, and the new product, service, or result that it is intended to satisfy. Which one of the following is NOT an input to this Develop Project Charter process?
   A. Project Statement of Work (SOW)
   B. Business case
   C. Agreements
   D. Project management plan

3. Which one of the following is FALSE about change management in a project?
   A. "Influencing the factors that affect change" means determining the source of changes and fixing the root causes.
   B. Whenever there is a change request, the project manager should evaluate the impact on project objectives such as scope, time, cost, quality, risk, resources, and other factors.
   C. The project manager should make all the effort to prevent unnecessary changes in the project.
   D. The project manager should make the change happen as soon as possible to meet and exceed customer expectations.

4. Your manager mentioned to you that the present value of a project is $350,000 and asked you to find out the future value that the project will have four years from now if the expected interest rate is 8 percent. What is the future value in this case?
   A. $350,000
   B. $400,000
   C. $476,000
   D. $257,352

5. Which one of the following statements is NOT true about the project management plan?
   A. It is a single-approved document that defines how the project is executed, monitored and controlled, and closed.
   B. It is developed through a series of integrated processes.
   C. It is progressively elaborated by updates and controlled and approved through the Perform Integrated Change Control process.
   D. It provides project inputs, tools & techniques, and outputs to be used on the project for the purpose of managing the product of the project.

6. You are a technical specialist and domain expert working on an IT project to implement a new console video game. There is a change control process in place, and the project scope is already signed off by the sponsor and key stakeholders. While having a casual conversation with one of the stakeholders, you realize that a simple change in the design will add a great feature to the project. Since there is no visible impact, you made the change to the project without informing the project manager. What kind of reaction should you expect from the project manager?

A. The project manager should simply ignore the change since it had no visible impact.
B. You should be informed that your action was inconsistent with the change management plan, and this kind of unauthorized action should not be repeated again.
C. The project manager should get the customer sign-off on the implemented change.
D. You should be recognized for exceeding customer expectations without affecting the project cost or schedule.

7. You are approaching the end of your project and have been asked to release the resources so that they can be assigned to other projects. Before releasing the resources, you want to make sure that you have completed the necessary actions. Which of the following is the correct order of actions that you take during the closing process?

A. Get formal acceptance, write lessons learned, release the team, and close the contract.
B. Get formal acceptance, release the team, write lessons learned, and close the contract.
C. Write lessons learned, release the team, get formal acceptance, and close the contract.
D. Release the team, get formal acceptance, close the contract, and write lessons learned.

8. While overseeing the implementation of a new computer infrastructure at the local hospital, you notice that a substantial amount of change requests have originated from one single key stakeholder. The stakeholder is also insisting that all of his requests should be implemented as soon as possible. What will be your BEST course of action?

A. Ask the sponsor to have a discussion with the key stakeholder and ask him not to request so many changes to the project.
B. Call the stakeholder and request him not to send any more change requests.
C. Have a meeting with the stakeholder to review the change process in the project and determine the causes of his changes.
D. Assign a team member to work solely with the stakeholder to understand his needs and expectations.

9. Which one of the following statements is FALSE about the Project Management Information System (PMIS)?

A. It is incorporated as part of the Enterprise Environmental Factors (EEFs) to several processes since it is part of the environment in which the project is performed.
B. It is an automated system that can serve as a repository for information and a tool to assist with communication and with tracking documents and deliverables.
C. It consists of the data sources and the tools & techniques used to gather, integrate, analyze, and disseminate the results of the combined outputs of the project management processes.
D. It defines how the project is executed, monitored and controlled, and closed.

10. Ashley is overseeing an IT project to implement a payroll system for a local doctor's office. The project has twelve team members and nine stakeholders, and it is supposed to be completed in six months. Ashley was unaware that a modification request to the product specifications by one of the stakeholders was immediately implemented by the project team. During the final testing, Ashley was surprised to find out that there was a major variance between the actual test results and the planned results. Which one of the following is a contribution to this kind of adverse consequence?

A. Poor quality management plan
B. Lack of commitment to the change control process
C. Poor definition of the test plan
D. Lack of adherence to the communication plan

11. You have just been assigned as a project manager to implement a web-based accounting software for one of your clients. You have chosen a specific change-driven product development life cycle for the implementation of your project. As you are expecting many changes during the course of the project, you want to establish a robust configuration management system to describe the different versions and characteristics of the product, service, or result of the project and to ensure the accuracy and completeness of the description. Which of the following statements is FALSE about configuration management?

A. It includes configuration identification, configuration status accounting, and configuration verification and audit.
B. It focuses on establishing and maintaining consistency of a product's requirements.
C. It compares the actual project performance against the project management plan and determines whether any corrective or preventive actions are required.
D. Its purpose is to maintain integrity of the work product.

12. You just received a change request from the customer, which will require an additional $2,000 and will also delay the project by two weeks. The customer mentioned that they were OK with the delay and were willing to pay for the extra amount as the new change will drastically improve their business automation. As per your organizational policy, you are supposed to get the project office's approval for any change that will extend the project duration by more than a week. What should you do in this situation?

A. Discuss the change with the project office.
B. Do not allow the change since it would extend the project duration by more than one week.
C. Allow the change and ask the team member to implement it since it will drastically help the customer and the customer is paying for the change anyway.
D. Advise the customer to take the change request to the project office and explain to them the importance of the change and his/her willingness to pay for it.

13. The Project Management Information System (PMIS), such as any automated system that can be utilized during the Direct and Manage Project Work process, will include all of the following EXCEPT:

A. A tool & technique to identify the internal and external stakeholders.
B. An information collection and distribution system.
C. A configuration management system.
D. A scheduling software tool.

14. One of your colleagues recently took over a project and expressed her concern to you about the new changes that may be streaming in from various sources. What is the best piece of advice you can offer her regarding changes and where she should devote most of her attention?

A. Implementing changes as accurately as possible
B. Tracking and recording all changes as accurately as possible
C. Preventing unnecessary changes in the project as much as possible
D. Informing the sponsor about all changes

15. Which one of the following is a subset of the Project Management Information System (PMIS) that describes the different versions and characteristics of the product, service, or result of the project and ensures accuracy and completeness of the description?

A. Quality Control
B. Configuration Management
C. Scope Change Control
D. Product Change Control

16. A project is just initiated under a contract in your organization, and you were assigned as the project manager. You were expecting a Statement of Work (SOW), which will describe the business need, product scope, and other elements. In this case, from whom should you expect the SOW?

A. The project sponsor
B. The buyer
C. The contractor
D. The Project Management Office (PMO)

17. While managing a data center project, you used a configuration management system to describe the different versions and characteristics of the product, service, or result of the project and to ensure the accuracy and completeness of the description. All of the following are configuration management activities in the Integrated Change Control process EXCEPT:

A. Configuration verification and audit
B. Configuration identification
C. Forecasting and variance analysis
D. Configuration status accounting

18. You are a project manager at a dairy farm that offers several dairy products to its clients in different states, especially on the West Coast. You have sent a few of your team members to China to get specialized training on a spectacular dairy food processing equipment recently introduced in the market. The team members just completed the training, and this is one of the work results you have collected and recorded. This output describes which of the following in the Direct and Manage Project Work process?

A. Deliverables
B. Work performance information
C. Change requests
D. Project management plan update

19. All of the following statements are true regarding assumptions EXCEPT:
   A. Assumptions are factors used for planning purposes and may be communicated to a project team by several different stakeholders.
   B. Assumptions are generally considered to be true, real or certain, and nonfactual.
   C. Assumptions are absolute and nonnegotiable.
   D. Failure to validate assumptions may result in significant risk events.

20. You are one of the members of the project prioritization and selection committee in your organization. The selection team is debating between two projects, which are both considered to be very important. The organization has to make an initial investment of $250,000 with expected cash inflows of $75,000 in the first year and $25,000 per quarter thereafter for the first project. The second project has a payback period of thirty-five months. Based solely on this information, which project should the selection committee recommend?
   A. First project as it has a smaller payback period
   B. Second project as it has a smaller payback period
   C. None of them since both of them have the same payback period
   D. Either of the two projects since payback period is not important

21. You are the project manager for a cable service provider that is providing Internet, TV, and phone service throughout the United States. Your company recently introduced its service in Canada and made you the project manager for a critical project, which is two months in execution at this time. You are reporting on project elements such as deliverable status, schedule progress, resource utilization, costs incurred, and others. Which of the following outputs of the Direct and Manage Project Work does this describe?
   A. Deliverables
   B. Work performance information
   C. Change requests
   D. Project management plan update

22. While managing a large construction project, you are ready to assign resources to the project using a work authorization system. All of the following statements are true about a work authorization system EXCEPT:
   A. It is a formal, documented procedure to describe how to authorize and initiate work in the correct sequence at the appropriate time.
   B. It is a tool & technique of the Monitor and Control Project Work process.
   C. It is a component of the enterprise environmental factors, which are inputs in the Monitor and Control Project Work process.
   D. It is used throughout the project executing process.

23. You are working as a project manager at a consulting firm and recently received a Statement of Work (SOW) from the client. As per your expectation, the SOW should contain or reference which of the following elements?
   A. Business need, product scope description or what is to be done, and how the project supports the strategic plan
   B. Measurable project objectives, business need, product scope description or what is to be done, and how the project supports the strategic plan
   C. Project purpose, business need, product scope description or what is to be done, and how the project supports the strategic plan
   D. Business need, product scope description or what is to be done, and project purpose

24. You are the project manager for ITPro Consultancy. You have a project in mind that will be able to meet the strategic objective of your organization. While evaluating the project, your team found out that the project would cost $600,000. Since you are introducing a new potential product in the market, you are very hopeful that your expected inflows will be $30,000 per quarter for the first two years and then $90,000 per quarter thereafter. What is the payback period of this project?
   A. Thirty-six months
   B. Thirty-eight months
   C. Forty-eight months
   D. Fifty-two months

25. While managing a data recovery project, you are performing the following activities: comparing actual project performance against the project management plan, analyzing, tracking, monitoring project risks, assessing performance to determine whether any corrective or preventive actions are required, providing information to support status reporting, monitoring implementation of approved changes, providing forecasts to update current costs and schedule information, and other things. Which process are you in at this time?
   A. Manage Stakeholder Expectations
   B. Monitor and Control Risks
   C. Direct and Manage Project Work
   D. Monitor and Control Project Work

26. Your company can accept one of three possible projects. Project A has a Net Present Value (NPV) of $30,000, it will take five years to complete, and the associated cost will be $10,000. Project B has a NPV of $60,000, it will take three years to complete, and the cost will be $15,000. Project C has a NPV of $80,000, it will take four years to complete, and it will cost $40,000. Based on the information, which project would you pick?
   A. They all have the same value
   B. Project A
   C. Project B
   D. Project C

27. A project manager for a pharmaceutical project is reviewing the project contract and going through the narrative description of products and services to be supplied under the contract. He is meeting with subject matter experts, key stakeholders, and business analysts to evaluate whether or not the project is worth the required investment of $1 million. He also asked the team members to carry out a feasibility study on the project and report to him the findings as soon as possible. Which of the following documents would be created as an output in the process?
   A. Project management plan
   B. Project statement of work
   C. Project charter
   D. Project requirement document

28. All of the following statements regarding integration management are true EXCEPT:
   A. The need for integration management is one of the major driving forces for communication in a project.
   B. Project integration is a key responsibility of the project team.
   C. The project manager's role as an integrator is to put all the pieces of a project into a cohesive whole.
   D. Project integration management is the set of combined processes implemented by the project manager to ensure all the elements of the project are effectively coordinated.

29. The scope management plan, schedule management plan, schedule baseline, process improvement plan, change management plan, and others are which one of the following to the project plan?
   A. Subsidiaries
   B. Appendixes
   C. Constraints
   D. Glossary

30. There are several potential projects in your organization. Unfortunately, the organization doesn't have the time, resources, or cash to work on all those projects. The senior management is particularly interested in two projects and ask you to identify the best one to work on based on the Net Present Value (NPV). While exploring those two projects, you discovered the following:

Project Alpha:

Investment needed: $ 135,000

Benefit: End of 1st year: $0, End of 2nd year: $75,000, End of 3rd year: 89,000

Project Beta:

Investment needed: $ 120,000

Benefit: End of 1st year: $55,000, End of 2nd year: 79,000

Assume an interest rate of 6%, which project should you recommend?
   A. Project Alpha
   B. Project Beta
   C. Neither of the projects should be recommended
   D. Both projects should be recommended

31. You are working on a construction project and successfully completed all the work. Your stakeholders were very pleased and recently communicated their final acceptance of the project. You are now meeting with your team to update the organizational process assets with a record of knowledge gained about the project to help future project managers with their projects. Once the lessons learned is completed, what should you do next?
   A. Release the team.
   B. Close the contract.
   C. Get formal acceptance.
   D. Write lessons learned.

Project Integration Management Answers

1. D: Only the project management plan contains the details about how to process, monitor, and control changes in a project.

2. D: The project management plan is developed later in the Develop Project Management Plan process, not in the Develop Project Charter process.

3. D: The project manager should not implement any change request prior to evaluating the impact of the change and receiving approval from the change control board.

4. C: We know $PV = \frac{FV}{(1+r)^n}$, FV = future value, r = interest rate, n = number of time periods
We can say that $FV = PV * (1+r)^n$
Thus, FV = $350,000 * (1+ .08) ^{4} = $350,000 * (1.08) ^{4} = $350,000 * 1.36 = $476,000

5. D: The project management plan, developed through a series of integrated processes, is a single-approved document that defines how the project is executed, how it is monitored and controlled, and how it is closed. Generally, the project plan is considered to be a guide that is expected to change throughout the project life cycle, and any such change should be controlled and approved through the Perform Integrated Change Control process.

6. B: It may seem like there is no visible impact on time and cost for a minor change, but it can result in significant scope creep and may impact other project constraints such as risk, customer satisfaction, quality, and other things. The change control process should be followed by everyone on the project team. A team member should consult with the project manager prior to making a design change to evaluate the possible impact on all the different constraints.

7. A: You should not release the team until the lessons learned are documented and added to the organizational process assets, as you need the team's help with the lessons learned. Most contracts have payment terms that allow for some period of time before full payment is required; thus, the last thing you do on the project is close the contract.

8. C: The most appropriate action is to ensure that the stakeholder fully understands the project scope of work and the change control process. It is also very important to identify the root causes of his changes. You should have a meeting with the stakeholder first and get all the details prior to meeting with the sponsor about your concern.

9. D: The project management plan defines how the project is executed, monitored and controlled, and closed (not the project management information system). The project management information system, which can be electronic or manual, is used to track project information and performance. Such information kept by these systems can include the tracking of time worked, project costs, and other factors that would be communicated to project stakeholders.

10. B: There is no indication that there is anything wrong with the quality plan, test plan, or communication plan. The change control process was not properly followed in this case. Failure to follow the agreed-upon change control processes may create adverse risk situations and jeopardize the entire project.

11. C: Comparing the actual project performance against the project management plan and determine whether any corrective or preventive actions are required is done as a part of the Monitor and Control Project Work process. All the other statements are true regarding the configuration management process.

12. A: Any kind of organizational policy, process, or guideline must be followed, and the project manager should discuss the change request with the project office. The project manager simply should not approve or deny a change request as the Change Control Board (CCB) is responsible for approving or denying a change request after evaluating it. The customer should not do the project manager's job and take the change request to the project office.

13. A: Stakeholder identification is a continuous, complex, and manual process carried on by the project manager and the team members throughout the project. The Project Management Information System (PMIS) can be used for collecting and distributing information; describing the different versions and characteristics of the product, service, or result (Configuration Management System); and scheduling.

14. C: The project manager should be focusing on all of these options, but he/she should be very proactive and always try to prevent the unnecessary changes as much as possible.

15. B: Configuration management system is a subset of the Project Management Information System (PMIS) and is specifically associated with changes to features, functions, and physical characteristics of a product or deliverable.

16. B: Usually the buyers come up with the SOW in a project that is initiated by a contract.

17. C: Configuration management activities in the Integrated Change Control process are configuration identification, configuration status accounting, and configuration verification and audit.

18. A: This output describes a deliverable. Note that deliverables can be intangibles, such as the completion of a training program.

19. C: Assumptions are not based on factual information, and failure to validate may result in significant risk events. Assumptions are documented mostly during the project initiating and planning processes. These assumptions are not absolute and can be negotiable.

20. A: The first project will have the cash inflows of $75,000 in the first twelve months, and for the rest of the investment ($250,000 – $ 75,000 = $175,000) it will take seven quarters to recapture it; thus, for the first project, the total payback period is 12 + 21 (each quarter has three months; thus, seven quarters have 7 * 3 = 21 months) = 33 months. The first project has a smaller payback period than that of the second project; thus, we should select the first project.

21. B: Work performance information describes how far along a deliverable is and how it is progressing against the plan. It can include several work performance data of interest, such as deliverable status, schedule progress, resource utilization, costs incurred, and quality standards.

22. B: A work authorization system is not a tool & technique of the project monitoring & controlling process. It is a subset of the Project Management Information System (PMIS) and is considered a component of the enterprise environmental factors, which are inputs in the Monitor and Control Project Work process. It is a formal, documented procedure to describe how to authorize and initiate work in the correct sequence at the appropriate time and is used throughout the executing process group.

23. A: The project SOW should contain the business need, product scope, and strategic plan.

24. A: The cash inflow is $30,000 per quarter, so in the first year the project will get back $120,000 in four quarters. In the first two years, the project will have a return of $240,000. The remaining investment will be $600,000 – $ 240,000 = $360,000. It will take four quarters or twelve months to have it back at a rate of $90,000 per quarter in the third year. The total amount of time it will take to get the entire investment back will be 24 months + 12 months = 36 months, or three years.

25. D: All these activities are performed in the Monitor and Control Project Work process.

26. D: The number of years and cost are not relevant as they are accounted for in the calculation of Net Present Value (NPV). You simply select the project with the highest NPV; in this case, it is Project C that has a NPV of $80,000.

27. C: The project manager is in the Develop Project Charter process in project integration management. The output of this process is a project charter, which is used to formally initiate a project. In this case, the project manager is using a Statement of Work (SOW) to understand the product requirements and descriptions. The project will be initiated under the contract, and the SOW was given to the project manager by the client.

28. B: Project integration is a key responsibility of the project manager.

29. A: The subsidiary plans are usually included to support the overall project management plan and are developed for the purpose of providing more detailed information, guidelines, and control processes for specifically defined project elements or planning components. These are the outputs of some of the other planning processes associated with scope, time, cost, quality, human resources, communications, risk, procurement, and stakeholder management. Additional plans such as change management, process improvement, and configuration management plans, can also be added to the project management plan.

30. A:

Project Alpha:

PV of $75,000 received at the end of 2nd year: PV = $\frac{\text{FV}}{(1+\text{r})^{\text{n}}} = \frac{\$75{,}000}{(1+.06)^2} = \frac{\$75{,}000}{(1.06)^2} = \frac{\$75{,}000}{1.123} = \$66{,}785$

PV of $89,000 received at the end of 3rd year: PV = $\frac{\$89{,}000}{(1+.06)^3} = \frac{\$89{,}000}{(1.06)^3} = \frac{\$89{,}000}{1.191} = \$74{,}727$

Therefore the NPV of project Alpha = ($66,785 + $74,727) – $135,000 = $6512

Project Beta:

PV of $55,000 received at the end of 1st year: PV = $\frac{\$55{,}000}{(1+.06)^1} = \frac{\$55{,}000}{1.06} = \$51{,}886$

PV of $79,000 received at the end of 2nd year: PV = $\frac{\$79{,}000}{(1+.06)^2} = \frac{\$79{,}000}{(1.06)^2} = \frac{\$79{,}000}{1.123} = \$70{,}347$

Therefore the NPV of project Beta = ($51,886 + $70,347) – $120,000 = $2233

Since project Alpha has a higher NPV than project Beta, you should recommend project Alpha.

31. A: You should release the team once the lessons learned are documented and added to the organizational process assets. Most contracts have payment terms that allow for some period of time before full payment is required; thus, the last thing you do on the project is close the contract. When closing the project, the order should be get formal acceptance, write lessons learned, release the team, and close the contract.

CHAPTER 5

PROJECT SCOPE MANAGEMENT

Project Scope Management

Project scope management includes the processes concerned with "all the work" and "only the work" required to successfully deliver to the stakeholders' expectations, manage changes, minimize surprises, and gain acceptance of the product in order to complete the project. During scope management, the project manager should always be in control of the scope and must make sure of the following:

- Each requirement is documented with the acceptance criteria defined
- All the work is being completed
- Define and control what is and is not in the project
- Guard against additional scope not covered under the project charter
- Prevent extra work or "gold plating," which increases risk and uncertainties and introduces problems into the project
- Proactively identify and influence the factors that cause changes
- Capture, evaluate, and manage the scope changes in a controlled, structured, and procedural manner

Key Terms in Project Scope Management

a. **Triple Constraints:** Scope is one of the "triple constraints;" thus, managing the scope of the project is one of the key ways in which project management performance can be measured. Since scope is usually owned by the project sponsor or the customer and managed by the project manager, project scope management is especially challenging.

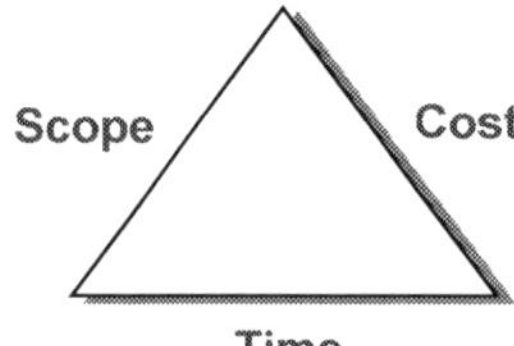

Figure 5-1: Triple Constraints

b. Scope Creeps: Scope creeps are unapproved and undocumented changes. Creeps occur when changes to the scope are not detected early enough or managed properly. All of these minor changes slowly add up and may have a drastic impact on budget, schedule, and quality.

Causes of creeps:

- **Unexpected scope-related issues:** These issues can change project requirements or increase its complexity.
- **Placating stakeholders:** Giving in to stakeholders' additional requests without following the proper procedures leads to scope creep.
- **Perfectionism:** Team members often try to improve the product without proper approval, which can lead to cost and time overruns.
- **Misunderstanding about the project scope:** Ambiguous and unclear scope that can cause the project team to misunderstand requirements also leads to scope creep.
- **Failure to identify key stakeholders:** The unidentified stakeholders will demand their missing requirements to be implemented.

c. Product Scope vs. Project Scope: Project scope management deals with managing both the product scope as well as the project scope.

Product Scope	Project Scope
Describes the features, functions, and physical characteristics that characterize a product, service, or result.	Describes work needed to deliver a product, service, or result with the specified features and functions.
May include subsidiary components.	Results in a single product, service, or result.
Completion measured against the product requirements to determine successful fulfillment.	Completion is measured against the project plan, project scope statement, and Work Breakdown Structure (WBS).

Table 5-1: Product Scope versus Project Scope

Example: In a cell phone project, customers are asking for browsing, multi-media, touch screen, and voice recognizing capabilities. All these features, functions, and physical characteristics that characterize the cell phone are product scope. On the other hand, the work needed to implement these capabilities is the project scope.

Project Scope Management Processes

The project scope management helps the project management team determine how the project scope will be defined, how the Work Breakdown Structure (WBS) will be created, how the scope will be validated by the customers and stakeholders, both at the end of the project and at the end of each project phase, and how the scope will be managed and controlled throughout the project. The project team must have a clear understanding of the project, the business need for the project, the requirements, and the stakeholders' expectations for the project.

Refer to the "Figure 3-16: Process Groups Key Inputs and Outputs" (See page 60) and you should realize that at this time you are in the planning process group and have completed working on the business case, feasibility study, a project charter, and a stakeholder register during the initiating process group. Obviously, all these documents can be used as inputs while you are working with project scope.

Now let's think about the real life scenario. The first thing you want to do is to plan how to define, validate, and control your project scope and come up with the scope and requirement management plan. You then ask your team members to work closely with the customers and other stakeholders to collect requirements from them. The team members will be working on a requirement document to document the quantifiable needs and expectations of the customers and stakeholders. Next, the team must work on a project scope statement to develop a comprehensive and detailed description of the project and product and identify all the work that needs to be done to complete project requirements. Now that the team has a clear understanding of the project deliverables, as a project manager you need to decompose these deliverables and project work into smaller, more manageable components so that you can easily assign resources, and create duration and cost estimates for all these components. At this stage, the team will develop a detailed Work Breakdown Structure (WBS). Developing the scope management plan, requirements management plan, requirement document, project scope statement, and WBS is all completed during the planning process group. During the executing process group, the team members will be working on the components you have assigned to them. You must obtain customers' and stakeholders' formal acceptance on the associated deliverables as needed through the monitoring & controlling process group via the Validate Scope process. Also, you need to continuously monitor the status of the deliverables, maintain control and manage changes to the scope baseline via the Control Scope process throughout the entire project.

PMI identifies six key processes that are associated with the scope management knowledge area. Since scope is one of the triple constraints, an understanding of these processes is vital to project success.

Process	Process Group	Detail	Key Outputs
1. Plan Scope Management	Planning	The process of developing a scope management plan that defines how project scope will be defined, validated, and controlled.	– Scope Management Plan – Requirements Management Plan
2. Collect Requirements	Planning	The process of collecting and documenting quantifiable needs and expectations of the sponsor, customer, and other stakeholders.	– Requirements Documentation – Requirements Traceability Matrix
3. Define Scope	Planning	The process of developing a comprehensive and detailed description of the project and product.	– Project Scope Statement
4. Create WBS	Planning	The process of decomposing project deliverables and project work into smaller, more manageable components.	Scope Baseline
5. Validate Scope	Monitoring & Controlling	The process of obtaining the stakeholders' formal acceptance of the completed project scope and associated deliverables.	– Accepted Deliverables – Change Requests
6. Control Scope	Monitoring & Controlling	The process of monitoring the status of the project and product scope, maintaining control over the project by preventing overwhelming scope change requests, and managing changes to the scope baseline.	– Work Performance Information – Change Requests

Table 5-2: Six Project Scope Management Processes and Key Outputs

Project Scope Management Processes, Inputs, Tool & Techniques, and Outputs

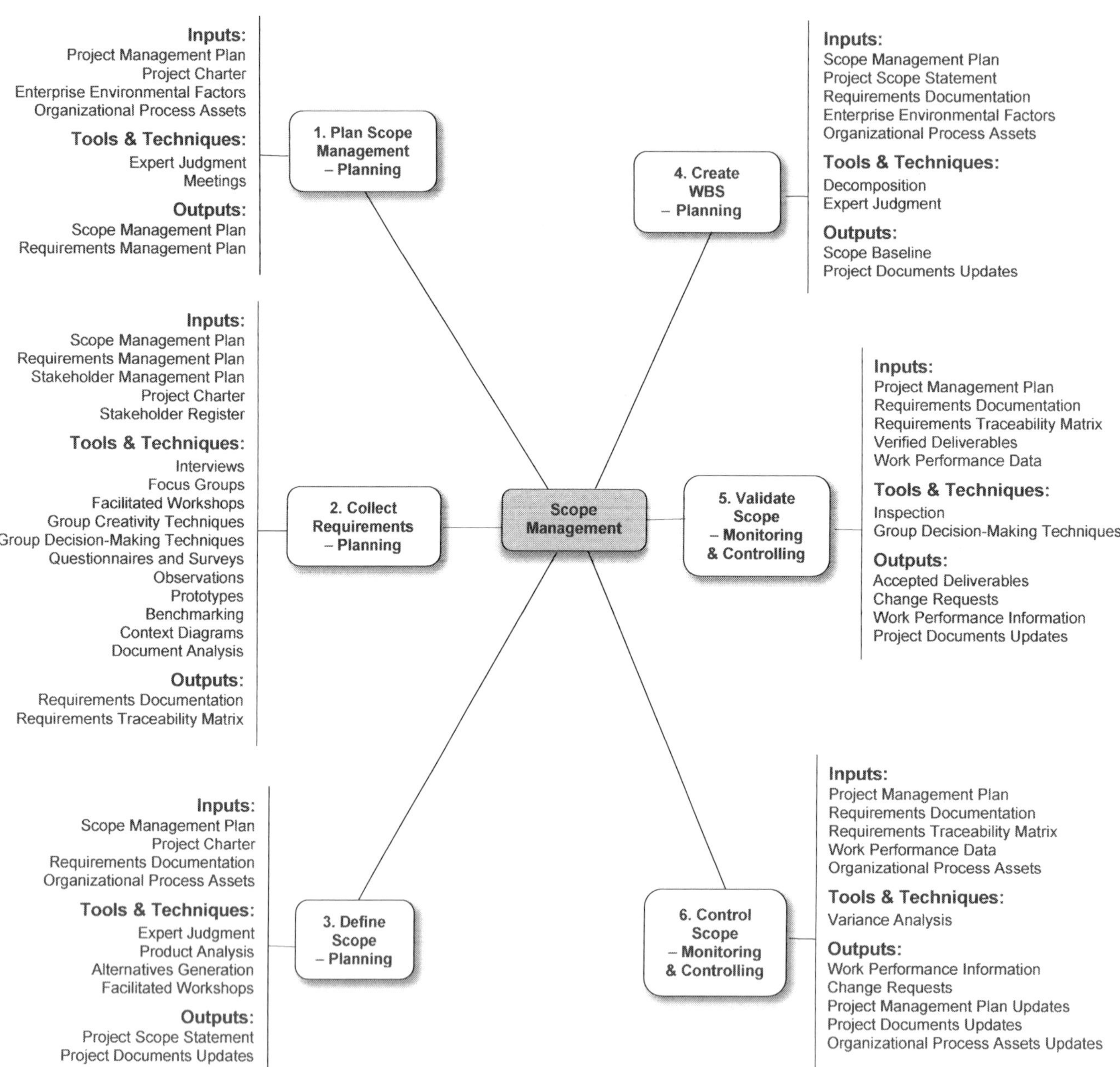

Figure 5-2: Project Scope Management Processes, Inputs, Tool & Techniques, and Outputs

Plan Scope Management

Plan Scope Management is the process of developing a scope management plan that defines how project scope will be defined, executed, validated, and controlled throughout the project life cycle.

The Plan Scope Management process defines the following:

- The plan for accomplishing the project scope
- The process of creating the WBS
- Required tools & techniques to achieve the scope
- Enterprise Environmental Factors (EEF) and Organizational Process Assets (OPA) that may have influence on the scope
- The process of defining, executing, validating, and controlling the scope as per the project management plan
- The process of obtaining acceptance of the deliverables from the customers and other stakeholders

As per the PMBOK®, the Plan Scope Management process has the following inputs, tools & techniques, and outputs:

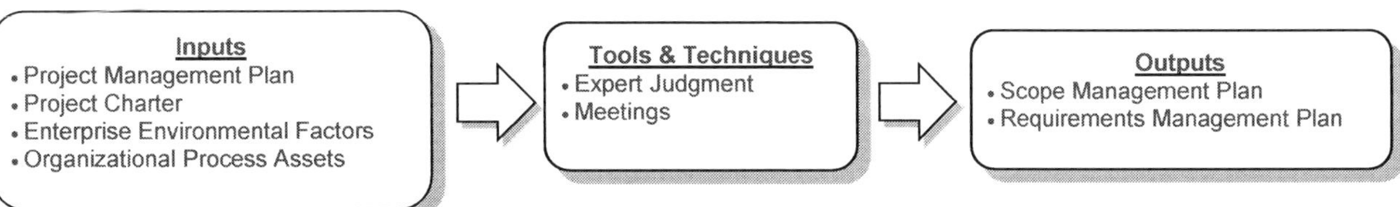

Figure 5-3: Plan Scope Management: Inputs, Tools & Techniques, and Outputs

Plan Scope Management: Inputs

- Project Management Plan
- Project Charter
- Enterprise Environmental Factors
- Organizational Process Assets

Project Management Plan: Various components of the project management plan are used to identify the approaches to plan and manage scope and to develop an overall scope management plan.

Project Charter: The project charter documents the high-level business objectives and current understanding of the stakeholders' needs of the new product, service, or result that may be used to create the scope management plan.

Enterprise Environmental Factors: Organizational structure and culture, market conditions, commercial databases, and other external factors that may influence the Plan Scope Management process.

Organizational Process Assets: Organizational process assets such as historical information and lessons learned from similar projects and organizational policies, procedures, and templates may influence the Plan Scope Management process.

Plan Scope Management: Tools & Techniques

- Expert Judgment
- Meetings

Expert Judgment: Other units within the organization, stakeholders including customers or sponsors, professional and technical associations, industry groups, subject matter experts, and consultants may provide expert opinion and judgments on the project scope management plan.

Meetings: Meetings with team members, the project manager, the sponsor, and other stakeholders will be beneficial to discuss and develop a scope management plan.

Plan Scope Management: Outputs

- Scope Management Plan
- Requirements Management Plan

Scope Management Plan: The scope management plan defines how project scope will be defined, validated, managed, and controlled throughout the project life cycle. The scope management plan contains information on the following:

- Process for developing a detailed project scope statement
- Process for developing the WBS from the detailed project scope statement
- Process for developing and approving the WBS
- Process for obtaining formal acceptance from customers and other stakeholders on completed project deliverables
- Process for managing and controlling changes to the project scope

Requirements Management Plan: The requirements management plan is a part of the overall project management plan and defines how requirements will be collected, analyzed, documented, and managed throughout the project. Components of the requirements management plan can include, but are not limited to, the following:

- How requirements activities will be planned, tracked, prioritized, and reported
- How changes to the requirements will be handled
- How requirements will be traced via a traceability structure
- Product metrics that will be used and the reasons for using them
- Configuration management activities

Collect Requirements

In the Collect Requirements process, quantifiable needs and expectations of the sponsor, customer, and other stakeholders are collected and documented. This process plays a significant role in the success of the overall project since project schedule, budget, risk factors, quality specifications, and resource planning are closely linked to the requirements. The success of this process is significantly influenced by the active participation and involvement of the stakeholders in the discovery and decomposition of the needs into requirements of the product, service, or result of the project.

Many organizations categorize requirements into project requirements and product requirements.

- Project requirements can include project management requirements, business requirements, and delivery requirements.
- Product requirements can include information on technical requirements, security requirements, and performance requirements.

As per the PMBOK®, the Collect Requirements process has the following inputs, tools & techniques, and outputs:

Figure 5-4: Collect Requirements: Inputs, Tools & Techniques, and Outputs

Collect Requirements: Inputs

- Scope Management Plan
- Requirements Management Plan
- Stakeholder Management Plan
- Project Charter
- Stakeholder Register

Scope Management Plan: The scope management plan defines how project scope will be defined, validated, managed, and controlled throughout the project life cycle. It will also help the team members to determine the type of requirements that needs to be collected for the project.

Requirements Management Plan: The requirements management plan defines how stakeholders' needs or requirements will be collected, analyzed, documented, and managed throughout the project.

Stakeholder Management Plan: The stakeholder management plan will assist in assessing the level of participation from the stakeholders in various requirements activities by analyzing stakeholders' communication requirements and level of engagement.

Project Charter: The project charter documents the high-level business objectives and current understanding of the stakeholders' needs of the new product, service, or result.

Stakeholder Register: The stakeholder register is used to identify all key internal and external stakeholders who will have an interest and influence on the project and who can provide information on detailed project and product requirements.

Collect Requirements: Tools & Techniques

- Interviews
- Focus Groups
- Facilitated Workshops
- Group Creativity Techniques
- Group Decision-Making Techniques
- Questionnaires and Surveys
- Observations
- Prototypes
- Benchmarking
- Context Diagrams
- Document Analysis

Interviews: An interview is a formal or informal approach usually conducted by the business analyst to discover information from stakeholders by having a face-to-face discussion with them.

Focus Groups: Focus groups bring together prequalified stakeholders and subject matter experts to discuss and learn the needs and expectations about a proposed product, service, or result.

Facilitated Workshops: The goal of the facilitated workshop is to bring key cross-functional stakeholders together to define product requirements with the help of a skilled facilitator. For example, this kind of session, called Joint Application Development (JAD), is used in the software development industry.

Group Creativity Techniques: Some of the group creativity techniques to identify project and product requirements are the following:

a. **Brainstorming:** Brainstorming focuses on "group thinking" as opposed to individual ideas. It involves individual idea generation, but the ideas are shared, discussed, synthesized, and improved upon by the entire group. This technique does not assure that all participants' ideas are captured; rather, it encourages a collaborative process of idea formation based upon sharing and building ideas as a group.

b. **Nominal Group Technique:** Usually done during the same session as brainstorming, this technique involves the participants meeting, voting, ranking, and prioritizing the most useful ideas generated during the brainstorming session.

c. **Delphi Technique:** This technique is mainly focused on preventing group thinking and discovering the true opinions of the participants by sending a request for information to the experts who participate anonymously. The responses are compiled, and results are sent back to them for further review until consensus is reached.

d. **Idea/Mind Mapping:** This is a technique to generate, classify, or record information in a graphical format. It looks like a tree with several branches to help the team visualize meaningful associations and relationships among ideas.

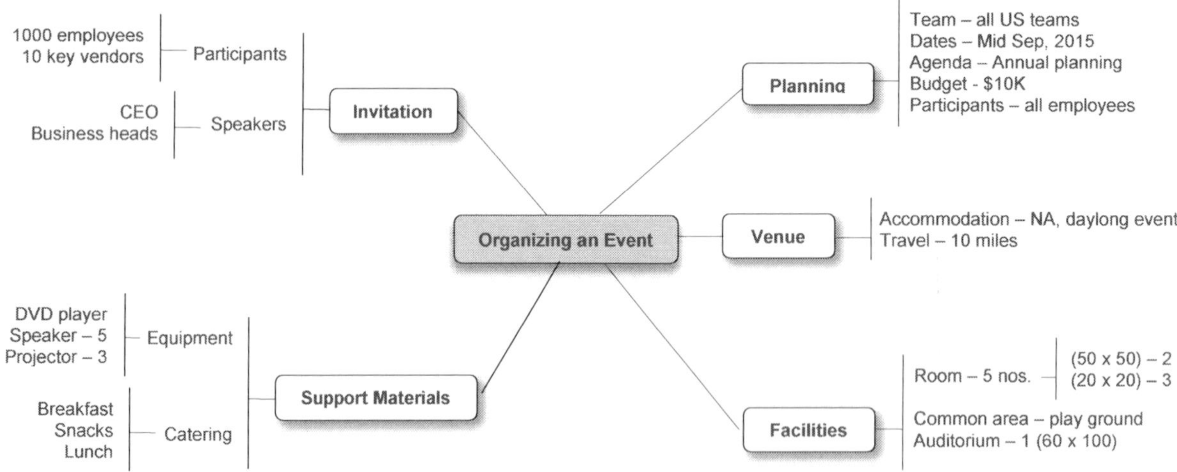

Figure 5-5: An Example of an Idea/Mind Map

e. **Affinity Diagram:** In this technique, the ideas generated from any other requirements gathering techniques are sorted into groups by similarities. Each group of requirements is then given a title. This sorting makes it easier to see additional scope (or risks) that have not been identified.

Planning	Venue	Facilities	Invitation	Support Materials
Team – all US teams	Accommodation – NA, daylong event	Room – 5 nos. – (50 x 50) – 2 – (20 x 20) – 3	Speakers – CEO, Business heads	Catering – Breakfast – Snacks – Lunch
Dates – Mid-Sep 2013	Travel – 10 miles	Common area – playground	Participants – – 1,000 employees – 10 key vendors	Equipment – Sound System – DVD player – Speakers - 5 – Projector - 2
Agenda – Annual planning		Auditorium – 1 (60 x 100)		
Budget - $10K				
Participants – all employees				

Table 5-3: Affinity Diagram for Organizing an Event

f. **Multi-Criteria Decision Analysis**: A technique to evaluate and rank ideas. This technique uses a decision matrix based on factors such as uncertainty, expected risk levels, cost and benefit estimates, and time estimates to quantify requirements.

Questionnaires and Surveys: Usually used for large groups, these tools present questions to help team members identify opinions and requirements from respondents rapidly. This method is easier and more convenient than other methods, as it is usually presented in a predefined, standard format and furthermore, aggregation and analysis are comparatively easier.

Observations: This technique involves "job shadowing," which comprises of watching a potential user of the product at work, and in some cases, participating in the work to help identify requirements that may not be obvious through other requirement collection methods.

Prototypes: A prototype is a working model or mockup of the proposed end product and is presented to the stakeholders for interaction and feedback. This is an iterative process, and the prototype may be modified numerous times to incorporate the feedback until the requirements have been finalized for the product.

Group Decision-Making Techniques: This technique makes an assessment of multiple alternatives with an expected outcome in the form of future actions resolution. A project manager can utilize these techniques to generate, classify, prioritize, and drive decisions forward. As per the PMBOK®, there are multiple methods of reaching a decision, for example:

- **Unanimity:** Occurs when a decision is based on a single course of action decided by everyone in the group.
- **Majority:** Occurs when a decision is based on the support from more than 50 percent of the members of the group.
- **Plurality:** Occurs when a decision is based on the largest block in a group even if a majority is not achieved.
- **Dictatorship:** Occurs when a decision is made for the group by one individual.

Benchmarking: Benchmarking is comparing actual or planned practices to those of other projects both in and beyond the performing organization to provide a basis for measuring performance, generating improvement ideas, and identifying best practices. This approach helps to identify and define requirements by comparing what the competitors are doing.

Context Diagrams: A context diagram represents a high-level view of the overall business or system boundary of interest. It defines the system's domain that is under investigation within an organization's environment. Within the domain, the diagram depicts the top process as a "black box" together with its major incoming and outgoing data flows linked to participating external entities. It is a popular diagrammatic tool for process modeling and scoping systems.

The diagram, therefore, can be a useful tool for helping identify the project scope and securing stakeholder agreement (sign-off) on the project scope. Below is an example of a context diagram for an online community tool.

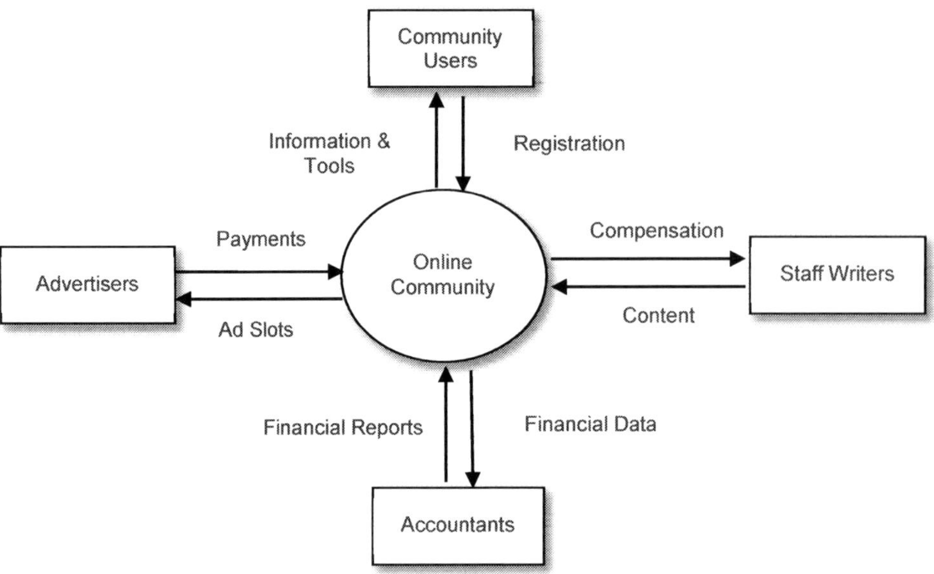

Figure 5-6: Context Diagram

Document Analysis: Various documents such as agreements, business plans, requests for proposals, application software documentation, business process documentation, use cases, issue logs, logical data models, and documentation for policies, procedures, and regulations may be reviewed to identify relevant requirements information.

Exercise 1: What tools & techniques will you use to collect requirements in the following situations?

1. To rank and prioritize the most useful ideas generated during the brainstorming session.	
2. To find out the true opinions of the participants anonymously.	
3. To come up with ideas as a group.	
4. To generate, classify, or record information in a graphical format.	
5. To sort ideas generated from any other requirements gathering techniques into groups by similarities.	
6. To watch a potential user of the product at work, and in some cases, participate in the work to help identify requirements.	
7. To compare actual or planned practices to those of other projects both in and beyond the performing organization.	
8. To represent a high-level view of the overall business or system boundary of interest.	
9. To develop a working model or mockup of the proposed end product.	

Collect Requirements: Outputs

- Requirements Documentation
- Requirements Traceability Matrix

Requirements Documentation: Requirements documentation describes how individual requirements meet the business needs and the expectations of the project sponsor and stakeholders. It should include a description of the following:

- Business need or opportunity to be seized
- Source of the requirement for traceability
- Functional requirements, business processes, information, and interaction with the product
- Nonfunctional requirements such as the level of service, performance, safety, security, compliance, supportability, retention/purge, etc.
- Quality requirements
- Acceptance criteria
- Business rules stating the guiding principles of the organization and how they will interact with the requirements
- Anticipated impacts of the requirements to others inside and outside the performing organization
- Support and training requirements
- Requirements assumptions and constraints

The project manager should make sure the requirements can be met within the project objectives by prioritizing competing requirements and resolving any conflicts between them. If needed, the project manager should look for options to adjust the contesting demands of scope, time, cost, quality, resources, risk, and customer satisfaction. A project manager should resolve competing requirements by accepting those that best comply with the business case, the project charter, the project scope statement, and project constraints.

Requirements Traceability Matrix: The requirements traceability matrix is like a requirements mapping that links requirements to their origin and traces them throughout the project life cycle. This process includes, but is not limited to, tracing the following:

- Requirements to business needs, opportunities, goals, and objectives
- Requirements to project objectives
- Requirements to project scope/WBS deliverables
- Requirements to product design
- Requirements to product development
- Requirements to test strategy and test scenarios
- High-level requirements to more detailed requirements

Example: Below is a template of a requirements traceability matrix:

Project Name											
Project Manager:											
Project Description:											
ID	**Technical Assumption(s) and/or Customer Need(s)**	**Functional Req**	**Status**	**Arc/ Design Doc**	**Tech Spec**	**SW Module**	**Test Case #**	**Tested In**	**Implemented In**	**Verification**	**Additional Comments**

Table 5-4: Requirements Traceability Matrix

Define Scope

Define Scope is the process of developing a comprehensive, detailed description of the project (the project management work) and the product (the features and characteristics of the product, service, or result of the project).

A detailed project scope statement is critical to project success and builds upon the additional analysis of requirements, major deliverables, assumptions, and constraints that are documented earlier in the project.
As per the PMBOK®, the Define Scope process has the following inputs, tools & techniques, and outputs:

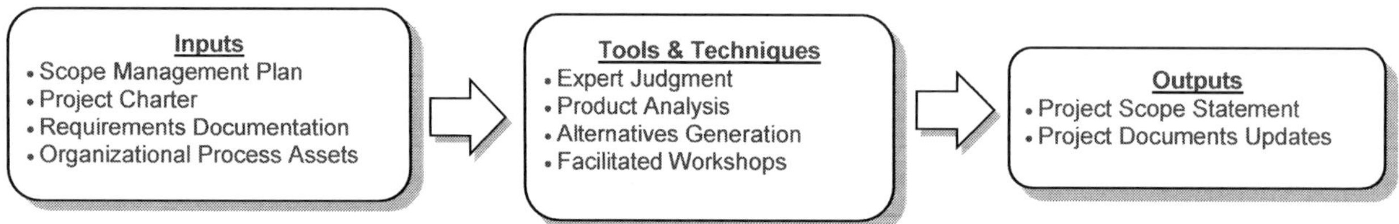

Figure 5-7: Define Scope: Inputs, Tools & Techniques, and Outputs

Define Scope: Inputs

- Scope Management Plan
- Project Charter
- Requirements Documentation
- Organizational Process Assets

Scope Management Plan: The scope management plan defines how project scope will be defined, validated, managed, and controlled throughout the project life cycle.

Project Charter: The project charter documents the high-level business objectives, product characteristics, and current understanding of the stakeholders' needs of the new product, service, or result.

Requirements Documentation: This document describes how individual requirements meet the business need and expectations of the project sponsor and stakeholders.

Organizational Process Assets: Policies, procedures, and templates for a project scope statement, in addition to project files from previous projects and lessons learned from previous phases or projects, may influence the Define Scope process.

Define Scope: Tools & Techniques

- Expert Judgment
- Product Analysis
- Alternatives Generation
- Facilitated Workshops

Expert Judgment: Other units within the organization, stakeholders including customers or sponsors, professional and technical associations, industry groups, subject matter experts, and consultants may provide expert opinion and judgments on the project scope.

Product Analysis: Product analysis techniques such as product breakdown, systems analysis, system engineering, value engineering, value analysis, and functional analysis are among the many techniques that may be used to perform a detailed analysis of the product, service, or result. This technique translates project objectives into tangible deliverables and requirements by improving the project team's understanding of the product.

Alternatives Generation: The most common techniques such as brainstorming, pair-wise comparisons, and lateral thinking may be used to properly identify different approaches or methods to execute and perform the project work.

Facilitated Workshops: These workshops are focused sessions that bring key cross-functional stakeholders together to define product requirements.

Define Scope: Outputs

- Project Scope Statement
- Project Document Updates

Project Scope Statement: It describes project deliverables and the work required to create them in detail, enables the project team to perform more detailed planning, guides the project team's work during execution, and provides the baseline for evaluating changes. As per the PMBOK®, the project scope statement contains many details pertaining to the project and product deliverables, such as:

Element	Detail	Example – Nursing Home Project
Project Objectives	Specifies the goals and needs of the project.	The team must release the application in six months. The project must return at least a 6 percent revenue increase.
Project Scope Description	Specifies all the features and functions a product must have.	A computerized database with connections throughout the organization that allows end users to input data and automate day-to-day activities in the nursing home.
Project Deliverables	Specifies all the work that needs to be done to complete the project.	– Functional requirements document – Technical & design specifications document – Quality assurance test plans – Development – Deployment of solution to production environment
Product Acceptance Criteria	Outlines requirements a project must meet before stakeholders accept the final product or service.	– Able to handle twenty concurrent connections – Should be available 99 percent of the time – Able to handle 10,000 transactions a day
Project Constraints	Specifies the limitations and restrictions such as constraints on time, budget, scope, quality, schedule, resource, and technology that a project faces.	– Must run on Microsoft Windows servers – Must meet 508 compliance regulations for disabled end users
Project Assumptions	Factors that are considered to be true in a project.	– All end users have basic computer knowledge – Existing infrastructure supports new system
Project Exclusions	The project scope statement must clearly specify what is not included in the project.	The application will be used only by administrative and emergency departments.

Table 5-5: Project Scope Statement Elements

Project Documents Updates: Project documents such as the stakeholder register, requirements documentation, requirements traceability matrix, risks, estimates, and issues may be updated as the scope is defined and elaborated.

Create WBS

The goal of the Create WBS process is to develop a deliverable-oriented decomposition of the work specified in the current approved project scope statement. The WBS defines the total scope of the project and subdivides the project work into smaller, more manageable pieces. It is the most important component of the project plan as activities, cost, risk, quality attributes, human resource, procurement decisions, and more are all based on the WBS.

As per the PMBOK®, the Create WBS process has the following inputs, tools & techniques, and outputs:

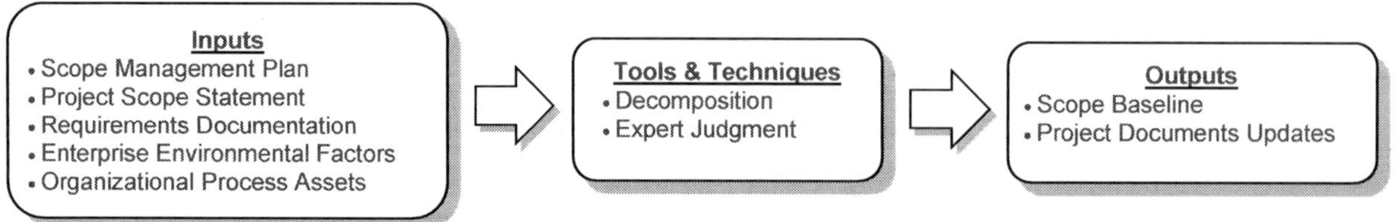

Figure 5-8: Create WBS: Inputs, Tools & Techniques, and Outputs

Create WBS: Inputs

- Scope Management Plan
- Project Scope Statement
- Requirements Documentation
- Enterprise Environmental Factors
- Organizational Process Assets

Scope Management Plan: The scope management plan defines how project scope will be defined, validated, managed, and controlled throughout the project life cycle. The scope management plan also specifies how the WBS will be created from the detailed project scope statement and its management and approval.

Project Scope Statement: This document describes project deliverables and the work required to create them in detail. This statement will act as the primary starting point for the WBS.

Requirements Documentation: This document describes how individual requirements meet the business needs and details the expectations of the project sponsor and stakeholders.

Enterprise Environmental Factors: Relevant industry-specific WBS template and standards may be beneficial for WBS creation.

Organizational Process Assets: Lessons learned, project files of old projects that are similar, policies, procedures, WBS templates, and software tools to create the graphical chart are among the resources that may be used.

Create WBS: Tools & Techniques

- Decomposition
- Expert Judgment

Decomposition: The technique of subdividing project deliverables into progressively smaller, more manageable components. The goal here is to break down the deliverables to a point so that planning, executing, monitoring & controlling, and closing become a lot easier.

How to Decompose: The WBS can be created to very low levels at a higher cost of time and effort, but it will make the project too difficult to understand and manage. The following steps can be performed while decomposing:

- Identify the deliverables, related work, and components to be decomposed.
- Structure and organize the WBS.
- Decompose upper WBS levels into lower-level detailed components. The top layer may be as general as major deliverables, product or project names, and the lowest level of the work packages.
- Verify the degree of decomposition that is necessary and sufficient by following these three steps:
    - Make sure that the work packages are small enough for time and cost estimation.
    - Make sure that the current level of detail is enough to proceed with the subsequent project activities.
    - Make sure that work packages are small enough to be assigned to a single person or group.
- Develop and assign identification codes to WBS components.

Three approaches: The following three approaches are most common in developing a WBS:

a. Phases
b. Major Deliverables or Subprojects
c. External Subprojects

a. Phases: Phases of the project life cycle are used as the first level of decomposition, and their deliverables will be the next level and so on.

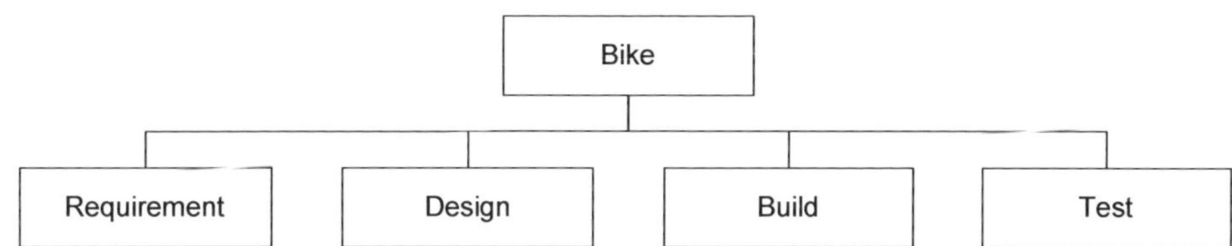

Figure 5-9: WBS – First Level of Decomposition

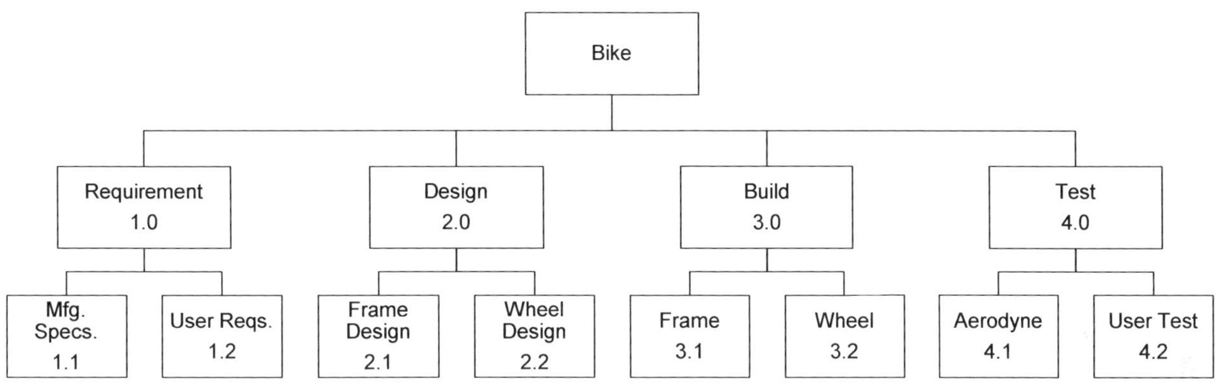

Figure 5-10: WBS – Further Decomposition

b. **Major Deliverables or Subprojects:** Major deliverables and subprojects are used as the first level of decomposition, and these deliverables are then further decomposed into smaller components

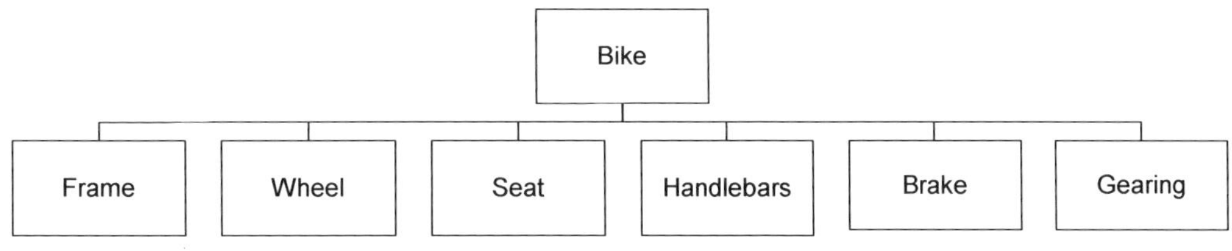

Figure 5-11: WBS – First Level of Decomposition

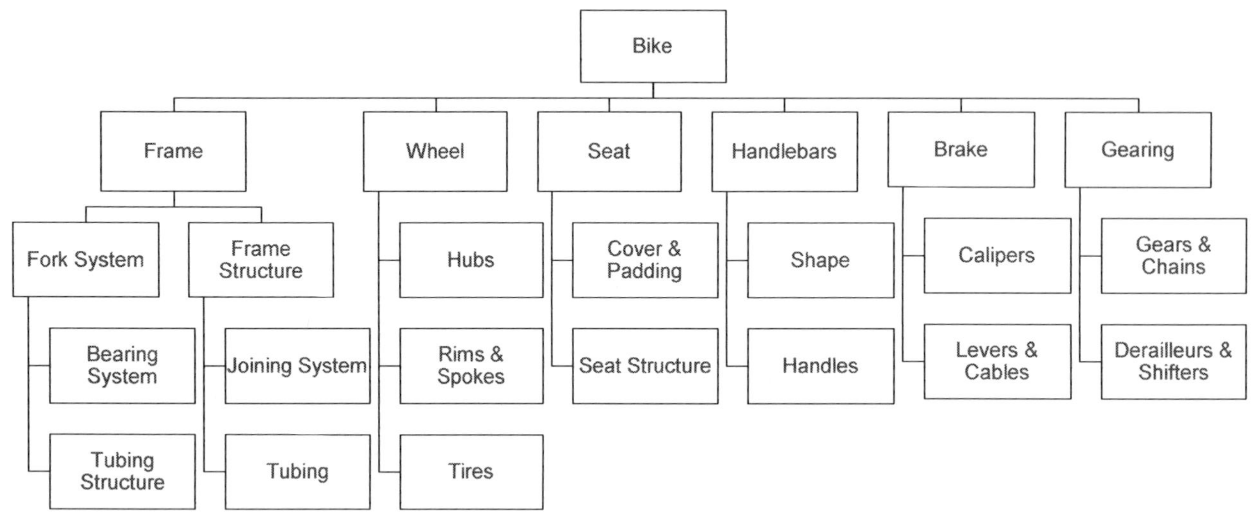

Figure 5-12: WBS – Further Decomposition

c. External Subprojects: If external companies or teams will be contracted to complete different aspects of the project work, a WBS can be structured into separate, external subprojects. For instance, if different segments of a road work project are contracted to cable, gas, electricity, water, and drainage and piping companies, each of these companies will create its own WBS.

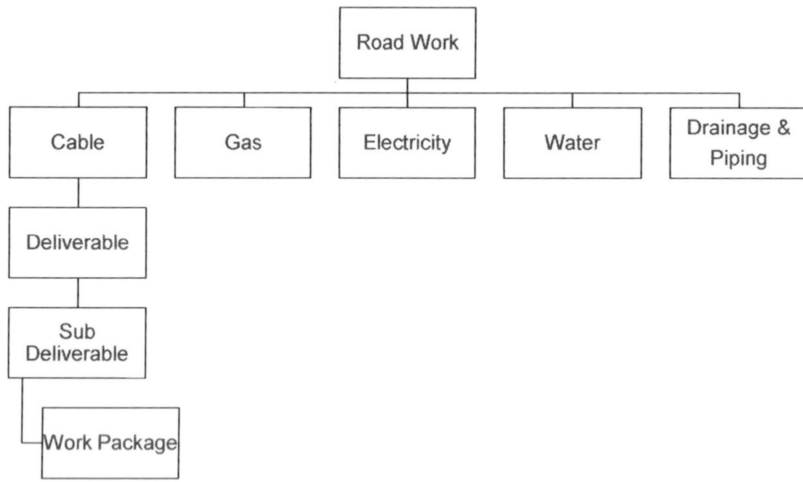

Figure 5-13: WBS – External Subproject

Expert Judgment: Stakeholders, including customers or sponsors, professional and technical associations, industry groups, subject matter experts, and consultants may provide expert opinion and judgments on how to efficiently break down common deliverables into discrete work packages.

Create WBS: Outputs

- Scope Baseline
- Project Documents Updates

Scope Baseline: Project scope baseline includes the approved project scope statement, WBS, and WBS dictionary.

Project Scope Statement: It describes project deliverables, assumptions, and constraints and the work required to create them in detail and will act as the primary starting point for the WBS.

Work Breakdown Structure: A Work Breakdown Structure (WBS) is the foundational block to the initiating, planning, executing, monitoring & controlling, and closing phases. Normally presented in chart form, it is a deliverable-oriented hierarchical decomposition of the work to be executed by the project team to accomplish project objectives and create required deliverables. It organizes and defines the total scope of the project. Deliverables not in the WBS are beyond the scope of the project. A WBS is the foundation of a project and forces team members to think through all aspects of the project.

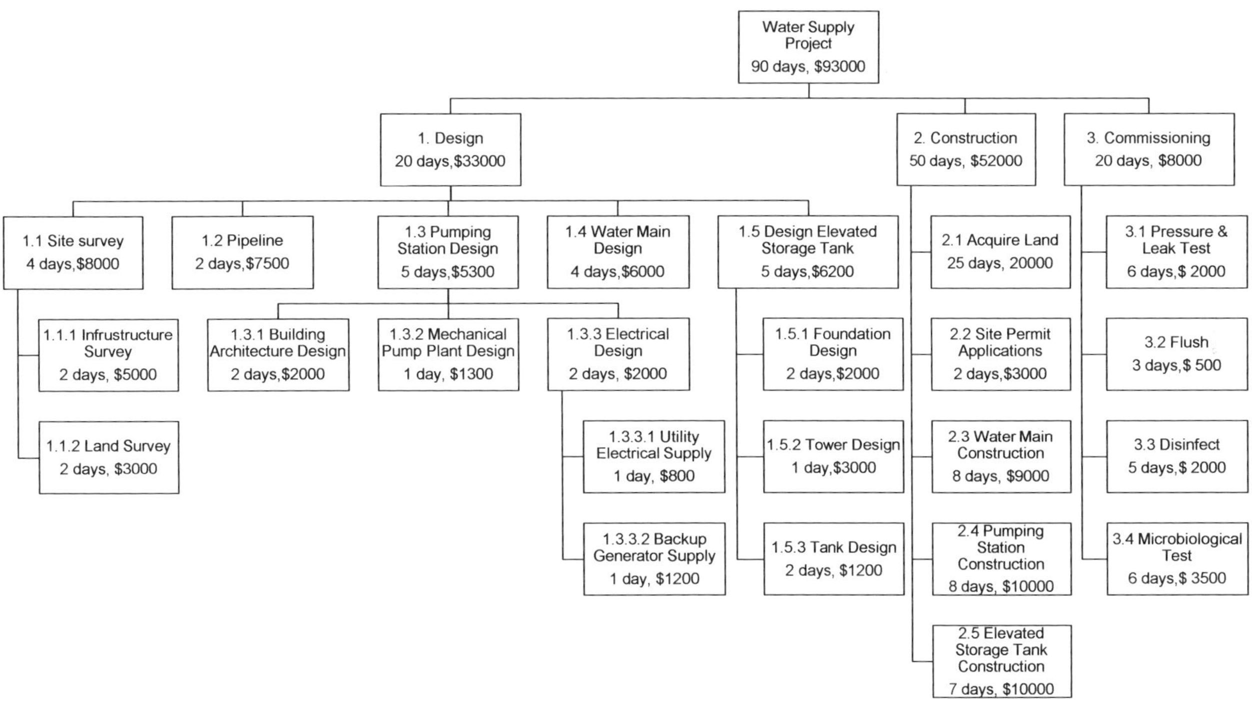

Figure 5-14: A Work Breakdown Structure (WBS)

Exercise 2: Many project managers make a list of "things to do" to capture the activities in the project and have no knowledge about the Work Breakdown Structure (WBS). Remember that a WBS is the foundation of a project and there are extensive benefits of using this kind of hierarchical structure instead of a simple list.
Provide reasons as to why a WBS is more effective than a simple list.

WBS	List

Benefits of WBS: A WBS is the foundation of a project as it:

- Provides a basis for estimating staff, cost, and time as well as helps to identify risks and define quality attributes.
- Helps prevent work from slipping.
- Helps the team to see where their pieces fit into the overall project plan and helps them to understand their role.
- Facilitates communication with all stakeholders.
- Helps prevent unnecessary changes.
- Focuses the team's attention on what needs to be done.
- Obtains team members' consent and helps build the team.
- Helps team justify the need for time, resources, and budget.
- Helps manage stakeholders' expectations and needs.

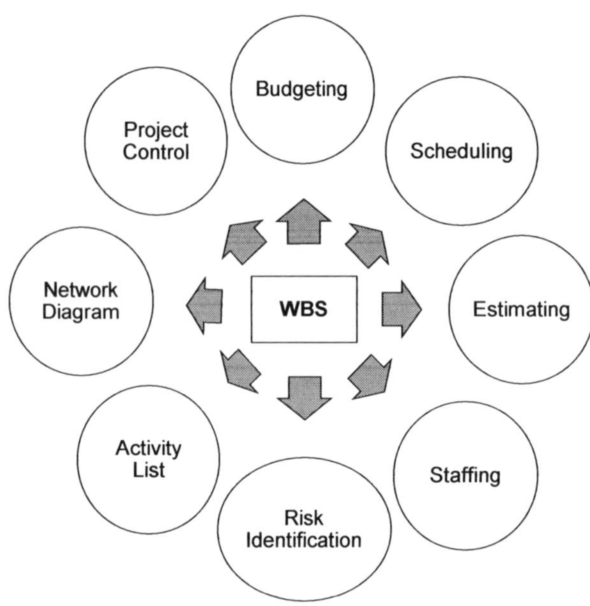

Figure 5-15: Benefits of WBS

Exercise 3: You are experiencing the following in your project:

- More changes than you expected
- Changes are costing more than you expected
- You met the requirements but your product is still being rejected

What would be the root causes of all these unexpected situations?

Exercise 4: Customers usually approve the project scope or product scope?

Poorly designed WBS: Component or full-project failure can often be indicative of a poorly developed or nonexistent WBS. A poorly constructed WBS can result in any of the following:
- Adverse project outcomes including ongoing, repeated project replans and extensions
- Unclear work assignments
- Budget overrun
- Scope creep or an unmanageable and frequently changing scope
- Missed deadlines
- Unusable new products or delivered features

WBS Dictionary: The WBS dictionary documents the detailed description of the work to be done for each work package. The WBS dictionary contains the following items:
- A number identifier (code of accounts)
- Related control account (for cost)
- A statement of the work to be done
- Who is responsible for doing the work
- Any scheduled milestones

Control Account:	
Work Package ID:	
Date of Update:	
Department:	
Work Package Description:	
Acceptance Criteria:	
Deliverables:	
Assumptions:	
Resources Assigned:	
Duration:	
Schedule Milestones:	
Estimated Cost:	
Date Assigned:	
Interdependencies:	**Predecessor work package:**
	Successor work package:
Approved by:	

Figure 5-16: A Sample WBS Dictionary

Usually, project title goes at the top of the WBS; the level below is called the control account or cost account, and the following lower levels are the work packages. The work packages are decomposed further into schedule activities in the Define Activities process of time management, but these activities are not usually included in the WBS, especially for the large projects. The WBS dictionary documents the details of the work packages as described earlier.

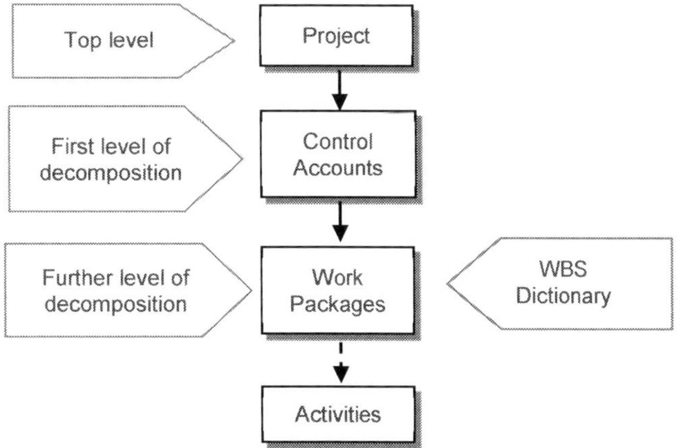

Figure 5-17: Levels of the WBS

Project Documents Updates: Project documents such as the requirements document, the requirements management plan, and the requirements traceability matrix may be updated.

Validate Scope

The Validate Scope is the process of obtaining the stakeholders' formal acceptance of the completed project scope and associated deliverables. This process is similar to the Control Quality process as it compares the product with the scope to ensure they match the specification; however, some of the key differences are as follows:

- Both the Control Quality and the Validate Scope processes can be performed simultaneously, but the Control Quality is usually performed prior to the Validate Scope.
- The Control Quality verifies correctness of the work, whereas the Validate Scope confirms completeness.
- The Control Quality is focused on measuring specific project results against quality specifications and standards, whereas the Validate Scope is mainly focused on obtaining acceptance of the product from the sponsor, customers, stakeholders, and others.

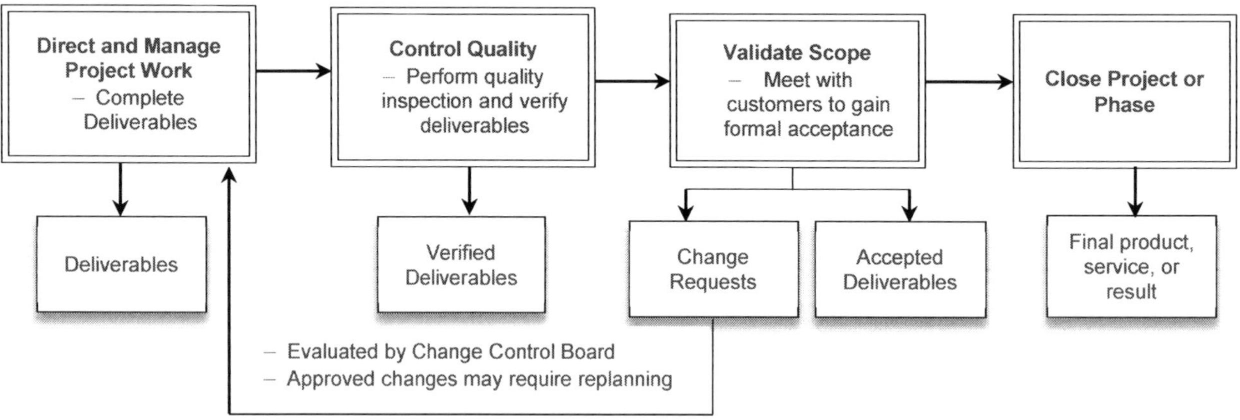

Figure 5-18: Relationship Between Validate Scope and Other Processes

Scope validation can be carried out throughout the project and at the end of each phase to get the formal acceptance of the phase deliverables. If the project is canceled or terminated, it is necessary to perform Validate Scope to identify where the product was at that time in relation to the scope, as this information can be used if the project is ever restarted.

As per the PMBOK®, the Validate Scope process has the following inputs, tools & techniques, and outputs:

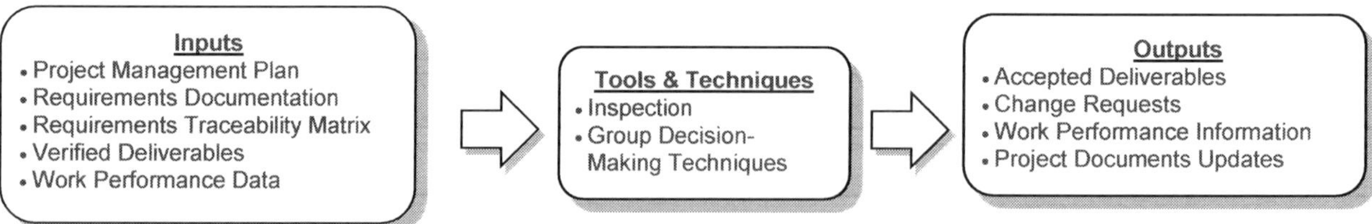

Figure 5-19: Validate Scope: Inputs, Tools & Techniques, and Outputs

Validate Scope: Inputs

- Project Management Plan
- Requirements Documentation
- Requirements Traceability Matrix
- Verified Deliverables
- Work Performance Data

Project Management Plan: The project management plan contains the scope baseline, which includes the project scope statement, the WBS, and the WBS dictionary.

Requirements Documentation: This document describes how individual requirements meet the business need and the expectations of the project sponsor and stakeholders while also providing useful information on the sources of the requirements for verification.

Requirements Traceability Matrix: The requirements traceability matrix is a mapping for requirements that links them to their origin and traces them throughout the project life cycle.

Verified Deliverables: These deliverables have been completed as per the documented scope and checked for defects by the project team members in the Control Quality process.

Work Performance Data: Various work performance data such as the degree of compliance with requirements, number of nonconformities, severity of the nonconformities, and number of validation cycles, among others, may influence the Validate Scope process.

Validate Scope: Tools & Techniques

- Inspection
- Group Decision-Making Techniques

Inspection: This lone tool in the Validate Scope process includes activities such as measuring, examining, and verifying to determine whether work and deliverables meet requirements and product acceptance criteria. Reviews, product reviews, walkthroughs, and audits are all types of inspection. User acceptance testing in a software development project to verify that deliverables match the documented scope can serve as an example of inspection.

Group Decision-Making Techniques: Various decision-making techniques such as unanimity, majority, plurality, etc., are used to reach a decision on the timing of the validation by the project team and other stakeholders.

Validate Scope: Outputs

- Accepted Deliverables
- Change Requests
- Work Performance Information
- Project Documents Updates

Accepted Deliverables: Customers or sponsors approve and formally sign off on some of the deliverables that meet their acceptance criteria. These accepted deliverables are then forwarded to the Close Project or Phase process.

Change Requests: Customers or sponsors do not approve and formally sign off on some of the deliverables if they do not meet the acceptance criteria. The reasons for non-acceptance are documented, and a change request for defect repairs may be generated through the Perform Integrated Change Control process.

Work Performance Information: Various work performance and progress information such as which deliverables are started, which are completed, which are pending, and which are accepted, among other things, are documented and communicated to the stakeholders.

Project Documents Updates: Any document defining the product or reporting the status on product completion may be updated.

Exercise 5: What are the items a project manager should focus on during the Validate Scope process?

Exercise 6: What is the relationship between the Control Quality process and the Validate Scope process?

Control Scope

This is the process of monitoring the status of the project and product scope, maintaining control over the project by preventing major scope change requests, and managing changes to the scope baseline. It also assures that underlying causes of all requested changes and recommended corrective actions are understood and processed through the Integrated Change Control process.

One of the key focuses in the process may be dispute resolution related to project scope. It is important to note that customers are one of the most important stakeholders, and all other things being equal, disputes should be resolved in their favor.

As per the PMBOK®, the Control Scope process has the following inputs, tools & techniques, and outputs:

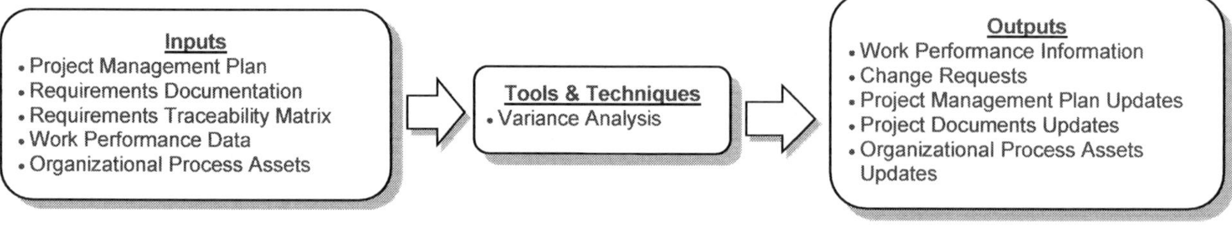

Figure 5-20: Control Scope: Inputs, Tools & Techniques, and Outputs

Control Scope: Inputs

- Project Management Plan
- Requirements Documentation
- Requirements Traceability Matrix
- Work Performance Data
- Organizational Process Assets

Project Management Plan: The scope baseline and management plan, the change management plan, the configuration management plan, and the requirements management plan may play key roles in the Control Scope process.

Requirements Documentation: Requirements documentation describes how individual requirements meet the business need for the project and should be evaluated whenever there is a change in the requirements.

Requirements Traceability Matrix: The requirements traceability matrix is a mapping for the requirements that links requirements to their origin and traces them throughout the project life cycle. It should be used whenever there is a change in the requirements.

Work Performance Data: Information about the number of changes requested, the number of changes accepted, which deliverables have started and their progress, and which deliverables have finished as per the project plan.

Organizational Process Assets: Policies, procedures, guidelines, and monitoring and reporting methods may influence the Control Scope process.

Control Scope: Tools & Techniques

- Variance Analysis

Variance Analysis: This tool is used to investigate and assess the magnitude of variation between what was defined and what was created and determine the cause relative to the scope baseline. It also helps to determine whether defect repairs, corrective and/or preventive actions are needed.

Control Scope: Outputs

- Work Performance Information
- Change Requests
- Project Management Plan Updates
- Project Documents Updates
- Organizational Process Assets Updates

Work Performance Information: Scope performance or technical performance measurements compared to the planned measurements are documented and communicated to the stakeholders and others. Work performance information such as the identified scope variance and causes, impact of the variances on schedule and cost, the categories of the changes received, and the future scope performance forecast are among elements that may assist in making scope-related decisions.

Change Requests: Change requests to the scope baseline or other components of the project's management, which can include defect repairs and corrective and preventive actions, are processed according to the Perform Integrated Change Control process. If a change request results in a new scope, the work should be decomposed to the work package level and then incorporated to the appropriate processes.

Project Management Plan Updates: The project scope statement, the WBS, and the WBS dictionary, along with other corresponding cost and schedule baselines in the project management plan, may be updated.

Project Documents Updates: Project documents such as the requirements document, the requirements management plan document, and the requirements traceability matrix may be updated.

Organizational Process Assets Updates: Organizational process assets such as lessons learned, causes of variances, and corrective actions may be updated.

Exercise 7: List items a project manager should focus on during the Control Scope process.

Exercise 8: Identify which process group each process belongs to.

Process Groups				
Initiating	Planning	Executing	Monitoring & Controlling	Closing

Process Names:

- Create WBS
- Control Scope
- Plan Scope Management
- Collect Requirements
- Define Scope
- Validate Scope

Exercise 9: Crossword

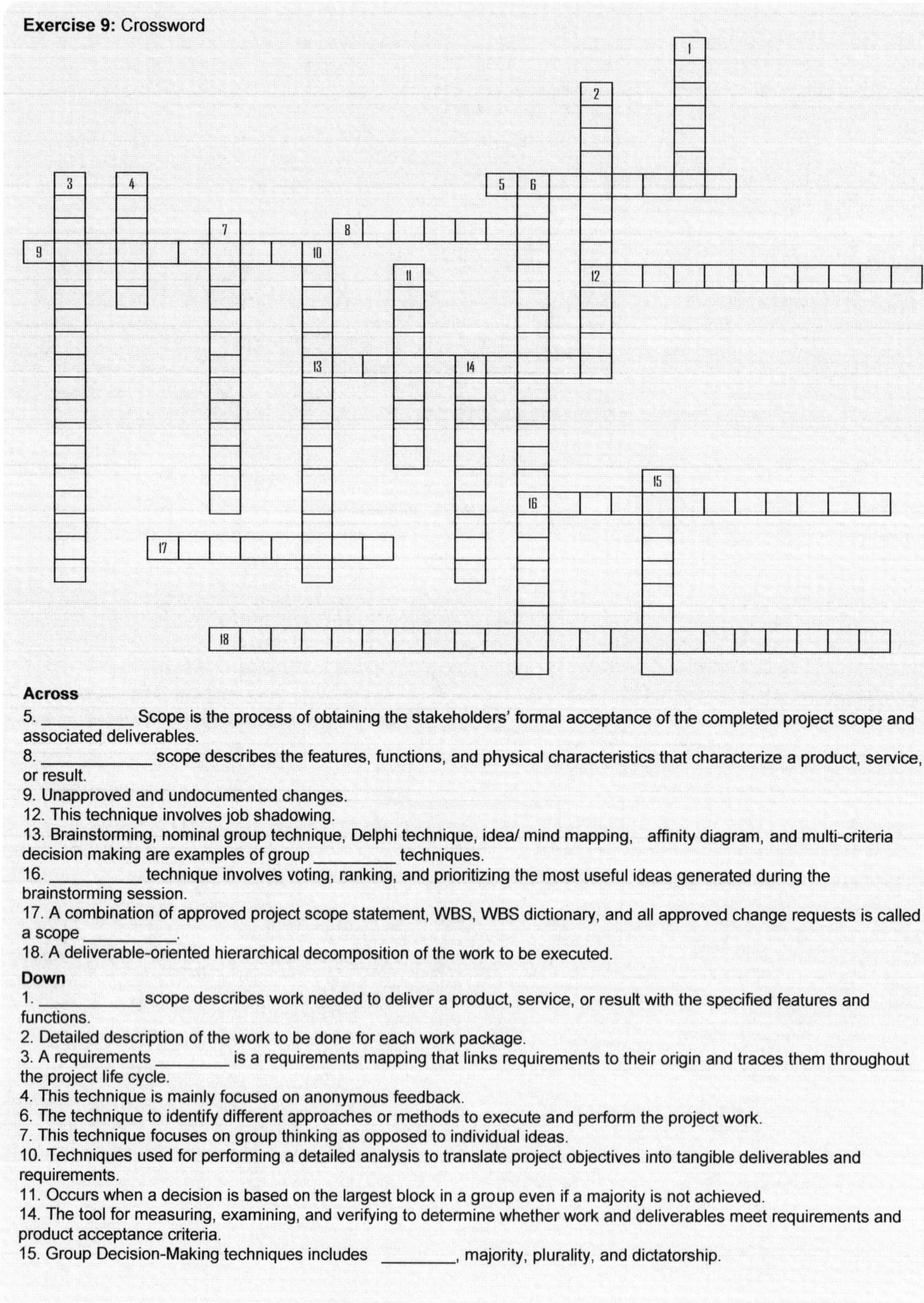

Across

5. __________ Scope is the process of obtaining the stakeholders' formal acceptance of the completed project scope and associated deliverables.
8. ____________ scope describes the features, functions, and physical characteristics that characterize a product, service, or result.
9. Unapproved and undocumented changes.
12. This technique involves job shadowing.
13. Brainstorming, nominal group technique, Delphi technique, idea/ mind mapping, affinity diagram, and multi-criteria decision making are examples of group _________ techniques.
16. __________ technique involves voting, ranking, and prioritizing the most useful ideas generated during the brainstorming session.
17. A combination of approved project scope statement, WBS, WBS dictionary, and all approved change requests is called a scope __________.
18. A deliverable-oriented hierarchical decomposition of the work to be executed.

Down

1. ___________ scope describes work needed to deliver a product, service, or result with the specified features and functions.
2. Detailed description of the work to be done for each work package.
3. A requirements ________ is a requirements mapping that links requirements to their origin and traces them throughout the project life cycle.
4. This technique is mainly focused on anonymous feedback.
6. The technique to identify different approaches or methods to execute and perform the project work.
7. This technique focuses on group thinking as opposed to individual ideas.
10. Techniques used for performing a detailed analysis to translate project objectives into tangible deliverables and requirements.
11. Occurs when a decision is based on the largest block in a group even if a majority is not achieved.
14. The tool for measuring, examining, and verifying to determine whether work and deliverables meet requirements and product acceptance criteria.
15. Group Decision-Making techniques includes ________, majority, plurality, and dictatorship.

Exercise 10: Answer the following:

1. This technique focuses on "group thinking" as opposed to individual ideas.
2. The process of obtaining the stakeholders' formal acceptance of the completed project scope and associated deliverables.
3. _________ describes the features, functions, and physical characteristics that characterize a product, service, or result.
4. __________ describes work needed to deliver a product, service, or result with the specified features and functions.
5. The process of collecting and documenting quantifiable needs and expectations of the sponsor, customer, and other stakeholders.
6. The technique of subdividing project deliverables into progressively smaller, more manageable components or work packages.
7. Brainstorming, nominal group technique, Delphi technique, Idea/mind mapping, and affinity diagram are examples of ________.
8. The tool for measuring, examining, and verifying to determine whether work and deliverables meet requirements and product acceptance criteria.
9. This technique is mainly focused on preventing group thinking and finding out the true opinions of the participants by sending a request for information to the experts who participate anonymously.
10. This tool is used to investigate and assess the magnitude of variation between what was defined and what was created and determine the cause relative to the scope baseline.
11. This knowledge area includes the processes concerned with "all the work" and "only the work" required to successfully deliver to the stakeholders' expectations.
12. Group Decision-Making Techniques includes unanimity, majority, plurality, and ___________.
13. _________ documents the detail description of the work to be done for each work package.
14. The _________is like a requirements mapping that links requirements to their origin and traces them throughout the project life cycle.
15. _________ includes the approved project scope statement, WBS, and WBS dictionary.
16. The process where a project scope statement is created is called the ________ Scope.
17. This document describes how individual requirements meet the business need and the expectations of the project sponsor and stakeholders.
18. A Joint Application Development (JAD), used mostly in the software development industry, is an example of a facilitated __________.
19. The most common in developing a WBS are by phases and ________.
20. Watching a potential user of the product at work, and in some cases, participating in the work to help identify requirements that may not be obvious through other requirement collection methods is called observation or _________.
21. The technique to vote, rank, and prioritize the most useful ideas generated during the brainstorming session.
22. The technique to identify different approaches or methods to execute and perform the project work.
23. The six processes of scope management are ________.
24. The key outputs of scope management processes are ________.
25. The key components of a project scope statement are ________.
26. The difference between Project Scope Statement and Project Statement of Work (PSOW).
27. A numbering system used to uniquely identify each component of the WBS is called _______.
28. The level above the work package level in a WBS is called _______.

Project Scope Management Summary

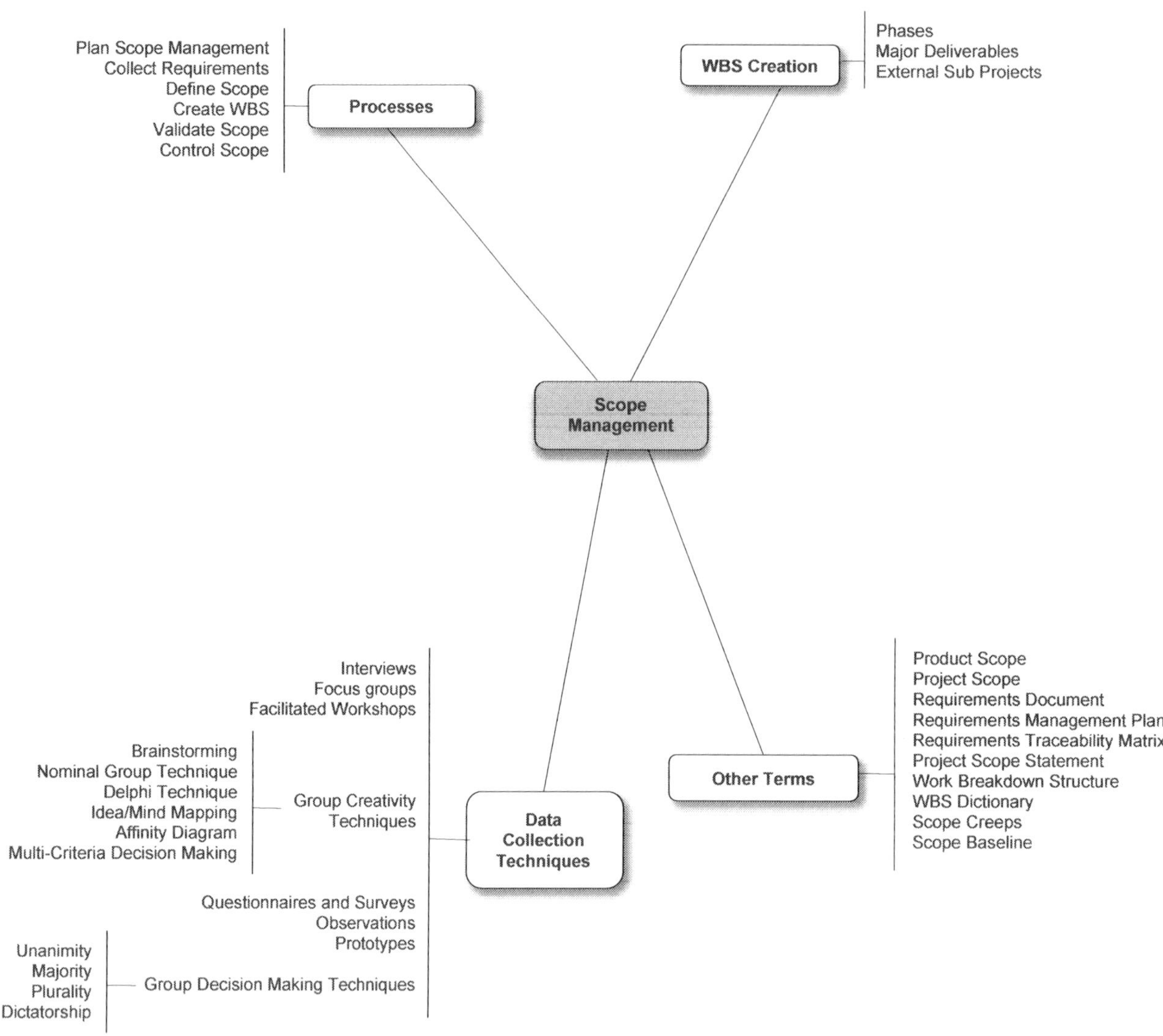

Figure 5-21: Project Scope Management Summary

Project Scope Management Key Terms

Data Collection Techniques

Interviews, focus groups, facilitated workshops, questionnaires and surveys, observations, prototypes

Group Creativity Techniques: Brainstorming, nominal group technique, Delphi technique, idea/ mind mapping, affinity diagram, multi-criteria decision making

Group Decision Making Techniques: Unanimity, majority, plurality, dictatorship

Other Terms

Product Scope: Describes the features, functions, and physical characteristics that characterize a product, service, or result

Project Scope: Describes work needed to deliver a product, service, or result

Requirements Document: Describes how individual requirements meet the business needs and expectations of the project sponsor and stakeholders

Requirements Traceability Matrix: A requirements mapping that links requirements to their origin and traces them throughout the project life cycle

Project Scope Statement: Describes project deliverables and work required to create them in detail

Scope Creeps: Unapproved and undocumented changes

Scope Baseline: A combination of approved project scope statement, WBS, WBS dictionary, and all approved change requests

Product Analysis: Techniques used for performing a detailed analysis to translate project objectives into tangible deliverables and requirements

Work Breakdown Structure (WBS): A deliverable-oriented hierarchical decomposition of the work to be executed. The lowest level of the WBS are the work packages, which are decomposed further into activities, but activities are not usually included in the WBS

WBS Dictionary: Detailed description of the work to be done for each work package

WBS Creation Methods: By project phases, by major deliverables or subprojects, or by external subprojects

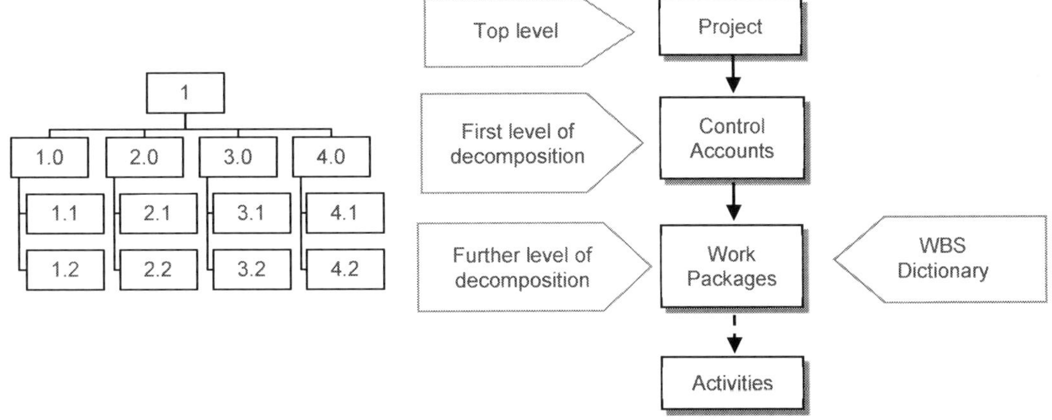

Work Breakdown Structure (WBS)

Project Scope Management Exercise Answers

Exercise 1:

1. Nominal group technique
2. Delphi technique
3. Brainstorming
4. Idea/Mind mapping
5. Affinity diagram
6. Observation/Job shadowing
7. Benchmarking
8. Context diagram
9. Prototype

Exercise 2:

WBS	List
Shows a complete hierarchy of the project.	Shows only list of items in the project.
Difficult to overlook a deliverable.	Easy to overlook a deliverable.
Allows breaking down the work into smaller work packages.	Does not allow the team to clearly break down a large project into smaller components.
Helps the team members see where their pieces fit into the overall project plan and helps them to understand their roles.	Difficult to understand the roles and overall project.
Makes it easier to show how one deliverable relates to another.	Does not really explain the relationship among deliverables.
A WBS is created with inputs from team members and stakeholders.	A list is usually created by one person.
Helps team members better understand the project.	Does not help team members much understand the entire project.
Involving team members and stakeholders helps gain their approval on deliverables.	Does not have approval of the team members and stakeholders on deliverables.
The project execution is much easier and less risky with a WBS.	The project execution is difficult and risky with a simple list.
Obtains team member's consent and helps build the team.	Does not really help build the team as the list is mostly created by one person.
Helps team justify the need for time, resources, and budget.	Does not help team justify the need for time, resources, and budget.
Water Supply Project Design: Site survey; Pipeline; Pumping Station Design; Water Main Design; Design Elevated Storage Tank Construction: Acquire Land; Site Permit Applications; Water Main Construction; Pumping Station Construction; Elevated Storage Tank Construction Commissioning: Pressure & Leak Test; Flush; Disinfect; Microbiological Test	**<u>Water Supply Project</u>** Design – Site survey – Pipeline – Pumping Station Design – Water Main Design – Design Elevated Storage Tank Construction – Acquire Land – Site Permit Applications – Water Main Construction – Pumping Station Construction – Elevated Storage Tank Construction Commissioning – Pressure & Leak Test – Flush – Disinfect – Microbiological Test

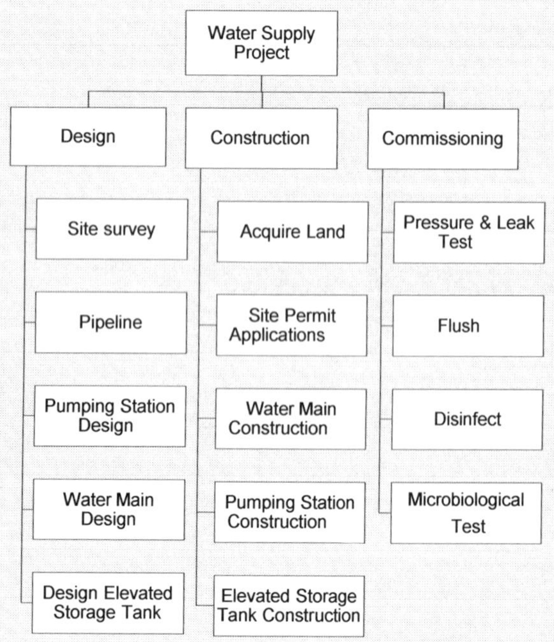

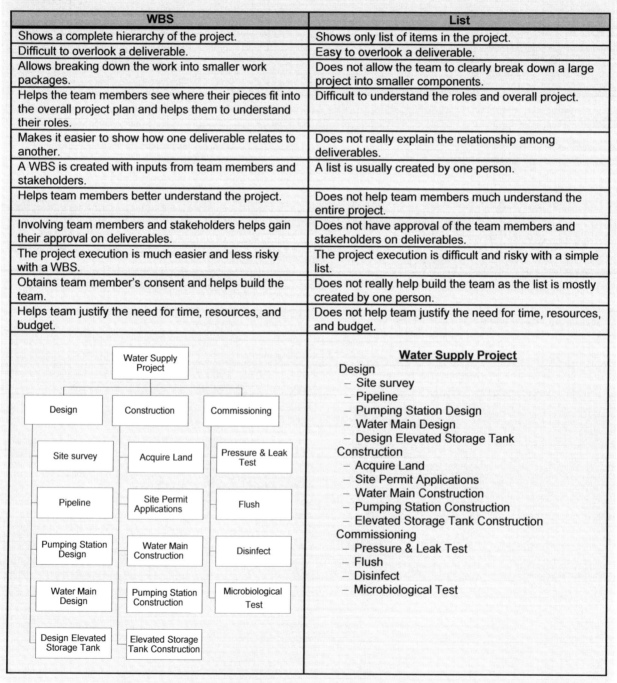

Exercise 3:
You did not have a quality requirement document as you did not understand the requirements of your customers. There is a huge gap between your understanding and customers' understanding about the scope of the project. In addition to this, you did not identify the stakeholders early enough or you did not identify the right stakeholders.

Exercise 4: Customers generally approve the product scope or their requirements and not the project scope or what you are going to do to complete their requirements.

Exercise 5:
- Frequently meet with the sponsor and customer to gain formal acceptance on deliverables.
- Refer to the scope baseline for approved scope while meeting with the customers.
- Refer to the requirement traceability matrix to track the requirements.
- Refer to scope management plan of methods on gaining formal acceptance from the customers.
- Make sure to communicate the work performance information on the deliverables.
- Update the scope management plan and other relevant documents as appropriate.
- Make sure to implement the approved changes on deliverables.

Exercise 6: The Validate Scope is the process of obtaining the stakeholders' formal acceptance of the completed project scope and associated deliverables. This process is similar to the Control Quality process as it compares the product with the scope to ensure they match the specification. The relationship between these two processes is as follows:
- Both the Control Quality and the Validate Scope processes can be performed simultaneously, but the Control Quality is usually performed prior to the Validate Scope process.
- The Control Quality verifies correctness of the work, whereas the Validate Scope confirms completeness.
- The Control Quality is focused on measuring specific project results against quality specifications and standards, whereas the Validate Scope is mainly focused on obtaining acceptance of the product from the sponsor, customers, stakeholders, and others.

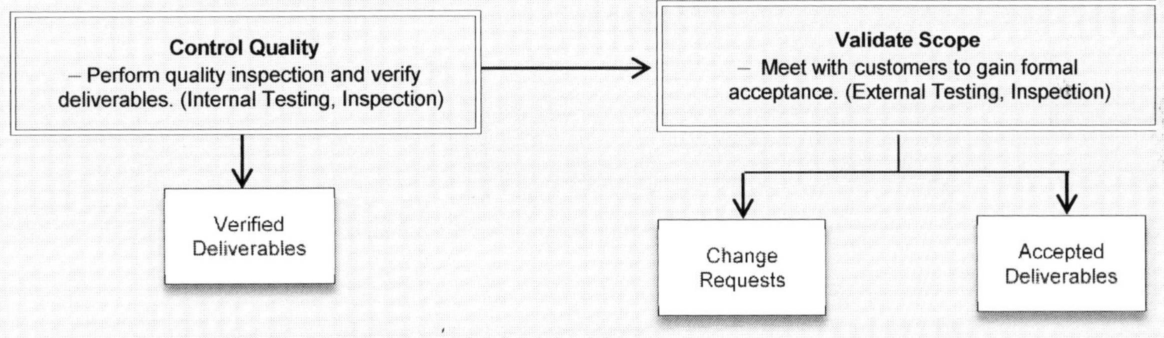

Exercise 7:
- Monitor the status of the project and product scope.
- Analyze any variances to see whether they warrant changes.
- Frequently meet with the sponsor and customers to gain formal acceptance on deliverables.
- Refer to the scope baseline for approved scope while meeting with the customers.
- Refer to the requirement traceability matrix to track the requirements.
- Refer to scope management plan of methods on gaining formal acceptance from the customers.
- Make sure to communicate the work performance information on deliverables.
- Update the scope management plan and other relevant documents as appropriate.
- Make sure to implement approved changes on deliverables.
- Manage changes to the scope baseline.
- Prevent or remove the need for any more changes from the source.
- Maintain control over the project by preventing overwhelming scope change requests.
- Assure that underlying causes of all requested changes and recommended corrective actions are understood and processed through the Integrated Change Control process.

Exercise 8:

Process Groups				
Initiating	Planning	Executing	Monitoring & Controlling	Closing
	– Plan Scope Management – Collect Requirements – Define Scope – Create WBS		– Validate Scope – Control Scope	

Exercise 9:

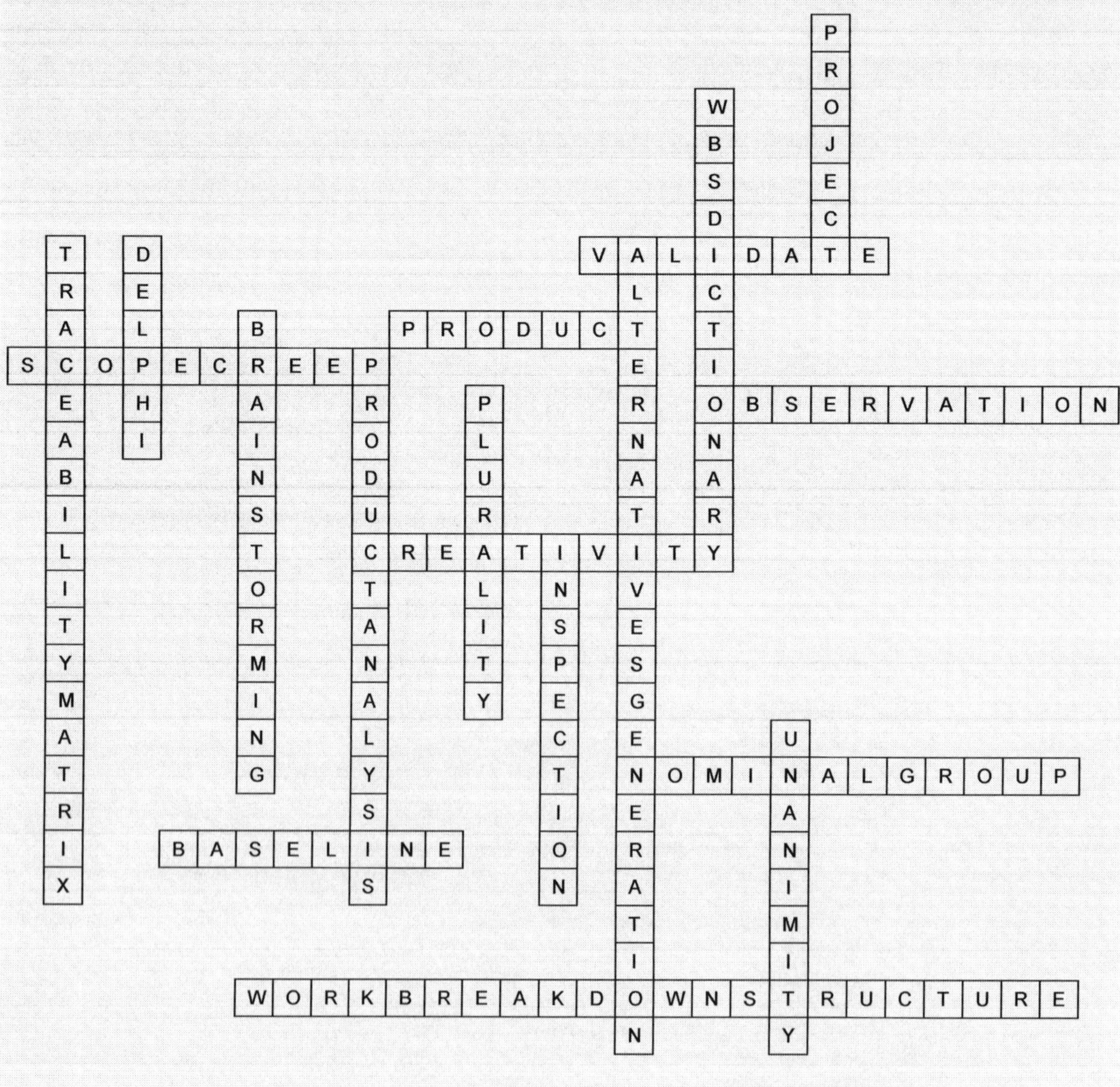

Exercise 10:

1. Brainstorming
2. Validate Scope
3. Product scope
4. Project scope
5. Collect Requirements
6. Decomposition
7. Group creativity techniques
8. Inspection
9. Delphi technique
10. Variance analysis
11. Project scope management
12. Dictatorship
13. WBS dictionary
14. Requirements traceability matrix
15. Scope baseline
16. Define
17. Requirements documentation
18. Workshop
19. Major deliverables
20. Job shadowing
21. Nominal group technique
22. Alternatives generation
23. Plan Scope Management, Collect Requirements, Define Scope, Create WBS, Validate Scope, and Control Scope
24. Plan Scope Management – Scope Management Plan, Requirements Management Plan
    Collect Requirements – Requirements Documentation, Requirements Traceability Matrix
    Define Scope – Project Scope Statement
    Create WBS – Scope Baseline
    Validate Scope – Accepted Deliverables, Change Requests
    Control Scope – Work Performance Information, Change Requests
25. Project objectives, project scope description, project deliverables, product acceptance criteria, project constraints, project assumptions, project exclusions
26. The scope statement is developed by the team to describe the work they are going to do on the project to deliver what is described in the Project Statement of Work (PSOW).
27. The code of accounts
28. The control account level or cost account level

Project Scope Management Exam Tips

- Be able to define the processes, major inputs, tools & techniques, and outputs of scope management.
- Understand the purpose of the project scope statement and the scope management plan.
- Be able to define the WBS and its components.
- Be able to answer questions where you will need to analyze a specific situation and determine what you should do next.
- Be familiar with the concepts and terms in the project scope management summary table, Figure 5-21: Project Scope Management Summary.

Project Scope Management Questions

1. You have been assigned as the project manager for a web-based application project to automate the sales and marketing processes for one of your clients. You have decided to utilize a group creativity technique to identify the project and product requirements during the Collect Requirements process. All of the following are valid group creativity techniques EXCEPT:
   A. Nominal group technique
   B. The Delphi technique
   C. Affinity diagram
   D. Tornado diagram

2. The project scope statement that describes project deliverables and the work required to create them in detail, enables the project team to perform more detailed planning, guides the project team's work during execution, and provides the baseline for evaluating changes includes all of the following EXCEPT:
   A. Detailed Work Breakdown Structure (WBS)
   B. Project constraints
   C. Project deliverables
   D. Product acceptance criteria

3. Which one of the following are the unapproved and undocumented changes and what occurs when changes to the scope are not detected early enough or are not managed?
   A. Scope baseline
   B. Residual risks
   C. Scope creeps
   D. Variances

4. You are the project manager for a cashier system project to produce cashier applications and software for the retail industry. You have recently discovered that one of your key competitors is also working on a similar project, but their new applications will include a computer-aided program and a web-based interface that your project does not offer. You have implemented a change request to update your project in order to include these exciting missing features. This is an example of which of the following?
   A. A change due to an error and omission in the business case
   B. A change due to a legal requirement and constraint
   C. A change due to an error or omission in the planning phase
   D. A change due to an external event

5. While trying to obtain the formal acceptance of the completed project scope and associated deliverables, with whom should the project manager validate the product?
   A. The sponsor, key stakeholders, and customers
   B. The customers
   C. The quality control team members
   D. The change control board members

6. The scope baseline, which consists of the project scope statement, the WBS, and the WBS dictionary, is used as an input in all of the following processes EXCEPT:
   A. Determine Budget process
   B. Plan Procurement Management process
   C. Define Activities process
   D. Sequence Activities process

7. Determining if the project scope has been completed by describing project deliverables and the work required to create them in detail, enabling the project team to perform more detailed planning, guiding the project team's work during execution, providing the baseline for evaluating changes, and other factors relies mostly upon the use of:
   A. Statement of work
   B. Project plan
   C. Project charter
   D. Project scope statement

8. You are working as a project manager for an Enterprise Resource Planning (ERP) application to automate the accounting and financial processes for one of your key customers. Due to a mismatch with the customer's requirement, you have been forced to redesign one of the major components. This is a significant setback since a substantial amount of code that has already been developed will have to be recoded to match the updated design. This rework has caused huge expenses, and you noticed a sign of extremely low morale among team members. Which of the following is TRUE in this situation?
   A. The team discovered this issue as a result of the Identify Risks process.
   B. The team did a poor job while creating the WBS.
   C. This problem was a result of poor scope definition.
   D. The team carried on a rigorous Control Quality process and discovered the issue.

9. While overseeing a construction project, you discovered that one of the team members, on her own initiative, added extra windows to increase air circulation and light in the basement. The original plan did not include the cost of these extra windows, but the team member thought they were absolutely required due to poor air circulation and low light in the basement. This is an example of which of the following?
   A. Value-added change
   B. Self-motivated team member
   C. Team member exceeding expectations
   D. Inefficient change control

10. After a major milestone release, some of the key stakeholders are not happy and complain that their requirements are not met. The project manager should have involved them in which of the following processes to ensure their approval for the release?
   A. Project Management Plan Development
   B. Identifying Constraints
   C. Validate Scope
   D. Schedule Management

11. Which one of the following mostly includes the product acceptance criteria that outline requirements a project must meet before stakeholders accept the final product or service?
   A. Quality management plan
   B. Project scope statement
   C. Scope management plan
   D. Requirements management plan

12. ITPro Consultancy, LLC has been offering cable TV, Internet, and phone services to its East Coast customers for almost five years now. Recently, they have initiated a project to introduce their service to the West Coast and have assigned a project manager. The project manager left the company, and you took over the project, as per the instruction of the CEO, when the project is almost ready to enter in execution. While reviewing the existing documents, you discovered that the team had done a great job in developing the requirements document and the project scope statement, but there was no WBS. What should you do FIRST in this situation?
   A. Immediately inform management and provide them with relevant oversight.
   B. Politely request to be excused from the project.
   C. You should not enter execution until the WBS is created for the project.
   D. You should refer to the WBS dictionary for the required detail needed to continue to execution.

13. While discussing the scope in your project with the stakeholders and team members, you realized that all of the following statements are TRUE about scope EXCEPT:
   A. Product scope describes the features and functions that characterize a product, service, or result.
   B. Project scope management includes the processes concerned with "all the work" and "only the work" required to successfully deliver to the stakeholders' expectations, manage changes, minimize surprises, and gain acceptance of the product in order to complete the project.
   C. Project scope describes work needed to deliver a product, service, or result with the specified features and functions.
   D. The project team should go above and beyond the defined scope and impress the customers by implementing extra features that will be beneficial for them.

14. Which one of the following is NOT true about the Define Scope process?
   A. It is the process of developing a comprehensive, detailed description of the project and product.
   B. Alternatives generation is used as a tool & technique in this process.
   C. The requirements document is the key output in this process.
   D. A detailed project scope statement that is created in this process is critical to project success and builds upon the additional analysis of requirements, major deliverables, assumptions, constraints, and other factors that are documented earlier in the project.

15. You have been assigned as the project manager for a web-based application project to automate the recruiting process for one of your clients. You have decided to utilize a group decision-making technique to generate, classify, prioritize, and drive decisions forward. All of the following are valid group decision-making techniques EXCEPT:

A. The decision is based on the most influential block in a group even if a majority is not achieved.
B. The decision is based on a single course of action decided by everyone in the group.
C. The decision is based on the support from more than 50 percent of the members of the group.
D. The decision is made for the group by one individual, mostly the project manager.

16. Product scope describes the features, functions, and physical characteristics that characterize a product, service, or result. Completion of the product scope is measured against which one of the following?

A. Scope statement
B. Project requirements
C. Project objectives
D. Product requirements

17. As per the project manager's instruction, the team has decomposed project deliverables and project work into smaller, more manageable components to develop a WBS and WBS dictionary. The team finalized the WBS by establishing control or cost accounts and unique identifiers for the lower-level components of the WBS called work packages. Normally presented in the chart form, this WBS provides a structure for hierarchical summation of:

A. Cost and schedule information
B. Cost and requirements information
C. Cost, resource, and schedule information
D. Schedule and requirements information

18. A project manager managing a data center project had the opportunity to attend several meetings about the project prior to the creation of the project charter. In one of the meetings, the sponsor specifically denied funding for two very specific items. Two months into the project, a couple of stakeholders requested the project manager add work for one of the items that was strongly denied by the sponsor. What will be the best thing the project manager can do in this situation?

A. Add the work if it does not have much impact on the schedule.
B. Inform the stakeholders that the work cannot be added.
C. Evaluate the impact of adding the work on time, cost, quality, risk, human resource, and other elements.
D. Immediately inform the sponsor about the request that was denied by him.

19. Verified deliverables are inputs in which of the following scope management processes?

A. Define Scope
B. Create WBS
C. Validate Scope
D. Control Scope

20. All of the following are true regarding the Control Scope process EXCEPT:

A. It assures that underlying causes of all requested changes and recommended corrective actions are understood and processed through the Integrated Change Control process.
B. One of the key focuses in the process may be dispute resolution related to project scope.
C. It monitors the status of the project and product scope, maintains control over the project by preventing overwhelming scope change requests, and manages changes to the scope baseline.
D. It verifies the correctness of work results.

21. Your project is approaching completion, and you were able to release some of the team members from the team to be assigned to other projects. Your team has successfully resolved all the issues in the issue log except for one, which will be fixed in the next version of the application as per the agreement with the client. You are ahead of schedule but $3,500 over budget due to an unexpected price increase for one of the major pieces of equipment. Your team also successfully performed quality control inspections and met quality requirements for all of the items except one. You called a meeting and requested the client for product verification, and surprisingly the client mentioned that they wanted to make a major change to the scope. In this situation, the project manager should:

A. Immediately inform management about this surprising new change
B. Have an urgent meeting with the team members to explore the feasibility of making the change
C. Inform that it is too late now to make a major change
D. Request the client for a description of the change

22. Your company, ITPro Consultancy, has assigned you as the project manager to upgrade the call center in your organization. The number of calls the customer support agents have to answer each month has increased drastically in the last five months, and the phone system is approaching the maximum load limit. Your team has worked on the requirements document and the project scope statement, and you are now ready to create the WBS with the help of your team members. All of the following are true regarding the WBS EXCEPT:

A. The WBS represents all the work required to be completed in the project.
B. Each level of the WBS represents a verifiable product or results.
C. Activities in the WBS should be arranged in the proper sequence they will be performed.
D. The WBS should be decomposed to a level called the work package level where cost and schedule can easily be calculated.

23. The sponsor has recently assigned you as a project manager to design and develop a custom video conferencing tool. As per the sponsor, the project must be completed in four months and should integrate with the existing infrastructure and applications in the organization. This is an example of which of the following?

A. Constraints
B. Assumptions
C. Expert judgment
D. High-level planning

24. All of the following are TRUE about the Validate Scope process EXCEPT:

A. Customer acceptance of the project deliverables is a key output of this process.
B. It is an input to the Develop Project Management Plan process and an output of the Control Quality process.
C. It should be performed at the end of each phase of the project.
D. This process is closely related to the Control Quality process.

25. A project manager is in the Control Scope process of monitoring the status of the project and product scope, maintaining control over the project by preventing overwhelming scope change requests, and managing changes to the scope baseline. Which one of the following is NOT true about this process?

A. The Control Scope process must be integrated with other control processes.
B. It should be performed prior to scope planning.
C. Variance analysis is used as a tool & technique in this process.
D. Work performance information and change requests are the key deliverables in this process.

26. Your project to build a new substation to supply power to a newly developed industrial park is not going too well. You are overwhelmed with numerous issues in the project and got really frustrated when the city conducted an inspection and reported a building code violation. You were asked by management to ensure full compliance to the mandatory city and construction industry standards. At this time, you are also approaching the final deadline of the project in two weeks. You have identified a couple of changes that will drastically enhance performance and make your clients very happy. While trying to sort all these messes out, you received a call from the senior engineer informing you that he would be leaving the company soon. Which is the MOST critical issue you should address first?

A. Notify the customers about the possible delay in the project.
B. Initiate the change control process to implement new changes.
C. Find a replacement for the senior engineer.
D. Ensure compliance with the city and construction industry standards.

27. Sarah, a project manager, is in the Define Scope process of developing a comprehensive, detailed description of the project and product. Which of the following is NOT a tool & technique used in this Define Scope process?

A. Product analysis
B. Alternatives generation
C. Facilitated workshops
D. Group decision-making techniques

28. You have been selected as the project manager for a major data center upgrade at your company headquarters. The sponsor has handed you a project charter and wished you best of luck. What should you do next as the first step?

A. Instruct the team to work on a project scope statement.
B. Instruct the team to work on the WBS.
C. Review the charter and make sure that all key stakeholders have inputs into the scope.
D. Start working on planning the project.

29. Walkthroughs, reviews, product reviews, and audits are examples of which one of the following methods of examining work or a product to determine whether it conforms to documented standards or not?

A. Observation
B. Verification
C. Inspection
D. Group decision-making techniques

30. A project manager is in the Collect Requirements process of collecting and documenting quantifiable needs and expectations of the sponsor, customer, and other stakeholders. Which of the following is NOT true regarding this process?

A. It describes project deliverables and the work required to create them in detail as well as deliverables description, product acceptance criteria, requirements assumptions and constraints, and exclusions from requirements.
B. Requirements documentation and requirements traceability matrix are the key outputs in this process.
C. Group creativity techniques and group decision-making techniques are used as tools & techniques in this process.
D. The scope management plan and requirements management plan are inputs in this process.

31. The team members are analyzing the objectives and description of the product stated by the customer or sponsor and turning them into tangible deliverables and finally creating the project scope statement. Which of the following BEST describes what the team members are doing?

A. Performing the product analysis
B. Performing the plan quality management
C. Conducting a multi-criteria decision analysis
D. Determining the product description

32. Your project to build a new substation to supply power to a newly developed industrial park is not going too well. The Net Present Value (NPV) of the project is $560,000 and the payback period is 3 years. After six-and-a-half months of work, the project is on schedule and budget, but requirements have been changing throughout the project. You became extremely worried to find out that a substantial amount of new change requests are coming from your key stakeholders, customers, and even from your manager. You are anxious that these changes will drastically increase the cost and time of the project. Which of the following will MOST likely happen in your project?

A. You may need to add additional resources
B. You may need to cut cost
C. You may need to terminate the project
D. You may not be able to measure completion of the product of the project

Project Scope Management Answers

1. D: A Tornado diagram is not a component of the Group Creativity technique. It is mostly used during the Perform Quantitative Risk Analysis process to display the sensitivity analysis data in order to determine which risks have the most potential impact on a project. This diagram can be used to determine sensitivity in cost, time, and quality objectives and will be helpful to determine a detailed response plan for the elements with greater impacts.

2. A: The detailed Work Breakdown Structure (WBS) is developed after the project scope statement has been defined and accepted. The scope baseline consists of the project scope statement, WBS, and WBS dictionary.

3. C: Scope creeps are the unapproved and undocumented changes, and they occur when changes to the scope are not detected early enough or managed. All these minor changes slowly add up and may have drastic impact on budget, schedule, and quality.

4. D: This is a change due to an external event mainly to remain competitive. The features that the competitors are offering were not included in the scope of the project; thus, they were never discussed during the initiation or planning phases. Due to the risk of losing a potential market, the project manager decided to include them in the project. Also, there was no legal requirement or constraint to include the missing features in this case.

5. A: The project manager should get the approval from the sponsor, key stakeholders, and the customers.

6. D: Except for the Sequence Activities process, scope baseline is used as an input in all of the listed processes.

7. D: The statement of work generally precedes a contract and provides a narrative description of work to be completed. The project plan is derived from the project scope statement. Once a project is selected or a contract is signed to perform a project, a project charter is created to formally authorize a project or a phase but is not a detailed plan. The scope statement answers the questions of what, why, who, where, and how and in combination with the work breakdown structure provides a detailed description of what must be accomplished.

8. C: This problem was a direct result of scope misunderstanding due to poor scope definition. Obviously, the team did not utilize all the tools & techniques to collect requirements from the customers and also did not spend quality time defining and developing a detailed description of the project and product.

9. D: This is an example of inefficient change control as the team should be focused on "all the work" and "only the work" needed to complete the project, not extra. The key objective should be to complete the project with the agreed-upon deliverables in time, with quality, and within budget. This kind of "gold plating" increases risk and uncertainties and introduces problems into the project and should be monitored and controlled by the project manager.

10. C: Validate Scope is the process of formal acceptance of completed project scope and deliverables by stakeholders through a signature on paper or via an e-mail that specifically states project approval. Prior scope validation would have avoided the dissatisfaction of stakeholders after the milestone release.

11. B: The project scope statement documents the characteristics and boundaries of the project and its associated products, results, and services in addition to the acceptance criteria.

12. C: You should inform management and provide relevant oversight, but doing so will not resolve the issue immediately. You can refuse to manage a project in case there is a conflict of interest or an ethical concern but not in this kind of situation. A WBS dictionary is the detail of the work packages, so a WBS should be created first. You should always have a WBS since it is the foundational block to the initiating, planning, executing, monitoring & controlling, and closing phases. Creating the WBS should not be a lengthy process that will require a long time; thus, you should take the time to create it prior to entering the execution.

13. D: The project team should be concerned with "all the work" and "only the work" required to successfully complete the project and try to avoid extra work or gold plating in every way possible.

14. C: The requirements document is the output in the Collect Requirements process, not in the Define Scope process.

15. A: The decision may be based on the largest block, not the most influential block in a group even if a majority is not achieved.

16. D: Completion of the product scope is measured against the product requirements to determine successful fulfillment. The project requirements, project objectives, and the project scope statement are associated with project scope.

17. C: A Work Breakdown Structure (WBS) is the foundational block to the initiating, planning, executing, monitoring & controlling, and closing phases. Normally presented in chart form, it is a deliverable-oriented hierarchical decomposition of the work to be executed by the project team to accomplish the project objectives and create the required deliverables. It provides a structure for hierarchal summation of cost, schedule, and resource information.

18. B: The most appropriate thing to do in this kind of situation is to find out the root cause of the problem, but the option is not presented here. Based on the information provided, there is no reason to find out the details and try to

convince the sponsor to add the work (C & D). The project manager should inform the sponsor, but the best course of action will be to inform the stakeholders that the work could not be added. Even though there is no impact on the schedule, there may be impact on other areas. A project manager should not implement a change request without performing an impact analysis and must get the approval for the change from the change control board.

19. C: Verified deliverables are the deliverables that have been completed as per the documented scope and checked for defects by the project team members in the Control Quality process. These deliverables are inputs in the Validate Scope process and are given to the customers and stakeholders for their acceptance.

20. D: Verifying the correctness of work is associated with the Control Quality process.

21. D: Note that in this kind of situation you should always try to gather as much information as possible if the time allows. You simply should not say no without knowing the details of the change and its possible impact on the project (C). The client only mentioned that they wanted a change but did not provide you with any description of it. You may inform management (A) and also have a meeting with the team if their inputs are needed (B) but not before understanding what the change is all about.

22. C: Note that we do not usually include the activities in the WBS, especially for the large projects, even though we decompose the WBS work packages to get our activities during the Define Activities process in time management. Once the activities are defined, sequencing is done in the Sequence Activities process. Note that WBS has no particular sequence to it.

23. A: Constraints specify the limitations and restrictions, such as constraints on time, budget, scope, quality, schedule, resources, and technology that a project faces. By specifying a time limit and technology compliance, the sponsor is limiting the options for the project.

24. B: The output of the Validate Scope process is the customer acceptance of the project deliverables. This process is performed during the monitoring & controlling process group. To get approval of the phase deliverables, it is done at the end of each project phase in addition to other points to get approval for the interim deliverables. Both the Control Quality and Validate Scope processes can be performed simultaneously, but Control Quality is usually performed prior to Validate Scope. Control Quality verifies correctness of the work, whereas Validate Scope confirms completeness. Control Quality is focused on measuring specific project results against quality specifications and standards, whereas Validate Scope is mainly focused on obtaining acceptance of the product from the sponsor, customers, and other stakeholders. It is not an input to the Develop Project Management Plan or an output of the Control Quality process.

25. B: Scope planning should be performed prior to the Control Scope process. A change in one control process impacts the others; thus, the Control Scope process is integrated with other control processes.

26. D: A project manager is responsible for prioritizing the most critical issue to concentrate on. The situation here does not really specify whether the senior engineer is playing a vital role in the project or not. "Gold Plating," or giving customers extra, is not actually required in the project. The project manager should evaluate the current situation and then determine if the project will require additional time or not to complete. The most critical item for the project manager is to ensure full compliance with the city and construction industry standards.

27. D: Group decision-making techniques are used as a tool & technique in the Collect Requirements process, not in the Define Scope process.

28. C: You should review the project charter and make sure that you have inputs from all key stakeholders in order to avoid confusion and unnecessary change requests in the future. You should then concentrate on creating the project scope statement, the WBS, and the project plan.

29. C: Inspection includes activities such as measuring, examining, and verifying to determine whether work and deliverables meet requirements and product acceptance criteria. Inspections are sometimes called walkthroughs, reviews, product reviews, and audits.

30. A: The project scope statement describes project deliverables and the work required to create them in detail as well as the deliverables description, product acceptance criteria, requirements assumptions and constraints, and exclusions from requirements.

31. A: The team members are gaining a better understanding of the product of the project to create the project scope statement by performing the product analysis. The team must have a product description before they can perform product analysis. The level of quality desired is analyzed in the plan quality management, not in product analysis. The multi-criteria decision analysis is a technique to evaluate and rank ideas. This technique uses a decision matrix based on factors such as uncertainty, expected risk levels, cost and benefit estimates, and time estimates to quantify requirements.

32. D: Nothing in this question is suggesting that you may need to cut cost, add resources, or terminate the project. Not having complete requirements will make it difficult to measure as requirements are used to measure the completion of the product of the project.

CHAPTER 6

PROJECT TIME MANAGEMENT

Time Management

Project time management involves the processes required to manage timely completion of the project. This knowledge area is primarily concerned with resources, activities, developing a realistic project schedule, and controlling changes to that schedule.

In the PMI model, time is the only one of the "triple constraints" typically owned by the project manager. The outputs of time management are elements of keen interest to senior management and other stakeholders.

Important Points to Consider: The following points are very important for a project manager to consider during project time management:

- All estimates should be based on the Work Breakdown Structure (WBS). Estimates are more accurate when applied to smaller-sized work components.
- The project manager should not come up with the estimates for the activities; rather, for accuracy, the estimation should be formulated by the people performing the work.
- Padding should be discouraged, and the project manager should ask for justification of estimates from the team members, as needed.
- Historical information such as activity duration estimation, resource estimation, and other factors from previous and similar projects can drastically improve estimates.
- The schedule baseline should be used to track project progress, and the only time it should be modified is when an approved change request is implemented.
- All changes impacting time, cost, risk, human resources, and scope should be approved through the Integrated Change Control process.
- Corrective and preventive actions should be recommended if the project is not progressing according to the schedule.
- The project manager should not just accept the requirements but should also analyze them, as required.
- Plans and all applicable documents should be revised as per the findings in the project.
- The project manager should try to keep the estimates realistic and accurate as much as possible and maintain the integrity of the estimates throughout the project life cycle by revisiting and recalculating them on a regular basis.

Exercise 1: What do you need to develop a project schedule?

Project Time Management Processes

Project time management is focused on planning, developing, managing, executing, and controlling a project schedule. Refer to the "Figure 3-16 Process Groups Key Inputs and Outputs" and you should realize that you have completed working on the business case, feasibility study, a project charter, and a stakeholder register in the initiating process group, and developed a scope management plan, a requirements management plan, a requirements document, a project scope statement, and a Work Breakdown Structure (WBS) in planning process group while working on the scope management. Obviously, all these documents can be used as inputs while you are working with project schedule.

Now, let's think about a real life scenario. When a project manager starts working on the project schedule, he/she will consider, along with her project team, all of the activities that will need to be completed based on the project's WBS. When all the project work has been identified and the activity list has been generated, it is time to put the activities in the order necessary to reach the project completion. Once the work has been organized and visualized, it is time to staff it. Project resource estimating considers people, as well as materials and equipment that your project will need. Of course, management and the project's stakeholders will want to know how long the project work will take to complete. A project manager must control the project schedule by applying the method of schedule compression and fast tracking.

PMI identifies seven key processes that are associated with the time management knowledge area. Since time is one of the triple constraints, an understanding of these processes is vital to a project success.

Processes	Process Groups	Detail	Key Outputs
1. Plan Schedule Management	Planning	The process of defining how the project schedule will be planned, developed, managed, executed, and controlled.	– Schedule Management Plan
2. Define Activities	Planning	The process of decomposing the WBS work packages into schedule activities that are at a level small enough for estimating, scheduling, monitoring, and changing.	– Activity List – Activity Attributes – Milestone List
3. Sequence Activities	Planning	The process of identifying and documenting relationships among defined activities and arranging them in the order they must be performed.	– Project Schedule Network Diagram
4. Estimate Activity Resources	Planning	The process of estimating the resources (such as material, equipment, manpower, and supplies) required to perform activities in the project.	– Activity Resource Requirements – Resource Breakdown Structure
5. Estimate Activity Durations	Planning	The process of estimating durations for the activities of the project by utilizing scope and resource information such as who will be doing the work, resource availability, number of resources assigned, etc.	– Activity Duration Estimates
6. Develop Schedule	Planning	The iterative process of analyzing activity sequence, dependency, logical relationships, durations, resources (such as materials, manpower, equipment, supplies, etc.), constraints, and assumptions to develop the project schedule with planned dates for project activities completion.	– Schedule Baseline – Project Schedule
7. Control Schedule	Monitoring & Controlling	The process of monitoring the status of the project by comparing the result to the plan, updating project progress, and managing changes to the project schedule baseline.	– Work Performance Information – Change Requests – Schedule Forecasts

Table 6-1: Seven Project Time Management Processes and Key Outputs

Project Time Management Processes, Inputs, Tool & Techniques, and Outputs

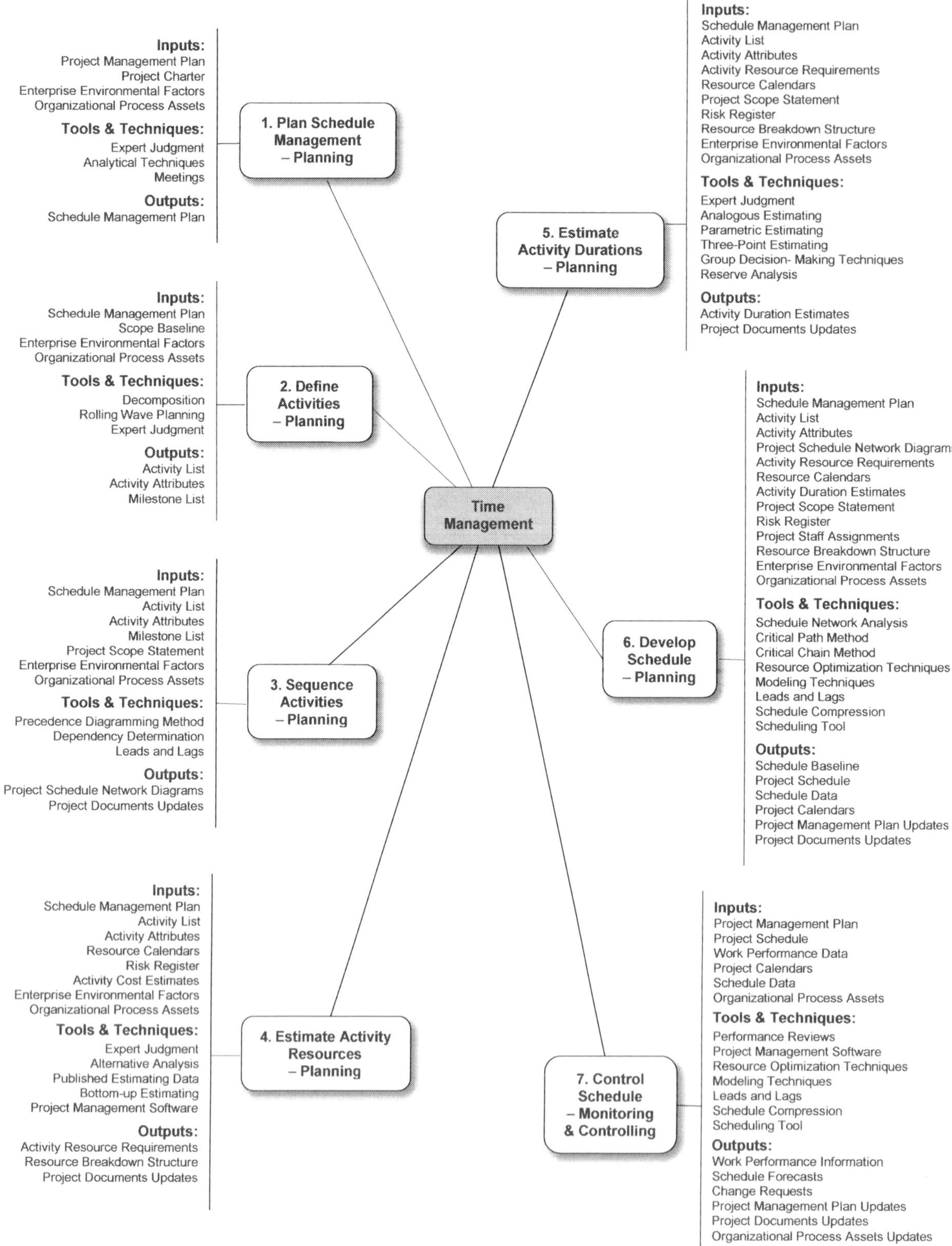

Figure 6-1: Project Time Management Processes, Inputs, Tool & Techniques, and Outputs

Plan Schedule Management

Plan Schedule Management is the process of defining how the project schedule will be planned, developed, managed, executed, and controlled throughout the project life cycle.

This process helps with the following:

- Establishes the policies and procedures that will be used for schedule development
- Defines the approach that will be taken to plan schedule development
- Identifies any existing work authorization system or software to use for schedule development
- Defines ways to manage and control the project to the schedule baseline
- Defines ways to manage and control schedule variances
- Defines the process of measuring schedule performance
- Identifies the team members and other stakeholders who will be involved in schedule development

As per the PMBOK®, the Plan Schedule Management process has the following inputs, tools & techniques, and outputs:

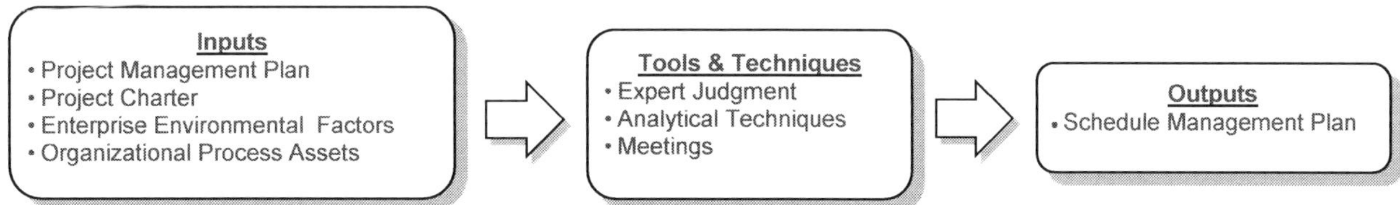

Figure 6-2: Plan Schedule Management: Inputs, Tools & Techniques, and Outputs

Plan Schedule Management: Inputs

- Project Management Plan
- Project Charter
- Enterprise Environmental Factors
- Organizational Process Assets

Project Management Plan: The following components of the project management plan may be used to plan schedule management.

Scope Baseline: Scope baseline consists of the project scope statement, the WBS, and the WBS dictionary. It also contains the deliverables, constraints, and assumptions that are considered while defining activities. Each schedule activity should be linked to a specific deliverable in the scope baseline. Other components such as cost, risk, communication, and management plans are also used.

Project Charter: The project charter contains high-level milestones and a roadmap as well as schedule approval requirements that may influence the Plan Schedule Management process.

Enterprise Environmental Factors: Work authorization system, Project Management Information System (PMIS), resource availability, and skill sets are among a variety of factors that may influence the Plan Schedule Management process.

Organizational Process Assets: Activity-related policies, procedures, lessons learned, historical information, and records on activities used by similar projects may influence the Plan Schedule Management process.

Plan Schedule Management: Tools & Techniques

- Expert Judgment
- Analytical Techniques
- Meetings

Expert Judgment: Team members or other individuals with expertise and experience in defining requirements, developing detailed scope, and creating the WBS and schedule can contribute to the Plan Schedule Management process.

Analytical Techniques: Various analytical techniques such as scheduling tools & techniques, scheduling methodologies, project management software, rolling wave planning, alternative analysis, estimating approaches, and formatting are used to plan the schedule management.

Meetings: Meetings with team members, the project manager, the sponsor, and other stakeholders will be beneficial for developing a schedule management plan.

Plan Schedule Management: Outputs

- Schedule Management Plan

Schedule Management Plan: The schedule management plan defines how the project schedule will be planned, developed, managed, executed, and controlled throughout the project life cycle. The schedule management plan may establish the following:

- Scheduling methodology and tools that will be used in the schedule development
- Schedule baseline against which performance will be measured
- Unit of measurement for resources such as hour, day, and week for time estimates, and meters, liters, tons, square feet, etc., for quantity measurements
- Acceptable and unacceptable variances
- Schedule change control procedures
- Schedule reporting formats and frequencies
- Guidelines on schedule variance identification and control
- Rules of performance measures such as earned value measurement techniques, Schedule Variance (SV), and Schedule Performance Index (SPI)

Exercise 2: Identify which process group each process belongs to.

Process Groups				
Initiating	Planning	Executing	Monitoring & Controlling	Closing

Process Names:

- Sequence Activities
- Estimate Activity Resources
- Plan Schedule Management
- Control Schedule
- Define Activities
- Estimate Activity Durations
- Develop Schedule

Define Activities

In the Define Activities process, once the scope baseline has been created and the WBS work packages have been decomposed into a level small enough for estimating, scheduling, monitoring, and changing, the activity list can be built. The activity list is the key output of this process and represents all the schedule activities required to complete the project. The activity list is also the foundation of all the remaining processes in this knowledge area. This process requires the participation of the project team and coordination with the project manager.

As per the PMBOK®, the Define Activities process has the following inputs, tools & techniques, and outputs:

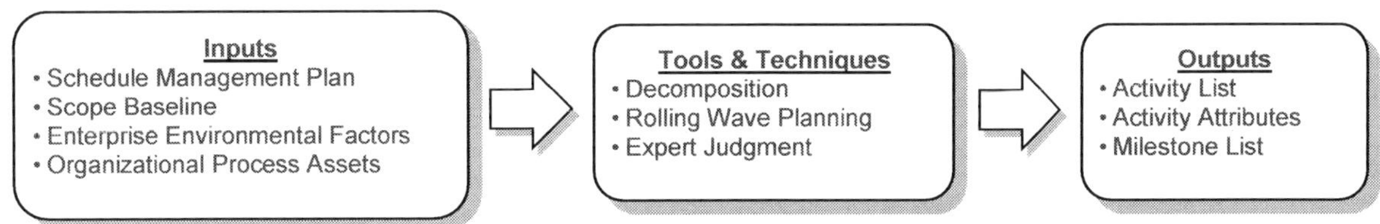

Figure 6-3: Define Activities: Inputs, Tools & Techniques, and Outputs

Define Activities: Inputs

- Schedule Management Plan
- Scope Baseline
- Enterprise Environmental Factors
- Organizational Process Assets

Schedule Management Plan: The schedule management plan contains details on the schedule management guidelines, policies, procedures, and activities.

Scope Baseline: The scope baseline consists of the project scope statement, the WBS, and the WBS dictionary, and it contains the deliverables, constraints, and assumptions that are considered while defining activities. Each schedule activity should be linked to a specific deliverable in the scope baseline.

Enterprise Environmental Factors: Organizational structure, a commercial database, and a Project Management Information System (PMIS) may influence the Define Activities process.

Organizational Process Assets: Activity-related policies, procedures, lessons learned, historical information, and records on activities used by similar projects may influence the Define Activities process.

Define Activities: Tools & Techniques

- Decomposition
- Rolling Wave Planning
- Expert Judgment

Decomposition: Decomposition is the technique of breaking the work packages into smaller and more manageable components called activities. Participation from team members and the functional manager will play a vital role in defining the activities. In the example below, a "Work Package" is decomposed into several schedule activities:

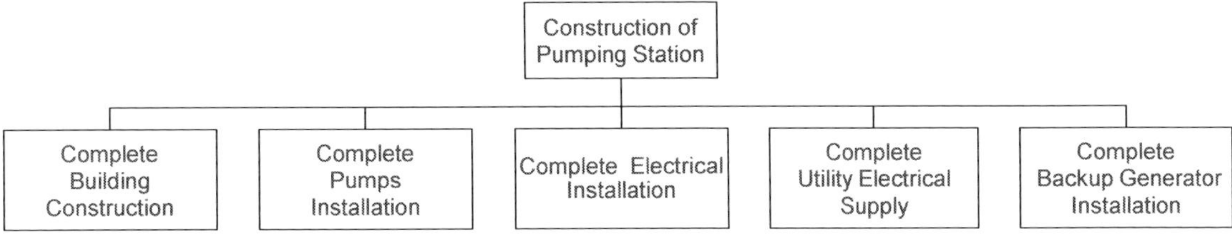

Figure 6-4: WBS Work Package Decomposition

Rolling Wave Planning: This planning utilizes the progressive elaboration approach by planning the work of the near term in detail and future work at a higher level. During the early strategic planning phase, work packages may be decomposed into less defined milestone levels since all details are not available, and later they are decomposed into detailed activities. This kind of planning is frequently used in IT and research projects where unknowns tend to be intangibles but less so in construction projects where unknowns are generally extremely expensive and destructive.

Expert Judgment: Team members or other individuals with expertise and experience in defining requirements, developing detailed scope, and creating the WBS and schedule can contribute in defining activities.

Define Activities: Outputs

- Activity List
- Activity Attributes
- Milestone List

Activity List: This list should have all the scheduled activities that are required to complete the project work. These activities should be as complete and as accurate as possible and should be mapped back to one or more work packages.

The major difference between activities and work packages is that activities are usually work that needs to be completed to execute the work package; work packages are based upon and tied to deliverables and are focused on the scope of the project. The WBS is a part of the scope baseline, and activities are an extension of the WBS but not a part of it.

Activity Attributes: Additional attribute information such as Activity ID, WBS ID, activity name, completion date, description, predecessor and successor activities, resource assignment, constraints and assumptions, and level of effort, are called attributes and may be stored with the activity list or in a separate document.

Milestone List: Milestones are considered to be major significant events or points in the project. All mandatory milestones that are required by contract as well as optional ones that are based on historical information and past projects should be listed in the milestone list.

Sequence Activities

Sequence Activities is the planning process of identifying and documenting relationships among defined activities and arranging them in the order they must be performed. This can be accomplished through PM software and active participation of team members.

In this process, the project network diagram represents activities and their logical relationships; through this process, dependencies and sequences are created.

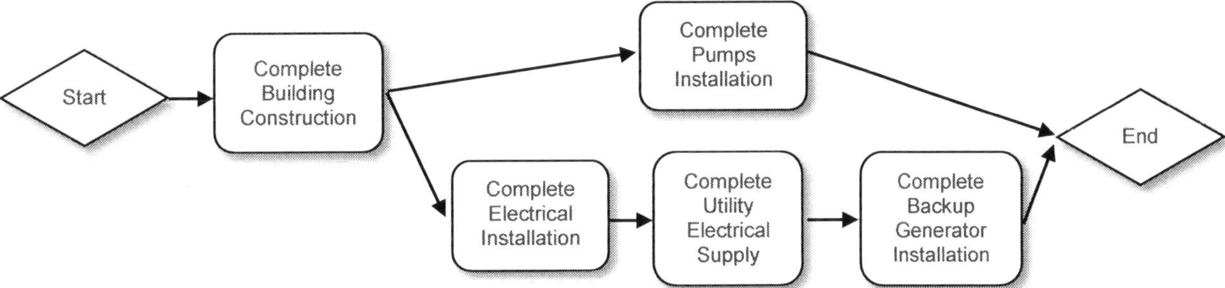

Figure 6-5: Work Package “Construction of Pumping Station” Activities Logically Sequenced

As per the PMBOK®, the Sequence Activities process has the following inputs, tools & techniques, and outputs:

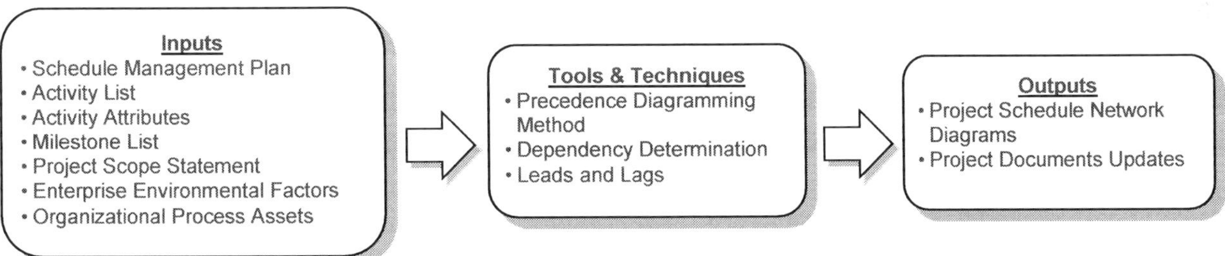

Figure 6-6: Sequence Activities: Inputs, Tools & Techniques, and Outputs

Sequence Activities: Inputs

- Schedule Management Plan
- Activity List
- Activity Attributes
- Milestone List
- Project Scope Statement
- Enterprise Environmental Factors
- Organizational Process Assets

Schedule Management Plan: The schedule management plan contains the details on the schedule management guidelines, policies, procedures, methods, and tools that may be used to sequence activities.

Activity List: Activities from the Define Activities process will be arranged and sequenced in this process.

Activity Attributes: Additional information about activities from the Define Activities process may influence how activities will be sequenced.

Milestone List: This list will contain schedule dates for specific milestones.

Project Scope Statement: The product scope description found in the project scope statement will have detailed information on product characteristics that may determine activity sequencing. For instance, constructing a software application may require procurement and configuration of the hardware and servers prior to coding, testing, and implementing the software components.

Enterprise Environmental Factors: The company work authorization system, industry standards, scheduling tools, and the Project Management Information System (PMIS) are among factors that may influence the Sequence Activities process.

Organizational Process Assets: Any relevant historical information and past project records on activities may be useful.

Sequence Activities: Tools & Techniques

- Precedence Diagramming Method
- Dependency Determination
- Leads and Lags

Precedence Diagramming Method: This method creates a schematic display of the sequential and logical relationships of the activities that comprise a project. Usually it shows dependencies and the order in which activities in a project must be performed. If activity duration estimates are included, then this method will show the critical path or the duration of the project.

This diagramming method uses the Activity-on-Node (AON) convention where boxes/nodes are used to represent activities and arrows show dependencies.

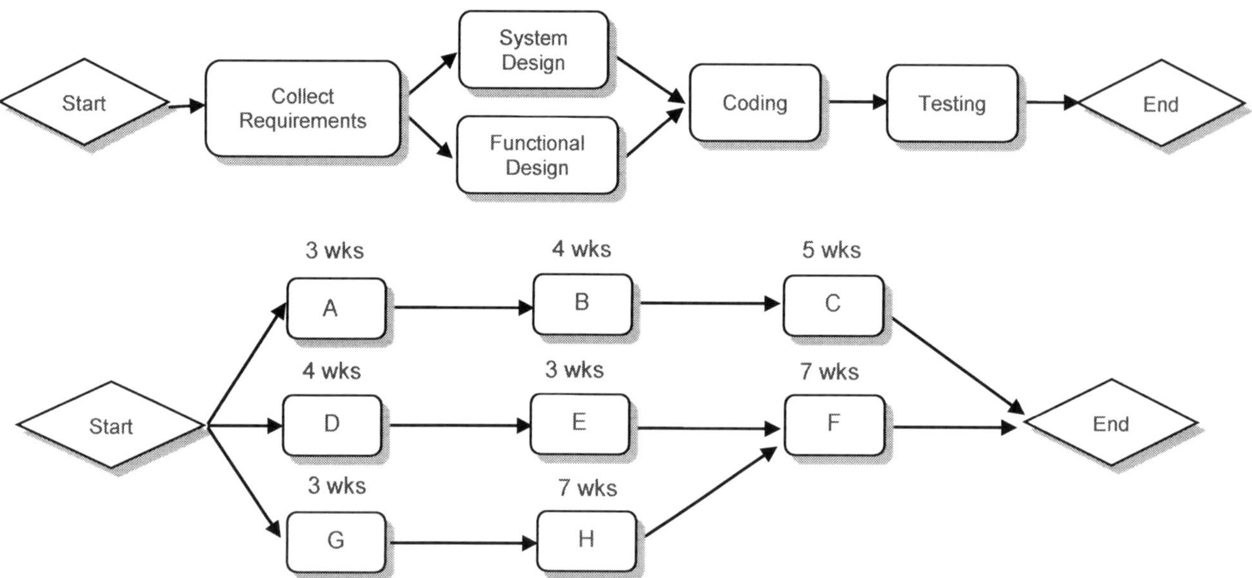

Figure 6-7: Activity on Node (AON) or a Network Diagram Created Using Precedence Diagramming Method

The Precedence Diagramming Method (PDM) can have four types of dependencies or logical relationships:

Dependency	Detail	Example
Finish-to-Start (FS)	Predecessor activity must be completed before the successor activity can be initiated.	Water pipes must be installed inside the walls before painting the walls. It would be much faster and less expensive to put the pipes in first, then to actually build the walls around the pipes, and then finally paint the walls.
Finish-to-Finish (FF)	Predecessor activity must be completed before the successor activity is completed.	Design activity must be completed before the coding activity is completed.
Start-to-Start (SS)	Predecessor activity must be started before the successor activity is started.	Design activity must be started before the coding activity is started.
Start-to-Finish (SF)	Predecessor activity must be started before the successor activity is completed.	A new shift must be started for a previous shift to be finished.
Note: Finish-to-Start is the most common and Start-to-Finish is the least common type of precedence relationship.		

Table 6-2: Logical Relationships

Graphical Evaluation and Review Technique (GERT): GERT is a modified network diagram drawing method that allows conditional branches and loops between activities. For example, you may have two activities to design a software component and test it. Depending on the result of the testing, you may or may not redesign the component.

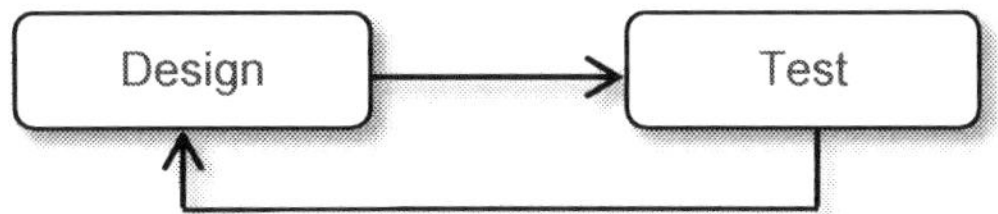

Figure 6-8: Graphical Evaluation and Review Technique (GERT)

Dependency Determination: Determining dependencies helps to identify which activities should be performed first.

Example: If we are working on a software development project, we may want to collect our requirements first, then complete the design, and lastly, perform the coding.

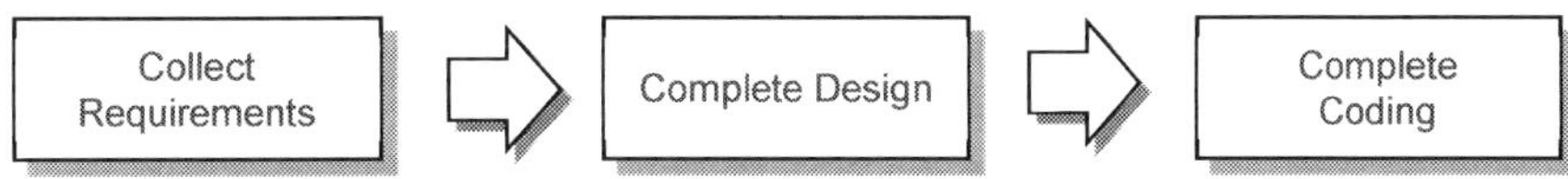

Dependency	Detail	Examples
Mandatory	These are mandatory and unavoidable dependencies that are inherent in the nature of the work or are contractually required. They are like laws of nature and are also called "hard logic."	– Pouring the foundation must precede raising the roof. – Requirements must be collected from the clients prior to completion of design.
Discretionary	These "preferred logic" or "soft logic" are the preferences of the project planner and the team members. These dependencies may be determined by best practices or local methodology and may vary from project to project. In order to fast-track the project, these kinds of dependencies should be modified or removed to perform activities in parallel.	You may originally plan to complete all the design work prior to coding but later decide not to work in sequential order but to work on items in parallel.
External	These dependencies are driven by circumstances or authority outside the project and must be considered during the process of sequencing the activities.	You are managing a project to build a multistory complex and waiting for the clearance from the city to start construction of a building.
Internal	These dependencies are based on the needs of the project and are mostly under the control of the project team.	The development team cannot start coding until the development and testing servers are configured by the support team.

Table 6-3: Four Types of Dependencies

Leads and Lags:

Lead: A lead is an acceleration of a successor activity, or in other words, a successor activity getting a jump start. A lead may be added to start an activity before the predecessor activity is completed.

Example: There may be a finish-to-start relationship between design and coding in a software development project, but coding may start five days before the design is completed. This can be shown as a finish-to-start with five days lead.

Lag: A lag is an inserted waiting time between activities.

Example: You must wait three days after pouring concrete before you can construct the frame for the house. This can be shown as a finish-to-start with three days lag.

Sequence Activities: Outputs

- Project Schedule Network Diagrams
- Project Documents Updates

Project Schedule Network Diagrams: This diagram, which was explained earlier, can be produced manually or by using project management software to display the project activities and the relationships or dependencies among them. A narrative of the diagram can be used to illustrate the approach used to sequence the activities; in this narrative, any unusual activity sequence or dependency should be clearly explained.

Project Documents Updates: Activity list, activity attributes, and the risk register can be updated.

Estimate Activity Resources

Estimate Activity Resources is the process of estimating the resources (such as materials, equipment, manpower, and supplies) required to perform activities in the project. This process is closely coordinated with the Estimate Costs process as type, quantity, and availability of the resources are identified for activities.

As per the PMBOK®, the Estimate Activity Resources process has the following inputs, tools & techniques, and outputs:

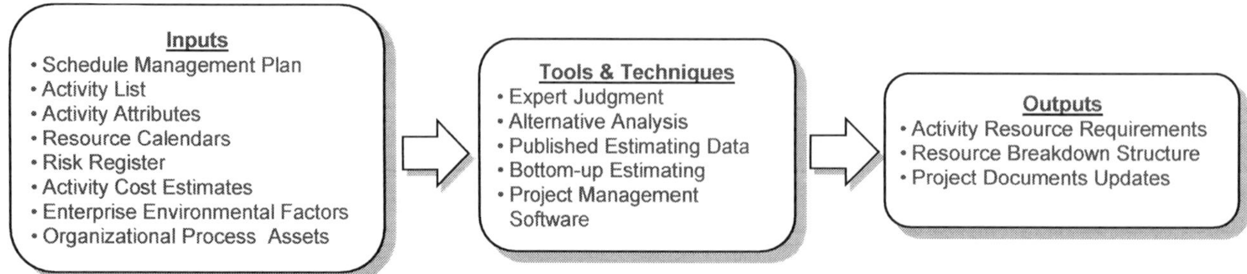

Figure 6-9: Estimate Activity Resources: Inputs, Tools & Techniques, and Outputs

Estimate Activity Resources: Inputs

- Schedule Management Plan
- Activity List
- Activity Attributes
- Resource Calendars
- Risk Register
- Activity Cost Estimates
- Enterprise Environmental Factors
- Organizational Process Assets

Schedule Management Plan: The schedule management plan contains details on the schedule management guidelines, policies, procedures, methods, tools, etc., as well as the level of accuracy and the units of measure that that may be used to estimate activity resources.

Activity List: This list will identify activities that will be evaluated for resource requirements.

Activity Attributes: Attributes give additional details of the activities to assist with identifying resource requirements.

Resource Calendars: These calendars show when and how long resources (such as materials, equipment, manpower, and supplies) will potentially be available during the project life cycle. Resource calendars may consider attributes such as experience, skill level, expertise, capabilities, geographical locations, and other factors necessary for human resources to identify the best resources and their availability.

Expense Type	Feb	Mar	Apr	May	Jun	Jul	Aug	Sep
Labor								
Project Manager								
Quality Reviewer								
Systems Architect								
Database Administrator								
Systems Trainer								
IT Support Analyst								
Equipment								
Application & Database Servers								
Communications Equipment								
Backup & Power Supply Equipment								
Operational Support Software								

Figure 6-10: A Resource Calendar

Risk Register: The risk register contains the list of identified risks and their probability, impact, priority, and response plan. Resource selection and availability may be impacted by these various risk events in the project.

Activity Cost Estimates: Resource selection criteria such as number, type, experience, and expertise are based on the cost of the resources.

Enterprise Environmental Factors: Enterprise environmental factors such as resource availability and skills, location, experience, and expertise may influence the Estimate Activity Resources process.

Organizational Process Assets: Policies and procedures regarding staffing and procurement as well as the historical information on the type of resources used in similar previous projects may influence the Estimate Activity Resources process.

Estimate Activity Resources: Tools & Techniques

- Expert Judgment
- Alternative Analysis
- Published Estimating Data
- Bottom-up Estimating
- Project Management Software

Expert Judgment: Any individual or group with relevant experience in resource planning and estimating can bring insight into the resource requirements of the activities.

Alternative Analysis: There can be several approaches to perform the same task, and the project team should spend time exploring the alternatives to identify the best one for the project whenever possible. Actions such as purchasing an off-the-shelf software component instead of building it, outsourcing a critical activity, adapting a new creative approach to complete a task, using various types and levels of expertise, using different sizes and types of equipment, or using different types of automated tools can be examples of alternatives.

Published Estimating Data: There are extensive, quality, up-to-date data on production rates and unit costs of resources available through well-known, recognized sources that can help in estimating resource requirements.

Bottom-up Estimating: If the resource requirements for an activity cannot be estimated due to the complex nature of the activity, then this activity can be further broken down into smaller pieces of work until the resources can be estimated for these pieces and later summed up from the bottom back up to an activity level.

Project Management Software: Different types of project management software can be extremely useful in organizing and storing information, quickly performing routine calculations, and exploring the various alternatives to develop resource estimates. In order to optimize resource utilization, software can be used to define the resource breakdown structure, resource calendars, and resource availability.

Estimate Activity Resources: Outputs

- Activity Resource Requirements
- Resource Breakdown Structure
- Project Documents Updates

Activity Resource Requirements: Resource requirements such as resource types and quantities for each activity in the work package are the key outputs. In order to determine the requirements for the work package, all of the requirements for the activities under that package can be aggregated. The resource requirements documentation should contain the basis of estimates, the decision-making process used to arrive at the estimates, and the assumptions, availability, and quantity for the activities.

Resource Breakdown Structure: A RBS is a graphical and hierarchical structure of the identified resources arranged by resource category (such as labor, material, equipment, and supplies) and type (such as expertise level, grade, and experience).

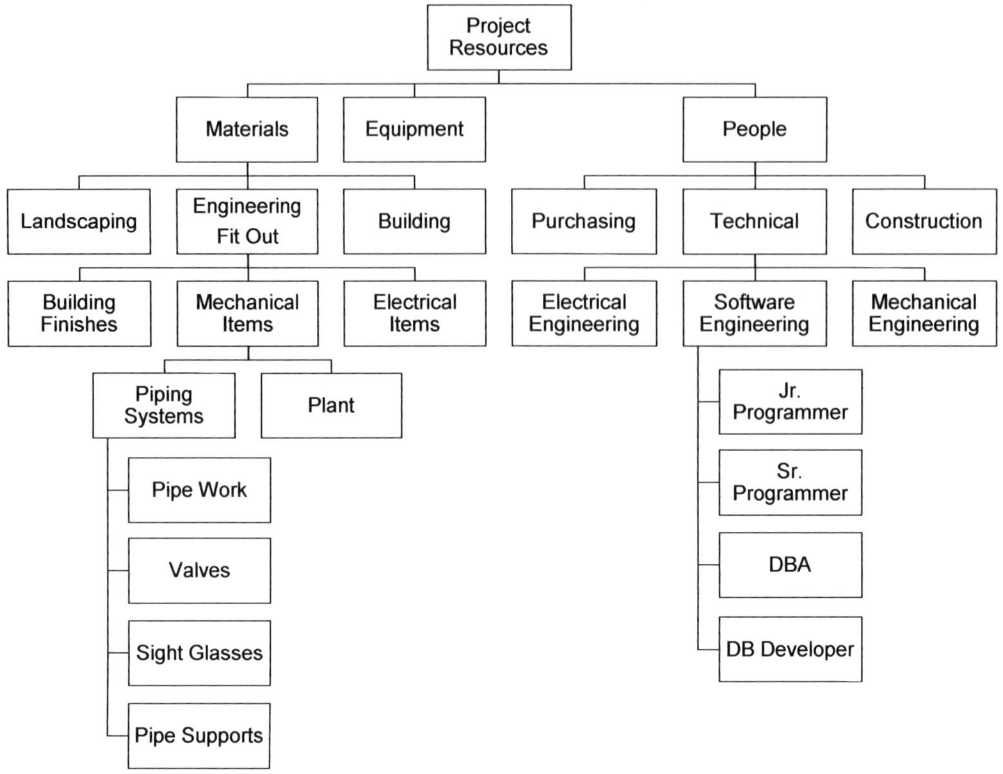

Figure 6-11: A Resource Breakdown Structure (RBS)

Project Documents Updates: The activity list, activity attributes, and resource calendars should be updated.

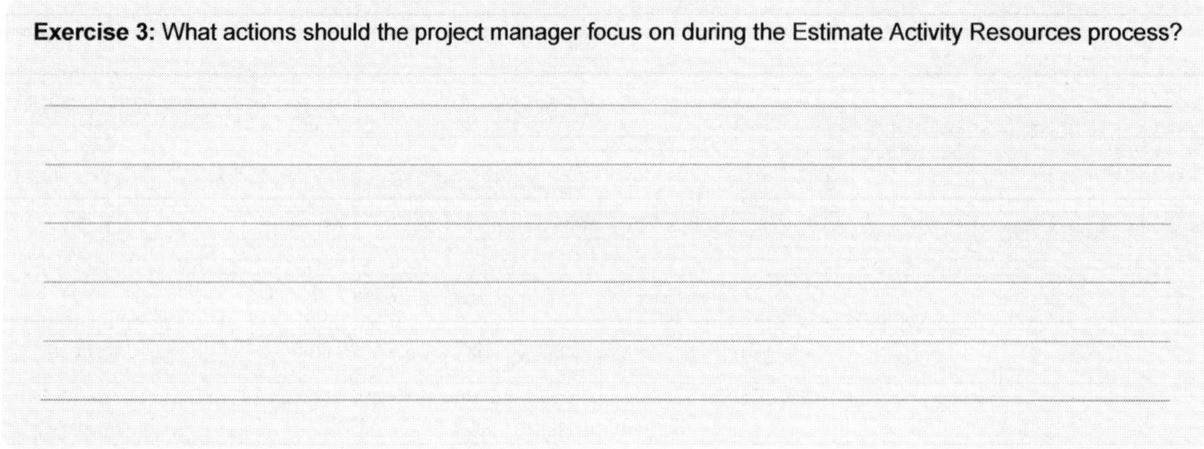

Exercise 3: What actions should the project manager focus on during the Estimate Activity Resources process?

Estimate Activity Durations

The Estimate Activity Durations process utilizes scope and resource information such as who will be doing the work, resource availability, and number of resources assigned to estimate durations for the activities of the project.

Estimates usually originate from project team members most familiar with the activity and then progressively elaborate. It is important that all estimates use a common work unit/period.

As per the PMBOK®, the Estimate Activity Durations process has the following inputs, tools & techniques, and outputs:

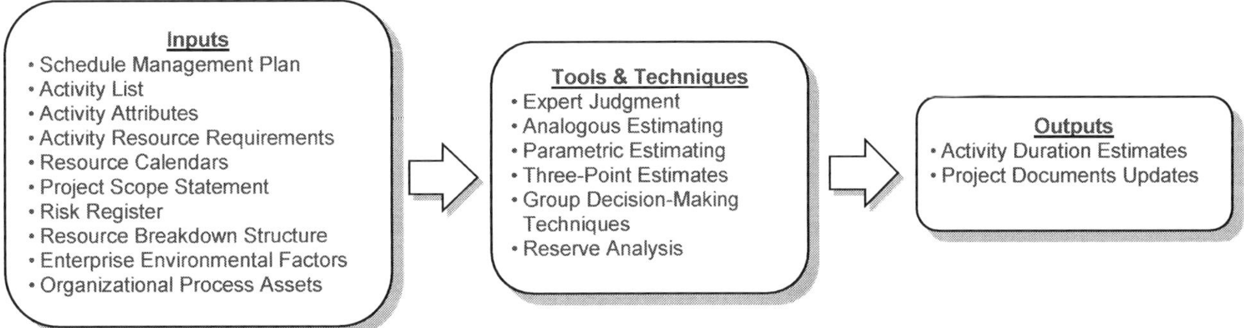

Figure 6-12: Estimate Activity Durations: Inputs, Tools & Techniques, and Outputs

Estimate Activity Durations: Inputs

- Schedule Management Plan
- Activity List
- Activity Attributes
- Activity Resource Requirements
- Resource Calendars
- Project Scope Statement
- Risk Register
- Resource Breakdown Structure
- Enterprise Environmental Factors
- Organizational Process Assets

Schedule Management Plan: The schedule management plan contains the details on the schedule management guidelines, policies, procedures, methods, tools, etc., as well as the level of accuracy and the units of measure that may be used to estimate activity durations.

Activity List: Activities in the activity list should be evaluated to estimate duration.

Activity Attributes: Additional details of the activities will help in determining duration.

Activity Resource Requirements: The type and number of resources as well as resource skills, capability, and availability will influence the duration of the activities.

Resource Calendars: These calendars will display the physical and manpower usage throughout the project life cycle and can also include information such as type, availability, capability, and other factors that can influence duration.

Project Scope Statement: This document contains critical information such as constraints and assumptions that can be used in estimating activity duration. For instance, a constraint that software components will be developed locally and need to be tested by the foreign team will influence the duration. Likewise, an assumption that more skilled and experienced resources will be available for quick development of software components during the implementation phase will be helpful in estimating duration.

Risk Register: The risk register contains the list of identified risks and their probability, impact, priority, and response plan. Activities and their durations may be impacted by these various risk events in the project.

Resource Breakdown Structure: A Resource Breakdown Structure (RBS) is a graphical and hierarchical structure of the identified resources arranged by resource category (such as labor, material, equipment, and supplies) and type (such as expertise level, grade, and experience).

Enterprise Environmental Factors: Public commercial information, productivity metrics, a duration estimating database, and other reference data, safety standards, and regulations may influence the Estimate Activity Durations process.

Organizational Process Assets: Organizational process assets such as lessons learned, scheduling methodology, project calendars, and historical duration estimates of similar projects that can provide structure and guidance to the Estimate Activity Durations process should be considered.

Estimate Activity Durations: Tools & Techniques

- Expert Judgment
- Analogous Estimating
- Parametric Estimating
- Three-Points Estimates
- Group Decision-Making Techniques
- Reserve Analysis

Expert Judgment: Experts with experience in defining activities and estimations can recommend methods of estimating and identify required duration estimation based on prior similar projects and historical information.

Estimating Techniques
One-Point Estimate or Bottom-Up Estimate This is the most time-consuming and generally the most accurate estimate. In this technique one estimate per activity is received from the team members. This estimate can be based on expert judgment, historical information, or an educated guess. Bad impacts: – Forces people into padding. – Hides risks and uncertainties from project manager, which are needed for better planning and control. – Results in an unrealistic schedule. – Estimators protect themselves. – Early completion makes team members look untruthful. To get a reliable estimate, the WBS, the WBS dictionary, and the activity list should be used.
Analogous Estimate or Top-Down Estimate This occurs when the overall project estimate is given to the project manager from management or the sponsor. This type of estimate measures the project parameters such as budget, size, complexity, and duration based on the parameters of a previous, similar project and historical information. It is usually done during the early phase of the project when not much information is available; thus, it is less accurate even though it is less costly and less time consuming.
Parametric Estimate This estimate uses mathematical models based on historical records from other projects. It utilizes the statistical relationship that exists between a series of historical data and a particular delineated list of other variables. Depending upon the quality of the underlying data, this estimate can produce higher levels of accuracy and can be used in conjunction with other estimates to provide estimates for the entire project or specific segments of a project. Measures such as time per line of code, time per installation, and time per linear meter are considered in this type of estimate.
Heuristics Estimate This type of estimation is based on rule of thumb. The 80/20 rule suggests that 80 percent of all the accidents are caused by 20 percent of the drivers. Using a similar approach, a rule of thumb of 40/40/20 may suggest that 40 percent of the time will be allocated for project design, 40 percent for coding, and 20 percent for testing.

Three-Point Estimate or Program Evaluation & Review Technique (PERT)

This estimate takes Optimistic, Pessimistic, and Most Likely estimates from the estimator and provides a risk-based expected duration estimate by taking a weighted average of the three estimates using the following formulas:

- Optimistic estimate: O
- Most likely estimate: M
- Pessimistic estimate: P

Depending on the assumed distribution of values, we may have the following two formulas:

- **Triangular Distribution (Simple Average):** Expected Activity Duration (EAD) = $\frac{(O + M + P)}{3}$
- **Beta Distribution (Weighted Average):** Expected Activity Duration (EAD) = $\frac{(O + 4M + P)}{6}$

The project manager should also make an effort to analyze the risks, identify uncertainties, measure the deviation from the plan, and take appropriate actions to bring the project back on track. Analyzing the expected range of each activity and its effects on the overall project duration can provide an improved perspective of the overall project estimate.

The following formulas are used to calculate standard deviation, variance, and range for the activities:

- Standard Deviation (SD) = $\frac{P - O}{6}$
- Variance = $[\frac{P - O}{6}]^2$
- Range = EAD +/– SD

Where the lower end of the range is the value of (EAD – SD) and higher end of the range is the value of (EAD + SD).

Example: Suppose you have the following activities in your project with the listed estimates in days. Find out the Expected Activity Duration (EAD) – beta distribution, Standard Deviation (SD), Activity Variance (AV), and Activity Range (AR) for each activity using the formulas listed above.

Activities	O	M	P	EAD	SD	AV	AR
Completion of Requirements Collection	13	26	46	27.16	5.50	30.25	27.16+/–5.50 or 21.66 to 32.66
Completion of Design	28	35	41	34.83	2.16	4.66	34.83 +/– 2.16 or 32.67 to 36.99
Completion of Coding	40	59	87	60.5	7.83	61.30	60.5 +/– 7.83 or 52.67 to 68.33
Completion of Testing	10	21	33	21.16	3.83	14.66	21.16 +/– 3.83 or 17.33 to 24.99

Now you may need to find out the overall project duration estimate, which consists of the following steps:

1. Determine the expected project duration by adding all the EAD estimates of all activities. In our case it will be (27.16 + 34.83 + 60.5 + 21.16) = 143.65.
2. Now calculating the standard deviation for the entire project is bit tricky. Instead of adding all the Standard Deviations of all activities (5.50 + 2.16 + 7.83 + 3.83 = 19.32), we need to add the activity variances (30.25 + 4.66 + 61.30 + 14.66 = 110.87). Standard deviation of the overall project will be the square root of the sum of all activity variances, which is the square root of 110.87 or 10.52, not 19.32.
3. Calculate the project duration estimate range using
   Expected project duration (The sum of EADs in step #1) +/– Standard Deviation from step #2.
   The lower end of the range will be 143.65 – 10.52 = 133.13 and
   The higher end of the range will be 143.65 + 10.52 = 154.17

	Expected Project Duration	Project Standard Deviation	Project Variance	Project Duration Estimate Range
Project	143.65	19.32 – is not the SD for the project. It will be 10.52 or the square root of 110.87.	110.87	143.65 +/– 10.52 or 133.13 to 154.17

Group Decision-Making Techniques: Various group creativity and decision-making techniques are beneficial in involving the team members in duration estimation. These members have a clear understanding of the time required to complete the activities and should have a role in these estimations. Involving the team members in the estimating process increases the accuracy of the estimate, helps to gain their approval on the resulting schedule, and also increases their commitment.

Reserve Analysis: This kind of reserve is also called time reserve or buffer and may be included into the overall project schedule to accommodate schedule uncertainty. This additional time can be calculated using quantitative methods or by taking a percentage of the estimated duration or a fixed number of work periods and should be modified, reduced, or even eliminated based on the precise information as it becomes available.

Estimate Activity Durations: Outputs

- Activity Duration Estimates
- Project Documents Updates

Activity Duration Estimates: These are the estimates of the likely number of work periods required for each activity. It will most likely represent a range such as optimistic, pessimistic, and most likely as identified in the three-point estimate.

Project Documents Updates: As more precise information becomes available, activity attributes and assumptions in duration estimation may be updated.

Develop Schedule

Develop Schedule is a relatively complex iterative process of analyzing activity sequence, dependency, durations, logical relationships, resources (materials, manpower, equipment, supplies, etc.), requirements, constraints, and assumptions to develop the project schedule with planned dates for the completion of project activities.

This process produces the most vital and visible project schedule that determines the planned start and finish dates for project milestones and activities. Once approved after several reviews and revision of the duration and resource estimates, it serves as a baseline to track project progress.

As per the PMBOK®, the Develop Schedule process has the following inputs, tools & techniques, and outputs:

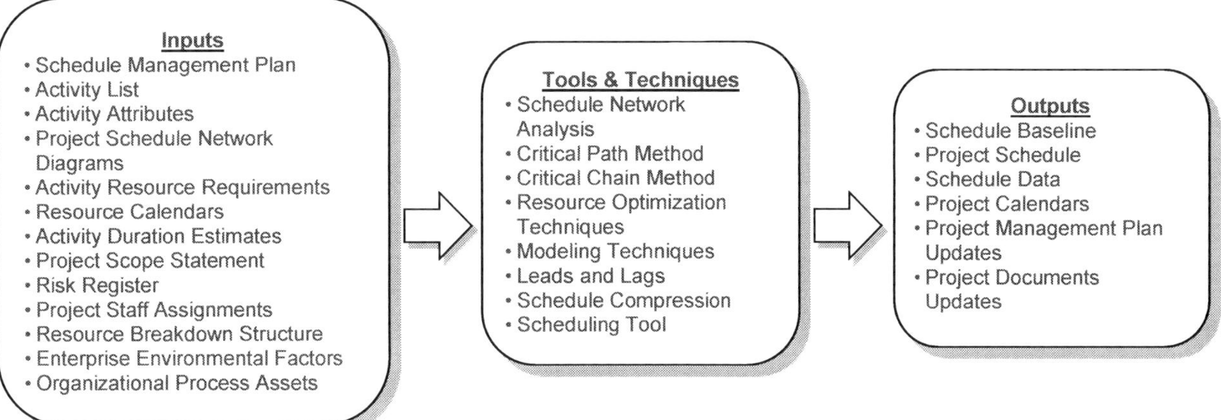

Figure 6-13: Develop Schedule: Inputs, Tools & Techniques, and Outputs

Develop Schedule: Inputs

- Schedule Management Plan
- Activity List
- Activity Attributes
- Project Schedule Network Diagrams
- Activity Resource Requirements
- Resource Calendars
- Activity Duration Estimates
- Project Scope Statement
- Risk Register
- Project Staff Assignments
- Resource Breakdown Structure
- Enterprise Environmental Factors
- Organizational Process Assets

Schedule Management Plan: The schedule management plan contains the details on the schedule management guidelines, policies, procedures, methods, and tools that may be used to develop the schedule.

Activity List: This is a list of all scheduled activities.

Activity Attributes: Detailed information about the activities will be helpful in scheduling the activities.

Project Schedule Network Diagrams: Network diagrams show the logical relationship, dependency, and order of activities, which will be essential for assigning dates to each activity.

Activity Resource Requirements: Information on resource (materials, manpower, equipment, supplies, etc.) requirements is essential to developing the schedule.

Resource Calendars: This calendar shows the resource usage across the organization and has information on resource availability and constraints that are useful in developing the project schedule.

Activity Duration Estimates: The information on how long the activity will take to complete is essential for schedule development.

Project Scope Statement: This document contains information on assumptions and constraints that are extremely helpful in schedule development.

Risk Register: The risk register contains the list of identified risks and their probability, impact, priority, and response plan. The project schedule may be impacted by these various risk events in the project.

Project Staff Assignments: Project staff assignments define resource allocation for each scheduled activity.

Resource Breakdown Structure: A Resource Breakdown Structure (RBS) is a graphical and hierarchical structure of the identified resources arranged by resource category (such as labor, material, equipment, and supplies) and type (such as expertise level, grade, and experience).

Enterprise Environmental Factors: A scheduling tool, such as Microsoft Project, can be used to develop the schedule.

Organizational Process Assets: Scheduling methodology and project calendar may influence the schedule development.

Develop Schedule: Tools & Techniques

- Schedule Network Analysis
- Critical Path Method
- Critical Chain Method
- Resource Optimization Techniques
- Modeling Techniques
- Leads and Lags
- Schedule Compression
- Scheduling Tool

Schedule Network Analysis: Schedule Network Analysis uses the following analytical techniques to generate the project schedule:

- Critical Path Method (CPM)
- Critical Chain Method
- What-if Analysis
- Resource Leveling

Critical Path Method (CPM): The critical path is the longest path through a network diagram and determines the shortest time to complete the project as well as any scheduling flexibility. It is not the project schedule, but it indicates the time period within which an activity could be scheduled considering activity duration, logical relationships, dependencies, leads, lags, assumptions, and constraints.

A few important points about the critical path:

- Identifies how much individual activities can be delayed without delaying the project.
- It is the path with zero float, so none of the activities in the critical path can slip.
- It is calculated using either single-point or PERT-weighted average estimates.
- Delays experienced with any activity on the critical path translate directly into delays of project completion date.
- **Near-Critical Path:** These are the paths in the network diagram with very small float (a slight delay can shift the critical path). Projects with more than one critical path or several near-critical paths are very risky projects as any delay in the near-critical path can introduce a new critical path or even delay the project.

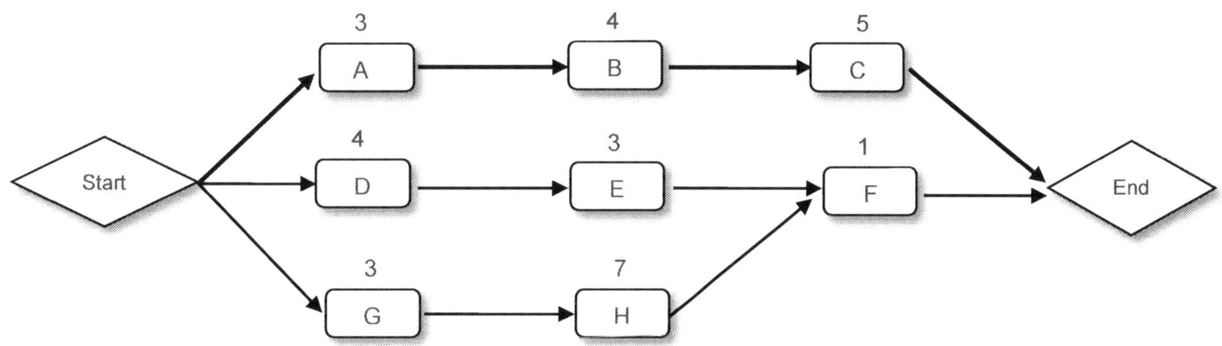

Figure 6-14: A Network Diagram

Let's look at the paths:

- Start, A, B, C, End = 12 wks, critical path
- Start, D, E, F, End = 8 wks
- Start, G, H, F, End = 11 wks, near-critical path

If the longest or critical path is twelve weeks long, the estimated duration of our project is also twelve weeks.

Float/Slack/Buffer Calculation: Float is the maximum amount of time an activity can be delayed without delaying the entire project.

Activities on the critical path have no float as any delay will increase the duration of the project. To calculate the float or buffer for activities not on the critical path, we can use the following techniques:

a. Find out the largest path the activity is on and
b. Subtract the largest path duration of that activity from critical path duration

So, Float/ buffer = Critical Path Duration – Longest Path Duration of the Activity

Example: In order to find out the buffer/float for Activity G, we need to find the largest path G is on. G is only on Start, G, H, F, End; thus, the longest path is eleven weeks. Now the duration of critical path Start, A, B, C, End is twelve weeks; thus, the buffer/float of G is 12 – 11 = 1 week.

Let's calculate the buffer/float for Activity F. Activity F is on the following two paths:
Start, D, E, F, End and Start, G, H, F, End. The duration of the first path is eight weeks, and the duration of the second path is eleven weeks. Thus, the second path is the longest path for F. So F has a buffer of 12 – 11 = 1 week. We can delay activity F by one week and still our project will not be delayed.

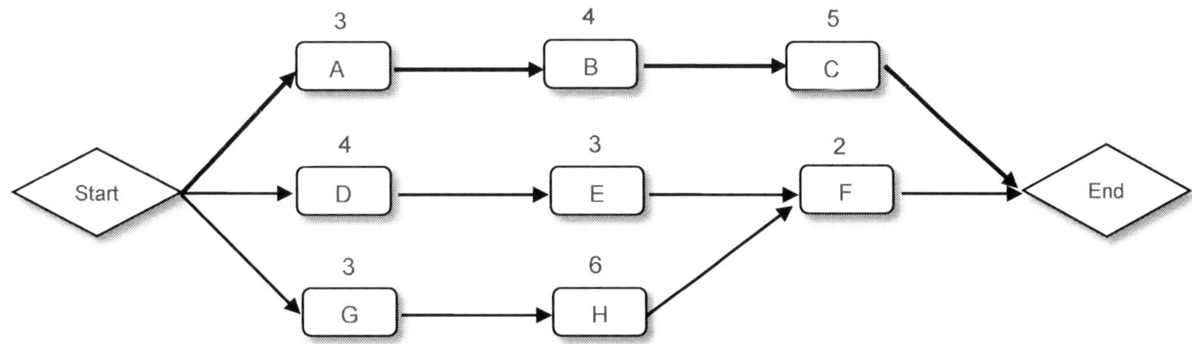

Figure 6-15: Calculating Buffer/Float for Any Activity

Exercise 4: What is the float/buffer for Activity B and Activity D in the diagram above?

Other values calculated in CPM include:

- **Early Start:** The soonest a task can begin.
- **Early Finish**: The soonest a task can end.
  Early Finish = Early Start + Duration – 1
- **Late Start:** The latest a task can begin without affecting the project duration.
  Late Start = Early Start + Float/Buffer
- **Late Finish**: The latest a task can end without affecting the project duration.
  Late Finish = Late Start + Duration – 1
  Buffer/Float/Slack = Late Finish – Early Finish or Late Start – Early Start

- A **Forward Pass** is used to calculate early start and early finish.
- A **Backward Pass** is used to calculate late start and late finish.

Example: The following network diagram is the same as the previous one we used for float/slack or buffer calculation. We know that the buffers are as below for the activities:

A = 0 week, on the critical path
B = 0 week, on the critical path
C = 0 week, on the critical path
D = 3 weeks, E = 3 wks, F = 1 wk, G = 1 wk, H = 1 wk

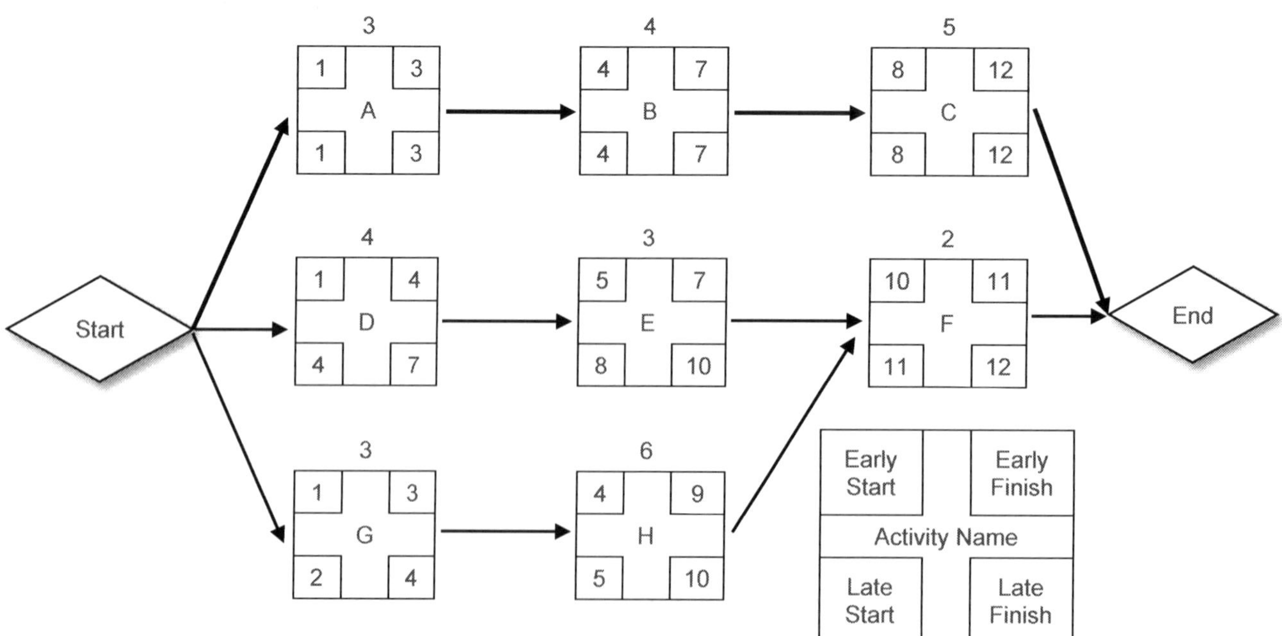

Figure 6-16: Calculating Early Start, Early Finish, Late Start, and Late Finish

Now the earliest we can start Activity A will be the first the day of work week (ww) 1; thus, for Activity A
Early Start = 1 and
Early Finish = (1 + 3) – 1 = 3, Early Finish = Early Start + Duration – 1
We have no buffer for Activity A; thus, for Activity A
Late Start = 1 + 0 = 1, Late Start = Early Start + Float/Buffer
Late Finish = (1 + 3) – 1 = 3, Late Finish = Late Start + Duration – 1
Note that for activities on the critical path Early Start = Late Start and Early Finish = Late Finish.

Since Activity B is depending on Activity A and it is also on the critical path, the earliest we can start Activity B will be ww4; thus, for Activity B
Early Start = 4, Early Finish = (4 + 4) – 1 = 7, Late Start = 4, and Late Finish = 7.

Activity C depends on Activity B; thus, for Activity C
Early Start = 8, Early Finish = (8 + 5) – 1 = 12, Late Start = 8, and Late Finish = 12.

We can also start Activity D on ww1; thus, for Activity D
Early Start =1, Early Finish = (1 + 4) – 1 = 4, Late Start = 1 + 3 = 4 (we have three weeks float/buffer for Activity D), Late Finish = (4 + 4) – 1 = 7.

Activity E depends on Activity D and has a buffer of three weeks; thus, for Activity E
Early Start = 5, Early Finish = (5 + 3) – 1 = 7, Late Start = 5 + 3 = 8, and Late Finish = (8 + 3) – 1 = 10.

Activity G can be started on ww1, and it has a buffer/float of one week; thus, for Activity G
Early Start = 1, Early Finish = (1 + 3) – 1 = 3, Late Start = 1 + 1 = 2, and Late Finish = (2 + 3) – 1 = 4.

Activity H depends on Activity G, and it has a buffer/float of one week; thus, for Activity H
Early Start = 4, Early Finish = (4 + 6) – 1 = 9, Late Start = 4 + 1 = 5, and Late Finish = (5 + 6) – 1 = 10.

Exercise 5: Find out the early start, early finish, late start, and late finish for Activity F.

Exercise 6: If the Early Start = 9, Early Finish = 13, Late Start = 17, and Late Finish = 21 for an activity, then what is the buffer/float of this activity?

Types of Float/Slack

Free Float: Amount of time an activity can be delayed without affecting the early start of its successor.

Total Float: Amount of time an activity can be delayed without affecting the project completion date.

Project Float: Amount of time a project can be delayed without delaying an externally imposed project completion date (e.g., customer-requested delivery date).

Negative Float: A negative float indicates that the amount of time required for the project is greater than the amount of time allocated.
Example: Consider a project is supposed to be completed in 30 weeks, but after 35 weeks, it is still in progress. In this case, the float is negative five weeks because the project should have been completed five weeks earlier.

Example: Let's calculate the total float and free float of Activity E.

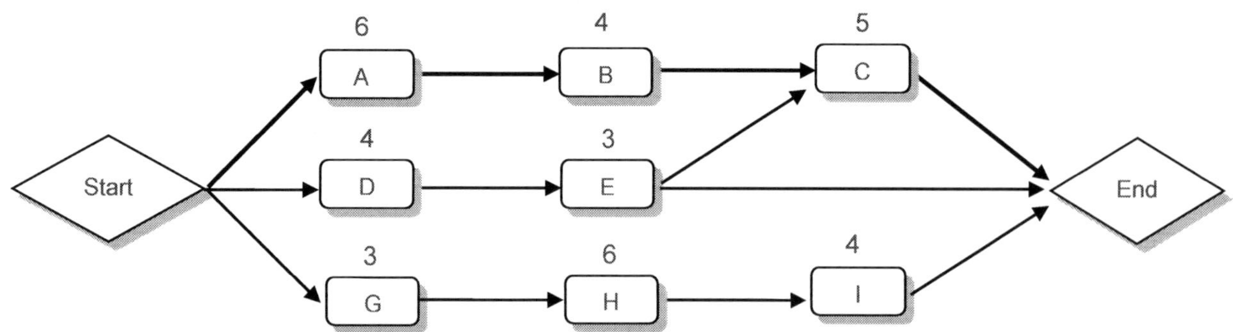

Figure 6-17: Calculating Free Float and Total Float

We have four paths in the network diagram:
Start, A, B, C, End = 15 weeks, the critical path
Start, D, E, C, End = 12 weeks, Start, D, E, End = 7 weeks, Start, G, H, I, End = 13 weeks.

Now Activity E is on the following paths:
Start, D, E, End = 7 weeks
Start, D, E, C, End = 12 weeks, the longest path

So total buffer/float of Activity E is 15 – 12 = 3 weeks. We can delay Activity E by three weeks and still our project will not be delayed.
To calculate the free float of Activity E, we need to find out the early start of its successor C. Let's only focus on the early start and early finish of the following activities since Activity C depends on Activities B and E, and Activity B depends on Activity A, and Activity E depends on Activity D.

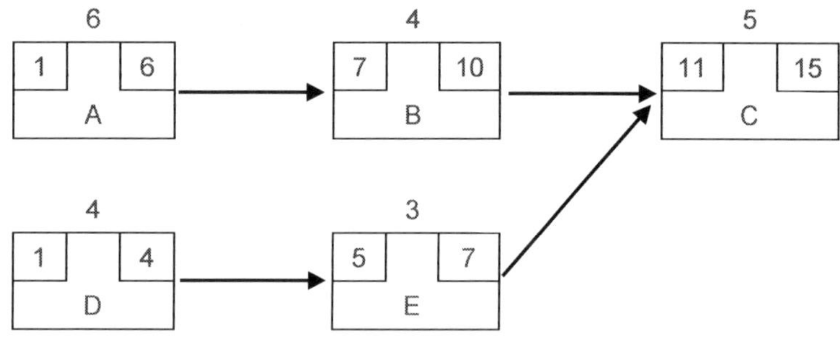

Figure 6-18: Calculating Free Float

Use the following formula to calculate early start and early finish for Activities A, B, D, E, and F.
Early Start: The soonest a task can begin.
Early Finish: The soonest a task can end. Early Finish = Early Start + Duration – 1

Since Activity A has no dependency, we can start Activity A on ww1; thus, for Activity A
Early Start = 1 and Early Finish = (1 + 6) – 1 = 6.

Activity B depends on Activity A; thus, for Activity B
Early Start = 7 and Early Finish = (7 + 4) – 1 = 10.

Again, Activity D has no dependency, so we can start Activity D on ww1; thus, for Activity D
Early Start = 1 and Early Finish = (1 + 4) – 1 = 4.
Activity E depends on Activity D, so the earliest we can start Activity E will be ww5. So for Activity E Early Start = 5 and Early Finish = (5 + 3) – 1 = 7.
Now that Activity C depends on both Activities B and E, and the earliest we can finish Activity B is on ww10 and E on ww7. Even though we are finishing Activity E on ww7, we cannot start Activity C on ww8 because we need to wait for Activity B to be completed on ww10. Thus, the earliest we can start Activity C will be ww11.

In order to not delay Activity C's early start of ww11, we need to complete Activity E by ww10. So we can delay Activity E by 10 – 7 = 3 weeks. Therefore, the free float of Activity E will be three weeks.

Critical Chain Method: The critical chain method is another way to develop an approved, realistic, resource-limited, and formal schedule. It provides a way to view and manage uncertainty when building the project schedule.

- Initially, the project schedule network diagram is built using duration estimates with required dependencies and defined constraints as inputs, and the critical path is then calculated. In addition, buffer may be added to high-risk activities to manage uncertainty.
- The critical chain method modifies this by estimating each activity as aggressively as possible, building the schedule network and adding one lump-sum buffer to the end of the network before the finishing date. This lump-sum buffer is then used to manage any individual activity on the critical path.
- The team is unaware, and therefore, they are kept on an aggressive schedule.
- Buffer is under the PM's control.

Example: Suppose as a project manager, you negotiated and decided, along with your project sponsor and client, that the expected duration of the project would be twenty-four months. Now, this is a strategically important project and no delay will be acceptable. From your experience with your team members, you know that if they are given only twenty-four months, then there is very little chance that the project will be completed on time. In order to mitigate the risk of delaying the project, you work on an aggressive schedule with the team members and come up with the duration of twenty-one months for the project, which is less than what you have discussed with the sponsor and client. Now the additional three months of buffer time that you have is kept secret from the team members can be used to deal with any unexpected delay in the project.

Resource Optimization Techniques:

Resource Leveling: Resource leveling is used to produce a resource-limited schedule by letting the schedule slip and cost increase in order to deal with a limited amount of resources, resource availability, and other resource constraints.

It can be used when shared or critically required resources are only available at certain times or are in limited quantities or when resources have been over allocated.

We may have several peaks and valleys in our resource histogram listed below. In order to level the resources, to evenly utilize them as much as possible, or to keep resource usage at a constant level, we can move some of our activities from the week when we are using a lot of resources to a week when we are hardly using any.

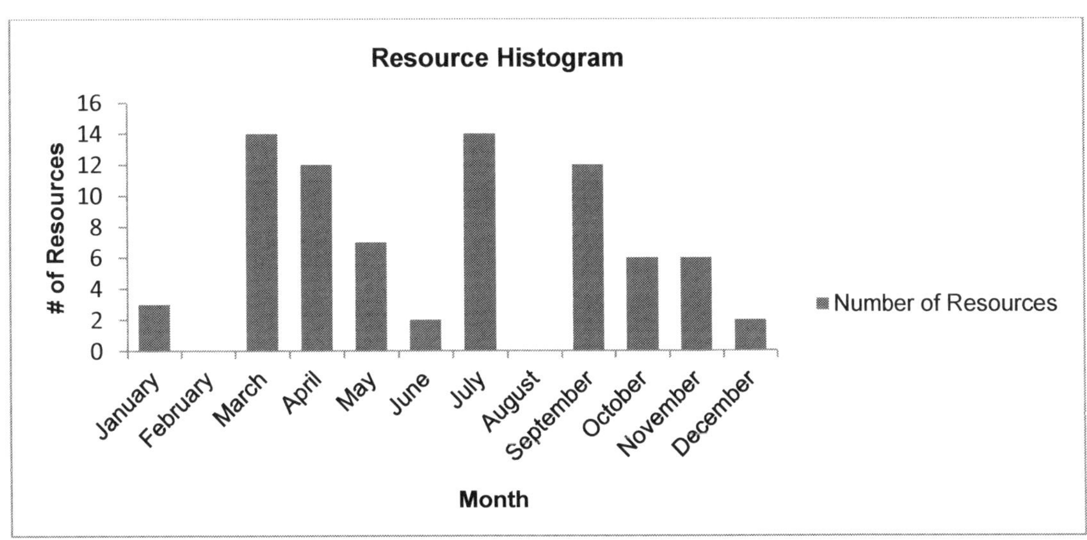

Figure 6-19: A Resource Histogram

Resource leveling is done to adjust the resource need to meet up with the organization's capability of providing required resources to the project. In order to resource level the project,

1. Calculate and analyze all the network paths for the project using the critical path method.
2. Apply resources to the analysis in Step 1 to figure out the impact on your schedule.

Assume that you have the following network diagram after performing your Estimate Activity Resources and Estimate Activity Durations processes.

ID	Activity	Dependency	Resources	Duration (Days)	Number of Resources
R	Collect Requirements	–	Business Analyst	5	2
D	Complete Design	R	System Designer	12	3
C	Complete Coding	R	Programmer	12	9
T	Complete Testing	D,C	Tester	3	2
P	Deploy in Production	T	System Admin	1	1

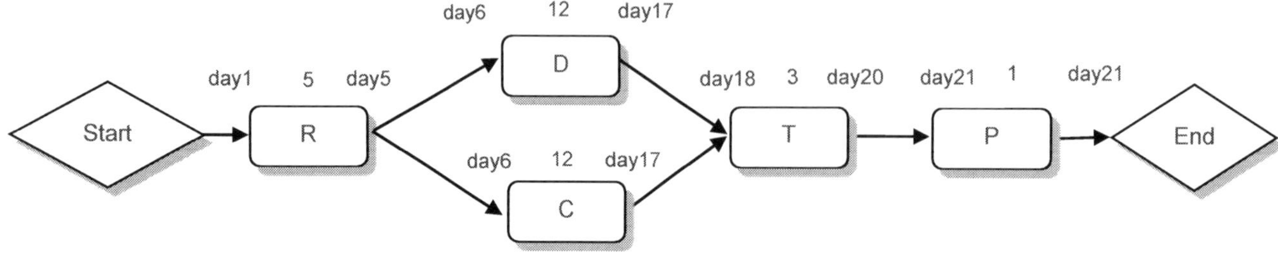

Figure 6-20: Initial Network Diagram

In this case, we are expecting the project to be completed in twenty-one days. Now consider that management has informed you that they could only supply three resources instead of the nine that you asked for to use in coding activities. You calculated that your activity would take thirty-six (12 * 3) days now since you are getting only one-third of the resources. This can often cause the original critical path to change, and the result will be an updated network diagram with a longer duration of forty-five days as illustrated in the following diagram.

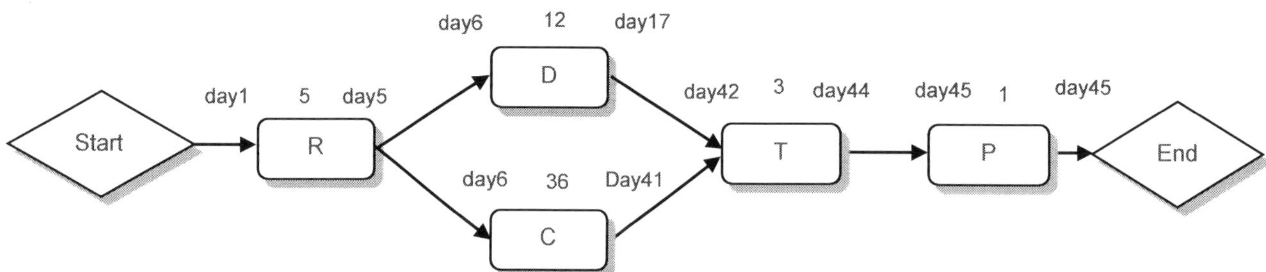

Figure 6-21: Network Diagram with the New Critical Path

Resource Smoothing: Resource smoothing is a modified form of resource leveling that levels the resources without modifying the critical path or delaying the completion dates of the activities. As resource smoothing only allows activities to be delayed within their limits of the total and free float, it may not be able to optimize all the resources.

Modeling Techniques:

What-if Scenario Analysis: This type of analysis usually uses Monte Carlo simulation to simulate the outcome of a project, making use of three-point estimates (optimistic, pessimistic, most likely) for each activity, a huge number of simulated scheduling possibilities, a few selected scenarios that are most likely, and the network diagram.

The outcome of this analysis may be used to evaluate the project schedule under adverse conditions and to develop the preventive and contingency action plans to reduce the impact and probability of unexpected situations.

This analysis can identify the following:

- Risky activities and their probabilities
- The possibility of completing the project on any specific day
- The possibility of completing the project for any specific cost
- Any particular task actually being on the critical path
- A project duration more accurate than PERT or CPM
- "Path convergence" (where multiple paths converge into one or more activities in the network diagram and add risk to the project)

Leads and Lags: This technique ensures that leads and lags are applied to the schedule appropriately and adjusted as needed.

Schedule Compression: Schedule compression is the process of shortening the project schedule without changing the project scope or sacrificing desired quality. Two main techniques used in schedule compression are fast-tracking and crashing.

Fast-Tracking: The technique of doing critical path activities in parallel when they were originally planned in series.

- Usually results in rework, increases risks, and requires more communication.
- Most of the time, it will not increase cost, but it will increase risk to the project since discretionary dependencies will be ignored to perform activities simultaneously.

Example: In a software development project, initially you planned to complete the activities in the following sequential order:

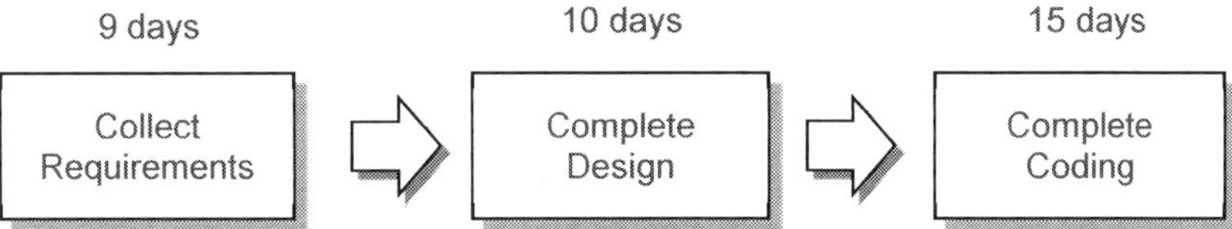

In this case, your project duration is 9 + 10 + 15 = 34 days. To shorten the duration of the project, you decided to work on the design and coding in parallel. Performing these two activities will add some complication, so they may take a little extra time individually, but overall it will save time. Suppose design work will now take an additional day and coding work will take a couple of additional days when we perform them in parallel due to additional complexity.

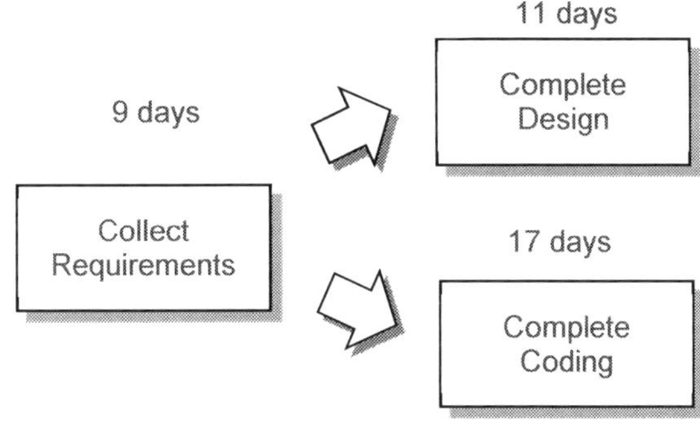

Figure 6-22: Fast-Tracking

By applying the fast-tracking, the project duration became 9 + 17 = 26 days from 34 days.

Crashing: The technique of adding additional resources to a critical path activities to complete them more quickly.

Original Estimate		
Activity	**Number of Resources**	**Duration**
Completion of Design	2	6
Completion of Coding	2	12
Crashed Estimate		
Completion of Design	4	3
Completion of Coding	6	4

- Examples of crashing could include approving overtime, bringing in additional resources, or paying to expedite delivery to activities on the critical path.
- Crashing does not always produce a viable alternative and may result in increased risk and/or cost. Increasing the number of resources may decrease time but not in a linear amount, as activities will often encounter the law of diminishing returns.

Exercise 7: What kind of scheduling shortening options will have the following impacts?

General Impacts	Schedule Shortening Options
1. Could possibly save time and cost, but it is not an option the project manager should consider	
2. May increase risk drastically	
3. Adds additional risks to the project	
4. Always adds cost as resources are added to the activities	
5. May add additional management time for the project manager	
6. Will have substantial negative impact on customer satisfaction	
7. May add management time for project manager due to increase in resources working together in multiple parallel activities	
8. Requires good metrics to make sure that quality will not be affected too much	

Exercise 8: Referring to the following table, determine the cost to crash the project schedule to seven days.

Task	Details	Duration	Predecessor	Normal Cost	Crash Cost	Max Crash Days
A	Collect Requirements	3	–	$3,000	$200/day	1
B	Complete Design	5	A	$1,700	$100/day	2
C	Complete Coding	4	A	$5,400	$400/day	2
D	Complete Testing	3	B	$2,100	$150/day	1
E	Complete User Testing	2	C	$ 4000	$250/day	1

Scheduling Tool: This kind of tool helps to perform routine schedule analysis. It also expedites the scheduling process by generating start and end dates for the activities based on the network diagram, dependencies, duration, assigned resources, and other factors. Other manual methods and project management software applications can also be used in conjunction with this kind of scheduling tool.

Develop Schedule: Outputs

- Schedule Baseline
- Project Schedule
- Schedule Data
- Project Calendars
- Project Management Plan Updates
- Project Documents Updates

Schedule Baseline: A schedule baseline is a specific version of a project schedule used to manage the project. It is also what the project team's performance is measured against. It is the original schedule, plus any approved changes and any schedule change requests that are approved as they become part of the schedule baseline.

Project Schedule: The project schedule is the result of schedule network analysis and includes a planned start date and planned end date for each activity. It can be presented in a summary form or in detail, and it is typically represented graphically. There can be several schedule formats as discussed below:
- Bar Charts
- Network Diagram
- Milestone Charts

Bar Charts/Gantt Charts: A bar chart is a time-phased graphical display of activity start dates, end dates, and durations. It is also referred to as a Gantt chart.
- Useful for tracking progress and reporting to the team.
- Relatively easy to understand and may be used in management presentations.
- Can be easily modified to show the percentage of completed work.

Example: Suppose you are working on the following tasks and listed the start date, duration, the number of days completed, and the number of days remaining. A bar chart/Gantt chart can be created to graphically display the activities.

ID	Task List	Start Date	Duration	# of Days Completed	# of Days Remaining
1	Plan Course	16-Mar-13	2	2	0
2	Collect Requirements	17-Mar-13	10	10	0
3	Functional Design	27-Mar-13	2	2	0
4	System Design	29-Mar-13	10	2	8
5	Simulations & Prototype	29-Mar-13	10	3	7
6	Integration & Unit Testing	8-Apr-13	2	0	2
7	Group Review	10-Apr-13	5	0	5
8	User Acceptance Testing	16-Apr-13	3	0	3
9	Release	19-Apr-13	1	0	1

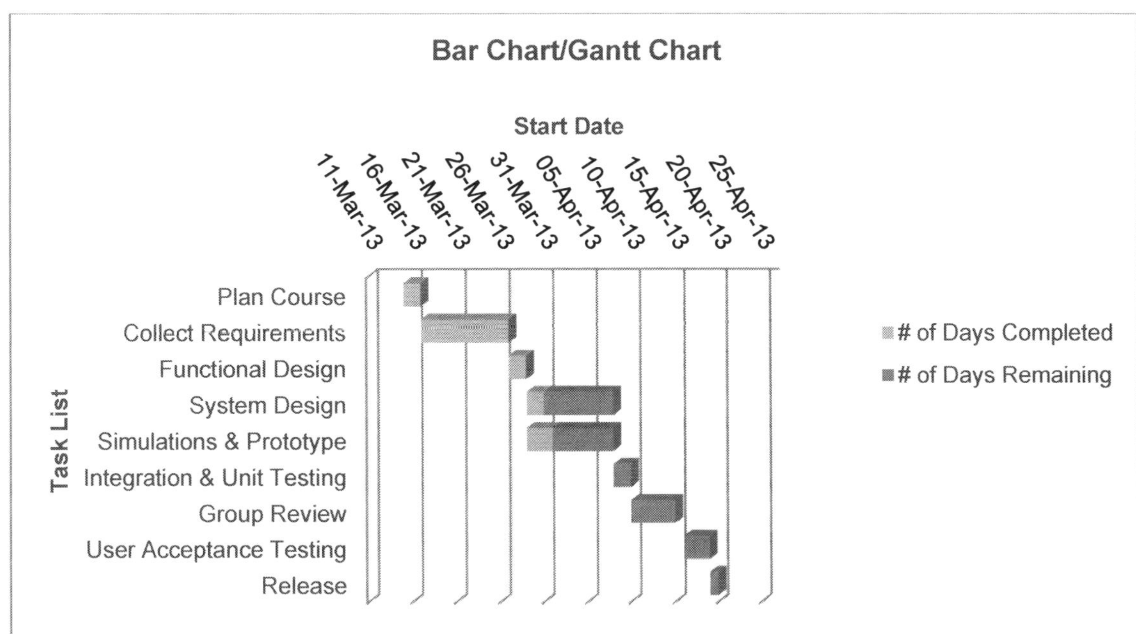

Figure 6-23: Graph: A Bar Chart/Gantt Chart

Network Diagram: A network diagram is a schematic display of the sequential and logical relationships of the activities that comprise a project. The network diagram shows dependencies and the order in which activities in a project must be performed. If activity duration estimates are added, then this method will show the critical path or the duration of the project.

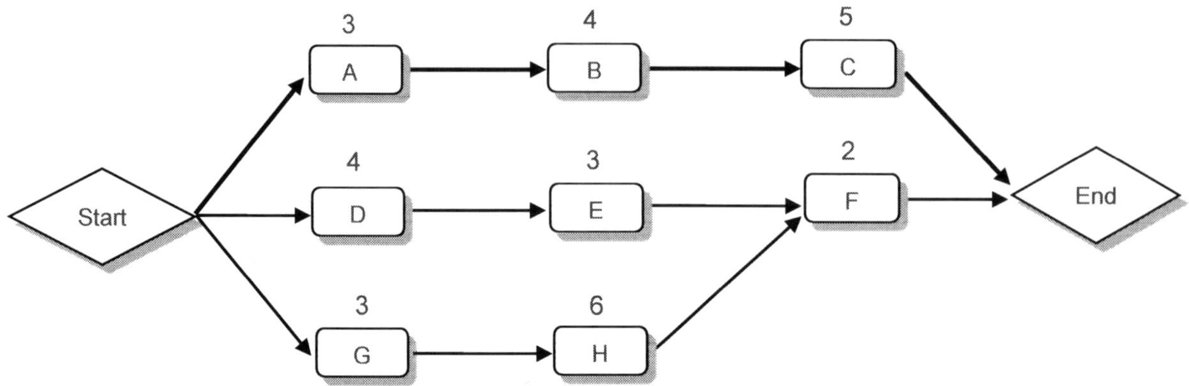

Figure 6-24: A Network Diagram

The network diagram can be beneficial in the following ways as it:
- Shows the interdependencies of all activities
- Shows the order in which activities will be performed
- Shows workflow, so sequence is known
- Aids in effectively planning, organizing, and controlling the project
- May be used for schedule control and reporting
- Helps justify time estimates
- Helps optimize or compress the schedule
- Helps to calculate critical path and near critical paths
- Helps to identify critical path activities
- Helps to calculate free and total floats for all activities
- Helps to calculate early start, early finish, late start, and late finish for all activities

Exercise 9: Identify which of the following statements are true and which are false about a network diagram.

Statement	
1. Shows interdependencies of all activities.	
2. Helps to develop the WBS.	
3. Shows the order in which activities will be performed.	
4. Shows workflow, so the sequence of activities is known.	
5. Helps to estimate the range of an activity.	
6. Helps in planning, organizing, managing, and controlling the project effectively.	
7. Shows project progress if used for schedule controlling and reporting.	
8. Helps justify time estimates.	
9. Helps develop a schedule management plan.	
10. Helps to optimize or compress the schedule.	
11. Helps to decompose the WBS work packages into the activity list.	
12. If duration is estimated, then it can be used to calculate the critical path, total float, free float, early start, early finish, late start, and late finish.	
13. The major difficulty encountered when developing a network diagram is that there are no feedback loops or alternative paths in it.	

Milestone Chart: This chart is similar to a bar chart but only shows major events.

- Milestones have no duration; they are simply the completion of activities.
- It is a good tool for reporting to management and customers.
- This type of chart is reserved for brief, high-level presentations as too much detail may be undesirable and distracting to senior management.

ID	Major Milestones	Jan	Feb	Mar	Apr	May	Jun	Jul
1.	Completion of Business Case and Feasibility Study	◆24						
2.	Completion of Project Charter		◆31					
3.	Completion of Requirements Collection			◆12				
4.	Completion of Design					◆30		
5.	Completion of Coding						◆4	
6.	Completion of User Acceptance Testing						◆15	
7.	Completion of Production Implementation							◆5
8.	Production Handover							◆14

Figure 6-25: A Milestone Chart

Schedule Data: Schedule data refers to information such as schedule templates, activities and their attributes, estimated duration, constraints and assumptions, resource requirements, and alternative schedules—best case or worst case, resource leveled or not leveled, with or without imposed dates—and/or schedule reserve that are used to model and create the project schedule.

Project Calendars: A project calendar identifies the available and unavailable working days and shifts for scheduling project activities. A customized project calendar or more than one calendar may be required for some projects to schedule different work periods for some activities.

Project Management Plan Updates: Components of the project management plan such as the schedule management plan and the schedule baseline may be updated.

Project Documents Updates: Updates to activity resource requirements, activity attributes, the risk register, the risk log, the calendar, and other documents is very common.

Exercise 10: What kind of scheduling tool will you be using in the following situations?

Situations	Scheduling Tools
1. To report to the customers and senior management	
2. To show interdependencies, logical relationships between activities, and the order in which activities will be performed	
3. To report to the team and track progress.	

Exercise 11: What actions should the project manager focus on to develop a realistic, formal, and approved final schedule?

Control Schedule

Control Schedule is the process of monitoring the status of the project by comparing the result to the plan, updating project progress, and managing changes to the project schedule baseline.

This process is focused on the following:

- Current status and changes to the project schedule
- Influential factors that create schedule changes
- Management of actual changes as they occur
- Identification of corrective and preventive actions
- Integration with the other control processes

As per the PMBOK®, the Control Schedule process has the following inputs, tools & techniques, and outputs:

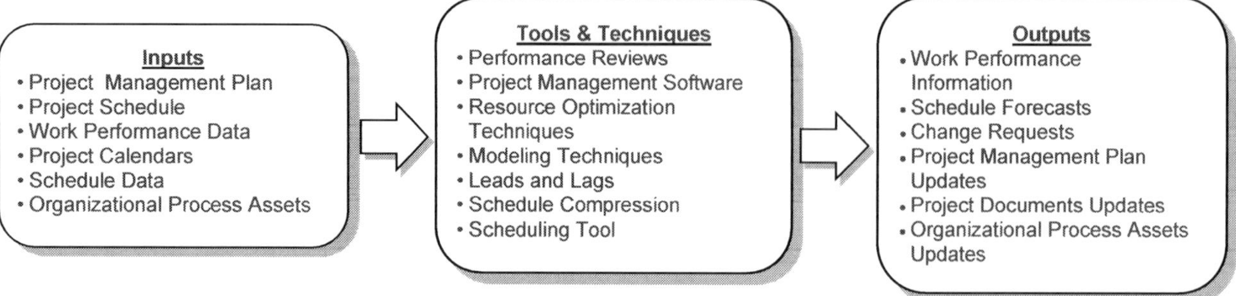

Figure 6-26: Control Schedule: Inputs, Tools & Techniques, and Outputs

Control Schedule: Inputs

- Project Management Plan
- Project Schedule
- Work Performance Data
- Project Calendars
- Schedule Data
- Organizational Process Assets

Project Management Plan: Both the schedule management plan and the schedule baseline in the project management plan are essential components in this process. How the schedule will be managed and controlled is specified in the schedule management plan, while the schedule baseline helps to determine necessary changes and corrective and preventive actions, as it is used to compare with actual results.

Project Schedule: This schedule is the primary input against which the results are controlled.

Work Performance Data: Information about project progress against schedule such as activities that have started and finished and the percentage of activities completed.

Project Calendars: A customized project calendar or more than one calendar may be required for some projects to schedule different work periods for some activities and to calculate schedule forecasts.

Schedule Data: Schedule data refers to information such as schedule templates, activities and their attributes, estimated duration, constraints and assumptions, resource requirements, and alternative schedules—best case or worst case, resource leveled or not leveled, with or without imposed dates—and schedule reserve. These are among the items used to model and create the project schedule. All these schedule data will be reviewed and updated in the Control Schedule process.

Organizational Process Assets: Any relevant assets such as schedule control tools, schedule control-related policies, procedures and guidelines, monitoring and reporting methods, and tools may be useful.

Control Schedule: Tools & Techniques

- Performance Reviews
- Project Management Software
- Resource Optimization Techniques
- Modeling Techniques
- Leads and Lags
- Schedule Compression
- Scheduling Tool

Performance Reviews: Performance review is used to measure project progress against the schedule. Earned value management measurements such as Schedule Variance (SV) and Schedule Performance Index (SPI), trend analysis, critical path method, and critical chain method are used to identify the magnitude of schedule variance and determine if any corrective actions are required or not.

Project Management Software: Different project management software can be used to track planned dates versus actual dates, forecast the effect of changes to the project schedule, and simplify and automate the schedule analysis.

Resource Optimization Techniques: Whenever there is a schedule change, resources may need to be leveled again to ensure proper execution of the project schedule.

Modeling Techniques: These techniques are used with multiple scenarios to identify the best approach for bringing the schedule into alignment with the plan.

Leads and Lags: Project activities that are behind schedule can be brought back into track by utilizing leads and lags.

Schedule Compression: Project activities that are behind schedule can be brought back into track by utilizing different techniques of schedule compression.

Scheduling Tool: Scheduling tools and supporting data are used to perform schedule network analysis and to manage large numbers of options and decisions to optimize, manage, and generate an updated project schedule.

Control Schedule: Outputs

- Work Performance Information
- Schedule Forecasts
- Change Requests
- Project Management Plan Updates
- Project Documents Updates
- Organizational Process Assets Updates

Work Performance Information: Earned value measurements such as Schedule Variance (SV), Schedule Performance Index (SPI), and other relevant measurements need to be calculated and communicated to the stakeholders.

Schedule Forecasts: Schedule forecasts are future estimates or the anticipation of future events and conditions based on the project's past performance, earned value performance indicators, expected future performance, and available knowledge and expertise. These forecasts are updated and reissued based on the work performance information as the project is executed.

Change Requests: Change requests can be generated to the schedule baseline or to other components of the project management plan from schedule variance analysis, progress reports, performance measurements, or modification to the project schedule. In order to reduce the probability of negative schedule variances, recommended change requests may be included in the preventive action plan.

Project Management Plan Updates: Any schedule change can impact project scope and budget; thus, the scope baseline, schedule management plan, and cost baseline may be updated as needed.

Project Documents Updates: Project schedule, schedule data, and risk register may be updated.

Organizational Process Assets Updates: Causes of variances, selected corrective actions, and lessons learned may be updated.

Project Schedule Development Example for a Construction Project

A project manager recently took over a construction project to build a house for one of her clients. The project manager created a schedule management plan to define how the project schedule will be planned, developed, managed, executed, and controlled. The team then focused on developing the activity list by decomposing the WBS work packages. A network diagram was developed for identifying and documenting relationships and dependencies among defined activities. The project manager identified the resource requirements for the project activities and received duration estimations from each team member for the activities. The project manager developed the following preliminary schedule based on the activity list, dependency, resource need, and duration estimates from the team members.

Major Milestones	Duration (days)	Start Date	End Date	Resources	Dependency
1. Initiating					
1.1. Create the Project Charter and Stakeholder Register	5	1/1	1/5	PM	
1.2. Appoint the Project Team	3	1/6	1/8	SP	1.1
1.3. Perform Initiating Phase Review	1	1/9	1/9	PM	1.2
2. Planning					
2.1. Create Detailed Project Plans	15	1/10	1/25	PM	1.3
2.2. Negotiate and Finalize Contract with the Suppliers	10	1/20	1/30	PM	
2.3. Obtain Relevant Construction Permits	10	2/1	2/12	PM	2.1
2.4. Gain Final Council Planning Approval	6	2/14	2/20	PM	2.3
2.5. Perform Planning Phase Review	1	2/22	2/22	PM	2.4
3. Executing					
3.1. Site Preparation					
3.1.1 Clear the Lot	5	2/23	2/27	Team	2.5
3.1.2. Construct Temporary Construction Utilities	10	2/28	3/8	Team	3.1.1
3.1.3. Construct Boundary Fence	5	3/9	3/14	Team	3.1.2
3.2. Install Services					
3.2.1. Install Water, Electric, Telephone, Drainage, and Gas Services	15	3/15	3/30	Team	3.1.3
3.3. Create Access					
3.3.1. Construct Roadways	10	4/1	4/11	Team	3.2.1
3.3.2. Install Street Lighting	6	4/5	4/11	Team	
3.4. Foundation Work					
3.4.1. Complete Excavation, Forming, and Placement of the Concrete for the Basement	15	4/12	4/27	Team	
3.5. Framing					
3.5.1. Construct Basic Wooden Frame of the House	15	4/28	5/13	Team	3.4.1
3.6. Dry-in					
3.6.1. Complete Sheathing, Roofing, Windows, and Doors	15	5/14	5/30	Team	3.5.1
3.7. Exterior Finishes					
3.7.1. Complete Installation of Brick, Siding, and Exterior Trim	15	6/1	6/15	Team	3.6.1
3.8. Interior Finishes					
3.8.1. Complete Insulation, Drywall, Paint, and Wallpaper	15	6/1	6/16	Team	3.5.1
3.8.2. Complete Cabinets, Carpet, and Tile	10	6/17	6/27	Team	3.8.1
3.8.3. Complete the Installation of the Plumbing, Electrical, and HVAC Systems	10	6/17	6/27	Team	3.8.1
3.9. Landscaping and Grounds Work					
3.9.1. Create Recreational Areas	10	6/28	7/8	Team	3.8.3
3.9.2. Complete Driveways, Sidewalks, Fences, and Plantings	10	6/28	7/8	Team	3.8.3
3.10. Perform Phase Review	1	7/9	7/9	PM	3.9.2

4. Closure					
4.1. Final Acceptance					
4.1.1.Conduct Final Inspection	1	7/12	7/12	Team	3.10
4.1.2. Gain Certification for Occupancy	2	7/13	7/14	PM	4.1.1
4.1.3. Conduct Final Cleanup	3	7/12	7/15	Team	3.10
4.1.4. Complete Walkthrough with the Owner	1	7/16	7/16	PM	4.1.3
4.1.5. Receive Owner's Final Acceptance	1	7/17	7/17	PM	4.1.4
4.2 Perform Post-Project Review	1	7/18	7/18	PM	4.1.5
4.3. Release Staff	1	7/20	7/20	PM	4.2
4.4. Close Supplier Contract	2	7/21	7/21	PM	

The preliminary schedule was given to the sponsor and stakeholders for their review and approval. The sponsor asked the project manager to explore options to shorten the duration of the project as much as possible. The project manager renegotiated the duration estimates with the team members and finalized the start date, end date, and duration. Once the dates were finalized they were renamed as baseline start date and baseline end date. The project manager also included two new fields called actual start date and actual end date to capture the actual dates from the team members during schedule monitoring and controlling.

Major Milestones	Duration (days)	Baseline Start Date	Baseline End Date	Resources	Dependency	Actual Start Date	Actual End Date
1. Initiating							
1.1. Create the Project Charter and Stakeholder Register	4	1/1	1/4	PM		1/2	1/5
1.2. Appoint the Project Team	2	1/5	1/7	SP	1.1	1/6	1/8
1.3. Perform Initiating Phase Review	1	1/8	1/8	PM	1.2	1/9	1/9
2. Planning							
2.1. Create Detailed Project Plans	14	1/9	1/23	PM	1.3		
2.2. Negotiate and Finalize Contract with the Suppliers	10	1/20	1/30	PM			
2.3. Obtain Relevant Construction Permits	10	2/1	2/12	PM	2.1		
2.4. Gain Final Council Planning Approval	6	2/14	2/20	PM	2.3		
2.5. Perform Planning Phase Review	1	2/22	2/22	PM	2.4		
3. Executing							
3.1. Site Preparation							
3.1.1 Clear the Lot	4	2/23	2/26	Team	2.5		
3.1.2. Construct Temporary Construction Utilities	10	2/27	3/7	Team	3.1.1		
3.1.3. Construct Boundary Fence	5	3/8	3/13	Team	3.1.2		
3.2. Install Services							
3.2.1. Install Water, Electric, Telephone, Drainage, and Gas Services	12	3/15	3/27	Team	3.1.3		

3.3. Create Access							
3.3.1. Construct Roadways	10	4/1	4/11	Team	3.2.1		
3.3.2. Install Street Lighting	6	4/5	4/11	Team			
3.4. Foundation Work							
3.4.1. Complete Excavation, Forming and Placement of the Concrete for the Basement	15	4/12	4/27	Team			
3.3. Create Access							
3.5.1. Construct Basic Wooden Frame of the House	15	4/28	5/13	Team	3.4.1		
3.6. Dry-in							
3.6.1. Complete Sheathing, Roofing, Windows, and Doors	15	5/14	5/30	Team	3.5.1		
3.7. Exterior Finishes							
3.7.1. Complete Installation of Brick, Siding, and Exterior Trim	15	6/1	6/15	Team	3.6.1		
3.8. Interior Finishes							
3.8.1. Complete Insulation, Drywall, Paint, and Wallpaper	15	6/1	6/16	Team	3.5.1		
3.8.2. Complete Cabinets, Carpet, and Tile	10	6/17	6/27	Team	3.8.1		
3.8.3. Complete the Installation of the Plumbing, Electrical, and HVAC Systems	10	6/17	6/27	Team	3.8.1		
3.9. Landscaping and Grounds Work							
3.9.1. Create Recreational Areas	8	6/28	7/6	Team	3.8.3		
3.9.2. Complete Driveways, Sidewalks, Fences, and Plantings	8	6/28	7/6	Team	3.8.3		
3.10. Perform Phase Review	1	7/7	7/7	PM	3.9.2		
4. Closure							
4.1. Final Acceptance							
4.1.1.Conduct Final Inspection	1	7/8	7/8	Team	3.10		
4.1.2. Gain Certification for Occupancy	2	7/9	7/10	PM	4.1.1		
4.1.3. Conduct Final Cleanup	3	7/8	7/10	Team	3.10		
4.1.4. Complete Walkthrough with the Owner	1	7/11	7/11	PM	4.1.3		
4.1.5. Receive Owner's Final Acceptance	1	7/12	7/12	PM	4.1.4		
4.2. Perform Post Project Review	1	7/18	7/18	PM	4.1.5		
4.3. Release Staff	1	7/20	7/20	PM	4.2		
4.4. Close Supplier Contract	2	7/21	7/21	PM			

The following seven time management processes were used to develop, execute, manage, and control this construction project schedule.

1. **Plan Schedule Management** – Develops the schedule management plan

7. Control Schedule – Monitors the status of the project by comparing the result to the plan, updating project progress, and managing changes to the project schedule baseline

2. Define Activities – Decomposes WBS work packages into schedule activities

Major Milestones	Duration (days)	Baseline Start Date	Baseline End Date	Resources	Dependency	Actual Start Date	Actual End Date
1. Initiating							
1.1. Create the Project Charter and Stakeholder Register	4	1/1	1/4	PM		1/2	1/5
1.2. Appoint the Project Team	2	1/5	1/7	SP	1.1	1/6	1/8
1.3. Perform Initiating Phase Review	1	1/8	1/8	PM	1.2	1/9	1/9

5. Estimate Activity Durations – Estimates durations for activities

4. Estimate Activity Resources – Estimates resources (such as material, equipment, manpower, and supplies) required to perform activities

3. Sequence Activities – Identifies relationships among activities and arranges them in order

6. Develop Schedule – Develops project schedule

Exercise 12: Draw the network diagram as per the information provided in the following table and answer the questions below.

Activity	**Duration** (Weeks)	**Predecessor** Activity
A	3	Start
B	5	Start
C	8	A, B
D	7	B
E	5	C
F	2	D
G	4	E
H	3	E, F
End	0	G, H

1. What is the duration of the critical path?
2. What is the float/buffer for Activity H?
3. What is the float for Activity A?
4. What is the float for Activity B?
5. What is the float for Activity D?
6. What is the float for Activity F?
7. If we remove Activity D, making Activity B the predecessor of Activity F, what impact will it have on the project?
8. Find out early start, early finish, late start, and late finish for Activity H.
9. What is the free float for Activity E?
10. What is the free float for Activity F?

Exercise 13: Which of the following statements are true and which are false about critical path?

1. The longest path through a network diagram.	
2. Determines the shortest time to complete the project.	
3. It is actually the project schedule.	
4. Helps to identify how much individual activities can be delayed without delaying the project.	
5. It is the path with zero float, so none of the activities in the critical path can slip.	
6. It is same as critical chain.	
7. Helps to compress the project schedule.	
8. Delays experienced with any activity on the critical path will not necessarily delay the project.	
9. Used to produce a resource-limited schedule by letting the schedule slip and cost increase in order to deal with a limited amount of resources, resource availability, and other resource constraints.	
10. Helps level the resources.	

Exercise 14: Draw a network diagram and answer the questions.

- Activity A can start immediately and has an estimated duration of three weeks.
- Activity B can also start immediately and has an estimated duration of nine weeks.
- Activity C can start after Activity A is completed and has an estimated duration of five weeks.
- Activity D can start after Activity B is completed and has an estimated duration of four weeks.
- Activity E can start after both Activities C and D are completed and has an estimated duration of seven weeks.
- Activity F can start after Activity D is completed and has an estimated duration of four weeks.

1. What is the duration of the critical path?
2. What is the float of Activity C?
3. What is the float of Activity E?
4. What is the float of Activity F?
5. What is the free float of Activity C?
6. Find the early start, early finish, late start, and late finish for Activity F.
7. A new activity G is added to the project which will take 8 weeks to complete and must be completed before activity F and after activity D. You are worried that the addition of the new activity will add an additional 8 weeks to the project, so you calculate how much it will actually delay the project. What amount of time will be added to your project in this case?

Exercise 15: List activities for controlling a project schedule.

Exercise 16: Crossword

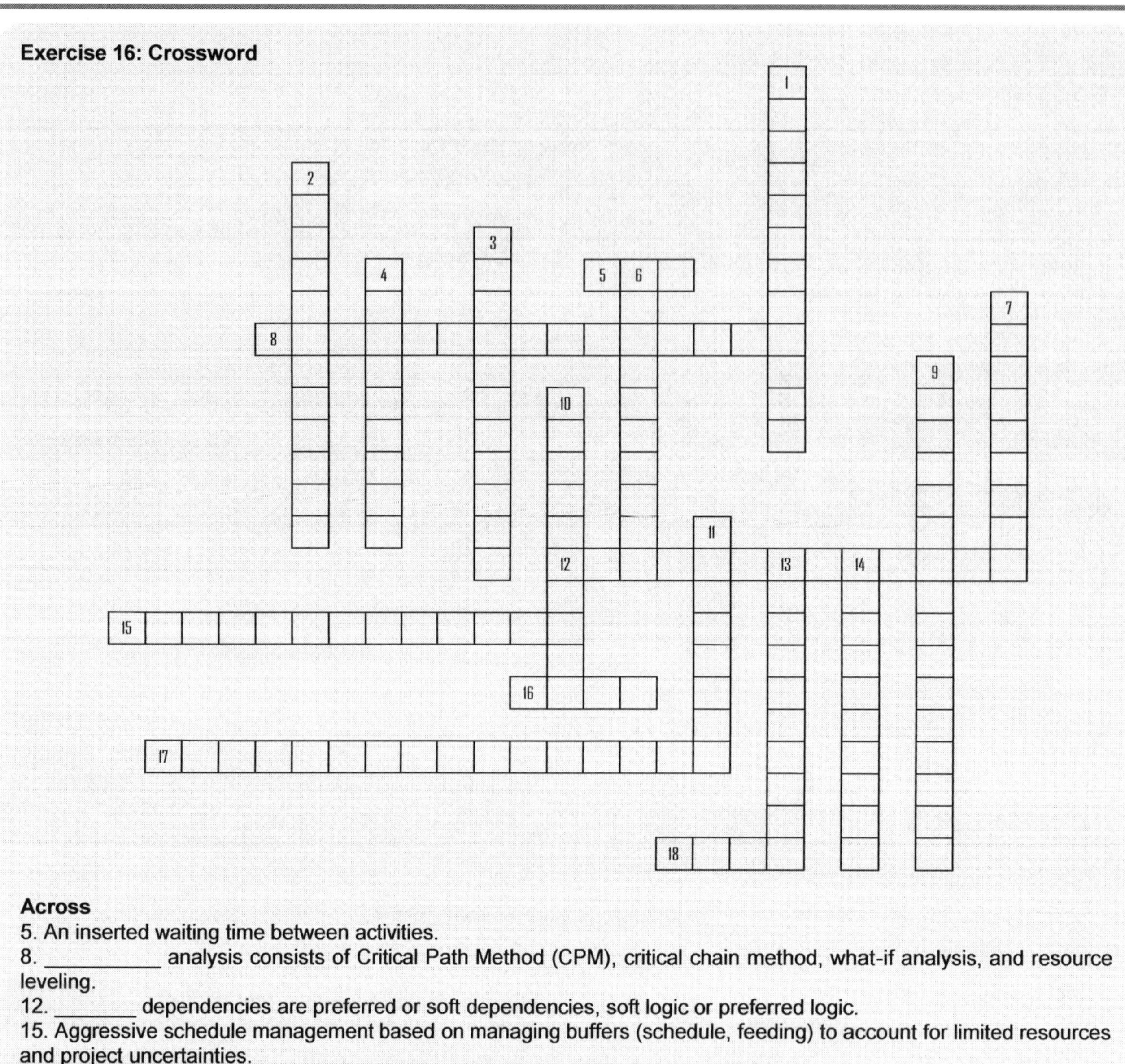

Across

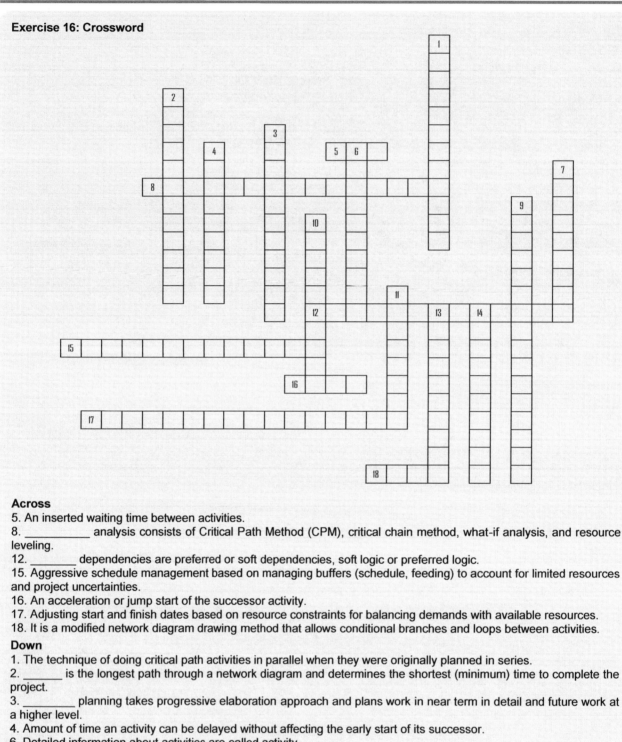

5. An inserted waiting time between activities.
8. __________ analysis consists of Critical Path Method (CPM), critical chain method, what-if analysis, and resource leveling.
12. _______ dependencies are preferred or soft dependencies, soft logic or preferred logic.
15. Aggressive schedule management based on managing buffers (schedule, feeding) to account for limited resources and project uncertainties.
16. An acceleration or jump start of the successor activity.
17. Adjusting start and finish dates based on resource constraints for balancing demands with available resources.
18. It is a modified network diagram drawing method that allows conditional branches and loops between activities.

Down

1. The technique of doing critical path activities in parallel when they were originally planned in series.
2. ______ is the longest path through a network diagram and determines the shortest (minimum) time to complete the project.
3. ________ planning takes progressive elaboration approach and plans work in near term in detail and future work at a higher level.
4. Amount of time an activity can be delayed without affecting the early start of its successor.
6. Detailed information about activities are called activity __________.
7. ________ dependencies are unavoidable dependencies, hard logic, and not in PM's control.
9. The process of decomposing the WBS work packages into schedule activities.
10. A method to create a schematic display of the sequential and logical relationships of activities is called a ___________ diagramming method.
11. The technique of adding additional resources to a project critical path activities to complete them more quickly.
13. Amount of time an activity can be delayed without effecting the project completion date.
14. The formula for three-point estimate is (_______ + 4 * most likely + pessimistic) /6.

Exercise 17: Answer the following:

1. Precedence diagramming method uses the Activity-on-Node (AON) convention where boxes/nodes are used to represent __________ and arrows show dependencies.
2. It is a modified network diagram drawing method that allows conditional branches and loops between activities.
3. This knowledge area is primarily concerned with resources and activities and developing a realistic project schedule and controlling changes to that schedule.
4. The process of decomposing the WBS work packages into schedule activities.
5. Amount of time an activity can be delayed without affecting the early start of its successor.
6. The technique of doing critical path activities in parallel when they were originally planned in series.
7. This schedule tool is useful for tracking progress and reporting to the team.
8. This planning takes the progressive elaboration approach and plans the work in the near term in detail and plans future work at a higher level.
9. Additional information such as Activity ID, WBS ID, activity name, completion date, description, predecessor and successor activities, resource assignment, constraints and assumptions, and level of effort, are called activity ___________.
10. The ___________ is the longest path through a network diagram and determines the shortest time to complete the project as well as any scheduling flexibility.
11. It is a good schedule tool for reporting to management and customers.
12. This estimate takes optimistic, pessimistic, and most likely estimates from the estimator and provides a risk-based expected duration estimate by taking a weighted average of the three estimates.
13. ________ is the maximum amount of time an activity can be delayed without delaying the entire project.
14. Pouring the foundation must precede raising the roof is an example of a ______________ dependency.
15. A ___________ is a graphical and hierarchical structure of the identified resources arranged by resource category and type.
16. The technique of adding additional resources to a project activity to complete it more quickly.
17. It is an inserted waiting time between activities.
18. An analysis where you review a lot of questions about different possibilities.
19. Design activity must be started before the coding activity is started is an example of ______________ relationship.
20. The process of monitoring the status of the project by comparing the result to the plan, updating project progress, and managing changes to the project schedule baseline.
21. Any delay in an activity on the _____________ path will cause the project to be delayed.
22. It is usually done during the early phase of the project when not much information is available; thus, it is less accurate even though it is less costly and less time consuming.
23. You are managing a project to build a multistory complex and waiting for the clearance from the city to start construction of a building is an example of an ________ dependency.
24. The formula for three-point estimate is (_______ + 4 * most likely + pessimistic) /6.
25. The seven processes of time management are ________.
26. The key outputs of time management processes are _______.
27. Name some of the tools and techniques used in the Define Activities process.
28. Name some of the tools and techniques used in the Develop Schedule process.
29. A technique of schedule analysis that considers activity durations, logical relationships, dependencies, leads, lags, assumptions, and constraints to identify the critical path with the least flexibility and the highest schedule risk so that it can be managed appropriately.
30. ________ have zero cost and zero duration.
31. When using a simulator such as Monte Carlo to simulate schedule risks we need activity durations as well as a ________ diagram.
32. A risk management technique to determine the impact of the identified risks by running simulations to identify the range of possible outcomes for a number of scenarios.

Project Time Management Summary

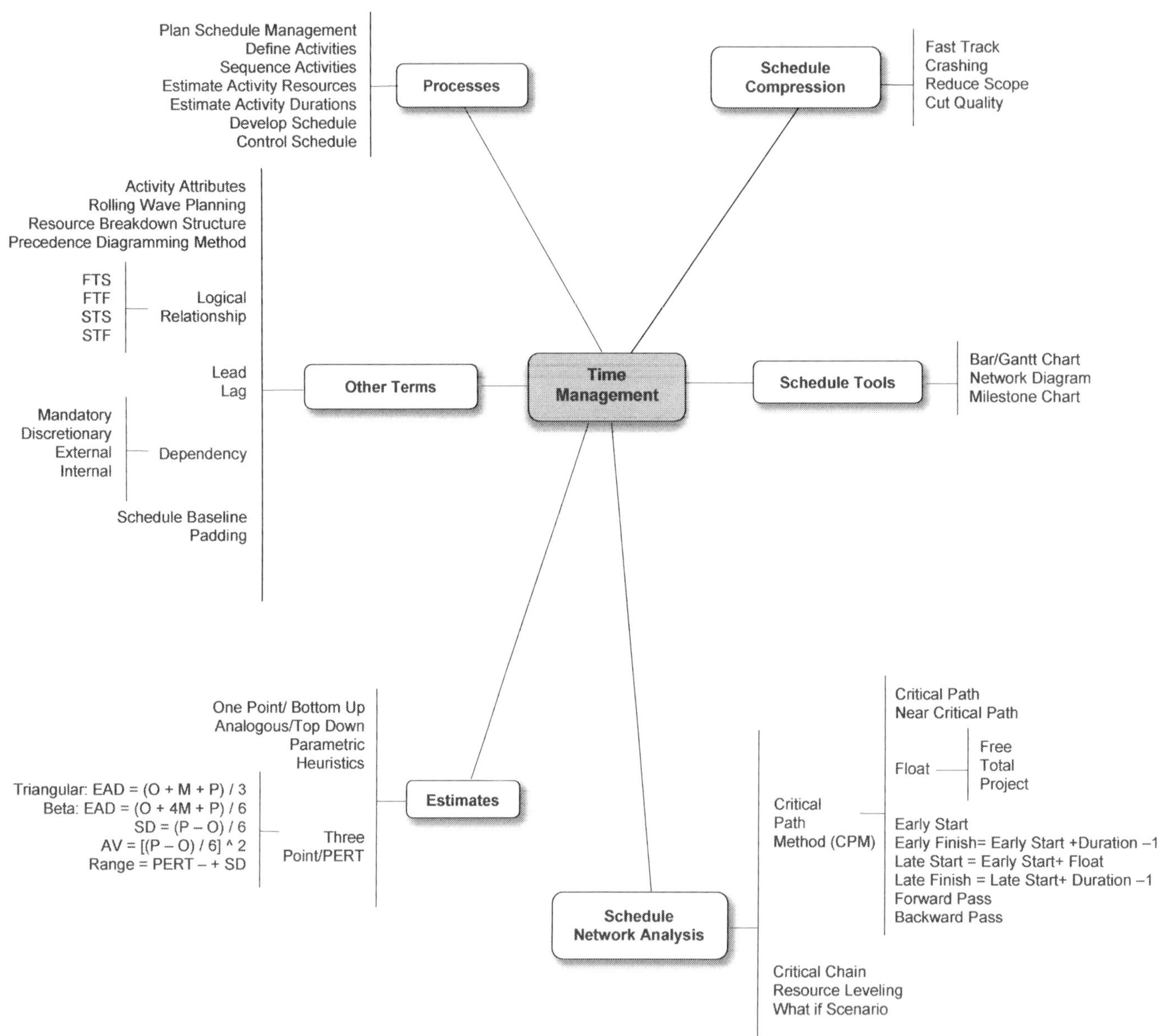

Figure 6-27: Project Time Management Summary

Project Time Management Key Terms

Activity Attributes: Detailed information about activities
Rolling Wave Planning: Taking progressive elaboration approach and planning work in near term in detail and future work at a higher level
Resource Breakdown Structure: A graphical and hierarchical structure of the identified resources arranged by resource category and type
Precedence Diagramming Method (PDM): A method to create a schematic display of the sequential and logical relationships of activities
Network Diagram: A schematic display of the sequential and logical relationships of the activities. Also called Activity-on-Node (AON)
Resource Histogram: A graphical display of the number of resources used in project throughout the project life cycle

Logical Relationship

Finish-to-Start (FS), Finish-to-Finish (FF), Start-to-Start (SS), Start-to-Finish (SF)

Dependencies

Mandatory: Unavoidable dependencies, hard logic, not in PM's control
Discretionary: Preferred or soft dependencies, soft logic or preferred logic
External: Driven by circumstances or authority outside the project
Internal: Based on the needs of project and under the control of project team

Estimates:

One-Point: Most time consuming but most accurate
Analogous: Less accurate. Mostly comes from higher management
Parametric: Uses mathematical models
Heuristic: Rule of thumb
Three-Point/PERT:
Expected Activity Duration (EAD) = Triangular: (O + M +P) / 3 or Beta: (O + 4M +P) / 6
Standard Deviation (SD) = (P – O) / 6
Activity Variance (AV) = $[(P - O)/6]^2$
Activity Range (AR) = EAD – + SD

Float

Free Float: Amount of time an activity can be delayed without affecting the early start of its successor
Total Float: Amount of time an activity can be delayed without effecting the project completion date

Other Terms

Lead: An acceleration or jump start of the successor activity
Lag: An inserted waiting time between activities

Schedule Baseline: Final schedule consists of original schedule plus all approved changes
Padding: Adding extras to estimates
Schedule Network Analysis: Critical Path Method (CPM), critical chain method, what-if analysis, and resource leveling
Critical Path Method (CPM): A schedule analysis to calculate critical path, scheduling flexibility, and overall schedule
Critical Path: The longest path through a network diagram and determines the shortest (minimum) time to complete the project; the path of highest risk

Early Start: The soonest a task can begin, WW01
Early Finish: Early Start + Duration – 1
Late Start: Early Start + Float/Buffer
Late Finish: Late Start + Duration – 1

Buffer/Float/Slack = Late Finish – Early Finish or Late Start – Early Start or
Critical path duration – the longest path of the activity we are calculating the buffer for
Critical Chain: Aggressive schedule management based on managing buffers (schedule, feeding) to account for limited resources and project uncertainties
Resource Leveling: Adjusting start and finish dates based on resource constraints for balancing demands with available resources
What-if Scenario Analysis: Usually uses Monte Carlo simulation to simulate the outcome of a project – computes large number of scenarios related to schedule

Schedule Compressions

Fast-Tracking: Performing critical path activities in parallel
Crashing: Adding additional resources to the critical path activities

Project Time Management Exercise Answers

Exercise 1:

Answer: Refer to the "Figure 3-16: Process Groups Key Inputs and Outputs" and you will conclude that we need the following items before we can develop a project schedule.

- Historical records of previous, similar projects
- Project scope statement: An understanding of the work required, including assumptions, milestones, and constraints
- Work Breakdown Structure (WBS): Hierarchical decomposition of the work required
- Components of a schedule:
  - Activity list and attributes
  - Network diagram: The order of how the work will be done
  - Resource requirements
  - Duration estimates
  - Resource calendar: An understanding of the availability of resources
  - Company calendar: An understanding of working and nonworking days
  - A list of pre-assigned team members
  - A list of potential schedule risk items
  - Start date and end date of all activities

Exercise 2:

Process Groups				
Initiating	**Planning**	**Executing**	**Monitoring & Controlling**	**Closing**
	– Plan Schedule Management – Define Activities – Sequence Activities – Estimate Activity Resources – Estimate Activity Durations – Develop Schedule		– Control Schedule	

Exercise 3:

- Review schedule management plan.
- Review the scope baseline, which contains the project scope statement, WBS, and WBS dictionary as well as the activity list, activity attributes, and activity cost estimates.
- Review organization resource calendars to identify resource availability and also to evaluate resources' experience and skill sets.
- Review the risk register.
- Estimate the resources (such as materials, equipment, manpower, and supplies) required to perform activities in the project.
- Consult with experts on the type, quantity, and required skillsets for the human resources on the project.
- Refer to similar past projects to learn about the detail of the resources used in those projects.
- Identify alternative approaches to better utilize the resources in the project.
- Understand organizational policies and guidelines on resource use.

Exercise 4: Since Activity B is on the critical path, the buffer/float of Activity B is zero.
Now D is only on one path→Start, D, E, F, End, and the duration of this path is nine weeks. So D has a buffer/float of 12 – 9 = 3 weeks. We can delay Activity D by three weeks and still our project will not be delayed.

Exercise 5: In order to find out the early start and early finish for Activity F, we need to perform a forward pass. Note that F is depending on both Activities E and H. The earliest we can finish Activity E is 7, but we cannot start working on the activity right away on ww8 since we are still waiting for Activity H to be completed. Now the earliest that Activity H can be completed is ww9; thus, the earliest we can start Activity F will be ww10. So in case of forward pass, we will take the larger value to calculate early start for the successor activity. Now that we know F has a buffer/float of one week, we can easily calculate the Early Finish, which is (10 + 2) – 1 = 11.
Late Start is 10 + 1 = 11, and Late Finish is (11 + 2) – 1 = 12.

Exercise 6: We know Buffer/Float = Late Start – Early Start or Late Finish – Early Finish, so the buffer for this activity will be 17 – 9 = 8 or 21 – 13 = 8.

Exercise 7:

1. Reducing scope and cutting quality
2. Reducing scope and cutting quality
3. Fast-tracking and crashing
4. Crashing
5. Fast-tracking and crashing
6. Reducing scope and cutting quality
7. Fast-tracking
8. Cutting quality

Exercise 8:

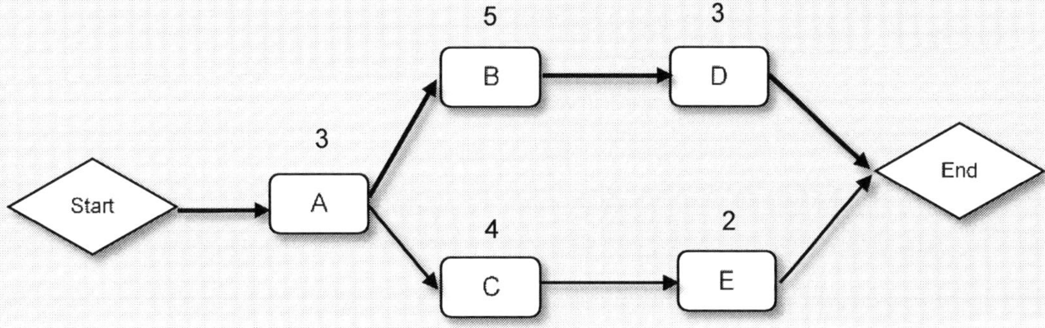

1. Create the network diagram and identify all paths.
   Start, A, B, D, End = 11 days, critical path
   Start, A, C, E, End = 9 days
2. To crash the schedule, start crashing the days from the critical path. Task A can be crashed one day at an additional cost of $200. Task B can be crashed two days for a total cost of $200. Task D is also on the critical path and can be crashed one day at a cost of $150. This reduces the critical path to seven days and adds a total of ($200 + $200 + $150) = $550 to the project cost.
3. Recalculate the new critical path Start, A, C, E, End, which is eight days since we already crashed one day from Activity A. Since crashing E is a cheaper option, we will crash E one day at a cost of $250. This reduces the total project duration to seven days, but the project now has two critical paths. The total cost to crash the project to seven days is ($550 + $250) = $800, which is added to the initial project cost.

Exercise 9:

1. True
2. False
3. True
4. True
5. False
6. True
7. True
8. True
9. False
10. True
11. False
12. True
13. True

Exercise 10:

1. Milestone chart
2. Network diagram
3. Bar chart/ Gantt chart

Exercise 11:

- Meet and negotiate with the resource managers for the required resources in the project.
- Understand stakeholders' expectations, priorities, and acceptance criteria.
- Look for alternative and better approaches to complete project activities.
- Gain formal approval of the functional and resource managers on resource allocation in the project.
- Collect duration estimates for activities from the team members and negotiate and ask for justification if appropriate.
- Develop a realistic project schedule and apply leads and lags.
- Apply all kinds of schedule compression techniques such as fast-tracking, crashing, and reestimating to optimize the schedule.
- Gain approval from the team members on the final schedule.
- Gain approval from the stakeholders and management on the final schedule.

Exercise 12:

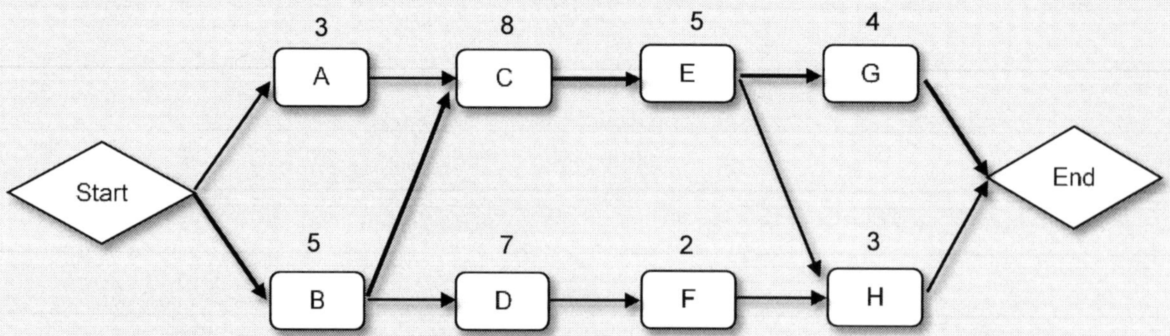

1. We have the following five paths in the network diagram:
Start, A, C, E, G, End = 20 wks
Start, A, C, E, H, End = 19 wks
Start, B, D, F, H, End = 17 wks
Start, B, C, E, G, End = 22 wks, critical path
Start, B, C, E, H, End = 21 wks

2. Activity H is on the following three paths:
Start, A, C, E, H, End = 19 wks
Start, B, D, F, H, End = 17 wks
Start, B, C, E, H, End = 21 wks
So the longest path for Activity H is twenty-one weeks. Activity H has a float/buffer of (22 – 21) = 1 wk.

3. Activity A is on the following two paths:
   Start, A, C, E, G, End = 20 wks
   Start, A, C, E, H, End = 19 wks
   So the longest path is twenty weeks. Activity A has a float/buffer of (22 – 20) = 2 wks.
4. Since Activity B is on the critical path it has zero float.
5. Activity D is only on one path—Start, B, D, F, H, End = 17 wks. So it has a float of (22 – 17) = 5 wks.
6. Activity F is also on one path—Start, B, D, F, H, End = 17 wks. So it also has a float of (22 – 17) = 5 wks.
7. Since Activity D is not on the critical path removing it will not have any schedule impact on the project.
8. To calculate early start, early finish, late start, and late finish for Activities A, B, C, D, E, and F to calculate them for Activity H:

   We know Early Start is the soonest we can start an activity:
   Early Finish = Early Start + Duration – 1
   Late Start = Early Start + Float
   Late Finish = Late Start + Duration – 1
   We also now know that float for Activity A= 2 wks, Activity B = 0 wks, Activity C= 0 wks, Activity D = 5 wks, Activity E = 0 wks, Activity F = 5 wks, and Activity H = 1 wk.

   For Activity A: Early Start = 1, Early Finish = (1 + 3) – 1 = 3, Late Start = 1 + 2 = 3, and Late Finish = (3 + 3) – 1 = 5.

   For Activity B: Early Start = 1, Early Finish = (1 + 5) – 1 = 5, Late Start = 1 + 0 = 1, and Late Finish = (1 + 5) – 1 = 5. Note that Activity B has no dependency on any other activity.

   For Activity C: Early Start = 6, Early Finish = (6 + 8) – 1 = 13, Late Start = 6 + 0 = 6, and Late Finish = (6 + 8) – 1 = 13. Note that Activity C is depending on both Activities A and B; thus, even though we are completing Activity A on ww3, we cannot start working on Activity C until activity is completed on ww5. Also Activity C has a float of zero weeks.

   For Activity D: Early Start = 6, Early Finish = (6 + 7) – 1 = 12, Late Start = 6 + 5 = 11, and Late Finish = (11 + 7) – 1 = 17. Note that Activity D is depending on Activity B and has a float of five weeks.

   For Activity E: Early Start = 14, Early Finish = (14 + 5) – 1 = 18, Late Start = 14 + 0 = 14, and Late Finish = (14 + 5) – 1 = 18. Note that Activity E is depending on Activity C and has a float of zero weeks.

For Activity F: Early Start = 13, Early Finish = (13 + 2) – 1 = 14, Late Start = 13 + 5 = 18, and Late Finish = (18 + 2) – 1 = 19. Note that Activity F is depending on Activity D and has a float of five weeks.

For Activity H: Early Start = 19, Early Finish = (19 + 3) – 1 = 21, Late Start = 19 + 1 = 20, and Late Finish = (20 + 3) – 1 = 22. Note that Activity H is depending on Activity E, and Activity F and has a float of one week. We cannot start working on Activity H right after completing activity on ww14 since the earliest we can complete Activity E is ww18.

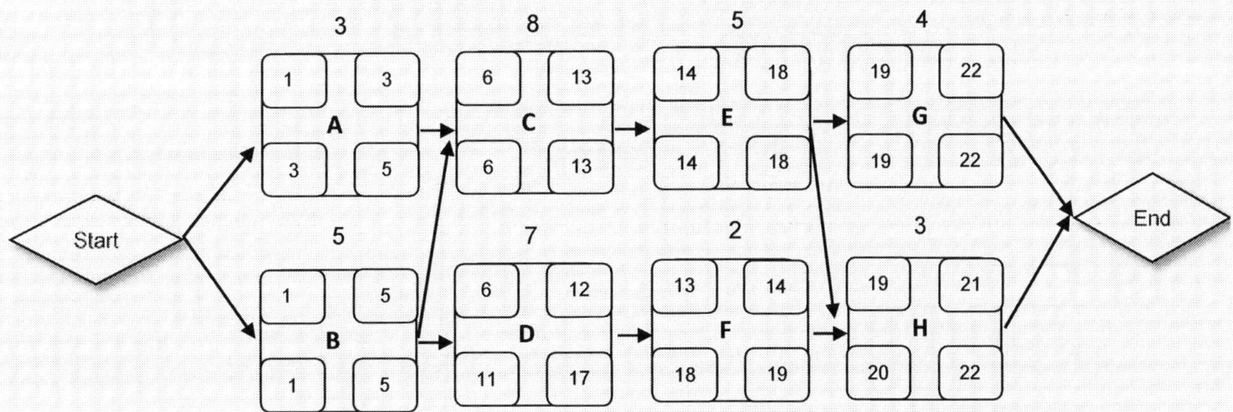

9. The early start of Activity H is ww19; therefore, we must finish Activity E by ww18 or the early start of Activity H will be delayed. Since we cannot delay Activity E, the free float of Activity E is zero.

10. The early finish of Activity F is ww14; therefore, we can delay Activity F till ww18, and still the early start of Activity H on ww19 will not be impacted. Thus, Activity F has a free float of (18 – 14) = 4 weeks.

Exercise 13:

1. True
2. True
3. False
4. True
5. True
6. False
7. True
8. False
9. False
10. False

Exercise 14:

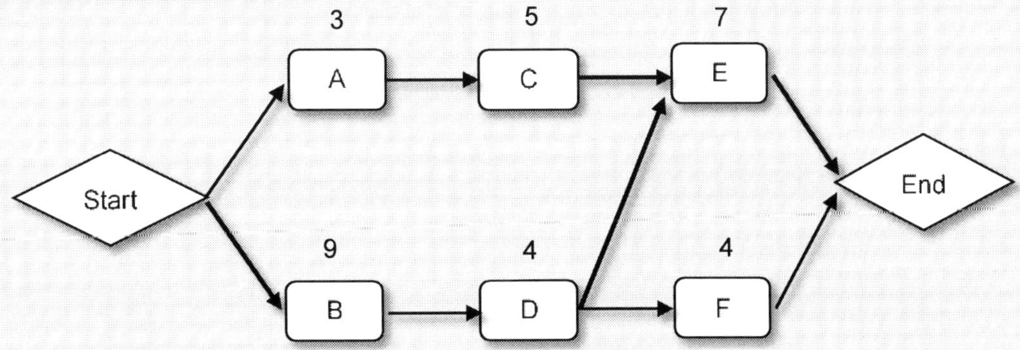

We have three paths in the network diagram:
Start, A, C, E, End = 15 wks
Start, B, D, F, End = 17 wks
Start, B, D, E, End = 20 wks

1. The duration of the critical path is twenty weeks.
2. Activity C is only on one path; thus, the longest path of Activity C is Start, A, C, E, End, which is fifteen weeks. Thus, the float/buffer for Activity C is (20 – 15 = 5) five weeks.
3. Activity E is on the critical path, so the float/buffer for Activity E is zero.
4. Activity F is on one path—Start, B, D, F, End = 17 wks. So the float/buffer for Activity F is (20 – 17 = 3) three weeks.
5. In order to calculate the free float of Activity C, we need to know the early start of Activity E.
   Since Activity E is depending on both Activities C and D, Activity C is depending on Activity A, and Activity D is depending on Activity B, we need to find out the early start and early finish for all of these activities.

For Activity A: Early Start = ww1, Early Finish = (1 + 3) – 1 = ww3
For Activity C: Early Start = ww4, Early Finish = (4 + 5) – 1 = ww8
For Activity B: Early Start = ww1, Early Finish = (1 + 9) – 1 = ww9
For Activity D: Early Start = ww10, Early Finish = (10 + 4) – 1 = ww13
For Activity E: Early Start = ww14, Early Finish = (14 + 7) – 1 = ww20 as we need to wait for both Activity C and Activity D to be completed to start working on Activity E.

Now in order not to delay the early start ww14 of Activity E, we need to complete Activity C by ww13. We know Activity C will be completed on ww8; thus, we can delay Activity C by (13 – 8) = 5 wks and still start Activity E on ww14. So Activity C has a free float of five weeks.

6. Activity F is depending only on Activity D. We know for Activity D
Early Start = ww10, Early Finish = (10 + 4) – 1 = ww13, so for Activity F
Early Start = ww14, Early Finish = (14 + 4) – 1 = ww17.
We found out earlier that float/buffer for Activity F is three weeks. So for Activity F
Late Start = 14 + 3 = ww17, Late Finish = (17 + 4) – 1 = ww20.

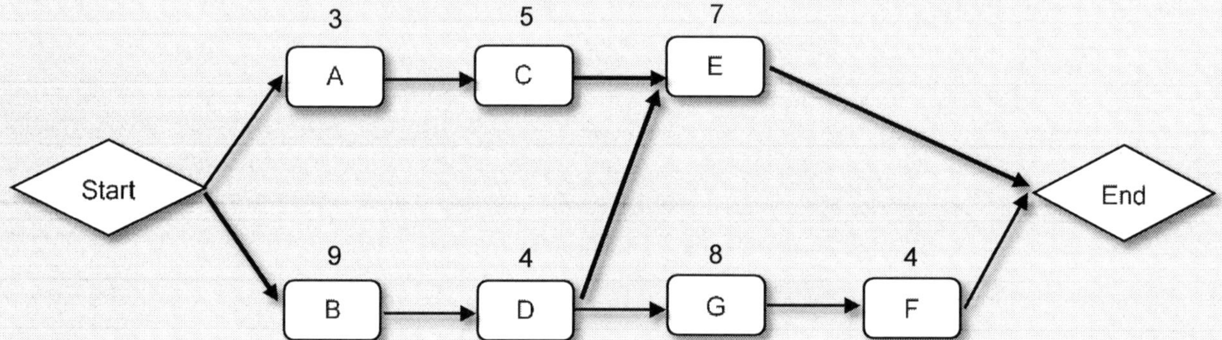

After adding the new Activity G, we have a new Critical Path – Start, B, D, G, F, End = 25 wks. The old duration of the project was twenty weeks; thus, an additional (25 – 20 = 5) five weeks will be added to the project to complete the new Activity G.

Exercise 15: The following activities are involved in controlling a project schedule:
- Review current project performance information.
- Re-estimate the entire remaining part of the project to confirm the end date, budget, and other project objectives are still achievable.
- Review all sorts of reports such as performance, trend, status, progress, earned value, etc.
- Consider optimizing resources.
- Identify the need for changes, including corrective and preventive actions.
- Strictly follow the change control process.
- Perform activities in parallel when they were originally planned in sequential order if needed.
- Add additional resources to the critical path activities if needed.
- Modify metrics to properly manage the project if needed.
- Make necessary adjustment to future parts of the project to deal with unavoidable delays and other consequences.
- Conduct a variance analysis by comparing the actual work completed to the planned work.
- Identify and manage changes as they arise.

Exercise 16:

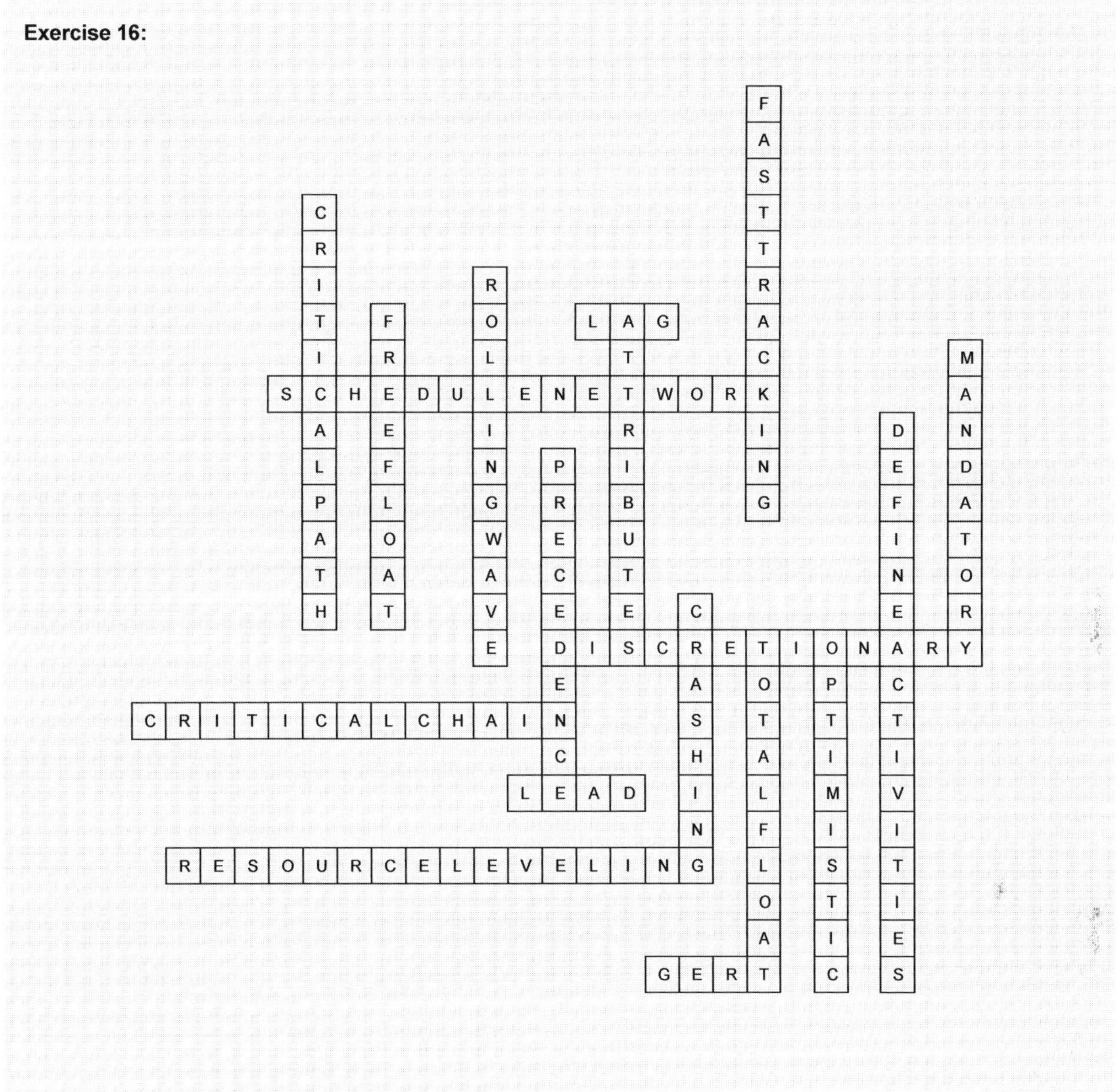
FASTTRACKING
CRITICALPATH
ROLLINGWAVE
LAG
ATTRIBUTE
FREEFLOAT
MANDATORY
SCHEDULENETWORK
DEFINEACTIVITIES
PRECEDENCE
DISCRETIONARY
CRASHING
TOTALFLOAT
OPTIMISTIC
CRITICALCHAIN
LEAD
RESOURCELEVELING
GERT

Exercise 17:

1. Activities
2. GERT
3. Time management
4. Define Activities
5. Free float
6. Fast-tracking
7. Bar chart/Gantt chart
8. Rolling wave planning
9. Attributes
10. Critical path
11. Milestone chart
12. Three-point estimate
13. Float
14. Mandatory
15. Resource Breakdown Structure (RBS)
16. Crashing
17. Lag
18. What-if analysis
19. Start-to-start
20. Control Schedule
21. Critical
22. Analogous estimate
23. External
24. Optimistic
25. Plan Schedule Management, Define Activities, Sequence Activities, Estimate Activity Resources, Estimate Activity Durations, Develop Schedule, and Control Schedule
26. Plan Schedule Management – Schedule Management Plan
    Define Activities – Activity List, Activity Attributes, Milestone List
    Sequence Activities – Project Schedule Network Diagram
    Estimate Activity Resources – Activity Resource Requirements, Resource Breakdown Structure
    Estimate Activity Durations – Activity Duration Estimates
    Develop Schedule – Schedule Baseline, Project Schedule
    Control Schedule – Change Request, Schedule Forecasts
27. Decomposition, rolling wave planning, expert judgment
28. Schedule network analysis, critical path method, critical chain method, resource optimization techniques, modeling techniques, lead and lags, schedule compression, scheduling tools
29. Critical Path Method (CPM)
30. Milestones
31. Network
32. Monte Carlo analysis

Project Time Management Exam Tips

- Be able to name all seven processes of project time management and their key activities.
- Be able to differentiate among all different estimating techniques.
- Be able to calculate PERT duration estimates.
- Be able to name the schedule compression techniques.
- Be able to calculate total float, free float, ES, EF, LS, and LF.
- Be able to answer questions where you will need to analyze a specific situation and determine what you should do next.
- Be familiar with the concepts and terms in the project time management summary table, Figure 6-27: Project Time Management Summary.

Project Time Management Questions

1. One of your team members working on the project informed you that a work package will most likely require ten weeks to complete. In the best case scenario, if everything goes well and there are no surprises, it will take eight weeks. Since he is involved in more than two projects and has several pending deliverables, this specific work package may take eighteen weeks to complete. Based on this information, what is the range of the work package?

   A. Eleven weeks to twelve weeks
   B. Eight weeks to ten weeks
   C. 9.34 weeks to 12.66 weeks
   D. Ten weeks to eighteen weeks

2. Your project sponsor is extremely disappointed with the project as it is over budget by $15,000 and also behind schedule by several weeks. The sponsor has asked you to take care of the situation immediately and do whatever it takes. While exploring different options to shorten the project duration, you decide to put some of the noncritical activities on hold so that some of the resources working on these activities can be assigned to the activities with the most schedule risk. You also asked for a couple of additional external resources to be added to the project. The sponsor agrees to pay the additional cost since time is now a critical factor. This is an example of which of the following?

   A. Crashing
   B. Fast-tracking
   C. Critical chain method
   D. Resource leveling

3. A project manager is in the Sequence Activities process of identifying and documenting relationships among defined activities and arranging them in the order they must be performed. While in this process, the project manager decided to utilize a software tool to create a Precedence Diagramming Method (PDM) network diagram. This network diagram creates a schematic display of the sequential and logical relationships, dependencies, and the order in which activities in a project must be performed. The project manager also added the duration of each activity in the network diagram to calculate the critical path. Which one of the following is FALSE about the critical path?

   A. It is the longest duration path through a network diagram.
   B. It determines the shortest time to complete the project.
   C. The activities on the critical path represent the highest schedule risk in the project.
   D. The activities on the critical path represent critical functionality.

4. While reviewing your project resource histogram, you notice several peaks and valleys, as resources are not evenly distributed in your project. In order to evenly utilize resources as much as possible, you decide to move some activities from the week when you are using a lot of resources to the week when you are hardly using any. Which technique are you using in this case?

   A. Resource leveling
   B. Overtime
   C. Schedule compression
   D. Schedule control

5. Which one of the following takes the progressive elaboration approach and plans the work in the near term in detail and future work in a higher level?

   A. Scope definition
   B. Rolling wave planning
   C. Decomposition
   D. SWOT analysis

6. Your team just finished the design activities for a software development project. You have ordered a server and a couple of PCs to set up the development environment and are waiting for the vendor to deliver to you so that the team can start the development work. The vendor informs you that it will take twelve days for the equipment delivery, set up, and configuration. The twelve days waiting time can be defined as:

A. Mandatory dependency
B. Lag
C. Lead
D. Internal dependency

7. Which one of the following estimating techniques uses mathematical models based on historical records from other projects and can produce higher levels of accuracy?

A. One point estimating
B. Analogous estimating
C. Parametric estimating
D. Three-points estimating

8. One of your team members is always late completing his deliverables. In order to help him out with proper planning for his activities, you like to explore different options with him. You asked the team member to send you information about the total float and free float for all of his activities if there is any. How does free float differ from total float?

A. Total float and free float are the same thing.
B. Free float affects only the early start of the successor activities.
C. Total float is the accumulated amount of free float.
D. Subtracting the total float from the critical path duration will give the free float.

9. You are managing a project that has the following activities:

- Activity A can start immediately and has an estimated duration of eight weeks.
- Activity B can also start immediately and has an estimated duration of seven weeks.
- Activity C can start after Activity A is completed and has an estimated duration of one week.
- Activity D can start after Activity B is completed and has an estimated duration of six weeks.
- Activity E can start after both Activities C and D are completed and has an estimated duration of seven weeks.
- Activity F can start after Activity D is completed and has an estimated duration of two weeks.

Your sponsor is very disappointed that the project is taking longer than he expected and asked you to shorten the project duration by at least two weeks. You decided to shorten Activity A first as it is not a very critical activity in the project and has the longest duration. What will be the impact of your decision?

A. It will not shorten the duration of the project.
B. It will shorten the duration of the project.
C. It will create a new critical path.
D. The project duration will be eighteen weeks now.

10. A project manager is managing a web-based application project to automate the accounting processes of his organization. The project has an estimated budget of $120,000 and a duration of nine months. While reviewing the project, the project manager notices that activities were scheduled in sequential order but coding work was initiated twelve days earlier than planned. What type of relationship represents the start of the coding work to the completion of the design work?

A. Finish-to-start relationship with a twelve-day lag
B. Finish-to-start relationship with a twelve-day lead
C. Start-to-finish with a twelve-day lag
D. Start-to-finish with a twelve-day lead

11. While working with your team members on activity sequencing, a team member identifies that even though a series of activities are planned to be completed in a specific sequence, they can be performed in parallel. What type of activity sequencing method may be utilized in this situation?

A. Critical path
B. Resource leveling method
C. Monte Carlo simulation
D. Precedence Diagramming Method (PDM)

12. You are the project manager overseeing the implementation of a new computer infrastructure at the local hospital. Your sponsor has informed you that all the existing applications must work in the new infrastructure, and the project should be completed in three months. These are examples of:

A. A lag
B. A lead
C. An estimation
D. A constraint

13. One of your team members is always late completing his deliverables. You decided to keep an eye on this team member's activities to avoid any delay in the project. While reviewing one of the activities of this team member, you found out that the activity has an early start of day 5, an early finish of day 12, a late start of day 15, and a late finish of day 22. The team member tells you that he needs an additional four days to complete the activity due to various reasons he can think of. Which one of the following statements is TRUE?
   A. This activity will delay the project.
   B. This activity will most probably not delay the project.
   C. The activity has a lag.
   D. The successor activity will be delayed.

14. Which one of the following analysis methods usually uses Monte Carlo simulation to simulate the outcome of a project by making use of three-point estimates (Optimistic, Pessimistic, Most Likely) for each activity, a huge number of simulated scheduling possibilities, or a few selected scenarios that are most likely, and the network diagram?
   A. Precedence Diagramming Method (PDM)
   B. What-if scenario analysis
   C. Critical chain method
   D. Resource leveling

15. A project manager managing a recruitment automation application project just completed developing the schedule and requested stakeholders and the client for their approval. The sponsor has expressed her frustration about the unexpected long duration of the project and has demanded the schedule be compressed as much as possible. While exploring different options, you find out that you cannot really change the network diagram due to various constraints, but the sponsor has agreed to pay for additional personnel resources if needed. What will be your BEST option in this situation?
   A. Apply the critical chain method
   B. Fast-track the project and also apply the resource leveling method
   C. Crash the project
   D. Crash and fast-track the project

16. Your project sponsor is extremely disappointed with the project as it is over budget by $20,000 and also behind schedule by several weeks. The sponsor has asked you to take care of the situation immediately. While exploring different options to shorten the project duration, you decide, with management's approval, to perform several activities in parallel rather than in sequential order as originally planned. You know your option will possibly result in rework, increase risks, and require more communication, but you decide to go for it any way. This is an example of which of the following?
   A. Critical chain method
   B. Crashing
   C. Resource leveling
   D. Fast-tracking

17. You have recently been assigned as a program manager to implement an ERP solution in your organization. Initially, the team will only work on five key modules in the first phase of the project. The second phase of the project has not been approved yet. You have estimated that three of the modules will take ten days each, and the remaining two will be completed in fifteen days each. It is not possible to work on these modules in parallel. What would be the approximate duration for the first phase of your project?
   A. Fifty-five to sixty-five days
   B. Fifty days
   C. Ten days
   D. Ninety days

18. You are in the Control Schedule process of monitoring the status of the project by comparing the result to the plan, updating project progress, and managing changes to the project schedule baseline. You are mainly focused on the current status and changes to the project schedule, influential factors that create schedule changes, and management of actual changes as they occur. Which of the following is NOT a tool or technique in this time management process?
   A. Schedule compression
   B. Scheduling tools
   C. Resource optimization techniques
   D. Schedule forecasts

19. Steve has just been assigned as a project manager for a newly approved software development project. The sponsor is interested in knowing a high-level estimation on the total duration of the project and asks Steve to send him the information by the end of the day. What kind of estimate should Steve use in this kind of situation?
   A. An analogous estimate
   B. A heuristic estimate
   C. A three-point estimate
   D. A bottom-up estimate

20. You are in the Estimate Activity Durations process to estimate durations for the activities of the project. These estimates usually originated from project team members most familiar with the activity and then progressively elaborated. Which one of the following is TRUE about this process?

A. This process must be performed after the Develop Schedule process.
B. Padding is a common practice and the project manager should not be too worried about it.
C. The activity duration estimates are outputs in this process.
D. It is not important that all estimates in this process should use a common work unit/period.

21. You just completed developing the schedule for your project and got the approval from stakeholders and the sponsor. One of the team members assigned to work on a critical component informs you that she needs additional time to complete her activities as several relevant pieces were missed during planning. Her updated estimate would have no impact on the critical path; thus, the project duration would be the same. The best approach the project manager may take in this situation will be:

A. Find a replacement for the resource who can complete the task within the allocated time.
B. Inform the resource that it is too late for any kind of change in the project schedule.
C. Inform her that it is OK as you have sufficient schedule reserve to handle this kind of situation.
D. Update the project schedule and other relevant plans to reflect the new estimate.

22. You are overseeing a data center project for one of your clients. The team members have finished creating the Work Breakdown Structure (WBS) and work breakdown structure dictionary. The team members also submitted their activity duration estimates to you. What should you focus on NEXT?

A. Sequence the activities using the precedence diagramming method.
B. Create the activity list.
C. Determine high-level project assumptions and constraints.
D. Develop the project schedule.

23. You are overseeing a data center project for one of your clients. The team members have finished creating the Work Breakdown Structure (WBS) and work breakdown structure dictionary. The team members also completed activity sequencing and submitted their activity duration estimates to you. Recently, you developed the project schedule. What should you focus on NEXT?

A. Finalize the schedule
B. Control the schedule
C. Compress the schedule
D. Gain approval

24. Your IT project is progressing well and is on schedule when a vendor sends you an e-mail stating that the equipment delivery will be delayed by a week due to severe snow storm on the East Coast. Which of the documents would best capture the impact of the delay on the project schedule?

A. Risk register
B. Issue log
C. Network diagram
D. Work breakdown structure

25. Your IT project has ten team members, and recently you have hired three more database developers. You are using a time-phased graphical display of activity start dates, end dates, and durations for tracking progress and reporting to the team. Which chart are you using?

A. Milestone chart
B. Work breakdown structure
C. Network diagram
D. Gantt chart

26. You are overseeing a project to implement a web-based traffic monitoring system. You have requested three programmers, three database developers, and two testers; senior management only approved five team members for your project. Which one of the following may you use to produce a resource-limited schedule by letting the schedule slip and cost increase in order to deal with a limited amount of resources, resource availability, and other resource constraints?

A. Resource leveling
B. Fast-tracking
C. Crashing
D. Critical path method

27. Steve is the project manager for a construction project to convert an old nursing home into a new multistory office complex. The architectural design and site surveys are completed, and Steve is now waiting for the clearance and permit from the city to start the construction. This is an example of which kind of dependency?
   A. Mandatory dependency
   B. Internal dependency
   C. External dependency
   D. Discretionary dependency

28. Your team has been working with the WBS for a while and has completed the decomposition of the work packages. After a week, the team finalized the estimates of all activities and completed the network diagram. Which of the following activities will be the next to concentrate on for the project manager?
   A. Develop a preliminary schedule and get the approval from the team members
   B. Finalize the project scope statement
   C. Use the precedence diagramming method for sequencing the activities
   D. Develop the risk management plan and add it to the total project management plan document

29. Which of the following is FALSE about analogous estimating?
   A. It measures the project parameters such as budget, duration, size, complexity, and duration based on the parameters of a previous similar project and historical information.
   B. It is usually done during the early phase of the project when not much information is available.
   C. It uses a bottom-up approach.
   D. It usually is the overall project estimate given to the project manager from management or the sponsor.

30. You recently took over a project from another project manager. While reviewing the network diagram, you find that there are four critical paths and three near-critical paths. What can you conclude about the project?
   A. The project will likely be completed on time and within budget.
   B. The project is at high risk.
   C. The project will require more people and additional budget.
   D. The project should be terminated.

Project Time Management Answers

1. C: PERT allows the estimator to include three estimates: optimistic, pessimistic, and most likely, given by the equation:
Expected Activity Duration (EAD) – Beta distribution = $\frac{(O + 4M + P)}{6}$
= (8 + 4*10 + 18) / 6 = 11 weeks
STD Dev = (P – O) / 6 = (18 – 8) / 6 = 1.66
Range = EAD – / + Std Dev
Thus, the range is 11 – / + 1.66 = 9.34 to 12.66

2. A: The best option here is to add additional resources to the project activities on the critical path to complete them quickly. Fast-tracking is the technique of doing critical path activities in parallel when they were originally planned in series. Resource leveling is used to produce a resource-limited schedule by letting the schedule slip and cost increase in order to deal with a limited amount of resources, resource availability, and other resource constraints. The critical chain method is another way to develop an approved, realistic, and resource-limited formal schedule. It provides a way to view and manage uncertainty when building the project schedule.

3. D: The activities on the critical path do not necessarily represent the critical functionalities in the project. The critical path is the longest duration path in the network diagram, and this duration is the shortest time needed to complete the project. The activities on the critical path have no buffer, and any delay in the critical path activities will delay the project; thus, the critical path activities represent the highest schedule risk.

4. A: Resource leveling is used to produce a resource-limited schedule by letting the schedule slip and cost increase in order to deal with a limited amount of resources, resource availability, and other resource constraints. It can be used when shared or critically required resources are only available at certain times, are in limited quantities, or when resources have been over allocated. We may have several peaks and valleys in our resource histogram. In order to level the resources, evenly utilize them as much as possible, or to keep resource usage at a constant level, we can move some of our activities from the week when we are using a lot of resources to the week when we are hardly using any.

5. B: The rolling wave planning takes the progressive elaboration approach and plans the work in the near term in detail and future work in a higher level. During the early strategic planning phase, work packages may be decomposed into less-defined milestone levels since all details are not available, and later they are decomposed into detailed activities. This kind of planning is usually used in IT and research projects but is very unlikely in construction projects where any unknowns are extremely expensive and destructive.

6. B: A lag is an inserted waiting time between activities.

7. C: This estimate uses mathematical models based on historical records from other projects. It utilizes the statistical relationship that exists between a series of historical data and a particular delineated list of other variables. Depending upon the quality of the underlying data, this estimate can produce higher levels of accuracy and can be used in conjunction with other estimates to provide estimates for the entire project or for specific segments of the project.
Measures such as time per line of code, time per installation, and time per linear meter are considered in this type of estimate.

8. B: Total float is the amount of time an activity can be delayed without affecting the project completion date. Free float is the amount of time an activity can be delayed without affecting the early start of its successor.

9. A: Shortening Activity A will have no impact on the project duration as it is not on the critical path.
We have three paths here:
Start, A, C, E, End = 16 wks
Start, B, D, F, End = 15 wks
Start, B, D, E, End = 20 wks

We should not always look for the longest duration activity to cut as it will not shorten the duration of the project if the activity is not on the critical path. Shortening Activity A will not shorten the project duration as it is not on the critical path, and neither will a new critical path be created. To shorten the project duration, we should always try to shorten the duration of the activities on the critical path.
Here the critical path is Start, B, D, E, End, which has a duration of twenty weeks. We can explore the option to shorten the duration of Activities B, D or E, but it is better to go for the first option and shorten the duration of Activity B.

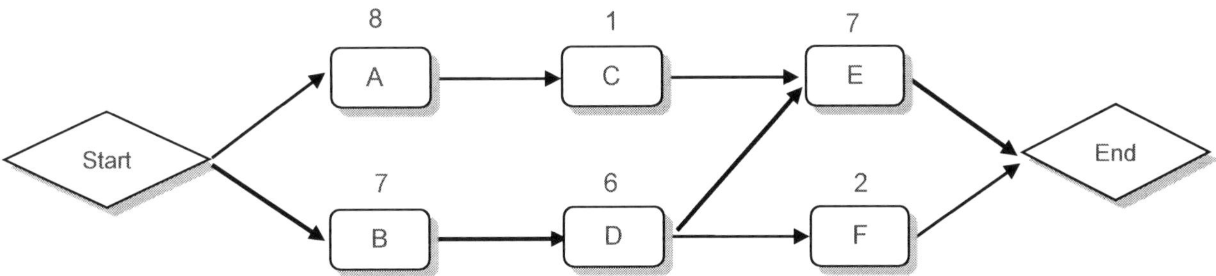

10. B: A lead is an acceleration of the successor activity, or in other words, a successor activity getting a jump start. A lead may be added to start an activity before the predecessor activity is completed. There is a finish-to-start relationship between the design and coding, meaning that design work should be completed prior to starting coding. But in this case, coding work had a jump start as it was initiated twelve days before the design was completed. This can be shown as a finish-to-start relationship with twelve days lead.

11. D: The precedence diagramming method creates a schematic display of the sequential and logical relationships of the project activities. Usually, it shows dependencies and the order in which activities in a project must be performed. Critical path is not a diagramming method.

12. D: These are examples of a constraint or limitation that limits options and eliminates alternatives in the project.

13. B: There is not much information to determine if the activity has a lag or not. The float/buffer of this activity is Late Finish – Early Finish = 10 days. The activity is not on the critical path because it has a float or buffer of ten days. Even if the team member takes four additional days to complete the activity, it probably will have no impact on the project schedule or on the successor activity.

14. B: What-if scenario analysis usually uses Monte Carlo simulation to simulate the outcome of a project by making use of three-point estimates (optimistic, pessimistic, most likely) for each activity, a huge number of simulated scheduling possibilities, or a few selected scenarios that are most likely, and the network diagram. The outcome of this analysis may be used to evaluate the project schedule under adverse conditions and to develop the preventive and contingency action plan to reduce the impact and probability of the unexpected situations.

15. C: Fast-tracking is the technique of doing critical path activities in parallel when they were originally planned in series. Fast-tracking will not be an option in this case since you cannot change the network diagram, or in other words, you cannot perform activities in parallel that were originally planned to be completed in sequence. The best option here is to add additional resources to the project activities on the critical path to complete them quickly. Resource leveling is used to produce a resource-limited schedule by letting the schedule slip and cost increase in order to deal with a limited amount of resources, resource availability, and other resource constraints. The critical chain method is another way to develop an approved, realistic, resource-limited, and formal schedule. It provides a way to view and manage uncertainty when building the project schedule.

16. D: Fast-tracking is the technique of doing critical path activities in parallel when they were originally planned in series.

17. A: The duration of three modules is 10 * 3 = 30 days, and the remaining two modules is 2 * 15 = 30 days. The first phase of the project will take 30 + 30 = 60 days, or approximately between fifty-five and sixty-five days.

18. D: The schedule forecasts are outputs of the Control Schedule process, not tools & techniques.

19. A: An analogous estimate is usually done during the early phase of the project when not much information is available about the project. It is less accurate even though it is less costly and less time consuming. In a bottom-up approach, one estimate per activity is received from the team members; it requires significant time to develop. A heuristic estimate is based on rule of thumb. A PERT estimate, also known as a weighted average estimate, is usually associated with specific project activities and requires significant time to develop as well.

20. C: The activity duration estimates are outputs in the Estimate Activity Durations process. This process should be performed before the Develop Schedule process. Adding additional time or padding the estimate is a common practice in this process, so the project manager should make sure that the estimates from the team members are realistic. It is important that all estimates in this process should use a common work unit/period.

21. D: The best course of action will be to update the project schedule and other relevant plans to reflect the new estimate.

22. A: Your team has created the WBS, WBS dictionary, and activity list and has submitted the activity durations. The next step should be to sequence the activities by creating a network diagram using the precedence diagramming method. Determining high-level project assumptions and constraints is done as part of project initiation and is completed much earlier. The Develop Schedule process follows the Sequence Activities process. Note that sequencing activities can be done before or after the activity duration estimation is done.

23. C: The Control Schedule process is the next process after the Develop Schedule process, but all the activities of the Develop Schedule process are not completed yet. Once the schedule is developed, it should be compressed, finalized, and approved by the stakeholders. Then you should start controlling the schedule.

24. C: The project network diagram represents activities and their logical relationships, dependencies, and sequence; thus, the network diagram will best capture the impact of the delay on the project schedule. The work breakdown structure is a deliverable-oriented hierarchical decomposition of the work to be executed by the project team to accomplish the project objectives and create the required deliverables, but it does not focus on the duration of the project activities. The risk register would show an increase in project risk but would not help to determine the impact of a delay on the project schedule. An issue log will also capture the root cause, person assigned, due date, and other factors but will not give out much information about the impact of the delay on the project schedule.

25. D: A bar chart or Gantt chart is a time-phased graphical display of activity start dates, end dates, and durations. It is useful for tracking progress and reporting to the team and can be easily modified to show the percentage of completed work. As the project progresses, bars are shaded to show which activities are now complete. The work breakdown structure is a deliverable-oriented hierarchical decomposition of the work to be executed by the project team to accomplish the project objectives and create the required deliverables, but it does not focus on the duration of the project activities. A milestone chart is similar to a bar chart but only shows major events. It is a good tool for reporting to management and customers. This type of chart is reserved for brief, high-level presentations as too much detail may be undesirable and distracting to senior management. A network diagram is a schematic display of the sequential and logical relationships of the project activities. It shows dependencies and the order in which activities in a project must be performed.

26. A: Resource leveling is used to produce a resource-limited schedule by letting the schedule slip and cost increase in order to deal with a limited amount of resources, resource availability, and other resource constraints. It can be used when shared or critically required resources are only available at certain times, are in limited quantities, or when resources have been over allocated. Fast-tracking is the technique of doing critical path activities in parallel when they were originally planned in series. Crashing is the technique of adding additional resources to a project activity to complete it more quickly. The critical path is the longest path through a network diagram and determines the shortest time to complete the project as well as any scheduling flexibility. It is not the project schedule, but it indicates the time period within which an activity could be scheduled considering activity duration, logical relationships, dependencies, leads, lags, assumptions, and constraints.

27. C: External dependencies are driven by circumstances or authority outside the project and must be considered during the process of sequencing the activities. Internal dependencies are based on the needs of the project and are mostly under the control of the project team. Mandatory dependencies are mandatory and unavoidable dependencies that are inherent in the nature of the work or are contractually required. They are like laws of nature and are also called "hard logic." Discretionary dependencies are also called "preferred logic" or "soft logic" as they are the preference of the project planner and the team members. These dependencies may be determined by best practices or by local methodology and may vary from project to project.

28. A: The project manager should now focus on developing the preliminary schedule and get the approval from the team members. Finalizing the project scope statement should have been completed prior to completing the WBS. The team members have completed the network diagram, which suggests that the activities sequencing is also completed. Since the project schedule is an input to risk management, developing the risk management plan should be done once the schedule is completed.

29. C: Analogous estimates take a top-down approach, and the overall project estimate is usually given to the project manager from the management or the sponsor. It is usually done during the early phase of the project when not much information is available. It is less accurate even though it is less costly and less time consuming. In a bottom-up approach, one estimate per activity is received from the team members.

30. B: The project is definitely at high risk because activities on critical path and near critical path can be delayed anytime causing the entire project to be delayed. Having more than one critical path and several near-critical paths does not necessarily mean that more resources and additional budget will be required to complete the project. There is no valid reason to terminate the project just because it is at high risk of schedule delay.

CHAPTER 7

PROJECT COST MANAGEMENT

Cost Management

Project cost management is focused on planning, estimating, budgeting, financing, funding, managing, and controlling costs so that the project can be completed within the sanctioned budget.

Every project should have a budget. Part of the success of a project is defined by executing project cost management. This includes processes required to estimate, budget, and control costs so that the project can be completed within the approved budget. Managing the cost of the project is one of the key ways in which project management performance can be measured, since cost is one of the "triple constraints".

Many organizations perform fiscal year planning and determine a high-level budget far in advance of their project planning and prior to knowing costs. The project manager should review the project scope, its resources and duration estimates, and then reconcile them to the scope and projected cost instead of simply accepting whatever budget is specified by management.

A well-defined, bottom-up approach should be utilized to estimate costs and create a budget for the project. The overall approach should be to define the scope first and have a robust Work Breakdown Structure (WBS), then define the activities with resources and duration estimates, develop a schedule, apply rates, and schedule against resources and activities to create activity cost estimates and a cost baseline.

The project manager should be concerned with both of the following:

Life Cycle Costing: Life Cycle Costing (LCC) is also known as cradle-to-grave costing. The purpose of this type of accounting is to provide a complete record of all the costs associated with the product or service. This type of costing is commonly found in manufacturing, product development, construction, and software companies. It looks at the total cost of ownership from purchase or creation through operations, maintenance, support, and finally to disposal of the product, service, or result of the project.

For example, while calculating the cost of a project, a project manager should estimate the cost from project initiating to closing in addition to the associated operational cost and maintenance and support cost, which may be 2 to 3 percent of the total project cost per year.

Life cycle costing not only considers the cost of the project, but it also considers the entire life of the product. For example, a decision to produce a lower quality product could save the company a certain amount, but it will cost the company a whole lot more in maintenance and support once the project is completed.

Value Analysis/Engineering: Value engineering is mainly focused on finding a less costly way to do the same work and on achieving more out of the project in every possible way. This includes increasing bottom line, decreasing costs, improving quality, and optimizing the schedule without reducing or impacting the scope.

Exercise 1: What documents and items do you need to estimate your project costs?

____

____

____

____

____

Exercise 2: List the steps that you will take to deal with an unrealistic end date and a total cost constraint from management for your project.

____

____

____

____

____

Important Points to Consider: The following points are very important for a project manager to consider during project cost management:

- All kinds of estimates should be based on the WBS, and estimates are more accurate if smaller-sized work components are estimated.
- The project manager should not come up with the estimates for the activities; rather, for accuracy, the estimation should be formulated by the people performing the work.
- Historical information can drastically improve estimates.
- Schedule baseline should be used to track project progress, and the only time it should be modified is when an approved change request is implemented.
- All changes impacting time, cost, risk, human resources, or scope should be approved through the Integrated Change Control process.
- Corrective and preventive actions should be recommended.
- The project manager should not just accept the requirements but should also analyze them as required.
- Plans should be revised as per the findings in the project.
- Padding should be discouraged, and the project manager should ask for justification on estimates from the team members as needed.
- The project manager should try to keep the estimates realistic and accurate as much as possible and maintain the integrity of the estimates throughout the project life cycle by revisiting and recalculating the estimates on a regular basis.
- The project manager should consider life cycle costing.

Important Accounting Terms

Although project managers are not expected to be accountants, understanding several accounting concepts and terms are essential in project cost management.

Four Main Types of Cost:

Variable Cost: This type of cost varies with the amount of work/production (e.g., buy more → lower cost per unit). For example, the cost of materials, supplies, and wages can be considered variable costs.

Fixed Cost: This type of cost does not change throughout the life of a project. For instance, rental cost may be unchanged during the project.

Direct Cost: This type of cost is directly attributable to the project work. For instance, wages and materials used in the project can be direct costs.

Indirect Cost: This is an overhead cost or cost that is incurred for the benefit of more than one project. For instance, cafeteria services, facilities, and fringe benefits are indirect costs.

Two other accounting terms use the word "cost" but are concepts related to analysis rather than types of cost:

Sunk Cost: The amount of cost that has been invested or paid for a project. It is often used to describe what is written off from a canceled project. For instance, you are halfway through a project with an initial budget of $1 million and have spent $2 million. Do you consider the $1 million over budget when determining whether to continue with the project? No. Accounting standards say that if the cost is unrecoverable it should be treated as irrelevant and should not be considered while deciding whether to continue with a troubled project.

Opportunity Cost: It is the value of a project that is not undertaken so that another project can be executed. It is the cost of a lost opportunity, missing the benefit of the project not selected. In other words: If Company A decides to do Project 1 instead of Project 2, then Project 1 has an opportunity cost equal to the value of Project 2.

While selecting a project, the smaller the opportunity cost the better, since it is not desirable to miss out on a great opportunity.

Exercise 3: You have two projects to choose from: Project A with an NPV of $53,000 or Project B with an NPV of $79,000. What is the opportunity cost of selecting Project B?

____

____

Working Capital: Working capital is calculated by taking current assets and subtracting the current liabilities, or the amount of money the company has available to invest, including investment in projects.

Working Capital = Current Assets – Current Liabilities

Project Cost Management Processes

Projects require resources and time, both of which cost money. Projects are estimated, or predicted, on how much the project work will likely cost to complete.

Refer to the "Figure 3-16: Process Groups Key Inputs and Outputs" and you should realize that you have completed several items while working on scope and time management. Obviously, all these documents can be used as inputs while you are working with the project budget. Now, let's think about the real life scenario. First of all, as a project manager you should develop the policy, procedures, direction, and guidance on how the project cost will be planned, managed, expended, and controlled. You may now refer to your project schedule and develop an approximation of the costs of all resources such as labor, materials, equipment, services, facilities, and any other special items associated with each schedule activity. The next process, Determine Budget, refers to the cost aggregation as the "roll-up" of the costs associated with each work package. The project manager and the project team work together to control the project costs and monitor the performance of the project work. The most comprehensible method to monitor the project cost is through earned value management, which demonstrates the performance of the project and allows the project manager to forecast where the project is likely going to end up financially.

PMI identifies four key processes that are associated with the cost management knowledge area. Since cost is one of the triple constraints, an understanding of these processes is vital to project success.

Processes	Process Groups	Detail	Key Outputs
1. Plan Cost Management	Planning	The process of developing the policy, procedures, direction, and guidance on how the project cost will be planned, managed, expended, and controlled throughout the project life cycle.	– Cost Management Plan
2. Estimate Costs	Planning	The process of developing an approximation of the costs of all resources such as labor, materials, equipment, services, facilities, and any other special items associated with each schedule activity.	– Activity Cost Estimates
3. Determine Budget	Planning	The process of utilizing the cost aggregation method by which activity costs are rolled up to the work packages' cost; work package costs are then rolled up to the "control account" or "cost account" costs and finally to the authorized project cost baseline.	– Cost Baseline – Project Funding Requirements
4. Control Costs	Monitoring & Controlling	The process of monitoring the project budget and managing changes to the cost baseline.	– Work Performance Information – Cost Forecasts – Change Requests

Table 7-1: Four Project Cost Management Processes and Key Outputs

Project Cost Management Processes, Inputs, Tool & Techniques, and Outputs

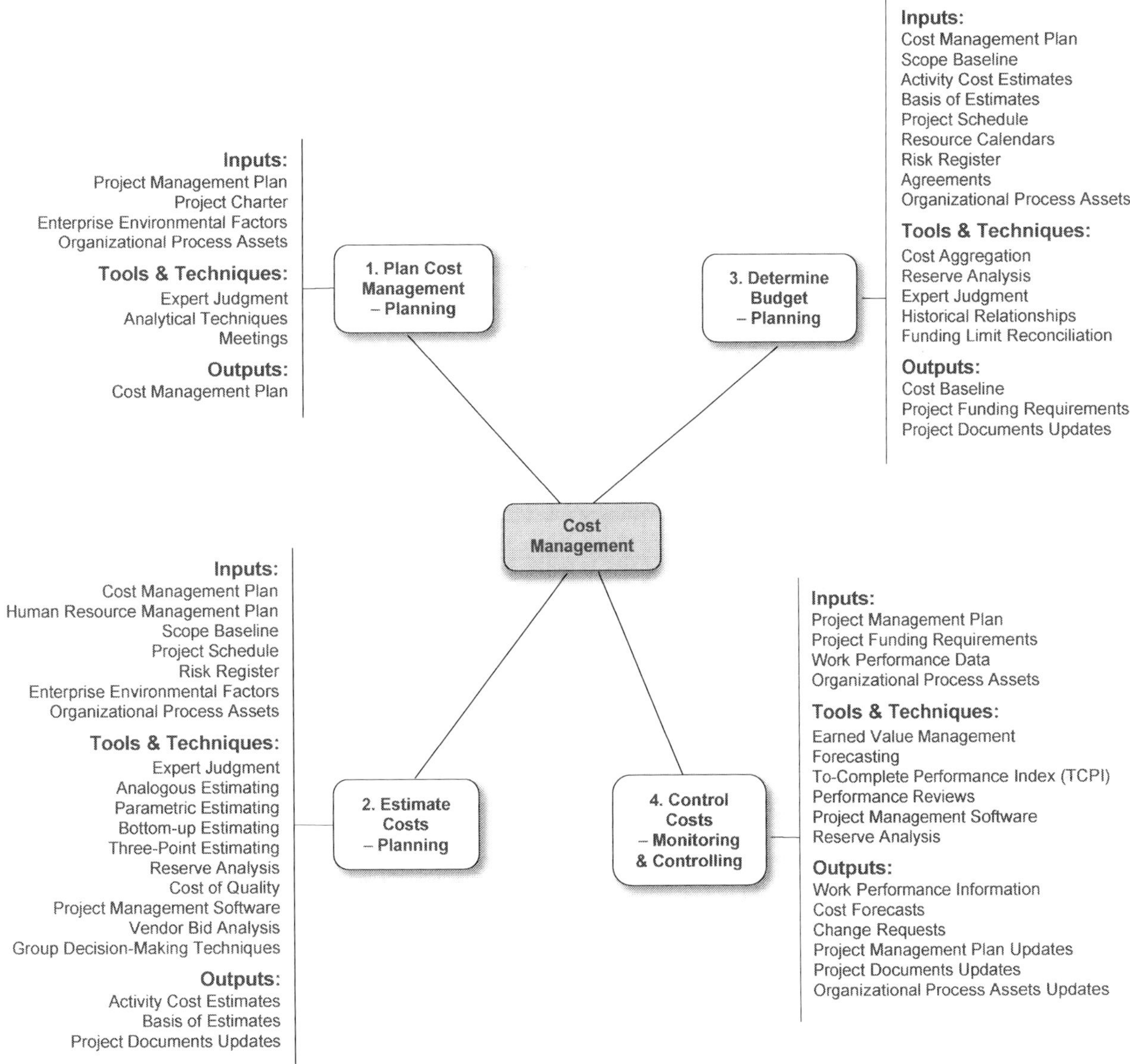

Figure 7-1: Project Cost Management Processes, Inputs, Tool & Techniques, and Outputs

Plan Cost Management

Plan Cost Management is the process of developing the policy, procedures, direction, and guidance on how the project cost will be planned, managed, expended, and controlled throughout the project life cycle.

As per the PMBOK®, the Plan Cost Management process has the following inputs, tools & techniques, and outputs:

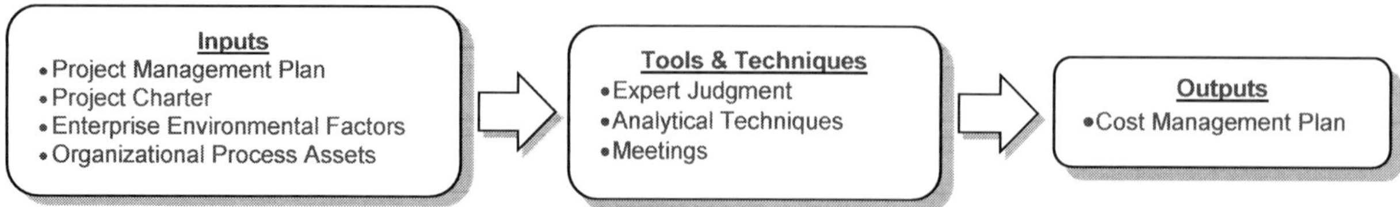

Figure 7-2: Plan Cost Management: Inputs, Tools & Techniques, and Outputs

Plan Cost Management: Inputs

- Project Management Plan
- Project Charter
- Enterprise Environmental Factors
- Organizational Process Assets

Project Management Plan: The project management plan includes the following information that is used to develop the cost management plan.

Scope Baseline: Scope baseline consists of the project scope statement, the WBS, and the WBS dictionary.

Schedule Baseline: Schedule baseline will provide the required timeline on cost occurrences.

Other Information: Other cost-related information such as cost risk, cost schedule, and cost-related communication from the project management plan will be used in developing the cost management plan.

Project Charter: The project charter contains the high-level budget that can be used to develop detailed project cost. It also defines the project objective and approval requirements that have influence on how cost is managed in the project.

Enterprise Environmental Factors: Marketplace conditions describing the source, availability, vendors' terms and conditions of the product or service, published commercial information on standard cost of material and equipment, published seller prices, and organizational culture and structure are among factors that may influence the Plan Cost Management process.

Organizational Process Assets: The financial database, financial control procedures, and existing formal and informal cost estimating-related policies, procedures, lessons learned, and guidelines may influence the Plan Cost Management process.

Plan Cost Management: Tools & Techniques

- Expert Judgment
- Analytical Techniques
- Meetings

Expert Judgment: Expert judgment guided by historical information on labor rates, material cost, risk factors, inflation, and other variables may influence the Plan Cost Management process.

Analytical Techniques: Various analytical techniques such as Return on Investment (ROI), payback period, Discounted Cash Flow, Present Value (PV), and Net Present Value (NPV) may be used to develop a cost management plan. Developing a cost management plan may require identifying strategic options to fund (self, with equity, or debt) or finance (make, purchase, rent, or lease) the project and may significantly impact the project schedule and risk.

Meetings: Meetings with team members, the sponsor, stakeholders, and anyone responsible for cost-related activities will be beneficial in order to discuss and develop a cost management plan.

Plan Cost Management: Outputs

- Cost Management Plan

Cost Management Plan: The project cost management plan is a component of the overall project management plan. It defines how the project cost will be planned, managed, expended, and controlled throughout the project life cycle. According to the PMBOK®, the cost management plan can establish the following:

Level of accuracy: Based on the scope, complexities of the activities, and magnitude of the project, activity cost estimates will be rounded to a prescribed precision: for example, $100, $1,000, and so on.

Unit of measure: This refers to the unit of measurements, such as hours, days, weeks, or a lump sum amount that will be used to estimate resources.

Organizational procedures links: The WBS provides a framework for the cost management plan, and a control account (CA) in the WBS is used to monitor and control project cost. Each control account is assigned a unique code or account number called the code of account that links directly to the performing organization's accounting system.

Control thresholds: Thresholds are usually expressed as percentage deviations from the cost baseline that the sponsor or stakeholders are willing to allow before any action is required.

Rules of performance measurement: This portion of the cost management plan documents how earned value management measurements are set, such as where the control accounts exist within the WBS, earned value management techniques that will be used to measure performance, specific tracking methodologies, and the equations that will be used for calculating Estimate at Completion (EAC) and other measurements.

Reporting format: This refers to the format, type, and frequency for various cost reports that will be created in the project.

Process description: This refers to the three cost management processes—Estimate Costs, Determine Budget, and Control Costs—and how these processes will be utilized to manage project cost.

Additional details: Other additional details on cost management activities such as procedures for cost recording, details on strategic funding options, and procedures and policies on dealing with fluctuations in currency exchange rates are documented.

Estimate Costs

The Estimate Costs process is focused on the development of an approximation of the costs of all resources, such as labor, materials, equipment, services, facilities, and any other special items associated to each schedule activity.

In order to achieve optimal cost for the project, different options such as sharing resources, buy versus lease, or make versus buy should be considered.

Cost estimates are predicted based on the available information at a given point of time and should be reevaluated and refined as cost-associated risk, alternatives, cost trade-off, and other factors are identified and more details become available. The accuracy of the cost estimates will gradually improve as the project progresses. For example, in the initial phase, a project may have a rough order of magnitude estimate in the range of –25 percent to +75 percent, but later on, the budget and definitive estimates will narrow the range of accuracy. Some organizations have more specific guidelines on expected degrees of confidence and accuracy in estimation and when and how cost estimate refinement should be done in the project. However, for the most part, the following three estimates are used for cost estimation:

- **Definitive Estimates (–5 percent to +10 percent):** Used for bids, contract changes, legal claims, and permit approvals.
- **Budget Estimates (–10 percent to +25 percent):** Prepared from flow sheets and used to establish funds required and to obtain approval for the project.
- **Rough Order of Magnitude Estimates (–25 percent to +75 percent):** This type of estimate is an approximate estimate made without detailed data. It is used during the formative stages for initial evaluation of a project's feasibility.

As per the PMBOK®, the Estimate Costs process has the following inputs, tools & techniques, and outputs:

Figure 7-3: Estimate Costs: Inputs, Tools & Techniques, and Outputs

Estimate Costs: Inputs

- Cost Management Plan
- Human Resource Management Plan
- Scope Baseline
- Project Schedule
- Risk Register
- Enterprise Environmental Factors
- Organizational Process Assets

Cost Management Plan: The project cost management plan is a component of the overall project management plan, and it defines how the project cost will be planned, managed, expended, and controlled throughout the project life cycle. It also defines the degree of confidence and accuracy expected in cost estimation and methods that will be used to estimate project activity cost.

Human Resource Management Plan: Project staffing attributes, personnel rates, and related rewards and recognitions found in the human resource management plan are essential components for developing the project cost estimates.

Scope Baseline: Scope baseline consists of the project scope statement, the WBS, and the WBS dictionary. Additional information on contractual and legal implications with property rights, licenses, permits, safety, security, performance, insurance, intellectual property, and the environment should be considered when estimating costs.

Project Scope Statement: The project scope statement contains deliverables, product description, acceptance criteria, constraints, and assumptions about the project.

Work Breakdown Structure: A Work Breakdown Structure (WBS) is the foundational block to the initiating, planning, executing, monitoring & controlling, and closing phases. Normally presented in the chart form, it is a deliverable-oriented hierarchical decomposition of the work to be executed by the project team to accomplish the project objectives and create the required deliverables.

WBS Dictionary: The WBS dictionary documents the detailed descriptions of the work to be done for each work package.

Project Schedule: A project schedule contains schedule activities. It also contains the type, quantity, amount of time that resources are required, and the quantity of materials and equipment needed to complete these activities. These are major factors in determining the project cost.

Risk Register: Risks found in the risk register are either threats or opportunities and can influence both project schedule activities and overall project costs. The risk register should be analyzed during cost estimation to consider risk prevention and mitigation costs.

Enterprise Environmental Factors: Marketplace conditions describing the source, availability, vendors' terms and conditions for the product or service, published commercial information on standard cost of materials and equipment, and published seller price may influence the Estimate Costs process.

Organizational Process Assets: Existing formal and informal cost estimating-related policies, procedures, lessons learned, and guidelines may influence the Estimate Costs process.

Estimate Costs: Tools & Techniques

- Expert Judgment
- Analogous Estimating
- Parametric Estimating
- Bottom-up Estimates
- Three-Points Estimates
- Reserve Analysis
- Cost of Quality
- Project Management Software
- Vendor Bid Analysis
- Group Decision-Making Techniques

Expert Judgment: Expert judgment guided by historical information on labor rates, material costs, risk factors, inflation, and other variables may influence the Estimate Costs process.

Analogous Estimating (Top-Down Estimating): The overall project estimate given to the project manager from management or the sponsor. This type of estimate measures the project parameters such as budget, size, complexity, and duration based on the parameters of a previous, similar project and on historical information. It is usually done during an early phase of the project when not much information is available; thus, it is less accurate even though it is less costly and less time consuming.

Parametric Estimating: This estimate uses a mathematical model based on historical records from other projects. Depending upon the quality of the underlying data, this estimate can produce a higher level of accuracy and can be used in conjunction with other estimates to provide the estimate for the entire project or for segments of a project. This kind of estimating may include measures such as time per line of code, time per installation, and time per linear meter.

There are two ways to create a parametric estimation:

Regression Analysis (Scatter Diagram): This diagram analyzes two variables to see if there is any interdependency between them and creates a mathematical formula to use in future parametric estimating.

Learning Curve: According to the learning curve theory, when a large number of items are produced repetitively, productivity will increase, but at a diminishing rate. Learning curve data indicates that as work is repeated, the time required to complete the work is reduced, but the rate of improvement decreases. For instance, installing carpet in the fiftieth room in a construction project will take less time than it did in the first room due to increased efficiency as workers become more efficient with the installation procedure.

Bottom-up Estimates: This technique, which is usually very accurate but costly in terms of time and labor to develop, is based on rolling up the cost of individual activities. In this technique, estimates for each schedule activity are calculated and then aggregated up to the summary nodes of the WBS.

Three-Point Estimates: This estimate takes optimistic, pessimistic, and most likely estimates from the estimator and provides a risk-based expected activity cost estimate by taking a weighted average of the three estimates using the following formulas:

- Optimistic estimate: O
- Most likely estimate: M
- Pessimistic estimate: P

Depending on the assumed distribution of values, we may have the following two formulas:

Triangular Distribution: Expected Activity Cost Estimate = $\frac{(O + M + P)}{3}$

Beta Distribution: Expected Activity Cost Estimate = $\frac{(O + 4M + P)}{6}$

Reserve Analysis: This analysis accommodates the cost and time risk associated with the project estimate through the use of reserve. This contingency is simply a buffer against any unexpected slippage on the project and may be a percentage of the estimated cost or a fixed amount, or it may be created using a quantitative analysis method such as Expected Monetary Value (EMV).

Cost of Quality (COQ): Work added to the project to accommodate quality planning also needs to be added.

Project Management Estimating Software: Estimating software such as computerized spreadsheets, simulations, and statistical tools can speed up the cost calculation.

Vendor Bid Analysis: Bids, especially the winning ones from qualified vendors, should be analyzed during cost estimation.

Group Decision-Making Techniques: Several group decision-making techniques such as brainstorming, mind mapping, nominal group technique, and Delphi technique, may be used to obtain detailed cost-related information and more accurate estimations.

Estimate Costs: Outputs

- Activity Cost Estimates
- Basis of Estimates
- Project Documents Updates

Activity Cost Estimates: Cost estimates address the cost of each schedule activity on the project considering all relevant cost items, such as labor, materials, equipment, services, facilities, interest charges, currency exchange rate, contingency reserves, inflation allowance, and administrative items, among other items. The estimate is expressed in units of currency and usually gets refined during planning.

Basis of Estimates: A clear and detailed description of cost estimation may include the following:

- A description of the work estimated (reference the WBS)
- Explanation of the estimation development process
- Documentation on known constraints and assumptions made
- Indication of the range of results (±5 percent, $100K ± $5K, etc.)

Project Documents Updates: The risk register and the cost management plan, which describes how cost and changes to cost will be managed, may be updated.

Determine Budget

A budget, also known as the cost baseline, takes the estimated project expenditures and maps them back to dates on the calendar to help plan for cash flow and likely expenditures.

To calculate the budget, the project manager utilizes the cost aggregation method by which activity costs are rolled up to the work packages' costs; work packages' costs are then rolled up to the control accounts' or cost accounts' costs, and finally to the project cost.

There are two types of reserves that can be added to this estimate: contingency reserves and management reserves. The project manager determines, manages, and controls the contingency reserves, which will address the cost impact of the risks remaining during the Plan Risk Responses process. On the other hand, management reserves are funds to cover unforeseen risks or changes to the project.

The cost baseline is the project cost plus the contingency reserves, and the cost budget, or how much money the company should have available for the project, is cost baseline plus the management reserves. The project manager should compare cost baseline and cost budget estimates to parametric estimates, expert judgment, or historical record to confirm accuracy. If there is a significant difference between reference data and project estimates, the project manager should investigate and justify the discrepancy.

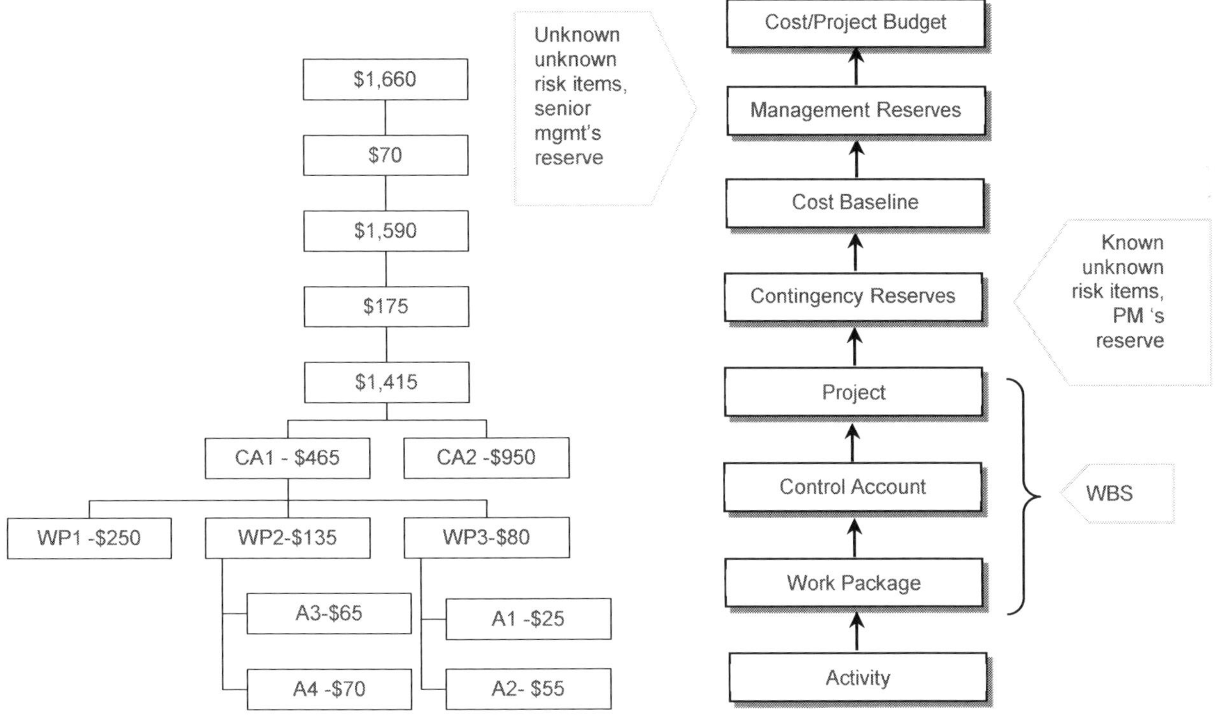

Figure 7-4: Cost Aggregation and Reserves

As per the PMBOK®, the Determine Budget process has the following inputs, tools & techniques, and outputs:

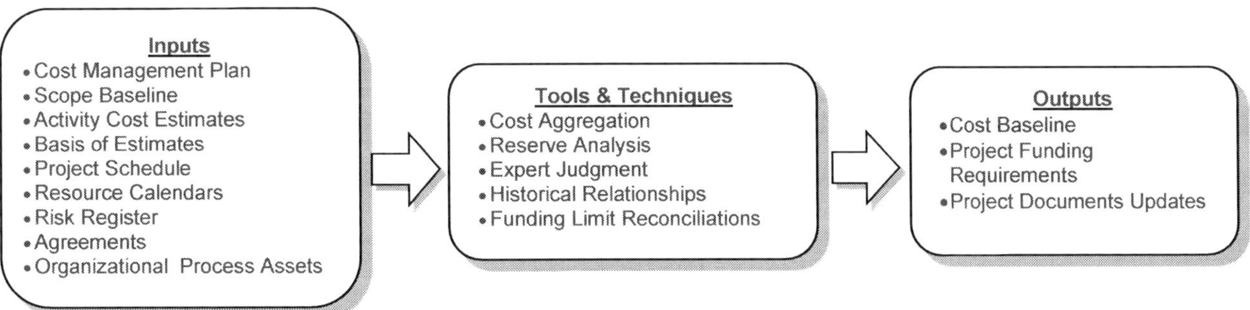

Figure 7-5: Determine Budget: Inputs, Tools & Techniques, and Outputs

Determine Budget: Inputs

- Cost Management Plan
- Scope Baseline
- Activity Cost Estimates
- Basis of Estimates
- Project Schedule
- Resource Calendars
- Risk Register
- Agreements
- Organizational Process Assets

Cost Management Plan: The project cost management plan is a component of the overall project management plan, and it defines how the project cost will be planned, managed, expended, and controlled throughout the project life cycle.

Scope Baseline: Scope baseline consists of the project scope statement, the WBS, and the WBS dictionary.

Activity Cost Estimates: Estimates for each schedule activity are calculated and then aggregated up to the summary nodes of the WBS.

Basis of Estimates: A clear and detailed description of cost estimation and description of any basic assumptions for inclusion or exclusion of indirect, variable, and other costs in the project budget.

Project Schedule: A project schedule contains schedule activities, milestones, work packages, and control accounts and the type, quantity, and amount of time resources are required to complete these activities, which are major factors in determining the project budget.

Resource Calendars: Resource calendars provide information on resource assignment and can help calculate project cost over the duration of the project.

Risk Register: In order to aggregate the risk response, the costs risk register should be reviewed.

Agreements: Information on applicable agreements and costs associated to products, services, or results that have been or will be purchased are used when determining the budget.

Organizational Process Assets: Cost budgeting tools, reporting methods, and cost budgeting-related policies, procedures, and guidelines are among factors that may influence the Determine Budget process.

Determine Budget: Tools & Techniques

- Cost Aggregation
- Reserve Analysis
- Expert Judgment
- Historical Relationships
- Funding Limit Reconciliations

Cost Aggregation: Cost estimates are aggregated first by work packages. These estimates are then aggregated for the higher component levels of the WBS and then for the entire project.

Reserve Analysis: This analysis accommodates the cost and time risks associated with the project estimate through the use of contingency and management reserves.

Expert Judgment: Consultants, stakeholders, technical and professional associations, industry groups, and other units within the performing organization may provide valuable input in determining the budget.

Historical Relationships: This relationship refers to a parametric estimating model based on historical data. It performs best when there are significant similarities between the project currently being undertaken and past projects with a substantial amount of organizational and industrial historical information available. An example of parametric estimating would be estimating the cost of laying tracks in a railway project based on historical projects with similar track lengths.

Funding Limit Reconciliation: The technique of reconciling the expenditure of funds with the funding limits set for the project. As per the variance between the expenditure of funds and the planned limit, the activities can be rescheduled to level out the rate of expenditures.

Determine Budget: Outputs

- Cost Baseline
- Project Funding Requirements
- Project Documents Updates

Cost Baseline: A time-phased budget used to monitor, measure, and control cost performance during the project. It is developed by summarizing costs over time and is usually displayed in the form of an S-curve. This suggests that the cost starts off low, then accelerates throughout the later phases of the project, and gradually slows down during closing.

ID	Resource Type	Jan	Feb	Mar	Apr	May	Jun	Jul	Aug
1.	**Labor**	$5,000	$6,000	$6,000	$5,500	$5,000	$4,000	$3,000	$2,000
2.	**Equipment**	$2,000	$9,000	$0	$4,000	$0	$0	$3,000	$1,000
3.	**Suppliers**	$1,000	$3,000	$0	$2,000	$1,000	$0	$1,000	$0
4.	**Administrative**	$500	$600	$450	$700	$700	$550	$600	$0
5.	**Travel**	$800	$1,000	$5,000	$0	$0	$1,200	$2,000	$0
6.	**Other**	$500	$500	$500	$500	$500	$500	$500	$500
	Monthly Total	$9,800	$20,100	$11,950	$12,700	$7,200	$6,250	$10,100	$3,500
	Grand Total								**$81,600**

Table 7-2: Project Cost Baseline

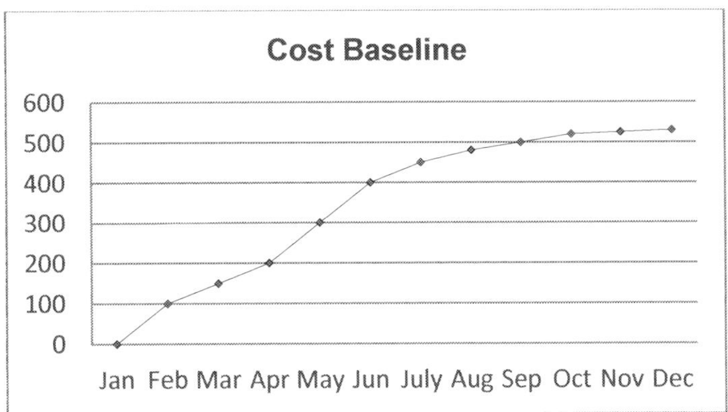

Figure 7-6: S-Curve

Project Funding Requirements: Total and periodic funding requirements are derived from the cost baseline. Total funds consist of the cost baseline and any management contingency reserves.

Project Documents Updates: The risk register, cost estimates, and the project schedule may be updated in this process.

Control Costs

Control Costs is a facilitating process of the monitoring & controlling process group that is focused on monitoring the project budget and managing changes to the cost baseline. As with the other controlling factors, it ensures that cost changes are understood, approved, communicated, implemented, and documented.

The following activities should be carried out during this process:

- Influence the factors that cause changes to the approved cost baseline.
- Understand the variance from cost baseline.
- Monitor changes to cost baseline.
- Resolve cost changes in a timely manner.
- Communicate with stakeholders on approved changes and their associated costs.
- Ensure that the project budget does not exceed acceptable limits.
- Ensure that all budget changes are agreed to and approved by the project sponsor where applicable.

As per the PMBOK®, the Control Costs process has the following inputs, tools & techniques, and outputs:

Figure 7-7: Control Costs: Inputs, Tools & Techniques, and Outputs

Control Costs: Inputs

- Project Management Plan
- Project Funding Requirements
- Work Performance Data
- Organizational Process Assets

Project Management Plan: The cost baseline and cost management plan portions of the project management plan are used to control costs.

Cost Baseline: Cost baseline describes what costs are projected and when they are supposed to incur. The variance between the cost baseline and the actual cost determines if changes or corrective or preventive actions are necessary.

Cost Management Plan: This plan describes how cost and changes to cost will be managed and controlled throughout the life of the project.

Project Funding Requirements: Total and periodic funding requirements are derived from the cost baseline. Total funds consist of the cost baseline (project cost + contingency reserves) and any management contingency reserves.

Work Performance Data: Information on the project status and cost of activities such as deliverables completed and not yet completed, costs authorized and incurred, estimates to complete the schedule activities, and percent completion of schedule activities will be used to control costs.

Organizational Process Assets: Cost budgeting tools, reporting methods, and cost budgeting-related policies, procedures, and guidelines may influence the Control Costs process.

Control Costs: Tools &Techniques

- Earned Value Management
- Forecasting
- To-Complete Performance Index (TCPI)
- Performance Reviews
- Project Management Software
- Reserve Analysis

Earned Value Management: A commonly used method of project performance and progress measurement that integrates project scope, cost, and schedule measures. This will be covered in further detail in the next section of this chapter. The Earned Value Management (EVM) develops and monitors the following three key dimensions for work packages and control accounts in a WBS:

- Planned Value (PV)
- Earned Value (EV)
- Actual Cost (AC)

Variances from the approved baseline will also be monitored by the following measurements:

- Schedule Variance (SV)
- Cost Variance (CV)
- Schedule Performance Index (SPI)
- Cost Performance Index (CPI)

Forecasting: Making estimates or predictions of conditions in the project's future, including Estimate to Complete (ETC) and Estimate at Completion (EAC).

To-Complete Performance Index (TCPI): To-Complete Performance Index (TCPI) is the calculated projection of cost performance that must be achieved on the remaining work to meet a specified management goal or earned value targets, such as the Budget at Completion (BAC) or the Estimate at Completion (EAC).

Performance Reviews:

- **Variance Analysis**: This type of analysis is used to compare actual project performance to planned or expected performance. Cost and schedule variances are the most frequently analyzed.
- **Trend Analysis:** This type of analysis examines project performance over time to determine if performance is improving or deteriorating.
- **Earned Value Performance:** This type of analysis compares the baseline plan to the actual schedule and cost performance.

Project Management Software: Project management software is often used to perform "what-if" analysis, to monitor the three EVM dimensions (PV, EV, and AC), to display graphical trends, and to forecast a range of possible final project results.

Reserve Analysis: Reserve analysis is performed to monitor the contingency and management reserves in order to find out if these reserves are still needed or if there is a need for additional reserves in the project. Unutilized contingency reserves may be released from the budget so that they can be used in other projects or operations.

Control Costs: Outputs

- Work Performance Information
- Cost Forecasts
- Change Requests
- Project Management Plan Updates
- Project Documents Updates
- Organizational Process Assets Updates

Work Performance Information: These measurements show how the project is performing against the plan. The calculated CV, SV, CPI, SPI, cumulative CPI, and cumulative SPI values for the WBS components are documented and communicated to stakeholders.

Cost Forecasts: Cost forecasts indicate how much total funding will be needed as well as how much more funding will be needed from this point on and when that funding will be needed. The Estimate at Completion (EAC) and the Estimate to Complete (ETC) values are documented and communicated to stakeholders.

Change Requests: Analysis of project performance can result in change requests to the project cost baseline to bring the project back on track. If there is significant deviation from the cost baseline, changes could take the form of cutting the scope, increasing the budget, or changing other factors related to execution.

Project Management Plan Updates: The cost baseline and cost management plan portions of the project management plan may be updated.

Project Documents Updates: Cost estimates and basis of estimates may be updated.

Organizational Process Assets Updates: Causes of cost variances, corrective actions chosen, and their reasons are among some of the types of lessons learned from project cost control that may be updated.

Exercise 4: List actions that you will take to control costs in your project.

Exercise 5: What are the three basic principles of learning curves?

Exercise 6: Identify which process group each process belongs to.

Process Groups				
Initiating	**Planning**	**Executing**	**Monitoring & Controlling**	**Closing**

Process Names:

- Control Costs
- Plan Cost Management
- Determine Budget
- Estimate Costs

Cost Management Example for an ERP Implementation Project

ITPro Consultancy, LLC has recently initiated an Enterprise Resource Planning (ERP) project. The ERP will need to support over three thousand users throughout fifty branches across the country. This cost plan itemizes the expenditures required to successfully undertake this project within a six-month time frame.

In the planning process group, we go through the Estimate Costs process where we look into all our activities to develop an approximation of the costs of each activity. We need to look at the manpower, equipment, suppliers, administrative costs, and other cost items and their unit costs in order to come up with the cost estimation. Once we have the estimation of the activities, we go through the process of Determine Budget and come up with the cost baseline and funding requirements. In the monitoring & controlling process group, we carefully monitor and control our costs to ensure that costs stay on track and that change is detected whenever it occurs.

Estimate Costs: The following section lists the major types of expenses involved.

Manpower: ITPro Consultancy will purchase the new ERP from an external supplier, who will install and customize the system in the ITPro Consultancy business environment. The following team members from ITPro Consultancy will be working closely with the supplier, who will be responsible for providing their consulting expertise to install and configure the ERP platform.

Number	ManPower	Unit Cost (US $/Hour)
1.	Project manager, IT team	$70
2.	Quality assurance lead, QA team	$50
3.	ERP acquisition administrator, procurement team	$45
4.	Contract administrator, procurement team	$45
5.	Systems architect, installation team	$60
6.	Systems programmer, ERP installation team	$60
7.	Database administrator, ERP installation team	$45
8.	Tester, QA team	$35
9.	Business analyst, IT team	$35

Suppliers: The following table lists the general items ITPro Consultancy, LLC will need to procure from the external supplier and their unit costs.

Number	Procurement Item	Unit cost (US $/Unit)
1.	ERP solution for all required modules	$300,000
2.	ERP consulting services for ERP solution installation & configuration	$150/hour
3.	ERP support services for the first six months of operation	$30,000
4.	ERP training courses for users	$5,000/course
5.	ERP documentation	$4,000

Equipment: The ITPro Consultancy, LLC project team is responsible for sourcing the following equipment needed to successfully implement and support the solution.

Number	Equipment	Unit Cost (US Dollar)
1.	Two application servers	$14,000
2.	Database server	$12,000
3.	Communication equipment – routers, switches, firewall, etc.	$8,500
4.	Backup & power supply equipment	$8,000
5.	Operational support software	$3,500
6.	One PC per branch (50 branches)	$500

Administrative and other items: The ITPro Consultancy, LLC project team will consume expenditures for administrative and other items as summarized in the following table:

Number	Administrative Item	Unit Cost (US $/month)
1.	Rental of office space	$4,500
2.	Rental of general equipment (PCs, laptops, phones)	$3,780
3.	Rental of office equipment (photocopiers, faxes)	$3,250
4.	Rental of office furniture (tables, desks, chairs)	$1,800
5.	Office consumables (printing paper, stationery)	$750
6.	Communication services (mobile and land line)	$1,200
7.	Other services (power, water, gas)	$250
8.	Broadband Internet service	$200
9.	Entertainment expenses	$400
10.	Miscellaneous expenses	$500

Determine Budget: Based on the unit costs listed above, the following financial schedule provides a breakdown of total monthly expenses budgeted within the project life cycle. In total, the project will require an approved budget of $891,420 + $80,000 as reserves, equivalent to $971,420, to successfully produce the required deliverables.

Number	Expense Type	Mar	Apr	May	Jun	Jul	Aug
Manpower							
1.	Project manager	$11,200	$11,200	$11,200	$11,200	$11,200	$11,200
2.	Quality assurance lead				$8,000	$8,000	$8,000
3.	ERP acquisitions administrator	$7,200	$7,200				$7,200
4.	Contract administrator	$7,200	$7,200			$7,200	$7,200
5.	Systems architect	$9,600	$9,600	$9,600	$9,600	$9,600	$9,600
6.	Systems programmer	$9,600	$9,600	$9,600	$9,600	$9,600	$9,600
7.	Database administrator	$7,200	$7,200	$7,200	$7,200	$7,200	$7,200
8.	Tester				$5,600	$5,600	$5,600
9.	Business analyst	$5,600	$5,600			$5,600	$5,600
Procurement Items		$57,600	$57,600	$37,600	$51,200	$64,000	$71,200
1.	ERP solution				$300,000		
2.	ERP consulting services	$6,000	$6,000	$6,000	$6,000	$6,000	$6,000
3.	ERP support services						$30,000
4.	ERP training courses	$2,500					$2,500
5.	ERP documentation	$2,000					$2,000
	Procurement Items Total	10,500	$6,000	$6,000	$306,000	$6,000	$40,500
Equipment							
1.	Application servers		$28,000				
2.	Database server		$12,000				
3.	Communication equipment			$8,500			
4.	Backup & power supply equipment			$8,000			
5.	Operational support software					$3,500	
6.	PCs				$25,000		
	Equipment Total		$40,000	$16,500	$25,000	$3,500	

Administrative and Other Items							
1.	Rental of office space	$4,500	$4,500	$4,500	$4,500	$4,500	$4,500
2.	Rental of general equipment			$3,780	$3,780	$3,780	$3,780
3.	Rental of office equipment	$3,250	$3,250	$3,250	$3,250	$3,250	$3,250
4.	Rental of office furniture	$1,800	$1,800	$1,800	$1,800	$1,800	$1,800
5.	Office consumables	$750	$750	$750	$750	$750	$750
6.	Communication services	$1,200	$1,200	$1,200	$1,200	$1,200	$1,200
7.	Other services	$250	$250	$250	$250	$250	$250
8.	Broadband Internet service	$200	$200	$200	$200	$200	$200
9.	Entertainment expenses	$400	$400	$400	$400	$400	$400
10.	Miscellaneous expenses	$500	$500	$500	$500	$500	$500
Administrative Items Total		$12,850	$12,850	$16,630	$16,630	$16,630	$16,630
Monthly Total (Funding Requirements)		**$80,950**	**$116,450**	**$76,730**	**$398,830**	**$90,130**	**$128,330**
Subtotal / Project Cost							$891,420
Contingency Reserve							$60,000
Cost Baseline							$951,420
Management Reserve							$20,000
Grand Total/Cost Budget/Project Budget							**$971,420**

Earned Value Management

In order to have full control over a project, it is extremely important to know how the project is really progressing. Lack of control over the project will result in the need to work overtime and spend additional money to complete the project. Earned Value Management (EVM) will be very beneficial in this situation as it is an industry standard way to do the following:

- Measure a project's progress against the project scope, cost, and schedule baselines
- Forecast future performance and the project's completion date and final cost
- Provide schedule and budget variances during the project

There are several formulas associated with earned value that we need to understand and memorize.

EVM is performed on the work packages and the control accounts of the WBS, and it continuously monitors Planned Value (PV), Earned Value (EV), and Actual Cost (AC) to produce the work of the project. Because these three measurements are key to EVM, let's try to understand them first. We also need to be familiar with the following outdated names of the three measurements as you may still hear them from time to time.

Planned Value	Earned Value	Actual Cost
Budgeted Cost of Work Scheduled	Budgeted Cost of Work Performed	Actual Cost of Work Performed

Suppose you are currently managing a construction project where four rooms will be fully renovated. Each room will take one day to complete, and $2,000 is budgeted per room. In your project, you decided to have a finish-to-start relationship, meaning that the rooms will be completed one after another.

Today is the end of day three and Room 1 and Room 2 are completed, but Room 3 is only 50 percent done. Also $2,000 was spent for Room 1, $2,200 for Room 2, and $1,400 for Room 3.

Room1	Room2	Room3	Room4
Duration=1 day Budget = $2,000 Status: 100% completed Cost = $2,000	Duration=1 day Budget = $2,000 Status: 100% completed Cost = $2,200	Duration=1 day Budget = $2,000 Status: 50% completed Cost = $1,400	Duration=1 day Budget = $2,000 Status: Not started yet

Planned Value (PV) is the estimated value of the work planned to be done. In this case we planned to complete Room 1, Room 2, and Room 3 in the first three days; thus, we planned to complete ($2,000 + $2,000 + $2,000) = $6,000 worth of work, meaning that our Planned Value (PV) is $6,000.

Earned Value (EV) is the estimated value of the work actually accomplished. In this case we have completed 100 percent of Room 1 ($2,000 worth of work), 100 percent of Room 2 ($2,000 worth of work), and 50 percent of Room 3 ($1,000 worth of work). The Earned Value (EV) or the total value of the work actually completed is $2,000 + $2,000 + $1,000 = $5,000.

Even though we planned to complete $6,000 worth of work in the first three days, we only completed $5,000 worth of work.

Actual Cost (AC) is the cost incurred for the work accomplished. In this case we spent $2,000 for Room 1, $2,200 for Room 2, and $1,400 for Room 3; thus, our Actual Cost (AC) is ($2,000 + $2,200 + $1,400) = $5,600.

Now that we understand PV, EV, and AC, let's find out how we can get all the cost formulas from the graph on the next page. We will look into details of all these formulas later on as we will only learn how to come up with the formulas first.

In the graph Planned Value (PV), Earned Value (EV), and Actual Cost (AC) are shown at a given point of time during the project. In our room project example above, if we spend $2,000 per room and complete one room a day, then the project will cost us $8,000, which is our original budget, or Budget at Completion (BAC). Note that if we can progress according to our Planned Value (PV), then at the end of the project, it will cost as per our Budget at Completion (BAC); thus, the end point is indicated as BAC.

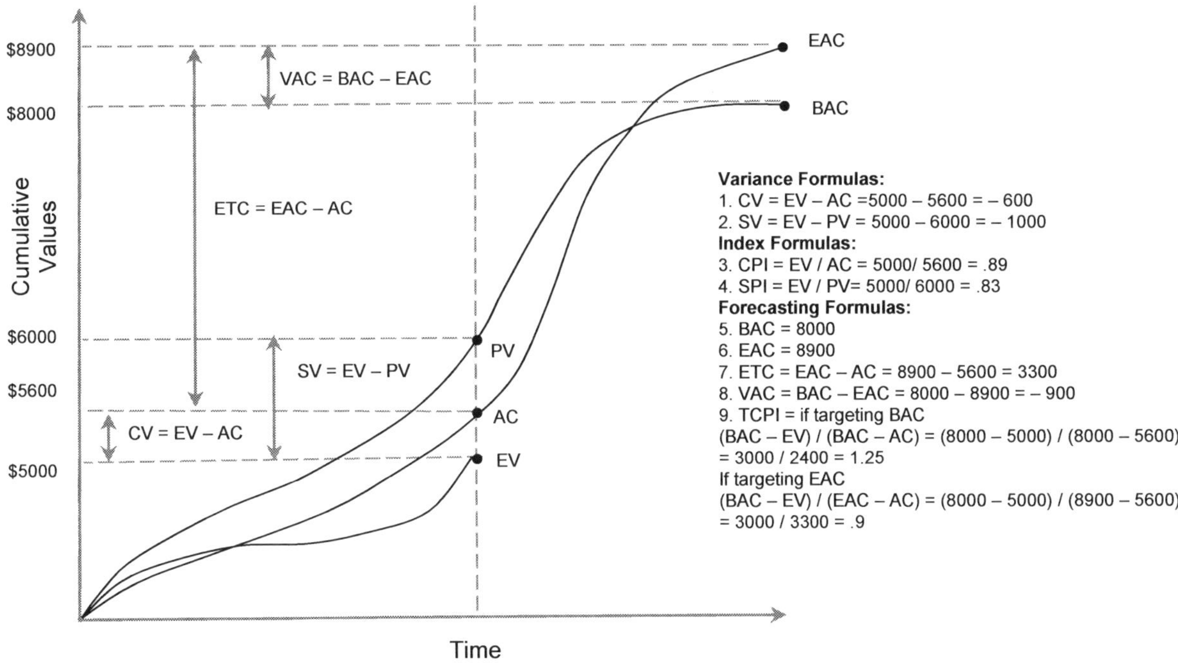
$8900
$8000
$6000
$5600
$5000
Cumulative Values
Time
EAC
BAC
VAC = BAC – EAC
ETC = EAC – AC
SV = EV – PV
CV = EV – AC
PV
AC
EV
Variance Formulas:
1. CV = EV – AC =5000 – 5600 = – 600
2. SV = EV – PV = 5000 – 6000 = – 1000
Index Formulas:
3. CPI = EV / AC = 5000/ 5600 = .89
4. SPI = EV / PV= 5000/ 6000 = .83
Forecasting Formulas:
5. BAC = 8000
6. EAC = 8900
7. ETC = EAC – AC = 8900 – 5600 = 3300
8. VAC = BAC – EAC = 8000 – 8900 = – 900
9. TCPI = if targeting BAC
(BAC – EV) / (BAC – AC) = (8000 – 5000) / (8000 – 5600)
= 3000 / 2400 = 1.25
If targeting EAC
(BAC – EV) / (EAC – AC) = (8000 – 5000) / (8900 – 5600)
= 3000 / 3300 = .9

Figure 7-8: Earned Value Management

Now if we spend as per our Actual Cost (AC), then we can say that the end point will be our Estimate at Completion (EAC), that is, how much we are expecting the total project to cost. We can also think of Budget at Completion (BAC) as our old budget and Estimate at Completion (EAC) as our new budget. Obviously the difference between Budget at Completion (BAC) and Estimate at Completion (EAC) will be the Variance at Completion (VAC), or how much over or under budget we expect to be at the end of the project. So we can use the formula:

Variance at Completion (VAC) = Budget at Completion (BAC) – Estimate at Completion (EAC)

Let's consider Estimate at Completion (EAC) to be around $8,900; thus, in the room project, Variance at Completion (VAC) will be $8,000 – $8,900 = –$900.

In the room project example, we know our Actual Cost (AC) is $5,600, so we already spent $5,600 in the project. If we assume that the Estimate at Completion (EAC) is around $8,900, then we will need ($8,900 – $5,600) = $3,300 more to complete this project from this point on. How much more the project will cost us from this point on till the completion is called the Estimate to Complete (ETC). So we can use the formula:

Estimate to Complete (ETC) = Estimate at Completion (EAC) – Actual Cost (AC)

In this case, our Estimate to Complete (ETC) = $3,300.

We will have two variance formulas, two index formulas, and few forecasting formulas. Below is how we will remember the variance and index formulas. We will be using Planned Value (PV), Earned Value (EV), and Actual Cost (AC) to come up with these four formulas. We will always start with Earned Value (EV), and if it is related to cost, then we will use Actual Cost (AC) or else we will use Planned Value (PV) in the formulas.

Variance Formulas:

1. Schedule Variance (SV) = Earned Value (EV) – Planned Value (PV)
2. Cost Variance (CV) = Earned Value (EV) – Actual Cost (AC)

Index Formulas:

1. Schedule Performance Index (SPI) = Earned Value (EV) / Planned Value (PV)
2. Cost Performance Index (CPI) = Earned Value (EV) / Actual Cost (AC)

Forecasting Formulas:

We already discussed a couple of forecasting formulas using the above graph.

1. Budget at completion (BAC); no formula.
2. Estimate at Completion (EAC) = Budget at Completion (BAC)/Cost Performance Index (CPI); this is the only formula you may need to remember. If you spend too much money, your project will cost you more than your original budget since you will have a poor Cost Performance Index (CPI).
3. Variance at Completion (VAC) = Budget at Completion (BAC) – Estimate at Completion (EAC); we got it from the graph.
4. Estimate to complete (ETC) = Estimate at Completion (EAC) – Actual Cost (AC); we got it from the graph.
5. To-Complete Performance Index (TCPI) = (BAC – EV) / (BAC – AC); for now just remember that To-Complete Performance Index (TCPI) is the performance that must be achieved in order to meet financial or schedule goals. In order to remember this formula, just write down the formula for Cost Performance Index (CPI) first (which is EV/AC). Now subtract these two values from Budget at Completion (BAC) to get the formula for To-Complete Performance Index (TCPI).

In your construction project example, we have a Budget at Completion (BAC) of $8,000 and our Actual Cost (AC) is $5,600 since we already spent $5,600. Your remaining balance or how much money you are left with at this time is Budget at Completion (BAC) – Actual Cost (AC) or $8,000 – $5,600 = $2,400.

So, we can say To-Complete Performance Index (TCPI) = (BAC – EV) / Remaining balance

In this project, your Estimate at Completion (EAC) is $8,900 since you are expecting this project to cost you $8.900 when it is completed. If management already gave you the additional $900 that you need to complete the project, then the remaining balance will be Estimate at Completion (EAC) – Actual Cost (AC) or $8, 900 – $5,600 = $3,300. In that case if we are targeting Estimate at Completion (EAC),

To-Complete Performance Index (TCPI) = (BAC – EV) / (EAC – AC), when targeting EAC.

Acronym	Term	Formula	Interpretation
PV or BCWS	Planned Value or Budgeted Cost of Work Scheduled	BAC * (Time Passed/Total Scheduled Time) or BAC * Planned % Complete	What is the estimated value of the work planned to be done?
EV or BCWP	Earned Value or Budgeted Cost of Work Performed	BAC * (Work Completed/Total Work Required) or BAC * Actual % Complete	What is the estimated value of the work actually accomplished?
AC or ACWP	Actual Cost or Actual Cost of Work Performed		What is the actual cost incurred for the work accomplished?
SV	Schedule Variance	SV = EV – PV	A comparison of the amount of work performed during a given period of time to what was scheduled to be performed. Negative = behind schedule Neutral = on schedule Positive = ahead of schedule
CV	Cost Variance	CV = EV – AC	A comparison of the budgeted cost of work performed with actual cost. Negative = over budget Neutral = on budget Positive = under budget
CPI	Cost Performance Index	CPI = EV/AC	Measures the value of the work completed against actual cost. CPI <1= over budget CPI >1= under budget CPI = 1= on budget
CPI^c	Cumulative CPI	$CPI^c = EV^c/AC^c$	Represents the cumulative CPI of the project at the point the measurement is taken.
SPI	Schedule Performance Index	SPI = EV/PV	Measures the progress to date against the planned progress. SPI <1 = behind schedule SPI >1= ahead of schedule SPI = 1 = on schedule
SPI^c	Cumulative SPI	$SPI^c = EV^c/PV^c$	Represents the cumulative SPI of the project at the point the measurement is taken.
BAC	Budget at Completion		How much did we BUDGET for the TOTAL project effort?
EAC	Estimate at Completion	If CPI is expected to be the same EAC = BAC/CPI If current variances are thought to be atypical of the future EAC = AC + (BAC – EV) If both CPI and SPI influence the remaining work EAC = AC+[(BAC–EV) / (CPI * SPI)]	What do we currently expect the TOTAL project to cost?
ETC	Estimate to Complete	ETC = EAC – AC	From this point on, how much MORE do we expect it to cost to finish the project?
VAC	Variance at Completion	VAC = BAC – EAC	How much over or under budget do we expect to be at the end of the project?
TCPI	To-Complete Performance Index	If targeting the current plan TCPI = (BAC – EV) / (BAC – AC) If targeting the current EAC TCPI = (BAC– EV) / (EAC – AC)	Performance that must be achieved in order to meet financial or schedule goals. TCPI >1 = harder to complete TCPI <1 = easier to complete

Table 7-3: Cost Management Formulas

Exercise 7: Match the terms in the left column to the description in the right column.

Acronym	Interpretation
1. PV/ BCWS	A. Performance that must be achieved in order to meet financial or schedule goals.
2. EV/ BCWP	B. A comparison of the budgeted cost of work performed with actual cost.
3. AC/ ACWP	C. How much did we BUDGET for the TOTAL project effort?
4. SV	D. How much over or under budget do we expect to be at the end of the project?
5. CV	E. What is the estimated value of the work actually accomplished?
6. CPI	F. From this point on, how much MORE do we expect it to cost to finish the project?
7. CPI^c	G. It represents the cumulative SPI of the project at the point the measurement is taken.
8. SPI	H. What do we currently expect the TOTAL project to cost?
9. SPI^c	I. It represents the cumulative CPI of the project at the point the measurement is taken.
10. BAC	J. What is the actual cost incurred for the work accomplished?
11. EAC	K. It measures the progress to date against the planned progress.
12. ETC	L. It measures the value of the work completed against actual cost.
13. VAC	M. A comparison of the amount of work performed during a given period of time to what was scheduled to be performed.
14. TCPI	N. What is the estimated value of the work planned to be completed?

Exercise 8: Find out the values for CV, SV, CPI, SPI, EAC, ETC, VAC, and TCPI for the following graph.

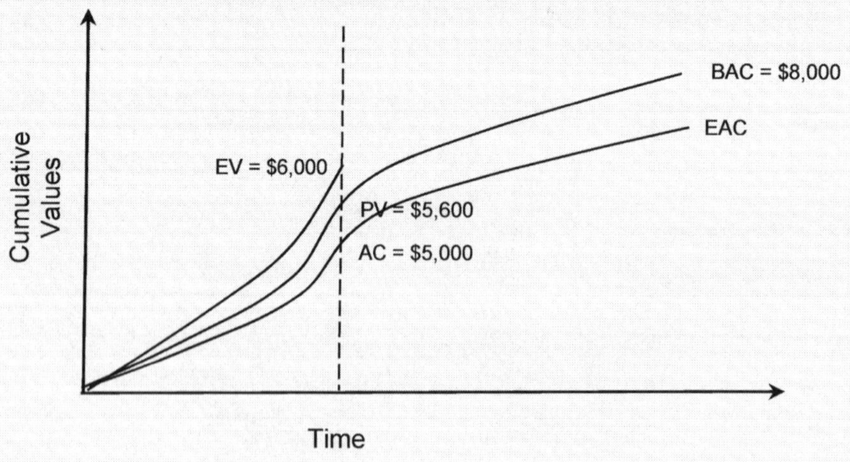

Exercise 9: You are the project manager of a software development project. The team members will be working on five different components. Each of the components is budgeted to be $2,625, and all components are supposed to be completed in five weeks. Using the status below in the following table, find PV, EV, AC, SV, CV, CPI, SPI, BAC, EAC, ETC, VAC, and TCPI values at the end of week four.

Project	Planned End Date	Planned Budget	Actual Amount Spent by week Four	Planned Completion by Week Four	Actual Completion by Week Four
Software Development Project	End of 5th week	$13,125 for total project or $2,625 for each component	$9,000	Four out of five components	Three out of five components

Exercise 10: Your project, which has a budget of $800,000, is running well. In the latest earned value report, you see the CPI = 1.1, the SPI = 0.9, and the PV = $600,000. You cannot find the EAC, VAC, and CV in the report, so you calculate them based on the information given. What are the values for EAC, VAC, and CV?

Exercise 11: You are currently managing a construction project where four rooms will be fully renovated. Each room will take one day to complete, and $2,000 is budgeted per room. In your project you decided to have a finish-to-start relationship, meaning that the rooms will be completed one after another. Today is the end of day three and Room 1 and Room 2 are completed, but Room 3 is only 50 percent done. Also $2,000 was spent for Room 1, $2,200 for Room 2, and $1,400 for Room 3. Find out AC, PV, EV, SV, CV, SPI, CPI, BAC, EAC, VAC, ETC, and TCPI.

Exercise 12: You are currently managing a construction project where four rooms will be fully renovated. Each room will take one day to complete, and $2,000 is budgeted per room. In your project, you decide to have finish-to-finish relationship, meaning that Room 1 should be completed before Room 2, Room 2 before Room 3, and so on, but your work can go on in any number of rooms simultaneously. Today is the end of day three and you found out that Room 1 and Room 2 are completed, Room 3 is 50 percent completed, and Room 4 is 75 percent completed. Also $2,000 was spent for Room 1, $2,200 for Room 2, $1,400 for Room 3, and $1,100 for Room 4. Find out AC, PV, EV, SV, CV, SPI, CPI, BAC, EAC, VAC, ETC, and TCPI.

Exercise 13: You are the project manager of a construction project that will take six months to complete and will cost $85,000 per month. At the end of the third month, you were asked to find out the cumulative CPI for the project and report it to management. While reviewing the project status, you found that you have spent $90,000 in the first month, $88,000 in the second month, and $87,000 in the third month. You also found that the project was 15 percent complete at the end of first month, 35 percent complete at the end of second month, and 45 percent complete at the end of third month. What is the cumulative CPI at the end of month three?

Exercise 14: While reviewing the status of your project, you found out the following EV, AC, and PV.

Month	PV	EV	AC
Month 1	$30,000	$27,000	$25,000
Month 2	$35,000	$40,000	$45,000
Month 3	$90,000	$80,000	$70,000
Month 4	$150,000	$125,000	$89,000

Answer the following:

1. What is the SPI for Month 3?
2. What is the cumulative SPI for Month 3?
3. What is the CPI for Month 4?
4. What is the cumulative CPI for Month 4?

Exercise 15: Three different types of performance reports are listed below. Which terms from the left column can be utilized in each report?

1. Schedule Variance (SV)
2. Cost Variance (CV)
3. Planned Value (PV)
4. Earned Value (EV)
5. Actual Cost (AC)
6. Estimate at Completion (EAC)
7. Variance at Completion (VAC)
8. Estimate to Complete (ETC)
9. Schedule Variance Index (SPI)
10. Cost Performance Index (CPI)

A. Status report
B. Progress report
C. Forecast report

Exercise 16: Fill in the blanks: Complete the report by filling the missing information.

Task #	Task	PV	EV	AC	SV	CV	SPI	CPI
1	Collect Requirements	?	200	120	–50	?	.8	?
2	Complete Design	300	?	200	?	150	?	1.75
3	Complete Coding	350	?	?	–50	50	.85	?
4	Complete Testing	?	380	410	?	–30	.?	.92
5	Complete Deployment	450	?	?	60	160	1.13	?
	Total	**1,750**	**1,740**	**?**	**–10**	**?**		

A. What will be your assessment for task 3 – "Complete Coding" once you review the earned value analysis for this task?
B. What will be your assessment for task 4 – "Complete Testing" once you review the earned value analysis for this task?
C. What are some of the possible causes for the variance in task 4?

Exercise 17: You are managing a software application project to develop an online PMP exam simulator to assist students to practice exam questions in similar real life environment. When asked by management what you currently expect the project to cost, you think that the costs you have incurred till now are an indicator of what will happen for the rest of the project. Which one of the following formulas will you use to get the most accurate Estimate at Completion (EAC)?

A. EAC = AC + (BAC – EV)
B. EAC = AC + Bottom-up ETC
C. EAC = (BAC – EV) / CPI * SPI
D. EAC = BAC/CPI

Exercise 18: Crossword

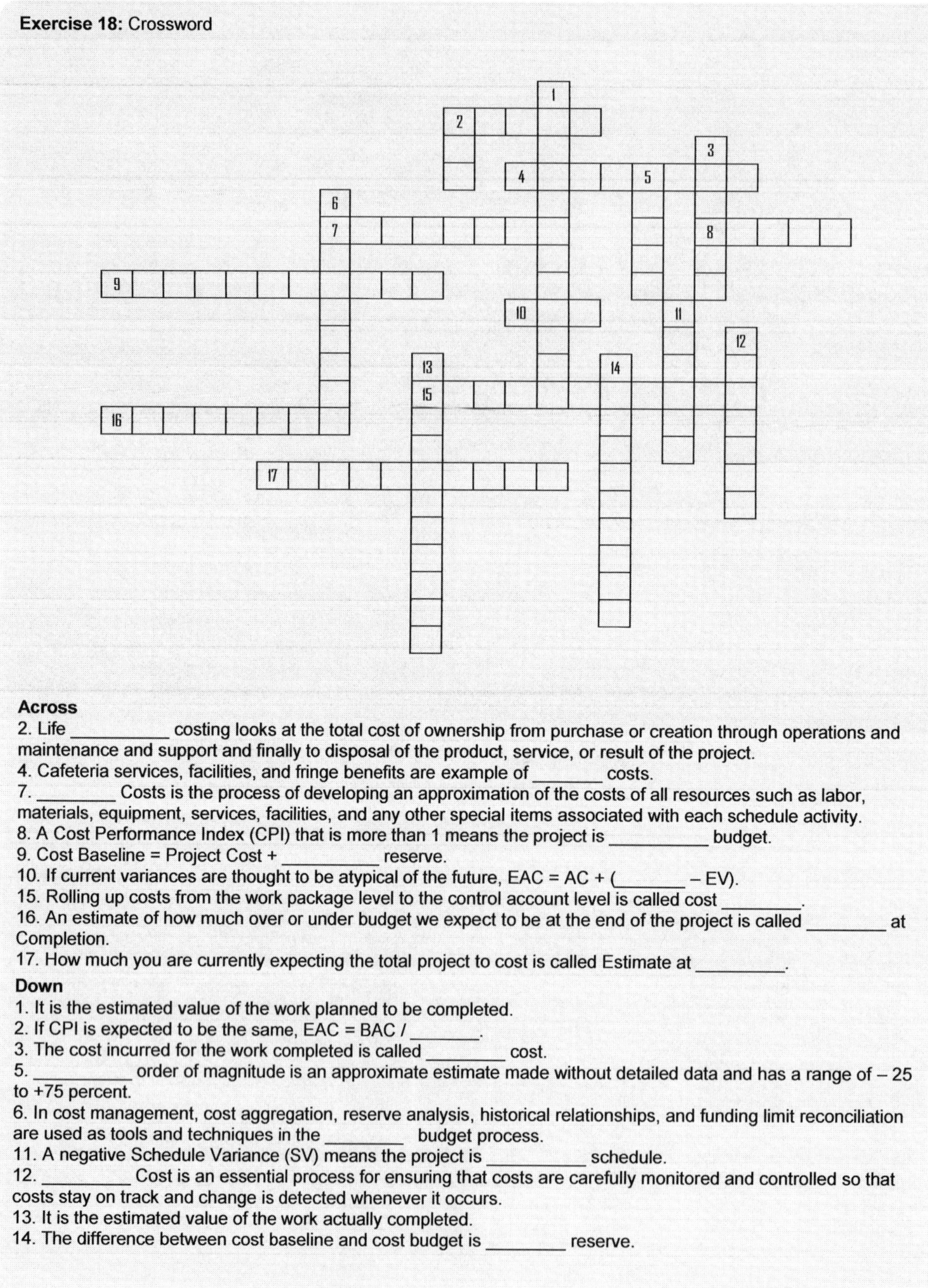

Across

2. Life __________ costing looks at the total cost of ownership from purchase or creation through operations and maintenance and support and finally to disposal of the product, service, or result of the project.
4. Cafeteria services, facilities, and fringe benefits are example of _______ costs.
7. ________ Costs is the process of developing an approximation of the costs of all resources such as labor, materials, equipment, services, facilities, and any other special items associated with each schedule activity.
8. A Cost Performance Index (CPI) that is more than 1 means the project is __________ budget.
9. Cost Baseline = Project Cost + __________ reserve.
10. If current variances are thought to be atypical of the future, EAC = AC + (_______ – EV).
15. Rolling up costs from the work package level to the control account level is called cost ________.
16. An estimate of how much over or under budget we expect to be at the end of the project is called ________ at Completion.
17. How much you are currently expecting the total project to cost is called Estimate at _________.

Down

1. It is the estimated value of the work planned to be completed.
2. If CPI is expected to be the same, EAC = BAC / _______.
3. The cost incurred for the work completed is called ________ cost.
5. __________ order of magnitude is an approximate estimate made without detailed data and has a range of – 25 to +75 percent.
6. In cost management, cost aggregation, reserve analysis, historical relationships, and funding limit reconciliation are used as tools and techniques in the ________ budget process.
11. A negative Schedule Variance (SV) means the project is __________ schedule.
12. _________ Cost is an essential process for ensuring that costs are carefully monitored and controlled so that costs stay on track and change is detected whenever it occurs.
13. It is the estimated value of the work actually completed.
14. The difference between cost baseline and cost budget is ________ reserve.

Exercise 19: Answer the following:

1. This estimate is an approximate estimate made without detailed data and has a range of – 25 to +75 percent.
2. How much you are currently expecting the total project to cost is called ________.
3. It looks at the total cost of ownership from purchase or creation through operations and maintenance and support and finally to disposal of the product, service, or result of the project.
4. It is mainly focused on finding a less costly way to do the same work and on achieving more out of the project in every possible way.
5. The cost is unrecoverable and should not be considered while deciding whether to continue with a troubled project.
6. A Cost Performance Index (CPI) that is less than 1 means the project is _______ budget.
7. It is the estimated value of the work actually completed.
8. From this point on, how much more do we expect it to cost to finish the project?
9. Rolling up costs from the work package level to the control account level is called _______.
10. It is the technique of reconciling the expenditure of funds with the funding limits set for the project.
11. It is the performance that must be achieved in order to meet financial or schedule goals.
12. The process of developing the policy, procedures, direction, and guidance on how the project cost will be planned, managed, expended, and controlled throughout the project life cycle.
13. This estimate has a range of –5 to +10 percent and is used for bids, contract changes, legal claims, and permit approvals.
14. Level of accuracy, organizational procedures links, control thresholds, rules of performance measurement, reporting format, and process description etc. are included in the _______.
15. A negative Schedule Variance (SV) means the project is _______ schedule.
16. It is the estimated value of the work planned to be completed.
17. If we are targeting the current EAC, the TCPI is (BAC – EV) / ________.
18. The four processes of cost management are _______.
19. The key outputs of cost management processes are ________.
20. If CPI is expected to be the same, EAC = ________.
21. If current variances are thought to be atypical of the future, EAC = _________.
22. In cost management, cost aggregation, reserve analysis, historical relationships, and funding limit reconciliation are used as tools and techniques in the _______ process.
23. Name some of the tools and techniques of the control costs process.
24. Cost forecasts are created as outputs in which cost management process?
25. The difference between cost baseline and cost budget is _______.
26. Cost budget = ________ + management reserve (unknown unknown risk items).
27. An estimate of how much over or under budget we expect to be at the end of the project.
28. An essential process for ensuring that costs are carefully monitored and controlled so that costs stay on track and change is detected whenever it occurs.
29. Name some of the forecasting formulas.
30. In project cost management, funding requirements are an input to the _______ process.
31. The cost incurred for the work completed.
32. Cost Baseline = Project Cost + _______.
33. When using a simulator such as Monte Carlo to simulate cost risks we need ________.

Project Cost Management Summary

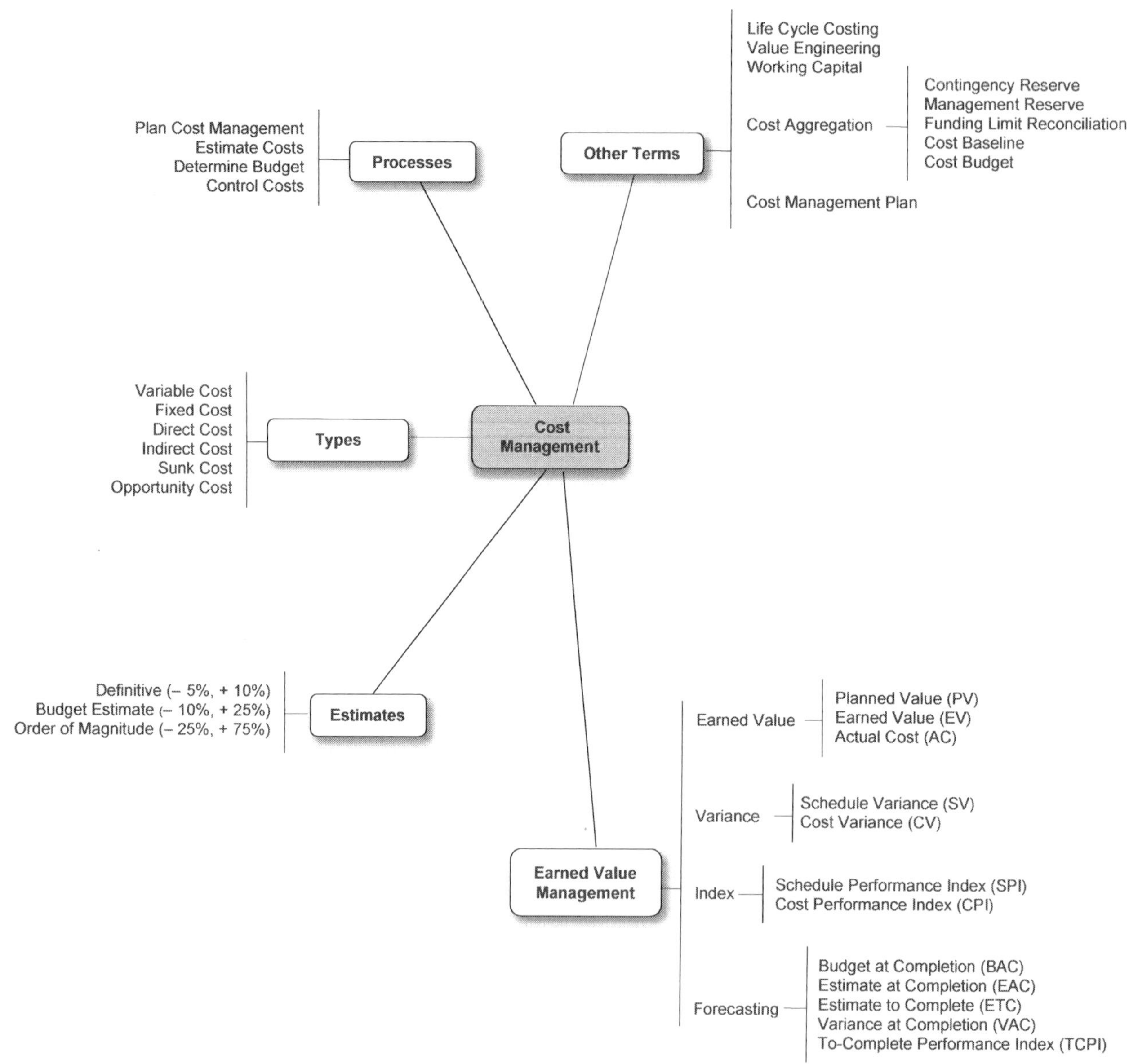

Figure 7-9: Project Cost Management Summary

Project Cost Management Key Terms

Cost Types

Variable Cost: Cost of materials, supplies, and wages
Fixed Cost: Rental cost, salary
Direct Cost: Wages and materials
Indirect Cost: Cafeteria services, facilities, and fringe benefits
Sunk Cost: What is written off from a canceled project – already spent
Opportunity Cost: Value of a project that is not chosen so that another project can be executed

Cost Estimates

Definitive (– 5%, + 10%)
Budget (– 10%, + 25%)
Rough Order of Magnitude (– 25%, + 75%)

Other Terms

Life Cycle Costing: Total cost of ownership from purchase or creation through operations and maintenance and finally to disposal
Value Engineering: Finding a less costly way to do the same work and on achieving more out of the project without reducing or impacting the scope
Working Capital = Current Assets – Current Liabilities
Cost Aggregation: Rolling up activity cost estimates to work packages; these estimates are then aggregated for the higher component levels of the WBS and then for the entire project
Contingency Reserve: Funds to address the cost impact of the remaining risks (known unknowns) that PM determines, manages, and controls
Management Reserve: Funds to cover unforeseen risks (unknown unknowns) or changes to the project. Not part of cost baseline
Funding Limit Reconciliation: A technique of reconciling the expenditure of funds with the funding limits set for the project
Cost Baseline = Project Cost + Contingency Reserve (Known unknowns)
Project Budget = Cost Baseline + Management Reserve (Unknown unknowns)

Earned Value Formulas

Term	Formula
Planned Value (PV)	BAC * Planned % Complete
Earned Value (EV)	BAC * Actual % Complete
Actual Cost (AC)	No formula
Schedule Variance (SV)	EV – PV , Negative = behind, Positive = ahead, Neutral = on schedule
Cost Variance (CV)	EV – AC , Negative = over, Positive = under , Neutral = on budget
Cost Performance Index (CPI)	EV/AC, CPI <1= over, >1= under, = 1= on budget
Cumulative CPI(CPI^c)	EV^c/AC^c
Schedule Performance Index(SPI)	EV/PV , SPI <1 = behind, >1= ahead, = 1 = on schedule
Cumulative SPI (SPI^c)	EV^c/PV^c
Budget at Completion (BAC)	No formula
Estimate at Completion (EAC)	BAC / CPI AC + (BAC – EV), If current variances are thought to be atypical of the future
Estimate to Complete (ETC)	EAC – AC
Variance at Completion (VAC)	BAC – EAC
To-Complete Performance Index (TCPI)	If targeting the current plan, (BAC – EV) / (BAC – AC) If targeting the current EAC, (BAC – EV) / (EAC – AC) TCPI >1 = harder to complete, <1 = easier to complete

Project Cost Management Exercise Answers

Exercise 1: All our estimates should be based on the Work Breakdown Structure (WBS). To calculate the project cost we can refer to the schedule since a schedule has all the work packages and activities listed for a project. If we identify the cost for all resources associated with each activity and add up costs for all activities, we will get the project cost. Refer to the "Figure 3-16: Process Groups Key Inputs and Outputs" and you will realize that we should have the following items before we estimate costs for our project.

- Project scope statement
- WBS
- Network diagram
- Schedule management plan
- Project schedule
- Organizational process assets: Policies on estimating, templates, processes, procedures, lessons learned, and historical information
- Enterprise environmental factors: Company culture and existing systems

The following items should be used when updating the cost estimates:

- Staffing management plan
- Risk management plan
- Risk register

Exercise 2: As project managers, we are responsible for properly managing the project schedule and budget. An unrealistic schedule or budget is the project manager's fault because a project manager should reconcile management's expectation to what can be achieved prior to committing to resources and wasting efforts on projects that will not be successful.

A project manager should:

1. Not put the blame on management for the impractical schedule or budget.
2. Understand that the proposed end date and budget from management are their expectations from the project manager.
3. Understand that it's the responsibility of the project manager to come up with the realistic schedule and budget.
4. Come up with a calculated end date and budget by estimating the time and cost of the work needed to complete the project.
5. Optimize the calculated schedule and budget as appropriate.
6. Compare the optimized schedule and budget to the end date and budget required by management. If there is a difference:
   - The project manager should scrutinize the project and provide options on how to change it to meet management's time and cost expectations.
   - Balance the constraints by negotiating a change to the end date or budget with management.

Exercise 3: The opportunity cost is $53,000 since it is the value of Project A that was not selected, or the opportunity that was missed out on.

Exercise 4: A project manager should take following actions to control costs in a project:

- Come up with required actions to control costs in the cost management plan and strictly follow the plan.
- Prevent changes and influence factors that cause changes to the approved cost baseline.
- Consider any organizational process assets (OPA) such as, policies, procedures, tools, or reporting formats related to controlling costs.
- Measure the variance from cost baseline and determine if these variances require changes, including corrective and preventive actions.
- Monitor changes to cost baseline.
- Resolve cost changes in a timely manner.
- Communicate with stakeholders on approved changes and their associated costs.
- Make sure that the project budget does not exceed acceptable limits.
- Make sure that all budget changes are agreed to and approved by the project sponsor where applicable.

Exercise 5: Learning curves stipulate that as the number of units produced increases, the time required for each unit decreases. The three basic principles of learning curves are:

a. As the task is repeated, the time required to perform a task decreases.
b. As more units are produced, the amount of improvement decreases.
c. The rate of improvement is consistent enough to allow its use as a prediction tool.

Exercise 6:

Process Groups				
Initiating	**Planning**	**Executing**	**Monitoring & Controlling**	**Closing**
	– Plan Cost Management – Estimate Costs – Determine Budget		– Control Costs	

Exercise 7: 1. N, 2. E, 3. J, 4. M, 5. B, 6 .L, 7. I, 8. K, 9. G, 10. C, 11. H, 12. F, 13. D, 14. A

Exercise 8:

1. CV = EV – AC = 6000 – 5000 = 1000
2. SV = EV – PV = 6000 – 5600 = 400
3. CPI = EV / AC = 6000/ 5000 = 1.2
4. SPI = EV / PV= 6000 / 5600 = 1.07
5. BAC = 8000
6. EAC = BAC / CPI = 8000 / 1.2 = 6666
7. ETC = EAC – AC = 6666 – 5000 = 1666
8. VAC = BAC – EAC = 8000 – 6666= 1334
9. TCPI =

if targeting BAC
(BAC – EV) / (BAC – AC) = (8000 – 6000) / (8000 – 5000) = 2000 / 3000 = .66
If targeting EAC
(BAC – EV) / (EAC – AC) = (8000 – 6000) / (6666 – 5000) = 2000 / 1666 = 1.2

Exercise 9:

Acronym	Term	Formula	Answer	Interpretation
PV	Planned Value	BAC * (Time Passed /Total Scheduled Time)	= $13,125 * (4/5) = $13,125 * 0.8 = $10,500	BAC is $13,125, and four weeks have passed out of five weeks.
EV	Earned Value	BAC * (Work Completed/Total Work Required)	= $13,125 * (3/5) = $13,125 * .6 = $7,875	We have completed three out of five components.
AC	Actual Cost		= $9,000	We spent $9,000 in the first four weeks.
SV	Schedule Variance	SV = EV – PV	= $7,875 – $ 10,500 = –$2,625	A negative schedule variance indicates that we are behind schedule.
CV	Cost Variance	CV = EV – AC	= $7875 – $9000 = –$1,125	A negative cost variance indicates that we are over budget by $1,125.
CPI	Cost Performance Index	CPI = EV/AC	= $7875/$9000 = 0.875	A less than one CPI indicates that we are over budget. We are getting $0.875 worth of performance for every one dollar we expend.
SPI	Schedule Performance Index	SPI = EV/PV	= $7875/$10,500 = 0.75	A less than one SPI indicates that we are behind schedule. We are progressing at 75 percent of the pace that we expected.
BAC	Budget at Completion		= $13,125	Total budget

EAC	Estimate at Completion	EAC= BAC/CPI	= $13,125/0.875 =$15,000	Our CPI is 0.875; thus, our EAC is higher than our original budget.
ETC	Estimate to Complete	ETC = EAC – AC	= $15,000 – $9,000 = $6,000	From this point on, we will need $6,000 more to complete this project.
VAC	Variance at Completion	VAC = BAC – EAC	= $13,125- $15,000 = –$1,875	We will be over budget by $1,875.
TCPI	To Complete Performance Index	TCPI = (BAC – EV) / (BAC – AC)	= ($13,125 – $7,875) / ($13,125 – $9,000) = $5,250/$4,125 = 1.27	TCPI is more than one, indicating that performance of the project is not good and we need to have a better performance to meet our schedule and financial goals.

Exercise 10: We know we need to use the following formulas:
CPI = EV/AC, CPI = 1.1
SPI= EV/PV, PV = $600,000 & SPI = 0.9
CV = EV – AC
EAC = BAC/CPI, BAC = $800,000 & CPI = 1.1
VAC= BAC – EAC, BAC = $800,000

Since we have all the values for EAC, we can calculate it first:
EAC = BAC/CPI = $800,000/1.1 = $727,272
We can easily find out the value of VAC since we now know the value of BAC and EAC
VAC= BAC – EAC = $800,000 – $727,272 = $72,728

Now we need to find out the value of CV, and we know that we need to find EV and AC to find the value of CV. We have the following:
SPI= EV/PV, PV = $600,000 & SPI = 0.9
Thus, 0.9 = EV/$600,000 or EV = 0.9 * $600,000 = $ 540,000

Again, we also have CPI = EV/AC, CPI = 1.1. Now that we just found out the value of EV = $540,000
1.1 = 540,000/AC or AC = 540,000/1.1 = $490,909
Now that we have both EV and AC, we can easily find out CV
CV = EV – AC
Thus, CV = $540,000 – $490,909 = $49,091

Exercise 11: Since we budgeted $2,000/room, our BAC is $2,000 * 4 = $8,000
PV = BAC * (Time Passed/Total Scheduled Time)
= $8,000 * (3/4) = $6,000
Note that so far we completed Room 1 and Room 2 and 50 percent of Room 3; thus, a total of (1 + 1 + .5) or two and a half out of four rooms.
EV = BAC * (Work Completed/Total Work Required)
= $8,000 * (2.5/4) = $5,000
AC = $2,000 + $2,200 + $1,400 = $5,600
SV = EV – PV = $5,000 – $6,000 = –$1,000 → Behind schedule
CV = EV – AC = $5,000 – $5,600 = –$600 →Over budget
SPI = EV/PV = 5,000/6,000 = 0.833 → Behind schedule
CPI = EV/AC = 5,000/5,600 = 0.892→ Over budget
EAC = BAC/CPI = $8,000/0.892 = $8,968
ETC = EAC – AC = $8,968 – $5,600 = $3,368
VAC = BAC – EAC = $8,000 – $8,968 = -$968 → Over budget by $968
TCPI = (BAC – EV) / (BAC – AC) = (8,000 – 5,000) / (8,000 – 5,600)
= 3,000/2,400 = 1.25 → Performance needs to be lot better to meet the schedule and cost objectives.

Exercise 12: Since we budgeted \$2,000/room, our BAC is \$2,000 * 4 = \$8,000
PV = BAC * (Time Passed/Total Scheduled Time)
= \$8,000 * (3/4) = \$6,000
Note that so far we completed Room 1 and Room 2, 50 percent of Room 3, and 75 percent of Room 4; thus, a total of (1 + 1 + 0.5 + 0.75) or three point two five out of four rooms.

EV = BAC * (Work Completed/Total Work Required)
= \$8,000 * (3.25 / 4) = \$6,500
AC = \$2,000 + \$2,200 + \$1,400 + \$1,100 = \$6,700
SV = EV – PV = \$6,500 – \$6,000 = \$500 → Ahead of schedule
CV = EV – AC = \$6,500 – \$6,700 = –\$200 → Over budget
SPI = EV/PV = 6,500/6,000 = 1.083 → Ahead of schedule
CPI = EV/AC = 6,500/6,700 = 0.970 → Over budget
EAC = BAC/CPI = \$8,000/0.970 = \$8,247 → Will cost us a little more at the end of the project
ETC = EAC – AC = \$8,247 – \$6,700 = \$1,547
VAC = BAC – EAC = \$8,000 – \$8,247 = –\$247→ Over budget by \$247
TCPI = (BAC – EV) / (BAC – AC) = (8,000 – 6,500) / (8,000 – 6,700)
= 1,500/1,300 = 1.15 → Performance needs to be better to meet the cost objective.

Exercise 13: We have a Budget at Completion (BAC) of (6 * \$85,000) = \$510,000.
In order to calculate the cumulative CPI, we need to find out cumulative EV and cumulative AC.
We spent \$90,000 in the first month, \$88,000 in the second month, and \$87,000 in the third month; thus, our cumulative AC is \$90,000 + \$88,000 + \$87,000 = \$265,000.

Note that the project was 15 percent completed in the first month, 35 percent completed in the second month, and 45 percent completed in the third month. It's obvious that 20 percent (35 percent minus 15 percent) of the work was completed in the second month and 10 percent (45 percent minus 35 percent) of the work was completed in the third month.

You can separately calculate the EV for each month and add them up to calculate the cumulative EV, or you can simply consider how much total work was completed at the end of the third month.

If we consider the EV for each month, then
EV for the first month was \$510,000 * 15 percent = \$76,500
EV for the second month was \$510,000 * 20 percent = \$102,000
EV for the third month was \$510,000 * 10 percent = \$51,000
So the cumulative EV is \$76,500 + \$102,000 + \$ 51,000 = \$229,500.

You can also consider the total work completed at the end of the third month and find out the same cumulative EV (\$510,000 * 45 percent) = \$229,500.

We know $CPI^c = EV^c/AC^c$
So CPI^c = \$229,500/\$265,000 or CPI^c = 0.86

Exercise 14:
1. We know SPI = EV/PV
For Month 3 EV = \$80,000 and PV = \$90,000; thus,
SPI = \$80,000/\$90,000 = 0.88

2. The cumulative PV for the first three months was \$30,000 + \$35,000 + \$ 90,000 = \$155,000.

The cumulative EV for the first three months was \$ 27,000 + \$ 40,000 + \$ 80,000 = \$147,000.

We know $SPI^c = EV^c/PV^c$, so SPI^c = \$ 147,000 / \$155,000 = 0.94

3. We know CPI = EV/AC, for Month 4 EV = \$125,000 and AC = \$ 89,000; thus, CPI = \$125,000/\$ 89,000 = 1.4

4. The cumulative AC for the first four months was \$25,000 + \$45,000 + \$ 70,000 + \$89,000 = \$229,000.
The cumulative EV for the first four months was \$ 27,000 + \$ 40,000 + \$ 80,000 + \$125,000 = \$272,000.
We know $CPI^c = EV^c/AC^c$, so CPI^c = \$ 272,000 / \$229,000 = 1.18

Exercise 15:
A. Status report: 1, 2, 9, 10
B. Progress report: 3, 4, 5
C. Forecast report: 6,7,8

Exercise 16:

Task #	Task	PV	EV	AC	SV	CV	SPI	CPI
1	Collect Requirements	250	200	120	–50	80	.8	1.66
2	Complete Design	300	350	200	50	150	1.16	1.75
3	Complete Coding	350	300	250	–50	50	.85	1.2
4	Complete Testing	400	380	410	–20	–30	.95	.92
5	Complete Deployment	450	510	350	60	160	1.13	1.4
	Total	1,750	1,740	1,330	–10	410		

A. Behind schedule and under budget.
B. Behind schedule and over budget.
C. Testing software costs more than expected, an external resource was hired to conduct the testing, there was a delay to start testing due to lack of resource.

Exercise 17: D: If CPI or past results are expected to continue, the correct EAC formula is EAC = BAC/CPI.

Exercise 18:

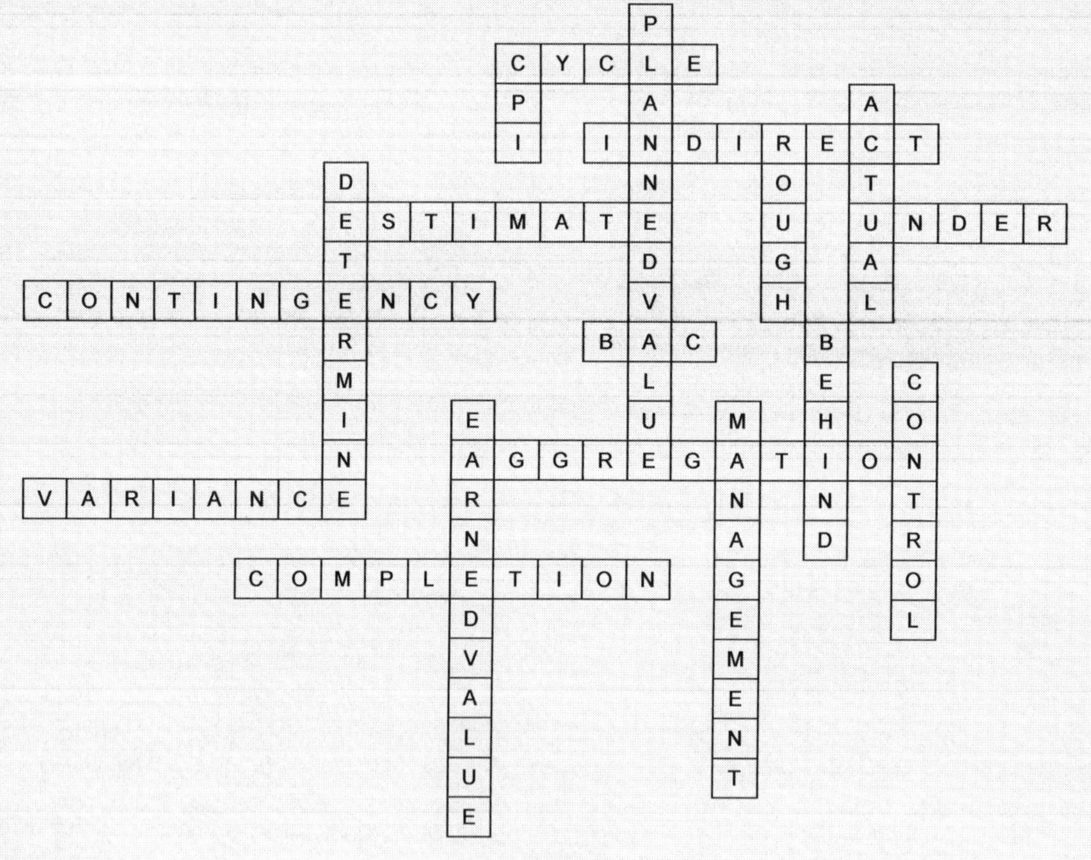

Exercise 19:

1. Rough order of magnitude
2. Estimate at Completion (EAC)
3. Life cycle costing
4. Value engineering
5. Sunk cost
6. Over
7. Earned Value (EV)
8. Estimate to Complete (ETC)
9. Cost aggregation
10. Funding limit reconciliation
11. To-Complete Performance Index (TCPI)
12. Plan Cost Management
13. Definitive estimate
14. Cost management plan
15. Behind
16. Planned Value (PV)
17. (EAC – AC)
18. Plan Cost Management, Estimate Costs, Determine Budget, and Control Costs
19. Plan Cost Management – Cost Management Plan
    Estimate Costs – Activity Cost Estimates
    Determine Budget – Cost Baseline, Project Funding Requirements
    Control Costs – Work Performance Information, Cost Forecasts, Change Requests
20. EAC = BAC/CPI
21. EAC = AC + (BAC – EV)
22. Determine budget
23. Earned value management, forecasting, To-Complete Performance Index (TCPI), performance reviews, project management software, reserve analysis
24. Control Costs
25. Cost budget adds management reserve to cost baseline.
    Cost budget = Cost baseline + management reserve
26. Cost baseline
27. Variance at Completion (VAC), VAC = BAC – EAC
28. Control Costs
29. Budget at Completion (BAC), Estimate at Completion (EAC), Estimate to Complete (ETC), Variance at Completion (VAC), To-Complete Performance Index (TCPI)
30. Control Costs
31. Actual Cost (AC)
32. Contingency reserve (known unknown risk items)
33. Cost Estimates

Project Cost Management Exam Tips

- Be able to name all four processes of project cost management and their key activities.
- Be able to differentiate among all different estimating techniques.
- Be familiar with all the formulas in Table 7-3 Cost Management Formulas and know how to use them.
- Be able to answer questions where you will need to analyze a specific situation and determine what you should do next.
- Be familiar with the concepts and terms in the project cost management summary table, Figure 7-9: Project Cost Management Summary.

Project Cost Management Questions

1. For an IT project your EV = $130,500, PV = $125,500, and AC = $129,000. Which one of the following statements is TRUE?
   A. The project is behind schedule and over budget.
   B. The project is ahead of schedule and under budget.
   C. The project is behind schedule and under budget.
   D. The project is ahead of schedule and over budget.

2. You recently took over a project from another project manager who left the organization. You find out that the project has a BAC = $45,000, PV = $30,000, cumulative AC = $25,000, and cumulative EV = $24,000. You decided to perform a forecasting analysis and calculated the values for EAC, ETC, TCPI, and VAC. Which of the following is NOT true?
   A. You will need $21,875 more to complete this project.
   B. The project will cost $46,875.
   C. The project performance is not good as TCPI is 1.05.
   D. The project will be under budget by $1,875.

3. You are in the Determine Budget process of developing a budget or cost baseline and project funding requirements. All of the following are inputs in this process EXCEPT:
   A. Work performance data
   B. Cost management plan
   C. Activity cost estimates
   D. Project schedule

4. To develop an online accounting application for your software development project, you are working on figuring out the total funding requirements and periodic funding requirements of the project. Which of the following will help you the MOST in this case?
   A. Project budget and contingency reserves
   B. Funding limit reconciliation
   C. Cost baseline and management reserves
   D. Management reserves and contingency reserves

5. You are in the Determine Budget process of developing a budget or cost baseline and project funding requirements. All of the following are tools & techniques in this process EXCEPT:
   A. Cost aggregation
   B. Reserve analysis
   C. Funding limit reconciliation
   D. Performance review

6. You are the project manager of a construction project that will take six months to complete and will cost $75,000/month. At the end of the third month, you were asked to find out the cumulative SPI for the project and report it to management. While reviewing the project status, you found that you have spent $80,000 in the first month, $72,000 in the second month, and $75,000 in the third month. You also found that the project was 15 percent complete at the end of first month, 35 percent complete at the end of second month, and 45 percent complete at the end of third month. If you planned to complete 50 percent of the work by this time, what is the cumulative SPI at the end of month three?
   A. 0.5
   B. 0.9
   C. 0.34
   D. 1.1

7. A project manager working on a construction project planned to install new carpets in all four rooms of the house. She measured the square footage of all the rooms and then multiplied that figure by a set cost factor to estimate the cost for installing the carpet. This is an example of:
   A. Bottom-up estimating
   B. Analogous estimating
   C. Parametric estimating
   D. Three-point estimating

8. With the help of your team members, you just finished the development of an approximation of the costs of all resources, such as labor, materials, equipment, services, facilities, and other special items associated with each schedule activity. What should you do NEXT?
   A. Control costs
   B. Resource leveling
   C. Bottom-up estimating
   D. Determine budget

9. Steve, a project manager, is trying to figure out the performance that must be achieved in order to meet the financial and schedule goals in his project. He is using a measurement that will give him the status on the remaining work with respect to the funds remaining. Which of the following measures is Steve using?
   A. Cost aggregation
   B. Variance analysis
   C. Trend analysis
   D. To-Complete Performance Index (TCPI)

10. You are overseeing a mobile application development project. While reviewing an earned value report, you observe that the SPI is 1.2 and the CPI is 0.9. Which statement can you make about the project?
   A. On track according to schedule and budget baselines.
   B. Behind the schedule and over budget.
   C. Ahead of the schedule and over budget.
   D. On schedule and under budget.

11. Your project has a budget of $900,000 and is running well. In the latest earned value report, the team reported that the CPI = 1.1, the SPI = 0.9, and the PV= $600,000. You want to know, from this point on, how much more the project will cost but could not find it in the report. What will be the estimate to complete, or ETC, be in this case?
   A. $300,000
   B. $327,272
   C. $818,181
   D. $490,909

12. You recently finalized your project cost estimate and cost baseline. The difference between the project cost estimate and the cost baseline can be BEST described as:
   A. The control account estimates
   B. The work package estimates
   C. The management reserves
   D. The contingency reserves

13. You asked one of your team members about the schedule variance (SV) for one of her key deliverables. She mentioned that she is behind schedule but there would not be any cost variance. Which of the following is NOT true in this case?
   A. EV and PV were the same
   B. EV and AC were the same
   C. EV is less than PV
   D. CPI is 1

14. There were eight potential projects in your organization, and your senior management wanted to select the best project that would meet and exceed the organizational strategic goals and objectives. As your organization has limited resources and time constraints, it developed business cases for these projects and compared the benefits to select the best project. Out of eight projects, management has selected two projects and later on decided to go for Project X, which would yield $250,000 in benefits instead of Project Y, which would yield $200,000. What is the opportunity cost for selecting Project X over Project Y?
   A. $250,000
   B. $200,000
   C. – $250,000
   D. – $200,000

15. You are overseeing a project to implement an accounting application for a dentist's office. In one of the performance meetings, you came up with the following measurement: AC = 500, PV = 600, and EV = 650. What is going on with this project?
   A. Both CV and SV are positive numbers; thus, you are under budget and ahead of schedule.
   B. You do not have enough information to calculate SPI and CPI.
   C. The CV is a negative number, which means you have spent more than planned.
   D. The SV is a negative number, which means the project is behind schedule.

16. The project manager and the team members have just finished working on the WBS and have almost finalized the project schedule. The project manager is also planning to start working on the project budget. Which document will be used for planning, estimating, budgeting, and controlling costs so that the project can be completed within the approved budget?

A. Earned value management
B. Cost baseline
C. Cost management plan
D. Funding limit reconciliation

17. The Earned Value Management (EVM) will NOT be very beneficial in which situation?

A. To measure a project's progress against the project scope, cost, and schedule baselines.
B. To forecast future performance and the project's completion date and final cost.
C. To provide schedule and budget variances during the project.
D. To develop the project cost baseline.

18. A project manager is working on a project designed to create an internal website for ITPro Consultancy, LLC that will allow them to schedule the conference room online. While reviewing the status of the project, the project manager found out the EV, AC, and PV (listed in the table below). What are the cumulative SPI and CPI for Week 5?

Week	PV	EV	AC
Week 1	$20,000	$20,000	$17,500
Week 2	$25,000	$24,000	$19,000
Week 3	$40,000	$36,000	$27,000
Week 4	$70,000	$64,000	$32,000
Week 5	$87,000	$80,000	$45,000

A. 0.925 and 1.59
B. 1.59 and .925
C. 0.919 and 1.77
D. 1.77 and 0.919

19. You are preparing a cost management plan for the data center project you are managing for ITPro Consultancy, LLC. All of the following is true regarding this plan EXCEPT:

A. Activity cost estimates will be rounded to a prescribed precision; for example, $100, $1,000, and so on.
B. Units of measurement such as hours, days, weeks, or a lump sum amount will be used to estimate resources.
C. The primary concern is determining the amount of resources needed to complete the project activities.
D. The WBS provides a framework for the cost management plan, and a control account (CA) in the WBS is used to monitor and control the project cost.

20. You estimated your project cost to be $80,000 with a timeline of eight months. After four months in the project, you found out that 40 percent of the project is completed; the actual cost is $25,000. What does the SPI tell you in this case?

A. There is not enough information to calculate the SPI.
B. The project is behind schedule.
C. The project is ahead of schedule.
D. The project is progressing as per the plan.

21. You estimated your project cost to be $80,000 with a timeline of eight months. As of today, you found out that 40 percent of the project is completed; the actual cost is $30,000. What does the CPI tell you in this case?

A. There is not enough information to calculate the CPI.
B. The project is over budget.
C. The project is under budget.
D. The project is costing as per the plan.

22. You just completed your cost management plan and defined how the project cost will be planned, managed, expended, and controlled throughout the project life cycle. You also looked into your variance threshold, which is usually expressed as percentage deviations from the cost baseline that the sponsor or stakeholders are willing to allow before any action is required. This threshold is called:

A. Approved threshold
B. Variance limit
C. Control threshold
D. Control limit

23. Which one of the following is FALSE about TCPI?
   A. TCPI calculates the performance that must be achieved in order to meet financial or schedule goals.
   B. TCPI usually determines the status on the remaining work with respect to the funds remaining.
   C. If the cumulative CPI falls below the baseline plan, all future work must be performed at the TCPI to achieve the planned BAC.
   D. If the cumulative CPI falls below the baseline plan, all future work must be performed below the TCPI to achieve the planned BAC.

24. All of the following statements are true about cost baseline EXCEPT:
   A. It is a time-phased budget used to monitor, measure, and control cost performance during the project.
   B. It is usually displayed in the form of an S-curve.
   C. It assigns cost estimates for expected future period operating costs.
   D. It aggregates the estimated costs of project activities to work packages, then to control accounts, and finally to the project.

25. While working on your project budget, you also calculated the contingency reserve. This contingency reserve is the estimated cost to be determined, managed, and controlled at your discretion to deal with which of the following?
   A. To compensate inadequacies in your original cost planning.
   B. To address the cost impact of the risks remaining during the Plan Risk Responses process.
   C. To handle anticipated and certain events in your project.
   D. To handle unanticipated events or surprises in your project.

26. Lori is the project manager for a software development firm and has been assigned to create an accounting automation application for a dentist's office. While reviewing the cost estimate with Lori, the sponsor expressed her frustration with the higher cost and asked to reduce the estimate by at least ten percent. The sponsor is not too worried about the project duration estimate and suggested that Lori seek her help with the schedule if needed. What is the best course of action for Lori in this kind of situation?
   A. Replace a couple of expensive resources with lower-cost resources.
   B. Continue with the project and constantly find an opportunity to save money for a total savings of 10 percent.
   C. Have an urgent meeting with the team members and ask them to be innovative and squeeze their estimate.
   D. Inform the sponsor of the activities to be cut.

27. Selina is a project manager involved in the Estimate Costs process in the early phase of her project when a limited amount of detail was available to her. The range of her estimate was $75,000 to $200,000, and the actual cost came to be around $150,000. What would you call such an estimate?
   A. A variable estimate
   B. A definitive estimate
   C. A rough order of magnitude estimate
   D. A budget estimate

28. You have fifteen components to work on in a software development project. As per your estimation, the first six components would cost $1,500 each, and the remaining nine would cost $1,400 each. Your schedule projected that you would be done with 40 percent of the components today. While collecting the status updates from the team members, you found out that the first five components were completed at a cost of $8,000. What is the SPI?
   A. 1.20
   B. 0.132
   C. 0.833
   D. Cannot be determined

29. You are working on a project to convert an old nursing home to a new office complex. While reviewing the progress of your project, you found out that your EV = $26,000 and AC = $27,000. One of your site supervisors calls to inform you that there are several damages in the foundation that were not discovered earlier, and it will result in a significant cost overrun. What will you do FIRST?
   A. Make sure that the contingency reserves you have will be sufficient enough to cover the cost overrun.
   B. Call the sponsor immediately and inform her that additional funds will be needed.
   C. Ask the supervisor to figure out why these damages were not discovered earlier.
   D. Evaluate the cause and size of this cost overrun.

30. You are managing a software application project budgeted for $90,000 to develop an online PMP exam simulator. The team has completed design work, received approval from technical review team, and initiated coding work. You think that the current variances are atypical, and that similar variances will not occur in the future. You found that AC = $30,000 and EV = $35,000. What is your Estimate at Completion (EAC)?

   A. $85,000
   B. $77,586
   C. $90,000
   D. $60,000

Project Cost Management Answers

1. B: The EV is greater than the PV, which indicates the project is ahead of schedule. The AC is smaller than the EV, which indicates the project is under budget.

2. D: We are given the following values:
BAC = $45,000
PV = $30,000
Cumulative AC = $25,000
Cumulative EV = $24,000.

We know

EAC = BAC/CPI^c
ETC = EAC – AC
VAC = BAC – EAC and
TCPI = (BAC – EV) / (BAC – AC)
$CPI^c = EV^c/AC^c$
Thus CPI^c = $24,000/$25,000 = 0.96
So EAC = BAC/CPI^c = $45,000/0.96 = $46,875
ETC = EAC – AC = $46,875 – $25,000 = $21,875
TCPI = (BAC – EV) / (BAC – AC) = (45,000 – 24,000) / (45,000 – 25,000) = 21,000 / 20,000 = 1.05
VAC= BAC – EAC = $45,000 – $46,875 = –$1,875

The project will cost $46,875 since the EAC is $46,875. The ETC is $21,875, so you will need $21,875 to complete the project. The VAC is –$1,875; thus, the project will be over budget by $1,875. The project performance is not good as TCPI is 1.05. All of the statements are true except D. The project is over budget by $ 1,875, not under budget.

3. A: Work performance data is not an input in the Develop Budget process but an input in the Control Costs process.

4. C: Total fund or cost budget = cost baseline + management reserves

Cost baseline = project cost + contingency reserves
The cost baseline is the project cost plus the contingency reserves, and the cost budget, or how much money the company should have available for the project, is the cost baseline plus the management reserves. The project manager determines, manages, and controls the contingency reserves, which will address the cost impact of the risks remaining during the Plan Risk Responses process. On the other hand, management reserves are funds to cover unforeseen risks or changes to the project. In this case, the cost baseline and the management reserves will be most helpful to calculate the total funding and periodic funding requirements. Funding limit reconciliation is the technique of reconciling the expenditure of funds with the funding limits set for the project. As per the variance between the expenditure of funds and planned limit, the activities can be rescheduled to level out the rate of expenditures.

5. D: Performance review is not a tool & technique in the Develop Budget process but a tool & technique in the Control Costs process.

6. B: We have BAC = 6 * $75,000 = $450,000
At the end of month three, we were supposed to finish 50 percent of the work.
Thus, PV = BAC * Planned % Complete or PV = $450,000 * 50 percent = $225,000
Also, project work is 45 percent completed at the end of three months.
Thus, EV = BAC * Actual % Complete or EV = $450,000 * 45 percent = $202,500
Both the PV and EV are cumulative values in three months.
We know $SPI^c = EV^c/PV^c$ or SPI^c = $202,500/$225,000 = 0.9

7. C: This estimate uses mathematical models based on historical records from other projects. It utilizes the statistical relationship that exists between a series of historical data and a particular delineated list of other variables. Depending upon the quality of the underlying data, this estimate can produce higher levels of accuracy and can be used in conjunction with other estimates to provide estimates for the entire project or specific segments of a project. Measures such as time per line of code, time per installation, and time per linear meter are considered in this type of estimate.

8. D: You just completed the Estimate Costs process and should be focusing on the Determine Budget process.

9. D: To-Complete Performance Index (TCPI) calculates the performance that must be achieved in order to meet financial or schedule goals.
If targeting the current plan, TCPI = (BAC – EV) / (BAC – AC)
If targeting the current EAC, TCPI = (BAC – EV) / (EAC – AC)
Here AC = Actual Cost, EV = Earned Value, EAC = Estimate at Completion, and BAC = Budget at Completion.

Here (BAC – EV) is the remaining work and (BAC – AC) or (EAC – AC) is the remaining fund.

10. C: A SPI of 1.2 means that the project is ahead of schedule, and a CPI of 0.9 or less than one means that the project is over budget.

11. B: We know ETC = EAC – AC, so we need to find out the values for Estimate at Completion (EAC) and Actual Cost (AC).

We are given the following values:
BAC = $900,000
CPI = 1.1
SPI = 0.9
PV = $600,000
We also know that EAC = BAC/CPI; thus EAC = $900,000/1.1 = $818,181
Now we have SPI = 0.9 or EV/PV = 0.9; thus EV = 0.9 * PV
So EV = 0.9 * 600,000 = $540,000
We also know that CPI = 1.1 or EV/AC = 1.1; thus, EV = 1.1 * AC
So AC = EV/1.1 or AC = 540,000/1.1 = $490,909
So ETC = EAC – AC or ETC = $818,181 – $490,909 = $327,272

12. D: The cost baseline is the project cost plus the contingency reserves; thus, the difference between the project cost estimate and the cost baseline can be best described as contingency reserves.

13. A: We know SV = EV – PV. Since SV has a negative value, EV must be less than PV.

Also CV = EV – AC. Since there will be no cost variance, EV and AC have the same value. CPI is also EV/AC = 1.

14. B: The opportunity cost is the value of the project that was not selected or the opportunity that was missed out on. In this case, the opportunity cost for Project X is the value of the Project Y, or $200,000.

15. A: We know SV = EV – PV and CV = EV – AC
So SV = 650 – 600 = 50 and CV = 650 – 500 = 150
A positive CV indicates that the project is under budget, and a positive SV indicates that the project is ahead of schedule.

16. C: The project cost management plan is a component of the overall project management plan, and it defines how the project cost will be planned, managed, expended, and controlled throughout the project life cycle.

17. D: Earned value analysis provides a means to determine cost and schedule variances, not to develop the project cost baseline.

18. A: We know that $SPI^c = EV^c/PV^c$ and $CPI^c = EV^c/AC^c$
At the end of Week 5, the cumulative EV = $20,000 + $24,000 + $36,000 + $64,000 + $80,000 = $224,000
Cumulative PV = $20,000 + $25,000 + $40,000 + $70,000 + $87,000 = $242,000
Cumulative AC = $17,500 + $19,000 + $27,000 + $32,000 + $45,000 = $140,500
$SPI^c = EV^c/PV^c$
= 224,000/242,000
= 0.925
$CPI^c = EV^c/AC^c$
= 224,000/140,500
= 1.59

19. C: The primary concern for project cost management is to determine the cost of resources, not the amount to complete the project activities.

20. B: Here we have BAC = $80,000
We know that EV = BAC * Actual % Complete
So EV = BAC * 40 percent completion = $80,000 x 40 percent = $32,000
Also PV = BAC * (Time Passed/Total Scheduled Time)
And PV = $80,000 * (4 months/8 months) = $40,000
So SPI = EV/PV = 32,000/40,000 = 0.8
SPI is less than one, which suggests that the project is behind schedule.

21. C: Here we have BAC= $80,000 and AC = $30,000
We know that EV = BAC * Actual % Complete
So EV = BAC * 40 percent completion
= $80,000 * 40 percent = $32,000
So CPI = EV/AC = 32,000/30,000 = 1.066
CPI is more than one, which suggests that the project is under budget.

22. C: Control thresholds are usually expressed as percentage deviations from the cost baseline that the sponsor or stakeholders are willing to allow before any action is required.

23. D: TCPI calculates the performance that must be achieved in order to meet financial or schedule goals and determines the status on the remaining work with respect to the funds remaining. If the cumulative CPI falls below the baseline plan, all future work must be performed at the TCPI to achieve the planned BAC.

24. C: Expected future period operation costs are considered to be ongoing costs and should not be part of the project costs.

25. B: The project manager determines, manages, and controls the contingency reserves, which will address the cost impact of the risks remaining (residual risks or known unknown risks).

26. D: The project manager is expected to come up with a realistic estimate that does not include padding. The project manager also should not simply reduce the estimate whenever asked by the sponsor or clients. If the project manager must reduce the estimate, she needs to explore other options such as cutting scope, reducing quality, or replacing expensive resources with lower-cost resources. In this case, Lori should inform the sponsor the activities to be cut in order to reduce the estimate by ten percent.

27. C: A rough order of magnitude (–25 percent to 75 percent) is an approximate estimate made without detailed data. This type of estimate is used during the formative stages for initial evaluation of a project's feasibility. In this example, $75,000 and $200,000 are –25 percent to +75 percent of $150,000.

28. C: The budget for the first six components is 6 * $1,500 = $9,000, and the budget for the remaining nine components is 9 * $1,400 = $12,600. So BAC = $9,000 + $ 12,600 = $21,600
We know PV = BAC * Planned % Complete
So PV = 21,600 * 40 percent = $8,640
We have a total of fifteen components and so far completed five components.
EV = BAC * (Work Completed/Total Work Required)
So EV = $21,600 * 5/15 = $7,200
So SPI = EV/PV = 7200/8640 = 0.833

29. D: The first step should be to get as much information as possible about the damages in the foundation by evaluating the cause and size of the damage and the amount needed for the fix. You can take other actions as appropriate once you have all the details.

30. A: If current variances are considered as atypical and you anticipate that similar variances will not occur in the future, the correct EAC formula is EAC = AC + (BAC – EV).
In this case, BAC = $90,000
EAC = $30,000 + ($90,000 – $35,000) = $85,000

CHAPTER 8

PROJECT QUALITY MANAGEMENT

Project Quality and Quality Management

Quality is a major concern in all projects as quality defines the stakeholders' expectations in the project. A project may be completed on time and within budget, but if the product is wrong or of inferior quality, the stakeholders will rightfully be dissatisfied.

There are several leading quality theories, including ISO 9000, Total Quality Management, Six Sigma, and more. Some of these early theories were mostly focused on inspection, but the current philosophy of quality is concentrated on prevention over inspection. This evolution of thought is based on the fact that with a focus on quality, we spend time preventing, rather than dealing with problems, as it costs a whole lot more to fix errors than to prevent them.

Quality is defined as the degree to which the project fulfills requirements. It is an agreed combination of the following attributes:

Attributes	Details
Conformity	The product has all the data, processes, and functionality specified.
Usability	The product is easy to use and understand from the client's perspective.
Efficiency	The product uses people, business processes, hardware, database, or other support efficiently.
Maintainability	The product is easy to maintain and support.
Flexibility	The product is easy to modify and include or add new functions and data.
Reliability	The product is free from errors and performs reliably.
Portability	The product can operate in different physical, business, software, and hardware environments.
Reusability	The product can be reused for a different purpose or application.
Security/Auditability	The product is secured from unauthorized access and modification, can be easily audited, and includes adequate controls.
Job impact	The product positively affects the existing workflows, control, and autonomy of the business area.

Table 8-1: Quality Attributes

A product that is produced at a high-level of quality but does not include many of the features of similar products is referred to as low grade. For instance, a software application can be of high quality, by having no obvious defects, but low grade, by having a limited number of features. Conversely, a product can be of low quality, by having a significant number of defects, but high grade, by having numerous features.

A project manager must determine the trade-offs of quality and grade and also determine the level of accuracy and precision. Accuracy indicates that the measured value is very close to the target value, whereas precision indicates that values of repeated measurements are clustered and have little scatter. A consistent outcome is the goal when focusing on precision. For example, if you are testing a procedure and the target is 500 liters output, accuracy deals with how close the measurement is to the 500 liters target. On the other hand, how many of the outputs are 500 liters is the focus of precision.

Project Quality Management: It includes the processes and activities to ensure that a project meets the defined needs from the customer's perspective and to ensure that there are no deviations from the project requirements. Quality management consists of the following processes:

1. Plan Quality Management
2. Perform Quality Assurance
3. Control Quality

Project Manager's Roles in Quality

Project quality management includes all processes required to ensure that the project will satisfy the needs for which it was undertaken. Throughout a project's life cycle, the project manager is responsible for assuring that process quality is maintained in order to guarantee meeting both specifications and customer needs. A project manager should:

- Understand the customer's definition and expectation of quality.
- Determine quality metrics to be used to measure quality prior to initiating the project work.
- Identify any quality standards that are applicable to the project.
- Identify the desired level of performance in the project.
- Recommend improvements to the performing organization's standards, policies, and processes.
- Consider the impact on quality whenever there is a change in the "triple constraints."
- Make sure that all activities and work packages are meeting the quality standard.
- Focus on improving quality in the project in every way possible.
- Make sure that authorized processes and approaches are followed in the project.
- Give quality the same importance as scope, time, and cost.
- Create other project standards and processes and identify ways of improving processes in the project.
- Hold regular meetings to identify and resolve quality issues.
- Evaluate the effectiveness of the quality control system.
- Make sure the team members understand the quality expectation in their deliverables.
- Perform quality assurance and quality control.
- Identify ways to stop problems, errors, and issues from reoccurring.
- Capture quality issues in lessons learned and make sure to feed lessons learned back into the project.

Quality Methodology: Crosby, Juran, and Deming

There are three prevailing theories for quality in the quality management literature:

Conformance to specifications: Phil Crosby popularized the concept of the cost of poor quality, advocated prevention over inspection and "zero defects," and defined quality as conformance to specification (project produces what it was created to produce).

Fitness for use: Joseph Juran developed the 80/20 principle, advocated top management involvement, and defined quality by fitness for use (product or service must satisfy the real need).

Plan-Do-Check-Act: Plan-Do-Check-Act is a cycle of iterative activities designed to drive continuous improvement. Initially implemented in manufacturing, it has broad applicability in business. First developed by Walter Shewhart, it was popularized by Edwards Deming.

This theory advocates that business processes should be scrutinized and measured to detect sources of variations that cause products to deviate from customer requirements. The recommendation is to place the business processes in an unremitting feedback loop so that managers can isolate and change the parts of the process that need improvements.

The four phases in the Plan-Do-Check-Act cycle involve the following:

- **Plan:** Design or revise business process components to improve results.
- **Do:** Implement the plan and measure its performance.
- **Check:** Assess the measurements and report the results to decision makers.
- **Act:** Decide on changes needed to improve the process.

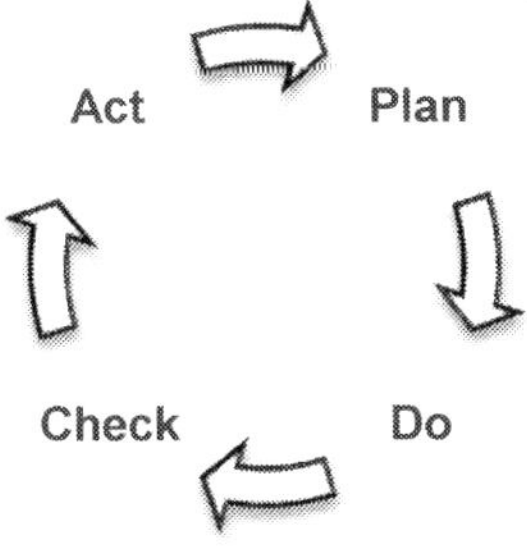

Figure 8-1: Plan-Do-Check-Act Cycle

There can be any number of iterations of the "Do" and "Check" phases as the solution is refined, retested, re-refined, and retested again.

Quality management recognizes the importance of the following:

Quality Methodologies	Details
Customer Satisfaction	To meet customer requirements we need to understand, define, evaluate, and manage expectations and combine fitness for use (product or service must satisfy the real need) and conformance to specifications (project produces what it was created to produce).
Total Quality Management (TQM)	Total quality management is a management strategy to embed awareness to focus on finding ways to improve quality in all organizational processes, business practices, and products. Everyone in the organization is responsible for quality and is capable of making a difference in the ultimate quality of the product.
ISO 9000 Series	ISO 9000 series is a collection of internationally accepted standards concerned with quality management compiled by the International Organization for Standardization. Eight quality management principles are defined in: – ISO 9000:2000, Quality Management Systems Fundamentals and Vocabulary – ISO 9004:2000, Quality Management Systems Guidelines for Performance Improvements
Six Sigma	Six Sigma is a disciplined quality process that strives to develop and deliver near-perfect products and services. The aim of Six Sigma is to measure how many defects are in a process and then systematically figure out how to eliminate them. It is a business process that allows companies to drastically improve their bottom line by designing and monitoring everyday business activities in ways that minimize waste and resources while increasing customer satisfaction. It guides companies into making fewer mistakes in everything they do, from filling out purchase orders to manufacturing airplane engines, eliminating lapses in quality at the earliest possible occurrence. It does not merely detect and correct errors; it provides specific methods to recreate processes so that errors never arise in the first place.
Continuous Improvement (Kaizen)	Plan-Do-Check-Act is the basis for continuous improvement defined by Deming. It is an ongoing effort to improve organizational quality and performance. Its aim is to improve customer satisfaction through continuous improvements to products, services, or processes. It's a philosophy that stresses constant process improvement in the form of small changes in products or services. Initiatives such as TQM and Six Sigma should improve the quality of project management as well as the quality of the product. Process improvement models such as Capability Maturity Model Integrated (CMMI) and Project Management Maturity Model (OPM3) also improve quality.
Cost of Quality	Cost of quality involves determining what costs will be needed to ensure quality. Prevention and appraisal costs include quality planning, quality control, and quality assurance. Other costs include training and quality control systems to ensure compliance with requirements.
Marginal Analysis	Sometimes added attention to quality may not produce added values, and when we reach that stage, we need to stop paying too much attention to quality. Marginal analysis refers to looking for the point where the benefits or revenue from improving quality equals the incremental cost to achieve that quality.
Prevention over Inspection	Quality should be planned, designed, and built in, not inspected in. It will cost much less to prevent mistakes than it will cost to correct them when they are found after the fact by inspection.

Just in Time (JIT)	Just in Time (JIT) is an inventory management method whereby materials, goods, and labor are scheduled to arrive or be replenished exactly when needed in the production process, thereby bringing inventory down to zero or almost near to a zero level. – It decreases costs by keeping only enough inventory on hand to meet immediate production needs. – Its planning, simplification, and standardization are aimed at reducing carrying costs by eliminating the expense of housing idle materials and lowering the costs of defective products, wasted space, extra equipment, overtime, warranty repair, and scrap. – It also speeds the production process, thereby eliminating long lead times and improving delivery performance. **Example:** Computer manufacturers like DELL use just-in-time inventory to control the manufacturing and ordering of their computer systems. Rather than a maintaining warehouse filled with pre-assembled computers, the company places orders for computer parts as customers make purchases. The computer firm buys its parts from various suppliers.
Management Responsibility	Although a project manager is responsible for the quality of the project's product, each team member should ensure the quality of his/her own deliverables. Senior management is responsible for the quality in the organization as a whole. As per W. Edwards Deming, 85 percent of the cost of quality is a management problem. All members of the project team should participate to ensure success, but providing the resources needed to succeed remains the responsibility of management. For instance, in a construction project, workers laying the foundation and constructing the building have very little control over the quality of the materials as the management team is responsible for purchasing and may propose to use inferior-grade materials to save money.
Possible Impacts of Poor Quality	– Increased Costs – Low Morale – Lower Customer Satisfaction – Increased Risk – Rework – Schedule Delay

Table 8-2: Quality Methodologies

Project Quality Management Processes

Project quality management warrants that the deliverables project teams create meet the expectations of the stakeholders. As a project manager you should not only plan quality before project work begins, but also as work is completed. Note that quality should be planned into a project, not solely inspected in a project. Quality planning can confirm the preexistence of quality or the need for quality improvements. During project execution, you should make sure that project activities are complying with organizational and project quality policies, standards, processes, and procedures. Moreover, you need to utilize the Quality Control process that uses inspections to prove the existence of quality within a project deliverable.

PMI identifies three key processes that are associated with the quality management knowledge area.

Processes	Process Groups	Details	Key Outputs
1. Plan Quality Management	Planning	The process of identifying all the relevant quality requirements, specifications, and standards for the project and product and specifying how the specifications will be met.	– Quality Management Plan – Process Improvement Plan – Quality Metrics
2. Perform Quality Assurance	Executing	The process of determining if the project activities are complying with organizational and project policies, standards, processes, and procedures.	– Organizational Process Assets Updates – Change Requests
3. Control Quality	Monitoring & Controlling	The process of monitoring specific project results to determine if they comply with relevant quality standards and identifying ways to eliminate causes of unsatisfactory results.	– Quality Control Measurements – Validated Changes – Validated Deliverables – Work Performance Information – Change Requests

Table 8-3: Three Project Quality Management Processes and Key Outputs

Project Quality Management Processes, Inputs, Tools & Techniques, and Outputs

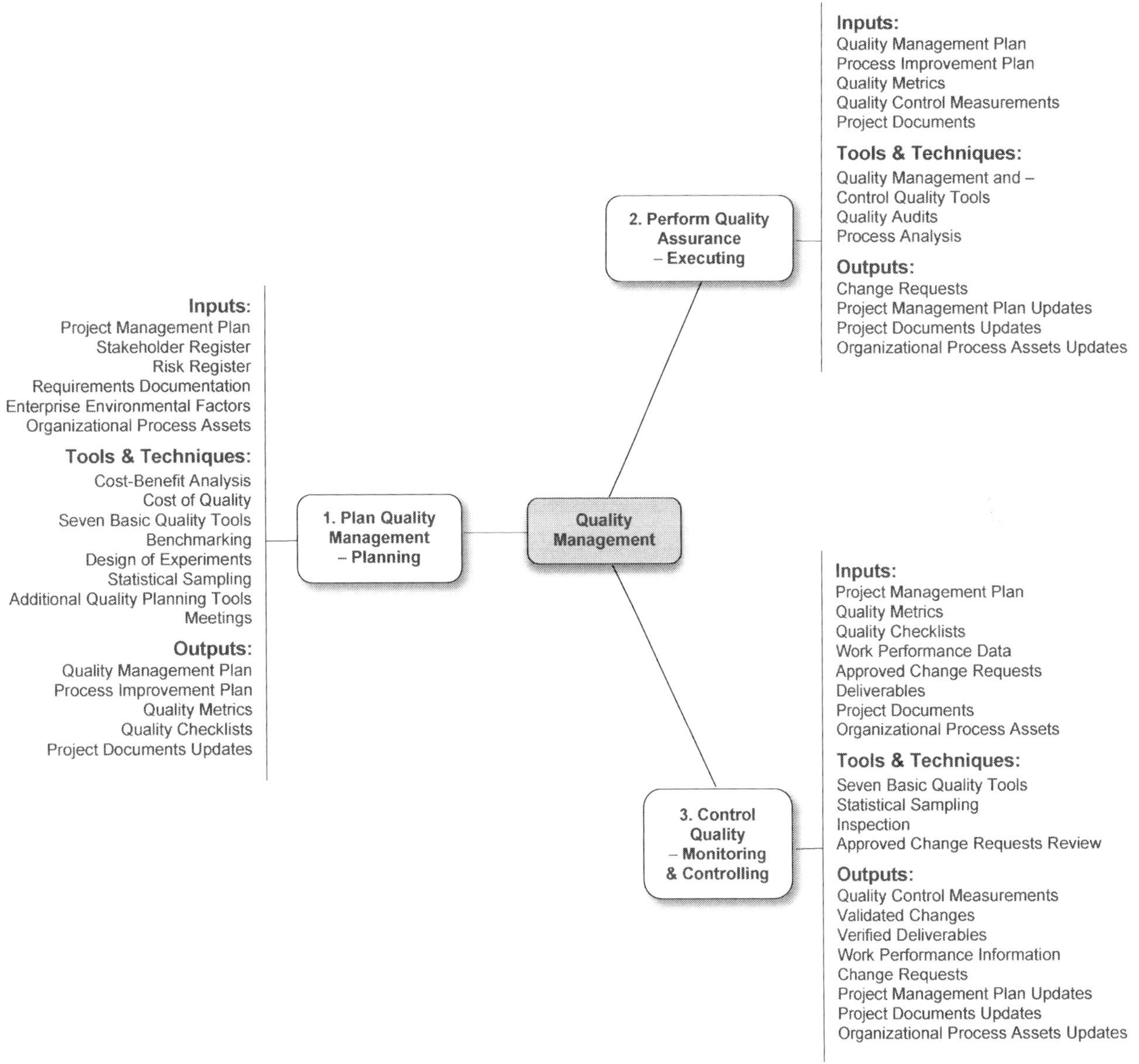

Figure 8-2: Project Quality Management Processes, Inputs, Tools & Techniques, and Outputs

Plan Quality Management

Plan Quality Management is the process of identifying all the relevant quality requirements, specifications, and standards for the project and product and specifying how the specifications will be met. It should begin in the early planning phase in parallel with other planning processes. Below are the key functionalities in this process:

- Identify existing quality standards for product and project management as appropriate
- Create additional project-specific standards as appropriate
- Determine actions needed to meet the quality standards
- Determine how to measure to make sure standards are met
- Balance the needs of quality with scope, cost, time, risk, and customer satisfaction
- Create a quality management plan and add it to the project management plan

As per the PMBOK®, the Plan Quality Management process has the following inputs, tools & techniques, and outputs:

Figure 8-3: Plan Quality Management: Inputs, Tools & Techniques, and Outputs

Plan Quality Management: Inputs

- Project Management Plan
- Stakeholder Register
- Risk Register
- Requirements Documentation
- Enterprise Environmental Factors
- Organizational Process Assets

Project Management Plan: The following components may be used along with others in the development of the quality management plan.

Scope Baseline: The scope baseline includes the following:

Project Scope Statement: Defines the project description, major deliverables, and acceptance criteria of project requirements. All these components affect quality planning, and by satisfying all acceptance criteria, it implies that customer quality requirements have been met.

WBS: Deliverables, work packages, and control accounts are used to measure project performance, and all these are identified by the WBS.

WBS Dictionary: Contains the technical information for the WBS elements.

Schedule Baseline: Scope is closely linked to quality, and changes in scope should be evaluated against the schedule.

Cost Performance Baseline: Changes in scope should also be evaluated against the cost performance baseline or budget.

Other Management Plans: Plans in other management areas will play major roles in defining actionable areas of concern with regard to quality.

Stakeholder Register: Contains information on stakeholders with specific interests, requirements, or expertise in quality.

Risk Register: Contains information on risks that are related to quality.

Requirements Documentation: Consists of product and quality requirements expected by the stakeholders and helps the team members to plan quality implementation in the project.

Enterprise Environmental Factors: Governmental agency regulations, rules, standards, and guidelines specific to the application area may affect the project. Some available standards include the following:

- The United Nations Convention on Contracts for International Sale of Goods (CISG), which governs international sales transactions
- Occupational Safety and Health Administration (OSHA) standards
- ISO 9000

Organizational Process Assets: Organizational quality policies, procedures, guidelines, historical databases, and lessons learned from previous projects specific to the application area may affect the project.

Plan Quality Management: Tools & Techniques

- Cost-Benefit Analysis
- Cost of Quality
- Seven Basic Quality Tools
- Benchmarking
- Design of Experiments
- Statistical Sampling
- Additional Quality Planning Tools
- Meetings

Cost-Benefit Analysis: A comparison of the cost of quality to the expected benefit. The benefit of quality must outweigh the cost of achieving it. The primary benefit of quality is increased stakeholders' satisfaction and less rework, which means higher productivity and lower cost.

The Cost of Quality (COQ): The cost of quality considers the expenses of all the activities within a project to ensure quality. It is broken down into two categories:

Cost of Conformance to Requirements: This approach is the cost of completing the project work to satisfy the project scope and the expected level of quality. Examples of this approach include prevention functions and appraisal functions.

Cost of Nonconformance: This approach is the cost of completing the project work without quality.

- The biggest issue posed by the scenario is the cost incurred as a result of project rework.
- It is always more cost effective to do the work right the first time.
- Other nonconformance costs include loss of customers, downtime, and corrective actions to fix problems caused by incorrect work.

Examples of this approach include internal failures, external failures, and legal implications.

Total COQ = Usually 15 percent to 25 percent of total product cost.

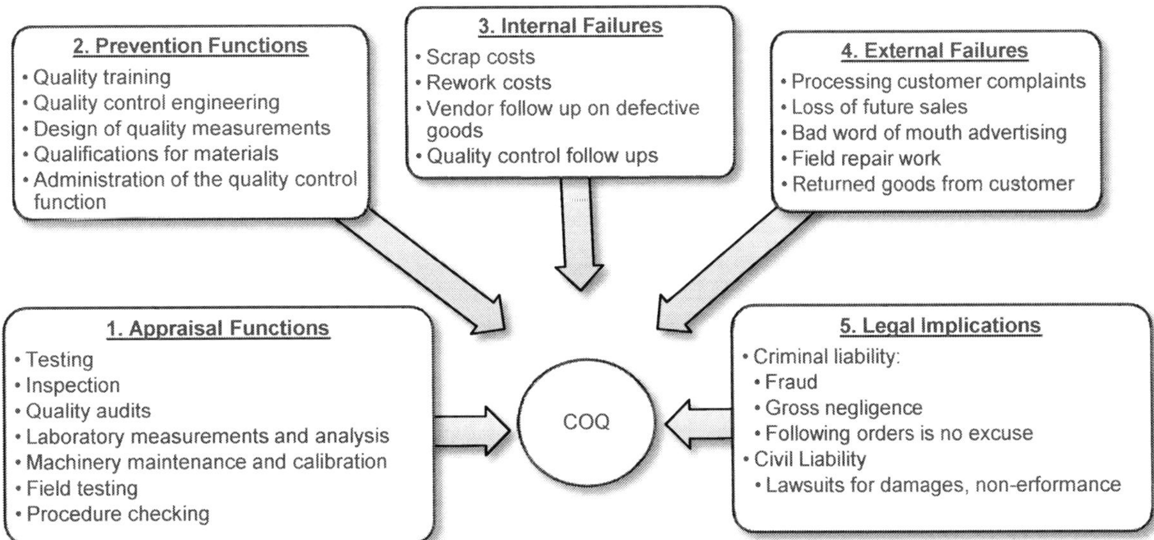

Figure 8-4: Cost of Quality – Cost of Conformance (1. Appraisal Functions and 2. Prevention Functions) and Cost of Nonconformance (3. Internal Failures, 4. External Failures, and 5. Legal Implications)

Seven Basic Quality Tools:

Seven basic quality tools, called 7QC tools, are used to identify and resolve quality-related problems in the project. They include:

1. Cause and effect diagram
2. Control chart
3. Flow chart
4. Histogram
5. Pareto chart
6. Scatter diagram
7. Checksheet

1. Cause and Effect (Ishikawa or Fishbone) Diagrams

The Cause and Effect (Ishikawa or Fishbone) diagram is a tool used for systematically identifying and presenting all the possible causes and sub-causes of a particular problem in a graphical format. It can help in quality control by identifying causes contributing to quality problems. Cause and effect diagrams are:

- Helpful in organizing thoughts and stimulating thinking and discussion.
- A creative way to look at causes/potential causes of an effect.
- Used to explore the factors that will result in a desired outcome.

Example: Suppose you are a project manager who has been working very hard to become a PMP. You sat for the exam twice, but unfortunately you have not managed to pass yet. Now you want to have a brainstorming session using the Ishikawa diagram as a tool to help illuminate issues that up to this point may have been unseen or not quite obvious. In the discussion, the following elements come into the spotlight as the major contributors to the problem:

1. People
2. Exam
3. Environment
4. Method
5. Material

The Ishikawa now looks like the following diagram:

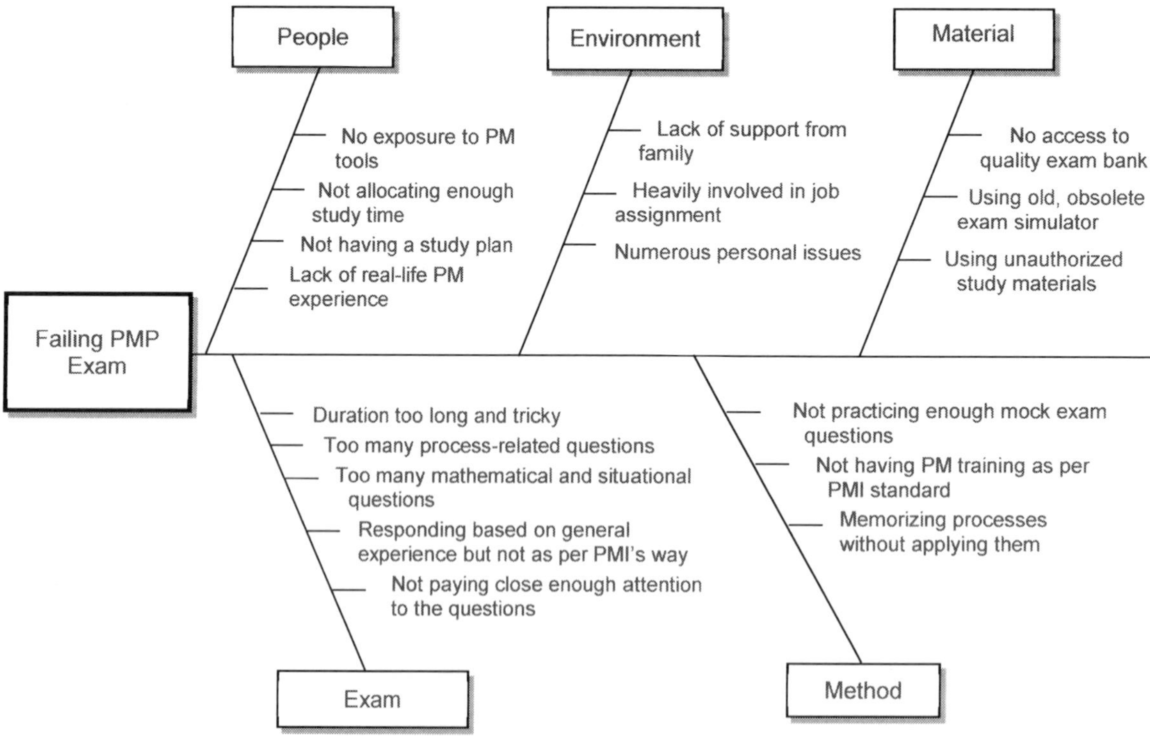

Figure 8-5: Cause and Effect Diagram or Fishbone Diagram

2. Control Charts

A control chart is a tool used to monitor processes and assure that they remain within acceptable limits or "in control." It helps distinguish process variation due to assignable causes from those due to unassignable causes, and if the process is "out of control," it must be brought statistically back in line.

Types of Variation	Variation Characteristics
Assignable Cause, also known as Special Cause	– Meaningful factors of process; not always present. – Cause can be avoided and should be investigated. – Not normal to process—rule of seven.
Unassignable Cause, also known as Common Cause	– Factors are always present. – Unavoidable and inherent in a process. – Normal and expected within a process.

Table 8-4: Variation Types and Characteristics

A control chart consists of the following:

Mean (Average): A line drawn through the average of all data points shows the middle of the range of acceptable variation in the process.

Upper and lower control limits: These limits define the acceptable range of variation of a process and are set by the project manager and stakeholders based on the expected quality standards.

For the samples chosen, at first, the mean and standard deviation are measured; then, upper and lower control limits are calculated by (Mean + 3 * Sigma) and (Mean – 3 * Sigma).

- The area between the upper and lower control limits represents the acceptable or normal distribution curve.
- The size of the distribution curve is typically three to six standard deviations or three to six sigmas. If it is three sigma, then 99.73 percent of the occurrences will fall within the acceptable range of the mean.

Specification Limits: Represent the customer's expectations or contractual requirements for performance and quality in the project and can appear either inside or outside of the control limit. The performing organization's standards must be stricter than those of the customers.

The process is "In Control" if: All process values are plotted within the upper and lower control limits and no particular tendency is noted (e.g., rule of seven).

The process is "Out of Control" if: Values are plotted outside the control limits and values show a particular tendency (e.g., rule of seven).

Rule of Seven:

It refers to nonrandom data points grouped together in a series that total seven on one side of the mean. This type of situation needs to be investigated and a cause should be found, because even though none of the points are out of the control limit, they are not random and the process may be out of control.

Example: Let's take the following data sample for the month of June to create a control chart.

Date	Sample Measures	Date	Sample Measures	Date	Sample Measures
June 1	12	**June 11**	18	**June 21**	12
June 2	11	**June 12**	14	**June 22**	15
June 3	15	**June 13**	10	**June 23**	14
June 4	11	**June 14**	6	**June 24**	15
June 5	10	**June 15**	10	**June 25**	13
June 6	13	**June 16**	8	**June 26**	15
June 7	10	**June 17**	10	**June 27**	9
June 8	1	**June 18**	11	**June 28**	13
June 9	15	**June 19**	19	**June 29**	8
June 10	16	**June 20**	14	**June30**	12

Table 8-5: Sample Measurements

1. First of all, we need to find out the mean, which is the average of all data points.
Mean =
(12 + 11 + 15 + 11 + 10 + 13 + 10 + 1 + 15 + 16 + 18 + 14 + 10 + 6 + 10 + 8 + 10 + 11 + 19 + 14 + 12 + 15 + 14 + 15 + 13 + 15 + 9 + 13 + 8 + 12)/30 = 12

2. We also need to find out the standard deviation, which can be calculated by doing the following:
   a. Calculate the difference between each data point and the mean, squaring each of the differences and then dividing the sum of the squared differences by the number of data points

(12–12)^2 + (12–11)^2 + (12–15)^2 + (12–11)^2 + (12–10)^2 + (12–13)^2 + (12–10)^2 + (12–1)^2 + (12–15)^2 + (12–16)^2 + (12–18)^2 + (12–14)^2 + (12–10)^2 + (12–6)^2 + (12–10)^2 + (12–8)^2 + (12–10)^2 + (12–11)^2 + (12–19)^2 + (12–14)^2 + (12–12)^2 + (12–15)^2 + (12–14)^2 + (12–15)^2 + (12–13)^2 + (12–15)^2 + (12–9)^2 + (12–13)^2 + (12–8)^2 + (12–12)^2 /30
= 382/30 = 12.73

   b. Calculate the square root of the average

standard deviation = Square root of 12.73 = 3.568

3. Upper control limit = Mean + 3 * standard deviation
= 12 + (3* 3.568) = 12 + 10.704 = 22.7

4. Lower control limit = Mean – 3 * standard deviation
= 12 – (3*3.568) = 12 – 10.704 = 1.3

Let's review the control chart below.

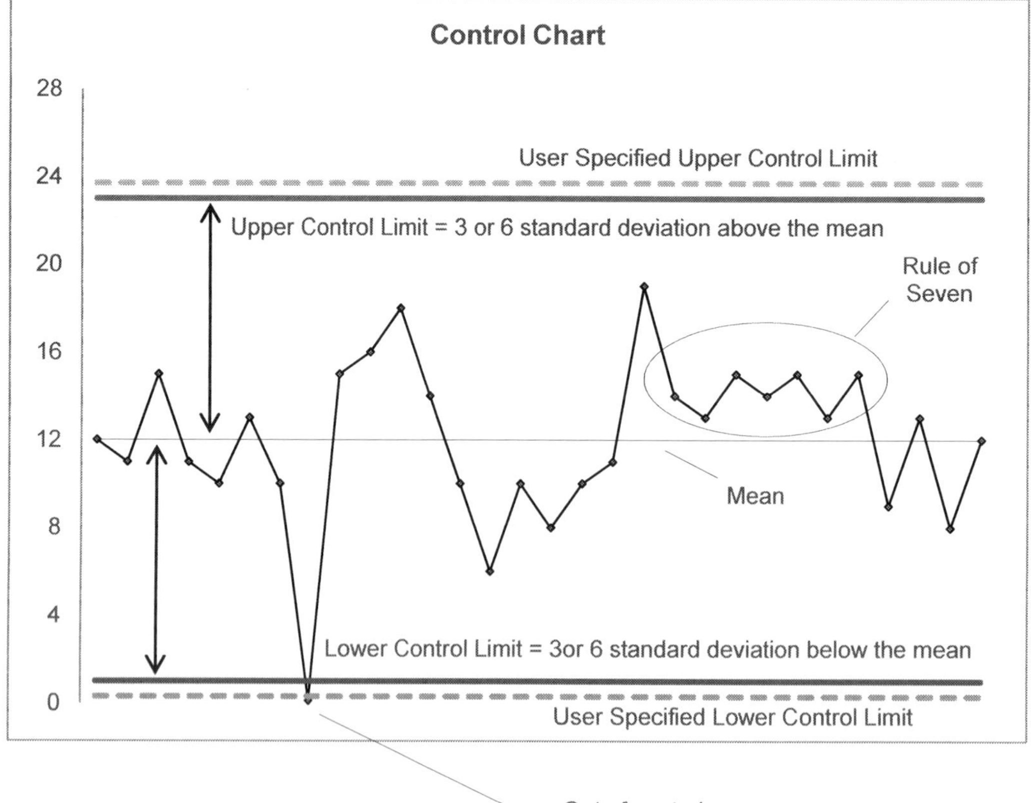

Figure 8-6: Control Chart

3. Flow Chart

A flow chart is a graphical representation of a process to help analyze how problems occur and identify potential process improvement opportunities. There are many styles, but all flow charts show activities, decision points, order of processing, points of complexity, and interrelationships between elements in the process.

Identifying risks and improving quality using flow charts:

To identify project risks and their causes from a flow chart, we need to ask the following questions:

1. What happens early in the process that could cause problems later on?
2. Which activities are out of our control?
3. Are there logical inconsistencies, bottlenecks, or complexities that could create delays, errors, or confusion?

In the house painting project flow chart diagram below, we notice that if there is lots of flaking paint, holes, or exposed wood, it will take longer than expected to paint the house. These items can easily act as bottlenecks, and things can go out of our control if we do not take precautions. Identifying these risk items and then coming up with viable solutions will help us improve the quality in the house painting project.

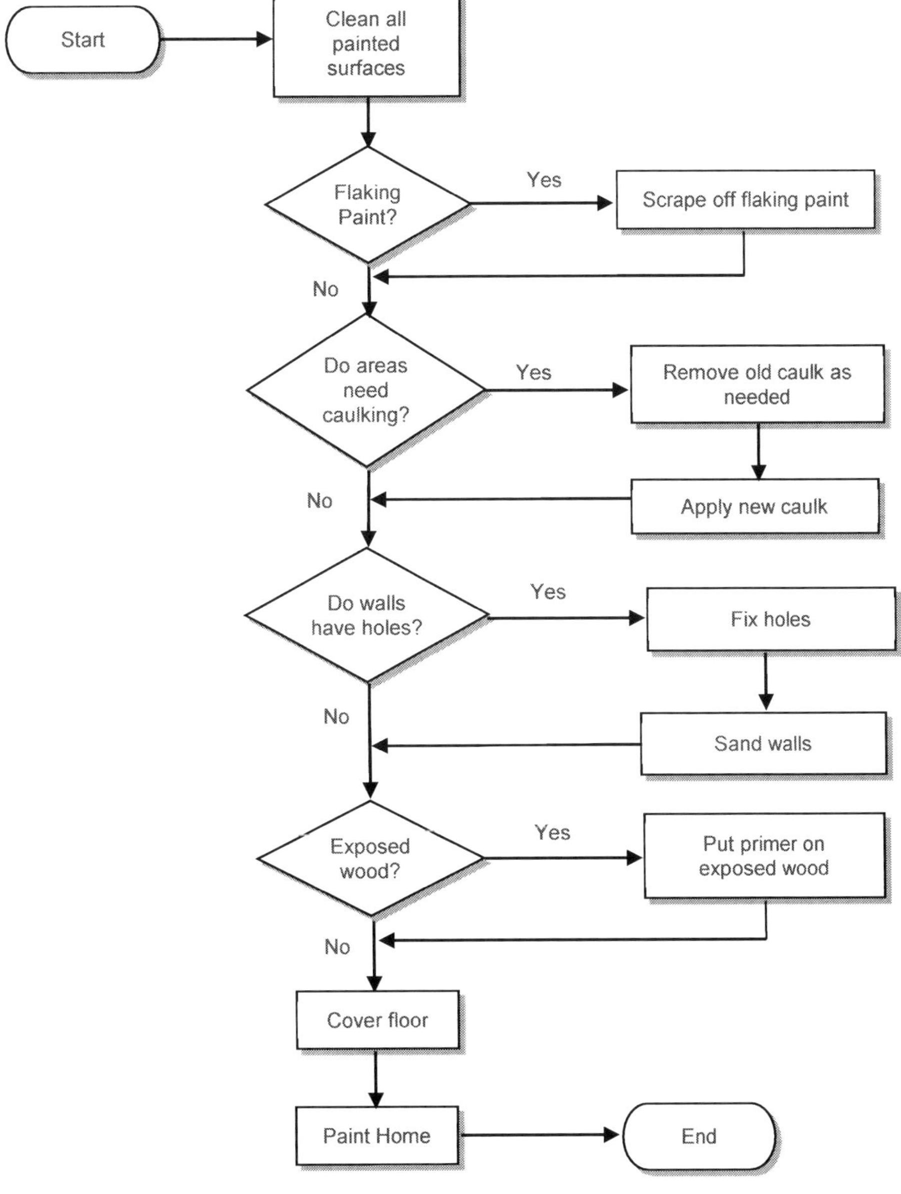

Figure 8-7: House Painting Flow Chart

4. Histogram

A histogram is a bar chart that shows the distribution of data. As it is designed to show the centering, dispersion (spread), and shape (relative frequency) of the data, it also shows a count of the data points falling in various ranges. Histograms can provide a visual display of large amounts of data that is difficult to understand in tabular or spreadsheet form.

The groups of data are called classes, and in the context of a histogram, they are known as bins, because one can think of them as containers that accumulate data and "fill up" at a rate equal to the frequency of that data class.

Example: Suppose you have the following students in an MBA class with their grades displayed in the table below. You want to find out how many grades fall into a certain category or range/interval (bin limits) and also if the chart represents a normal distribution or not. We can do this by defining a bin limit, or interval, and plotting the frequency or number of grades falling within each limit or interval in a histogram.

Student	Grade	Student	Grade	Student	Grade	Student	Grade
Arnold	45	Ian	51	Quezar	57	Ying Ping	60
Brenda	48	James	63	Romeo	48	Zanet	54
Chris	73	Keith	68	Steve	55		
David	54	Larry	36	Tim	43		
Eric	66	Max	48	Ujen	46		
Frank	62	Nancy	53	Vincent	53		
George	38	O'Neil	65	Wan Lee	58		
Harry	34	Patrick	29	Xeo Lee	56		

Table 8-6: Student Grades for an MBA Class

Now let's pick an interval of five and calculate the frequency in the following table:

Bin Limit	0	5	10	15	20	25	30	35	40	45	50	55	60	65	70	75	80	85	90	100
Frequency	0	0	0	0	0	0	1	1	2	2	4	6	4	3	2	1	0	0	0	0

As we can see, in the middle of the graph, we have around six students who received grades that fall between the range of fifty-five and sixty, and we almost have a normal distribution here.

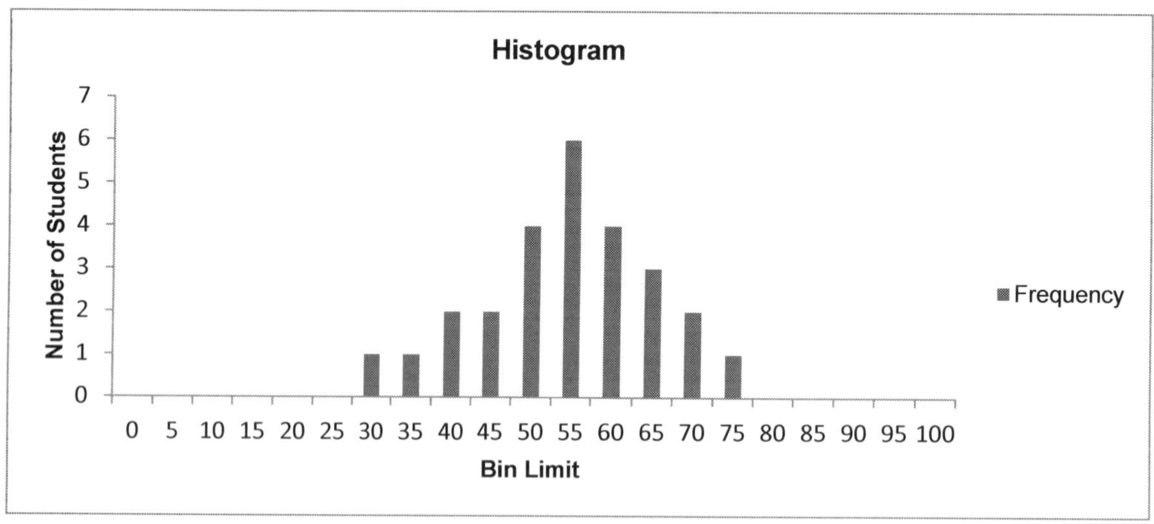

Figure 8-8: Histogram

5. Pareto Chart

A Pareto chart illustrates a prioritized list of causes of errors. It is displayed as a histogram and shows frequency of errors according to causes. The concept is based on the 80/20 rule: "80 percent of the problems come from 20 percent of the causes;" thus, it is important to pay close attention to the 20 percent of critical causes in order to resolve 80 percent of the problems. A Pareto chart:

- Helps concentrate awareness on the most critical issues.
- Prioritizes prospective causes of the problems.
- Determines priorities for quality improvement activities.
- Isolates the critical few causes of the problems from the uncritical many.

Example: Suppose you have gathered data on different complaints in a hotel and want to identify the critical causes of the problems. In order to draw a Pareto chart, you need to come up with the number of complaints in each complaint type, order them from largest to smallest, and calculate the cumulative number and cumulative percentage.

Complaint Types in a Hotel			
Complaint Type	**Number of Complaints**	**Cumulative Number**	**Cumulative Percentage**
Room Service	234	234	40.1%
Reservation	113	347	59.5%
Bed Linen	80	427	73.2%
TV Set	44	471	80.8%
Internet	44	515	88.3%
Furniture	32	547	93.8%
Heating	15	562	96.4%
Cleaning	7	569	97.6%
Towel	5	574	98.5%
Noise	4	578	99.1%
Décor	3	581	99.7%
Pillow	2	583	100.0%

Table 8-7: Complaint Types in a Hotel

If you pay close attention, you will notice that the first four complaints—room service, reservation, bed linen, and TV set—make up around 80 percent of the cumulative percentage. Thus, instead of focusing on all the complaints, we need to concentrate on these four complaints first, which will resolve 80 percent of the problems.

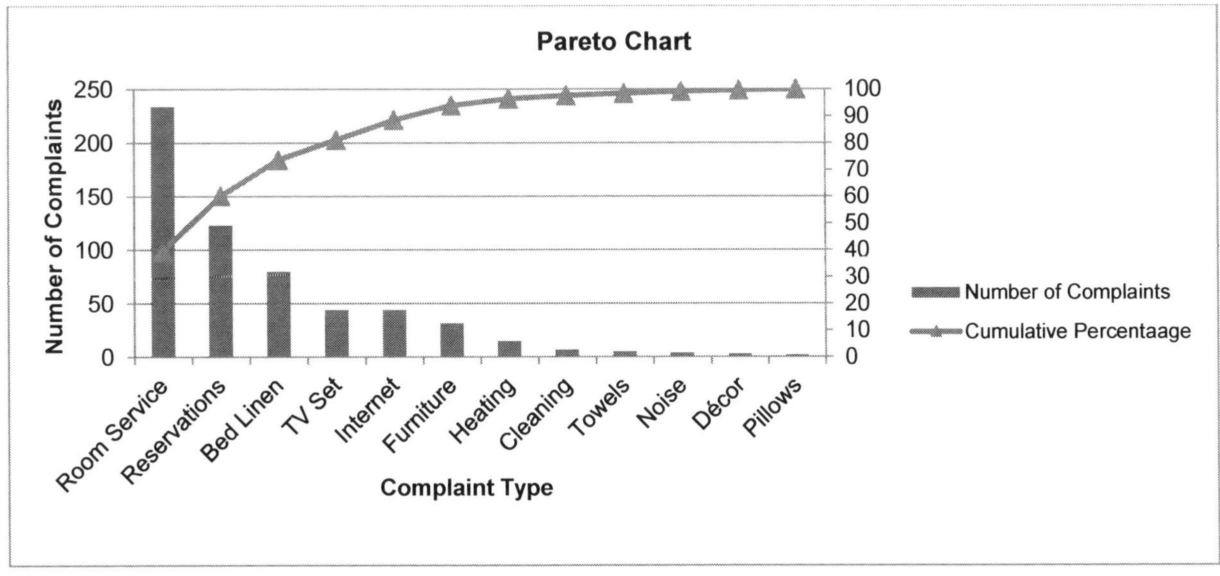

Figure 8-9: Pareto Chart

6. Scatter Diagram

This diagram is used to identify potential interdependencies that may exist between two variables.

- Observed data must be collected on both characteristics, and data being collected must be random with no time or other dependency present.
- The overall pool of data is then represented as a group of points set up on a plot of two variables.
- We can make a general conclusion if the two parameters correlate and if this is a positive versus negative as well as a strong versus weak correlation.

Example: Suppose you want to find out if there is any correlation between the PMP score and a project manager's salary. We identified ten project managers and their PMP scores and salary information in the following table. From the graph we can easily identify that there is a strong positive correlation between the PMP score and salary: the higher the PMP score, the more money project managers are likely to make.

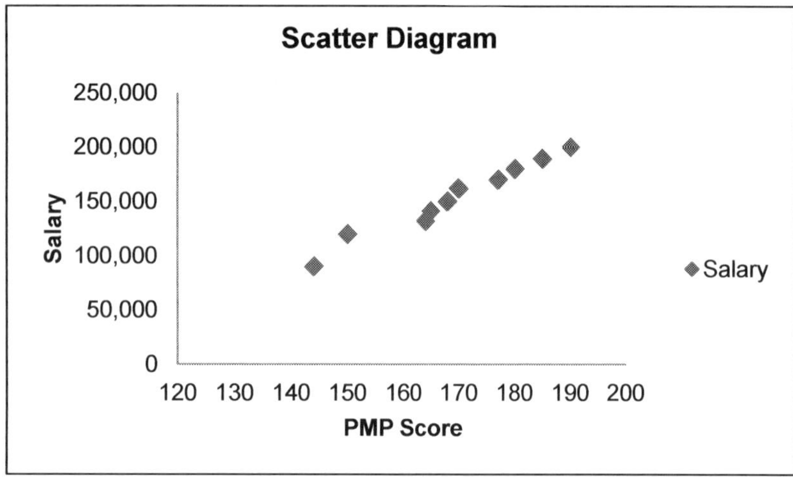

	PMP Score	Salary
1	190	$200,000
2	185	$189,000
3	180	$180,000
4	177	$170,000
5	170	$162,000
6	168	$150,000
7	165	$141,000
8	164	$132,000
9	150	$120,000
10	144	$90,000

Figure 8-10: Scatter Diagram (Positive Correlation)

Table 8-8: PMP Score and Salary

If we find out that PMP score has nothing to do with the project managers' salary, we can say that there is no correlation between the PMP score and a project managers' salary. Now consider the following scatter diagram and look at the scores and salary, and you will notice that there is a strong negative correlation between these two variables: the higher the PMP score, the less money project managers are likely to make.

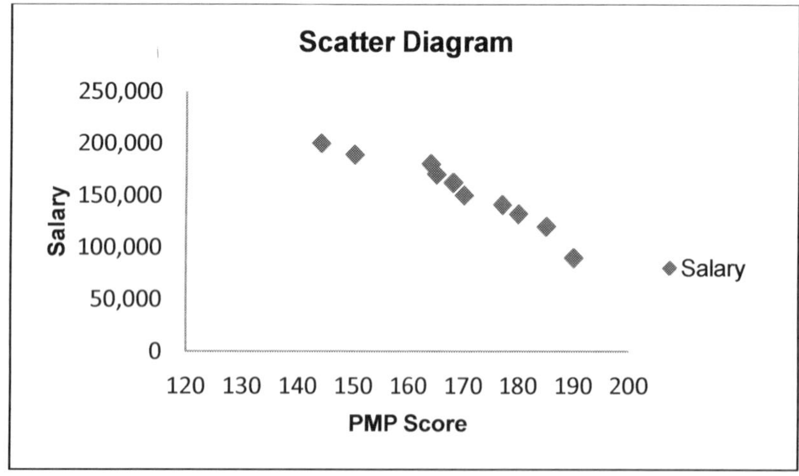

	PMP Score	Salary
1	190	$90,000
2	185	$120,000
3	180	$132,000
4	177	$141,000
5	170	$150,000
6	168	$162,000
7	165	$170,000
8	164	$180,000
9	150	$189,000
10	144	$200,000

Figure 8-11: Scatter Diagram (Negative Correlation)

Table 8-9: PMP Score and Salary

7. Checksheet (Tally Sheet)

A Checksheet, also called a Tally Sheet, is used as a form for collecting information about a process in an organized manner through observation and counting. Checksheets provide an easy way to keep track of the frequency of occurrences and are designed to answer the question "How often does this event occur and under what conditions?"

Checksheets are usually created in the Plan Quality Management process and used in Control Quality to keep track of useful data, such as quality problems uncovered during inspections. This data can be interpreted and exhibited into other formats such as a Pareto chart.

Example: The figure below shows a Checksheet used to collect data on telephone interruptions. The tick marks represent data that was collected over several weeks.

Telephone Interruptions

Reasons	Day							
	Sat	Sun	Mon	Tues	Wed	Thurs	Fri	Total
Information request	II	IIII	I	IIII	𝍸II	I	III	22
Wrong number	III	𝍸	II	I	𝍸	IIII	I	21
Senior management	𝍸	I	I	IIII	𝍸I	I	𝍸	23
Support team	II	II	I	III	I	II	III	14
Total	12	12	5	12	19	8	12	80

Table 8-10: A Checksheet Example

Benchmarking: Benchmarking involves comparing actual or planned practices to those of other projects, both in and beyond the performing organization. The objective is to provide a basis with which to measure performance, generate improvement ideas, and identify best practices.

Design of Experiments (DOE) / Taguchi method: A statistical method which is usually applied to the product of a project. This method provides a '"what-if" analysis of alternatives to identify which factors might improve quality. It provides statistical analysis for changing key product or process elements all at once to optimize the process.

Example: A plastic molding workshop wants to reduce injection molding rejects and so it performs a set of experiments that change injection pressure, mix, temperature, and setting times. Analysis of the results shows a combination of temperature and setting times as the most significant factors. Further experiments find the optimum combination of these factors.

Statistical Sampling: Statistical sampling involves choosing part of a population of interest for inspection instead of measuring the entire population.

Example: Selecting one hundred bottles to inspect at random from a list of ten thousand. This approach should be the best when we are confident that there are not many defects and measuring the entire population would be too expensive, time consuming, and destructive.

Additional Quality Planning Tools: There are several additional quality planning tools, such as brainstorming, affinity diagrams, force field analysis, nominal group techniques, matrix diagrams, and prioritization matrices. There are several proprietary approaches to quality, such as Six Sigma, Lean Six Sigma, Quality Function Deployment, CMMI®, and others.

Meetings: Meetings with team members, stakeholders, the sponsor, and others responsible for quality management activities in the project will be helpful to develop the quality management plan.

Plan Quality Management: Outputs

- Quality Management Plan
- Process Improvement Plan
- Quality Metrics
- Quality Checklists
- Project Documents Updates

Quality Management Plan: The quality management plan is a formal, approved document that includes quality control, quality assurance, and continuous process improvement approaches. It also describes how the project team will implement its quality policies.

Process Improvement Plan: Process boundaries, configuration, metrics, and targets for improved performance all help to identify how quality activities will be streamlined and improved.

Quality Metrics: The quality metric is an operational definition that specifically describes a project or product attribute (items associated with the actual physical product) and defines how quality will be measured. For instance, it is not adequate to specify that the application will generate all reports as quickly as possible. Instead, a quality metric might specify that the application will generate the reports within three seconds for 99.95 percent of all requests for up to two hundred concurrent users. Some other examples of quality metrics include failure rate, defect frequency, reliability, cost control, number of defects, availability, test coverage, and on-time performance.

Quality Checklists: The quality checklist is a component-specific, structured tool used to verify that a set of required steps have been performed in the proper sequence. It is often available from professional organizations or commercial service providers of the application area. Also, many organizations have their own checklists to ensure consistency in frequently performed tasks.

Project Documents Updates: Project documents such as WBS, WBS dictionary, stakeholder register, and responsibility assignment matrix may be updated during the Plan Quality Management process.

Exercise 1: Match the following principles with the appropriate inventor.

1. Top management involvement
2. Conformance to specifications (project produces what it was created to produce)
3. Cost of poor quality
4. Continuous improvement
5. Design of experiments
6. Prevention over inspection
7. Fitness for use (product or service must satisfy the real need)
8. Zero defects
9. 80/20 principle
10. Business processes should be scrutinized and measured to detect sources of variations that cause products to deviate from customer requirements
11. Quality should be designed into the product

A. Phil Crosby
B. Joseph Juran
C. W. Edwards Deming
D. Taguchi

Exercise 2: Identify which process group each process belongs to.

Process Groups				
Initiating	**Planning**	**Executing**	**Monitoring & Controlling**	**Closing**

Process Names:
- Control Quality
- Plan Quality Management
- Perform Quality Assurance

Internet Service Provider (ISP) Project

Let's go through one scenario where we will use all the seven key quality tools. Suppose you are a project manager in an ISP company that provides broadband Internet connectivity to its clients nationwide. Recently, you are getting many complaints about slow performance and downtime from your customers and would like to use all of these seven tools to identify the root causes and resolve the downtime problem.

ISP Project – Control Chart: You created a control chart to find out the downtime for a specific area last week. Your upper limit was one hour/day and the lower limit was fifteen minutes/day. As you can see, on most of the days, the service was out of your control limit. Therefore, you need to do an investigation to find out what happened in those days.

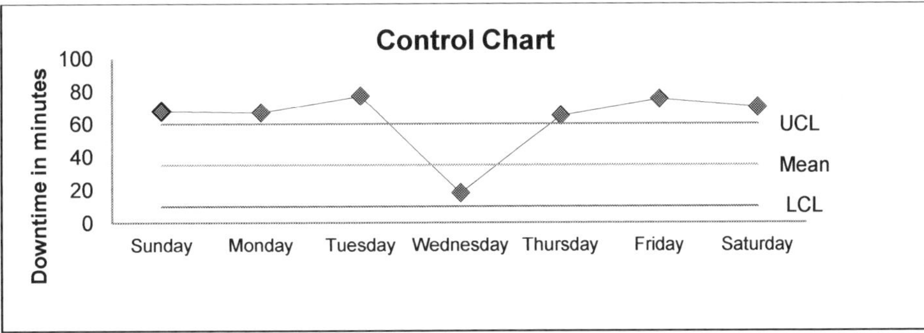

Figure 8-13: ISP Project – Control Chart

ISP Project – Checksheet: You created a Checksheet to keep track of the number of calls from customers for each complaint reason.

Reasons	Day							
	Sat	**Sun**	**Mon**	**Tues**	**Wed**	**Thurs**	**Fri**	**Total**
Information request	II	II	I	III	卌	I	I	15
Downtime	II	卌	II	I	卌	II	I	18
Slow performance	卌	I	I	II	卌 I	I	卌	21
Discontinue service	II	II	I	III	I	II	III	14
Total	11	10	5	9	17	6	10	68

Table 8-11: ISP Project – Checksheet

ISP Project – Scatter Diagram: You created a scatter diagram to identify if there is any interdependency between the time of the day and the connectivity downtime or slow performance. If it is found that issues occur mostly after office hours when many people are using home computers browsing the Internet, then they are experiencing downtime or slowness due to heavy traffic and bandwidth usage. This problem could be solved by increasing the bandwidth for the specific area after office hours.

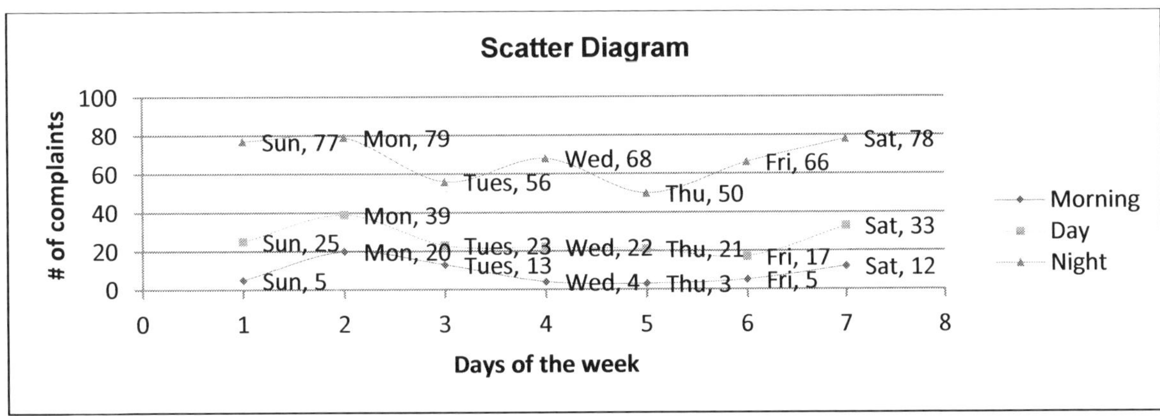

Figure 8-15: ISP Project – Scatter Diagram

ISP Project – Cause and Effect Diagram: You created a cause and effect diagram to systematically identify and present all the possible causes and sub-causes of the downtime problem. You discovered that the downtime issue is mostly caused by personnel, machine, material, management, technology, and design. Incompetent technicians, support agents, and operators are contributing to personnel problems; inefficient POPs, out-of-order switches, routers and old servers are contributing to machine problems; low-grade cables are contributing to a materials problem; too little involvement and wrong decisions from management are contributing to the downtime issue; and design problems due to the wrong POP and network design as well as a customer lack of knowledge are also causing the downtime.

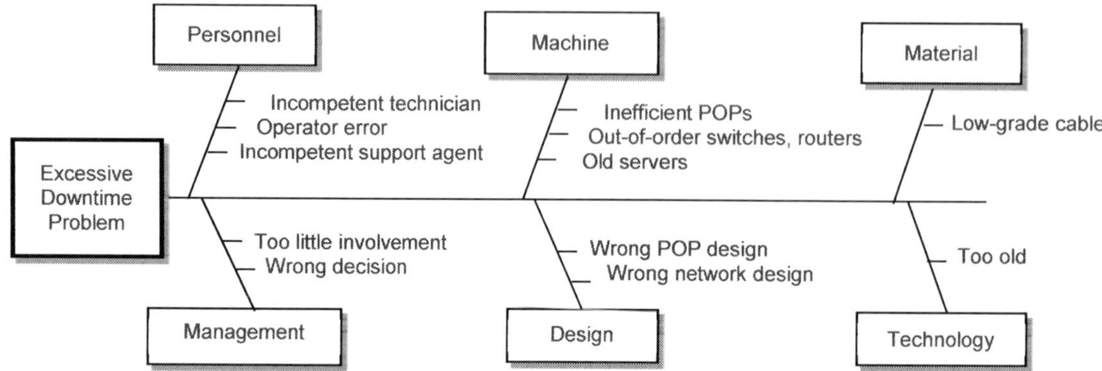

Figure 8-16: ISP Project – Cause and Effect Diagram

ISP Project – Flow Chart: You created a flow chart for the customer support service and identified where things can go wrong, what is out of your control, and where the bottleneck is. Once this information is available, you can take action to resolve the issue accordingly.

Start
Ticket/E-mail submitted by customer
Support case is created and assigned
Standard business hours?
Yes
No
Alert sent to support team
Alert sent to on-call technician
Ticket assigned?
No
Reminder is sent
Yes
Tickets are viewed & fixed as per priority
No
Issue fixed?
Yes
Ticket is closed & system sends follow-up e-mail
End

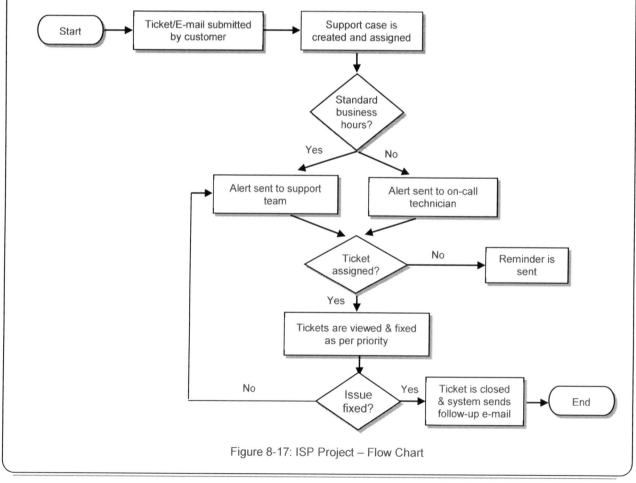

Figure 8-17: ISP Project – Flow Chart

ISP Project – Histogram: You created a histogram to find out how many issues were reported due to personnel, machine, design, material, management, and customer problems. Through this diagram you will be able to visually identify key problem areas.

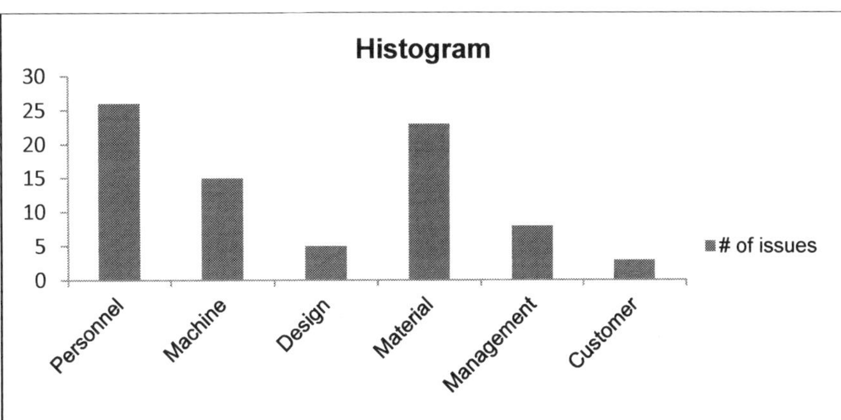

Figure 8-18: ISP Project – Histogram

ISP Project – Pareto Chart: You created a Pareto chart to identify which of the causes are behind 80 percent of the problems. You found out that cumulatively, personnel, material, and machines are causing 80 percent of the problem, so you decide to investigate and solve these causes first.

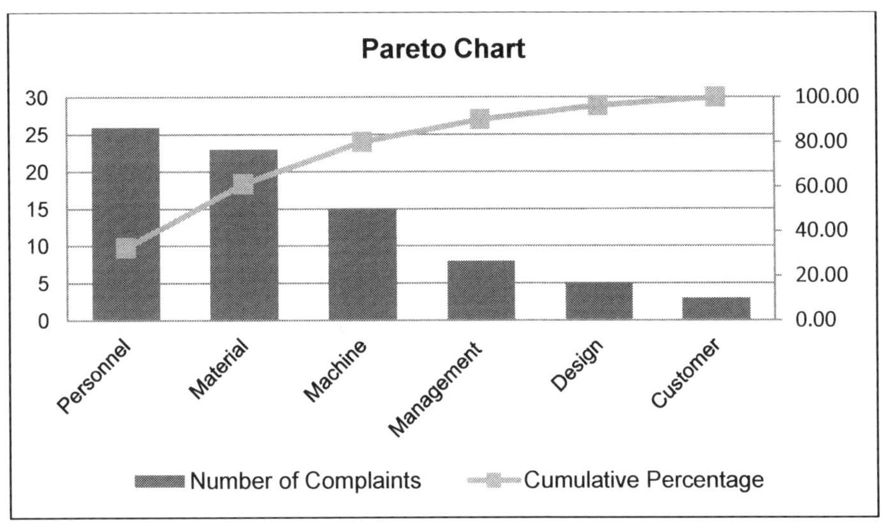

Figure 8-19: ISP Project – Pareto Chart

Perform Quality Assurance

Perform Quality Assurance is the process to determine if the project activities are complying with organizational and project policies, standards, processes, and procedures.

This process is primarily concerned with overall process improvement and does not deal with inspecting the product for quality or measuring defects. The primary focus is on steadily improving the processes and activities undertaken to achieve quality.

Below are the key functionalities in this process:

- Identify ineffective and inefficient activities or processes used in the project.
- Perform continuous improvement as appropriate.
- Perform quality audits to determine if project activities comply with organizational and project policies, processes, and procedures.
- Identify required improvements, gaps, and shortcomings in the processes.
- Identify and correct deficiencies.
- Recommend changes and corrective actions to Integrated Change Control.

As per the PMBOK®, the Perform Quality Assurance process has the following inputs, tools & techniques, and outputs:

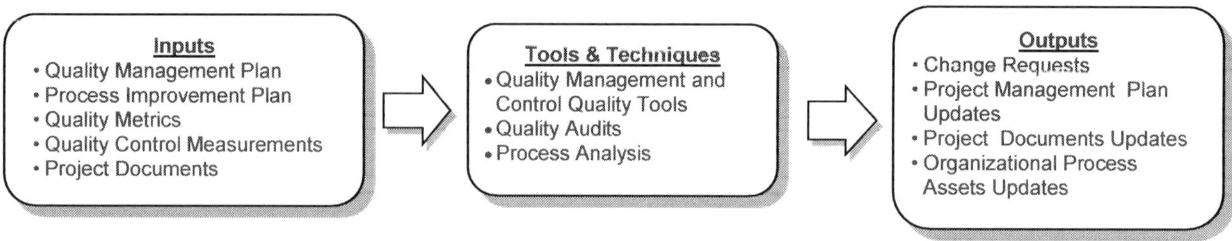

Figure 8-20: Perform Quality Assurance: Inputs, Tools & Techniques, and Outputs

Perform Quality Assurance: Inputs

- Quality Management Plan
- Process Improvement Plan
- Quality Metrics
- Quality Control Measurements
- Project Documents

Quality Management Plan: The quality management plan describes how quality assurance and continuous process improvements will be performed.

Process Improvement Plan: The process improvement plan looks at processes and what quality assurance activities will enhance their values.

Quality Metrics: An operational definition that specifically defines how quality will be measured.

Quality Control Measurements: Relevant quality level and compliance measurements. This data is the results of Control Quality activities, which is fed back into this process for analyzing and evaluating the quality standards and processes.

Project Documents: Several project documents may contribute to quality assurance activities. Performance information from project activities such as technical performance measures, project deliverables statuses, schedule progress, and costs incurred are collected on a regular basis.

Perform Quality Assurance: Tools & Techniques

- Quality Management and Control Quality Tools
- Quality Audits
- Process Analysis

Quality Management and Control Quality Tools: Tools & techniques used for Plan Quality Management and Control Quality can also be used for Perform Quality Assurance. In addition, the following tools are also used during this process:

Affinity Diagrams: Affinity diagrams can be utilized to structure and group the result of a root cause analysis in the Perform Quality Assurance process to decide if a change to quality policies, procedures, and standards is necessary.

Tree Diagram: The tree diagram is a representation of a tree structure, a way of representing the hierarchical nature of a structure in a graphical form. This diagram can be used for decision analysis and to represent decomposition hierarchy, such as Work Breakdown Structure (WBS), Risk Breakdown Structure (RBS), and Organizational Breakdown Structure (OBS). It can also be utilized for structuring data, plotting relationships, decomposing processes to ascertain a solution to a problem, and developing preventive and corrective procedures.

Process Decision Program Charts (PDPC): The Process Decision Program Chart (PDPC) is a technique designed to help formulate contingency plans. The emphasis of the PDPC is to identify the consequential impact of failure on activity plans and to create appropriate contingency plans to limit risks.

Prioritization Matrices: A prioritization matrix provides a way of sorting a diverse set of items into an order of importance. It also enables their relative importance to be identified by deriving a numerical value of the importance of each item. In Perform Quality Assurance, this tool is expended to prioritize both issues and appropriate solutions for implementation.

Interrelationship Digraphs: An interrelationship digraph is a graphical display that maps out the cause and effect links among complicated, multivariable problems or desired outcomes. It can be utilized to assess particular issues or general organizational concerns when it is difficult to identify the interrelationships between the concepts and it is ambiguous if the issue is the problem or the solution.

Activity Network Diagrams: In Perform Quality Assurance, the activity network diagram can be used with project scheduling methodologies, such as Program Evaluation and Review Technique (PERT), Critical Path Method (CPM), and Precedence Diagramming Method (PDM) to improve time management processes.

Matrix Diagrams: The matrix diagram is a graphical tool that shows the matrix's tabular format of connections or correlations between ideas or issues. A present or absent relationship exists at each intersection of rows and columns.

Quality Audits: Scheduled or randomly structured reviews performed by internal or third-party auditors to determine whether quality management activities comply with organizational and project processes, policies, and procedures. Such an audit identifies inefficient and ineffective activities, processes, and lessons learned. The lessons learned such as gaps and best practices can improve performance of the current project and future ones. Quality improvements are the results of quality audits since they correct any deficiencies in the quality processes. It should result in a reduced cost of quality and an increase in stakeholders' acceptance of the product.

Process Analysis: Process analysis is a part of the continuous improvement effort and looks at process improvement from an organizational and technical point of view. It identifies needed improvements by following the steps outlined in the process improvement plan, examining the problems and constraints experienced, and identifying non-value-added activities during process operations. One of the techniques used in process analysis is root cause analysis, which identifies the problem, discovers the underlying causes, and develops preventive actions. Fixing the process may be the best approach for solving a problem as an inefficient or faulty process could contribute to the problem or variance. Process analysis techniques from methodologies like Six Sigma, Len, and Kanban can help with this effort.

Perform Quality Assurance: Outputs

- Change Requests
- Project Management Plan Updates
- Project Documents Updates
- Organizational Process Assets Updates

Change Requests: The majority of the change requests in this process will be procedural changes and can be used to take corrective or preventive actions or to perform defect repairs.

Project Management Plan Updates: The quality management plan, schedule management plan, and cost management plan may be updated.

Project Documents Updates: Quality can impact any of the knowledge areas and corresponding plans, such as scope, budget, schedule, risk, and human resource, as well as quality audit reports, training plans, and process documentation. All these documents can be updated as part of the quality processes.

Organizational Process Assets Updates: Quality standards may be updated.

Control Quality

The Control Quality process is about monitoring specific project results to determine if they comply with relevant quality standards and identifying ways to eliminate causes of unsatisfactory results.

In this process, each deliverable is inspected, measured, and tested to ensure quality standards. This process typically occurs continuously throughout the project, beginning with the production of the first deliverable and continuing until all deliverables have been accepted. This process mostly uses statistical sampling and inspection to make sure the results of the activities are as expected.

Below are the key functionalities in this process:

- Measure specific project results against quality standards.
- Implement approved changes to the quality baseline.
- Repair any defects reported.
- Recommend changes, corrective and preventive actions, and defect repairs to Integrated Change Control to eliminate noncompliance in the project deliverables.
- Identify quality improvements as appropriate.
- Ensure the deliverables are correct and meet the relevant quality standards.

As per the PMBOK®, the Control Quality process has the following inputs, tools & techniques, and outputs:

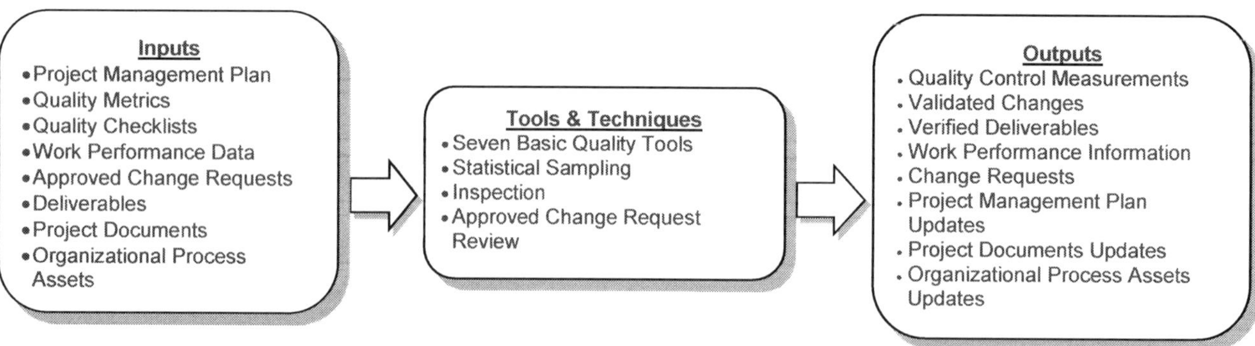

Figure 8-21: Control Quality: Inputs, Tools & Techniques, and Outputs

To better understand the Control Quality process, we need to understand the following terms.

Attribute Sampling: Attribute sampling is a method of measuring quality that consists of observing the presence (or absence) of some characteristics (attributes) in each of the units under consideration to determine whether to accept a lot, reject it, or inspect another lot.

Mutual Exclusivity: Two events are said to be mutually exclusive if they cannot both occur in a single trial.
Example: Painting the same wall white and pink cannot be done at the same time; thus, these two events are mutually exclusive.

Probability: The likelihood that something will occur, usually expressed as a decimal or a fraction on a scale of zero to one.

Normal Distribution: The most common probability density distribution chart. Certain data, when graphed as a histogram, create a bell-shaped curve known as a normal curve, or normal distribution. Normal distributions are symmetrical with a single central peak at the mean (average) of the data. The shape of the curve is described as bell-shaped with the graph falling off evenly on either side of the mean. 50 percent of the distribution lies to the left of the mean, and 50 percent lies to the right of the mean. The spread of a normal distribution is controlled by the standard deviation. See Figure 8-22 regarding standard deviation.

Statistical Independence: The likelihood of one event occurring that does not affect the likelihood of another event occurring. This is considered while identifying quality issues and resolutions.
Example: The probability of rolling a five on a die is statistically independent from the probability of rolling a six on the next roll.

Standard Deviation: It is used to set the level of quality that a company has decided to achieve and also to set upper and lower control limits to determine if a process is in control (control chart). Standard Deviation is a measure of how far the measurement is from the mean. One sigma is the lowest quality level, allowing 317,500 defects per million outputs. Approximately twenty-seven hundred out of one million products produced will have a problem in three sigma, whereas less than 3.4 in six sigma. As you can see, Six Sigma represents a higher quality standard than three. But even Six Sigma levels may not be sufficient enough for industries like pharmaceutical, airline, space, and power utilities.

Standard Deviation Calculation:

1. First of all, we need to calculate the mean, which is the average of all data points.
2. Then we need to calculate the difference between each data point and the mean, squaring each of the differences and then dividing the sum of the squared differences by the number of data points (–1).
3. We then calculate the square root of the average we found in Step 2.

If the dataset is "normally distributed," as in the following chart, then we will have the following statistics:

+ / – 1 Sigma	68.26 percent of the occurrences will fall within one sigma from the mean
+ / – 2 Sigma	95.46 percent of the occurrences will fall within two sigma from the mean
+ / – 3 Sigma	99.73 percent of the occurrences will fall within three sigma from the mean
+ / – 6 Sigma	99.99985 percent of the occurrences will fall within six sigma from the mean

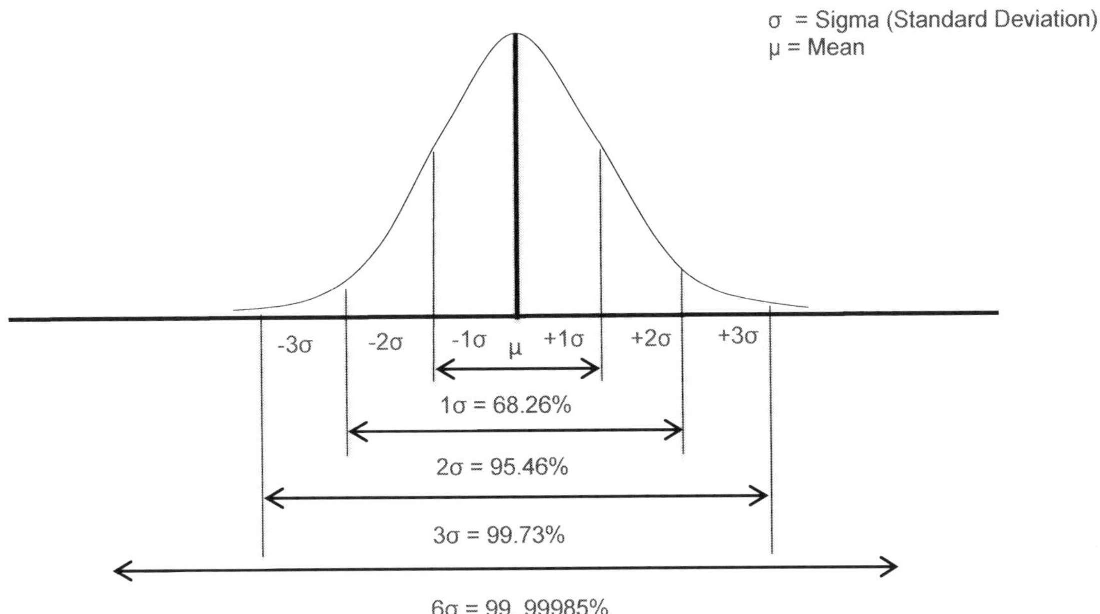

Figure 8-22: Standard Deviation

Control Quality: Inputs

- Project Management Plan
- Quality Metrics
- Quality Checklists
- Work Performance Data
- Approved Change Requests
- Deliverables
- Project Documents
- Organizational Process Assets

Project Management Plan: Describes how the project management team will implement quality assurance and quality control.

Quality Metrics: An operational definition that specifies how quality will be measured.

Quality Checklists: A component-specific, structured tool used to verify that a set of required steps have all been performed and that they were performed in the proper sequence.

Work Performance Data: Information relative to project status, performance, and results. It can include planned versus actual schedule, cost, and technical performance information.

Approved Change Requests: Approved change requests are documented, authorized changes to project parameters, such as scope, schedule, cost, or methodology.

Deliverables: Unique, verifiable products, results, or capabilities necessary for the successful completion of the project are inspected and measured to ensure that they conform to quality standards.

Project Documents: Several project documents such as process documents obtained using the seven basic quality tools or the quality management and control tools, agreements, training plans, quality audit reports, change logs with action plans, and assessments of effectiveness may be useful.

Organizational Process Assets: These include any informational assets relevant to quality standards and policies, standard work guidelines, communication policies, and issue and defect reporting procedures.

Control Quality: Tools & Techniques

- Seven Basic Quality Tools
- Statistical Sampling
- Inspection
- Approved Change Request Review

Seven Basic Quality Tools: The Control Chart, Checksheet, Flow Chart, Cause & Effect Diagram, Scatter Diagram, Histogram, and Pareto Chart are the seven basic tools and they are described in detail in the previous section.

Statistical Sampling: Part of a population of interest is selected for inspection and testing as defined in the quality management plan.

Inspection: An internal inspection such as a review, product review, walkthrough, or audit is the examination of a work product to determine whether or not it conforms to standards. Inspections can be conducted at any level to test or review the final product of the project or the results of an activity.

Approved Change Request Review: Approved change request review is the examination process used to ensure all approved changes are satisfactorily implemented.

Control Quality: Outputs

- Quality Control Measurements
- Validated Changes
- Verified Deliverables
- Work Performance Information
- Change Requests
- Project Management Plan Updates
- Project Documents Updates
- Organizational Process Assets Updates

Quality Control Measurements: Quality control measurements are the relevant quality level, compliance measurements, and documented results of the Control Quality activities.

Validated Changes: Validated changes are the inspection and acceptance of resolved defects as per quality standards.

Verified Deliverables: These are deliverables validated through the performance of Control Quality activities as per the quality standards. Validated deliverables are inputs for the Validate Scope process, which ends with formal acceptance.

Work Performance Information: Information such as causes for rejections, required rework, and required process adjustments is collected from various controlling processes.

Change Requests: Changes initiated through the defined Integrated Change Control process.

Project Management Plan Updates: The quality management plan and process improvement plan documents may be updated.

Project Documents Updates: Quality standards document, agreements, training plans, quality audit reports, change logs with action plans, and assessments of effectiveness may be updated.

Organizational Process Assets Updates: Completed checklists and lessons learned documents may be updated.

Exercise 3: What is the relationship between the Control Quality process and the Validate Scope process?

Exercise 4: Match the specific descriptions with the appropriate tools.

Details	Tools
1. A tool used to monitor processes and assure that they remain within acceptable limits.	A. Pareto Diagram
2. It provides an easy way to keep track of the frequency of occurrences.	B. Cause and Effect Diagram
3. The concept is based on the 80/20 rule.	C. Scatter Diagram
4. It is a bar chart that shows the distribution of data.	D. Control Chart
5. It can help in quality control by identifying causes contributing to quality problems.	E. Flow Chart
6. This diagram is used to identify potential interdependencies that may exist between two variables.	F. Histogram
7. It is a graphical representation of a process to help analyze how problems occur and identify potential process improvement opportunities.	G. Checksheet

Exercise 5: Match the specific descriptions with the appropriate quality methodologies.

Details	Methodologies
1. It refers to looking for the point where the benefits or revenue from improving quality equals the incremental cost to achieve that quality.	A. Just in Time (JIT)
2. It is a collection of internationally accepted standards concerned with quality management compiled by the International Organization for Standardization.	B. Continuous Improvement
3. Its goal is to bring inventory down to zero or almost near to a zero level.	C. Prevention over Inspection
4. It is a management strategy to embed awareness to focus on finding ways to improve quality throughout the organization.	D. Six Sigma
5. It states that quality should be planned, designed, and built in, not inspected in.	E. Total Quality Management (TQM)
6. It is also known as Kaizen.	F. Marginal Analysis
7. A statistical method to measure how many defects are in a process and then systematically figure out how to eliminate them.	G. ISO 9000 series

Project Quality Management Flow Chart

It is essential to comprehend how quality management fits into the overall project management process. Project managers with limited quality management experience struggle to visualize how quality management efforts fit into managing a real life project. The following scenario and diagram will help to clarify the concept:

1. Customers identify and determine their requirements.
2. Project team members work closely with the customers to clarify those requirements. Team members also determine work needed to meet those requirements.
3. With the help of the quality control and quality assurance department, the project manager determines the existing standards, policies, guidelines, and procedures. The project manager also creates additional standards and processes if needed and integrates all project needs.
4. Project team commences project planning work and execution.
5. Quality control team measures deliverables against the plan and quality metrics.
6. Quality assurance department audits to find out whether team is complying with standards, policies, plan, and procedures, looks for best practices, and also looks for organizational process improvement.
7. Change requests – preventive, corrective, and defect repairs are issued.
8. Project team members fine-tune plans and work as needed and return to Step 4 until project is completed.
9. Verified deliverables are moved to Validate Scope process to gain formal acceptance. Lessons learned are shared.
10. Work is completed, deliverables are accepted, project is completed, quality targets are accomplished, and customers are satisfied.
11. Organizational process assets are updated and improved.

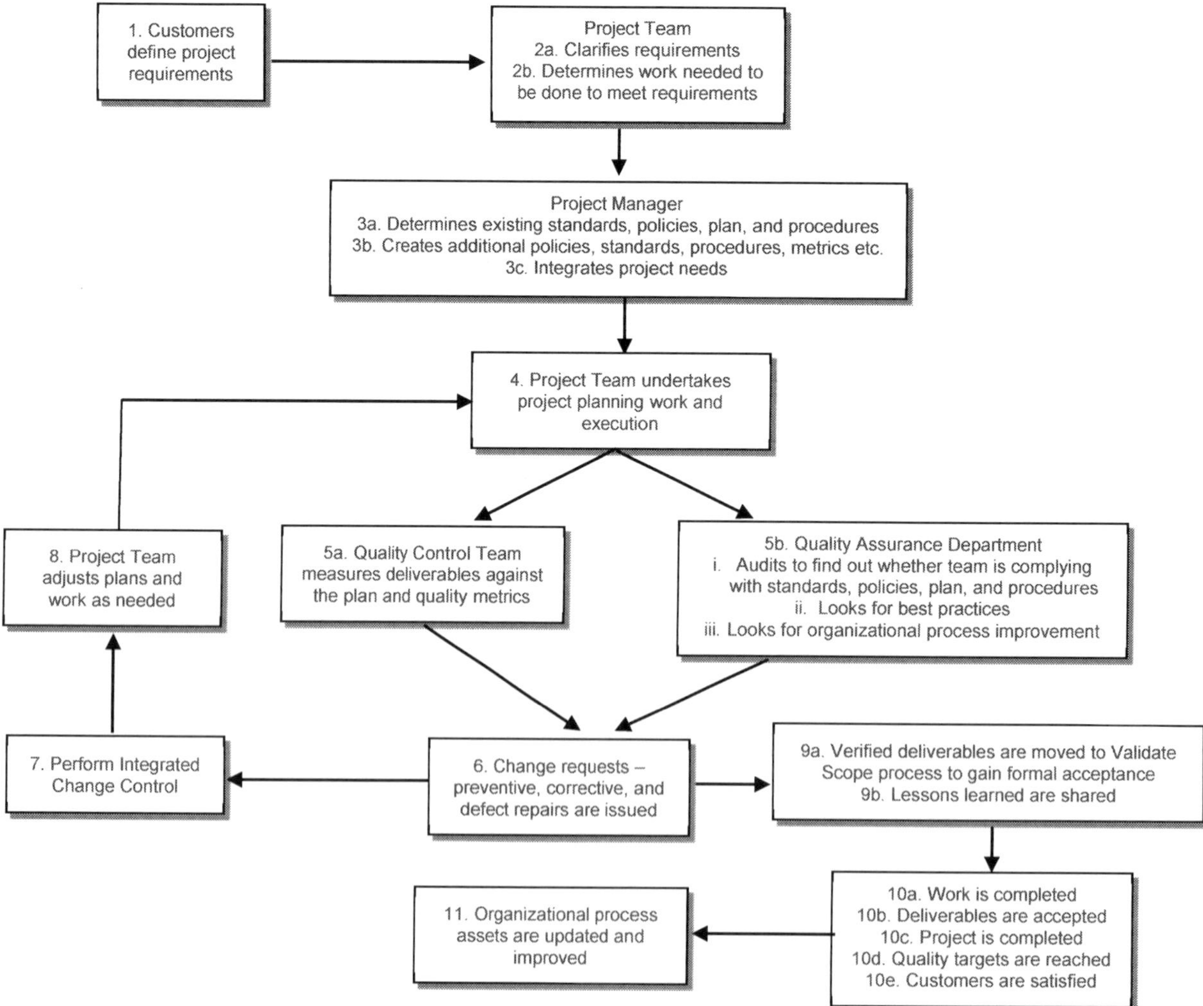

Figure 8-23: Project Quality Management Flow Chart

Exercise 6: Identify what quality tools/techniques are used in the following situations and in which process.

Situation	Tools/Techniques?	Process?
1. You are analyzing a chart of problems to find the most frequent one in order to determine if processes need to be improved.		
2. You are taking measurements and comparing them to the upper and lower thresholds of variance.		
3. You are showing data in the form of bars to measure and plot how frequently some problems occurred.		
4. You are analyzing two characteristics of a process to see if there is any interdependency between them.		
5. You are computing the cost of the effort needed to implement quality and comparing it with the benefit of the quality.		
6. You are determining the acceptable upper and lower thresholds of variance in your project.		
7. You are using a structured tool to verify that a set of required steps have all been performed and that they were performed in the proper sequence.		
8. You are graphically representing a process to determine where a process that is achieving a low-quality result might be failing.		
9. You are using a tool for systematically identifying and presenting all the possible causes and sub-causes that might have led to a defect or problem.		
10. You are using a statistical analysis for changing key product or process elements all at once (or some) to optimize the process.		
11. You are using a tool for systematically identifying and presenting all the possible causes and sub-causes of a particular problem in a graphical format to examine if the proper process was followed or if processes must be improved.		
12. As a supervisor in charge, you are inspecting ten windows in every one thousand.		
13. You are looking at the project practices of comparable projects both in and beyond the performing organization to identify best practices.		
14. You are using a bar chart to illustrate which causes of error are most serious and showing frequency of errors according to causes.		
15. You are creating a list of required steps with proper sequence to be checked during inspections.		

Exercise 7: The following table is an example of a:

A. Cause and effect diagram
B. Checksheet
C. Scatter diagram
D. Pareto chart

Issues	Vendor1	Vendor2	Vendor3	Vendor4	Total
Delay in delivery	II	IIII	I	IIII	11
Defective equipment	III	IIII	II	I	10
Damaged parts	III	I	I	IIII	9
Incorrect bills	II	II	I	III	8
Missing documents	I	III	II	IIII	10

Exercise 8: Identify items associated with Plan Quality Management, Perform Quality Assurance, or Control Quality.

Plan Quality Management	Perform Quality Assurance	Control Quality

A. Create additional project specific standards
B. Balance the needs of quality with scope, cost, time, risk, and satisfaction
C. Determine if project activities comply with organization and project policies, processes, and procedures
D. Correct deficiencies in quality policies and procedures
E. Determine how to measure to make sure standards are met
F. Perform internal quality inspection
G. Identify required improvements in quality policies and procedures
H. Measure specific project results against quality standards
I. Determine work needed to meet the standard
J. Repair defects
K. Recommend changes, corrective and preventive actions and defect repair to integrated change control
L. Find existing quality standards for product and project management
M. Perform quality audit

Exercise 9: Match the specific events or issues with the appropriate cost of quality element.

Events or Issues	Quality Cost (Prevention/Appraisal/ Internal/External/Legal Implication)	Category (Cost of Conformance/ Cost of Nonconformance)
1. Bad word of mouth advertising		
2. Returned goods from customer		
3. Inspection		
4. Quality Control Engineering		
5. Scrap costs		
6. Procedure Checking		
7. Laboratory measurements and analysis		
8. Loss of future sales		
9. Field repair work		
10. Machinery maintenance and calibration		
11. Rework costs		
12. Criminal Liability: Fraud, gross negligence		
13. Field testing		
14. Processing customer complaints		
15. Quality Training		
16. Quality control follow ups		
17. Testing		
18. Design of Quality Measurements		
19. Civil Liability: Lawsuits for damages, non-performance		
20. Vendor follow up on defective goods		

Quality Management Example for a Financial Management System Implementation Project

The board of directors of NetFinancial has decided to implement a new financial management system for handling a wider variety of products, suppliers, clients, and payment methods. By installing a suite of new accounting system functions, NetFinancial would not only replace most of the current manual administrative processes, but it would also generate the management report needed to better manage cash flow and create a sound strategy for growth. This solution requires the installation of at least the following system modules:

- General ledger (GL)
- Accounts receivable (AR) and
- Accounts payable (AP)

Quality Plan: To ensure that the quality targets specified in this document are achieved, NetFinancial will implement a suite of quality assurance and quality control methods. These methods will enable NetFinancial to monitor and control the actual quality of the deliverables produced for this financial management system implementation project. The following table lists the specific quality targets to be achieved by the project team:

Quality Target			
Project Requirements	**Project Deliverables**	**Quality Criteria**	**Quality Standards**
General Ledger	Implementation of Oracle Financial General Ledger (GL) to contain all the accounts for recording transactions related to company's assets, liabilities, owners' equity, revenue, and expenses.	GL thoroughly tested and successfully installed	– GL operational, no errors – 100 percent compliance with Oracle financial standard
Accounts Receivable	Implementation of Accounts Receivable (AR) to record money owed by customers (individuals or corporations) to NetFinancial in exchange for goods or services that have been delivered or used but not yet paid for.	AR thoroughly tested and successfully installed	– AP operational, no errors – Zero deviation from financial industry standard
Accounts Payable	Implementation of Accounts Payable (AP) to record the money owed by NetFinancial to its suppliers shown as a liability on its balance sheet.	AP thoroughly tested and successfully installed	– AR operational, no errors – Zero deviation from financial industry standard

Quality Assurance Plan: The following table lists the method the project manager and quality manager will wish to implement to assure the quality of deliverables on this project.

Technique	Frequency
Process checklists and project audits	At the completion of each key deliverable
Referencing historical data to understand areas where quality issues are likely to occur	Throughout the project
Reiterating the quality standards to be met to clarify the level of quality required	Throughout the project
Recruiting skilled staff to produce the deliverables and undertake the processes	Throughout the project
Undertaking quality reviews to provide confidence that the project is on track	At the completion of each key deliverable
Performing formal Change Control to minimize the likely number of quality issues	Throughout the project

Quality Control Plan: The following table lists the methods to be undertaken by internal team members to monitor and control the actual quality level of deliverables for this project.

Technique	Frequency
Peer Reviews	Weekly throughout the project
Deliverable Reviews	At the completion of each deliverable
Documentation Reviews	Throughout the project
Process Reviews	Weekly throughout the project
Stage-Gate Reviews	At the end of each project phase

Quality Control Review Form: This quality control review form will assist the quality manager in reviewing the physical deliverables produced by the project. This project will use the following form to assess the level of quality of the deliverables produced by the project.

Quality Achieved					
Requirements	**Quality Level**			**Quality Deviation**	**Improvement Recommendation**
	L	M	H		
General Ledger (GL)	x			Critical errors experienced during install	Reinstall GL system to remove critical errors.
Account Receivables (AR)		x		Implementation is only partially complete	Complete system implementation.
Account Payables (AP)			x	No deviation from quality standard	No further action is required.

Exercise 10: Crossword

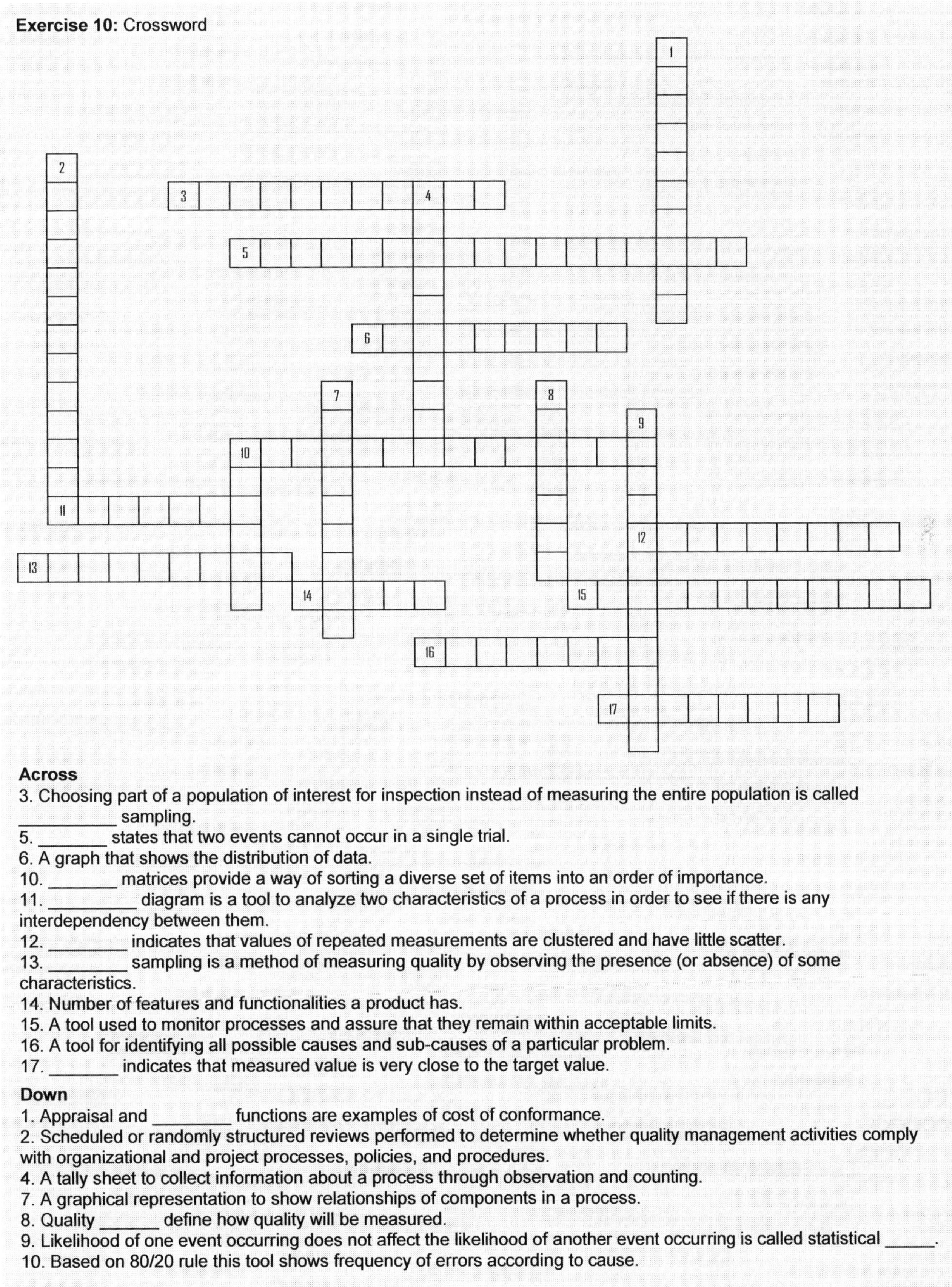

Across

3. Choosing part of a population of interest for inspection instead of measuring the entire population is called _________ sampling.
5. _______ states that two events cannot occur in a single trial.
6. A graph that shows the distribution of data.
10. _______ matrices provide a way of sorting a diverse set of items into an order of importance.
11. ________ diagram is a tool to analyze two characteristics of a process in order to see if there is any interdependency between them.
12. _______ indicates that values of repeated measurements are clustered and have little scatter.
13. _______ sampling is a method of measuring quality by observing the presence (or absence) of some characteristics.
14. Number of features and functionalities a product has.
15. A tool used to monitor processes and assure that they remain within acceptable limits.
16. A tool for identifying all possible causes and sub-causes of a particular problem.
17. ______ indicates that measured value is very close to the target value.

Down

1. Appraisal and ________ functions are examples of cost of conformance.
2. Scheduled or randomly structured reviews performed to determine whether quality management activities comply with organizational and project processes, policies, and procedures.
4. A tally sheet to collect information about a process through observation and counting.
7. A graphical representation to show relationships of components in a process.
8. Quality ______ define how quality will be measured.
9. Likelihood of one event occurring does not affect the likelihood of another event occurring is called statistical _____.
10. Based on 80/20 rule this tool shows frequency of errors according to cause.

Exercise 11: Answer the following:

1. This diagram is used when we need to analyze two characteristics of a process and see if there is any interdependency between them.
2. ________ quality is not acceptable, but low grade may be acceptable.
3. It is an operational definition that specifically describes a project or product attribute and defines how quality will be measured.
4. It is a method of measuring quality that consists of observing the presence (or absence) of some characteristics (attributes) in each of the units under consideration to determine whether to accept a lot, reject it, or inspect another lot.
5. These are scheduled or randomly structured reviews performed by internal or third-party auditors to determine whether quality management activities comply with organizational and project processes, policies, and procedures.
6. In this process, each deliverable is inspected, measured, and tested to ensure quality standards.
7. Internal failure, external failure, and legal implication are examples of cost of ________.
8. It is a part of the continuous improvement effort and looks at process improvement from an organizational and technical point of view.
9. The process of determining if the project activities are complying with organizational and project policies, standards, processes, and procedures.
10. The process is ________ if values are plotted outside the control limits and values show a particular tendency (e.g., rule of seven).
11. Comparing actual or planned practices to those of other projects, both in and beyond the performing organization.
12. A graph that shows the distribution of data.
13. Conformance to specifications was introduced by ________.
14. It is a tool used for systematically identifying and presenting all the possible causes and sub causes of a particular problem in a graphical format.
15. It decreases costs by keeping only enough inventory on hand to meet immediate production needs.
16. Two events are said to be ________ if they cannot both occur in a single trial.
17. A line drawn through the average of all data points shows the middle of the range of acceptable variation of the process.
18. ________ helps concentrate awareness on the most critical issues, prioritizes prospective causes of the problems, and determines priorities for quality improvement activities.
19. It involves choosing part of a population of interest for inspection instead of measuring the entire population.
20. It refers to nonrandom data points grouped together in a series that total seven on one side of the mean in a control chart.
21. Plan-do-check-act was introduced by ________.
22. It will cost much less to ________ mistakes than it will cost to correct them when they are found after the fact by inspection.
23. Kaizen is synonym for __________.
24. Prevention functions and appraisal functions are examples of cost of __________.
25. This diagram is a representation of a tree structure, a way of representing the hierarchical nature of a structure in a graphical form.
26. In the Perform Quality Assurance process, it is a technique designed to help formulate contingency plans.
27. It provides a way of sorting a diverse set of items into an order of importance.
28. It is a graphical display that maps out the cause and effect links among complicated, multivariable problems or desired outcomes.
29. This diagram is a graphical tool that shows the matrix's tabular format of connections or correlations between ideas or issues.
30. The three processes of quality management are ________.
31. The key outputs of quality management processes are ________.

Project Quality Management Summary

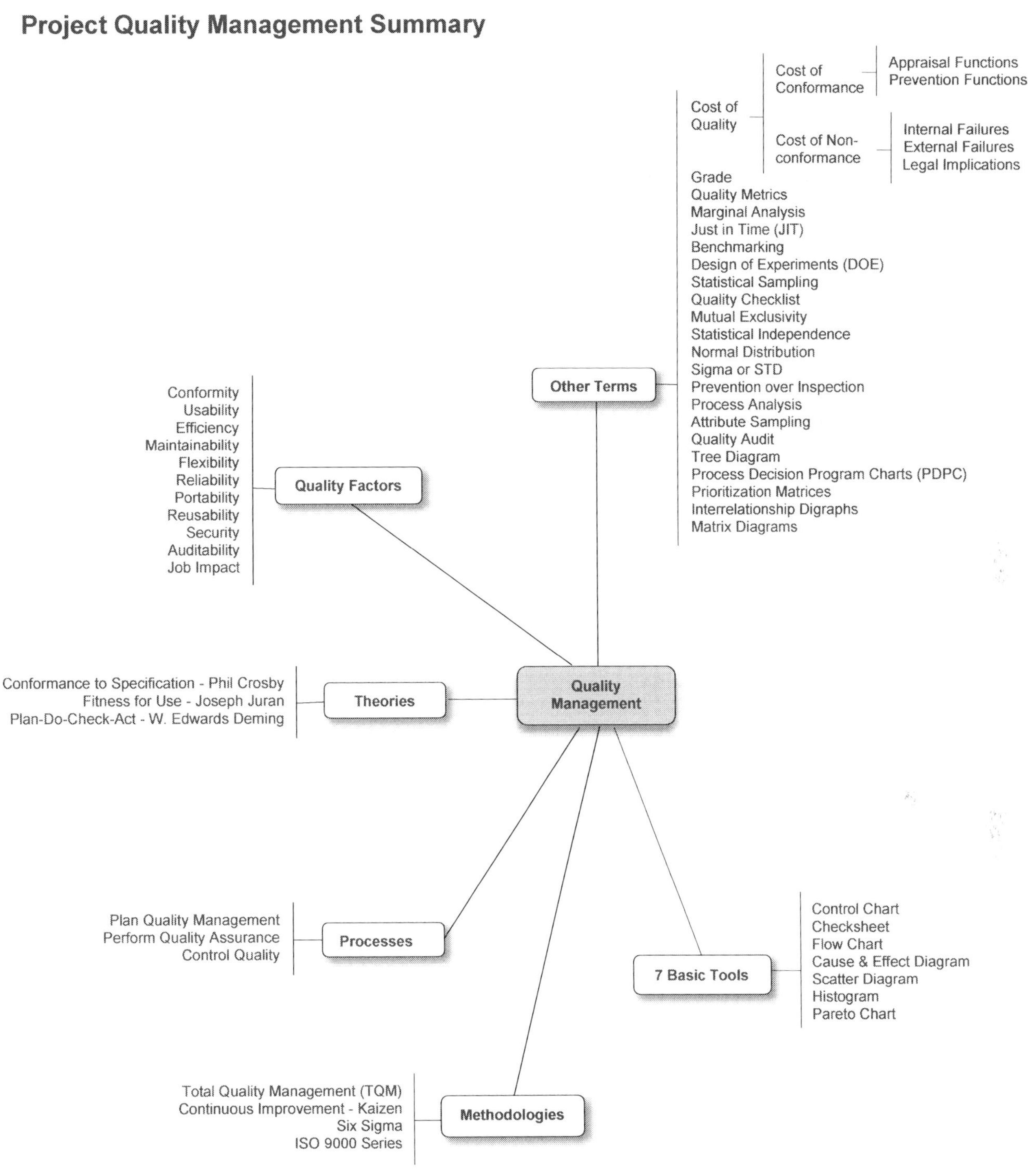

Figure 8-24: Project Quality Management Summary

Project Quality Management Key Terms

Grade: Number of features and functionalities a product has
Quality: Degree to which a project fulfills requirements
Accuracy: Measured value is very close to the target value
Precision: Values of repeated measurements are clustered and have little scatter

Methodologies

Total Quality Management (TQM): Everyone in the organization is responsible for quality
Continuous Improvement – Kaizen: An ongoing effort to improve quality
Six Sigma: A disciplined quality process to develop near-perfect products and services. 3.4 defect, 99.99985%
ISO 9000 Series: A collection of internationally accepted quality standards compiled by ISO. Companies document and do what they say

Theories

Conformance to Specification: Phil Crosby
Fitness for Use: Joseph Juran
Plan-Do-Check-Act: W. Edwards Deming

Cost of Quality

Cost of Conformance: Appraisal & prevention functions
Cost of Nonconformance: Internal failures, external failures, legal implications

7 Basic Tools

Control Chart: A tool used to monitor processes and assure that they remain within acceptable limits.
Out of Control – 1) A single point exceeds the control limit 2) 7 consecutive points below or above mean (Rule of 7)
Checksheet: A tally sheet to collect information about a process through observation and counting
Flow Chart: A graphical representation to show relationships of components in a process
Cause & Effect Diagram: A tool for identifying all possible causes and sub-causes of a particular problem
Scatter Diagram: A tool to analyze two characteristics of a process in order to see if there is any interdependency between them
Histogram: A graph that shows the distribution of data
Pareto Chart: Shows frequency of errors according to cause. Based on the 80/20 rule

Other Terms

Quality Metrics: An operational definition to describe a project or product attribute and to define how quality will be measured
Marginal Analysis: Looking for the point where benefits from improving quality equal the incremental cost to achieve that quality
Just in Time (JIT): Bringing inventory down to zero or almost near to a zero level
Benchmarking: Comparing actual or planned practices to those of other projects
Design of Experiments (DOE): A what-if analysis of alternatives to identify which factors might improve quality. Framework for changing all important factors, not just one at a time
Statistical Sampling: Choosing part of a population of interest for inspection instead of measuring the entire population
Quality Checklist: A component-specific, structured tool to verify all required steps have been performed in proper sequence
Mutual Exclusivity: Two events are mutually exclusive if they cannot both occur in a single trial
Statistical Independence: Likelihood of one event occurring does not affect the likelihood of another event occurring
Prevention over Inspection: Quality should be planned, designed, and built in, not inspected in
Process Analysis: A part of the continuous improvement effort to look at process improvement from an organizational and technical point of view
Attribute Sampling: A method of measuring quality by observing the presence (or absence) of some characteristics to determine whether to accept a lot, reject it, or inspect another lot
Quality Audits: Scheduled or randomly structured reviews performed to determine whether quality management activities comply with organizational and project processes, policies, and procedures
Normal Distribution: A bell-shaped curve; data points are evenly distributed
Sigma or STD: The level of quality that a company has decided to achieve
Tree Diagram: A way of representing the hierarchical nature of a structure in a graphical form
Process Decision Program Charts (PDPC): A technique designed to help formulate contingency plans
Prioritization Matrices: Provide a way of sorting a diverse set of items into an order of importance
Interrelationship Digraphs: A graphical display that maps out the cause and effect links among complicated, multivariable problems or desired outcomes
Matrix Diagrams: A graphical tool that shows the matrix's tabular format of connections or correlations between ideas or issues

Project Quality Management Exercise Answers

Exercise 1:

1. B
2. A
3. A
4. C
5. D
6. A
7. B
8. A
9. B
10. C
11. D

Exercise 2:

Process Groups				
Initiating	**Planning**	**Executing**	**Monitoring & Controlling**	**Closing**
	– Plan Quality Management	– Perform Quality Assurance	– Control Quality	

Exercise 3: The Validate Scope is the process of obtaining the stakeholders' formal acceptance of the completed project scope and associated deliverables. This process is similar to the Control Quality process as it compares the product with the scope to ensure they match the specification. The relationship between these two processes is as follows:

- Both the Control Quality and the Validate Scope processes can be performed simultaneously, but the Control Quality is usually performed prior to the Validate Scope.
- The Control Quality verifies correctness of the work, whereas the Validate Scope confirms completeness.
- The Control Quality is focused on measuring specific project results against quality specifications and standards, whereas the Validate Scope is mainly focused on obtaining acceptance of the product from the sponsor, customers, stakeholders, and others.

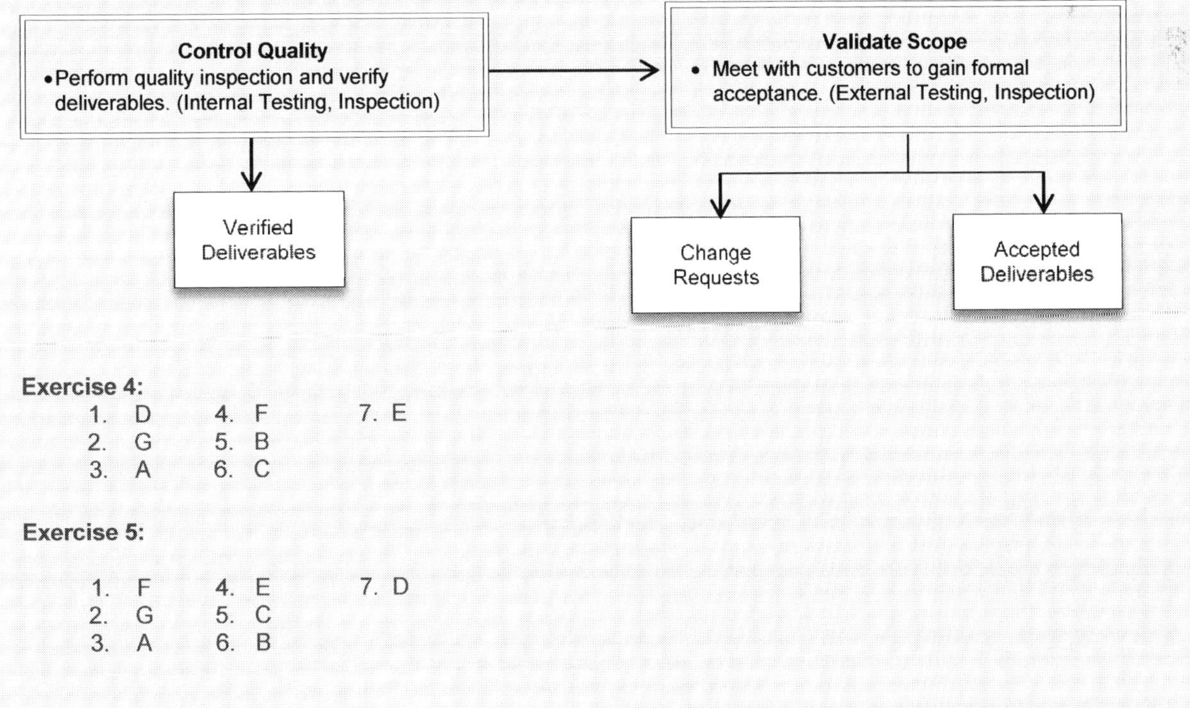

Exercise 4:

1. D	4. F	7. E
2. G	5. B	
3. A	6. C	

Exercise 5:

1. F	4. E	7. D
2. G	5. C	
3. A	6. B	

Exercise 6:

Situation	Tools/Techniques?	Process?
1.	Pareto chart	Perform Quality Assurance
2.	Control chart	Control Quality
3.	Histogram	Control Quality
4.	Scatter diagram	Perform Quality Assurance
5.	Cost benefit analysis	Plan Quality
6.	Control chart	Plan Quality
7.	Checklist	Control Quality
8.	Flow chart	Perform Quality Assurance
9.	Cause and effect diagram	Control Quality
10.	Design of experiments (DOE)	Perform Quality Assurance
11.	Cause and effect diagram	Perform Quality Assurance
12.	Statistical sampling	Control Quality
13.	Benchmarking	Plan Quality
14.	Pareto chart	Control Quality
15.	Checklist	Plan Quality

Exercise 7: B. Checksheet

Exercise 8:

Plan Quality Management	Perform Quality Assurance	Control Quality
A. Create additional project specific standards. B. Balance the needs of quality with scope, cost, time, risk and satisfaction E. Determine how to measure to make sure standards are met L. Find existing quality standards for product and project management I. Determine work needed to meet the standard	C. Determine if project activities comply with organization and project policies, processes, and procedures. D. Correct deficiencies in quality policies and procedures G. Identify required improvements in quality policies and procedures M. Perform quality audit.	F. Perform internal quality inspection. H. Measure specific project results against quality standards J. Repair defects K. Recommend changes, corrective and preventive actions and defect repair to integrated change control

Exercise 9:

Events or Issues	Quality Cost	Category
1.	External Failures	Cost of Nonconformance
2.	External Failures	Cost of Nonconformance
3.	Appraisal Function	Cost of Conformance
4.	Prevention Function	Cost of Conformance
5.	Internal Failure	Cost of Nonconformance
6.	Appraisal Function	Cost of Conformance
7.	Appraisal Function	Cost of Conformance
8.	External Failure	Cost of Nonconformance
9.	External Failure	Cost of Nonconformance
10.	Appraisal Function	Cost of Conformance
11.	Internal Failure	Cost of Nonconformance
12.	Legal Implication	Cost of Nonconformance
13.	Appraisal Function	Cost of Conformance
14.	External Failure	Cost of Nonconformance
15.	Prevention Function	Cost of Conformance
16.	Internal Failure	Cost of Nonconformance
17.	Appraisal Function	Cost of Conformance
18.	Prevention Function	Cost of Conformance
19.	Legal Implication	Cost of Nonconformance
20.	Internal Failure	Cost of Nonconformance

Exercise 10:

Exercise 11:

1. Scatter diagram
2. Low
3. Quality metric
4. Attribute sampling
5. Quality audits
6. Control Quality
7. Nonconformance
8. Process Analysis
9. Perform Quality Assurance
10. Out of control
11. Benchmarking
12. Histogram
13. Phil Crosby
14. Cause and effect (Ishikawa or Fishbone) diagram
15. Just in Time (JIT)
16. Mutually exclusive
17. Mean
18. Pareto chart
19. Statistical sampling
20. Rule of seven
21. W. Edwards Deming
22. Prevent
23. Continuous improvement
24. Conformance
25. Tree Diagram
26. Process Decision Program Charts (PDPC)
27. Prioritization matrices
28. Interrelationship digraphs
29. Matrix diagrams
30. Plan Quality Management, Perform Quality Assurance, and Control Quality
31. Plan Quality Management – Quality Management Plan, Process Improvement Plan, Quality Metrics
    Perform Quality Assurance – Organizational Process Assets Updates, Change Requests
    Control Quality – Quality Control Measurements, Validated Changes, Validated Deliverables, Work Performance Information, Change Requests

Project Quality Management Exam Tips

- Be able to name all three processes of project quality management and their key outputs.
- Be able to name all seven basic quality tools and know how to use them.
- Be able to answer questions where you will need to analyze a specific situation and determine what you should do next.
- Be familiar with the concepts and terms in the project quality management summary table, Figure 8-24: Project Quality Management Summary.

Project Quality Management Questions

1. You have been asked to identify the primary reasons for the substantial amount of customer complaints your company is experiencing every day. Which of the following tools will most effectively assist you in further identifying the reasons for the failures?

   A. Cause and effect diagram
   B. Run chart
   C. Statistical sampling
   D. Design of experiments

2. You are in the Perform Quality Assurance process to determine if project activities are complying with organizational and project policies, processes, and procedures. You are using process analysis as a tool & technique in this process to identify process improvements from an organizational and technical point of view. Which one of the following relates to process analysis?

   A. Quality control measurements
   B. Root cause analysis
   C. Work performance information
   D. Quality metrics

3. While trying to isolate the root cause of a critical problem in the production process, your team has detected two variables—temperature and humidity—as the conceivable contributors to the problem. There is a concern that these two variables are complicating the problem by affecting each other. Which of the following tools or techniques will assist to see if there is any interdependency between them?

   A. Cause and effect diagram
   B. Influence diagram
   C. Scatter diagram
   D. Pareto chart

4. Control Quality is the process of monitoring specific project results to determine if they comply with applicable quality standards and identifying ways to eradicate causes of unsatisfactory results. All of the following are tools & techniques used in the Control Quality process EXCEPT:

   A. Inspection
   B. Flow chart
   C. Quality metrics
   D. Statistical sampling

5. While using a control chart to monitor processes and to assure that they remain within acceptable limits or "in control," you noticed that seven data points are grouped together in a series on one side of the mean. All of the following are false about this situation EXCEPT:

   A. This type of situation needs to be investigated and a cause should be found.
   B. This trend is normal and expected within process.
   C. This is a random cause of variation and can be ignored.
   D. The process is stable and in control as none of the data points are outside control limits.

6. The project to build a ship that you are supervising is not progressing well. You were notified by the quality lead that the system design team has to redesign the ship due to poor quality and significant shortcomings in the design. Also during a walkthrough inspection, you have discovered that a considerable amount of scrap material has been generated by a team of newly hired engineers. The scrap material and rework are examples of:

   A. External failure
   B. Cost of conformance
   C. Prevention costs
   D. Internal failure

7. Your team is using a particular method of measuring quality and approving only a tiny portion of the outputs as per an unyielding pass/fail standard. Which of the following techniques is your team using?
   A. Product analysis
   B. Process analysis
   C. Attribute sampling
   D. Statistical sampling

8. A project manager is working on a project to install a generator in a local power company. She is anxious that her project practices are not robust enough and asked for your expert opinion. You advised her to compare her actual or planned practices to those of other projects both in and beyond the performing organization to identify a basis for performance measurement, improvement ideas, and best practices. Which of the following tools & techniques have you asked her to utilize?
   A. Design of experiments
   B. Cost-benefit analysis
   C. Statistical sampling
   D. Benchmarking

9. You are the project manager of a project to implement a golf simulator for a local golf club. Quality is the first thing in your mind, and you hired a Subject Matter Expert (SME) to ascertain if the project activities comply with organizational and project policies and procedures. The SME is particularly interested in identifying ineffective and inefficient activities or processes used in the project as well as gaps and deficiencies in your processes. You have initiated which of the following?
   A. Design of experiments
   B. Develop quality control measurements
   C. Quality audit
   D. Prevention functions

10. You discovered a pattern of flaws in several projects you are working on as a senior project manager. You have the impression that some kind of deficiency in the process your organization is using may be contributing to these repetitive defects. You conducted a cause and effect analysis and formulated a few recommendations for process change to avoid this recurring problem in future projects. You are in which of the following processes?
   A. Perform Qualitative Risk Analysis
   B. Plan Quality
   C. Perform Quality Assurance
   D. Control Quality

11. A plastic molding workshop wants to reduce injection molding rejects and performs a set of experiments that change injection pressure, mix, temperature, and setting times. Analysis of the results shows a combination of temperature and setting times as the most significant factors. Which of the following techniques is being used?
   A. Statistical sampling
   B. Brainstorming
   C. Nominal group technique
   D. Design of experiments

12. You are the project manager supervising a project to develop a new wireless media streaming device. The client asked you to have vigorous quality as it is one of their major concerns. You are in the Plan Quality Management process of identifying all the pertinent quality requirements, specifications, and standards for the project and product and specifying how those specifications will be met. You will be using all of the following as inputs of the Plan Quality Management process EXCEPT:
   A. Scope baseline
   B. Stakeholder register
   C. Quality metrics
   D. Schedule baseline

13. Costs associated with inspection, laboratory measurements and analysis, machinery maintenance and calibration, field testing, and procedure checking are examples of which of the following?
   A. Opportunity costs
   B. Sunk costs
   C. Prevention costs
   D. Appraisal costs

14. Plan-Do-Check-Act is a cycle of activities designed to drive continuous improvement. This theory was popularized by which of the following quality theorists?
   A. W. Edwards Deming
   B. Ishikawa
   C. Joseph Juran
   D. Philip Crosby

15. You are the project manager for one of a top wood furniture producers in the world. You are currently overseeing a project to create and manufacture a large amount of custom furniture for several major local retailers. Your organization has decided to practice just-in-time management and asked you to explore the practice. You found out that all of the following are FALSE about just-in-time EXCEPT:
   A. The project team will have no control over the inventory.
   B. It will allow less range of deviation than other inventory solutions.
   C. It will decrease the inventory investment.
   D. The organization will have lower quality of parts.

16. Monitoring specific project results to determine if they comply with relevant quality standards and identifying ways to eliminate causes of inadequate results is:
   A. Quality assurance
   B. Quality planning
   C. Quality control
   D. Quality management

17. Conformance to specifications—or making sure a project produces what it was created to produce—prevention over inspection, and zero defects are key items emphasized by:
   A. W. Edwards Deming
   B. Phil Crosby
   C. Joseph Juran
   D. None of the above

18. You are planning to hire a third-party auditor to perform a scheduled or random structured review to determine whether your quality management activities comply with organizational and project processes, policies, and procedures. All of the following will be done in this quality audit EXCEPT:
   A. Identify ineffective and inefficient activities or processes used on the project.
   B. Identify required improvements, gaps, and shortcomings in the processes.
   C. Create quality metrics.
   D. Recommend changes and corrective actions to Integrated Change Control.

19. You are overseeing a software application project to implement a custom accounting and financial system for medium to large-sized corporations. The quality assurance team submitted a defect report that has relevant information on the description, severity, root causes, possible resolutions, owner, due date, and reporter of the defects. You intend to know which causes of defects are most serious so that you can prioritize the potential causes of the problems. Which of the following tools should you use to isolate the critical few causes of defects from the uncritical many?
   A. Control chart
   B. Pareto chart
   C. Scatter diagram
   D. Fishbone diagram

20. Control Quality is the process of monitoring specific project results to determine if they comply with relevant quality standards and identifying ways to eliminate causes of unsatisfactory results. All of the following are tools & techniques used in Control Quality EXCEPT:
   A. Expert judgment
   B. Inspection
   C. Control chart
   D. Cause and effect diagram

21. A project manager was recently recognized for delivering a high-quality product with no noticeable defects. Some of the stakeholders were skeptical about limited features offered by the product. This kind of product that has a high-level of quality but does not include many of the features of comparable products is referred to as:
   A. Low quality
   B. Low grade
   C. Inaccurate
   D. Sketchy

22. Plan Quality Management is the process of identifying all the relevant quality requirements, specifications, and standards for the project and product and detailing how the specifications will be met and should be performed:
    A. During the initial phase of the project.
    B. Prior to the approval of the project charter.
    C. After the work breakdown structure has been developed.
    D. In parallel with the other planning processes.

23. A project manager working on implementing WIMAX connectivity in a rural area has to deploy several network devices and set up POPs to house those devices. She performed a cost-benefit analysis and was apprehensive about the high cost of nonconformance, or cost that will incur if proper quality is not implemented in her project. In quality management, which one of the following is NOT an attribute of the cost of nonconformance?
    A. Processing customer complaints
    B. Machinery maintenance and calibration
    C. Bad word-of-mouth advertising
    D. Field repair work

24. As a project manager, you are trying to decide the trade-offs between quality and grade in your project. Which one of the following is correct with respect to a product developed or a service performed?
    A. There is no difference between quality and grade.
    B. Neither low grade nor low quality is acceptable.
    C. Low quality is acceptable, but low grade is not.
    D. Low quality is not acceptable, but low grade is.

25. A project manager is in the Plan Quality Management process of identifying all the applicable quality requirements, specifications, and standards for the project and product and detailing how the specifications will be met. All of the following are true about the Plan Quality Management process EXCEPT:
    A. It should begin in the early planning phase in parallel with other planning processes.
    B. It should balance the needs of quality with scope, cost, time, risk, and customer satisfaction.
    C. Design of Experiments (DOE) is a tool & technique of this process that provides statistical analysis for changing product or process elements one at a time for process optimization.
    D. Inputs of this process are Scope Baseline, Stakeholder Register, Cost Performance Baseline, Schedule Baseline, Risk Register, Enterprise Environmental Factors, and Organizational Process Assets.

26. A project manager for a business automation project is working with the quality assurance department to improve stakeholders' confidence that quality management activities will comply with organizational and project processes, policies, and procedures. Which of the following MUST the project manager and assurance team have prior to initiating this Perform Quality Assurance process?
    A. Quality control measurements
    B. Change requests
    C. Validated changes
    D. Quality improvement

27. Proprietary quality management methodologies are used as tools & techniques in which of the following quality processes?
    A. Plan Quality Management
    B. Perform Quality Assurance
    C. Control Quality
    D. Perform Quality Management

28. You are using standard deviation to set the level of quality that your company has decided to achieve and also to set upper and lower control limits to determine if a process is in control. Standard deviation is a measure of how:
    A. Accurate the sample data is.
    B. Close the estimate is from the lowest estimate.
    C. Far the measurement is from the mean.
    D. Far apart the upper and lower control limits are.

29. While developing the quality metrics, you have defined the product attributes and ascertained how quality will be measured in your project. You have spent a substantial amount of time defining key attributes that are crucial to you and your stakeholders. Which of the following is NOT an example of a product attribute?
    A. Number of defects
    B. Desirability
    C. Availability
    D. Defect frequency

30. A project manager supervising a project to develop an auto crash video simulator for a local auto maker recently created a project budget, formalized a communications management plan after identifying all major stakeholders and their information needs, and was about to contemplate on completing the work packages. As per the instruction of senior management, the project manager has to move to a higher-priority project, leaving the simulator project to another project manager. What should the new project manager do NEXT?

A. Enter in the executing process group.
B. Initiate the Identify Risks process.
C. Facilitate completion of work packages.
D. Identify quality standards.

31. Which one of the following statements is TRUE about verified deliverables? Verified deliverables are:

A. Outputs of the Control Quality process and inputs to the Validate Scope process.
B. Inputs to the Control Quality process and outputs of the Validate Scope process.
C. Tools and techniques of the Control Quality and Validate Scope processes.
D. Outputs of the Control Quality and Validate Scope processes.

Project Quality Management Answers

1. A: A cause and effect diagram or fishbone diagram is a root cause analysis tool. A run chart is a line graph that displays process performance over time. Upward and downward trends, cycles, and large aberrations may be spotted and investigated further using a run chart. Statistical sampling involves choosing part of a population of interest for inspection instead of measuring the entire population. Design of Experiments (DOE) is a statistical method, usually applied to the product of a project, and provides a '"what-if" analysis of alternatives to identify which factors might improve quality.

2. B: One of the techniques used in process analysis is root cause analysis, which identifies the problem, discovers the underlying causes, and develops preventive actions.

3. C: The scatter diagram is used to determine the correlation between two variables.

4. C: Quality metrics are an output of the Plan Quality Management process and an input to both the Perform Quality Assurance and Control Quality processes.

5. A: The rule of seven refers to nonrandom data points grouped together in a series that total seven on one side of the mean. This type of situation needs to be investigated and a cause should be found, because even though none of the points are out of the control limit, they are not random and the process may be out of control.

6. D: Internal failure results in defects, repairs, scrap, and rework, vendor follow-up on defective goods, and quality control follow-ups. External failure is associated with quality issues experienced by the customer such as processing customer complaints, loss of future sales, bad word-of-mouth advertising, field repair work, and returned goods from customer. Cost of conformance refers to the costs incurred to ensure compliance. Prevention costs are included in the cost of conformance.

7. C. Attribute sampling is a method of measuring quality that consists of observing the presence (or absence) of some characteristics (attributes) in each of the units under consideration to determine whether to accept a lot, reject it, or inspect another lot.

8. D: Benchmarking is comparing actual or planned practices to those of other projects, both in and beyond the performing organization, to provide a basis for performance measurement, to generate improvement ideas, and to identify best practices. Design of Experiments (DOE) is a statistical method usually applied to the product of a project and provides a '"what-if" analysis of alternatives to identify which factors might improve quality. Statistical sampling involves choosing part of a population of interest for inspection instead of measuring the entire population. Cost-benefit analysis is a comparison of the cost of quality to the expected benefit. The benefit of quality must outweigh the cost of achieving it. The primary benefit of quality is increased stakeholders' satisfaction and less rework, which means higher productivity and lower cost.

9. C: A quality audit during the Perform Quality Assurance process is performed to determine if project activities comply with organizational policies and procedures.

10. C: You are in the Perform Quality Assurance process. This is the process to determine if the project activities comply with organizational and project policies, standards, processes, and procedures. This process is primarily concerned with overall process improvement and does not deal with inspecting the product for quality or measuring defects. The primary focus is on steadily improving the processes and activities undertaken to achieve quality.

11. D: Design of Experiments (DOE) is a statistical method usually applied to the product of a project. This method provides a '"what-if" analysis of alternatives to identify which factors might improve quality. It provides statistical analysis for changing key product or process elements all at once to optimize the process. Statistical sampling is performed after products have been produced. Brainstorming and nominal group techniques are tools & techniques associated with defining requirements or identifying problems.

12. C: Quality metric is an operational definition that specifies how quality will be measured. It is an output of the Plan Quality Management process, not an input.

13. D: Appraisal costs are associated with the cost of conformance and include inspection, laboratory measurements and analysis, machinery maintenance and calibration, field testing, and procedure checking.

14. A. Plan-Do-Check-Act is a cycle of iterative activities designed to drive continuous improvement. Initially implemented in manufacturing, it has broad applicability in business. First developed by Walter Shewhart, it was popularized by Edwards Deming. This theory advocates that business processes should be scrutinized and measured to detect sources of variations that cause products to deviate from customer requirements. The recommendation is to place the business processes in an unremitting feedback loop so that managers can isolate and change the parts of the process that need improvement. The four phases in the Plan-Do-Check-Act cycle involve the following:

- Plan: Design or revise business process components to improve results.
- Do: Implement the plan and measure its performance.
- Check: Assess the measurements and report the results to decision makers.
- Act: Decide on changes needed to improve the process.

15. C: Just-in-Time (JIT) is an inventory management method whereby materials, goods, and labor are scheduled to arrive or to be replenished exactly when needed in the production process; this brings inventory down to zero or to a near-zero level. It decreases costs by keeping only enough inventory on hand to meet immediate production needs.

16. C: Quality control is utilized to monitor and record results during execution of quality activities.

17. B: Phil Crosby popularized the concept of the cost of poor quality, advocated prevention over inspection and "zero defects," and defined quality as conformance to specification (project produces what it was created to produce).

18. C: A quality audit is done in the Perform Quality Assurance process, and quality metrics, which are the outputs in the Plan Quality Management process, are used as inputs in the Perform Quality Assurance process.

19. B: A Pareto chart illustrates which causes of error are most serious. It is displayed as a histogram and shows frequency of error according to cause. The concept is based on the 80/20 rule: "80 percent of the problems come from 20 percent of the causes;" thus, it is important to pay close attention to the 20 percent of critical causes in order to resolve 80 percent of the problems. A Pareto chart:

- Helps focus attention on the most critical issues
- Prioritizes potential causes of the problems
- Is used to determine priorities for quality improvement activities
- Separates the critical few from the uncritical many

20. A: Expert judgment is not listed as a tool & technique for any of the quality management processes.

21. B: Products that are produced at an acceptable level of quality and meet the desired requirements of the customer but have limited functionality and features compared to similar products are referred to as low grade.

22. D: Quality management is integrated with many other project planning processes, especially cost and time management.

23. B: Machinery maintenance and calibration is an appraisal function that is included in the cost of conformance. All other costs listed are costs of nonconformance.

24. D: A product that is produced at a high-level of quality but does not include many of the features of comparable products is referred to as low grade. A low grade product with limited features may be acceptable, but a low quality product or service is unacceptable.

25. C: DOE is a statistical method usually applied to the product of a project and provides a "what-if" analysis of alternatives to identify which factors might improve quality. It provides statistical analysis for changing key product or process elements all at once (<u>not one at a time</u>) to optimize the process.

26. A: Quality control measurements are relevant quality level and compliance measurements. These measurements are inputs to the Perform Quality Assurance process. Change requests are outputs for both the Perform Quality Assurance and Control Quality processes, and validated changes are outputs for the Control Quality process. Quality improvement is the result of the Perform Quality Assurance process.

27. A: Proprietary quality management methodologies such as Six Sigma, Lean Six Sigma, Quality Function Deployment, and CMMI® are used as tools & techniques in the Plan Quality Management process.

28. C: Standard deviation is a measurement of range around the mean.

29. B: Attributes are those items associated with the actual physical product or deliverable. Failure rate, defect frequency, reliability, cost control, number of defects, availability, test coverage, and on-time performance are product attributes, but desirability is not.

30. D: The previous project manager did not complete the planning; thus, planning should be completed first followed by executing. Identifying risks and quality standards are both done in the planning process group, but quality standards are identified prior to risk identification in the project.

31. A: Verified deliverables are Outputs of the Control Quality process and inputs to the Validate Scope process.

CHAPTER 9

PROJECT HUMAN RESOURCE MANAGEMENT

Project Human Resource Management

Project human resource management includes the processes that define the roles of all the team members and the responsibilities of each role. It also defines how to organize, manage, and lead the project team.

A project manager is not usually given full control over resources and budget. The project manager should utilize leadership skills and power to motivate and convince people to act in the best interest of the project.

The project team or project staff is made up of people who have assigned roles and responsibilities for assisting the project manager with planning and decision making as well as completing the project.

The project management team is the subset of the project team responsible for project leadership and management activities. The management team should be aware of professional and ethical behaviors and ensure that team members are following them.

The project sponsor typically works with the project management team and is responsible for project funding. To benefit the project, the project sponsor also assists in clarifying scope questions, approving the project plan, preventing unnecessary changes, monitoring project progress, and influencing others.

A few activities such as creating business cases, completing the feasibility study, and developing the Work Breakdown Structure (WBS) will be done by the initial or pre-assigned team members. Additional team members will be added to the team as needed later in the project. Risk planning may need to be revisited and updated as additional team members with different levels of expertise and experience or lack of required expertise are added to the team. These additional team members will decrease or increase the project risk.

Again, activity duration estimates may need modification since during the Estimate Activity Durations process these durations are sometimes estimated, budgeted, or planned prior to identifying all team members and their expertise and experience levels.

Important Project Roles and Responsibilities

It is essential to understand all the roles and responsibilities in a project. The project manager has the responsibility to clearly identify the specific roles and responsibilities for everyone involved in the project, including the roles for management, project team members, and other stakeholders. Below is the list of key roles and responsibilities of some of the key players in a project:

Project Sponsor: One who provides the financial resources for the project.
Responsibilities:

- Plays key role in formal acceptance.
- May provide key milestones and due dates.
- Provides input into risk thresholds.
- Gives the project manager authority as outlined in project charter.
- Determines the priorities between triple constraint components.
- Provides expert judgment.
- Prevents unnecessary changes.
- Protects the project form external changes and influences.
- Gathers the required support for the project.

Senior Management: Individuals in higher management who have higher authority.
Responsibilities:

- Allocates resources to projects.
- Sets priorities among projects.
- Approves final project plan.
- Signs project charter.
- Resolves issues beyond the project manager's control.

Project Manager: Individual responsible for managing the project to meet the project objectives.
Responsibilities:

- Is accountable for success/failure of project.
- Is in charge of projects, but possibly not resources.
- Leads planning efforts.
- Deals with conflicts in scope, schedule, quality, risk, etc.
- Determines and delivers required level of quality.
- Creates a change control system.
- Leads the team.
- Integrates the project components into a cohesive whole that meets customers' need.
- Maintains control over the project.
- Enforces professional and social responsibilities.

Functional Manager: Individual who manages and owns the resources in a specific department, such as IT, Finance, HR, Admin, etc., and generally directs the technical work of the individuals working in the project from the functional area.

Responsibilities:

- Assigns specific individuals to project team.
- Assists with resolving resource issues.
- Involved in planning until specific work units are assigned.
- Assists with planning corrective actions.
- Optimizes utilization of functional staff.
- Approves the final project management plan and final schedule during plan development.
- Manages activities within functional areas.

Project Team: A group of people who will complete the work on the project to achieve its objectives. The structure and characteristics of a project team may vary based on organizational culture, location, management strategies, etc. The following are examples of basic project team types:

Dedicated: Most of the team members are assigned full-time to work on the project. This kind of structure is most common in projectized organizations. The team members are committed to the project and usually report directly to the project manager.

Part-Time: The team members spend a portion of their time working on the project while remaining in their existing departments and carrying on their normal functions. This type of structure is most common in functional and matrix organizations. The functional managers control the team members and the resources allocated to the project.

Partnership: In the case of a partnership, joint venture, or alliance, several organizations may undertake a project. In this structure, teams will have members from all participating organizations, but one organization assigns a project manager to coordinate and lead the efforts. This kind of structure offers cost savings but faces difficulties of managing resources due to the project manager's lower degree of control.

Virtual: A virtual team is often required for projects where resources are located onsite or offsite or both. A virtual team can exist with any type of organizational structure and team composition. There are numerous challenges associated with virtual teams, such as language barriers, less bonding, time differences, cultural differences, complex communication, and other factors (See the virtual teams section of this chapter).

Responsibilities:

- Identify project requirements.
- Identify relationship and dependencies between activities.
- Create the work breakdown structure.
- Help identify and manage stakeholders.
- Help create the change control system.
- Attend project meetings.
- Make some project decisions.
- Comply with quality and communication plans.
- Provide time and cost estimates.
- Identify risks.
- Work on deliverables.
- Assist in project management plan development.
- Recommend corrective and preventive actions.
- Execute the project management plan.

Stakeholders: One who can positively or negatively impact the project or who will be impacted by the project.

Responsibilities:

- Have their knowledge, skills and requirements assessed.
- Receive performance reports.
- Approve project plan changes.
- Can become risk managers.
- Identify constraints.
- Approve project changes as a change control board member.
- Assist in project management plan development.

Exercise 1: List few characteristics and personality traits you will be looking for when selecting your project team members.

____

____

____

____

____

Exercise 2: Write the initials of the key person/group responsible for solving each of the problems in the following chart. Only consider team members, project manager, sponsor, senior management, and functional manager. Also consider yourself working in a matrix organization.

Situation	Key Person(s)
1. A couple of additional resources and two weeks of extra time will be needed for additional work.	
2. The team members are having conflict over priorities between work packages.	
3. After receiving the green light from the project manager, the functional manager is pulling a resource off the project.	
4. The team members are not sure who is really in charge of the project as no one is leading and managing the project.	
5. Project is lacking resources.	
6. The team members are not sure about their deliverables and when they are due.	
7. One of the work packages is taking an unexpectedly long time and will delay the project.	
8. One of the team members in the project team is having a performance issue.	
9. The project manager does not have the proper authority to lead the team and get things done.	
10. The project can be terminated any time.	
11. A team member comes up with a new method to complete an activity.	
12. One of several potential projects needs to be selected.	
13. The project is running behind schedule.	
14. Team members are not motivated.	
15. Additional funds are needed for the project.	
16. Two of the team members are arguing over a disagreement.	
17. A resource with the right expertise from one of the functional areas is needed, but the functional manager does not want to assign the resource to the project due to other priorities, despite several requests and extensive negotiation.	
18. There is no information on what, when, and how to communicate with stakeholders.	
19. Appropriate processes have not been selected for the project.	
20. The project is not meeting the organizational objective.	
21. There are extensive outside influences and changes in the project.	
22. The required level of quality has not been identified in the project.	
23. There is no activity list.	
24. Stakeholders are not happy or satisfied with the project.	
25. Stakeholders are not fully involved in the project.	
26. An unrealistic schedule and budget were given by the sponsor.	

Project Human Resource Management Processes

The project manager plans for the staffing requirements of the project to complete project activities. In addition, the project manager also determines how the human resources will be managed, trained, motivated, and led throughout the entire project life cycle.

A staffing management plan is an important component of the Plan Human Resource Management process. It defines how the project team will be acquired, managed, trained, motivated, led, rewarded for the work, and then released from the project team. The project team is acquired as per the staffing management plan. Note that the team, however, isn't always selected - it's often preassigned to the project. Sometimes, the project manager has to negotiate with the functional managers, the sponsor, and other project managers to get the best resources on the project. Also, when the resources aren't available inside the organization, the project manager often has to deal with outside contractors. However, in many cases, the project team is not at the same physical location and a virtual team is created. Whatever conditions surround the project team, the project manager must develop the project team and focus to enhance project performance by building a sense of team and improving competencies, interaction, and overall environment. Team development focuses on building team cohesiveness through team building exercises, training, and team involvement. Through conversations, observations, performance appraisals, conflict management, and the issue log, the project manager will manage the project team.

PMI identifies four key processes that are associated with the Human Resource Management knowledge area in the planning and executing process groups.

Processes	Process Groups	Detail	Key Outputs
1. Plan Human Resource Management	Planning	The process of identifying and documenting project roles, responsibilities, required skills, competencies, and reporting structure, among other things.	– Human Resource Management Plan
2. Acquire Project Team	Executing	The process of carrying out the Plan Human Resource Management process. The primary goal is to secure the best possible resources through negotiation or appropriate organizational processes to build the project team for carrying out the project activities efficiently.	– Project Staff Assignments
3. Develop Project Team	Executing	The process of enhancing project performance by building a sense of team and improving competencies, interaction, and overall team environment.	– Team Performance Assessments
4. Manage Project Team	Executing	The process of managing the team through observing, using issue logs, keeping in touch, providing feedback, completing performance appraisals, and resolving issues and conflicts.	– Change Requests

Table 9-1: Four Project Human Resource Management Processes and Key Outputs

Project Human Resource Management Processes, Inputs, Tool & Techniques, and Outputs

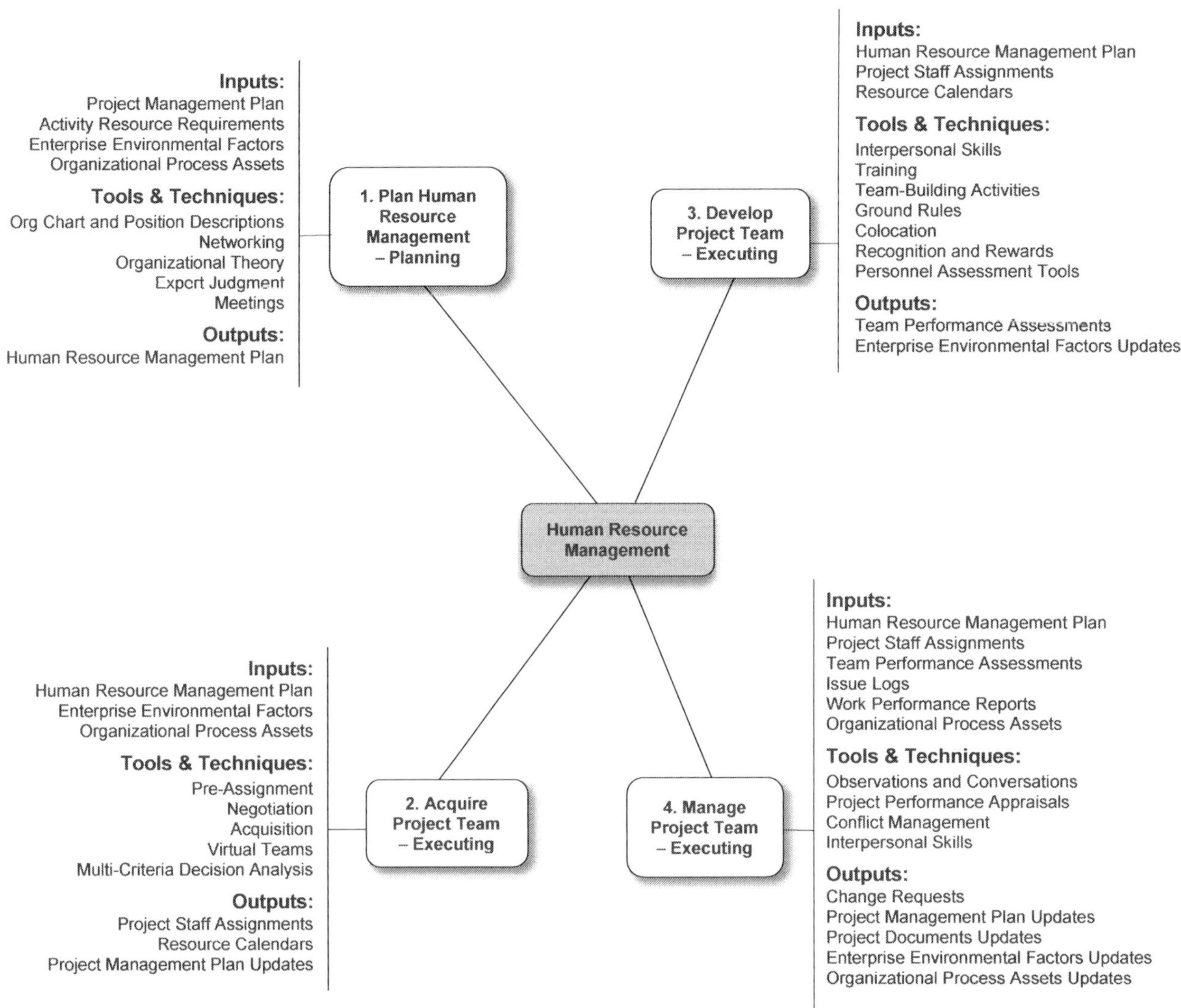

Figure 9-1: Project Human Resource Management Processes, Inputs, Tool & Techniques, and Outputs

Plan Human Resource Management

Plan Human Resource Management is the process of identifying and documenting project roles, responsibilities, required skills, competencies, reporting structure, and other related factors.

This process creates an overall staffing management plan by identifying the availability of resources, skill levels, training needs, team-building strategies, plan for recognition and reward programs, compliance considerations, safety issues, timetable for staff acquisition and release, and the impact of a staffing management plan on the organization. Each of these factors can have an impact on the schedule, cost, and quality of the project and may introduce risks not previously considered.

As per the PMBOK®, the Plan Human Resource Management process has the following inputs, tools & techniques, and outputs:

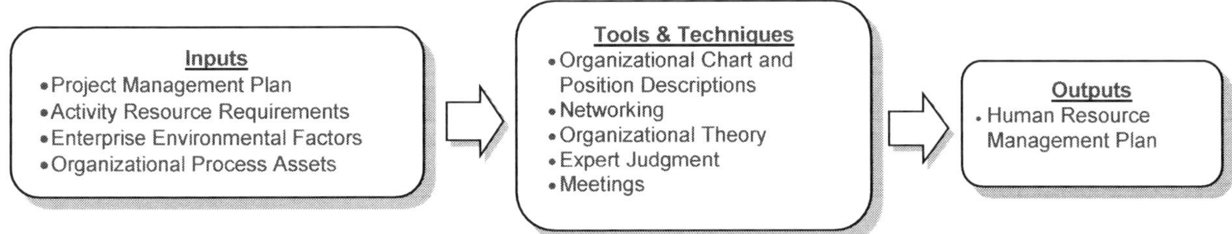

Figure 9-2: Plan Human Resource Management: Inputs, Tools & Techniques, and Outputs

Plan Human Resource Management: Inputs

- Project Management Plan
- Activity Resource Requirements
- Enterprise Environmental Factors
- Organizational Process Assets

Project Management Plan: A human resource management plan is developed as a component of the overall project management plan using information such as the change and configuration management plan, how activities will be executed, stakeholders' communication needs, how project baselines will be maintained, and processes that will be applied to each phase of the project life cycle.

Activity Resource Requirements: Human resource planning uses activity resource requirements to determine the human resource needs to complete the work on the project. Human resource needs that were developed in the time management planning process are now thoroughly evaluated in this process.

Enterprise Environmental Factors: Enterprise environmental factors such as organizational culture and structure, existing human resources, location and logistics, administrative procedures, market conditions, and other aspects may influence the Plan Human Resource Management process.

Organizational Process Assets: Organizational process assets such as organizational standard processes and procedures, historical information, templates for organizational charts and position descriptions, lessons learned, and other elements may influence the Plan Human Resource Management process.

Plan Human Resource Management: Tools & Techniques

- Organizational Chart and Position Descriptions
- Networking
- Organizational Theory
- Expert Judgment
- Meetings

Organizational Chart and Position Descriptions: To document team members' roles and responsibilities, various types of formats are available, such as:

- Hierarchical-Type Charts
- Matrix-Based Charts
- Text-Oriented Formats

Hierarchical-Type Charts:

a. **Organizational Breakdown Structure (OBS):** This diagram is similar to a company's standard organizational chart. It looks like a WBS but only includes the positions and relationships in a top-down, graphic format. It is arranged according to an organization's existing departments, units, or teams with their respective work packages. Any operations department such as manufacturing or engineering can identify all of its project responsibilities by looking at its portion of the OBS.

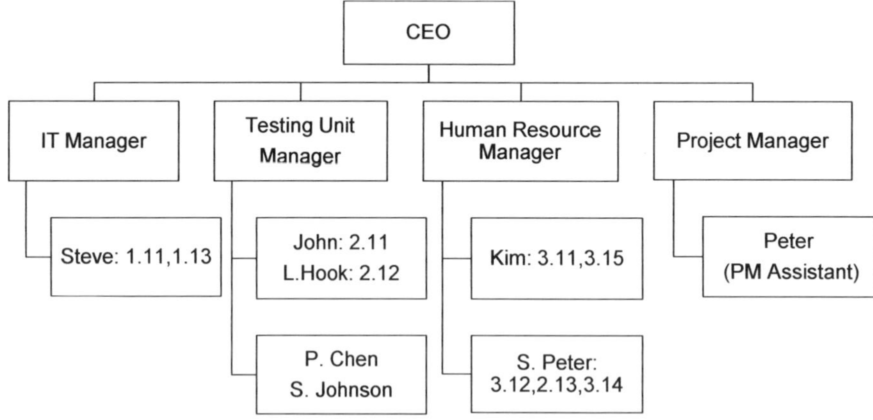

Figure 9-3: An Organizational Breakdown Structure (OBS) with Positions and Relationships

b. **Resource Breakdown Structure (RBS):** This diagram looks like a typical organizational chart, but this one is organized by types of resources. A RBS can help track project cost as it ties to the organization's accounting system. All resources have a cost associated with them, so it's easy to see that by identifying the resources needed and the respective quantities required to deliver the project's scope, we are working towards establishing a base cost for the whole project. For instance, you may have junior, midlevel, and senior QA testers working on your project. These testers have an average salary recorded in the organization's accounting system that can be used to calculate the cost of these resources.

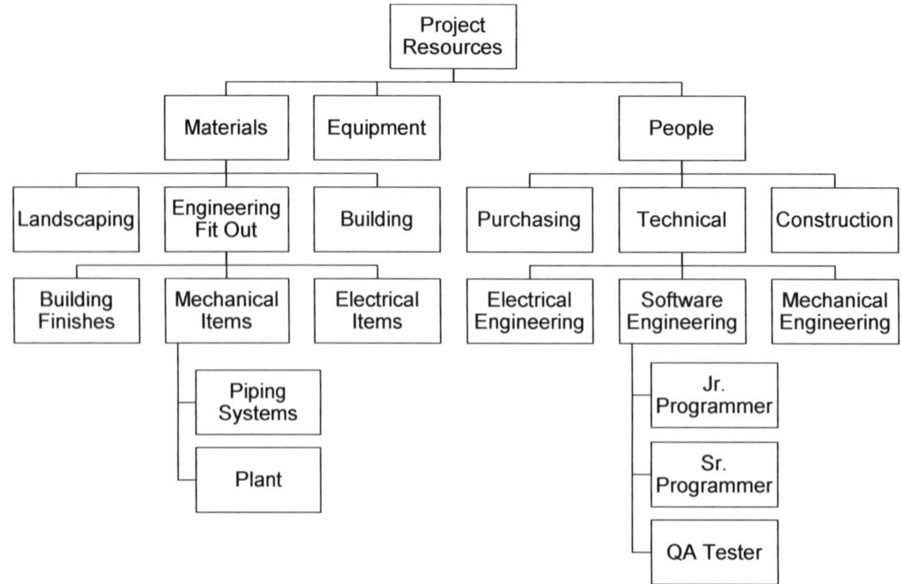

Figure 9-4: A Resource Breakdown Structure (RBS)

Matrix-Based Charts:

a. **Responsibility Assignment Matrix (RAM):** This chart cross-references team members with the activities or work packages they are to accomplish. One example of a RAM is a RACI (Responsible, Accountable, Consult, and Inform) chart, which can be used to ensure clear divisions of roles and responsibilities.

WBS Element	Project Team Member					Other Stakeholder		
	John	Paul	Don	Mark	Rick	Dick	Nick	Ron
Requirements	I				R			
System Design		R	C					
Functional Design	R					A		C
Develop			R					A
Test and Integrate			R			I	p	
User Acceptance				R				
Production Implementation								
Support		R			C	I		

Table 9-2: A RACI Chart - **R**=Responsible **A**=Accountable **C**=Consult **I**= Inform

Text-Oriented Formats:

a. **Position Description:** This text-oriented position description or role-responsibility-authority form is particularly important in recruiting. It is used to describe a team member's position title, responsibilities, authority, competencies, and qualifications in detail.

b. **Other sections of a project management plan:** Other sections include some responsibilities related to managing the project such as risk register (includes risk owners), quality plan (includes owners for quality assurance and quality control activities), and communication plan (lists members responsible for communication activities).

Networking: Networking is the process of formal and informal interaction with others in an organization, industry, or professional environment. A project manager can identify the political and organizational forces that will influence the project by networking within the organization.

Organizational Theory: Understanding organizational theory is extremely important as it provides information regarding the way in which people, teams, and organizational units behave.

Expert Judgment: Consultants, other units within the organization, industry groups, subject matter experts, professional and technical associations, stakeholders, the Project Management Office (PMO), customers, the sponsor, and others who have relevant specialized knowledge, training, and expertise can provide expert judgment to develop a human resource management plan.

Meetings: Planning meetings with team members, stakeholders, the sponsor, and others responsible for human resources in the project will be helpful to develop a human resource management plan.

Plan Human Resource Management: Outputs

- Human Resource Management Plan

Human Resource Management Plan: This plan is a subset of the project management plan and the sole output of the Plan Human Resource Management process.

a. **Roles and Responsibilities:** This component defines each role and specifies a title, authority, level of responsibility, and skill level or competency needed to be able to perform each specific role.

b. **Project Organization Charts:** These are graphical displays of project team members and their reporting relationships.

c. **Staffing Management Plan:** This is a document that describes how you plan to develop team members as well as when and how human resource requirements will be met. It has the following components:
   - Number of pre-assigned team members the project already has, number of additional team members that are needed, and when project team members will be acquired
   - Timetable for adding staff using a resource histogram
   - Identification of training needs and certification requirements
   - Plan for recognition and rewards to motivate team members
   - Compliance considerations, safety issues and how resources will be protected from safety hazards
   - Criteria for releasing team members

Acquire Project Team

Acquire Project Team is the process of carrying out the Human Resource Management plan. The primary goal is to secure the best possible resources through negotiation or appropriate organizational processes to build the project team for carrying out the project activities efficiently. Lack of necessary human resources may affect the project risks, quality, customer satisfaction, budget, and schedule. If the human resources are not available due to various constraints, it may be required to assign alternative resources, perhaps with lower expertise and competencies, considering that there is no regulatory, legal, mandatory, or other type of violation. This process is focused on the following:

- Identifying pre-assigned team members
- Negotiating for the best possible resources
- Confirming human resource availability
- Hiring of new employees
- Creating virtual team if needed

As per the PMBOK®, the Acquire Project Team process has the following inputs, tools & techniques, and outputs:

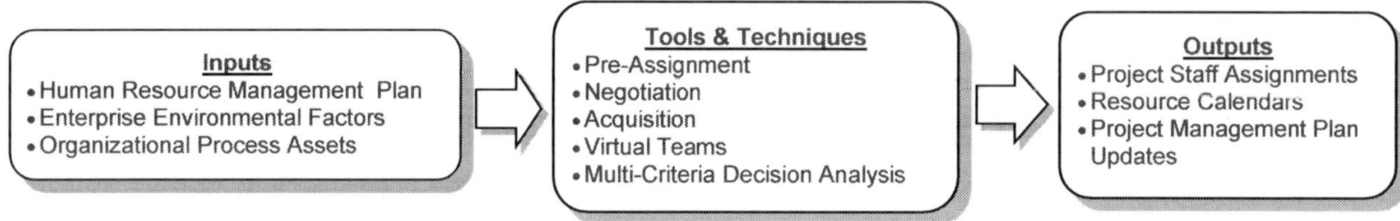

Figure 9-5: Acquire Project Team: Inputs, Tools & Techniques, and Outputs

Acquire Project Team: Inputs

- Human Resource Management Plan
- Enterprise Environmental Factors
- Organizational Process Assets

Human Resource Management Plan: The human resource management plan includes the following:

- Roles and responsibilities are defined, and for each role, title, authority, level of responsibility, and skill level or competency needed is made clear.
- The project organizational chart is a graphical display of project team members and their reporting relationships.
- The staffing management plan describes how you plan to develop team members as well as when and how human resource requirements will be met.

Enterprise Environmental Factors: Information on existing human resource availability, competency, prior experience, salary information, interest on projects, and other facets may influence the Acquire Project Team process.

Organizational Process Assets: The organizational standard policies, procedures, and processes may influence the Acquire Project Team process.

Acquire Project Team: Tools & Techniques

- Pre-Assignment
- Negotiation
- Acquisition
- Virtual Teams
- Multi-Criteria Decision Analysis

Pre-Assignment: Under most circumstances a role is defined first, and then the resource is assigned to perform the role and fulfill the responsibilities. However, some of the team members will be selected in advance and considered as pre-assigned to fill roles before the human resource management plan has been created or the project has been formally initiated.

Resources can be pre-assigned as a part of a competitive proposal, as per some staff assignment defined in the project charter, or for dependency on the experience and expertise of particular individuals.

Negotiation: Staff assignments are negotiated on many projects. To gain resources from within the organization and in contract situations, a project manager has to negotiate frequently. In order to successfully negotiate, a project manager should:

- Know the objectives, goals, and needs of the project and its priority in the organization.
- Convince the resource manager to assist in the project by assigning resources.
- Understand that a resource manager has his/her own priorities and may not gain any benefit from supporting a project.
- Justify why better resources are needed with the help of the network diagram and project schedule.
- Be focused on building a good relationship with the resource manager.
- Work with the resource manager to deal with problems with resources working within the project since most of the resources will be reporting to the resource manager.
- Not seek the best resources if they are not needed.

Acquisition: The performing organization may acquire services from outside sources if it lacks the in-house staff with the required skills and competencies to work on the project. This can involve subcontracting work to another organization or hiring individual consultants to help during the course of the project or project phase or for specific activities.

Virtual Teams: A virtual team consists of a group of people who never or rarely meet but who have a shared goal to complete the project successfully. Communication planning becomes increasingly important in a virtual team environment due to the availability of electronic communication, such as e-mail, audio and video conferencing, web-based meetings, and other mediums. The use of virtual teams creates new possibilities and makes it possible to achieve the following items:

- Carry on with projects that would have never been initiated due to heavy travel expenses.
- Include members of the team who live in widespread geographic areas, employees who work from home or have different shifts/hours, and people with mobility limitations or disabilities.
- Add special expertise and competency to a project team from outside of the project's geographic area.

There are numerous challenges associated with virtual teams, such as language barriers, less bonding, time differences, cultural differences, complex communication, and other factors. Caution must be taken to set clear expectations, develop protocols for conflict resolution, set up a robust decision-making procedure, and set up a proper recognition and reward system.

Multi-Criteria Decision Analysis: Potential team members are often rated and scored by various selection criteria during the Acquire Project Team process. These selection criteria are weighted according to their relevant importance and are developed using the multi-criteria decision analysis tool.

A project team member's abilities or competencies, communication capabilities, relevant knowledge, skills, experience, cost (for adding the team member), attitude or ability to work with others, and availability. Other factors such as time zone and geographical location are some examples of selection criteria that can be used to rate and score team members.

Acquire Project Team: Outputs

- Project Staff Assignments
- Resource Calendars
- Project Management Plan Updates

Project Staff Assignments: This is the primary output in this process. The project is staffed when appropriate people have been assigned as per their defined roles and previously described methods.

Resource Calendars: Resource calendars document the time periods that project team members can work on the project considering their schedule conflicts, vacation time, and bandwidth allocated to other projects.

Project Management Plan Updates: Elements of the project management, such as the human resources management plan, may be updated to reflect replanning and corrective actions to change the team structure, roles, and responsibilities.

Exercise 3: As a project manager, you may encounter the following difficulties when attempting to staff your project team. Identify actions that you may take to respond to these difficulties.

Difficulties	Actions
1. Lack of resources with technical or subject matter expertise and experience.	
2. Multiple projects are fighting for limited resources.	
3. Critical resources may not be available as per the project needs.	
4. Performance appraisals are mostly done by the functional managers.	
5. Resources are not too enthusiastic to accept project assignments due to the temporary nature of projects.	
6. Functional managers are reluctant to release their highly skilled resources.	

Exercise 4: Project managers are compelled to influence functional managers and may be forced to compete with other project managers as multiple projects compete for limited resources and priority. What actions should project managers take to influence functional managers and convince them to provide the necessary resources?

Exercise 5: Take few minutes to discuss the benefits and complexities of virtual teams. What factors are important for an effective virtual team?

Exercise 6: What factors are frequently used to indicate successful completion of a project?

Develop Project Team

The Develop Project Team process is performed throughout the project. The focus is to enhance the project performance by building a sense of team and improving the competencies, team interaction, and the overall team environment.

The Develop Project Team process may have the following objectives:

- Improve individual and team productivity, cooperation, trust, and spirit by creating a cohesive, dynamic, and friendly team environment.
- Assist in sharing knowledge and expertise by arranging cross-training and mentoring between team members.
- Reduce conflicts, increase teamwork, and raise morale by improving trust and understanding among team members.
- Increase the ability of the team members to complete project deliverables by improving their skill sets and knowledge.
- Lower the project cost, improve quality, and reduce project duration by improving overall team performance.

In order to meet project objectives and goals, the project manager should have the skill sets to build, motivate, lead, and inspire the project team effectively. A project manager needs to take the following actions to develop a project team:

- Hold team building activities throughout the project
- Provide required training to all team members
- Establish ground rules
- Give recognition and rewards
- Place team members in the same physical location
- Encourage and motivate team members
- Assess team members' performance
- Discuss and find mutual solutions to problems
- Make decisions via group discussion if appropriate
- Assess team members' strengths, weaknesses, preferences, personalities, needs, and learning styles to assist team cohesiveness.

As per the PMBOK®, the Develop Project Team process has the following inputs, tools & techniques, and outputs:

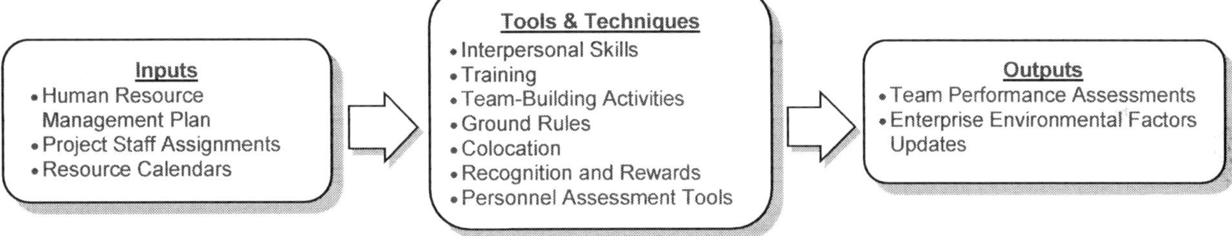

Figure 9-6: Develop Project Team: Inputs, Tools & Techniques, and Outputs

Develop Project Team: Inputs

- Human Resource Management Plan
- Project Staff Assignments
- Resource Calendars

Human Resource Management Plan: This plan outlines the training strategies and plans for developing the project team. As a result of ongoing team performance assessments and other forms of project team management, items such as rewards, feedback, additional training, flex time, bonus pay, options for telecommuting, disciplinary actions, and other elements can be added to the plan.

Project Staff Assignments: Team development starts with a list of the project team members found in the project staff assignments documents.

Resource Calendars: Resource calendars identify times when the project team members will be available to participate in team development activities.

Develop Project Team: Tools & Techniques

- Interpersonal Skills
- Training
- Team Building Activities
- Ground Rules
- Colocation
- Recognition and Rewards
- Personnel Assessment Tools

Interpersonal Skills: These are sometimes known as "soft skills," such as empathy, influence, creativity, and group facilitation. These skills are particularly important for project team members to get along with others, to ensure their support and cooperation, and to motivate them to give their best effort for the project.

It's a thorny area for the project manager, but it's important to realize that team productivity can be greatly increased and conflicts can be reduced by understanding the sentiments of the team members, acknowledging their concerns, following up on their issues, and anticipating their actions.

Training: Training includes a wide range of activities, such as classroom, online, computer-based, on-the-job training, and other mediums designed to enhance the competencies of the project team members.

Team-Building Activities: Team building is forming the project team into a cohesive group working for the best interest of the project. Team building cannot be forced; although it may be a special event, it can occur while performing regular project activities as the project progresses. Below are the responsibilities of the project manager:

- Guide, manage, and improve the bonds, relationships, and interactions of team members
- Improve the trust and cohesiveness among the team members
- Incorporate team-building activities in all project activities
- Start team-building activities in the early phases of every project

Team-building activities can include the following:

- Holiday and birthday celebrations
- Milestone parties
- Trips outside of work
- Project planning that gets everyone involved in some way

Tuckman's theory states that there are five stages of development that teams may go through:

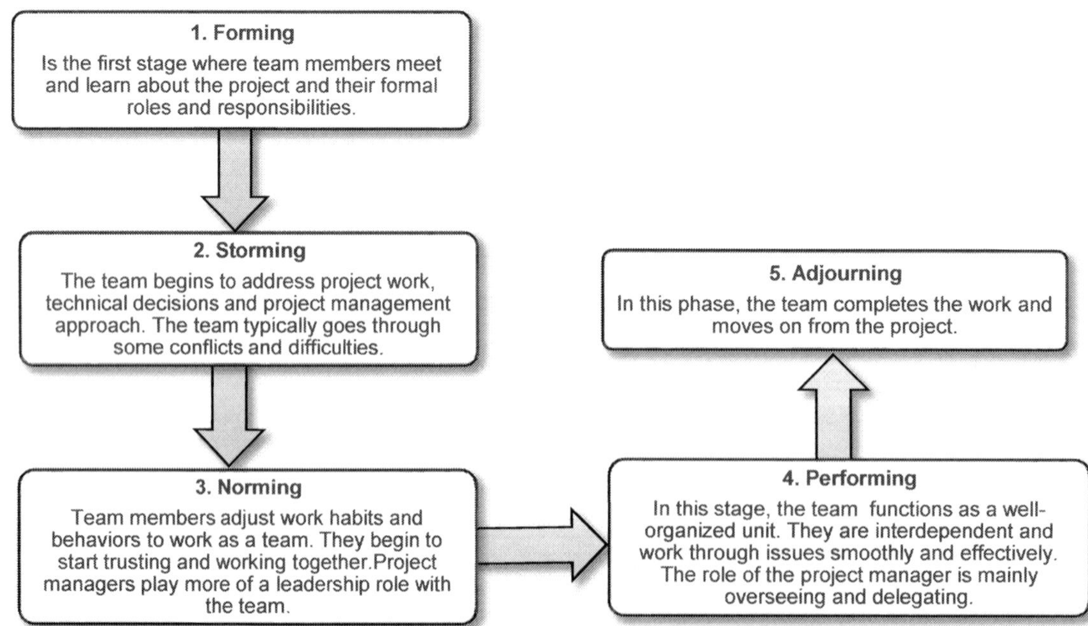

Figure 9-7: Tuckman's Five Stages of Team Development

Ground Rules: Ground rules identify acceptable and unacceptable behaviors on the project and try to minimize the negative impacts of bad behaviors. Some of the ground rules include the following:
- Methods of resolving conflicts
- Ways to treat sensitive data in the project
- Methods of notifying the project manager about difficulties, issues, and concerns
- Acceptable ways to interrupt someone talking at a meeting
- Methods to stop talking over a team member inappropriately
- Rules for joining meetings and consequences of being late
- Guidelines to talk to higher management
- Rules to give direction to contractors

Colocation (Tight Matrix): Colocation involves placing many or all of the most active project team members in the same physical location to enhance their ability to perform as a team. Examples of colocation can be the creation of a war room where all team members can work or colocating the project team at the customer's site.

Recognition and Rewards: Recognition and rewards play a vital role in improving a team's performance and keeping team members motivated to work more efficiently and produce a better result for the project. The project manager should give the team members all the possible recognition during the project life cycle rather than after completion of the project. The right motivational tools, along with clear expectations and defined procedures, will help team members excel drastically.

It is important to note that lack of an established method or criteria for giving out recognition and rewards can destroy the morale of team members. If team members feel that the reward is win-lose and that only certain members are rewarded, this will significantly hurt their morale and negatively impact team cohesiveness. Recognition and rewards should be win-win and proportional to the performance and achievement of the individuals and team. A project manager should also consider cultural differences and individual preferences while giving out recognition and rewards.

Some of the recognition and rewards can be as follows:
- Award prizes such as "Employee of the Month" or cash prizes for good performance.
- Send notes to senior management and the functional manager about a team member's good performance.
- Plan milestone parties or other celebrations to celebrate the successful completion of a major milestone.
- Recommend team members for raises, bonuses, or promotion.
- Send a team member for training which is paid from the project budget.
- Assign a team member to a noncritical path activity so that he/she can gain more knowledge in that area.
- Say "thank you" for great contributions to the project more often and whenever possible.
- Appreciate project members' contributions and dedications during meetings and other times.

Personnel Assessment Tools: Various personnel assessment tools such as structured interviews, focus groups, ability tests, attitudinal surveys, specific assessments, and others, provide the project manager and team with insight into areas of strength, weakness, and required improvements.

The project manager may use these tools to assess the performance of team members, identify their preferences, and have a better understanding of how well they organize and process information, interact with others, and make decisions. Assessing and understanding team members will increase trust, commitment, understanding, and communication among team members; as a result, there will be more productivity throughout the project.

Develop Project Team: Outputs

- Team Performance Assessments
- Enterprise Environmental Factors Updates

Team Performance Assessments: The goal of team performance assessments is to identify the specific training, coaching, mentoring, assistance, or other changes required to improve the team's performance and effectiveness. The project management team makes formal or informal assessments of the project team's effectiveness while team development efforts such as training, team building, and colocation are implemented. A team's performance is measured against the agreed-upon success criteria, schedule, and budget target.

The evaluation of a team's effectiveness may include the following indicators:
- How well the team is performing, communicating, and dealing with conflicts
- Areas of improvement in skills that will help individuals to perform assignments more efficiently and areas of improvement in competencies that will help the team perform better
- Increased cohesiveness where team members will work together to improve overall project performance by sharing information and experiences openly and by helping each other more frequently
- Reduced staff turnover rate

Enterprise Environmental Factors Updates: Personnel administration, including employee training records and skills assessments, may be updated.

Exercise 7: Identify which of the following are NOT the roles of a project manager.

- Establish project controls
- Motivate the team members
- Provide staffing
- Estimate activity durations
- Define how tasks will be completed
- Remain flexible and in control
- Develop plans
- Control each project task
- Organize resources
- Estimate each activity cost
- Set objectives

Exercise 8: As a project manager, you will be spending 90% of your time communicating with several individuals involved in your project. What information and expectations should you communicate to the project team?

Exercise 9: The project manager is often faced with substantial amount of obstacles. Describe some of the obstacles and provide suggestions for overcoming them to achieve the desired performance benefits.

Manage Project Team

Manage Project Team is the process of managing the team through observing, using issue logs, keeping in touch, providing feedback, completing performance appraisals, and resolving issues and conflicts. The management team requires a combination of communication, conflict management, negotiation, problem solving, influencing, and leadership skills to ensure teamwork and to create a high-performance project team.

As per the PMBOK®, the Manage Project Team process has the following inputs, tools & techniques, and outputs:

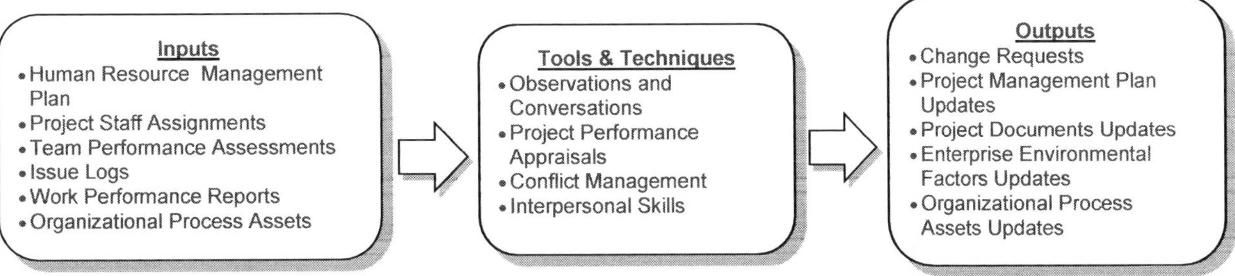

Figure 9-8: Manage Project Team: Inputs, Tools & Techniques, and Outputs

Manage Project Team: Inputs

- Human Resource Management Plan
- Project Staff Assignments
- Team Performance Assessments
- Issue Logs
- Work Performance Reports
- Organizational Process Assets

Human Resource Management Plan: The human resource management plan has information on roles and responsibilities, project organization, and staffing management plans and guides regarding how project human resources are defined, acquired, managed, controlled, and released from the project.

Project Staff Assignments: Project staff assignments are an output of the Acquire Project Team process and the key input in Manage Project Team process. It provides documentation, which includes the list of project team members.

Team Performance Assessments: The goal of team performance assessments is to identify the specific training, coaching, mentoring, assistance, or changes required to improve the team's performance and effectiveness. The project management team makes formal or informal assessments of the project team's effectiveness while team development efforts such as training, team building, and colocation are implemented. A team's performance is measured against the agreed-upon success criteria, schedule, and budget target.

Issue Logs: An issue is an obstacle that threatens project progress and can block the team from achieving its goals. An issue log is a written log to record issues that require solutions. It helps monitor who is responsible for resolving specific issues by a target date. There should be one owner assigned for each issue reported within the project.

ID	Issue Description	Date Added	Priority	Raised By	Owner	Due Date	Status	Date Resolved	Issue Resolution
01	Chris was moved to a higher priority project – need an urgent replacement.	3/3/2014	High	Steve	Project manager	3/15/2014	Closed	3/10/2014	Miguel was assigned for next three months to replace Chris.
02	Equipment (PCs, servers, digital storages) were delivered late.	3/6/2014	High	Rony	Project manager	3/20/2014	Closed	3/15/2014	A change request was issued and approved for a three week time extension.

Table 9-3: Issue Log

Work Performance Reports: These include documentation about current project status compared to project forecasts in scope, time, cost, and other factors. The information received from performance reports and forecasts will be beneficial to determine future human resource requirements and updates to the staffing management plan.

Organizational Process Assets: Relevant organizational process assets can include certificates of appreciation, perquisites, corporate apparel, bonus information, newsletters, websites, and other elements.

Manage Project Team: Tools & Techniques

- Observations and Conversations
- Project Performance Appraisals
- Conflict Management
- Interpersonal Skills

Observations and Conversations: These informal tools are used by the project management team to stay in touch with the work, morale, and attitudes of project team members. These tools help to monitor progress toward project deliverables, accomplishments, interpersonal issues, and potential or actual problems.

Project Performance Appraisals: This is an evaluation of individual team member's effectiveness. The project management team meets with the team members and provides feedback about team member's performance and how effectively he/she is performing his/her tasks.

A 360-degree feedback system is used to receive feedback from all directions, including from peers, from superiors and subordinates, and sometimes from vendors and external contractors. Team members not only evaluate other team members, but they should evaluate the project manager as well. Individual comments should not be disclosed, but the general feedback results should be shared with each team member in a private session. In order to have complete and honest feedback, it is vital that the participants remain anonymous.

Conflict Management: Conflict is inevitable, and managing it in a constructive way can be beneficial for the project as it may actually present opportunities for improvement and help improve team morale and performance. It is essential to get familiar with the new concepts on conflicts.

Old Views	New Views
Conflicts are destructive and mostly caused by leadership failure or due to personality differences.	Conflicts are inevitable due to the need for frequent interactions among team players.
Every effort should be made to avoid conflicts.	Conflicts can be constructive, as differences in opinion can lead to better decision making and increased creativity. Successful conflict management also results in positive working relationships and greater productivity.
Conflicts should be resolved by physically separating the parties having the conflicts. Upper management should also intervene whenever needed to resolve conflicts.	Conflicts are resolved through identifying the causes and solving problems. If a conflict cannot be resolved among the parties involved, it should be escalated to the appropriate authority. Solid project management practices such as role definition and a robust communication plan, ground rules, group norms, and other elements can reduce the amount of conflicts in a project.

Conflict is natural, and it is unavoidable due to the following reasons:

- A project manager has limited power, and most of the time a project manager is not given full control over resources and budget.
- In projects, we need to address the needs and requirements of many stakeholders and prioritize the needs of one individual over another.
- Functional managers may not gain much from the project, but they have to give up resources for the projects.

The success of project managers in managing their project teams often depends substantially on their ability to resolve conflict. When handing conflict in a team environment, the project manager should be familiar with the relative importance, intensity, time pressure, players involved, and other items of the conflict. To avoid conflict, the project manager should take the following actions:

- Follow robust project management policies and practices.
- Inform the team members about the exact project direction, project objectives, assumptions and constraints, content of the project charter, and all major decisions, issues, and changes.

- Make the expectations and work assignments clear to the team members and get their buy-in.
- Make work assignments as interesting and as challenging as possible.

Sources of Conflict: There are several sources of conflict including schedule priorities, scarce resources, personal work style, cost, and other causes. It is important to note that personality differences are not the root cause of conflict; in fact, they are rarely the case. Below are the seven sources of conflict in order of frequency.

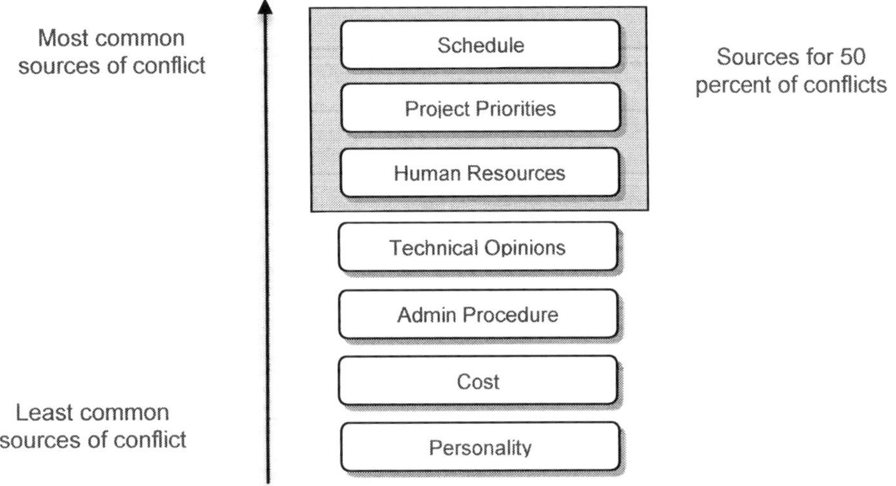

Figure 9-9: Primary Sources of Conflict in a Project

Conflict Resolution Techniques: There are several techniques to resolve conflict, and five of them are discussed below. To successfully resolve conflict, project managers need to create an open environment, and their conflict resolution should focus on issues (not personalities) and on the present (not the past).

Style	Description	Best Outcome
Withdrawing/Avoiding	Retreating from conflict, avoiding or postponing resolution.	LOSE/LOSE
Forcing/Directing	Exerting one opinion over another. It destroys team morale, does not help resolve the problem, and almost never provides a long-term solution.	WIN/LOSE
Smoothing/Accommodating	Emphasizing areas of agreement, downplaying differences of opinion to maintain harmony.	YIELD/LOSE
Compromising/Reconciling	Bargaining to some level of mutual (dis)satisfaction to both parties. Parties are asked to give up something to gain something.	YIELD/YIELD
Collaborating/Problem Solving	Focusing on working to combine multiple differing perspectives into one shared perspective for resolving the real problem so that the problem goes away.	WIN/WIN

Note: Collaborating or problem solving is the most favorable approach. PMI does not favor withdrawal as with this approach conflict is never resolved.

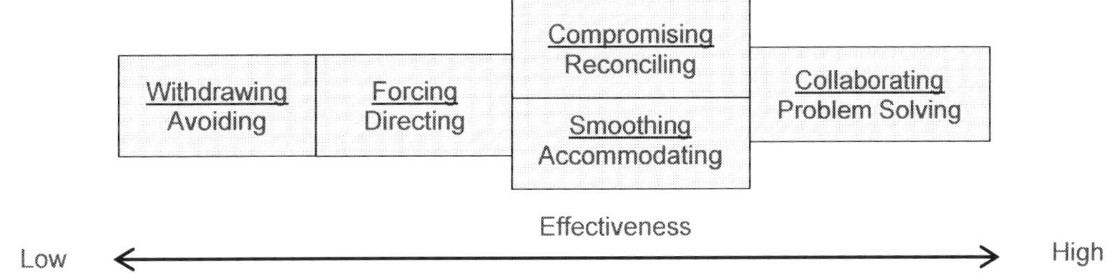

Figure 9-10: Conflict Management Effectiveness

Interpersonal Skills: Interpersonal skills such as leadership, team building, motivation, communication, influencing, decision making, political and cultural awareness, negotiation, trust building, conflict management, and coaching are of significant importance for project managers. Among the most important of these are the following:

Leadership: Leadership skills are essential to communicate the vision as well as to inspire the project team to achieve high performance.

Influencing: Project managers should be persuasive and have the capability to influence stakeholders and others to address critical issues. Moreover, project managers need to be able to reach agreements while upholding mutual trust by illustrating points and positions considering the various perspectives in any situation.

Effective decision making: To negotiate and influence the organization and project management team in effective decision making, project managers should focus on goals, study environmental factors, analyze information, manage risk, stimulate team creativity, and follow a decision-making process.

Manage Project Team: Outputs

- Change Requests
- Project Management Plan Updates
- Project Documents Updates
- Enterprise Environmental Factors Updates
- Organizational Process Assets Updates

Change Requests: Dealing with staffing changes due to people moving to different assignments, outsourcing some of the work, replacing over- or under-qualified team members, or dealing with a team member leaving the organization, in addition to other factors, should be done during the Integrated Change Control process.

Project Management Plan Updates: The human resource management plan portion of the project management plan will be updated as well as any other relevant portions.

Project Documents Updates: Documents such as staff assignments, role descriptions, and issue logs, among others, may be updated.

Enterprise Environmental Factors Updates: Some of the factors that may need to be updated are inputs to organizational performance appraisals and personnel skills.

Organizational Process Assets Updates: Some of the assets that may need to be updated are historical information and lessons learned, templates, standard processes, and other items.

Exercise 10: List actions a project manager should take to manage the team.

____

____

____

____

____

Exercise 11: What actions can a project manager take to deal with a difficult person?

____

____

____

____

Exercise 12: Determine which of the conflict resolution techniques is being used in the following situations:

Description	Technique
1. "There is a lack of understanding about the deliverables and their due dates. Let's review the detailed project plan and project schedule to figure out when the deliverables are due and what is expected from each of you."	
2. "Look, I am in charge. We're sticking with whatever I have decided."	
3. "Let's listen to what everyone has to say and come up with a solution to the problem together."	
4. "Come on, dudes. It may seem like we cannot make it, but look—we are ahead of schedule and under budget."	
5. "OK, man, I am willing to accept the late delivery of the equipment in exchange for a 20 percent discount."	
6. "I am busy now, so let's deal with this concern next week."	
7. "Look. There needs to be some give-and-take from both of you so that we can carry on with our lives and finish the project."	
8. "OK, I will be releasing Steve a week early as you promised to assign John to the project for a couple of weeks."	
9. "I am not interested in discussing the topic, and I also do not have time for this right now. Let's just have it your way and forget I ever said anything."	

Exercise 13: You want to create a positive environment that is conducive to teamwork so that your team members will contribute more to the project. List actions that you will take to develop a high performing team in a positive environment.

Exercise 14: Describe how a difficult person may disrupt the entire team and jeopardize the project.

Types of Power Available to the Project Manager

Project managers almost always have difficulties getting people to cooperate and perform, especially in a matrix organization. A project manager is rarely given complete and unquestioned authority on a project, thus the philosophy of power is based on the realization that the project manager must be able to persuade and motivate people to act in the best interest of the project and to give their best efforts to the project.

Getting people to cooperate requires the project manager to understand and utilize the five types of available authority/power:

Reward: This type of power imposes positive reinforcement. It's the ability of giving rewards and recognition. It is any type of reward that will motivate a team member, such as good performance review, pay raise, bonus, time off, or any other type of perquisite.

Formal (Legitimate): A position in the organization and/or formal authority.

Penalty (Coercive/Punishment): This type of power is predicated on fear and gives the project manager the ability to penalize a team member for not meeting the project goal and objective.

Expert: This type of power is based on the knowledge or skill of the project manager on a specific domain. Being the subject matter expert or project management expert will give the project manager substantial power to influence and control team members.

Referent: This type of power is based on the respect or the charismatic personality of the project manager or on referring to someone in a higher position to leverage some of the superior's power.

Note: Reward and Expert are the most effective forms of power, and Punishment/Penalty/Coercive should be used as the last resort after all other forms have been exhausted.

Project Manager's Qualities

A project manager is expected to have all kinds of managerial and interpersonal skills to be successful. An effective project manager should have a combination of interpersonal, ethical, and conceptual skills to analyze various situations and to interact appropriately. Some of the most important qualities that a project manager should have are listed below:

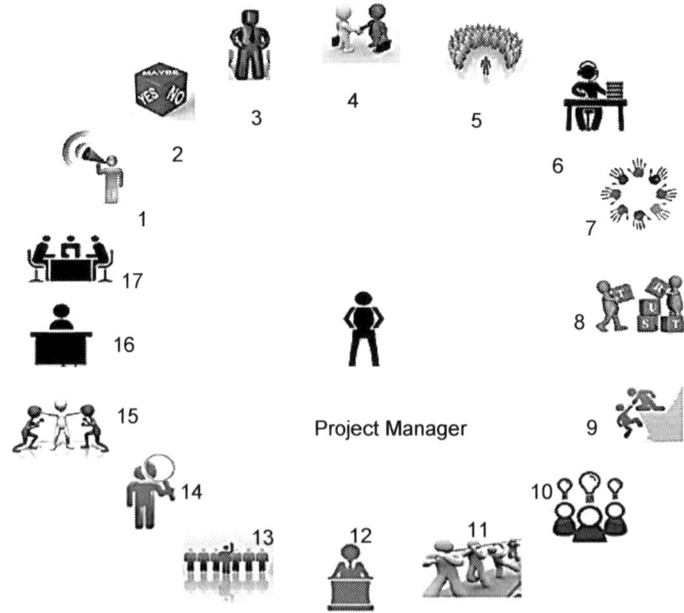

Figure 9-11: Qualities of a Successful Project Manager

1. Motivational skill
2. Decision making skill
3. Professionalism
4. Negotiating skill
5. Team building skill
6. Writing skill
7. Political and cultural awareness
8. Trust building skill
9. Coaching
10. Knowledge of PM
11. Team player skill
12. Presentation skill
13. Leadership skill
14. Problem solving skill
15. Conflict management skill
16. Administrative skill
17. Communication skill

Principle Leadership Styles

Project management is heavily dependent on managing people, which has been defined as being able to produce key results. On the other hand, leadership is all about establishing mission and vision, aligning team members to the established direction, motivating individuals, and inspiring them.

The most effective leadership style varies according to situation and project phase. While the particular style of leadership varies from one project to another, during the initial phase of a project, a project manager usually directs the activities and takes a significant active leadership role. As the project progresses, a project manager may take less heavy-handed leadership approaches such as coaching, facilitating, or other supporting styles.

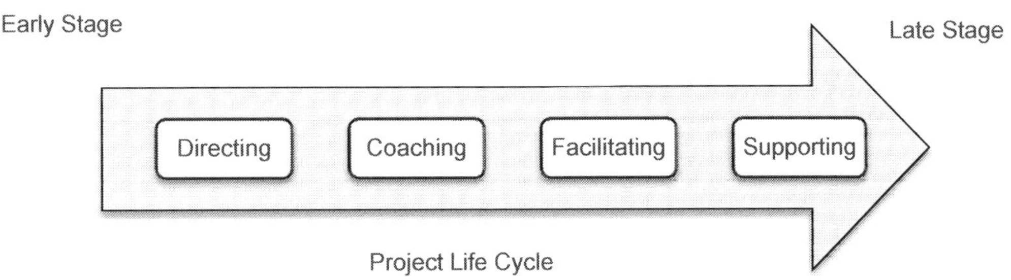

Figure 9-12: Leadership Styles in Different Phases of a Project

Some of the leadership and management styles are listed below:

Leadership Style	Details
Directing	Management tells others what to do.
Facilitating	Management coordinates input from others.
Coaching	Management guides or instructs others.
Supporting	Management provides help.
Autocratic	Management makes decisions alone without any input.
Consultative	Management invites suggestions before making decisions.
Consensus	Management decides via group agreement.
Consultative Autocratic	Management solicits team members' input but retains decision-making authority.
Delegating	Management establishes the goal and gives the team sufficient authority to carry on work.
Bureaucratic	Management is focused on following procedures rigorously.
Charismatic	Management encourages and energizes.
Democratic or Participative	Management encourages team participants in the decision-making process.
Laissez-Faire	Management is not directly involved but manages and consults as required. The French term means "allow to act" or "leave alone."
Analytical	Depends on management's technical ability and knowledge.
Driver	Management constantly gives directions.
Influencing	Management stresses team building, teamwork, and team decision making.

Constructive and Destructive Team Roles

Initiator: Initiates ideas.
Information Seeker: Actively seeks to gain more information and knowledge.
Information Giver: Shares information.
Encourager: Encourages team members and always maintains a positive attitude.
Clarifiers: Makes sure everyone is at the same level of understanding.
Harmonizer: Enhances information in such a way that understanding is increased.
Summarizer: Summarizes the overwhelming detail to a simple level for everyone to understand.
Gate Keeper: Draws others in or judges whether the project should continue at different stages.

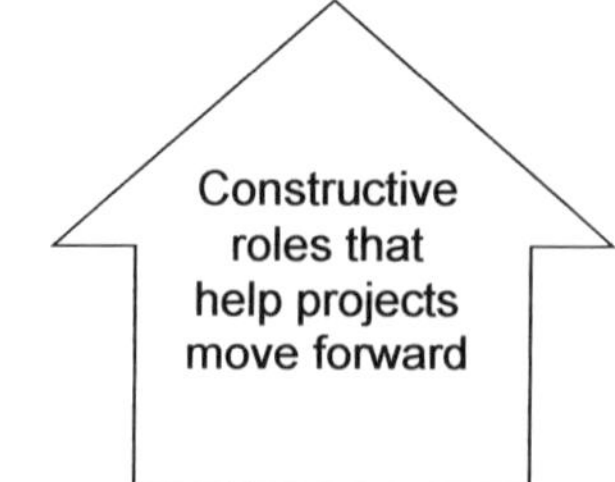

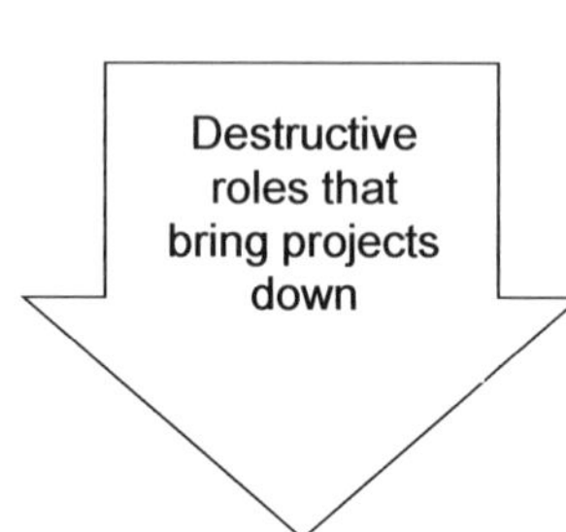

Aggressor: Opposed to the project and very hostile.
Blocker: Interrupts the communication flow and blocks access to information.
Withdrawer: Doesn't participate in any discussion.
Recognition Seeker: Prioritizes own benefits over the project and can jeopardize the project if there is any benefit.
Topic Jumper: Constantly changes topics and brings up unrelated facts.
Dominator: Presents opinions forcefully.
Devil's Advocate: Takes an opposite view to most ideas and disrupts communication.

Figure 9-13: Constructive and Destructive Team Roles

Exercise 15: Identify which process group each process belongs to.

Process Groups				
Initiating	**Planning**	**Executing**	**Monitoring & Controlling**	**Closing**

Process Names:
- Manage Project Team
- Develop Project Team
- Acquire Project Team
- Plan Human Resource Management

Exercise 16: Tuckman's theory states that there are five stages of development that teams may go through. Match the description with the appropriate stage.

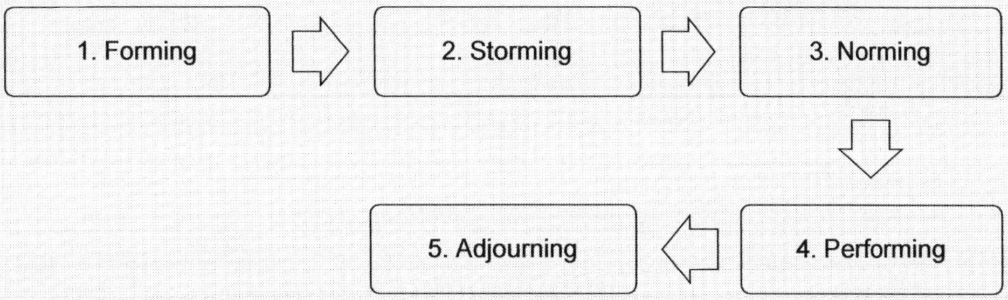

1. Forming → 2. Storming → 3. Norming → 4. Performing → 5. Adjourning

A. In this stage, the team functions as a well-organized unit. They are interdependent and work through issues smoothly and effectively. The role of project manager is mainly overseeing and delegating.
B. The team begins to address project work, technical decisions and project management approach. The team typically goes through some conflicts and difficulties.
C. In this phase, the team completes the work and moves on from the project.
D. In this stage, the team meets and learns about the project and their formal roles and responsibilities.
E. Team members adjust work habits and behaviors to work as a team. They begin to start trusting and working together. Project managers play more of a leadership role with the team.

Exercise 17: List the type of power or interpersonal influence that is being used in each of the following situations:

Situations	Type of Power
1. The project manager has extensive experience in project management and authored several books. The team highly respects him for the depth of his knowledge.	
2. I will be forced to replace you with someone and cut your bonus by 50% if you fail to complete all your deliverables by the end of the week.	
3. We will be sending you for a paid vacation for your spectacular contribution to the project.	
4. It would not be a good idea to challenge her decision as she is a very close friend of the chairman.	
5. The project manager started putting the resources together as soon as she was assigned as the project manager in the project charter by the sponsor.	

Exercise 18: As a project manager, you will be managing a variety of personality types. Match the following personality types with the characteristics of each type.

Characteristic	Personality Type	Constructive/ Destructive Characteristics?
1. Interrupts the communication flow and blocks access to information.	A. Recognition Seeker	
2. Constantly changes topics and brings up unrelated facts.	B. Clarifiers	
3. Takes an opposite view to most ideas and disrupts communication.	C. Harmonizer	
4. Prioritizes own benefits over the project and can jeopardize the project if there is any benefit.	D. Withdrawer	
5. Actively seeks to gain more information and knowledge.	E. Initiator	
6. Draws others in or judges whether the project should continue at different stages.	F. Information Seeker	
7. Opposed to the project and very hostile.	G. Devil's Advocate	
8. Enhances information in such a way that understanding is increased.	H. Information Giver	
9. Initiates ideas.	I. Gate Keeper	
10. Shares information.	J. Topic Jumper	
11. Summarize the overwhelming detail to a simple level for everyone to understand.	K. Dominator	
12. Presents opinions forcefully.	L. Summarizer	
13. Doesn't participate in any discussion.	M. Blocker	
14. Makes sure everyone is at the same level of understanding.	N. Aggressor	
15. Encourages team members and always maintains a positive attitude.	O. Encourager	

Theories of Motivation

In simple words, motivation is the psychological feature that arouses an individual to action toward a desired goal. In other words, motivation is an incentive that generates goal-directed behaviors.

The phrase "Theories of Motivation" is concerned with the processes that illustrate why and how human behavior is activated and directed. It is regarded as one of the most important areas of study in the field of organizational behavior.

There are several motivation theories. However none of them are universally accepted. No single theory can account for all aspects of motivation, but each of the major approaches contributes something to our understanding of motivation. Some of the theories of motivation are traditional PMP exam favorites. We need to thoroughly understand these theories to be fully prepared for the exam. Some of the theories are discussed below:

1. Abraham Maslow's Hierarchy of Needs
2. Alderfer's Existence, Relatedness, Growth (ERG) Needs
3. Herzberg's Motivator-Hygiene
4. McClelland's Achievement Motivation
5. McGregor's Theory X and Theory Y
6. Willam Ouchi's Theory Z
7. Fred E. Fiedler's Contingency Theory
8. Victor Vroom's Expectancy Theory
9. Geert Hofstede National Culture and Context Theory

1. Abraham Maslow's Hierarchy of Needs

This theory groups human needs into five basic categories, and Maslow insists that one proponent need must be relatively satisfied before an individual can move on to the next level. At some point, people do not work for security or money; rather, they work to contribute and to use their skills. Maslow calls this "self-actualization."

Self-Actualization: Self-fulfillment, growth, and learning. Living and working at full potential.

Esteem: Accomplishment, respect, attention, and appreciation.

Social: Love, affection, approval, friends, and association.

Safety: Security, stability, and freedom from harm.

Physiological: Need for air, water, food, housing, and clothing.

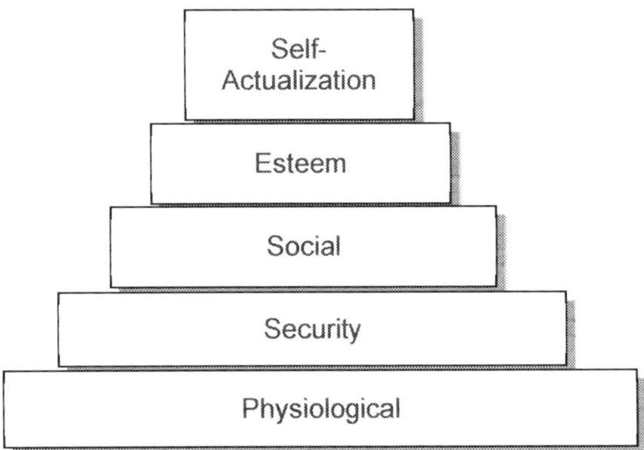

Figure 9-14: Maslow's Hierarchy of Needs

A project manager should understand the different needs of the team members to help them perform at their full potential.

2. Alderfer's Existence, Relatedness, Growth (ERG) Needs

Alderfer argues that individuals have the need for existence, relatedness, and growth and points out:

- There is no hierarchy.
- Although a need may be satisfied, that need may continue to dominate.

Existence	Relatedness	Growth
– Hunger – Thirst – Sleep – Reproduction	– Family – Friends – Co-workers	– Productivity – Creativity – Meaningful Tasks

Table 9-4: Alderfer's Existence, Relatedness, Growth (ERG) Needs

Exercise 19: Identify the 5 Levels of Maslow's Hierarchy of needs:
Level 5: Self-fulfillment, growth, and learning
Level 4: Accomplishment, respect, attention, and appreciation
Level 3: Love, Affection, approval, friends, and association
Level 2: Security, stability, and freedom from harm
Level 1: Need for air, water, food, housing, and clothing

3. Herzberg's Motivator-Hygiene

Herzberg identified the following hygiene factors and motivating agents to illustrate his theory:

Hygiene Factors

- Compensation
- Personal life
- Working conditions
- Relationships with peers, subordinates, and supervisors
- Security
- Status

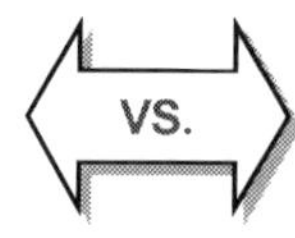

Motivating Agents

- Opportunity for advancements
- Opportunity for achievement
- Variety of work
- Sense of responsibility
- Recognition
- Professional growth

Figure 9-15: Herzberg's Hygiene Factors and Motivating Agents

- Herzberg classified needs under two much larger categories of motivators (belongingness/esteem/self-actualization) and hygiene (physiological and safety) needs.
- Hygiene factors can destroy motivation, but improving them under most circumstances will not improve motivation.
- Hygiene factors are not sufficient to motivate people, and motivating agents provide the best positive reinforcement.
- Motivating people is best done by rewarding people and letting them grow.

4. McClelland's Achievement Motivation

This theory suggests that people are most motivated by one of the three needs listed below. A person who falls into one category would be managed differently than a person who falls into another category.

Primary Need	Behavioral Style
Need for achievement	– These people should be given projects that are challenging but reachable. – These people may prefer to work alone and also like recognition.
Need for affiliation or association	– These people work best when cooperating with others and working in a team. – They seek to maintain good relationships and approval rather than recognition. – These people perform well in a customer-facing team position.
Need for power	– These people like to organize and influence others. – Their need for power can be socially oriented or personally oriented. – People whose power is socially oriented are effective leaders and should be given management roles.

5. McGregor's Theory X and Theory Y

McGregor posits that there are two basic models/belief theories about workers.

Theory X: Average workers are incapable, avoid responsibility, have an inherent dislike of work, and are only interested in their own selfish goals.
The workers must be forced to do productive work as they dislike their work and are not devoted and motivated.

Theory X managers believe that constant supervision or micromanagement is essential to achieve expected results in a project. These managers are like dictators and impose very rigid and rigorous controls over their subordinates.

Theory Y: Workers are creative and committed to the project objectives and goals. They are willing to work without supervision, need very little external motivation, can direct their own efforts, and want to achieve. Theory Y is difficult to put into practice on the shop floor in large mass production operations, but it can be used initially in the managing of managers and professionals.

McGregor's research demonstrates that staff will contribute more to the organization if they are treated as responsible and valued employees.

6. Willam Ouchi's Theory Z

Theory Z was introduced by Dr. Willam Ouchi. This theory is concerned with increasing employee loyalty to his/her organization. This theory emphasizes the well-being of employees both at work and outside of work, it suggests that steady employment leads to high employee satisfaction, morale, and overall it results in increased productivity.

7. Victor Vroom's Expectancy Theory

The expectancy theory, first proposed by Victor Vroom, demonstrates that employees who believe their efforts will lead to effective performance and who expect to be rewarded for their accomplishments remain productive as rewards meet their expectations.

8. Fred E. Fiedler's Contingency Theory

It is a combination of Motivator-Hygiene theory and Theory Y behaviors. This theory illustrates that the effectiveness of a leadership style is contingent upon two key factors. The first factor evaluates workplace situation, such as how successful or unsuccessful the environment is. The second factor measures if the leader is relationship-oriented or task-oriented.

9. Geert Hofstede's National Culture and Context Theory

Professor Geert Hofstede conducted one of the most comprehensive studies of how values in the workplace are influenced by culture. He defines culture as "the collective programming of the mind distinguishing the members of one group or category of people from others".

Dimensions of national culture

a. **Power Distance Index (PDI):** This dimension expresses the degree to which the less powerful members of a society accept and expect that power is distributed unequally. The fundamental issue here is how a society handles inequalities among people. People in societies exhibiting a large degree of power distance accept a hierarchical order in which everybody has a place and which needs no further justification. In societies with low power distance, people strive to equalize the distribution of power and demand justification for inequalities of power.

b. **Individualism versus Collectivism (IDV):** The high side of this dimension, called individualism, can be defined as a preference for a loosely-knit social framework in which individuals are expected to take care of only themselves and their immediate families. Its opposite, collectivism, represents a preference for a tightly-knit framework in society in which individuals can expect their relatives or members of a particular in-group to look after them in exchange for unquestioning loyalty.

c. **Masculinity versus Femininity (MAS):** The masculinity side of this dimension represents a preference in society for achievement, heroism, assertiveness and material rewards for success. Society at large is more competitive. Its opposite, femininity, stands for a preference for cooperation, modesty, caring for the weak and quality of life. Society at large is more consensus-oriented.

d. **Uncertainty Avoidance Index (UAI):** The uncertainty avoidance dimension expresses the degree to which the members of a society feel uncomfortable with uncertainty and ambiguity. The fundamental issue here is how a society deals with the fact that the future can never be known: should we try to control the future or just let it happen?

e. **Long Term Orientation versus Short Term Normative Orientation (LTO):** Every society has to maintain some links with its own past while dealing with the challenges of the present and the future. Societies prioritize these two existential goals differently. Societies who score low on this dimension, for example, prefer to maintain time-honored traditions and norms while viewing societal change with suspicion. Those with a culture which scores high, on the other hand, take a more pragmatic approach: they encourage thrift and efforts in modern education as a way to prepare for the future.

f. **Indulgence versus Restraint (IND):** Indulgence stands for a society that allows relatively free gratification of basic and natural human drives related to enjoying life and having fun. Restraint stands for a society that suppresses gratification of needs and regulates it by means of strict social norms.

Few Other Important Terms

Perquisites (Perks): Perks are special rewards, such as assigned parking spaces, corner offices, executive dining, and other incentives, given to some specific employee for his/her excellent performance and contribution.

Fringe Benefits: The standard benefits formally given to all employees, such as education benefits, insurance, and profit sharing.

Halo Effect: The tendency to rate high or low on all factors due to the impression of a high or low rating on some specific factor. This kind of action has negative impacts on projects and the performing organization.
Example: Someone is a good programmer; thus, he was made a project manager and was expected to do great.

Problem Solving: Even though the project manager spends a great deal of energy and time preventing problems, there are still problems that need to be resolved. Below is the problem-solving technique:

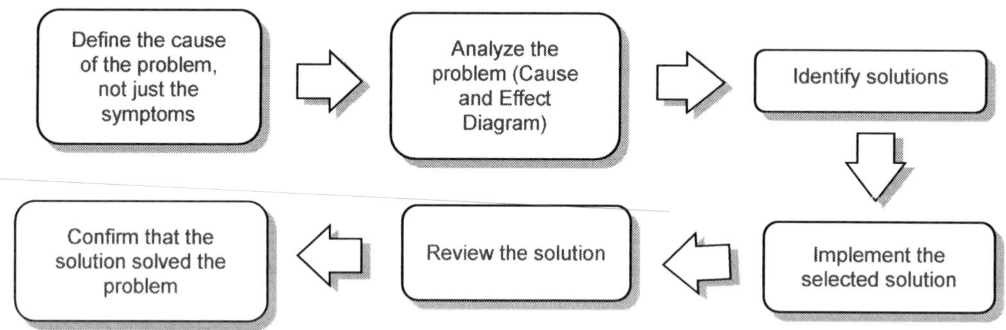

Figure 9-16: Problem Solving

Exercise 20: What are the differences between Team Performance Assessment and Project Performance Appraisal?

____

____

____

____

Exercise 21: Herzberg's Motivator-Hygiene Theory: Review the following list and identify which ones are hygiene factors and which ones are motivating agents.

- Compensation
- Opportunity for advancements
- Recognition
- Personal life
- Variety of work
- Working conditions
- Relationships with peers, subordinates, and supervisors
- Professional growth
- Security
- Sense of responsibility
- Status
- Opportunity for achievement

____

____

____

____

Human Resource Planning Example for a Data Center Project

ITPro Consultancy, LLC, a networking service provider company, has been providing customers with cutting-edge, turnkey data center solutions and services for the last ten years for consolidating IT infrastructure, distributed processes, and applications.

Recently ITPro Consultancy has been awarded five data center projects by five different companies. The following human resource management plan was developed to implement all five data centers in eight months.

Resource Listing: It is critical to use the right resources with the right skills at the right time in order to successfully deliver this extremely challenging data center project. This human resource management plan, not only itemizes the resources required, but it also provides a schedule of resource utilization throughout the project life cycle.

Manpower: The following table lists the key roles and the skills and expertise ITPro will need:

Role	# of Resources	Start Date	End Date	Responsibilities	Skills
Systems Engineer	3	Jan 1	Mar 30	Responsible for managing the server life cycle from installation to troubleshooting and decommissioning. Also in charge of monitoring and managing remote access systems.	Experienced with storage, virtualization, VMware, cloud computing, and infrastructure management solutions.
Infrastructure Network Engineer	3	Jan 1	Apr 30	Responsible for enterprise network design and implementation, data center migration, Windows servers, firewalls, and switches maintenance and support.	Experienced with storage, virtualization, routers, firewalls, and switches.
Operations Specialist	4	Apr 1	Aug 30	Responsible for tasks associated with operation of the data center.	Experienced with data center storage, virtualization, and computing solutions.
Technician	4	May 1	Aug 30	Responsible for hardware installation, storage, operating systems, and test lab configuration.	Experienced with data center storage, virtualization, and computer hardware solutions.
Planning Manager	3	Jan 1	Mar 30	Responsible for participating in the site selection process for new data centers from start to finish as well as actively driving capacity management work for the existing footprint.	Experienced with designing and executing international site selection initiatives.
Project Manager	3	Jan 1	Aug 30	Responsible for taking projects from original concept through final implementation.	Experienced with PM skills, data center operations, server storage, networking, database systems, help desk, and DR/business recovery practices.
Pre-Sales Consultant	4	Jan 1	Mar 30	Responsible for working with end clients and internal project teams to identify business and technical requirements for data center services as well as providing tier-three support.	Experienced with sales and marketing, data center storage, virtualization, cloud computing, and computing solutions.

Solution Architect	4	Jan 1	Mar 30	Responsible for presenting and explaining various storage technologies to customers and formulating a solution consisting of hardware, software, licensing, and engineering services.	Experienced with data center storage, virtualization, computing solutions, VMware-based technologies, and cloud computing.
Marketing Director	2	Jan 1	Mar 30	Responsible for developing sales and account strategies to win and acquire new clients as well as providing insight to market trends for product management and development.	Experienced with sales and marketing, data center storage, virtualization, cloud computing, and computing solutions.

Resource Plan

Schedule: The following resource schedule provides a breakdown of the quantity of each type of resource required to undertake all five data center projects:

Resource Type	Jan	Feb	Mar	Apr	May	Jun	Jul	Aug
Labor								
Systems Engineer	3	3	3					
Infrastructure Network Engineer	3	3	3	3				
Operations Specialist				4	4	4	4	4
Technician					4	4	4	4
Planning Manager	3	3	3					
Project Manager	3	3	3	3	3	3	3	3
Pre-Sales Consultant	4	4	4					
Solution Architect	4	4	4					
Marketing Director	2	2	2					
	22	22	22	10	11	11	11	11

Exercise 22: Match the following situations to the associated level of Maslow's Hierarchy of Needs.

Situation	Level of Maslow's Hierarchy of Needs
1. The team members expect to be recognized and rewarded for their hard work and dedication.	
2. The friendly project environment provides an excellent opportunity to work in a team, network with others, and actively participate in group discussion.	
3. The entire team is worried about the temporary nature of the project and their employment at the project completion.	
4. During the economic slowdown, the team members became worried about their basic needs.	
5. A project manager articulates personal achievements and feelings of self-satisfaction.	

Exercise 23: Matching exercise:

Description	Theory
1. This theory illustrates that the effectiveness of a leadership style is contingent upon two key factors. The first factor evaluates workplace situation, such as how successful or unsuccessful the environment is. The second factor measures if the leader is relationship-oriented or task-oriented.	A. Geert Hofstede's National Culture and Context Theory
2. This theory illustrates that average workers are incapable, avoid responsibility, have an inherent dislike of work, and are only interested in their own selfish goals.	B. Victor Vroom's Expectancy Theory
3. This theory groups human needs into five basic categories and insists that one proponent need must be relatively satisfied before an individual can move on to the next level.	C. Theory Y
4. This theory is concerned with increasing employee loyalty to his/her organization. This theory emphasizes the well-being of employees both at work and outside of work, it suggests that steady employment leads to high employee satisfaction, morale, and overall it results in increased productivity.	D. McClelland's Achievement Motivation
5. This theory illustrates that workers are creative and committed to the project objectives and goals. They are willing to work without supervision, need very little external motivation, can direct their own efforts, and want to achieve.	E. Theory X
6. This theory demonstrates that employees who believe their efforts will lead to effective performance and who expect to be rewarded for their accomplishments remain productive as rewards meet their expectations.	F. Fred E. Fiedler's Contingency Theory
7. This theory suggests that people are most motivated by one of the three needs - need for achievement, need for affiliation or association, and need for power.	G. Abraham Maslow's Hierarchy of Needs
8. This theory classifies needs under two much larger categories of motivators (belongingness/esteem/self-actualization) and hygiene (physiological and safety) needs.	H. Theory Z
9. This theory defines culture as "the collective programming of the mind distinguishing the members of one group or category of people from others".	I. Herzberg's Motivator-Hygiene

Exercise 24: Crossword

Across

1. _______ of Needs theory groups human needs into self-actualization, esteem, social, safety, and physiological.
2. A conflict resolution technique that emphasizes areas of agreement and downplays differences of opinion to maintain harmony.
4. A written log to record issues that require solutions.
9. This theory suggests that the effectiveness of a leadership style is contingent upon the workplace situation and whether the leader is relationship oriented or task oriented.
11. It means “allow to act” or “leave alone”.
12. Feedback about team members’ performance via a 360-degree feedback is called _______ performance appraisal.
13. _______ managers believe supervision is essential.
15. Directing, facilitating, supporting, autocratic, consultative, consensus, laissez-faire are examples of ________ styles.
16. ________ managers believe workers are willing to work without supervision.
17. Identify specific training, coaching, mentoring, assistance, or other changes required to improve team’s performance is called team performance _________.
18. Special rewards given to some specific employee.
19. Leading, influencing, effective decision-making are examples of ________ skills.
20. This team consists of a group of people who never or rarely meet.

Down

1. Tendency to rate high or low on all factors due to the impression of a high or low rating on some specific factor.
3. The standard benefits formally given to all employees.
5. This theory suggests that employees who expect to be rewarded for their accomplishments remain productive.
6. This theory encourages steady employment as it leads to high employee satisfaction and morale.
7. Percentage of conflict comes from schedule, project priorities, and human resources.
8. This type of power is based on the respect or the charismatic personality of the project manager or on referring to someone in a higher position.
10. Placing project team members in the same physical location to enhance their ability to perform as a team.
14. Aggressor, blocker, withdrawer, recognition seeker, topic jumper, dominator, devil’s advocate are examples of ________ team roles.

Exercise 25: Answer the following:

1. Tuckman's theory states that a team typically goes through some conflicts and difficulties in this stage.
2. This theory demonstrates that employees who believe their efforts will lead to effective performance and who expect to be rewarded for their accomplishments remain productive as rewards meet their expectations.
3. The Acquire Project Team is part of the _________________ process group.
4. This type of team includes members who live in widespread geographic areas, employees who work from home or have different shifts/hours, and people with mobility limitations or disabilities.
5. This knowledge area includes the processes that define the roles of all the team members and the responsibilities of each role as well as defining how to organize, manage, and lead the project team.
6. This is similar to a company's standard organizational chart that looks like a WBS but only includes the positions and relationships in a top-down, graphic format.
7. This theory emphasizes the well-being of employees and encourages steady employment for increased productivity.
8. This is the process of managing the team through observing, using issue logs, keeping in touch, providing feedback, completing performance appraisals, and resolving issues and conflicts, among other methods.
9. The tendency to rate high or low on all factors due to the impression of a high or low rating on some specific factor.
10. The French term means "allow to act" or "leave alone." as management is not directly involved but manages and consults as required.
11. An example of a Responsibility Assignment Matrix (RAM).
12. According to Maslow's Hierarchy of Needs living and working at full potential is referred to as ______.
13. This power is based on the respect or the charismatic personality of the project manager or on referring to someone in a higher position to leverage some of the superior's power.
14. The goal is to identify the specific training, coaching, mentoring, assistance, or other changes required to improve the team's performance and effectiveness.
15. It is a written log to record issues that require solutions.
16. This hierarchical type chart can help track project cost as it ties to the organization's accounting system.
17. This chart cross-references team members with the activities or work packages they are to accomplish.
18. According to the Tuckman's theory, the role of project manager is mainly overseeing and delegating in _______ stage.
19. It involves placing many or all of the most active project team members in the same physical location to enhance their ability to perform as a team.
20. This motivational theory suggests that hygiene factors can destroy motivation, but improving them under most circumstances will not improve motivation.
21. This conflict resolution technique emphasizes areas of agreement and downplays differences of opinion.
22. The most effective forms of power are reward power and _____________ power.
23. According to this theory, people cannot achieve self-actualization until lower needs are satisfied.
24. The most critical tool for a project manager to use in Acquire Project Team process.
25. The four processes of human resource management are ________.
26. The key outputs of human resource management processes are _________.
27. Name some of the tools and techniques used in Plan Human Resource Management process.
28. This theory implies that a person good at technical skills would make a good project manager.
29. Ground rules and colocation are used as tools and techniques in which human resource management process?
30. Team performance assessments are _________ in the Develop Project Team process.
31. Project performance appraisals are _________ in the Manage Project Team process.
32. This management theory focuses on employees who want to be self-managed and direct themselves.
33. It is the worst form of power for a project manager to use.
34. If the training is specific to project needs, the _________ budget will cover the cost.
35. If the training is useful on other projects, often the __________ will cover the cost.
36. Logs and __________ are never tools & techniques.
37. Conflict management is used as a tool and technique in the _________ process.

Project Human Resource Management Summary

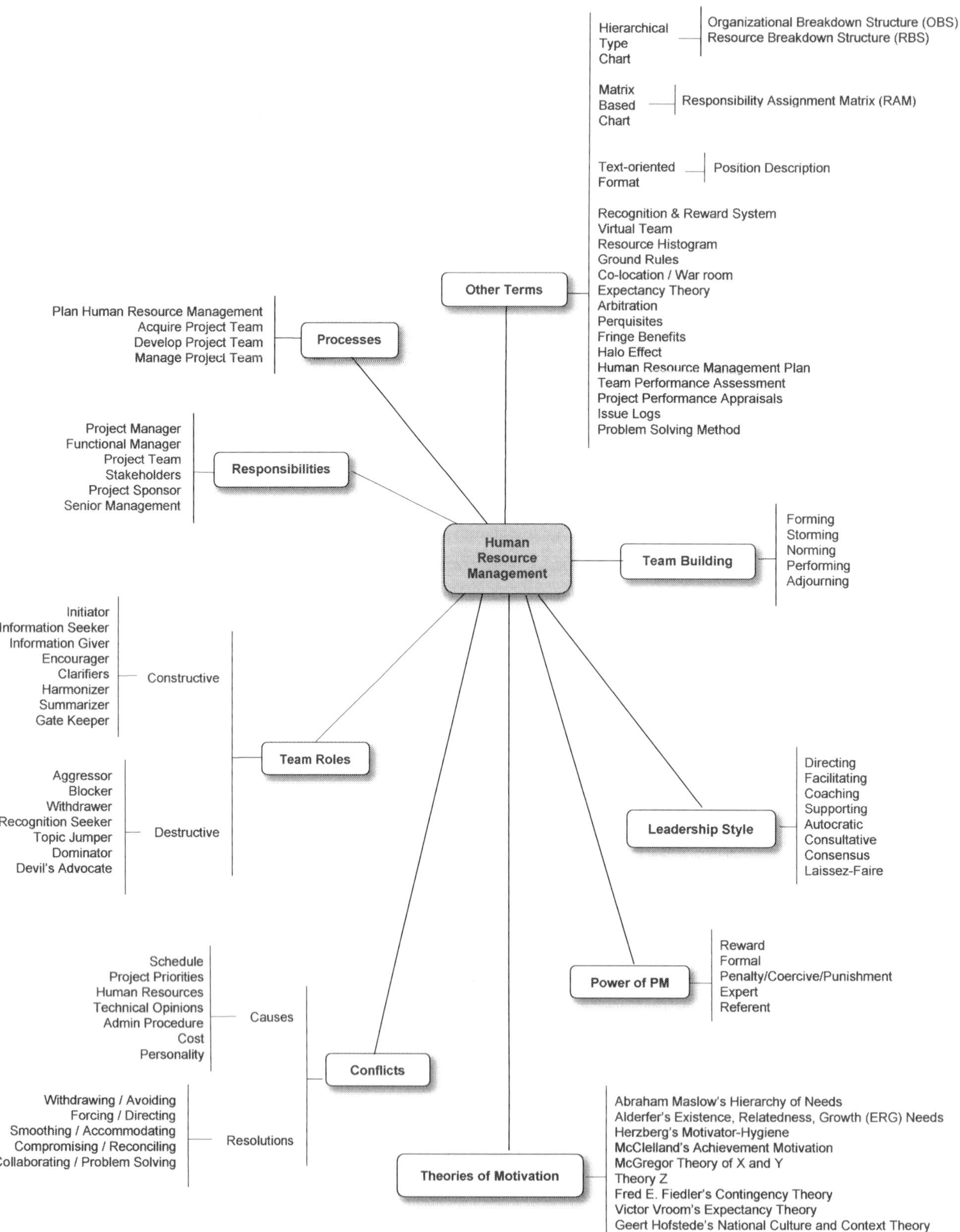

Figure 9-17: Project Human Resource Management Summary

Project Human Resource Management Key Terms

Hierarchical-Type Chart

Organizational Breakdown Structure (OBS): A chart arranged according to an organization's existing departments, units, or teams with their respective work packages
Resource Breakdown Structure (RBS): Helps track project cost as it ties to the organization's accounting system

Matrix-Based Chart

Responsibility Assignment Matrix (RAM): This chart cross-references team members with the activities or work packages. Example - Responsible, Accountable, Consult, and Inform (RACI) chart

Text-Oriented Format

Position Description: Text-oriented roles and responsibilities

Virtual Teams: Consists of a group of people who never or rarely meet but who have a shared goal of successful completion of the project
Staffing Management Plan: Describes how and when members will be acquired, timetable for adding staff, training needs, recognition and rewards, compliance considerations, criteria for releasing
Ground Rules: Identify acceptable and unacceptable behaviors
Colocation/War room: Placing project team members in the same physical location to enhance their ability to perform as a team
Perquisites (Perks): Special rewards given to some specific employee
Fringe Benefits: The standard benefits formally given to all employees
Halo Effect: Tendency to rate high or low on all factors due to the impression of a high or low rating on some specific factor
Team Performance Assessments: Identify specific training, coaching, mentoring, assistance, or other changes required to improve team's performance
Project Performance Appraisals: Feedback about team members' performance via a 360-degree feedback
Interpersonal skills: Leading, influencing, effective decision-making
Power of PM: Reward (best), formal, penalty (worst), expert (best), referent
Leadership Style: Directing, facilitating, coaching, supporting, autocratic, consultative, consensus, laissez-faire

Theories of Motivation

Abraham Maslow's Hierarchy of Needs: Groups human needs into self-actualization, esteem, social, safety, and physiological. One proponent need must be relatively satisfied before one can move to next level
Herzberg's Motivator-Hygiene: Destroying hygiene factors can destroy motivation, but improving them will not always improve motivation
McClelland's Achievement Motivation: People are most motivated by one of the three needs - achievement, affiliation, or power
McGregor's Theory of X and Y: X-managers believe supervision is essential; Y-managers believe workers are willing to work without supervision
Willam Ouchi's Theory Z: Encourages steady employment as it leads to high employee satisfaction and morale
Fred E. Fiedler's Contingency Theory: The effectiveness of a leadership style is contingent upon the workplace situation and whether the leader is relationship oriented or task oriented
Vroom's Expectancy Theory: Employees expect to be rewarded for their accomplishments remain productive
Geert Hofstede's National Culture and Context Theory: The collective programming of the mind distinguishing the members of one group or category of people from others

Conflicts

Causes: 50% (schedule, project priorities, human resources), technical options, admin procedure, cost, personality
Resolutions: Withdrawing/avoiding, forcing/directing, smoothing/accommodating, compromising/reconciling, and collaborating/problem solving

Team Roles

Constructive: Initiator, info seeker, info giver, encourager, clarifiers, harmonizer, summarizer, gate keeper
Destructive: Aggressor, blocker, withdrawer, recognition seeker, topic jumper, dominator, devil's advocate

Project Human Resource Management Exercise Answers

Exercise 1:

- Good team player and easy going
- Good listener
- Willingness to learn new things and take challenges
- Flexibility
- Honesty and reliability
- Technical competencies
- Domain knowledge and expertise
- Understanding of the job responsibilities
- Hard working and motivated

Exercise 2:

Situation	Key Person	Detail
1.	Sponsor	Extra funds required for additional time and work will be provided by the sponsor.
2.	Project manager	The project manager should resolve these types of work packages- and activities-related conflicts with the help of the network diagram and critical path.
3.	Team members	The team should get involved in knowledge and responsibility transfer. The project manager should give out all the details and proper instructions and should assign the workload accordingly to other team members' workloads to replace the team member who will be leaving soon.
4.	Sponsor	The sponsor assigns the proper authority to the project manager in the project charter.
5.	Sponsor/ Functional manager	The functional manager mainly controls human resources, and the sponsor controls funding; thus, he/she should take care of this situation.
6.	Project manager	The project manager should make the deliverables, the expectations from team members, and the due dates for the deliverables very clear to the team members so that there is no confusion.
7.	Sponsor	Once the team evaluates the impact of any such delay, it will be approved by the CCB and sponsor.
8.	Functional manager	In a matrix organization, both the project manager and functional manager direct resources, but resources are reporting directly to the functional manager. Any performance issue of the team members should be resolved by the functional manager.
9.	Sponsor	The sponsor assigns the proper authority to the project manager in the project charter.
10.	Sponsor	The project manager should bring up the urgent concern to the proper authority, but the sponsor should protect the project from any drastic change as critical as project termination.
11.	Team members	The team member should inform the project manager about any such changes so that the project manager can perform impact analysis. A team member controls his/her own activities as long as scope, risk, quality, time, and cost objectives are met.
12.	Senior management	Prioritizing potential projects and opportunities is the responsibility of senior management, as per the findings of the team about the opportunity, cost, risk, ROI, and other factors associated with the projects.
13.	Project manager	Developing a project schedule and controlling it is strictly the role of the project manager.
14.	Project manager	A project manager should encourage the team members, recognize and award them, and send them to required trainings to keep them motivated and productive.
15.	Sponsor	The sponsor provides the funds for the project.
16.	Team members	A project manager should not get involved every time team members have a disagreement unless team members seek guidance from the project manager or the situation is impacting the project. As professionals, the team members should be able to resolve their own conflicts and concerns by themselves.

Situation	Key Person	Detail
17.	Sponsor/Senior management	All effort should be made to resolve conflicts at the lowest levels of authority whenever possible. In some cases, conflict resolution requires involving the project sponsor or senior management, especially when there is a major concern regarding resource assignments.
18.	Project manager	A project manager is responsible to come up with a robust communications management plan.
19.	Project manager	A project manager is responsible to identify appropriate processes suggested by the industry or organization.
20.	Project Manager /Team members	The project manager and team members should execute the project management plan to meet organizational goals and objectives.
21.	Sponsor	A sponsor is responsible for the success of the project and must control all kinds of outside influences.
22.	Project manager	A project manager must make sure that team members are collecting quality expectations of stakeholders.
23.	Team members	Team members should decompose work packages into activities.
24.	Project manager	A project manager is fully responsible to keep stakeholders happy and satisfied.
25.	Project manager	A project manager is fully responsible to develop and execute strategies to keep stakeholders involved all the time.
26.	Sponsor	Once the project manager justifies the schedule and budget are not realistic, the sponsor should make an effort to change the project charter.

Exercise 3:

Difficulties	Actions
1.	– Provide required training. – Hire resources with adequate expertise. – Outsource the project if needed.
2.	– Understand the organizational priority. – Ensure everyone understands the importance and value of your project. – Negotiate and ensure that your project receives the appropriate resources.
3.	– Escalate to the sponsor. – Identify backup resources. – Adjust schedule as per the resources availability. – Negotiate availability of the resources with the functional manager.
4.	– Negotiate with the sponsor and senior management about joint performance appraisal and management responsibility. – Inform team members about the project manager's role in their performance evaluation.
5.	– Confirm the return of resources to the functional teams. – Plan bonus and rewards. – Provide job placement support if needed. – Provide training to develop expertise for other positions.
6.	– Minimize the length of time and bandwidth needed from the resources. – Confirm release dates of the resources with the functional manager. – Explain the value of the project to the organization. – Explain how the project will meet the organizational goals and objectives.

Exercise 4:

- Realize the priorities of the functional manager
- Evaluate the work environment
- Understand factors associated with the functional manager's position
- Be sympathetic with the functional manager's concerns and issues
- Negotiate a win-win situation

Exercise 5:
Benefits:
- Teams are made up of people who never or rarely meet.
- It usually reduces travel and save cost.
- It makes it possible to have a team when it's not physically possible.
- There are longer work hours if team members are in different geographic locations.

Complexities:
- Communication is complex and difficult.
- Conflicts are more frequent and a bit more difficult to resolve.
- There is a lack of dedication.
- There is less bonding.

Important Factors:
- Establishing trust and connection among team members is important.
- Consistent communication is critical.

Exercise 6:
Projects are completed on time, within budget, and with the desired quality. Other factors are customer satisfaction, minimum or mutually agreed upon scope changes, no interrupt of operations, minimal conflicts among team members and other organizational units, fully functional and accepted product or service, achievement of objectives, values, and benefits.

Exercise 7:
- Estimate activity durations
- Define how tasks will be completed
- Control each project task
- Estimate each activity cost

Exercise 8:
- Goals, objectives, and importance of the project
- Functional, nonfunctional, and quality requirements of the project
- Contractual requirements
- Acceptance criteria from the customers
- Assumptions and constraints
- How the project will meet and exceed organizational goals and objectives
- Key deliverables and dates
- Expectations from the team members
- Stakeholders' details (contact information, expectation, information need, influence level, interest level, and role).
- Change management processes
- Status of the project
- Project management processes, procedures, and policies

Exercise 9:
Organizational structure: Build good working relationships with management.
Project complexity: Ensure a detailed requirement doc with all the functional and nonfunctional requirements, and acceptance criteria is prepared. Also, a detailed project scope statement must be created.
Changing requirements: Establish a robust change control process. Make sure to have a well-defined configuration management system.
Other major obstacles can be internal politics, changing technologies, and organizational culture.

Exercise 10:
- Be a good leader.
- Have conversations with team members on a regular basis.
- Use negotiation and leadership skills.
- Observe what is happening in the project and with team members.
- Use an issue log.
- Always keep in touch.
- Evaluate individual team member's performance.
- Actively look for and help to resolve conflicts.
- Resolve issues and problems.
- Communicate with everyone on a regular basis.

Exercise 11:

- Make job assignments and expectations crystal clear to the team members.
- Define roles and responsibilities clearly.
- Provide adequate training.
- Empower the team members to perform their job responsibilities with ease.
- Provide required support and mentoring.
- Involve team members in decision making process.
- Do not claim credit for the work done by the team and avoid personal recognition.
- Do not act as a functional manager.
- Do not aggressively control or micromanage the team.
- Recognize and reward excellent job performance.
- Ensure the team gets the credit and recognition for achievements.
- Put all the team members in one location (co-location) when possible.
- Create team building activities.
- Demonstrate honesty and integrity all the time.

Exercise 12:

1. Collaborating
2. Forcing
3. Collaborating
4. Smoothing
5. Compromising
6. Withdrawing
7. Compromising
8. Compromising
9. Withdrawing

Exercise 13:

- Screen the individual before assigning him/her to the project
- Establish ground rules and expectation at an early stage in the project
- Explain roles and responsibilities clearly
- Set proper vision and goals
- Ensure the person understands the importance of teamwork
- Explain the project management process, policies, and guidelines
- Involve the person to the project activities as much as possible

Exercise 14:

- Not participating in team discussion and decision making
- Unwillingness to abide by rules, policies, and procedures set by the organization
- Delaying deliverables
- Unwillingness to complete assigned tasks on time
- Not contributing to the project success
- Nonacceptance of the established formal authority
- Ignoring the established ground rules
- Focusing on other aspects at the expense of the project schedule and budget

Exercise 15:

Process Groups				
Initiating	**Planning**	**Executing**	**Monitoring & Controlling**	**Closing**
	– Plan Human Resource Management	– Acquire Project Team – Develop Project Team – Manage Project Team		

Exercise 16:

1. D
2. B
3. E
4. A
5. C

Exercise 17:

1. Expert
2. Penalty
3. Reward
4. Referent
5. Formal or Legitimate

Exercise 18:

Characteristic	Personality Type	Constructive/ Destructive Characteristic?
1.	M. Blocker	Destructive
2.	J. Topic Jumper	Destructive
3.	G. Devil's Advocate	Destructive
4.	A. Recognition Seeker	Destructive
5.	F. Information Seeker	Constructive
6.	I. Gate Keeper	Constructive
7.	N. Aggressor	Destructive
8.	C. Harmonizer	Constructive
9.	E. Initiator	Constructive
10.	H. Information Giver	Constructive
11.	L. Summarizer	Constructive
12.	K. Dominator	Destructive
13.	D. Withdrawer	Destructive
14.	B. Clarifier	Constructive
15.	O. Encourager	Constructive

Exercise 19:
Level 5: Self-Actualization
Level 4: Esteem
Level 3: Social
Level 2: Safety
Level 1: Physiological

Exercise 20: Team Performance Assessment is the output in the Develop Project Team process. This is the evaluation of the entire team to identify the specific training, coaching, mentoring, assistance, or other changes required to improve the team's performance and effectiveness. On the other hand, Project Performance Appraisal is the tool & technique used in the Manage Project Team Process. This is an evaluation of individual team member effectiveness. The project management team meets with the team members and provides feedback about team members' performance and how effectively they are performing their tasks.

Exercise 21:

Hygiene Factors

- Compensation
- Personal life
- Working conditions
- Relationships with peers, subordinates, and supervisors
- Security

Motivating Agents

- Opportunity for advancements
- Recognition
- Variety of work
- Professional growth
- Sense of responsibility
- Status
- Opportunity for achievement

Exercise 22:

1. Esteem
2. Social
3. Security
4. Physiological
5. Self-Actualization

Exercise 23:

1. F. Fred E. Fiedler's Contingency Theory
2. E. Theory X
3. G. Abraham Maslow's Hierarchy of Needs
4. H. Theory Z
5. C. Theory Y
6. B. Victor Vroom's Expectancy Theory
7. D. McClelland's Achievement Motivation
8. I. Herzberg's Motivator-Hygiene
9. A. Geert Hofstede's National Culture and Context Theory

Exercise 24:

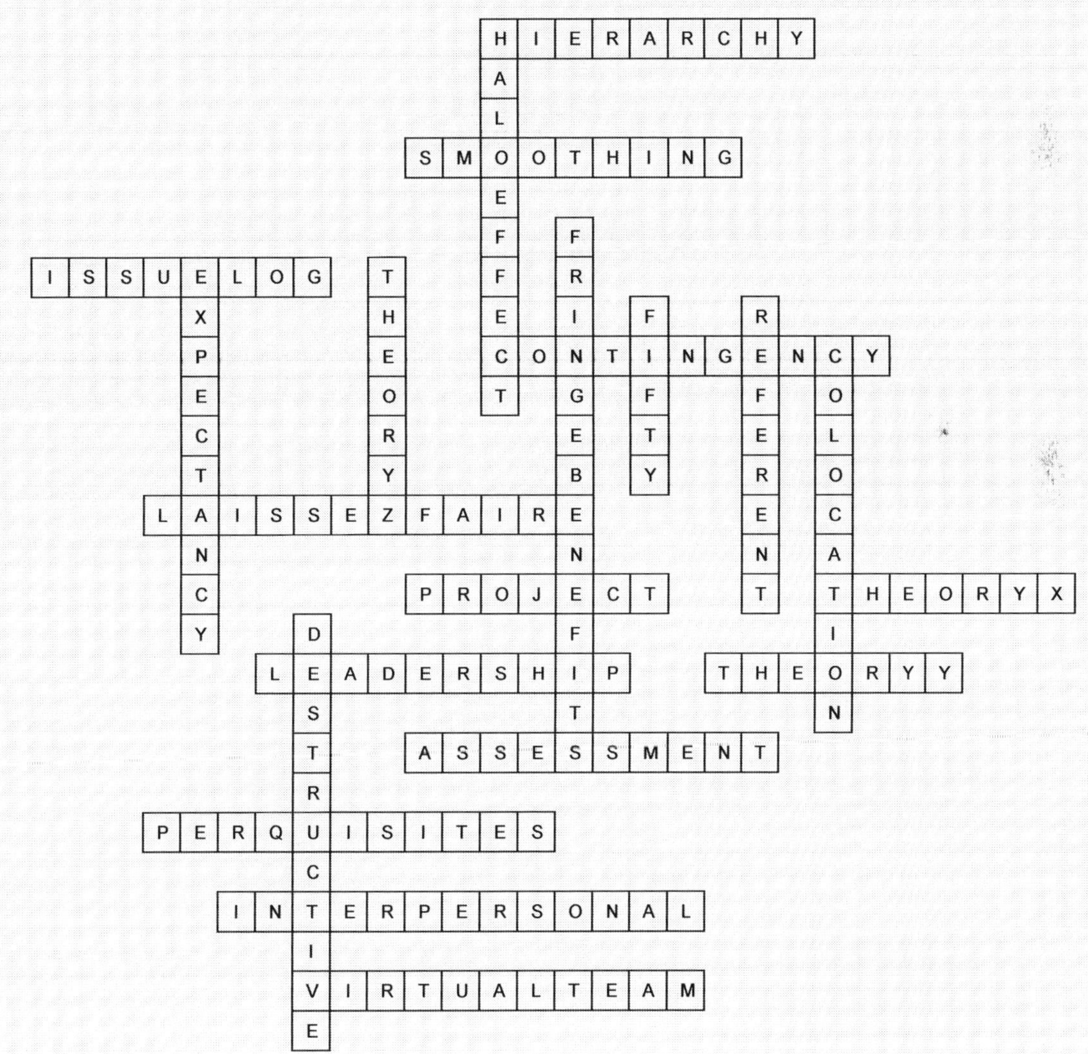

Exercise 25:

1. Storming
2. Victor Vroom's Expectancy Theory
3. Executing
4. Virtual team
5. Project human resource management
6. Organizational Breakdown Structure (OBS)
7. Theory Z
8. Manage Project Team
9. Halo Effect
10. Laissez-Faire
11. RACI (Responsible, Accountable, Consult, and Inform) chart
12. Self-actualization
13. Referent power
14. Team performance assessments
15. Issue log
16. Resource breakdown structure
17. Responsibility Assignment Matrix (RAM)
18. Performing
19. Colocation or war room
20. Herzberg's Motivator-Hygiene
21. Smoothing
22. Expert
23. Maslow's Hierarchy of Needs
24. Negotiation
25. Plan Human Resource Management, Acquire Project Team, Develop Project Team, and Manage Project Team
26. Plan Human Resource Management – Human Resource Management Plan
    Acquire Project Team – Project Staff Assignments
    Develop Project Team – Team Performance Assessments
    Manage Project Team – Change Requests
27. Organizational charts and position descriptions, networking, organizational theory, expert judgment, meetings
28. Halo Effect
29. Develop Project Team
30. Outputs
31. Tools and techniques
32. Theory Y
33. Penalty
34. Project
35. Organization
36. Reports
37. Manage Project Team

Project Human Resource Management Exam Tips

- Be able to describe the purpose of all four project human resource management processes.
- Be able to name the inputs, tools & techniques, and outputs of all the project human resource management processes.
- Be familiar with the five stages of group formation.
- Be familiar with different types of power available to the project manager.
- Be familiar with the causes of conflicts and their resolution techniques.
- Be able to answer questions where you will need to analyze a specific situation and determine next step.
- Be familiar with various theories of motivation.
- Be familiar with the concepts and terms in the project human resource management summary table, Figure 9-17: Project Human Resource Management Summary.

Project Human Resource Management Questions

1. You are in the Plan Human Resource Management process of identifying and documenting project roles, responsibilities, required skills, competencies, reporting structure, and other items. The structure that you are using is arranged according to an organization's existing departments, units, or teams with their respective work packages. Which of the following are you using?

A. Resource Breakdown Structure (RBS)
B. Responsibility Assignment Matrix (RAM)
C. Position descriptions
D. Organizational Breakdown Structure (OBS)

2. Project success is heavily dependent on the leadership and management style of the project manager. Even though we do not usually distinguish between leading and managing, it is generally believed that there is a difference between these two. Which of the following is typically considered to be a responsibility associated with managing?

A. Consistently producing key results expected by stakeholders
B. Establishing direction, mission, and vision
C. Aligning team members to the established direction
D. Motivating and inspiring

3. You made sure that one of the junior team members in your team received the required training to perform his activities. While assessing the team member, you were concerned to find out that the team member was still lacking the competency and required further improvement. What will be the BEST course of action?

A. Replace the team member with an experienced resource.
B. Have an urgent discussion with the team member and inform him that he will be out of the project if there is no immediate improvement.
C. Have a discussion with the functional manager about the lack of competency of the team member.
D. Identify the team member's current lacking and provide more focused training.

4. A project manager is overseeing a complex custom CSM solution that has rigorous quality standards and tight schedule constraints. The project manager just found out that one of the key deliverables in the project was not completed because the team member responsible for it was assigned to another higher-priority project by her functional manager. Who will be the person for the project manager to address the issue with in this kind of situation?

A. The sponsor
B. The president of the company
C. The customers
D. The team

5. A project manager recently got her PMP certification and joined a professional project management group. The group members meet on a regular basis to discuss new opportunities, trends, and issues in project management. The satisfaction that the project manager gains from the association with this group is MOST closely aligned with:

A. Victor Vroom's Expectancy theory
B. The third level of Maslow's Hierarchy of Needs
C. Herzberg's Motivator-Hygiene theory
D. Theory X

6. You are currently managing the team through observing, using issue logs, keeping in touch, providing feedback, completing performance appraisals, resolving issues and conflicts, and through other methods. You are in which of the following human resource management processes?

A. Plan Human Resource Management
B. Acquire Project Team
C. Develop Project Team
D. Manage Project Team

7. You are the project manager overseeing a project to build a navigation system for an auto company. You are in the Develop Project Team process, and your key focus is to enhance the project performance by building a sense of team and improving the competencies, team interaction, and overall team environment. You will be using all of the following tools & techniques in the process EXCEPT:

A. Acquisition
B. Ground rules
C. Colocation
D. Recognition and rewards

8. You are overseeing the implementation of a library management system for a local library. While in the execution phase, the functional manager informs you that his team needs to work on a higher-priority project and he will be pulling out two critical resources from your project. What should you do FIRST as a project manager?

A. Evaluate the impact by referring to the resource histogram.
B. Reassign activities of these two members to the other team members.
C. Immediately inform higher management.
D. Request the functional manager to assign two new resources first before pulling out the existing members.

9. You are a member of a management team overseeing a critical construction project of constructing the tallest building in town. Your team, which is a subset of the project team, is responsible for project leadership and management activities. Which of the following statements is FALSE about your team?

A. Your team is responsible for managing people, which has been defined as being able to produce key results.
B. Your team is responsible for establishing mission and vision, aligning team members to the established direction, motivating individuals, and inspiring them.
C. Your team is responsible for project funding.
D. The management team should be aware of professional and ethical behaviors and ensure that team members are following them.

10. A project manager is in the Develop Project Team process focusing on enhancing project performance by building a sense of team and improving competencies, team interaction, and overall team environment. While referring to Tuckman's model, she notices that the greatest level of conflict in the five different stages of team building is most likely to appear in which of the following stages:

A. Forming
B. Adjourning
C. Storming
D. Exploring

11. While in the Manage Project Team process, the project management team met with the team members and provided feedback on team members' performance and how effectively they were performing their tasks. A 360-degree feedback was used to provide feedback from all directions, including from peers, from superiors and subordinates, and sometimes from vendors and external contractors. This tool & technique is referred to as:

A. Team performance assessments
B. Project performance appraisals
C. Observations and conversations
D. Team-building activities

12. You just completed working on your staffing management plan and identified how human resources should be defined, staffed, managed, and eventually released from your project. Which portion of the staffing management plan will help you the most to determine when to release resources from your project?

A. Training needs and certification requirements
B. Recognition and rewards
C. Compliance considerations
D. Resource histogram

13. While in the Manage Project Team process, the project management team met with the team members and provided feedback on team members' performance and how effectively they were performing their tasks. A 360-degree feedback was used to receive feedback from all directions, including from peers, from superiors and subordinates, and sometimes from vendors and external contractors. Which of the following is the most important factor when utilizing 360-degree feedback?

A. All team players such as peers, superiors, subordinates, and vendors should participate in the evaluation.
B. Participants should remain anonymous.
C. Results of the evaluation should not be disclosed.
D. Only team members should evaluate other team members.

14. Which motivational theory below is concerned with increasing employee loyalty and support for the organization by emphasizing the well-being of employees both at work and outside of work and encouraging steady employment?

A. Expectancy theory
B. Theory Z
C. Theory Y
D. Theory X

15. A project team member's abilities or competencies, communication capabilities, relevant knowledge, skills, experience, cost (for adding the team member), attitude or ability to work with others, availability, and other factors such as time zone and geographical location are some examples of selection criteria that can be used to rate and score that team member. Which one of the following looks at all of these selection criteria while acquiring a team member for the project?

A. Multi-criteria decision analysis
B. Monte Carlo analysis
C. Team performance assessment
D. Project performance appraisal

16. You were asked by management to identify the root cause behind a project not performing well in your organization. You find out that the project manager is hardly in contact with the team members and often places one of his team members in charge for days at a time. The project manager also allows the team members to act as per their preferences and only gets involved with them if requested. This style of management is generally considered to be:

A. Delegating
B. Democratic or participative
C. Bureaucratic
D. Laissez-Faire

17. A project manager overseeing a data center deployment project just completed negotiation unsuccessfully for three additional resources and extra reserve money for her project. During the negotiation, two of the functional managers were very skeptical about the request for additional resources and were reluctant to assign their resources due to other priorities. In this case, the conflict will require the assistance of which of the following to reach a solution?

A. Functional manager
B. Contractor
C. Project sponsor
D. Key customer

18. You are in the Plan Human Resource Management process to create an overall staffing management plan by identifying the availability of resources and those resources' skill levels. Which of the following is NOT a tool & technique is this process?

A. Organizational charts and position descriptions
B. Networking
C. Organizational theory
D. Colocation

19. You are in the Plan Human Resource Management process of identifying and documenting project roles, responsibilities, required skills, competencies, reporting structure, and other items. Which of the following organizational charts and position descriptions tool can help you track project cost as it ties to the organization's accounting system?

A. Resource Breakdown Structure (RBS)
B. Organizational Breakdown Structure (OBS)
C. Responsibility Assignment Matrix (RAM)
D. Position descriptions

20. A project manager is in the Develop Project Team process, focusing on enhancing project performance by building a sense of team and improving the competencies, team interaction, and overall team environment. While referring to Tuckman's model, she notices that the team members begin to start trusting and working together as they adjust work habits and behaviors to work as a team. What stage of team development is the project manager referring to?

A. Forming
B. Adjourning
C. Storming
D. Norming

21. You are considering the idea of putting all team members in the same physical location for the first time. All of the following is true about colocation EXCEPT:
   A. The goal is to enhance team members' ability to perform as a team.
   B. It is also called a war room.
   C. It is meant to identify concerns and issues and to come up with mutually agreed-upon solutions.
   D. The goal is to identify the individual(s) or team responsible for project issues and inform them about it.

22. You are in the Plan Human Resource Management process of identifying and documenting project roles, responsibilities, required skills, competencies, reporting structure, and other items. Which one of the following will you NOT use as a tool & technique in this process?
   A. Hierarchical-type organizational charts
   B. Recognition and rewards
   C. A responsibility assignment matrix
   D. Organizational theory

23. You were informed by management that an external audit team will be auditing your project to make sure that the project complies with standard organizational project management policies and procedures. During the audit, the key auditor wants to review the training plan for the team members as well as their certification requirements. You should refer the auditor to which of the following?
   A. Staffing management plan
   B. RACI chart
   C. Training and certification management plan
   D. Resource breakdown structure

24. While overseeing a data center project, you notice that one of the team members is extremely dedicated to the project and a consistent overachiever. In order to appreciate her spectacular work and great contribution, you made her the 'team member of the month' three times in a row. What kind of impact will this have on the project team?
   A. This will initiate a healthy competition among the team members.
   B. This will drastically improve team cohesiveness.
   C. This will negatively impact team morale.
   D. Team members hardly care about recognition and rewards; thus, there will be no impact.

25. You are a project manager who believes steady employment leads to high employee satisfaction and morale, increased loyalty to the organization, and increased productivity. Which theory do you subscribe to?
   A. McGregor Theory X and Theory Y
   B. Fred E. Fiedler's Contingency theory
   C. Dr. Willam Ouchi's Theory Z
   D. Victor Vroom's Expectancy theory

26. Mary, a project manager, is in the Develop Project Team process, focusing on enhancing project performance by building a sense of team and improving the competencies, team interaction, and overall team environment. While referring to Tuckman's model, she notices that the team is in a stage where her role is mostly overseeing and delegating. The team is in which stage of team development?
   A. Forming
   B. Adjourning
   C. Storming
   D. Performing

27. A project manager overseeing a construction project notices that her team members are having constant conflicts over issues. The situation was causing her a lot of concern, and she decides to identify the key causes of the conflicts. While exploring the causes, she finds that the most common causes of conflicts among team members are project priorities, resources, and:
   A. Personality
   B. Schedule
   C. Technical options
   D. Administration procedures

28. A project manager is overseeing a complex custom CSM solution that has rigorous quality standards and tight schedule constraints. Since the project manager is working in a weak matrix environment, none of the resources are reporting to her functionally. She also does not have either the power or the budget to reward the team members to encourage and motivate them for their performance and contribution to the project. What kind of power should the project manager try to use in this type of situation?
   A. Formal
   B. Punishment
   C. Referent
   D. Expert

29. You are overseeing a video conferencing application project and just completed negotiation for three additional resources from different functional areas and extra reserve money for your project. During the negotiation, two of the functional managers were very skeptical about the request for additional resources and were reluctant to assign their resources to your project. At last a solution was reached in which you were allowed to obtain the resources you requested, but you had to agree to give up some other resources at an earlier date than you had originally planned. What type of conflict resolution technique was used in this situation?

A. Smoothing
B. Compromising
C. Forcing
D. Collaborating

30. Your data center project is in a mess, and the entire team is under enormous pressure from management to complete the project on time. At team meetings, team members are continuously pointing fingers at each other and blaming others for the delay in their deliverables. You had an urgent meeting with the sponsor to discuss the situation, and he expressed his interest to attend the meeting to evaluate the situation himself. What will be the BEST course of action for you in this type of situation?

A. Request the sponsor to provide help if possible but not to attend the meeting.
B. Inform the team members that the sponsor will be attending the meeting.
C. Remove the team member from the team who is most vocal and who is causing the most issues.
D. Create new ground rules for the meetings and introduce them to the team members.

Project Human Resource Management Answers

1. D: An OBS is similar to a company's standard organizational chart that looks like a WBS but only includes the positions and relationships in a top-down, graphic format. It is arranged according to an organization's existing departments, units, or teams with their respective work packages. Any operations department such as manufacturing or engineering, can identify all of its project responsibilities by looking at its portion of the OBS. An RBS also looks like a typical organizational chart, but this one is organized by types of resources. An RBS can help track project cost as it ties to the organization's accounting system. A RAM cross-references team members with the activities or work packages they are to accomplish. One example of a RAM is a Responsible, Accountable, Consult, and Inform (RACI) chart, which can be used to ensure clear divisions of roles and responsibilities. A text-oriented position description, or role-responsibility-authority form, is particularly important in recruiting. It is used to describe a team member's position title, responsibilities, authority, competencies, and qualifications in detail.

2. A: Project management is heavily dependent on managing people, which has been defined as being able to produce key results. On the other hand, leadership is all about establishing mission and vision, aligning team members to the established direction, and motivating and inspiring individuals.

3. D: The role of the project manager is to make sure that team members specially the junior members with limited experience get the required training and assistance to perform their activities.

4. A: It is one of the key roles of the sponsor to prevent unnecessary changes in the project in addition to providing funding for the project.

5. B: The third level of Maslow's Hierarchy of Needs is the need for social connections or belonging, such as love, affection, approval, friends, and association. The Expectancy theory, first proposed by Victor Vroom, demonstrates that employees who believe their efforts will lead to effective performance and who expect to be rewarded for their accomplishments remain productive as rewards meet their expectations. Herzberg's Motivator-Hygiene theory suggests that hygiene factors can destroy motivation, but improving them under most circumstances will not improve motivation. Motivating people is best done by rewarding people and letting them grow. Theory X managers believe that average workers are incapable, avoid responsibility, have an inherent dislike of work, and are only interested in their own selfish goals. The workers must be forced to do productive work as they dislike their work and are not devoted and motivated.

6. D: Manage Project Team is the process of managing the team through observing, using issue logs, keeping in touch, providing feedback, completing performance appraisals, resolving issues and conflicts, and other factors.

7. A: Acquisition is used as a tool & technique in the Acquire Project Team process, where the main goal is to secure the best possible resources to build the project team so that they can carry on the project activities efficiently.

8. A: In this sort of situation, a project manager should always evaluate the impact of the changes and gather as much information as possible prior to taking any further steps.

9. C: The project sponsor usually assists with funding, not the project management team. The project management team is the subset of the project team responsible for project leadership and management activities. Project management is heavily dependent on managing people, which has been defined as being able to produce key results. On the other hand, leadership is all about establishing mission and vision, aligning team members to the established direction, motivating individuals, and inspiring them. The management team should be aware of professional and ethical behaviors and should ensure that team members are following them.

10. C: Storming follows the Forming stage, and it is where the team begins to address project work, technical decisions, areas of disagreement, and project management approaches. The team typically goes through some conflicts and difficulties in this stage more than any other.

11. B: For the project performance appraisals, the project management team meets with the team members and provides feedback on team members' performance and how effectively they are performing their tasks. A 360-degree feedback is used to receive feedback from all directions, including from peers, from superiors and subordinates, and sometimes from vendors and external contractors. Here the focus is the individual, and in team performance assessments the focus is on the team performance, not on the individual. The goal of team performance assessments is to identify the specific training, coaching, mentoring, assistance, or changes required to improve the team's performance and effectiveness. The project management team makes formal or informal assessments of the project team's effectiveness while team development efforts such as training, team building, and colocation are implemented. A team's performance is measured against the agreed-upon success criteria, schedule, and budget target.

12. D: A resource histogram is a graphical display that shows the amount of time that a resource is scheduled to work over a series of time periods.

13. B: A 360-degree evaluation is an effective tool to evaluate team members' performance and effectiveness and to identify areas of improvement. Effort should be given to include all the team players in the evaluation process, but it is not mandatory. Team members not only evaluate other team members, but they should evaluate the project manager as well. Individual comments should not be disclosed, but the general feedback results should be shared with each team member in a private session. In order to have complete and honest feedback, it is vital that the participants remain anonymous.

14. B: Theory Z was introduced by Dr. Willam Ouchi. This theory is concerned with increasing employee loyalty to his/her organization. This theory emphasizes the well-being of the employees both at work and outside of work, it encourages steady employment, it leads to high employee satisfaction and morale, and overall it results in increased productivity and support for the organization. Theory X managers believe that average workers are incapable, avoid responsibility, have an inherent dislike of work, and are only interested in their own selfish goals. The workers must be forced to do productive work as they dislike their work and are not devoted and motivated. Theory Y managers believe that workers are creative and committed to project objectives and goals. They are willing to work without supervision, need very little external motivation, can direct their own efforts, and want to achieve. The Expectancy theory, first proposed by Victor Vroom, demonstrates that employees who believe their efforts will lead to effective performance and who expect to be rewarded for their accomplishments remain productive as rewards meet their expectations.

15. A: Potential team members are often rated and scored by various selection criteria during the Acquire Project Team process. These selection criteria are weighted according to their relevant importance and are developed using the multi-criteria decision analysis tool. A project team member's ability or competencies, communication capabilities, relevant knowledge, skills, experience, cost (for adding the team member), attitude or ability to work with others, availability, and other factors such as time zone and geographical location are some examples of selection criteria that can be used to rate and score team members.

16. D: A manager with a "hands-off" attitude toward the project is considered "Laissez-Faire." With this style, management is not directly involved but manages and consults as required. This French term means "allow to act" or "leave alone."

17. C: Customers and contractors should not be allowed to be involved in internal resource-related disputes in most cases. All efforts should be given to resolve the conflicts at the lowest levels or authority whenever possible. In some cases, conflict requires the involvement of the project sponsor or senior management, especially when there is a major concern regarding resource assignments.

18. D: Colocation is a tool & technique used in the Develop Project Team process, not in the Plan Human Resource Management process.

19. A: An RBS looks like a typical organizational chart, but it is organized by types of resources. An RBS can help track project cost as it ties to the organization's accounting system. An OBS is similar to a company's standard organizational chart that looks like a WBS but only includes the positions and relationships in a top-down, graphic format. It is arranged according to an organization's existing departments, units, or teams with their respective work packages. Any operations department such as manufacturing or engineering, can identify all of its project responsibilities by looking at its portion of the OBS. A RAM cross-references team members with the activities or work packages they are to accomplish. One example of a RAM is a Responsible, Accountable, Consult, and Inform (RACI) chart, which can be used to ensure clear divisions of roles and responsibilities. A text-oriented position description, or role-responsibility-authority form, is particularly important in recruiting. It is used to describe a team member's position title, responsibilities, authority, competencies, and qualifications in detail.

20. D: The team members are in the Norming stage as they are adjusting work habits and behaviors to work as a team. They begin to start trusting and working together.

21. D: The objective of collocation, or the war room, is to build a better relationship among the team members, enhance their ability to perform as a team, identify concerns and issues in the project, and figure out solutions for those issues. The idea is not to point fingers at other team members or get involved in any kind of argument.

22. B: Recognition and rewards are used as a tool & technique in the Develop Project Team process, not in the Plan Human Resource Management process. Hierarchical-type organizational charts, a responsibility assignment matrix (which is a matrix-type organizational chart), and organizational theory all are used as tools & techniques in the Plan Human Resource Management process.

23. A: The staffing management plan identifies the training needs and certification requirements of the team members. One example of a responsibility assignment matrix is a RACI (Responsible, Accountable, Consult, and Inform) chart, which can be used to ensure clear divisions of roles and responsibilities. Training and certification management plan is a fake term. A resource breakdown structure (RBS) looks like a typical organizational chart, but this one is organized by types of resources. An RBS can help track project cost as it ties to the organization's accounting system.

24. C: A project manager can kill the team morale by consistently rewarding the same individual repeatedly as it can be perceived that the project manager is playing favorites. If the team members believe that the rewards are win-lose and that only certain team members will be rewarded, it may demoralize them. In this kind of situation, the project manager can consider team awards, which is a win-win as all the team members are recognized for their contributions.

25. C: Theory Z was introduced by Dr. Willam Ouchi. This theory is concerned with increasing employee loyalty to his/her organization. This theory emphasizes the well-being of employees both at work and outside of work, it encourages steady employment, it leads to high employee satisfaction and morale, and overall it results in increased productivity.

26. D: As per Tuckman's model, in the Performing stage, the team functions as a well-organized unit. They are interdependent and work through issues smoothly and effectively. The role of the project manager is mainly overseeing and delegating.

27. B: There are several sources of conflict, including schedule priorities, scarce resources, personal work style, cost, and other elements, but it's important to note that personality differences are not the root cause of conflict; in fact, it's rarely the case. The three main causes of project conflicts are schedule, project priorities, and resources, as approximately 50 percent of all conflicts come from these three sources.

28. D: Reward and Expert are the most effective forms of power, and Punishment/Penalty/Coercive should be used as the last resort only after all other forms have been exhausted. Since the project manager has no power or budget to reward the team members, she should use her expert power in this situation.

29. B: Compromising is bargaining to some level of mutual (dis)satisfaction to both parties. Parties are asked to lose something to gain something. Smoothing is emphasizing areas of agreement and downplaying differences of opinion. Forcing is exerting one opinion over another. Collaborating focuses on working to combine multiple differing perspectives into one shared perspective and results in a win-win situation for all parties.

30. D: The most effective solution in this type of situation will be to create ground rules and introduce them to the team members. Ground rules identify acceptable and not acceptable behaviors on the project and try to minimize the negative impacts of bad behaviors. Some of the ground rules that will be applicable in this situation include the following:

- Methods of how conflict should be resolved
- Ways to treat sensitive data in the project
- Methods of notifying the project manager about difficulties, issues, and concerns
- Acceptable ways to interrupt someone talking at a meeting
- Methods to stop talking over a team member inappropriately
- Rules for joining meetings and consequences of being late

CHAPTER 10

PROJECT COMMUNICATIONS MANAGEMENT

Project Communications Management

Project communications management is a systematic approach to communicate efficiently and effectively with all the parties involved in the project, such as stakeholders, team members, the sponsor, senior management, vendors, and others. It also covers all activities required for producing, compiling, sending, storing, retrieving, distributing, and managing project records.

- A project manager spends 90 percent of his/her time communicating, and around 50 percent of that time is spent communicating with team members.
- It is mandatory to have a robust communications management plan for any project to be a success.
- Communications' need, frequency, and methods have to be identified and communicated to all parties.
- The communication plan needs to be revisited frequently at team meetings to limit communication problems.

Project Manager's Responsibilities in Communication

- Understand the organizational approach of communicating with a different organization and individuals.
- Make sure that everybody gets the right message at the right time.
- Develop a consistent approach to communications management, adhere to it, and regularly monitor and control it.
- Develop an environment of open and honest communication about all project management concerns.
- Commit to communicate project-related matters proactively and consistently throughout the project life cycle.

Key Terminology in Communications Management

Communications activity has many potential dimensions including:

- Internal and external
- Formal and informal
- Vertical and horizontal
- Official and unofficial
- Written and oral
- Verbal and nonverbal

It is crucial to note that communication is not one-sided, and information needs to be distributed to many internal (within the project team) and external (outside the project team) individuals:

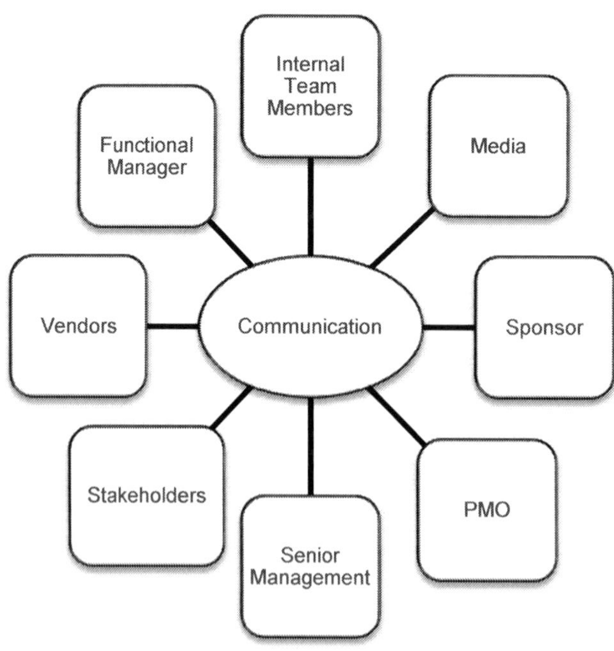

Figure 10-1: Communication among Internal and External Team Members

Communication Matrix: A communication matrix helps to identify the team players communicating with each other. Below is a simple communication matrix. The project manager is the one who mostly communicates with everyone involved in a project.

	Project Manager	Sponsor	PMO	Team	Functional Manager	Customer	Media	Vendors	Gov. Agency
Project Manager		X	X	X	X	X	X	X	X
Sponsor	X			X	X	X	X		
PMO	X	X			X				
Team	X	X		X	X	X		X	X
Functional Manager	X	X		X					
Customer	X			X					X
Media	X	X							
Vendors	X			X					
Gov. Agency	X			X		X			

Table 10-1: Communication Matrix

In addition to communication occurring internally and externally, it also occurs in the core project team, vertically (up and down the organization), and horizontally (with peers); thus, our planning should include communicating in all of the following directions:

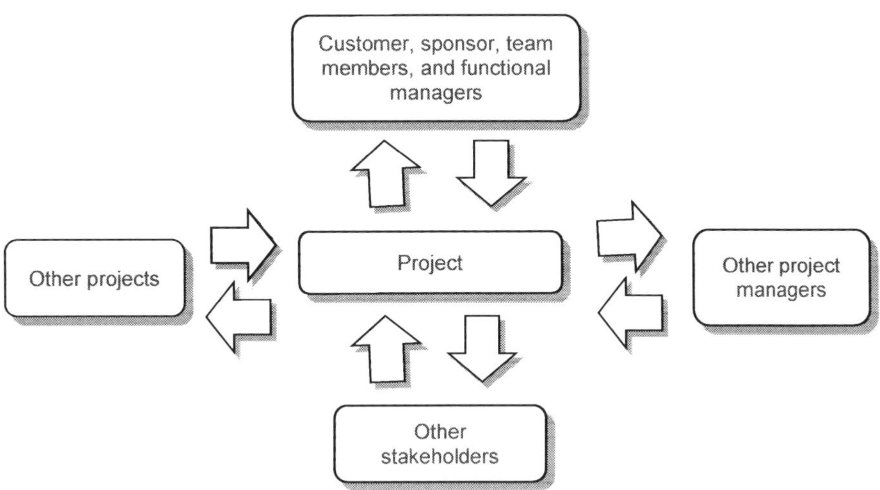

Figure 10-2: Communication Directions

The project manager should handle communication in a structured manner by selecting the best form of communication for a specific situation in order to have clear, concise communication. A decision on whether communication will be formal, informal, written, or verbal needs to be made for each instance of communication.

Exercise 1: What information and documents need to be communicated within a project?

Communication Types: Below are the different types of communication used in communications management:

Communication Type	When Used	Example
Formal Written	Used essentially for prominent documents that go into the project record	Complex problems, project management plan, project charter, important project communications, contracts, and legal notices
Formal Verbal	Used for special events, announcements, and public relations	Presentations, bidder conferences, and speeches
Informal Written	Frequently used to communicate and convey information	Memos, e-mails, and notes
Informal Verbal	Mostly used to communicate information efficiently and quickly	Meetings, conversations, discussions, and phone calls

Table 10-2: Communication Types

Exercise 2: What is the best type of communication in the following situations?

Situation	Communication Types
1. You are in the executing phase of your project, and several defects are reported as well as requests for corrective and preventive actions. As per the findings, you are updating your project management plans.	
2. Your vendor has raised a few concerns in the contract, and you are making changes to it.	
3. Your team is facing a very complex technical problem with one of the software components they are working on, and the team is now trying to solve it.	
4. You send out a meeting request and agenda to schedule a meeting.	
5. One of the critical deliverables is getting delayed in your project, and you are requesting additional resources to complete the deliverable on time.	
6. You are working on a complicated and technically challenging project, and the team is trying to clarify one of the most complicated work packages.	
7. You are having a meeting to discuss and find out the root cause of a problem.	
8. Your sponsor and a couple of senior management personnel are interested in knowing all the details of your project, and you are making presentations to them.	
9. You want to answer any queries that the vendors may have and conduct a bidder conference with all the potential vendors.	
10. Your team has just finished a major milestone. To celebrate the success, the team is holding a milestone party.	
11. Your project expeditor is making notes regarding a telephone conversation that you are having with one of the key stakeholders.	
12. You have encountered several issues in one of the support applications you are using and send an e-mail to the vendor to ask for clarification of the issues.	
13. One of your team members is not performing at all in your project, and you are having a meeting informing the team member of the poor performance and about your concern.	
14. You have discussed your concern about the poor performance of one of the team members and have also come up with an improvement plan. You do not really notice any performance improvement and decide to inform the team member about the poor performance for the second time.	

Communication Blockers

Anything that interferes with the meaning of a message is considered noise or a communication blocker. Some examples of the communication blockers are discussed below:

Communication Blockers	Detail
Frame of Reference	Different individuals often interpret the same information differently according to their own experience or frame of reference.
Cultural Differences	Cultural differences between the communicator and the receiver can create obstacles due to language differences or differences in beliefs, attitudes, or other practices.
Selective Listening	A receiver may be selective in his/her listening, allowing his/her prejudices or biases to influence his/her understanding of the message.
Value Judgment	Communicators and receivers place different value judgments on the message. The communicator may believe the message to be much more important than the receiver may feel it is.
Filtering	Information in a message may be manipulated for the communicator's purposes—for example, to make negative news seem more positive for the benefit of the receiver.
Source Credibility	The credibility of a message to its receivers may be influenced by their level of trust in the communicator.

Table 10-3: Communication Blockers

Blockers for Global Companies

Communication Blockers	Detail
Cultural Differences	Cultural differences such as variations in social and business practices, religious beliefs, and political differences significantly impact communication.
Language Barriers	Organizations often need to operate across international language barriers. Furthermore, communication even within some countries requires knowledge of several languages or dialects.
Time Differences	Operating across time zones can present communication challenges for an organization.
Geopolitical Factors	Geopolitical factors that may represent a risk to business communication include the probability of disasters and political unrest, financial instability in the region or industry, and predominant ethical and moral attitudes and customs.

Table 10-4: Communication Blockers for Global Companies

Project Communications Management Processes

Project communications management is all about keeping everyone involved in the project informed. Project managers spend 90 percent of their time communicating and have to communicate with management, customers, the project team members, and the rest of the stakeholders involved in the project.

The communications management plan organizes and documents the communication processes, types of communication, and the stakeholder expectations for communication. It also defines how information is gathered, organized, accessed, and dispersed. The plan should also provide a timeline of expected communication based on a calendar schedule, such as project status meetings. Some communications are prompted by conditions within the project, such as cost variances, schedule variances, or other performance-related issues. A project manager needs to accurately report on the project status, changes, performance, and earned values. A project manager should also pay close attention to controlling the information to ensure that the communications management plan is functioning as intended.

PMI identifies three key processes that are associated with the communications management knowledge area in the planning, executing, and monitoring & controlling process groups.

Processes	Process Groups	Used For	Key Outputs
1. Plan Communications Management	Planning	The process of identifying the information and communication needs of the people involved in a project by determining what needs to be communicated, when, to whom, with what method, in which format, and how frequently.	– Communications Management Plan
2. Manage Communications	Executing	The process of making relevant information available to project stakeholders in a timely manner as planned.	– Project Communications
3. Control Communications	Monitoring & Controlling	The process of ensuring that the information needs of stakeholders are met by monitoring and controlling communication throughout the project life cycle.	– Work Performance Information – Change Requests

Table 10-5: Three Project Communications Management Processes and Key Outputs

Project Communications Management Processes, Inputs, Tool & Techniques, and Outputs

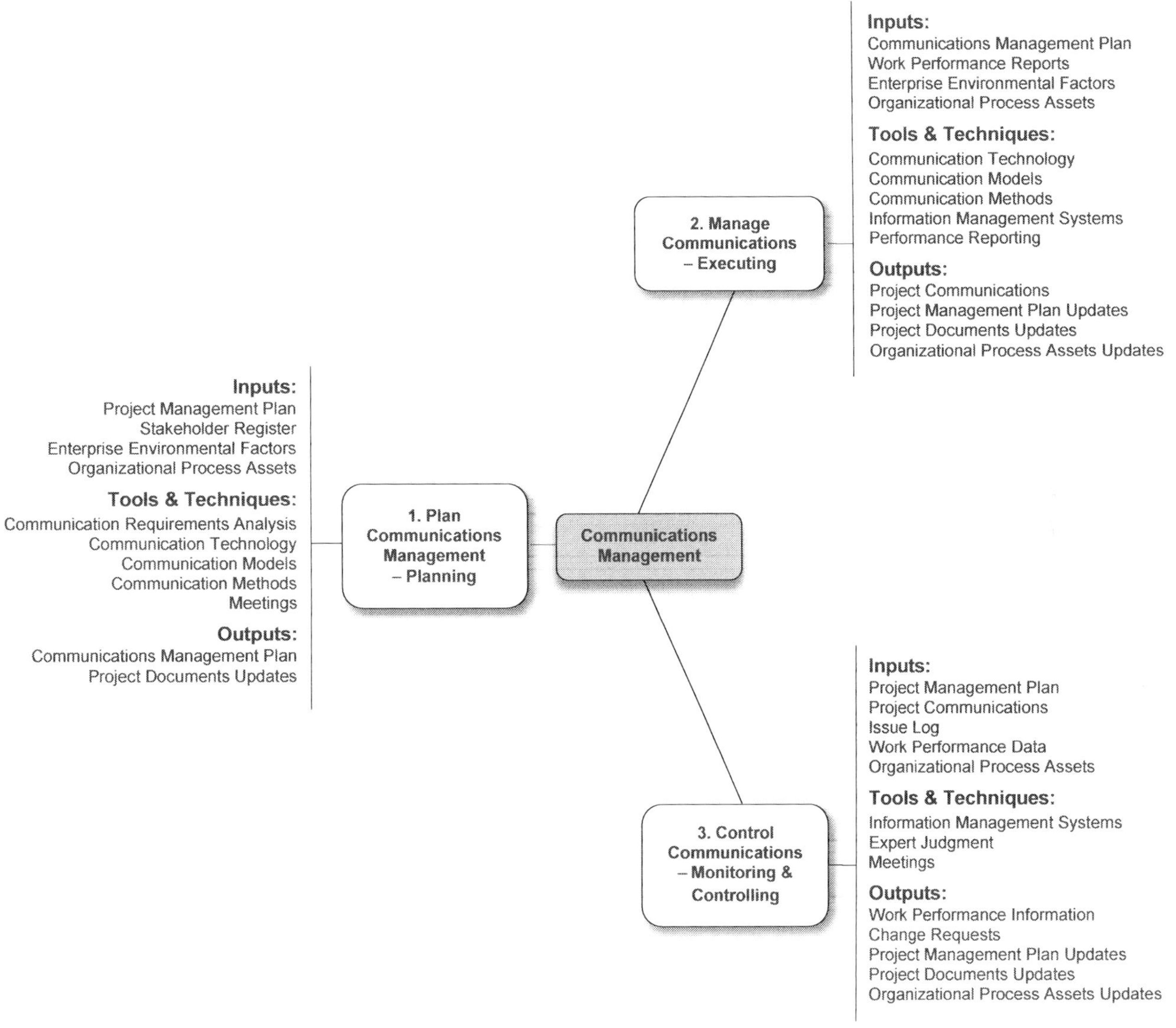

Figure 10-3: Project Communications Management Processes, Inputs, Tool & Techniques, and Outputs

Plan Communications Management

Communications planning involves identifying the information and communication needs of the people involved in a project by determining what needs to be communicated, when, to whom, with what method, in which format, and how frequently.

Developing a robust communications plan is essential for project success. A lack of planning will cause delay in message delivery, misinterpretation and misunderstanding of the message communicated, communication to the wrong audience, and other things. Communication planning should be performed at the early stage of project planning so that appropriate resources such as time and budget, can be allocated to the communication activities.

Subjects covered during the communications planning should include but not be limited to the following:

- Who needs the information?
- Why they need the information?
- When and at what frequency will they need the information?
- Who is authorized to access the information?
- Who will be sending the information?
- How the information will be stored and retrieved?
- What format the information should be stored and reported?
- What kind of impact will the time zone, cultural differences, and language barriers have on the communication?

As per the PMBOK®, the Plan Communications Management process has the following inputs, tools & techniques, and outputs:

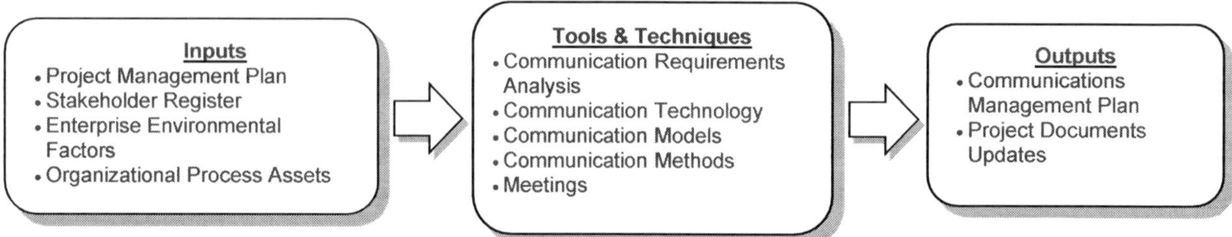

Figure 10-4: Plan Communications Management: Inputs, Tools & Techniques, and Outputs

Plan Communications Management: Inputs

- Project Management Plan
- Stakeholder Register
- Enterprise Environmental Factors
- Organizational Process Assets

Project Management Plan: The project management plan defines how the overall project will be executed, monitored, controlled, closed, and maintained.

Stakeholder Register: The stakeholder register contains all details related to the identified stakeholders, including identification information, assessment information, information need, and classification.

Enterprise Environmental Factors: All environmental factors are used, especially the company's organizational structure, culture, existing systems, and established communication channels.

Organizational Process Assets: All organizational process assets, especially historical information and lessons learned, are used.

Plan Communications Management: Tools & Techniques

- Communication Requirements Analysis
- Communication Technology
- Communication Models
- Communication Methods
- Meetings

Communication Requirements Analysis: Analysis of the communication requirements determines the type, format, value, and information needs of the project stakeholders. Resources in a project are allocated only upon communicating information that contributes to the success of the project or where a lack of communication will cause failure.

As per the PMBOK®, there are several sources that we can examine to determine project communications requirements, including the following:

- Department and company organizational charts
- Stakeholder information from the stakeholder register and the stakeholder management strategy
- Project organization and stakeholder responsibility relationships
- Disciplines, departments, business units, and specialties involved with the project
- Number of resources involved with the project and their locations
- Internal information needs (e.g., communicating within the project team) and external information needs (e.g., communicating with the media, public, government, industry group, or contractors)

Communication Channels: The communication network model defines the interactions needed between project participants. It consists of nodes with lines connecting the nodes that indicate the number of communication channels. Communications are complex and need to be managed properly as adding one more person makes the team communication channels grow exponentially. The communication channels can be calculated by using the following formula:

$$\text{Communication Channels} = n(n-1)/2 \text{ or } (n^2 - n)/2$$

n = number of people

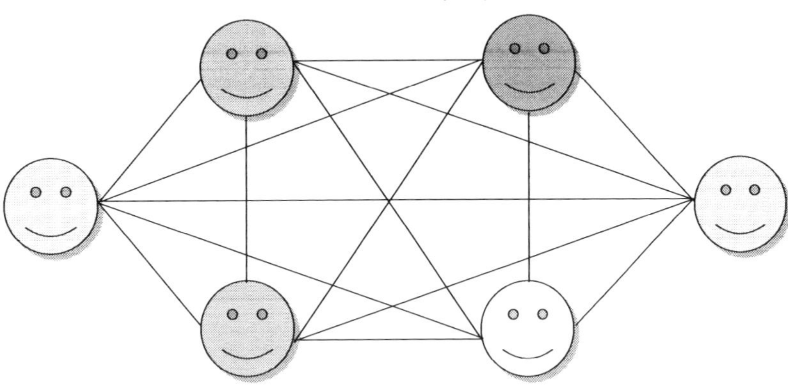

Figure 10-5: Communication Channels

Exercise 3: If you have four people on the team and you add two more, how many more communication channels will you have?

Communication Technology: The methods used to transfer information to, from, and among project stakeholders can vary significantly. Factors that can affect the project communications include the following:

- **Availability of technology:** Appropriate systems may already be in place, or new systems or technology may need to be procured.
- **Expected project staffing:** Project participants may already be experienced with the proposed communication systems, or extensive training and learning may be required.
- **Urgency of the need for information:** There may be a need to have frequently updated information available on a moment's notice, or regularly issued written reports may be sufficient.
- **Project environment:** Project team members are located together and may operate on a face-to-face basis, or they may be spread out in a virtual environment.
- **Duration of the project:** Technology will not likely change prior to the project's completion, or it may need to get updated at some point.
- **Sensitivity and confidentiality of the information:** Depending on the nature of the information, additional security measures may be required.

Communication Models: This is a basic model of communication that demonstrates how information is sent from the sender and how it is received by the receiver. The key components of the model include the following:

- Sender
- Message and feedback message
- Receiver
- Medium
- Noise

Each message is encoded by the sender and decoded by the receiver based on factors like the receiver's education, experience, language, and culture. Communication models often call these factors "noise" or "communication blockers."

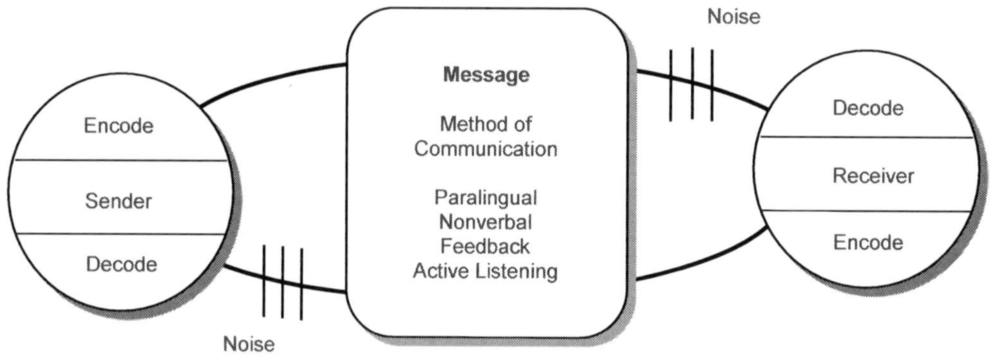

Figure 10-6: Communication Model

Effective Communication: The sender should encode a message carefully, determine the communication method used to send it, and confirm that the message is understood.

- **Nonverbal:** About 55 percent of all communications are nonverbal (e.g., based on physical mannerisms such as facial expressions, hand gestures, and body language).
- **Paralingual:** Pitch and tone of voice also help convey a message.
- **Feedback:** The sender tries to receive feedback or a comment about the message from the receiver.

Effective Listening: The receiver should decode the message carefully and confirm the message is understood. This includes the following:

- **Watching:** The speaker should pick up on physical gestures and facial expressions.
- **Repeating:** Repeat what the sender has communicated.
- **Feedback:** The listener should send feedback about the message.
- **Active Listening:** The receiver confirms he/she is listening, confirms agreement, or asks for clarification.
- **Paralingual:** The listener pays attention to the pitch and tone of the sender.

Communication Methods: There are several communication methods used to share information among all project stakeholders. These methods can be broadly classified into:

- Interactive communication
- Push communication
- Pull communication

Category	Detail	Example
Interactive Communication	It is between two or more parties who are performing a multidirectional exchange of thoughts and ideas. It is the most efficient way to ensure a common understanding of specified topics by all participants.	Meetings, phone calls, video conferencing, etc.
Push Communication	It is the way of sending information to specific recipients who need to know it. This ensures that the information is distributed, but it is not concerned with whether it reached, or was understood by, the intended audience.	Letters, memos, reports, e-mails, faxes, voice mails, press releases, etc.
Pull Communication	It is sort of the opposite of push communication. It is used for very large volumes of information or for very large audiences that require recipients to access the communication content at their own discretion.	Intranet sites, e-learning, knowledge repositories, etc.

Table 10-6: Communication Categories

Meetings: Meetings with team members, sponsors, and identified stakeholders will be beneficial to discuss the most effective ways of communicating information with the stakeholders in order to resolve problems and make decisions.

Plan Communications Management: Outputs

- Communications Management Plan
- Project Documents Updates

Communications Management Plan: The communications management plan is a subsidiary of the project management plan. It can be formal or informal, highly detailed or broadly framed, and is based on the needs of the project. As per the PMBOK®, the communications management plan typically describes the following:

- Purpose of communication
- Information needs of each stakeholder or stakeholder group
- Stakeholder communication requirements
- Format, method, time frame, and frequency of the distribution of required information
- Person responsible for communicating the information
- Methods for updating the communications management plan
- Persons or groups who will receive the information
- Glossary of common terms

Communication Type	Objective	Method	Person Responsible	Audience	Frequency
Status Report	Communicate current project status to everyone.	Soft copy	Project coordinator	All stakeholders	Weekly
Forecasting Report	Communicate future project status and performance to everyone.	Soft copy	Project coordinator	All stakeholders	Bi weekly
Team Meeting	Update on team members' activities, communicate messages from senior management, and team building	Face to face, net meeting, or video conferencing	Project manager	Team members	Weekly, Thursday 2-3 PM

Table 10-7: Communications Management Plan

Project Documents Updates: Project documents such as the project schedule, the stakeholder register, and the stakeholder management strategy may be updated.

Manage Communications

Manage Communications is the process of making relevant information available to project stakeholders in a timely manner as planned. In this process, the communications management plan that was created in the Plan Communications Management process is put into action by creating, collecting, distributing, storing, and retrieving the project information. It is performed throughout the entire project life cycle and in all management processes.

As per the PMBOK®, effective communication management includes a number of techniques:

- **Choice of media:** Selection of oral or written communication, formal reports or informal memos, and face-to-face or indirect communication.
- **Sender-receiver models:** Sender, receiver, feedback loops, message, and noise or barriers to communication.
- **Meeting management techniques:** Meeting agenda, ground rules, meeting minutes, and conflict resolution techniques.
- **Presentation techniques:** Visual aids, body language.
- **Listening techniques:** Watching, repeating, sending feedback, confirming understanding, and acknowledging, as well as other elements.
- **Facilitation techniques:** Building consensus and overcoming obstacles.
- **Writing style:** Sentence structure, word choice, and active versus passive voice.

As per the PMBOK®, the Manage Communications process has the following inputs, tools & techniques, and outputs:

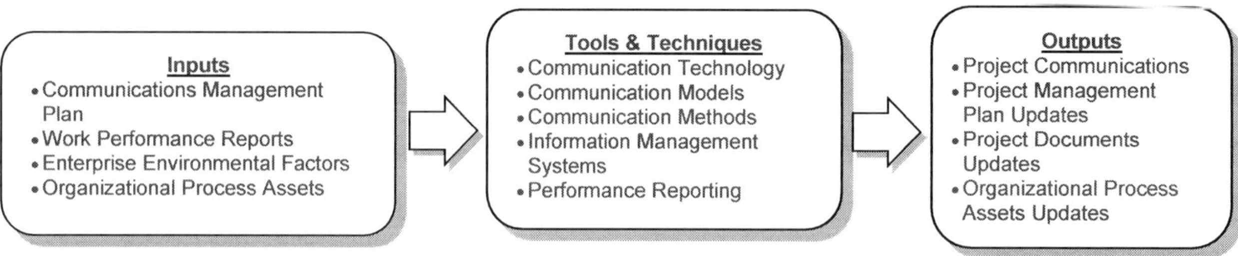

Figure 10-7: Manage Communications: Inputs, Tools & Techniques, and Outputs

Manage Communications: Inputs

- Communications Management Plan
- Work Performance Reports
- Enterprise Environmental Factors
- Organizational Process Assets

Communications Management Plan: The communications management plan portion of the project management plan is executed in this process.

Work Performance Reports: Performance reports are used to distribute project performance and status information; they should be made available prior to project meetings and should be as precise, accurate, and current as possible.

Enterprise Environmental Factors: Industry standards and regulations, organizational structure and culture, the project management information system, government regulations, and other things may influence the Manage Communications process.

Organizational Process Assets: Organizational process assets such as policies, procedures, and guidelines regarding information distribution; templates; historical information; and lessons learned may influence the Manage Communications process.

Manage Communications: Tools & Techniques

- Communication Technology
- Communication Models
- Communication Methods
- Information Management Systems
- Performance Reporting

Communication Technology: Various communication technologies such as e-mail, text (SMS), fax, phone, video and audio conferencing, computer chat, and other mediums are used to effectively communicate information within the project.

Communication Models: A basic model of communication that demonstrates how information is sent from the sender and how it is received by the receiver. In order to have effective communication, an appropriate communication model should be selected; any noise or communication blockers should be identified and properly managed.

Communication Methods: Various communication methods such as formal, informal, written, and verbal as well as interactive, push, and pull communications are used to deal with potential challenges and barriers in communication. In order to receive proper response and feedback from recipients, we need to make sure that the information has been received and understood properly.

Information Management Systems: Various tools are used to manage and distribute project information, such as:

- Focus group, fact sheet, media release, newsletter, shared-access electronic databases, manual filing systems, and hard-copy document distribution
- Electronic communication and conferencing tools such as video and web conferencing, websites and web publishing, e-mail, e-fax, SMS, chat, voice mail, and telephone
- Electronic tools for project management such as a meeting and virtual office support application, a web-based scheduling interface, an automated project management application, collaborative work management tools, and portals

Performance Reporting: Performance reports organize and summarize the information gathered and show how the project is progressing against various baselines, such as scope, time, cost, quality, and other elements. Various common formats for performance reports include bar charts, S-curves, histograms, and tables. Variance analysis, earned value analysis, and forecast data are often included as part of performance reporting.

- **Earned Value Management:**
  - **Earned Value Report:** Integrates scope, cost, and schedule measures to assess project performance. For instance, Planned Value (PV), Earned Value (EV), and Actual Cost (AC).
  - **Variance Report:** Compares actual project results with baselines. For instance, Schedule Variance (SV), Cost Variance (CV), Schedule Performance Index (SPI), and Cost Performance Index (CPI).
  - **Forecasting Report:** Analyzes and predicts future project status and performance. For instance, Budget at Completion (BAC), Estimate at Completion (EAC), Estimate to Complete (ETC), Variance at Completion (VAC), And To-Complete Performance Index (TCPI).
- **Status Report:** Describes in detail where the project now stands regarding performance measurement baselines in cost, schedule, scope, and quality.
- **Progress Report:** Describes what has been accomplished in the project so far.
- **Trend Report:** Examines project results over time to see if performance is improving or deteriorating.

Major Milestones	Values			Variance		Performance Index		
	Planned Value	Earned Value	Actual Cost	Schedule	Cost	Schedule	Cost	Cumulative CPI
Requirements Collection	73,000	69,000	72,500	– 4000	–3500	0.945	0.951	
Design Complete	94,000	89,000	95000	–5000	–6000	0.946	0.936	
Coding Complete	80,000	78,000	79,000	–2000	–1000	0.975	0.987	
Unit Testing Complete	22,000	20,000	22,500	–2000	–2500	0.909	0.888	
User Testing Complete	7,000	6,000	6,800	–1000	–800	0.857	0.882	
	276,000	262,000	275,800					0.949

Table 10-8: Performance Report Sample

Budget at Completion	Estimate At Completion	Estimate To Complete	Variance at Completion	To Complete Performance Index
$400,000	$421,496	$15,032	–$21,496	1.1

Table 10-9: Forecast Report Sample

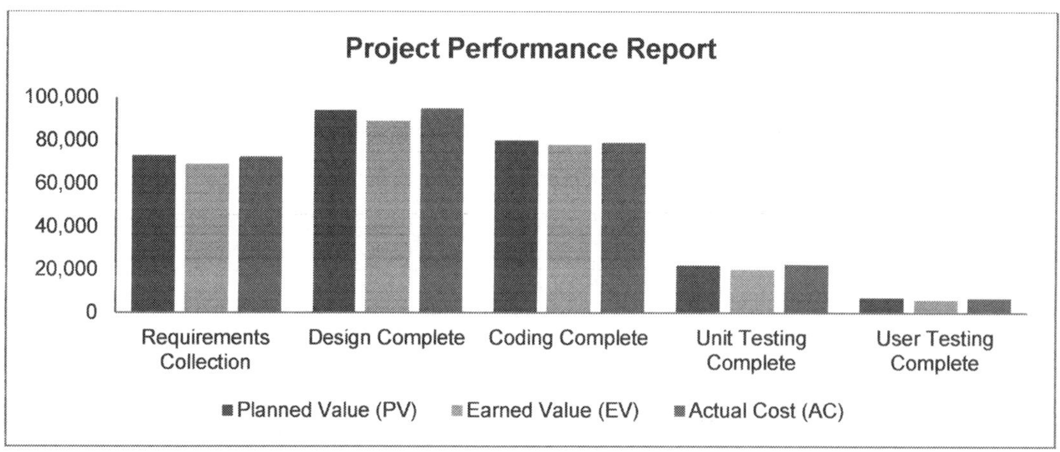

Figure 10-8: Project Performance Report Sample

Manage Communications: Outputs

- Project Communications
- Project Management Plan Updates
- Project Documents Updates
- Organizational Process Assets Updates

Project Communications: Depending on the urgency, impact, method of delivery, and level of confidentiality, project communications may include performance, status, progress, costs incurred, and other reports.

Project Management Plan Updates: Updates are based on the deviation between current performance and the performance measurement baseline. Various components of the project management plan such as project schedule, scope and cost baselines, communications management plan, and stakeholder management plan, among other things, may be updated.

Project Documents Updates: The project schedule, issue logs, project communication plan, project funding requirements, and other elements may be updated.

Organizational Process Assets Updates: Organizational process assets such as stakeholder notifications, project reports, project presentations, project records, feedback from stakeholders, lessons learned documentation, and other items may be updated.

Exercise 4: Identify which process group each process belongs to.

Process Groups				
Initiating	Planning	Executing	Monitoring & Controlling	Closing

Process Names:

- Manage Communications
- Control Communications
- Plan Communications Management

Control Communications

Control Communications is the process of ensuring that the information needs of the project stakeholders are met by monitoring and controlling communication throughout the project life cycle. This process determines if the communications management plan is being followed and if communication is meeting the needs of the stakeholders. The focus of this process is to ensure efficient information flow to all stakeholders at any moment in time within the project.

As per the PMBOK®, the Control Communications process has the following inputs, tools & techniques, and outputs:

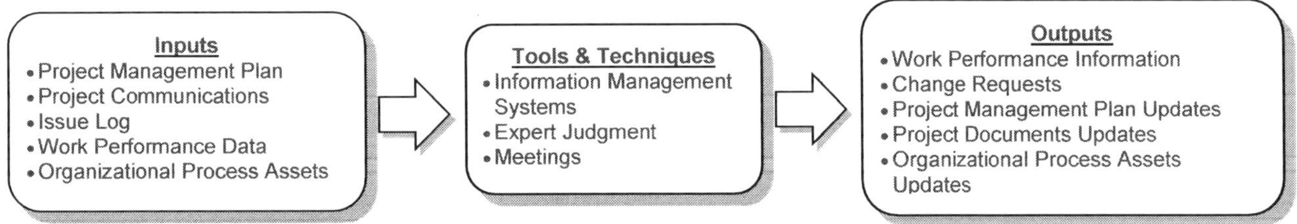

Figure 10-9: Control Communications: Inputs, Tools & Techniques, and Outputs

Control Communications: Inputs

- Project Management Plan
- Project Communications
- Issue Log
- Work Performance Data
- Organizational Process Assets

Project Management Plan: The communications management plan portion of the project management plan contains valuable information for the Control Communications process, such as:

- Purpose of communication
- Information needs of each stakeholder or stakeholder group
- Stakeholder communication requirements
- Format, method, time frame, and frequency of the distribution of required information
- Person responsible for communicating the information
- Methods for updating the communications management plan
- Persons or groups who will receive the information
- Glossary of common terms

Project Communications: Depending on the urgency, impact, method of delivery, and level of confidentiality, project communications may include performance, status, progress, costs incurred, and other reports.

Issue Log: An issue is an obstacle that threatens project progress and can block the team from achieving its goals. An issue log is a document to record issues that require a solution. It helps monitor who is responsible for resolving specific issues by a target date. There should be one owner assigned for each issue reported in the project.

ID	Issue Description	Date Added	Priority	Raised By	Owner	Resolution Due Date	Status	Date Resolved	Issue Resolution
01	Chris was moved to a higher priority project – need an urgent replacement.	3/3/2014	High	Steve	Project manager	3/15/2014	Closed	3/10/2014	Miguel was assigned for next three months to replace Chris.
02	Equipment (PCs, servers, digital storages) were delivered late.	3/6/2014	High	Rony	Project manager	3/20/2014	On going	3/15/2014	A change request is issued for a three week time extension.

Table 10-10: Issue Log

Work Performance Data: This raw data can help to measure the effectiveness and efficiency of communications against plan metrics. A root cause analysis using this raw data can be utilized to assess if poor communications could be the cause of a problem or to scrutinize a variance to conclude if a change is necessary.

Organizational Process Assets: Various organizational process assets such as policies and procedures for measures and indicators, variance limits defined by the organization, templates for reports, record retention policies, allowed communication media, and other elements may influence the Control Communications process.

Control Communications: Tools & Techniques

- Information Management Systems
- Expert Judgment
- Meetings

Information Management Systems: An information management system is an automated system that can serve as a repository of information, a tool to assist with communication, and to track documents and deliverables. An information management system also supports the project from beginning to end by collecting and distributing information to stakeholders regarding cost, schedule, and performance. Several reporting techniques such as spreadsheet analysis, table reporting, presentation, graphics for visual representations, and other items may be consolidated from various systems and communicated to the stakeholders.

Expert Judgments: Judgment and expert opinions can be gathered from senior management, project team members, specific stakeholders, project managers from similar projects, subject matter experts, industry groups and consultants, and other units within the organization to assess the impact of project communication, actions required, time frame allowed, and responsibilities for the actions.

Meetings: Meetings with team members, the sponsor, and identified stakeholders will be beneficial to determine the best approach to address stakeholders' concerns and communicate project performance.

Control Communications: Outputs

- Work Performance Information
- Change Requests
- Project Management Plan Updates
- Project Documents Updates
- Organizational Process Assets Updates

Work Performance Information: Information from project activities, such as resource utilization, deliverables status, schedule progress, costs incurred, and quality updates, is collected for performance results.

Change Requests: Recommended corrective actions for securing the future performance of the project and recommended preventive actions for reducing the probability and impact of future negative project performance will generate many change requests.

Project Management Plan Updates: Various components of the project management plan such as the human resource plan, the stakeholder management plan, and the communications management plan may be updated.

Project Documents Updates: Various project documents such as the issue log, performance reports, and forecasts may be updated.

Organizational Process Assets Updates: Organizational process assets such as report formats, lessons learned documents, reasons for corrective actions, and other elements can be updated.

Exercise 5: What are the specific actions or tasks a project manager should focus on during the Control Communications process?

____

____

____

Communications Management Example for a Construction Project

DreamHouse Properties, LLC would like to build a luxury housing complex called WonderHouse with twenty freestanding and fifty duplex three- and four-bedroom homes. The construction portion was outsourced to BestDeveloper, LLC to work on the following:

- Construction of two model houses and a marketing office, including landscaping and furnishings
- Installation of the infrastructure, including roads, drainage, services, and boundary walls
- Construction of each home with basic landscaping
- Construction of recreational areas, including a lake, a park, and two children's playgrounds

Stakeholder Information Needs: A stakeholder is identified here as any person or group who requires regular information about this project. Each of these stakeholder groups will require different types of information regarding the project. The following table lists the information required by each stakeholder to enable us to create a plan for meeting the stakeholders' requirements.

Stakeholder/Group	Description	Information Need
DreamHouse Properties project team members.	All project team members of DreamHouse Properties should be kept up-to-date with information regarding the project's progress.	– Detailed project status – List of key deliverables produced to date and identified project risks, issues, and changes – End-of-phase review results
Senior Management, DreamHouse Properties	This is a major undertaking for DreamHouse Properties. As such, the entire senior management team has asked to be kept fully informed of the project's progress. The CEO of DreamHouse Properties will be the project sponsor.	– Summarized project status – Immediate risks, issues, and changes – Imminent project milestone delivery dates
CEO, BestDeveloper	The CEO of BestDeveloper has a vested interest in the success of this project.	– Purpose of the project – Deliverables produced to date – Benefits to be received from project delivery – Immediate risks, issues, and changes
Finance Head, BestDeveloper	The finance head for BestDeveloper will be interested in ensuring that the cash flow for this project is extremely well managed.	– Project purpose, benefits, and proposed changes – Benefits to be delivered by changes – Current status of the project and next steps – Any cost change – Payment status
Housing Authority	The local government housing authority will be interested in ensuring that municipal standards and ordinances are upheld throughout the project.	– High-level project status – Any potential violations
Builders Union	The local building and construction union will be interested in ensuring that employment contracts and regulations are upheld throughout this project.	– High-level project status – Any potential violation

Communication Plan: The following communication activities are required to distribute information to the appropriate audience throughout the project life cycle. We need to identify information (what), stakeholders (to whom), person responsible (who), time frame (when), and method (how) regarding how communication will be carried out in the project.

Information	Stakeholders	Person Responsible	Time Frame	Method
Business case and project charter	All	Project manager	Mid-May	Advertisements placed in the local newspaper
Project status	Team members	Project manager	Weekly	Weekly release & team meetings
End-of-phase review	All	Project manager	End of phase	Newsletters & phase review
Forecasting reports	All	Project manager	Biweekly	Forecast reports
Risk items	Finance head, CEO, BestDeveloper and senior management, DreamHouse	Project manager	Biweekly	Risk register
Project budget	Finance head, CEO, BestDeveloper and senior management, DreamHouse	Project manager	At budget completion	Project budget
Issues, concerns, and violations	Finance head, CEO, BestDeveloper and senior management, DreamHouse, housing authority, builders union	Project manager	Biweekly	Issue logs
Payment status	CEO, finance head, BestDeveloper	Finance head, DreamHouse	Monthly	Payment status report

Exercise 6: Crossword

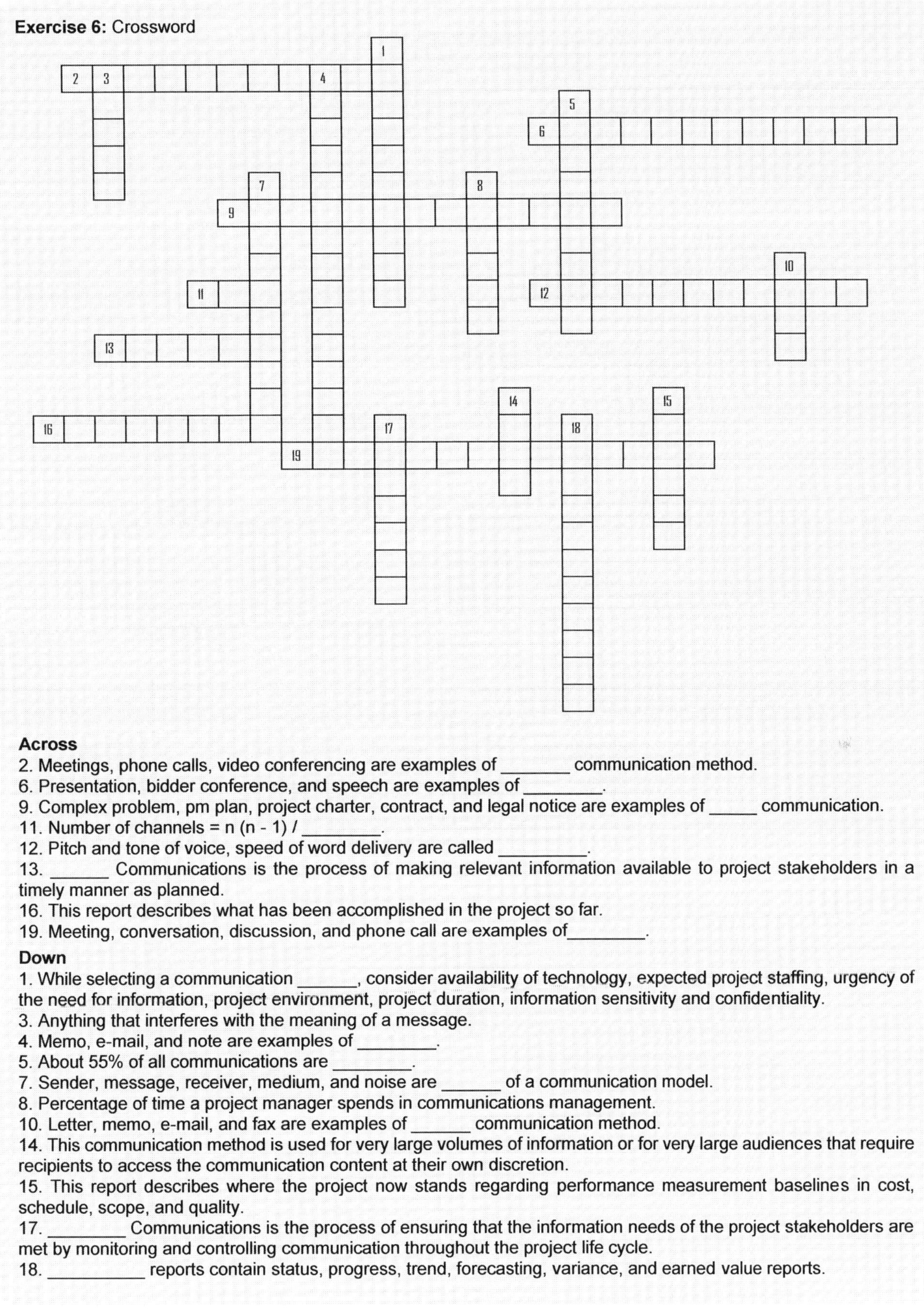

Across

2. Meetings, phone calls, video conferencing are examples of _______ communication method.
6. Presentation, bidder conference, and speech are examples of ________.
9. Complex problem, pm plan, project charter, contract, and legal notice are examples of _____ communication.
11. Number of channels = n (n - 1) / ________.
12. Pitch and tone of voice, speed of word delivery are called _________.
13. ______ Communications is the process of making relevant information available to project stakeholders in a timely manner as planned.
16. This report describes what has been accomplished in the project so far.
19. Meeting, conversation, discussion, and phone call are examples of________.

Down

1. While selecting a communication ______, consider availability of technology, expected project staffing, urgency of the need for information, project environment, project duration, information sensitivity and confidentiality.
3. Anything that interferes with the meaning of a message.
4. Memo, e-mail, and note are examples of ________.
5. About 55% of all communications are ________.
7. Sender, message, receiver, medium, and noise are ______ of a communication model.
8. Percentage of time a project manager spends in communications management.
10. Letter, memo, e-mail, and fax are examples of ______ communication method.
14. This communication method is used for very large volumes of information or for very large audiences that require recipients to access the communication content at their own discretion.
15. This report describes where the project now stands regarding performance measurement baselines in cost, schedule, scope, and quality.
17. ________ Communications is the process of ensuring that the information needs of the project stakeholders are met by monitoring and controlling communication throughout the project life cycle.
18. __________ reports contain status, progress, trend, forecasting, variance, and earned value reports.

Exercise 7: Answer the following:

1. This kind of communication includes vocal but nonverbal signals such as pitch and tone of voice to convey a message.
2. This report describes what has been accomplished in the project so far.
3. This communication method ensures that the information is distributed, but it is not concerned with whether it reached or was understood by the intended audience.
4. A project manager spends ___ percent of his/her time communicating, and around 50 percent of that time is spent communicating with team members.
5. Complex problems, project management plan, project charter, important project communications, contracts, and legal notices are example of ___________ communication.
6. Anything that interferes with the meaning of a message is considered _____ or a communication blocker.
7. The process of making relevant information available to project stakeholders in a timely manner as planned.
8. The communication channels can be calculated by using this formula.
9. This report describes where the project now stands regarding performance measurement baselines in cost, schedule, scope, and quality.
10. The key components of the communication model are sender, receiver, message and ______.
11. About ______ percent of all communications are nonverbal (e.g., based on physical mannerisms such as facial expressions, hand gestures, and body language).
12. Letters, memos, reports, and e-mails that are frequently used to communicate and convey information are examples of _________.
13. Most of the communication takes place in the ______________ process.
14. Each message is ________ by the sender and decoded by the receiver.
15. You are using _______ communication method as your stakeholders are getting information from your department's web site.
16. ___________ communication is used for special events, announcements, and public relations.
17. The process of ensuring that the information need of project stakeholders is met by monitoring and controlling communication throughout the project life cycle.
18. The three processes of communications management are ________.
19. The key outputs of communications management processes are ________.
20. Name some of the tools and techniques used in Plan Communications Management process.
21. In which communications management process is performance reporting used as a tool and technique?
22. The number of possible formal or informal communication paths exists in a project.
23. Performance reports can include several reports such as ______ .
24. The factors used in determining the communication technology for a project are _____.
25. The common formats of performance reports are ________.
26. Items typically required to determine the project communication requirement are ______.
27. This report examines project results over time to see if performance is improving or deteriorating.
28. Components of the communication management plan are _______.
29. The human resource management plan is associated with the team and the communications management plan is associated with ________.
30. This report shows the variance between the plan (baseline) and the actual results.

Project Communications Management Summary

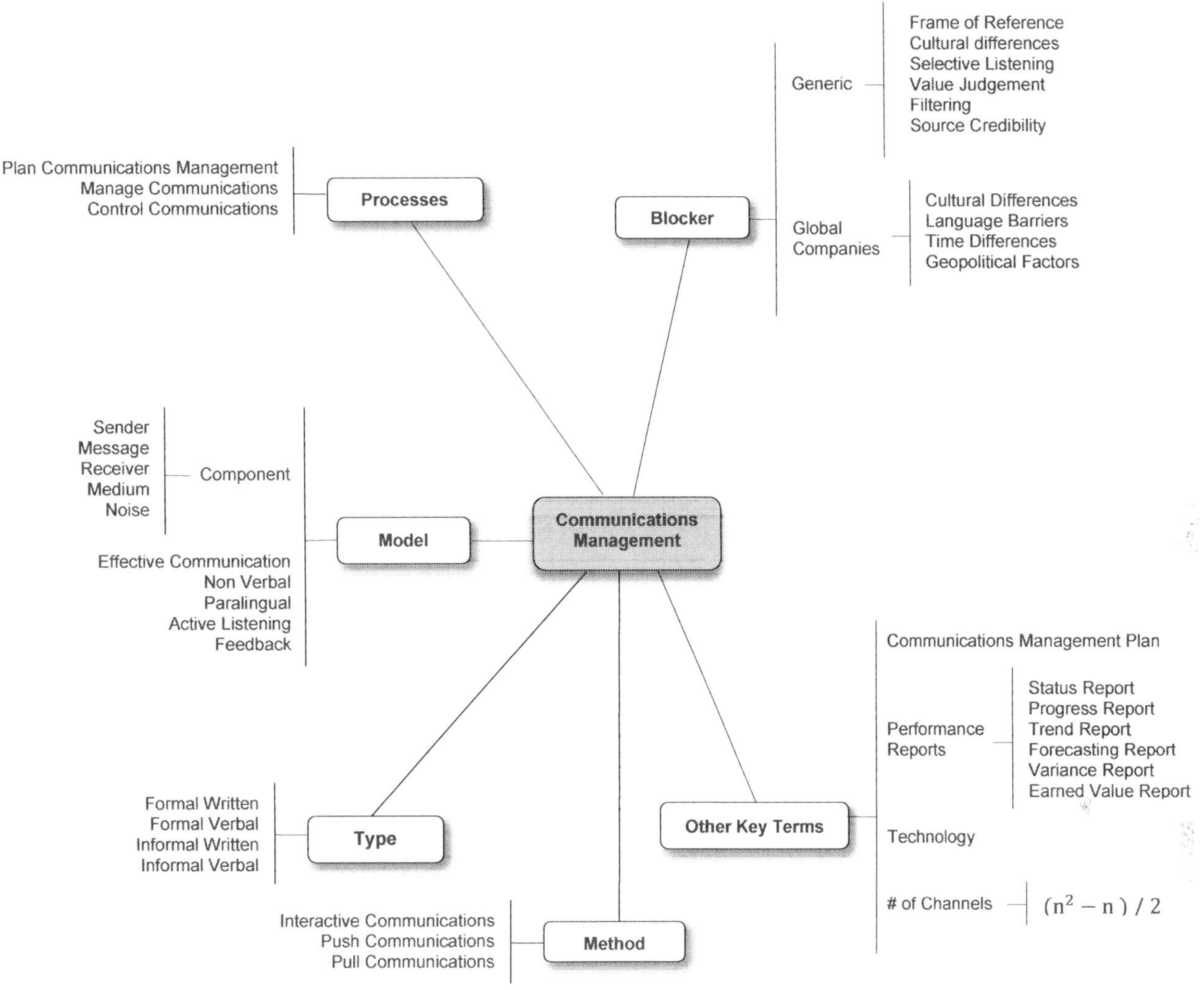

Figure 10-10: Project Communications Management Summary

Project Communications Management Key Terms

Communications Ideals

- A project manager spends 90% of time in communications management.
- A project manager should communicate project-related matters proactively and consistently throughout the project life cycle to the right audience in a timely manner.

Communication Model

Components: Sender, message, receiver, medium, and noise

Communication Types

Formal Written: Complex problem, project management plan, project charter, contract, and legal notice
Formal Verbal: Presentation, bidder conference, and speech
Informal Written: Memo, e-mail, and note
Informal Verbal: Meeting, conversation, discussion, and phone call

Communication Methods

Interactive: Interacting directly. Meeting, phone call, and video conferencing
Push: Sending information to specific recipients. Letter, memo, e-mail, and fax
Pull: Making information available. Intranet site, e-learning, and knowledge repository

Other Terms

Nonverbal Communication: About 55% of all communications. Physical mannerisms such as facial expressions, hand gestures, and body language

Paralingual: Pitch and tone of voice, and speed of word delivery

Communications Management Plan: Purpose for communication; stakeholders' information needs; format, method, time frame, and frequency for information distribution; person responsible; glossary of terms

Number of Channels = n (n – 1) / 2 or $(n^2 - n) / 2$, where n = number of team members

Performance Reports: Earned Value Management (earned value, variance, forecasting), status, progress, and trend
Communication Technology: While selecting a communication technology, it is important to consider the availability of the technology, the expected project staffing, urgency of the need for information, project environment, project duration, and information sensitivity and confidentiality.

Project Communications Management Exercise Answers

Exercise 1: Much information and many documents need to be communicated within a project. Refer to the "Figure: 3-16" for a comprehensive list, but listed below are some of the more important items that need to be communicated.

Initiating process group: Business case, feasibility study, project charter, project impact on other projects, and contact information of all stakeholders.

Planning process group: Project management plan, requirements document, project scope statement, WBS and WBS dictionary, project schedule, project budget, identified risks, resource needs, uncertainties, and work assignments.

Executing and Monitoring & Controlling process groups: Project success, project status, problems, quality audit results, scope changes, upcoming deliverables, delays, issue logs, and performance reports.

Closing process group: Final closure reports, Lessons learned.

Exercise 2:

1. Formal written
2. Formal written
3. Formal written
4. Informal written
5. Formal written
6. Formal written
7. Informal verbal
8. Formal verbal
9. Formal verbal
10. Informal verbal
11. Informal written
12. Informal written
13. Informal verbal
14. Formal written

Exercise 3: We know that for four team members the number of channels will be 4(4 – 1)/2 or (4 * 3)/2 = 6 Now since we added two more members to the team, we have six team members. For six members we will have 6(6 – 1)/2 or (6 * 5)/2 = 15 channels. Thus we will have 15 – 6 = 9 more channels now.

Exercise 4:

Process Groups				
Initiating	**Planning**	**Executing**	**Monitoring & Controlling**	**Closing**
	Plan Communications Management	Manage Communications	Control Communications	

Exercise 5:

- Determine if the communications management plan is being followed.
- Ensure that the information needs of the project stakeholders are met.
- Ensure efficient information flow to all stakeholders at any moment in time within the project.
- Meet with team members, the sponsor, and identified stakeholders to determine the best approach to address stakeholders' concerns and communicate project performance.
- Communicate project work performance information on a regular basis.
- Ensure implementation of approved change requests from stakeholders.
- Update the project management plan, other relevant project documents, and organizational process assets as appropriate.

Exercise 6:

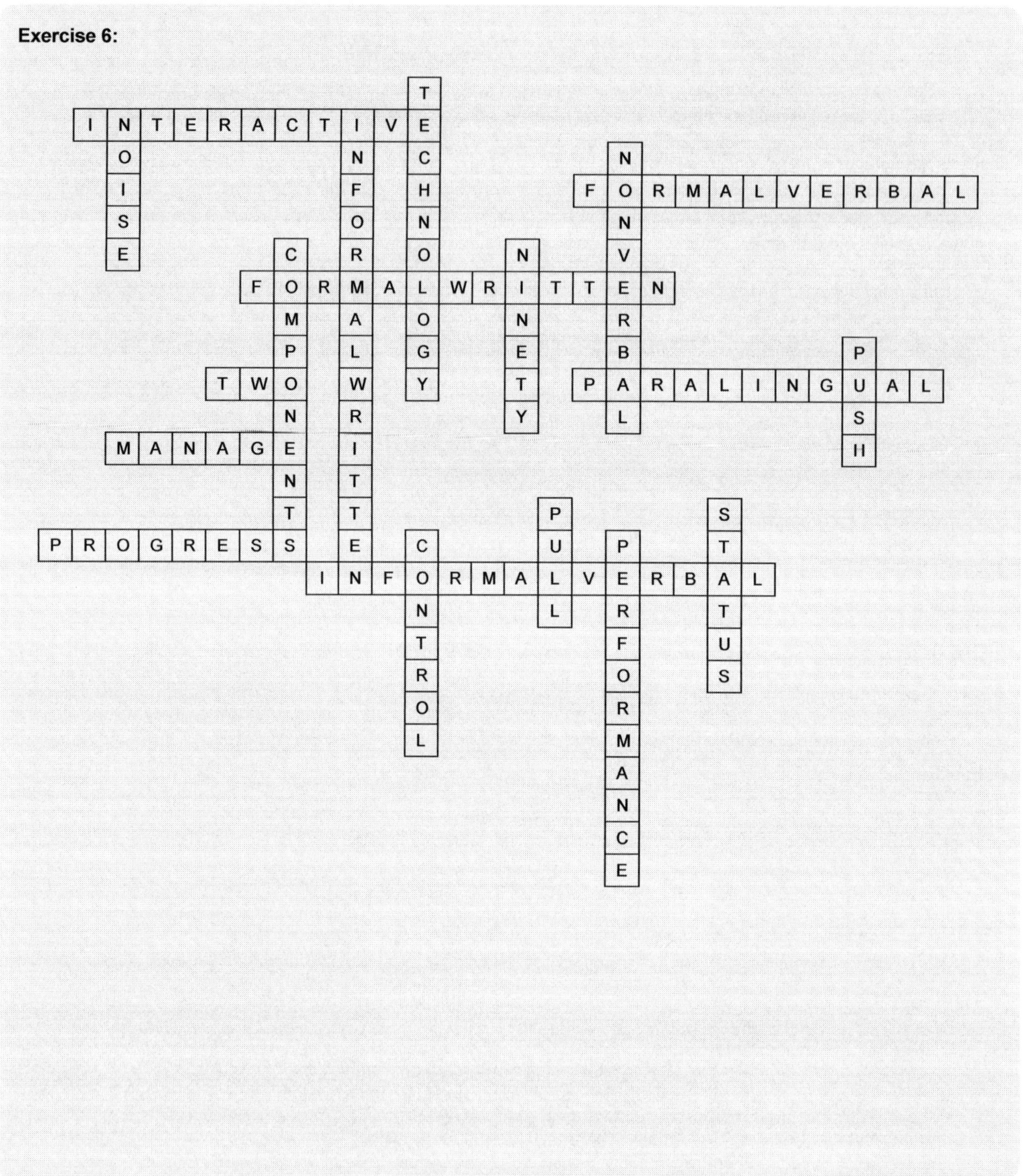
INTERACTIVE
NOISE
INFORMALWRITTEN
TECHNOLOGY
NONVERBAL
FORMALVERBAL
COMPONENT
NINETY
FORMALWRITTEN
PUSH
TWOWAY
PARALINGUAL
MANAGE
PROGRESS
PULL
STATUS
PERFORMANCE
CONTROL
INFORMALVERBAL

Exercise 7:

1. Paralingual
2. Progress Report
3. Push Communication
4. 90
5. Formal written
6. Noise
7. Manage Communications
8. (n^2 – n)/2, n = number of people
9. Status Report
10. Medium
11. 55
12. Informal written communication
13. Manage Communications
14. Encoded
15. Pull communication
16. Formal verbal
17. Control Communications
18. Plan Communications Management, Manage Communications, and Control Communications
19. Plan Communications Management – Communications Management Plan
    Manage Communications – Project Communications
    Control Communications – Work Performance Information, Change Requests
20. Communication requirements analysis, communication technology, communication models, communication methods, meetings
21. Manage Communications
22. Communication channels
23. Status, progress, trend, forecasting, variance, and earned value
24. Availability of the technology, expected project staffing, urgency for the need of information, project environment, duration of the project, sensitivity, and confidentiality of the information
25. Bar charts, s-curves, histogram, and tables
26. Project management plan, stakeholder register, enterprise environmental factors, organizational process assets
27. A Trend Report
28. Communication type, format, objective, method, person responsible, audience, frequency, glossary of terms
29. Stakeholders
30. A Variance Report

Project Communications Management Exam Tips

- Be able to describe the purpose of all three communications management processes.
- You should be able to name the inputs, tools & techniques, and outputs of all the communications processes.
- Be able to answer questions where you will need to analyze a specific situation and determine what you should do next.
- Be familiar with the concepts and terms in the project communications management summary table, Figure 10-10: Project Communications Management Summary.

Project Communications Management Questions

1. In your network infrastructure project XYZ, you have determined the type, format, value, and information needs of the stakeholders through communication requirements analysis. Project resources should be expended only on communicating information that:
   A. Originates from the sponsor or the project management office.
   B. Has been generated by the project team members only.
   C. Is relevant to the most influential and powerful stakeholders.
   D. Contributes to project success or where a lack of communication can lead to a failure.

2. A project manager is in the process of ensuring that the information needs of the project stakeholders are met by monitoring and controlling communication throughout the project life cycle. The project manager is involved in which process?
   A. Direct and Manage Project Work
   B. Monitor and Control Project Work
   C. Control Communications
   D. Manage Communications

3. As a project manager, Henry is cognizant of the importance of effective communication, and he always makes sure that he has the proper physical mannerisms such as facial expressions, hand gestures, and body language, while conveying a message. He is also particularly observant to the pitch and the tone of his voice, and he tries to receive comments and feedback from the receiver while communicating. What percentage of Henry's message is sent through nonverbal communication?
   A. Approximately 10 to 20 percent
   B. No more than 30 percent
   C. No more than 45 percent
   D. More than 50 percent

4. You are in the Plan Communications Management process to identify the information and communication needs of the people involved in your project by determining what needs to be communicated, when, to whom, with what method, in which format, and how frequently. Which of the following is MOST closely linked to this process?
   A. Communication requirements analysis
   B. Information management system
   C. Interpersonal skills
   D. Performance reporting

5. A project manager is leading a team of fifteen team members. One of the team members is not dedicated to the project and is having a performance issue. What form of communication can the project manager use to address this kind of situation?
   A. Informal written
   B. Informal verbal
   C. Formal written
   D. Formal verbal

6. You recently successfully completed a data center project that has been in production for more than a month. All the stakeholders have formally approved the project, and no issues have been reported since it has been in production. While reviewing one of the deliverables of your project with a project manager who is preparing for a similar project, you discover a problem in your project that may cause a minor safety issue in the future. What should you do under this circumstance?
   A. Communicate with your management about your finding both verbally and in writing.
   B. There is no need to bring this minor safety issue to the attention of the customers since no complaints have been filed.
   C. Call the customers immediately and inform them about the safety issue.
   D. Since it is a minor safety concern, it can be fixed without letting the customers know about it.

7. As a project manager, you know you will be spending 90 percent of your time communicating with all the players involved in your project. You need to make sure that you have the proper physical mannerisms such as facial expressions, hand gestures, and body language, while conveying a message. You also need to be particularly observant to the pitch and the tone of your voice, and you should try to receive comments and feedback from the receiver while communicating. Your communication skills will be utilized MOST during which of the following processes?

A. Communication Change Control
B. Manage Communications
C. Report Performances
D. Plan Communications Management

8. You are successfully managing a software project to automate the business processes for one of your clients. A key stakeholder articulates her concern to you about the lack of relevant information on her team's deliverables in the project status reports that you have been sending out. She is worried that her team has no visibility in this project and has requested you to look into the matter as soon as possible. What should you do FIRST in this situation?

A. Revisit the information distribution process in your project.
B. Have an urgent meeting with the stakeholders to understand what her team is working on.
C. Ask the stakeholder to send the status of her team so that you can incorporate them in your report.
D. Revisit your communications management plan.

9. A project manager overseeing an ERP implementation project planned to distribute large volumes of information about the project to a large audience. He decided to post the information in an online knowledge repository for access at the discretion of the stakeholders. This type of communication method is known as:

A. Interactive communication
B. Push communication
C. Pull communication
D. Expert judgment

10. As a project manager, you are required to report project performance to all your stakeholders on a regular basis. Which one of the following can utilize Earned Value Management (EVM) in its preparation for management?

A. Status reports
B. Trend reports
C. Progress reports
D. All of the above

11. Which communication method is used essentially for prominent documents that go into project records?

A. Informal verbal
B. Informal written
C. Formal verbal
D. Formal written

12. In your project you are facing many multifaceted problems that need to be discussed and resolved. You have explored different communication methods to use in solving complex problems. Extensive use of which of the following methods will most likely assist in solving complex problems in your project?

A. Nonverbal
B. Verbal
C. Written
D. Paralingual

13. A project manager supervising a video conferencing implementation project has several internal and external stakeholders whom she needs to send project progress, status, and forecast reports to on a regular basis. The project manager is making sure she is sending information to specific recipients who need to know it. Even though she ensures that the information is distributed, she is not concerned with whether it reached or was understood by the intended audience. This type of communication method is known as:

A. Interactive communication
B. Push communication
C. Expert judgment
D. Pull communication

14. A project manager is in the process of making relevant information available to project stakeholders in a timely manner as planned. The project manager is involved in which of the following processes?

A. Plan Communications Management process
B. Manage Communications process
C. Control Communications process
D. Distribute Information process

15. The sender-receiver model is a basic model of communication that demonstrates how information is sent from the sender and how it is received by the receiver. This model is designed to assist project managers and team members in improving their communication skills. This communication model highlights which one of the following?
   A. Horizontal communication
   B. Noise and feedback loops
   C. Downward communication
   D. Verbal and nonverbal communication

16. A project manager is in the Manage Communications process of collecting and distributing performance information and is especially focused on reporting against the performance baseline. Which one of the following is an output in this process?
   A. Performance reporting
   B. Information management system
   C. Communication methods
   D. Project communications

17. Your project currently has ten more people assigned to the team besides you. As your project is getting delayed, management wants you to add four additional team members to your project at the end of the month. How many more communication channels will you have once the additional team members are added?
   A. 55
   B. 50
   C. 105
   D. 160

18. You have been asked to provide information about your project's current performance in terms of the relationships between scope, schedule, and budget. The most appropriate type of report that will accomplish this is:
   A. Progress report
   B. Earned Value Management report
   C. Trend report
   D. Status report

19. Which one of the following is not a noteworthy factor in the determination of the method that may be used to transfer information to, from, and among project stakeholders?
   A. Availability of technology: Appropriate systems may already be in place, or you may need to procure a new system or technology.
   B. Urgency of the need for information: There may be a need to have frequently updated information available at a moment's notice, or regularly issued written reports may be sufficient.
   C. Stakeholder identification: It will provide a list of stakeholders affected by the project and who have interest in the project.
   D. Duration of the project: Technology will not likely change prior to the project's completion or it may need to be upgraded at some point.

20. You set up a project status meeting with key stakeholders and customers, but it is not going too well. Participants are discussing various topics at random, talking at the same time and interrupting each other, a few of the attendees are not participating in the discussion at all, and two of the customers are busy over the phone. To avoid this kind of situation and have an effective meeting, what meeting rules should you apply?
   A. You should have a real purpose of the meeting and invite the right people.
   B. You should always schedule your meeting in advance so that people have plenty of time to be prepared for the meeting.
   C. You should create and publish an agenda with specific topics to discuss and set up ground rules.
   D. You should control who is allowed to speak and who is not and ask everyone to demonstrate courtesy and consideration to each other.

21. You have several internal and external stakeholders involved in your construction project. As a project manager, you need to identify the information type, format, value, and needs for all these stakeholders. Which of the following tools & techniques is used to identify this type of information?
   A. Stakeholder management strategy
   B. Communications requirements analysis
   C. Trend analysis
   D. Value analysis

22. You have been managing a multi-year construction project for one of your most important clients. You requested your lead business analyst to develop a report that will capture project results for the last four years and illustrate whether project performance is improving or deteriorating. You are interested in which of the following reports?

A. Trend report
B. Variance report
C. Forecasting report
D. Progress report

23. You have fifteen identified internal and external stakeholders in the network infrastructure project you are supervising. You are sending out progress and status reports to all your stakeholders on a regular basis as per your communications management plan. One of the stakeholders needs a very specific progress report on her team's deliverables and sends you an urgent e-mail requesting you to send the report as soon as possible. Your bandwidth is almost fully occupied in various project-related activities, but you have to find some spare time to fulfill this unexpected request from the stakeholder. What will be your BEST course of action?

A. Consider it as part of the Manage Communications process and send out the requested report.
B. Consider it as gold plating and ignore the request from the customer.
C. Inform the stakeholder that you are unable to send out ad hoc reports as it is not included in the project communications management plan.
D. Complain to the sponsor about this unreasonable request from the stakeholder.

24. You are the project manager of a very important software development project in your organization. As you are closely monitoring and managing your project, you are happy that the project is progressing as per your plan. You reviewed the status of all the deliverables with your team members prior to having a project status update meeting with the stakeholders. Your team has developed a prototype, or a working model of the proposed end product, and it will be presented to the stakeholders for interaction and feedback. This will be an iterative process, and the prototype may be modified numerous times to incorporate the feedback until the requirements have been finalized for the product. Which one of the following will you do in your status meeting?

A. Do not mention anything about the prototype.
B. Demo the prototype to the stakeholders and obtain their formal approval.
C. Report on the progress of the prototype and point out that it's a completed task.
D. Review the technical documentation of the prototype and obtain the formal approval.

25. While planning communication for the network infrastructure project to which you have been assigned as project manager, you know you have to pay particular attention to your body's mannerisms, facial expressions, and the tone and pitch of your voice to communicate effectively. All of the following are FALSE about communication EXCEPT:

A. Acknowledge means the receiver has received and agreed with the message.
B. Encode means to translate ideas or thoughts so that others can understand them.
C. Noise has nothing to do with sending and receiving messages.
D. Verbal communication is more important than nonverbal communication.

26. While working on your communications plan, you have considered several communication technologies to transfer information among project stakeholders. Communication technology will take into account the following factors that can affect the project EXCEPT which one?

A. Urgency of the need for information: Are regularly issued written reports enough for the project, or is frequently updated information needed at a moment's notice?
B. Expected project staffing: Are the proposed communication systems compatible with the experience and expertise of the project participants, or is extensive training and learning required?
C. Duration of the project: Is the available technology likely to change before the project is over?
D. Reason for the distribution of information: What are the reasons for distributing information?

27. A project manager overseeing a construction project has several stakeholders involved in the project. During project implementation, the project manager is required to submit several reports that will communicate information about the project. The report that describes where the project now stands regarding performance measurement baselines in cost, schedule, scope, and quality is called:

A. Status report
B. Quality report
C. Progress report
D. Forecast report

28. You are managing a software development project and have worked on a stakeholder register and a communications management plan. Now you are about to execute your communications management plan. Which one of the following is TRUE regarding Manage Communications?

A. Manage Communications will end when the product has been accepted.
B. Communication methods such as individual and group meetings, video and audio conferences, computer chats, and other remote communication methods are used to manage communications.
C. Manage Communications is a monitoring & controlling process.
D. Manage Communications only carries out predetermined communication and does not respond to unplanned requests from stakeholders.

29. The project manager who has been managing a large, multi-year network infrastructure project recently left the company, and you were assigned as a project manager to continue with the project. There are more than five different vendors, fifteen team members, and several key stakeholders involved in this very important project. While trying to identify stakeholder communication requirements, format, method, time frame, and frequency for the distribution of required information, which of the following will you be referring to?

A. Communications management plan
B. The information distribution plan
C. Project management plan
D. Stakeholder management strategy

30. A Project Management Information System (PMIS) is used as a tool & technique in many of the forty-seven processes. Which statement describes a PMIS BEST?

A. A PMI certification for project management focused on information systems.
B. A necessary log for timekeeping.
C. A repository for project information used for future reference.
D. An automated system to support the project by optimizing the schedule and helping collect and distribute information.

Project Communications Management Answers

1. D: Communications requirements analysis determines the information type, format, value, and needs of the stakeholders and identifies information that is most critical to success or where a lack of communication can lead to failure.

2. C: Control Communications is the process of ensuring that the information needs of the project stakeholders are met by monitoring and controlling communication throughout the project life cycle. The focus of this process is to ensure efficient information flow to all stakeholders at any moment in time within the project.

3. D: About 55 percent of all communications are nonverbal (e.g., based on physical mannerisms such as facial expressions, hand gestures, and body language).

4. A: Communication Requirements Analysis is a tool & technique in the Plan Communications Management process. Performance reporting and information management systems are tools & techniques within the Manage Communications process. Interpersonal skills are associated with the Manage Stakeholder Engagement process (stakeholder management).

5. B: The project manager should have an informal verbal discussion with the team member about the lack of dedication and poor performance. The goal is to address the concern of the project manager and to identify areas for improvement as well as any training needs for the team member. If this method is not effective, then the project manager should consider a formal written approach as the next step.

6. A: Even though no complaints have been filed and the issue is relatively minor, the project manager should report this sort of finding to management and take action as per management's recommendation.

7. B: Communication Change Control and Report Performances are not valid processes. Communications planning involves identifying the information and communication needs of the people involved in a project by determining what needs to be communicated, when, to whom, with what method, in which format, and how frequently. Manage Communications is the execution of your communications management plan, which covers a broad range of topics such as what, how, when, and how frequently information will be communicated and requires an ample amount of communication ability and skills.

8. D: Since the stakeholder is receiving the status reports, there is no issue with the information distribution process. You should revisit your communications management plan first to understand the information need, communications requirements, format, method, time frame, and frequency for the distribution of required information for this specific stakeholder. You may want to have an urgent meeting with the stakeholder once you have the details.

9. C: Pull communication utilizes intranet sites, e-learning, knowledge repositories, and other types of accessible databases for a large volume of information or for a large audience who will be accessing the contents at their own discretion. Expert judgment generally refers to the input from subject matter experts. Interactive communication is between two or more parties performing a multidirectional exchange of information; in push communication, information is distributed, but it is not certified that the information reached its intended audience or was understood.

10. D: Earned Value Management (EMV) terms such as Actual Cost (AC), Earned Value (EV), Planned Value (PV), Estimate at Completion (EAC), Estimate to Complete (ETC), Variance at Completion (VAC), and Budget at Completion (BAC) can be used for all kind of performance reports such as, status, trend, and progress reports.

11. D: Prominent records such as complex problems, the project management plan, the project charter, important project communications, contracts, legal notices, and other items use the formal written method.

12. C: Both verbal and written communications should be used in solving complex problems. But in a written communication, your words will be documented and presented in the same form to everyone. In the case of the other methods listed, the same message will not be received by everyone; thus, they will not be as helpful as a written method.

13. B: Push communication is a way of sending information to specific recipients who need to know it. This ensures that the information is distributed, but it is not concerned with whether it reached or was understood by the intended audience.

14. B: Manage Communications is the process of making relevant information available to the project stakeholders in a timely manner as planned by creating, collecting, storing, retrieving, and distributing project information. It is performed throughout the entire project life cycle and in all management processes.

15. B: The sender-receiver model highlights awareness about the appropriate message to be delivered, the potential barriers or noises that may be encountered, and the significance of a feedback loop to improve delivery and understanding of a message.

16. D: Performance reporting, information management system, and communications methods are tools & techniques in the Manage Communications process; only project communications are the outputs.

17. B: Your team currently has eleven team members including you; thus, the number of communication channels is calculated by using the formula: # of Channels = n* (n – 1)/2
11 (11 – 1)/2 = 55
If you add four more resources, then you will have 11 + 4 = 15 team members. So the number of channels will be
15 (15 – 1)/2 = 105
So you will have 105 – 55 = 50 more channels after adding the new resources.

18. D: Earned Value Management provides an integrated view of project performance and compares work performed with work planned to be performed and the planned cost of work with the actual cost of work. Progress reports provide information about what has been accomplished so far; a trend report examines project results over time to see if performance is improving or deteriorating. A status report describes where the project now stands regarding performance measurement baselines in cost, schedule, scope, and quality.

19. C: The methods used to transfer information to, from, and among project stakeholders can vary significantly. Factors such as availability of technology, expected project staffing, urgency of the need for information, project environment, duration of the project, and other things may play a significant role in determining the method that may be used to transfer information among project stakeholders. Stakeholder identification will provide a list of stakeholders affected by the project and does not play much of a role in this situation.

20. C: 'A' and 'B' will not help too much in this kind of situation as there is no indication here that the right people were not invited to the meeting or the meeting was not scheduled in advance. 'D' is not a rule for a meeting. People discussing topics at random suggests that there was no set agenda for the attendees to follow. Imposing ground rules will restrict people from talking at the same time and interrupting each other or remaining busy over the phone.

21. B: Stakeholder communications requirements are determined during communications requirements analysis. The intention is to identify information that is most valuable to stakeholders. The stakeholder management strategy is an output to identify the stakeholder communication process, and it defines an approach to manage stakeholders and to increase support for and minimize negative impacts on stakeholders throughout the entire project life cycle. A trend analysis examines project results over time to see if performance is improving or deteriorating. Value analysis or value engineering is associated with product analysis, and it helps to find a less costly way to do the same work without loss of performance.

22. A: The trend report examines project results over time to see if performance is improving or deteriorating.

23. A: Accommodating to planned and ad hoc information requests is part of the Manage Communications process.

24. C: Usually the project manager reports on the progress of the project in a status meeting rather than demoing any prototype or reviewing any technical documentation.

25. B: Acknowledge means the receiver has received the message, but it does not mean that the receiver necessarily agrees with the message. Noise or communication blockers play a vital role in effective communication. 55 percent of all communication is nonverbal, and verbal communication is not more important than nonverbal communication. Encoding is translating ideas and thoughts.

26. D: Communication technology will take into account urgency of the need for information, expected project staffing, and duration of the project, but not reason for the distribution of information.

27. A. Status reports address the current condition of a project, including risks and issues. Progress reports refer to work that has been completed during a reporting period, and forecasts refer to future scheduled work. The quality report is a made-up term.

28. B: Some stakeholders will need information distributed even after the product has been accepted as they want to get information about the closure of the project and the contract. The Manage Communications is an executing process. Manage Communications carries out not only predetermined communication but also handles responses to unplanned requests from stakeholders. The listed communication methods are used in Manage Communications; thus, letter 'B' is the correct answer.

29. A: Even though the communications management plan is a part of the project management plan, the best option here will be the communications management plan, where the purpose for communication, communication requirements, method, time frame and frequency for distribution, person responsible for communication, methods for updating the communications management plan, and other communication related items can be found.

30. D: PMIS is an automated tool used to gather, integrate, and disseminate project information.

CHAPTER 11

PROJECT RISK MANAGEMENT

Project Risk

Project risk is an uncertain event or condition in the future, and if it occurs, it will have a positive or negative impact on one or more project objectives including: scope, schedule, cost, and quality. Risk may have one or more causes, such as requirements, assumptions, and constraints or conditions that create the possibility of negative or positive outcomes.

It is normal even for the extremely organized or most carefully planned project to run into unexpected troubles. Several factors such as inadequate resources, the project environment, the project management processes, and other facets can all contribute to project risks. We will be able to anticipate some risks in advance and come up with response plans; other risk events will occur unannounced during the project. Team members can get sick or quit unexpectedly, sudden weather change can drastically limit your options - even resources that you are depending on may become unavailable. The purpose of risk management is to identify potential problems that could cause concern for your project, analyze how likely and at what frequency they will occur, take preventive actions for the ones you can avoid, and minimize the impacts and probability for the ones you can't avoid.

There are two generalized types of risk:

- Business Risk: Risk of loss/threat or gain/opportunity.
- Pure Risk: Only a risk of a loss/threat. These risks are sometimes also called insurable risks. Events like fire, theft, personal injury, and other elements are pure risks.

Opportunities (Positive Risk): These are the risks with positive effects. It is a favorable situation in the organizational environment.

Example: Arrival of new technology, removal of an international trade barrier, and an unfulfilled customer need may have significant positive impact on your project.

Threats (Negative Risk): These are external elements in the environment that arise from Political, Economic, Social, and Technological (PEST) forces and can cause trouble for the business.

Example: New regulation, an increased trade barrier, or emergence of substitute products.

- A threat may be a barrier, a constraint, or anything external that might cause problems, damage, or injury.
- Technological developments may make your offerings obsolete.
- Market changes may result from the changes in customer needs, competitors' moves, or demographic shifts.
- The political situation determines government policy and the taxation structure.

The same event can be an opportunity for some organizations and a threat for others at the same time. NASA is working with several companies to send shuttles to a space station on a regular basis. NASA is also working with a few nanotech companies on building an elevator from the ground to the space station to transfer the equipment, manpower, and other materials more conveniently and cheaply. So far it has not been successful since no material that could be used to build the elevator can withstand the air pressure. These nanotech companies are working on a substance called carbon nanotube that is capable of withstanding the air pressure and will not break. This emergence of a substitute product or arrival of new technology is a huge opportunity for these nanotech companies but a huge threat for others working with NASA on the shuttles.

Project Risk Management

Project risk management is a systematic approach to identification, analysis, response, and control of project risk. The objectives of risk management are to increase the probability and impact of positive events and to decrease the probability and impact of adverse events.
Project risk management is an iterative, continuous process in which risks are identified, updated, added, and reassessed throughout the project life cycle.

Project Manager's Responsibilities

- Understand organizational attitude and project team's attitude toward risk
- Develop a consistent approach to risk management
- Develop an environment of open and honest communication about risk and risk handling
- Commit to addressing risk proactively and consistently throughout the project
- Focus on preventative instead of reactive problem solving

Important Risk Management Concepts

Project Risk Event: The actual occurrence of the risk. Example: Equipment failure.

Project Risk Condition: Related to the environment in which the project is run.

Risk Triggers: Symptoms or warning signs that a potential risk is about to occur in the project. For instance, a key team member searching for a better job opportunity is a warning sign that the person may be leaving the team soon, causing schedule delay, increased cost, and other adverse events.

Uncertainty: A state characterized by the absence of information related to an outcome. A risk has uncertainty in both the occurrence and the outcome. It is typical of most projects that uncertainty and risk diminish as the project proceeds.

Risk Factors: Aspects of risk that should be considered include the following:
- **Source:** Where is the risk coming from?
- **Probability:** What is the possibility of the risk event to happen?
- **Impact:** What are the possible outcomes?
- **Timing:** Expected timing of risk events in the project life cycle.
- **Frequency:** Anticipated frequency of risk events from the source.

Risk Averse: Someone who does not want to take risks.

Risk Appetites: A high-level, generic description of the acceptable level of risk in the project. For instance, a customer with a moderate risk appetite is OK with accepting some cost and schedule risk in the project.

Risk Tolerances: Areas of risks where risks can be acceptable or unacceptable. A risk that will affect the reputation of a company will not be tolerated, but a financial risk can be acceptable; thus, reputation is not an area of risk tolerance, but finance can be.

Risk Threshold: The amount of risk that is acceptable. For instance, a company is OK with a financial risk of $30,000 but not more than that; thus, the threshold here is the amount of financial risk the company is willing to consider.

Exercise 1: What information or documents will the project manager need to adequately perform risk management?

Key Tools & Techniques for Risk Management

The following tools & techniques are used in various risk management processes. They bear special consideration here due to either their importance or complexity.

1. Expected Monetary Value (EMV) Analysis
2. Decision Trees
3. Diagramming Technique
4. SWOT Analysis
5. Monte Carlo Analysis

1. Expected Monetary Value (EMV) Analysis

Expected Monetary Value (or simply Expected Value) is a statistical concept that calculates the average outcome of a decision. It is the product of the probability and consequences of an event or task.

Expected Monetary Value (EMV) = Probability * Impact

- EMV is calculated by multiplying the value of each possible outcome by its probability of occurrence and then adding them together.
- Values of consequences of opportunities are expressed as positive values while values of threats are expressed as negative values.
- A common use of this type of analysis is in decision-tree analysis.

Example: Suppose you are managing a construction project and you have identified the following two negative and one positive project risks:

Expected Monetary Value of Risks			
Risk	**Probability**	**Value of Consequences**	**Expected Monetary Value**
1. Bad weather	30 percent	$90,000	30/100 * (– $90,000) = – $27,000
2. Labor unrest	6 percent	$120,000	6/100 * (– $120,000) = – $7,200
3. Lower cost of construction materials	15 percent	$110,000	15/100 * ($110,000) = $16,500

Table 11-1: Expected Monetary Value (EMV)

Note: If the bad weather negative project risk occurs, the project loses $27,000; if the labor unrest negative project risk occurs, the project loses $7,200; and if the lower cost of construction materials positive project risk occurs, the project gains $16,500.

Though the highest impact is caused by the labor unrest, the expected monetary value is the lowest as its probability of occurring is very low.

The project's expected monetary value based on these project risks is

– $27,000 – $7,200 + $16,500 = – $17,700

Therefore, if all risks occur in the construction project, the project would lose $17,700. In this scenario, you can add $17,700 to the budget to compensate for this.

2. Decision Tree

A decision tree is usually used for risk events associated with time and cost. It takes into account future events in an attempt to make a decision today and typically includes calculations of the Expected Monetary Value (EMV) of the action(s) presented.

It is primarily used to make decisions regarding individual risks by taking into account the risks, probability, and impacts.

Suppose you are considering getting either a PMP certification or an MBA degree. Attending a boot camp session and studying really hard will help you to get your PMP certification, but on the other hand, you may need to take time off from your job for the MBA program. Also, the MBA program is expensive; thus, you have a better probability to get the PMP certification than the MBA. If you get your PMP certification, you will be getting a 15 percent increase in your $70,000 salary, and for the MBA you will be getting a 25 percent increase. The value of getting the PMP certification is $10,500, and for the MBA it is $17,500.

The EMV for getting a PMP is 90/100 * 10,500 = $9,450, and for an MBA it is 40/100 * 17,500 = $7,000. Since we are talking about opportunity, we will consider getting a PMP certification since it has a bigger EMV.

Expected Value of Tasks			
Task	**Probability**	**Value of Consequences**	**Expected Monetary Value**
Get PMP	90 percent	15 percent increase in $70,000 salary = $10,500	90% * 10,500 = $9,450
Get MBA	40 percent	25 percent increase in $70,000 salary = $17,500	40% * 17,500 = $7,000

Table 11-2: Expected Monetary Value (EMV)

Example:

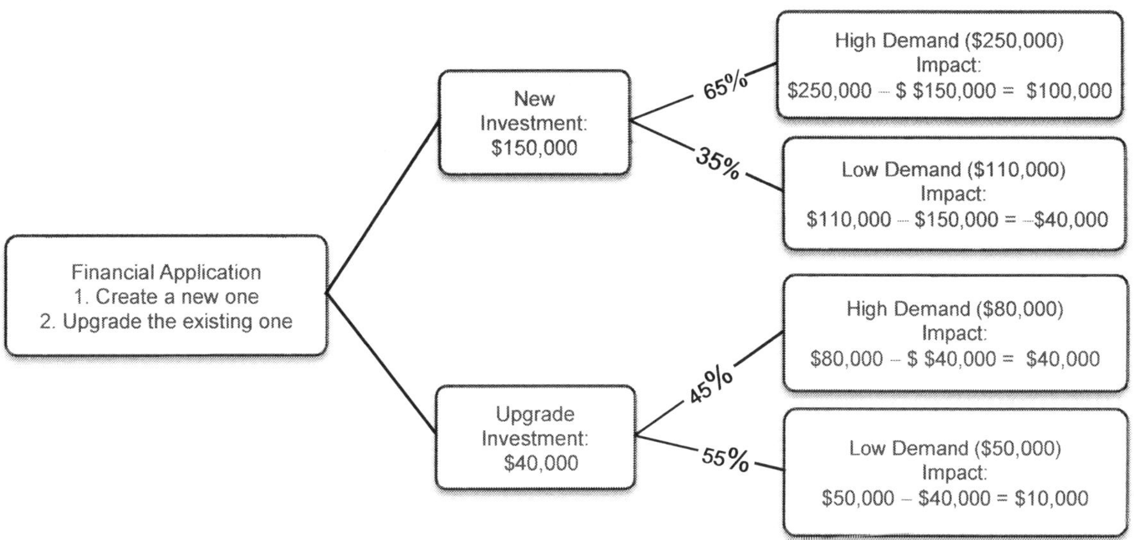

Figure: 11-1: Decision Tree

The Expected Monetary Value (EMV) for the new investment:
High Demand: 65 percent * $100,000 = $65,000
Low Demand: 35 percent * – $40,000 = – $14,000
So total EMV = $65,000 – $14,000 = $51,000

The Expected Monetary Value (EMV) for the upgrade investment:
High Demand: 45 percent * $40,000 = $18,000
Low Demand: 55 percent * $10,000 = $5,500
So total EMV = $18,000 + $5,500 = $23,500

Since we are getting a bigger EMV for the new investment, we should consider it over upgrading.

3. Diagramming Technique

A diagramming technique that's useful during the Identify Risks process is a system or process flow chart.

- This can help you recognize new risks.
- It graphically illustrates the logical sequence of steps in a process or system from start to finish.

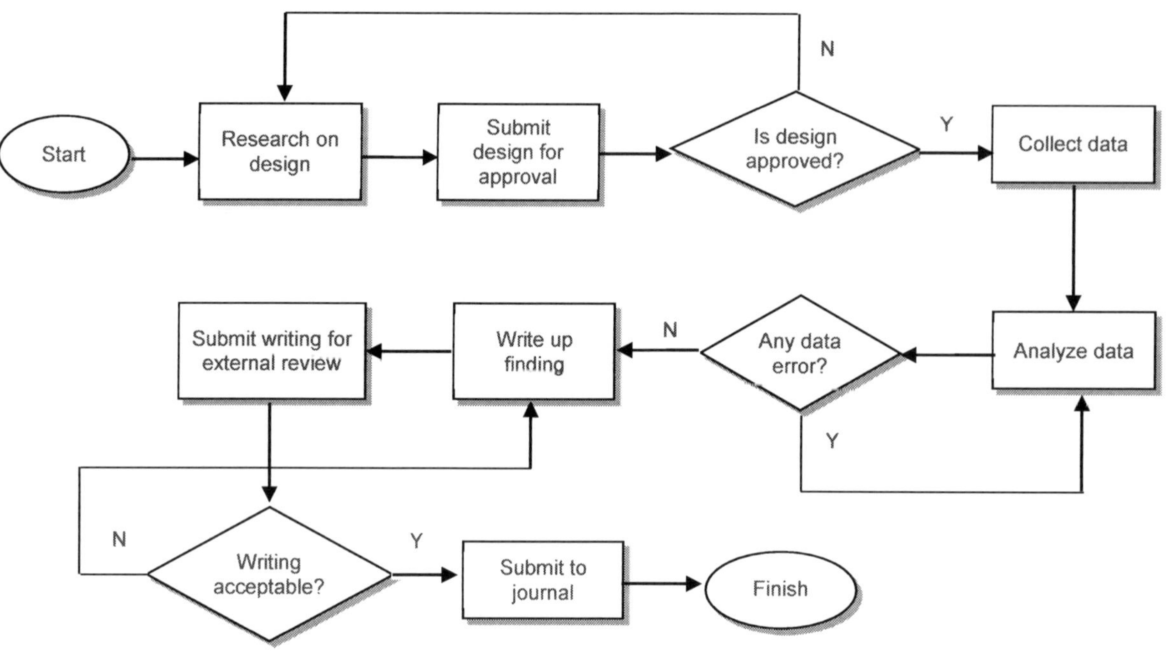

Figure 11-2: Diagramming Technique

Identifying risks using flow charts

To identify project risks and their causes from a flow chart, you need to ask the following questions:

a. What happens early in the process that could cause problems later on?
b. Which activities are out of your control?
c. Are there logical inconsistencies, bottlenecks, or complexities that could create delays, errors, or confusion?

In the above flow chart diagram, events such as "Design Approval" and "Writing Acceptance" may be out of your control since they may be performed by external parties. Any delay in these events will eventually delay your journal submission. Identifying these problems will help you identify a risk in your project.

4. SWOT Analysis

Strengths – Weaknesses – Opportunities - Threats Analysis: This is a brainstorming technique and a key component of strategic development. It can prompt actions and responses.

- **Strengths:** Characteristics of the business or team that give it an advantage over others in the industry
- **Weaknesses:** Characteristics that place the firm at a disadvantage relative to others
- **Opportunities:** External chances to make greater sales or profits in the environment
- **Threats:** External elements in the environment that could cause trouble for the business.

Successful businesses build on their strengths, resolve their weaknesses, exploit opportunities, and protect against or avoid internal and external threats.

STRENGTHS	OPPORTUNITIES
– What are our core competencies? – How strong are we in the market? – Do we have a skilled workforce? – Do we have a strong cash flow? – Do we have a superior reputation?	– What favorable circumstances are we facing? – Are we entering new markets? – Can we position ourselves for new opportunities? – What is the market attractiveness?
WEAKNESSES	**THREATS**
– What are our weak areas that affect the project? – What do we do poorly? – Is our management weak? – Is our organizational structure sufficient to take on the project? – Are we using obsolete technologies?	– What are our competitors doing? – What are potential obstacles? – How rapidly is technology changing our business efforts? – What are the regulatory and legislative aspects threatening the project? – What standards and specifications are potential threats?

Internal	**Build on Strengths** – Patent – Strong brand name – Favorable access to distribution network	**Exploit Opportunities** – Arrival of new technology – Removal of international trade barrier – An unfulfilled customer need
External	**Resolve Weaknesses** – Limited patent protection – Limited working cash – A weak brand name – Lack of experts – No support from management	**Avoid Threats** – New regulation – Increased trade barrier – Emergence of substitute products

5. Monte Carlo Analysis

Monte Carlo analysis involves determining the impact of the identified risks by running simulations to identify the range of possible outcomes for a number of scenarios. A random sampling is performed by using uncertain risk variable inputs to generate the range of outcomes with a confidence measure for each outcome. This is typically done by establishing a mathematical model and then running simulations using this model to estimate the impact of project risks. This technique helps in forecasting the likely outcome of an event and thereby helps in making informed project decisions.

Example: Suppose you are managing a project involving the creation of an accounting automation module. The creation of the module comprises three tasks: designing a database, writing code, and integrating all the components. Based on prior experience or other expert knowledge, you determine the best-case, most likely, and worst-case estimates for each of these activities as given below:

Tasks	Best-case estimate	Most likely estimate	Worst-case estimate
Design database	4 days	6 days	8 days
Write code	5 days	7 days	9 days
Components integration	2 days	4 days	6 days
Total duration	11 days	17 days	23 days

The Monte Carlo simulation randomly selects the input values for the different tasks to generate the possible outcomes. Let us assume that the simulation is run five hundred times. From the above table, we can see that the project can be completed anywhere between eleven and twenty-three days. When the Monte Carlo simulation runs are performed, we can analyze the percentage of times each duration outcome between eleven and twenty-three is obtained. The following table depicts the outcome of a possible Monte Carlo simulation:

Total Project Duration	# of times the simulation result was less than or equal to the Total Project Duration	Percentage
11	5	1%
12	20	4%
13	75	15%
14	90	18%
15	125	25%
16	140	28%
17	165	33%
18	275	55%
19	440	88%
20	475	95%
21	490	98%
22	495	99%
23	500	100%

This can be shown graphically in the following manner:

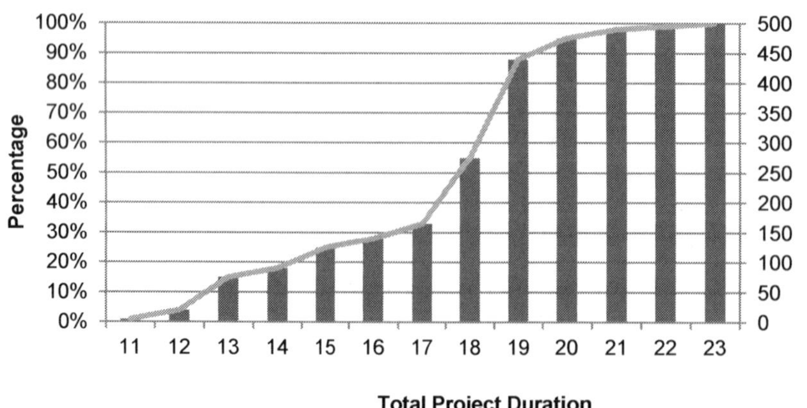

Figure 11-3: Monte Carlo Analysis

What the above table and chart suggest, for example, is that the likelihood of completing the project in seventeen days or less is 33 percent. Similarly, the likelihood of completing the project in nineteen days or less is 88 percent, etc. Note the importance of verifying the possibility of completing the project in seventeen days, as this, according to the most likely estimates, was the time you would expect the project to take. Given the above analysis, it looks much more likely that the project will end up taking anywhere between nineteen and twenty days.

Benefits of using Monte Carlo analysis

Whenever you face a complex estimation or forecasting situation that involves a high degree of complexity and uncertainty, it is best advised to use the Monte Carlo simulation to analyze the likelihood of meeting project objectives based on your risk factors. It is very effective as it is based on evaluation of data numerically, and there is no guesswork involved. The key benefits of using Monte Carlo analysis are listed below:

- It is an easy method for arriving at the likely outcome for an uncertain event and an associated confidence limit for the outcome. The only prerequisites are that you should identify the range limits and the correlation with other variables.
- It is a useful technique for easing decision making based on numerical data to back your decision.
- Monte Carlo simulations are typically useful while analyzing cost and schedule. With the help of Monte Carlo analysis, you can add the cost and schedule risk events to your forecasting model with a greater level of confidence.
- You can also use Monte Carlo analysis to find the likelihood of meeting your project milestones and intermediate goals as it provides the probability of completing the project on any specific day or for any specific amount of cost.
- It brings our attention to facts that are not always obvious by simply looking at the schedule.

Exercise 2: Match the following examples with the four components of Strength, Weaknesses, Opportunities, and Threats (SWOT) analysis.

- A weak brand name
- Favorable access to distribution network
- Limited working cash
- Arrival of new technology
- Emergence of substitute products
- An unfulfilled customer need
- New regulation
- Increased trade barrier
- Strong brand name
- Removal of international trade barrier
- Limited patent protection
- Patent

	Build on Strengths	**Resolve Weaknesses**
Internal		
	Exploit Opportunities	**Avoid Threats**
External		

Project Risk Management Processes

Project risk management is all about identifying, analyzing, responding, and controlling project risk. The risk management plan addresses the project's risk management approach, creates the boundaries, expectations, and general rules for managing risks in the project. The first step is to identify risks where the project team, the project manager, the project sponsor, vendors, stakeholders, end users, and even customers can contribute if required. The next step is to assess the probability and impact of all the risk items. Then it's off to quantitative analysis, where the risks' probability and impact are quantified. The team must make an effort to prevent the risk items from happening and should always identify preventive actions as well as contingency actions. Ongoing monitoring & controlling of the risk events and their impact is essential to effective risk management. The risk register is the project's journal and database of risks, their status, impact, and any supporting detail about the risk events and a key output for all these risk management processes.

PMI identifies six key processes that are associated within the risk management knowledge area.

Processes	Process Groups	Detail	Key Outputs
1. Plan Risk Management	Planning	The process of deciding how to approach, plan, and execute risk management activities.	– Risk Management Plan
2. Identify Risks	Planning	The iterative process of identifying all the risks that may impact the project, documenting them, and identifying their characteristics.	– Risk Register
3. Perform Qualitative Risk Analysis	Planning	The process of prioritizing risks for subsequent further analysis or action by assessing and combining their probability of occurrence and impact.	– Project Documents Updates
4. Perform Quantitative Risk Analysis	Planning	The process of numerically analyzing the effect of identified risks on overall project objectives.	– Project Documents Updates
5. Plan Risk Responses	Planning	The process of developing options and actions to enhance opportunities and reduce threats to project objectives.	– Project Documents Updates
6. Control Risks	Monitoring & Controlling	The process of identifying, analyzing, and planning for newly arising risks, keeping track of the identified risks, reanalyzing existing risks, monitoring trigger conditions, monitoring residual risks, and reviewing the execution and effectiveness of risk responses.	– Work Performance Information – Change Requests

Table 11-3: Six Project Risk Management Processes and Key Outputs

Project Risk Management Processes, Inputs, Tool & Techniques, and Outputs

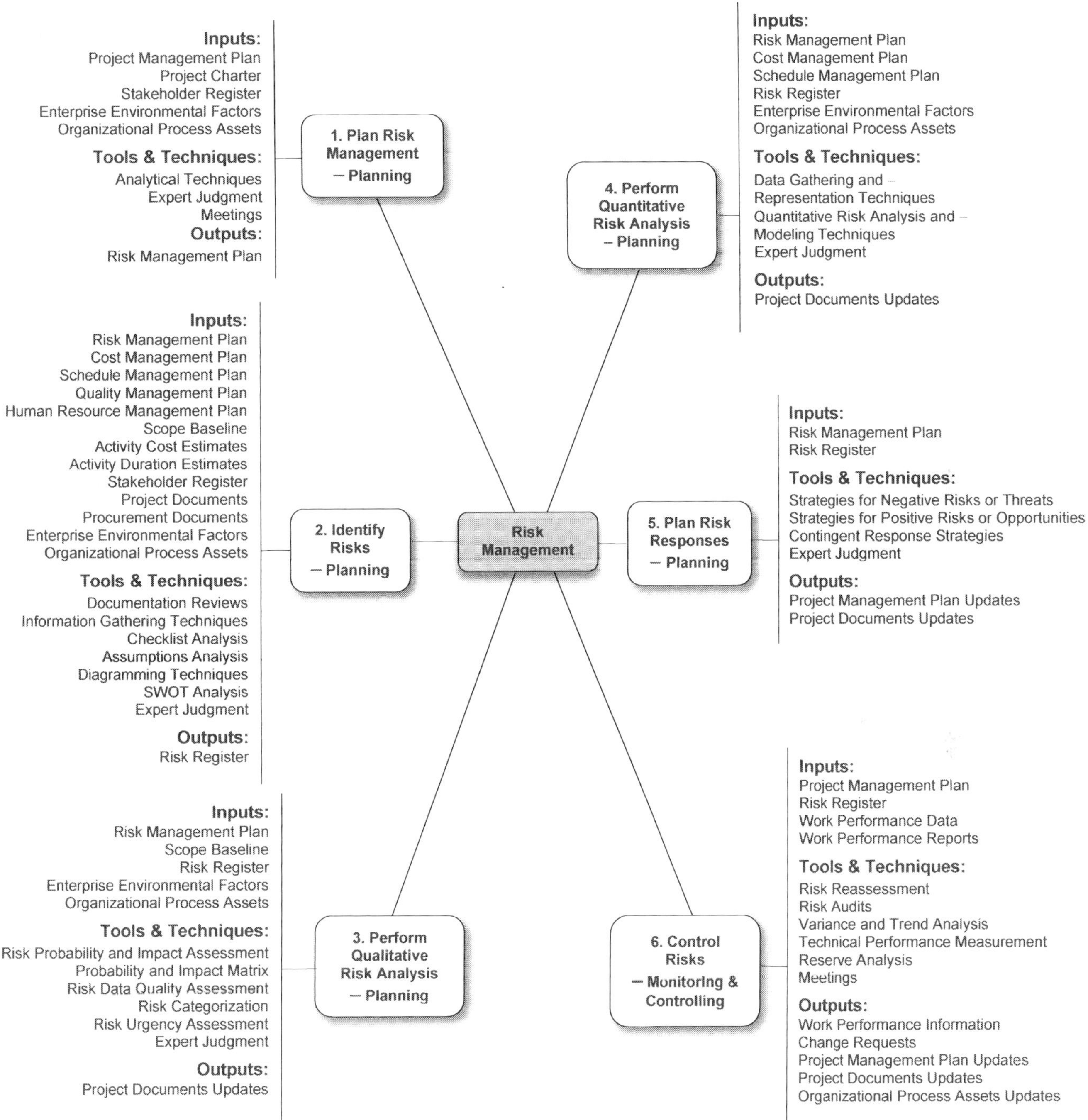

Figure 11-4: Project Risk Management Processes, Inputs, Tool & Techniques, and Outputs

Plan Risk Management

The Plan Risk Management process establishes the basis by which the project manager manages risk by deciding how to approach, plan, and execute risk management activities throughout the life of the project. In this process, all the other remaining five risk management processes are planned. The focus here is not identifying risks but rather how risks will be approached.

As per the PMBOK®, the Plan Risk Management process has the following inputs, tools & techniques, and outputs:

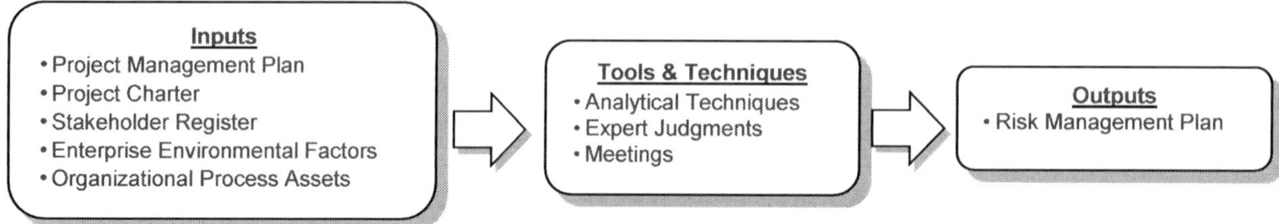

Figure 11-5: Plan Risk Management: Inputs, Tools & Techniques, and Outputs

Plan Risk Management: Inputs

- Project Management Plan
- Project Charter
- Stakeholder Register
- Enterprise Environmental Factors
- Organizational Process Assets

Project Management Plan: All the major components and baselines should be reviewed during risk management planning.

Project Scope Statement: Describes the details of the project's deliverables and may contain some early defined risks.

Cost Management Plan: Defines how risk budgets, contingencies, and management reserves will be reported and assessed.

Schedule Management Plan: Defines how schedule contingencies will be reported and assessed.

Communications Management Plan: Gives information about stakeholders' concerns for particular risks and also how, when, how frequently, and what should be communicated to them.

Project Charter: The project charter contains valuable information about high-level requirements, project description, project objectives, high-level risks, constraints, and assumptions.

Stakeholder Register: The stakeholder register lists all of the key stakeholders, their contact information, and their roles in the projects. These stakeholders may provide valuable input about project risks.

Enterprise Environmental Factors: Organizational risk attitudes, threshold, tolerances, and other relevant enterprise environmental factors may influence the Plan Risk Management process.

Organizational Process Assets: Predefined approaches to risk management such as standard templates or common definitions of terms, stakeholder registers, roles and responsibilities, risk categories, lessons learned, common definitions of concepts and terms, and historical information may influence the Plan Risk Management process.

Plan Risk Management: Tools & Techniques

- Analytical Techniques
- Expert Judgments
- Meetings

Analytical Techniques: Various analytical techniques such as stakeholder risk profile analysis, and strategic risk scoring may be used to identify stakeholder risk attitude, appetite, threshold, and tolerance. This kind of assessment will be helpful to develop an overall risk management approach and to allocate appropriate resources to execute risk management activities.

Expert Judgments: Judgment and expert opinions can be gathered from senior management, project team members, project managers from similar projects, subject matter experts, industry groups and consultants, other units within the organization, and additional people to develop the risk management plan.

Meetings: Project team members with responsibility to manage risk, along with key stakeholders, and others as needed discuss the approach and content of the Risk Management Plan in the planning meeting. Risk cost elements, contingency reserves, risk management responsibilities, definitions of terms and concepts, probability and impact, and other elements will be tailored to the project at hand.

Plan Risk Management: Output

- Risk Management Plan

Risk Management Plan: The risk management plan is like a roadmap to all other risk processes that describes how risk management will be structured and performed on the project.
The risk management plan may include the following:

Methodology: Defines approaches, tools, and data sources for risk management.

Roles and Responsibilities: Defines the roles and responsibilities and sometimes includes non-team members who may have certain roles in risk management.

Budgeting: Includes the cost for risk management activities.

Timing: Since new risks can be identified and the degree of risk may change as the project progresses, this section defines when and how often to take risk management measurements.

Risk Categories: A group of potential causes for risk, which can be grouped into categories such as technical, political, external, project, and environmental. In order to systematically identify risks to a consistent level of detail, we can use the form of a simple list of categories or a Risk Breakdown Structure (RBS). It's a comprehensive way of ordering risks according to their source.

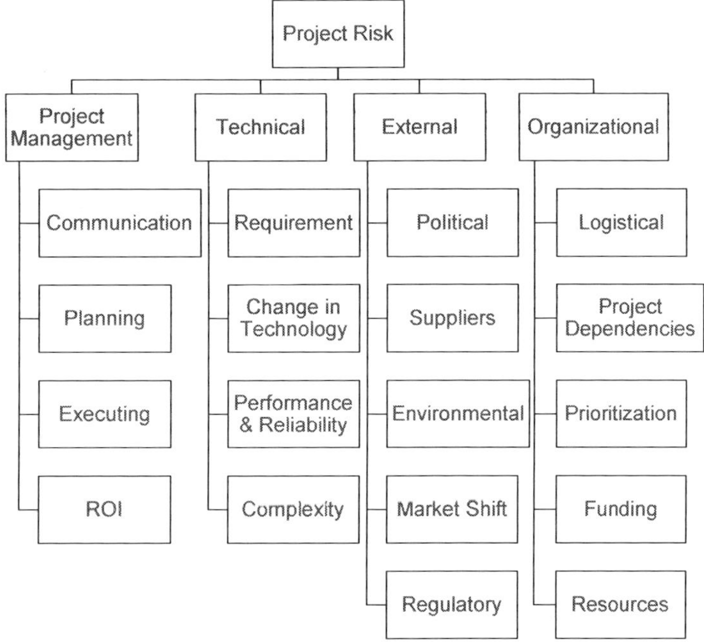

Figure 11-6: Risk Breakdown Structure (RBS)

Risk may be categorized into different types of industry or application areas in which the project is running. For instance, a construction project may have several risks in the external risk category, whereas IT projects will most likely have many risks that fall in the technical category.

Definition of risk probability and impact: The levels of probability and impact are tailored for use in the subsequent project. Risks are prioritized according to their probability and potential impact to meet project objectives.

Probability and Impact Matrix: This matrix is based on the principle that a risk has two primary dimensions:

- **Probability**: A risk is an event that "may" occur. The probability of it occurring can range anywhere from just above 0 percent to just below 100 percent.
- **Impact:** A risk, by its very nature, always has an impact. However, the size of the impact varies in terms of cost and impact on health, human life, or some other critical factor.
- Ratings are assigned to risks based on their assessed probability and impact. This rating helps to determine which risks warrant immediate responses and which ones should be put on the watch list for later review.
- Descriptive terms or numeric values are used depending on the organization.

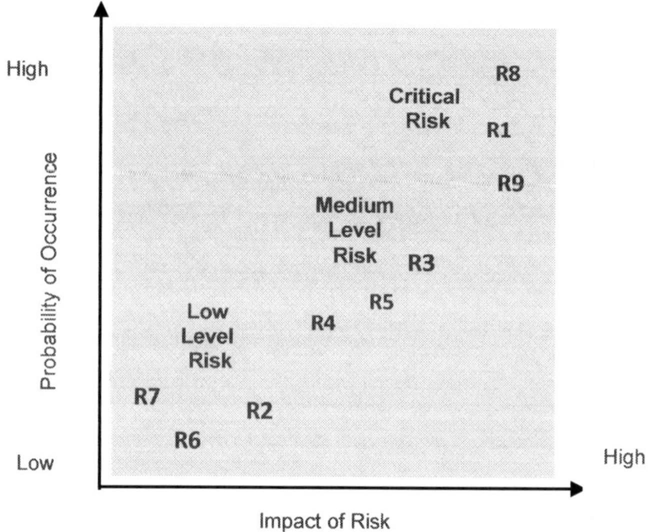

Figure 11-7: Probability/Impact Matrix

- **Low impact/Low probability:** Risks in the bottom left corner are low level and can be ignored most of the time.
- **Low impact/High probability:** Risks in the top left corner are of moderate importance, and we can cope with them and move on; however, we should try to reduce the likelihood that they'll occur.
- **High impact/Low probability:** Risks in the bottom right corner are of high importance, but they're very unlikely to happen. For these we should do what we can to reduce the impact and should have a contingency plan in place.
- **High impact/High probability:** Risks toward the top right corner are of critical importance with top priorities, and we must pay close attention to them.

Revised Stakeholder Tolerances: Stakeholder risk tolerances may be revised as they apply to the specific project and should not be implied but uncovered during initiation and clarified and refined continually.

Reporting Formats: Describes the content and format of the risk register or any other reports containing risk information.

Tracking: Defines how the risk process will be audited and documents how risk activities will be recorded for the benefit of current and future projects.

Identify Risks

Identify Risks is an iterative process of identifying all the risks that may impact the project, documenting them, and identifying their characteristics.

Risk identification is an iterative process as new risks will evolve throughout the project life cycle. Depending on the nature of the project and associated risks, the frequency of iteration and participation of project team members, stakeholders, subject matter experts, the risk management team, and others in risk identification activities will vary. In order to effectively analyze and develop risk response strategies, identified risks should be fully understood.

The single output in this process, the risk register (which is a list of all identified risks, causes, and potential responses to these risks), is developed at this point.

As per the PMBOK®, the Identify Risks process has the following inputs, tools & techniques, and outputs:

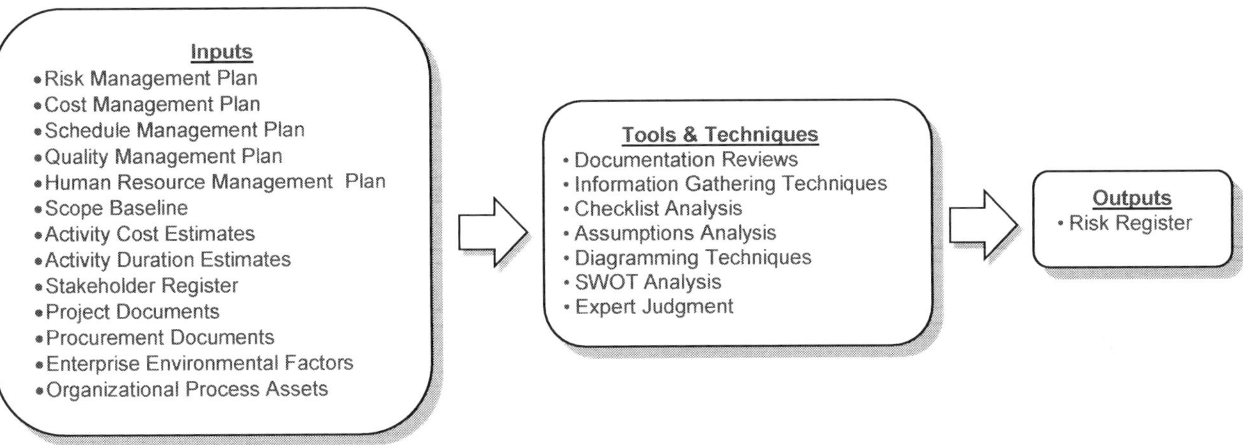

Figure 11-8: Identify Risks: Inputs, Tools & Techniques, and Outputs

Identify Risks: Inputs

- Risk Management Plan
- Cost Management Plan
- Schedule Management Plan
- Quality Management Plan
- Human Resource Management Plan
- Scope Baseline
- Activity Cost Estimates
- Activity Duration Estimates
- Stakeholder Register
- Project Documents
- Procurement Documents
- Enterprise Environmental Factors
- Organizational Process Assets

Risk Management Plan: Risk categories, Risk Breakdown Structure (RBS), roles and responsibilities, and provisions for risk management activities in the budget and schedule are key inputs.

Cost Management Plan: The project-specific approach, process, and controls to the cost management plan may generate or eliminate risk by its nature or structure.

Schedule Management Plan: The project-specific schedule objectives and expectations found in the schedule management plan may be impacted by risk in the project.

Quality Management Plan: The quality measures and metrics found in the quality management plan are used for identifying risks.

Human Resource Management Plan: Various components of the human resource management plan such as roles and responsibilities, organizational charts, the staffing management plan, and other items are key inputs in risk identification.

Scope Baseline: The project scope statement contains the assumptions and uncertainties in project assumptions that can be potential causes of risks. Also, risks can be identified and tracked at the control account and the work package levels of the WBS.

Activity Cost Estimates: These estimates provide a quantitative assessment of the likely cost to complete scheduled activities, and a review may help verify if the estimates are sufficient to complete activities.

Activity Duration Estimates: These estimates help to identify risks related to the time allocated for activities or for the entire project.

Stakeholder Register: The stakeholder register will provide information about the stakeholders who will be interviewed or who will otherwise participate in identifying risks.

Project Documents: Project documents proven to be valuable in identifying risks include but are not limited to assumptions log, work performance reports, earned value reports, network diagrams, baselines, and other project information.

Procurement Documents: Procurement documents will be a key input to the Identify Risks process if there is a need in the project to purchase or acquire goods, services, or results from outside the organization. It is essential to identify project risks and incorporate mitigation and allocation of these risks into the contract.

Enterprise Environmental Factors: These include a published checklist, benchmarking, industry studies, risk attitudes, academic studies, and other factors that are proven to be valuable in identifying risks.

Organizational Process Assets: The organizational process assets proven to be valuable in identifying risks include but are not limited to risk statement templates, lessons learned, project files including actual data, and organizational and project process controls.

Identify Risks: Tools & Techniques

- Documentation Reviews
- Information Gathering Techniques
- Checklist Analysis
- Assumptions Analysis
- Diagramming Techniques
- SWOT Analysis
- Expert Judgment

Documentation Reviews: A structured and organized review of project plans and assumptions, prior similar project files, contracts, lessons learned, articles, and other documents can help uncover risks and confirm completeness, correctness, and consistency.

Information Gathering Techniques: There are several techniques for gathering information for risk identification, such as:

Brainstorming:

- The most frequently used method of risk identification.
- One idea helps generate another.
- The goal is to create a comprehensive list of possible risks without consideration of probability or consequences.

Delphi Technique: The Delphi technique is an anonymously directed survey and a way to reach a consensus of experts.

Interviewing: Interviewing project participants, stakeholders, or subject matter experts helps to identify relevant risks.

Root Cause Analysis: Reorganizing risks by causes identifies more risks.

Checklist Analysis: This analysis uses a Risk Breakdown Structure (RBS) either from the current project or when available from historical information or industry resources to check off items and ensure all major risks and risk categories are being evaluated.

- It can be a quick and easy way to start building the list of risks.
- There is no such thing as a comprehensive checklist; thus, care should be taken to explore items not found on the checklist.
- It is important to review and revise checklists at the close of projects to improve them for future use.

Assumptions Analysis: This is the analysis of the validity of assumptions, hypotheses, and scenarios developed in project initiation to identify risks from inaccuracies, incompleteness, and inconsistencies of assumptions. The assumptions that turn out to be invalid should be evaluated, qualitatively and quantitatively analyzed, and planned for just like other risks.

Diagramming Techniques:

Cause and Effect Diagrams: Diagramming techniques include diagrams such as Ishikawa or fishbone diagrams and are useful for identifying causes of risks.

System or Process Flow Chart: This chart is a graphical representation of a complex process flow that shows how various elements of a system are interrelated and the mechanism of causation.

Influence Diagram: This chart shows how a set of influencers may influence others and affect outcomes. For instance, a delay in receiving equipment may influence other factors, such as triggering overtime work or triggering a quality issue due to lack of time to perform tasks.

SWOT Analysis: This technique examines the project from each of the SWOT (strengths, weaknesses, opportunities, and threats) perspectives to identify opportunities for the project arising from organizational strengths and to identify threats from organizational weaknesses.

Expert Judgment: Risks can be identified directly by experts with relevant experience of similar projects or business areas.

Identify Risks: Outputs

- Risk Register

Risk Register: This register contains primary outputs from the Risk Identification process and becomes an essential input into the remaining risk management processes. This register may be updated throughout the project life cycle.

List of identified risks: This list includes identified potential risks with reasonable descriptions.

List of potential responses: Potential responses to a risk may sometimes be identified at this stage and can be very useful as inputs to the Plan Risk Responses process.

Root causes: Root causes of the risks are documented to reassess risk later in the project as well as to be used as historical records in a future project.

Updated risk categories: The Risk Breakdown Structure (RBS) may need to be updated.

Category	Risk ID	Risk Description	Potential Response	Root Cause
Political	R01	A change in government in the upcoming elections leads to a reduction in project funding, scope, or sponsorship.	Secure project sponsorship from leaders of the political parties likely to come into power.	Change in government

Table 11-4: Fragment of a Risk Register

Exercise 3: List activities that you will perform to identify risks in your project.

Perform Qualitative Risk Analysis

Perform Qualitative Risk Analysis is the process of prioritizing risks by assessing and combining their probability of occurrence and impact to the project if they occur. This fast, relatively easy to perform, and cost effective process ensures that the right emphasis is on the right risk areas as per their ranking and priority and helps to allocate adequate time and resources for them.

Even though numbers are used for the rating in Perform Qualitative Risk Analysis, it is a subjective evaluation and should be performed throughout the project.

As per the PMBOK®, the Perform Qualitative Risk Analysis process has the following inputs, tools & techniques, and outputs:

Figure 11-9: Perform Qualitative Risk Analysis: Inputs, Tools & Techniques, and Outputs

Perform Qualitative Risk Analysis: Inputs

- Risk Management Plan
- Scope Baseline
- Risk Register
- Enterprise Environmental Factors
- Organizational Process Assets

Risk Management Plan: Key elements include the overall approach to the risk, roles and responsibilities for conducting risk management, budgets, schedule, risk categories, definition of probability and impact, and stakeholder risk tolerances.

Scope Baseline: Projects of a recurrent type tend to have better understood risks, but highly complex projects have more uncertainty; thus, it is recommended to examine the scope baseline to evaluate the uncertainty and complexity of the project.

Risk Register: The risk register contains information about identified risks that will be used to assess probability and impact.

Enterprise Environmental Factors: Commercial risk databases from a relevant industry or other proprietary sources and research and study of similar projects by risk specialists will provide useful context and insight to risk assessment.

Organizational Process Assets: Information about prior projects, internal or commercially available risk databases, and studies of similar projects by risk experts may be helpful.

Perform Qualitative Risk Analysis: Tools & Techniques

- Risk Probability and Impact Assessment
- Probability and Impact Matrix
- Risk Data Quality Assessment
- Risk Categorization
- Risk Urgency Assessment
- Expert Judgment

Risk Probability and Impact Assessment: Assessment is done for each risk to investigate the likelihood that each specific risk will occur and to assess the potential effect on the project objectives, such as time, cost, scope, or quality. It is done by interviews or meetings with participants selected for their familiarity with the risk categories.

Probability: Determining the risk probability is sometimes difficult as it is mostly defined using expert judgment. The probability is expressed as a number from 0.0 to 1.0.

Probability 0.0: There is no probability that the event will occur.

Probability 1.0: There is 100 percent certainty that the event will occur.

Impact: Impacts are the possible outcomes of the risk event. The risk impact scale can be of the following two types:

Ordinal scale: This scale assigns values as high, medium, low, or a combination of these.

Cardinal scale: This numeric scale is expressed as values from 0.0 to 1.0 and can be stated in equal (linear) or unequal (nonlinear) increments.

The following risk impact scale for scope, time, cost, and quality objectives is based on both ordinal and cardinal values.

Objectives	Very Low 0.05	Low 0.20	Medium 0.40	High 0.60	Very High 0.80
Scope	Barely noticeable	Minor areas are affected	Major areas are affected	Unacceptable to sponsor	End item is useless
Time	Barely noticeable	<5 percent time increase	>5 percent to <12 percent time increase	>12 percent to <20 percent time increase	>20 percent time increase
Cost	Barely noticeable	<5 percent cost increase	>5 percent to <12 percent cost increase	>12 percent to <20 percent cost increase	>20 percent cost increase
Quality	Barely noticeable	<5 percent of components are impacted	>5 percent to <10 percent of components are impacted	>10 percent to <20 percent of components are impacted	End item is useless

Table 11-5: Risk Impact Scale

Probability and Impact Matrix: It is a tool used to determine whether a risk is considered low, moderate, or high by combining the two dimensions of risk: its probability of occurring and its impact on objectives. Risks can be prioritized before further quantitative analysis, and each of these two values are given a ranking (such as high, medium, and low) and are multiplied together to get a risk score to set the priority.

Suppose your experts believe that there will be a 10 percent time increase in the project. According to the risk impact scale in Table 11-6, this risk carries a medium impact with a value of 0.40. Also, the team has determined that there is a 0.4 probability of the risk event occurring. According to the probability and impact matrix on the next page, the risk carries an overall score of 0.16 (0.4 x 0.4) and falls into the low threshold.

Probability	Very Low 0.05	Low 0.20	Medium 0.40	High 0.60	Very High 0.80
0.2	0.01	0.04	0.08	0.12	0.16
0.4	0.02	0.08	0.16	0.24	0.32
0.6	0.03	0.12	0.24	0.36	0.48
0.8	0.04	0.16	0.32	0.48	0.64

Table 11-6: Probability and Impact Matrix

Risk Data Quality Assessment: Risk data needs to be accurate, unbiased, and credible and should be objectively evaluated to find out how useful it is. This assessment examines how well the risk is understood and considers factors, such as accuracy, quality, reliability, and integrity about the risk. It may be necessary to gather better quality data if data quality is not up to standard.

Risk Categorization: Grouping risks by common causes (categories) can lead to developing effective risk responses. A Risk Breakdown Structure (RBS) is a common way to organize identified risks into categories.

Risk Urgency Assessment: Risks that cannot wait and require near-term responses may be considered more urgent to address. Indicators of priority can include time to affect a risk's response, symptoms and warning signs, and the risk rating. For instance, if you find out about a major concern with the foundation, it would require immediate attention while another risk such as a crack in the wall, might be less important.

Expert Judgment: Expert judgment is required to assess the probability and impact of each risk.

Perform Qualitative Risk Analysis: Outputs

- Project Documents Updates

Project Documents Updates: Various project documents will be updated such as the following:

Risk Register Updates:

Relative ranking or priority list of project risks: Uses the probability and impact matrix to focus attention on those items of high significance.

Risks grouped by categories: Reveals common root causes that require particular attention.

List of risks requiring response in the near term: Risks that require an urgent response and those that can be handled later can be put into different groups.

List of risks for additional analysis and response: Some risks may warrant more analysis.

Watch lists of low-priority risks: Keep an eye on risks not assessed as important.

Trends in qualitative risk analysis results: Trends for particular risks may become apparent—need to find out if the risk is increasing, decreasing, or staying the same.

Category	Risk ID	Risk Description	Potential Response	Root Cause	Probability	Impact
Political	R01	A change in government in the upcoming elections leads to a reduction in project funding, scope, or sponsorship.	Secure project sponsorship from leaders of the political parties likely to come into power.	Change in government	Medium	High

Table 11-7: Fragment of a Risk Register

Assumptions Log Updates: The assumptions log should be revisited as new information becomes available about risks during the Perform Qualitative Risk Analysis process. Assumptions made earlier could change or may no longer be valid; thus, the assumptions log needs to be updated to accommodate new changes.

Perform Quantitative Risk Analysis

Perform Quantitative Risk Analysis is the process of numerically analyzing the effect of identified risks on overall project objectives. It mostly performs numerical analysis of the probability and impact of risks moved forward from the Perform Qualitative Risk Analysis process.

The key objectives of this process are to:

- Perform sensitivity analysis to figure out which risks have the most impact.
- Perform further investigation on the highest-rated risks.
- Determine how much schedule and cost reserves are needed in the project.
- Determine which risks require the most attention and planning.
- Figure out the realistic, quantified probability of achieving project goals and objectives.
- Develop realistic scope, schedule, or cost targets that are achievable.

This numerical evaluation is not needed for all projects and may be skipped if required to move on to risk response planning. As per the PMBOK®, the Perform Quantitative Risk Analysis process has the following inputs, tools & techniques, and outputs:

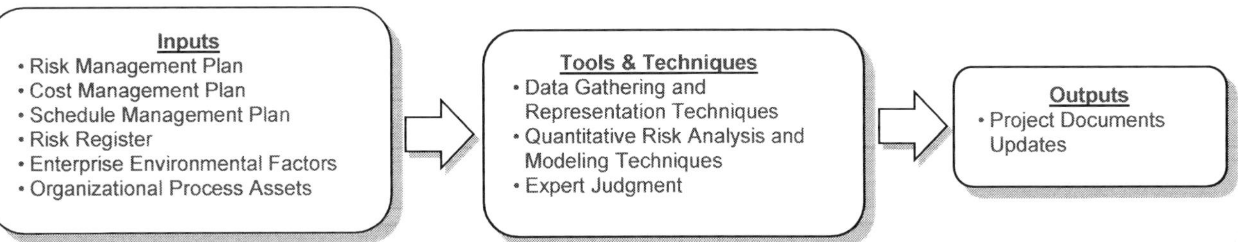

Figure 11-10: Perform Quantitative Risk Analysis: Inputs, Tools & Techniques, and Outputs

Perform Quantitative Risk Analysis: Inputs

- Risk Management Plan
- Cost Management Plan
- Schedule Management Plan
- Risk Register
- Enterprise Environmental Factors
- Organizational Process Assets

Risk Management Plan: Key elements include the overall approach to the risk, roles and responsibilities for conducting risk management, budgets, schedule, risk categories, definition of probability and impact, and stakeholder risk tolerances.

Cost Management Plan: Cost is easily quantified; thus, the cost management plan helps with quantitative analysis in establishing and managing risk reserves.

Schedule Management Plan: Schedule is easily quantified; thus, the schedule management plan helps in quantitative analysis in establishing and managing risk reserves.

Risk Register: The risk register contains information about identified risks that will be used to perform quantitative analysis.

Enterprise Environmental Factors: Commercial risk databases from a relevant industry or other proprietary sources, research and study of similar projects by risk specialists, and other elements will provide useful context and insight to risk assessment.

Organizational Process Assets: Risk information from prior projects, organizational internal risk databases, and studies of similar projects by risk experts may be helpful.

Perform Quantitative Risk Analysis: Tools &Techniques

- Data Gathering and Representation Techniques
- Quantitative Risk Analysis and Modeling Techniques
- Expert Judgment

Data Gathering and Representation Techniques:

Interviewing: Subject matter experts are interviewed about the probability and impact of risks on project objectives; pessimistic, optimistic, and realistic values associated with each risk may be created as per experts' feedback.

Probability distributions: It is a mathematical representation that shows the probability of an event occurring and is usually expressed as a table or a graph. It is beneficial as it looks at the real probability of an event occurring and helps to make an appropriate decision to approach it.

Example: A probability graph for getting tails when you flip a coin nine times will be something similar to the following graph.

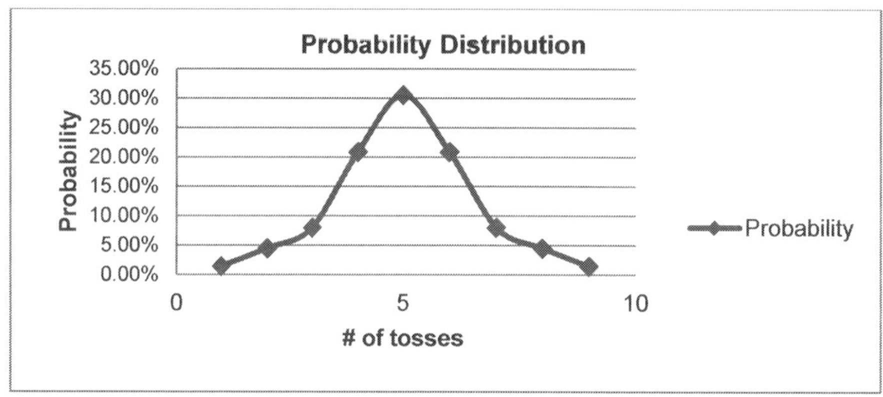

Figure 11-11: Probability Graph

Quantitative Risk Analysis and Modeling Techniques:

Sensitivity Analysis: It helps to determine which risks have the most potential impact on a project, or in other words, whether the occurrence of a particular threat would merely be an inconvenience or whether it would ruin the project.

A tornado diagram can be used to display sensitivity analysis data by examining all the uncertain elements at their baseline values. It gives a quick overview of how much the project will be impacted by various elements, and the element with the greatest impact on the project appears at the top. This diagram can be used to determine sensitivity in cost, time, and quality objectives and will be helpful to determine a detailed response plan for the elements with greater impacts.

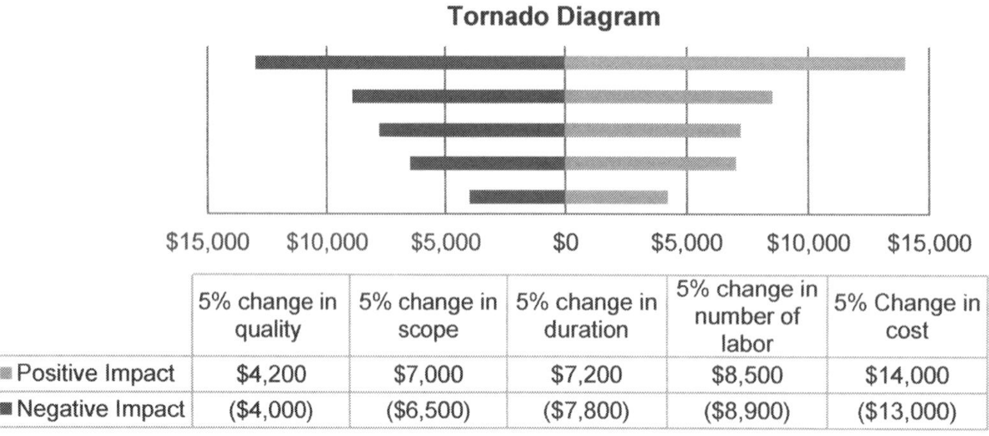

	5% change in quality	5% change in scope	5% change in duration	5% change in number of labor	5% Change in cost
Positive Impact	$4,200	$7,000	$7,200	$8,500	$14,000
Negative Impact	($4,000)	($6,500)	($7,800)	($8,900)	($13,000)

Figure 11-12: Tornado Diagram

Expected Monetary Value Analysis: A statistical concept that calculates the average outcome when the future includes scenarios that may or may not happen.

Decision Tree Analysis: Diagrams that show the sequence of interrelated decisions and the expected results of choosing one alternative over another.

Modeling and Simulation: Techniques such as Monte Carlo analysis may be helpful.

Expert Judgment: Experts with relevant, recent experience will be very helpful in reviewing data, tools, and methodologies used in risk analysis. Experts will help determine when and what appropriate tools to use by identifying their weaknesses and strengths.

Perform Quantitative Risk Analysis: Outputs

- Project Documents Updates

Project Documents Updates:

Risk Register Updates: The risk register is further updated in this process. Updates include the following main components:

Probabilistic analysis of the project: This includes estimates of potential project schedule and cost outcomes with their associated confidence levels.

Probability of achieving cost and time objectives: Understanding the risks facing the project, the probability of achieving the objectives under the current plan can be estimated.

Prioritized list of quantified risks: List of risks including those that pose the greatest threat or present the greatest opportunity to the project.

Trends in quantitative risk analysis results: Trends may become apparent that lead to conclusions affecting risk responses.

Plan Risk Responses

Plan Risk Responses is the process of figuring out options and actions needed to reduce threats and enhance opportunities to project objectives. It addresses risks by their priority and includes identification and assignment of a risk response owner for each risk item. Risk responses must be:

- Appropriate as per the significance of the risk
- Focused on eliminating threats before they happen
- Focused on making sure that opportunities happen
- Focused on decreasing the probability and impact of threats
- Focused on increasing the probability and impact of opportunities
- Cost effective
- Timely, realistic, and must have a contingency and fallback plan (if contingency plans are not effective or only partially effective)
- Approved from all parties involved

The Plan Risk Responses is an extremely beneficial process as you eliminate threats that can cause stress, delays, and additional cost to the project while still in the planning process. As a result, your project will go smoother and faster, with significantly fewer impediments, because preventable problems were solved before they happened.

As per the PMBOK®, the Plan Risk Responses process has the following inputs, tools & techniques, and outputs:

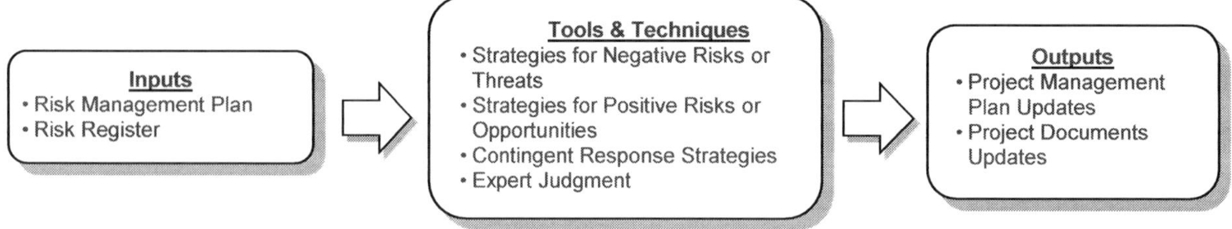

Figure 11-13: Plan Risk Responses: Inputs, Tools & Techniques, and Outputs

Plan Risk Responses: Inputs

- Risk Management Plan
- Risk Register

Risk Management Plan: Key elements include the overall approach to risk, roles and responsibilities for conducting risk management, budgets, schedule, risk categories, definition of probability and impact, and stakeholder risk tolerances.

Risk Register: The risk register refers to the list of identified risks with potential responses, root causes, categories, and probability and impact assessed.

Plan Risk Responses: Tools & Techniques

- Strategies for Negative Risks or Threats
- Strategies for Positive Risks or Opportunities
- Contingent Response Strategies
- Expert Judgment

Strategies for Negative Risks or Threats

Four strategies typically deal with threats or risks that may have negative impacts on project objectives if they occur.

Strategy	Detail	Example
Avoid	Eliminate the threat by eliminating the cause or changing the project management plan.	– Remove a work package or a person. – Use a slower but reliable technology instead of a cutting-edge one to avoid associated risk. – Extend the schedule, change the strategy, or cut scope.
Mitigate	Risk mitigation simply means taking actions to reduce the probability and/or impact of an adverse risk event to an acceptable threshold.	– Constructing the building outside of the rainy season to mitigate the risk of weather damage. – Designing redundancy in the system, taking early action, adopting less complex processes, conducting more tests, and developing prototypes to reduce the impact and probability.
Transfer	Transferring is shifting the negative impact of a threat, along with the ownership of the response, to a third party to make it their responsibility. It only gives another party responsibility for its management but does not eliminate the risk. It nearly always involves payment to the third party for taking on the risk.	Insurance bonds, warranties, guarantees, and contracts.
Accept	Since it is seldom possible to eliminate all risks, and also the cost or impact of avoiding, transferring, and mitigating is too high, acceptance can be the preferred strategy. It indicates that the project team is simply accepting the risk and will continue with the project. – Passive acceptance requires no action. – The active acceptance strategy is to establish contingency reserves to handle threats.	We are accepting the risk associated with getting out of bed and can have any kind of accident every day.

Table 11-8: Four Responses for Dealing with Threats

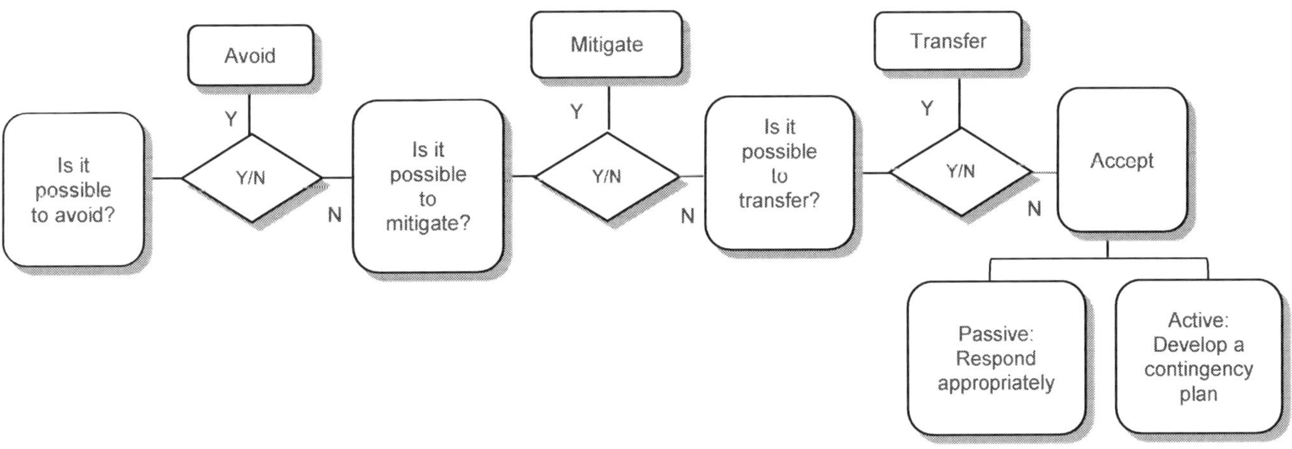

Figure 11-14: Threat or Negative Risks Decision Flow Chart

Strategies for Positive Risks or Opportunities

Four responses are suggested to deal with risks and positive impacts on project objectives.

Strategy	Detail	Example
Exploit (opposite of Avoid)	Seeks to eliminate the uncertainty by making the opportunity definitely happen.	Adding work or changing the project to make sure the opportunity occurs.
Enhance (opposite of Mitigate)	By influencing the underlying risk triggers, this strategy increases the size, probability, likelihood, and positive impact of an opportunity.	A cruise company might add tours to popular destinations during holidays in order to enhance traffic and profitability.
Share (opposite of Transfer)	Sharing a positive risk involves working with another party or allocating ownership to a third party who is best able to capture the opportunity for the benefit of the project.	Forming risk-sharing partnerships or joint ventures to secure a large project.
Accept	Accepting is not actively pursuing an opportunity but taking advantage of it if it comes along.	

Table 11-9: Four Responses for Dealing with Opportunities

Whenever we are responding to either threats or opportunities, we need to make sure that

1. Our strategy is timely and appropriate to the severity of the risk.
2. One response can be used to address many risks, and more than one response can be used to address the same risk.
3. We should always engage the experts, team members, and stakeholders in identifying and implemeting strategies.

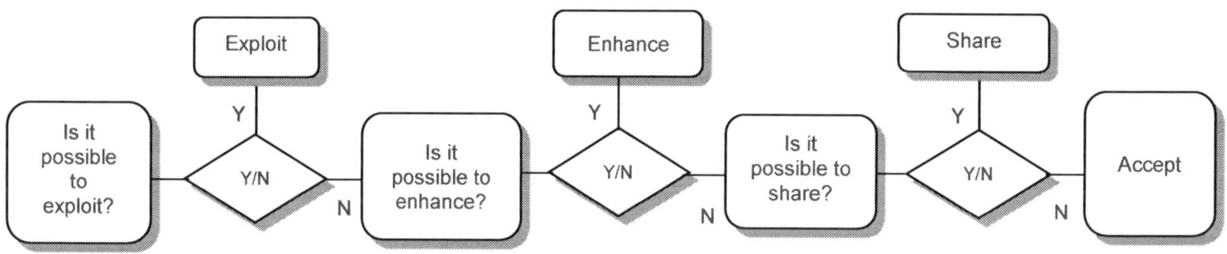

Figure 11-15: Opportunity or Positive Risk Decision Flow Chart

Contingent Response Strategy: Some responses are designed for use only if certain events occur, but that decision is contingent upon certain conditions.

Expert Judgment: Inputs from knowledgeable parties with specialized education, knowledge, skills, experience, or training in establishing risk responses to identify the actions to be taken on a specific and defined risk.

Plan Risk Responses: Outputs

- Project Management Plan Updates
- Project Documents Updates

Project Management Plan Updates: The creation of risk response strategies may result in modifications and updates to the schedule, cost, quality, human resource, and procurement management plans as well as to the scope, schedule, and cost baselines.

Risk response strategies, once agreed to, are fed back into the appropriate processes in other knowledge areas (e.g., budget and schedule).

Project Documents Updates: Project documents that may be updated include but are not limited to the assumptions log, technical documents, as well as the risk register.

Risk Register Updates:

Residual risks: Risks that remain after execution of risk response planning and for which contingency and fallback plans can be created.

Contingency plan: The specific action that will be taken if opportunities or threats occur.

Risk owners: The risk owner for a particular risk is responsible for implementing the actions defined by mitigation and the contingency plan in risk management.

Secondary risk: A new risk created due to the implementation of the selected risk response strategy.

Risk triggers: Risk triggers are symptoms or warning signs that a potential risk is about to occur in the project. For instance, a key team member searching for a better job opportunity is a warning sign that the person may be leaving the team soon, causing schedule delay, increased cost, and other issues.

Fallback plan: Specific action or Plan B that will be taken if the contingency plan or Plan A is not effective.

Workarounds: Unplanned responses developed to deal with the occurrence of unanticipated risk events.

Reserves: For time and cost management, there are contingency (known unknown—residual risk) and management reserves (unknown unknown). These reserves are calculated based on quantitative risk analysis, the organization's risk tolerance, and thresholds.

Category	Risk ID	Risk Description	Potential Response	Root Cause	Probability	Impact
Political	R01	A change in government in the upcoming elections leads to a reduction in project funding, scope, or sponsorship.	Secure project sponsorship from leaders of the political parties likely to come into power.	Change in government	Medium	High

Risk ID	Preventive Actions	Action Resource	Action Date	Contingent Actions	Action Resource	Action Date
R01	Secure project sponsorship from leaders of the political parties likely to come into power	Project Manager	Feb 5	Structure the project so that the scope can be reduced without having to close the project	Project Manager	Feb 20

Table 11-10: Updated Risk Register

Exercise 4: Determine the name of each risk response strategy described below.

Description of Strategy	Risk Response Strategy
1. Combine orders for the equipment to purchase over thirty-plus items at once so as to secure a lower price.	
2. You decide to outsource difficult components of a complex project to a more experienced company.	
3. You plan your way around the construction site and take another highway to go to your destination.	
4. Assign a team member to work closely with the members of the company working on your project to learn about potential project delays as early as possible.	
5. You have selected a new but more reliable and reputed vendor to avoid delay in delivery of equipment.	
6. One of your new team members is not performing well, and you send her for additional training.	
7. Your team members are continuously having issues and conflicts, and you decide to train the team on conflict resolution strategies.	
8. Modify the project plan in a way that a work package or activity will no longer be needed.	
9. You plan the trip using the original route and accept the risk of running into construction and possible delay.	
10. You decide to develop a prototype for a risky piece of equipment so that you can get better feedback from the stakeholders.	
11. A resource is having conflicts with several team members, and you remove the troublesome resource from the project.	
12. Move a work package to next month when a resource with more experience and a higher level of productivity is available to be assigned to the project.	
13. You do not have the cash flow required to bid for a project, so you form a joint venture with another organization.	

Exercise 5: You are working as a project manager on a construction project for a reputed builder. What is the cost contingency reserve that you would use if your analysis comes up with the following scenarios?

Risk	Probability	Impact
There is an architectural design defect.	10 percent	– $9,000
Construction may take less time than expected.	25 percent	$6,000
There is a delay in the receipt of construction materials.	35 percent	– $11,000
Construction materials will be cheaper than expected.	15 percent	$8,000
Seasonal labor will be more expensive than expected.	20 percent	– $4000

Control Risks

Control Risks is the process of identifying, analyzing, and planning for newly arising risks. The process also keeps track of the identified risks, reanalyzes existing risks, monitors trigger conditions, monitors residual risks, chooses alternative strategies, executes a contingency or fallback plan, takes corrective actions, and reviews the execution and effectiveness of risk responses. This process applies techniques such as variance and trend analyses.

The Control Risks process also determines if:

- Project assumptions are still valid.
- Risk, as assessed, has changed state and can be retired.
- Proper risk management policies are being followed.
- Contingency reserves of cost or schedule should be modified in line with the risks of the project.

As per the PMBOK®, the Control Risks process has the following inputs, tools & techniques, and outputs:

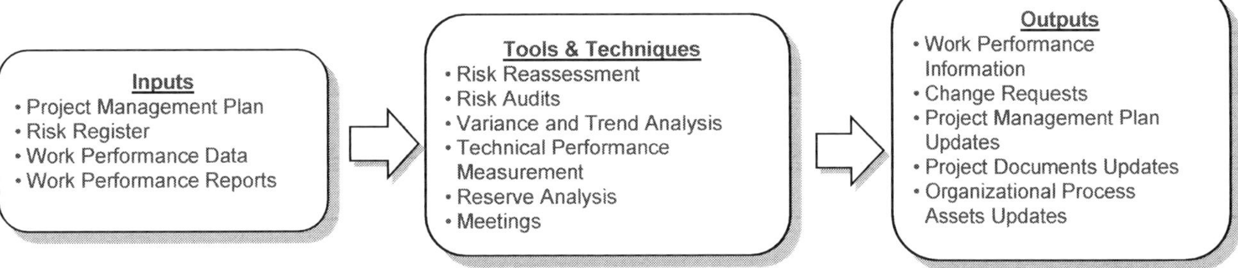

11-16: Control Risks: Inputs, Tools & Techniques, and Outputs

Control Risks: Inputs

- Project Management Plan
- Risk Register
- Work Performance Data
- Work Performance Reports

Project Management Plan: The risk management plan in the project management plan, which contains all risk-related information.

Risk Register: Identified risk and owners, risk responses, implementation actions, symptoms and warning signs, residual and secondary risks, a watch list of low-priority risks, and contingency reserves are key inputs.

Work Performance Data: Various performance data related to performance results such as deliverable status, schedule progress, costs incurred, and other elements will be key inputs.

Work Performance Reports: Reports such as variance analysis, earned value data, forecasting data, and others will be key inputs.

Control Risks: Tools & Techniques

- Risk Reassessment
- Risk Audits
- Variance and Trend Analysis
- Technical Performance Measurement
- Reserve Analysis
- Meetings

Risk Reassessment: Additional planning may be required if the impact of a risk differs from what was planned or expected as the response may not be adequate. The amount of detail and repetition depends on how the project progresses and the priority of the risk.

Risk Audits: These audits examine and document the effectiveness of risk responses as well as the overall risk management process. A separate risk audit meeting may be held in addition to reviewing risk in a regular review meeting.

Variance and Trend Analysis: Variance analysis concentrates on what was planned versus what was executed. Trend analysis focuses on the trends in performance, and a trend showing worsening time and cost performance indicates that a problem is imminent.

Technical Performance Measurement: Technical performance measurement focuses on functionality and shows how the project has met its delivery objective of the scope.

Reserve Analysis: This analysis determines if contingency reserves are adequate at any point in the project.

Meetings: Risk management becomes easier as it is practiced. Frequent discussions make identifying risks easier and more accurate.

Control Risks: Outputs

- Work Performance Information
- Change Requests
- Project Management Plan Updates
- Project Documents Updates
- Organizational Process Assets Updates

Work Performance Information: Various work performance information will assist in communicating and supporting project decision making.

Change Requests: A requirement to implement a change is submitted to the Integrated Change Control process.

Recommended corrective actions: These actions are used to bring the project into compliance with the project management plan and to reduce the probability of negative consequences associated with risks.

Recommended preventive actions: These actions include contingency and workaround plans that are essential to deal with emerging risks not previously identified.

Project Management Plan Updates: If approved change requests have an impact on the risk management processes, then the corresponding parts of the project management plan are revised to reflect the changes.

Project Documents Updates: Project documents that may be updated include but are not limited to the assumptions log, technical documents, risk register, and other materials.

Risk Register Updates: An updated risk register contains the following:

- Outcomes of risk reassessment, risk audits, and periodic risk reviews as well as updates to probability, impact, priority, response plans, and other elements of the risk register. Outcomes can also include closed risks that are no longer applicable.
- The actual outcomes of the project's risks and responses. This completes the record of risk management on the project and is an input to the Close Project process.

Organizational Process Assets Updates: Project Risk Management Processes produce information that can be used on future projects. The final versions of the risk register, risk management plan, probability and impact matrix, Risk Breakdown Structure (RBS), lessons learned are included.

Common Risk Management Errors

We have so many hiccups in our projects because of a lack of appropriate attention to risks in the project. Some of the common mistakes we make in risk management are as follows:

- Risk management is given the least attention during project execution compared to other project management areas.
- Risks are identified in the early phase when not much information is available about the project.
- Project managers do not spend sufficient time explaining the risk management process, tools & techniques, and other items to their team members during project planning.
- Mostly, a brief list of risks is created instead of an extensive one since risk identification is not given enough time and importance.
- Many facts that are certain are considered to be risks in the project.
- Not all relevant risk categories are considered, and whole categories of risks are missed, such as technology, culture, or marketplace.
- Only a few preferred methods are used to identify risks rather than a combination of methods, such as Expected Monetary Value (EMV) analysis, decision tree analysis, Monte Carlo analysis, SWOT analysis, diagramming techniques, and requirements gathering techniques.
- Not much options analysis is done while selecting a response strategy for the risk, and mostly the first strategy identified is selected.
- It is essential to identify risks and incorporate mitigation and allocation of risks into the contract as appropriate, but contracts are usually signed long before risks to the project are discussed.

Exercise 6: Identify best practices for planning effective risk responses.

Exercise 7: What risk-related work should the project manager be doing while project work is ongoing?

Exercise 8: What is the difference between qualitative risk analysis and quantitative risk analysis?

Risk Management Flow Chart

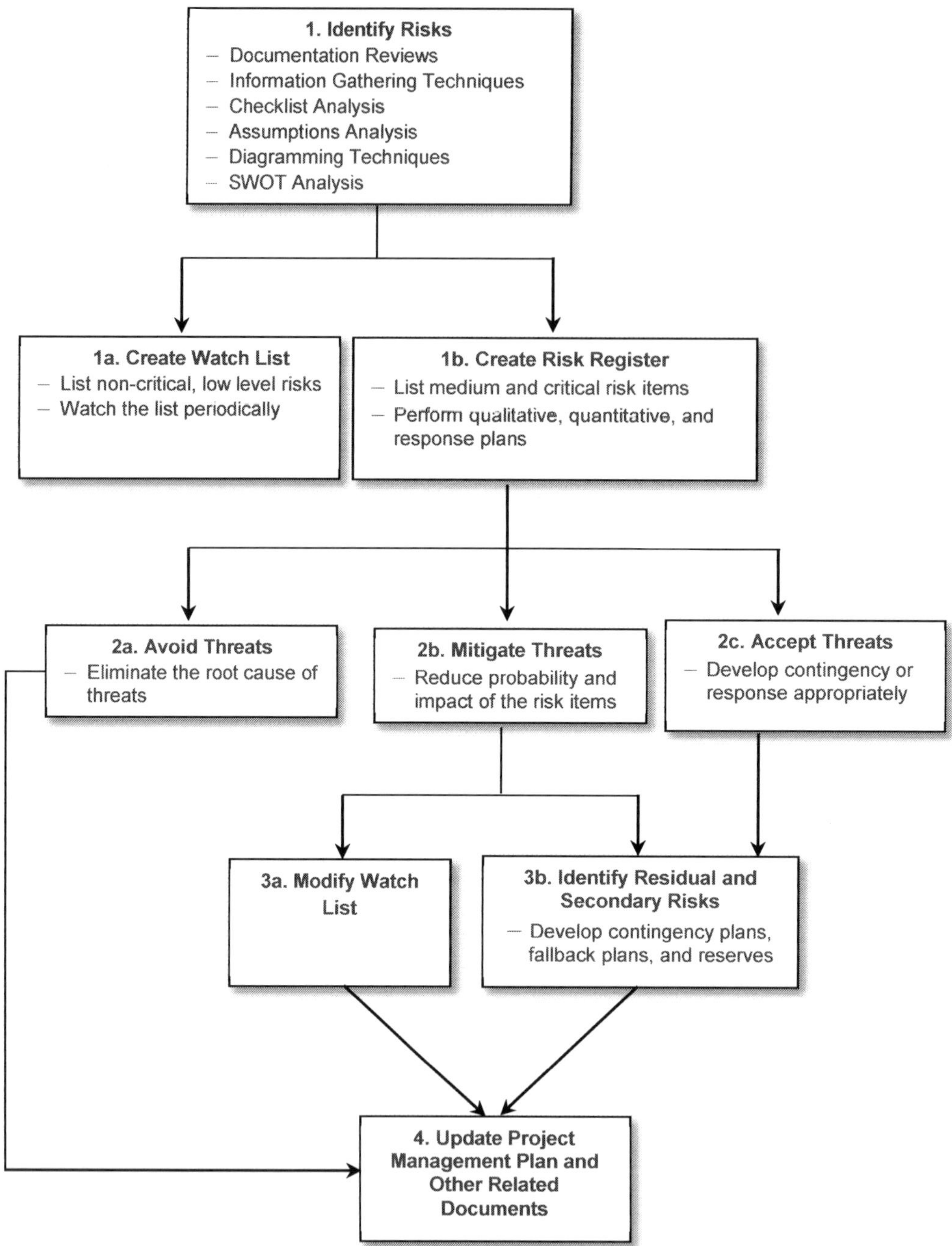

Figure 11–17: Risk Management Flowchart

Exercise 9: If you have to make a decision between two scenarios, which one will provide the greater potential payoff as per Expected Monetary Value (EMV)?

Scenario 1

Best case provides a 25 percent probability of making $185,000
Worst case provides a 15 percent probability of losing [–$22,000]
Most likely case provides a 60 percent probability of making $ 80,000

Scenario 2

Best case provides a 25 percent probability of making $210,000
Worst case provides a 30 percent probability of making $12,000
Most likely case provides a 45 percent probability of making $50,000

Exercise 10: Identify which process group each process belongs to.

Process Groups				
Initiating	**Planning**	**Executing**	**Monitoring & Controlling**	**Closing**

Process Names:

- Plan Risk Responses
- Plan Risk Management
- Identify Risks
- Perform Quantitative Risk Analysis
- Control Risks
- Perform Qualitative Risk Analysis

Exercise 11: Your team identified that there is a 35% probability that the project will be delayed and 40% probability that it will be over budget. What is the probability that the project will be completed on time and within budget?

Exercise 12: While assessing the probability of a design error in a software development project, the team members identified it as medium and assigned a numerical value of 0.7 to it. The team considers the impact of this risk to be high and assigns a value of 0.8. What is the rating for this risk item?

Exercise 13: While exploring the options whether to self-publish or go to an external publisher, you assessed that if there is a high demand, gross sales will be $500,000 and $40,000 if the demand is low. There is a 65% probability of high demand and a 35% probability of a low demand. If you self-publish the book, you will be able to keep the entire revenue. On the other hand, an external publisher will only give you 8% royalty on sales.
Note that the cost for self-publishing is $300,000.

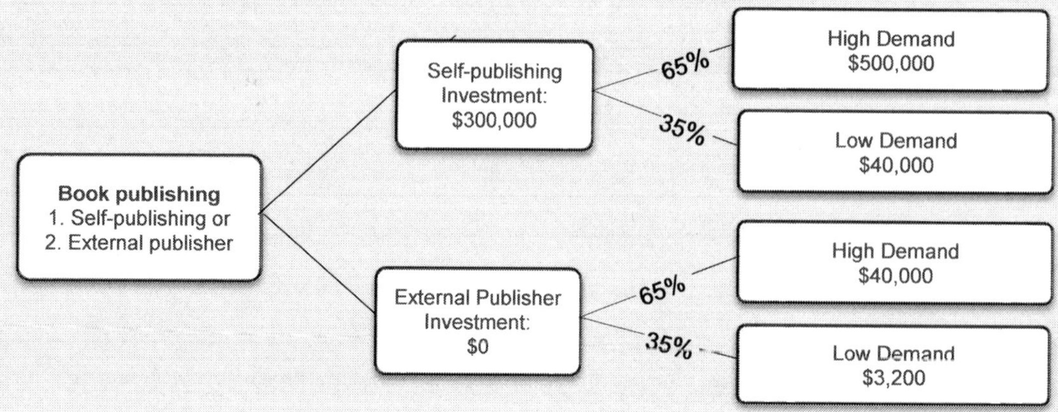

Based on the above scenario, which option should you select? What will happen if the demand is low?

Exercise 14: Match the following terms with the proper description.

1. **Residual risks**	A. The person responsible for implementing the actions defined by mitigation and the contingency plan in risk management.
2. **Risk owners**	B. Symptoms or warning signs that a potential risk is about to occur in the project.
3. **Secondary risk**	C. Specific action or Plan B that will be taken if the contingency plan or Plan A is not effective.
4. **Risk triggers**	D. Risks that remain after execution of risk response planning and for which contingency and fallback plans can be created.
5. **Fallback plan**	E. Unplanned responses developed to deal with the occurrence of unanticipated risk events.
6. **Workarounds**	F. The specific action that will be taken if opportunities or threats occur.
7. **Contingency plan**	G. A new risk created due to the implementation of the selected risk response strategy.

Project Risk Management Example for WIMAX Project

BestTech Consultancy, LLC, a telecommunications services company, has been providing customers with cutting-edge telecommunications services for the last ten years. BestTech's technical offering includes everything from frame relay, DSL, ADSL, and HDSL to video-on-demand and voice over IP using coaxial, fiber optic, and hybrid cabling systems. The company designs and installs customized solutions using wireless, broadband, voice, and telephony telecommunications technologies.

Recently, management decided to install a new WIMAX infrastructure to provide high-speed Internet connections at 120 designated "wireless hotspots" throughout a specific metropolitan area so that thousands of new individuals and corporate cellular customers can access the Internet. To ensure that all medium- and high-priority risks have been identified prior to the project execution phase, several risk workshops were undertaken with government staff, engineering specialists, and telecommunications experts. This report documents the risks identified during these risk workshops as well as actions needed to avoid, transfer, and/or mitigate them. The following risks have been identified under each risk category:

Risk Category	Risk ID	Risk Description
Return on Investment	1.1	Number of WIMAX users does not meet forecasts, thereby extending the payback period.
Delivery Time Frame	2.1	Significant time constraints to produce all of the project deliverables.
	2.2	Lack of time to make a complete evaluation of the existing networking infrastructure.
Political	3.1	A change in board membership leads to a reduction in project funding, scope, or sponsorship.
Resource	4.1	Lack of competent WIMAX resources in the market to undertake this complex project.
Planning	5.1	Existing network infrastructure data on POPS, MicroPOPS, electrical, power, and network (Canopy and CPEs) equipment is obsolete and inaccurate, making it challenging to know which assets require upgrading.
	5.2	The recent violations in the wireless industry compel the government to instigate new wireless standards and regulations, leading to project delays.
Execution	6.1	Unanticipated site conditions, such as unavailability, earth instabilities, or prior contamination lead to increased construction costs for towers, POPs, and MicroPOPs installation.
	6.2	Unrest or strike by WIMAX team may lead to project delays.

Each risk is assessed to investigate the likelihood that it will occur and to assess its potential effect on project objectives, such as time, cost, scope, and quality. Risk assessment is done by interviews or meetings with participants selected for their familiarity with the risk categories. Determining the risk probability is sometimes difficult as it is mostly defined using expert judgment. The probability is expressed as a number from 0.0 to 1.0. Probability 0.0: There is no probability that the event will occur. Probability 1.0: There is 100 percent certainty that the event will occur.

Impacts are the possible outcomes of the risk event. Ordinal scale assigns values as high, medium, low, or a combination of these. Cardinal scale is expressed as values from 0.0 to 1.0 and can be stated in equal (linear) or unequal (nonlinear) increments.

The following risk impact scale for scope, time, cost, and quality objectives is based on both ordinal and cardinal values.

Objectives	Very Low 0.05	Low 0.20	Medium 0.40	High 0.60	Very High 0.80
Scope	Barely noticeable	Minor areas are affected	Major areas are affected	Unacceptable to sponsor	End item is useless
Time	Barely noticeable	<5 percent time increase	>5 percent to <12 percent time increase	>12 percent to <20 percent time increase	>20 percent time increase
Cost	Barely noticeable	<5 percent cost increase	>5 percent to <12 percent cost increase	>12 percent to <20 percent cost increase	>20 percent cost increase
Quality	Barely noticeable	<5 percent of components are impacted	>5 percent to <10 percent of components are impacted	>10 percent to <20 percent of components are impacted	End item is useless

During the risk workshops undertaken, each risk identified was assigned a probability and impact score using the scoring mechanisms listed above. The overall priority score was calculated by multiplying the probability and impact scores. The following table lists the scores assigned to each risk identified for this WIMAX project:

Risk ID	Likelihood Score	Impact Score	Priority Score	Priority Rating
1.1	0.2	0.05	0.01	Very low
2.1	0.4	0.2	0.08	Very low
2.2	0.6	0.4	0.24	Low
3.1	0.8	0.6	0.48	Medium
4.1	0.2	0.8	0.16	Very low
5.1	0.4	0.05	0.02	Very low
5.2	0.6	0.8	0.48	Medium
6.1	0.8	0.4	0.32	Low
6.2	0.8	0.8	0.64	High

To safeguard the success of this WIMAX project, the team needs to execute a suite of actions to avoid, transfer, and/or mitigate the detected risks. The following table itemizes the preventive actions to be taken to downgrade the likelihood of each risk occurring as well as the contingent actions to be taken should the risk actually occur. The person designated to complete each action is identified as well as the date upon which the action needs to be completed.

Risk ID	Preventive Actions	Resource	Action Date	Contingent Actions	Resource
1.1	Assign a marketing budget to promote the spectacular features of WIMAX to meet the forecast.	Project manager	Jan 15	Offer discounted rate in the event of low customer numbers.	Project manager
2.1	Request an extension in the overall delivery timetable.	Project manager	Jan 15	Allocate 5 percent of elapsed time in the project schedule as contingency.	Project sponsor
2.2	Allocate additional time to assess the existing infrastructure.	Project manager	Feb 15	Utilize the 5 percent of elapsed time in the project schedule allocated as contingency.	Project manager
3.1	Approve a mandate to maintain the project scope.	Project board	Feb 15	Impose the approved project board mandate when required.	Project sponsor
4.1	Recruit additional competent WIMAX resources from overseas markets to assist with the completion of this project.	Project HR manager	Feb 15	Sign backup contracts for foreign competent resources from overseas should they be needed.	Project HR manager
5.1	Allocate time in the project schedule for the review of all existing assets.	Project asset manager	Jan15	Obtain asset information from telecommunications companies.	Project asset manager
5.2	Ensure that all existing industry regulations are adhered to. Appoint a full-time auditor.	Project regulatory team	Jul 15	Implement compliance actions immediately to prevent adverse consequences.	Project manager
6.1	Conduct geological surveys and contact landlords well ahead of construction.	Project site work manager	Feb 15	Rent POPs from other providers in case land is unavailable or not suitable.	Project planning manager
6.2	Resolve WIMAX team issues ahead of potential unrest.	Project logistics manager	Mar15	Take legal action if necessary.	Project logistics manager

Below is the final risk register for the WIMAX project. In addition to the preventive and contingent actions, some project managers may also consider adding fallback actions while planning for the risk responses.

Step 1: Plan Risk Management
- Develop the risk management plan

Step 2: Identify Risks
- Create a risk register
- Identity risk categories, risk ids, risk descriptions for all risk items.

Step 4: Perform Quantitative Risks Analysis
- Perform numerical analysis to analyze overall effect on project objectives of identified risks.

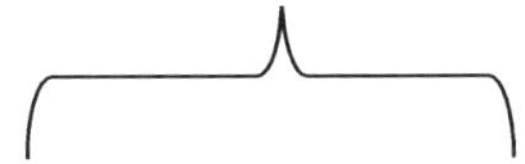

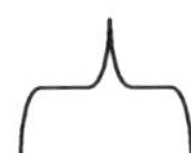

Risk Category	Risk ID	Risk Desc.	Probability	Impact	Severity	Preventive Actions	Action Date	Resource	Contingent Actions	Resource	Fallback Actions
	1.1										
	2.1										
	2.2										
	3.1										
	4.1										
	5.1										
	5.2										
	6.1										

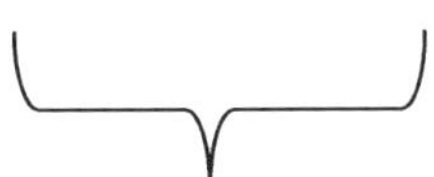

Step 3: Perform Qualitative Risks Analysis
- Find out the probability and impact of all risk items.

Step 5: Plan Risk Responses
- Identify preventive, contingent, and fallback plans for all risk items.

Step 6: Control Risks
- Compare the risk plan with actual.
- Make sure that all the preventive actions were executed as planned.
- Execute the contingent and fallback actions as appropriate.
- Reassess the probability, impact, priorities and response plan for all the risk items.

Exercise 15: Crossword

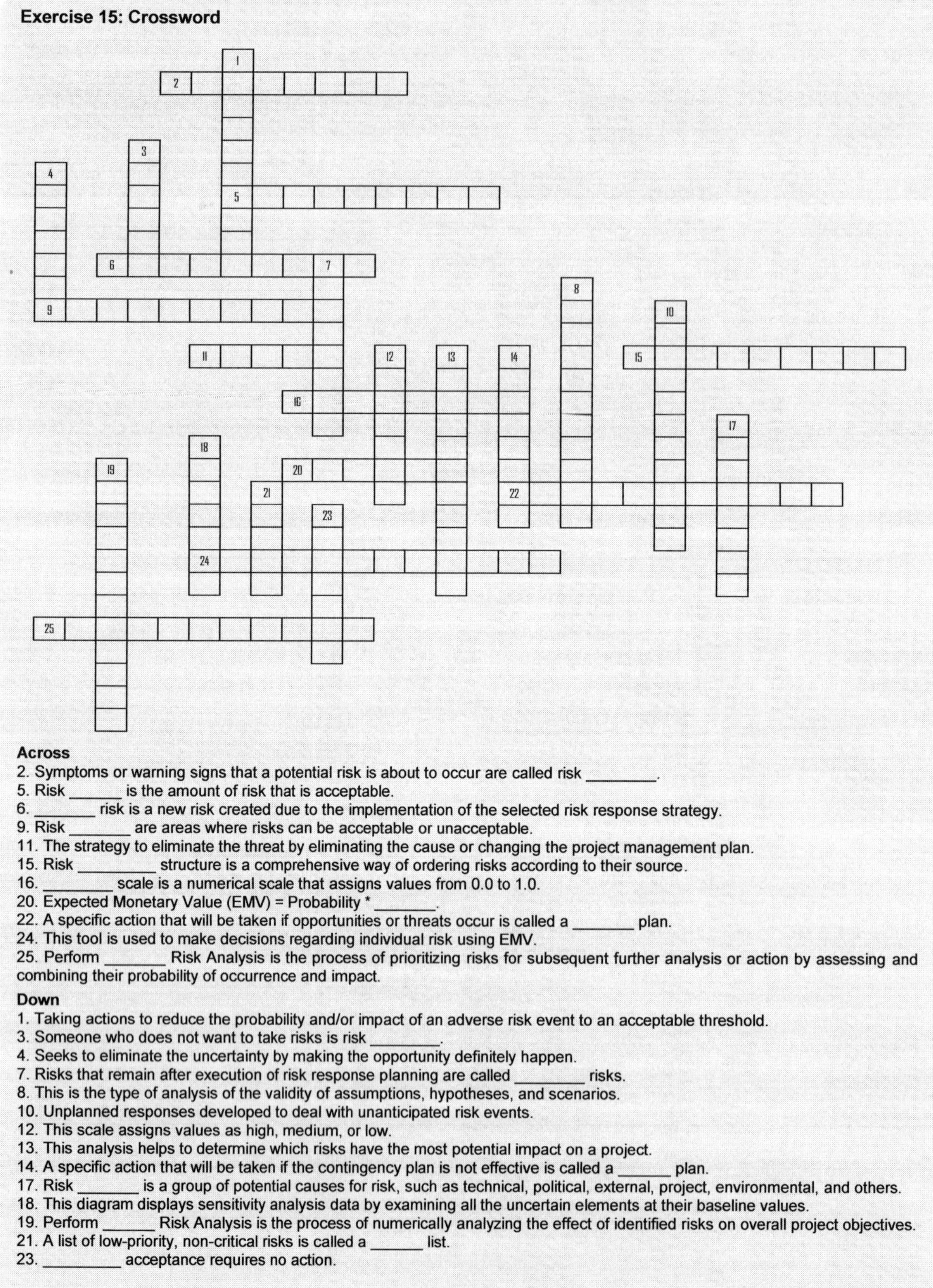

Across

2. Symptoms or warning signs that a potential risk is about to occur are called risk ________.
5. Risk ______ is the amount of risk that is acceptable.
6. _______ risk is a new risk created due to the implementation of the selected risk response strategy.
9. Risk _______ are areas where risks can be acceptable or unacceptable.
11. The strategy to eliminate the threat by eliminating the cause or changing the project management plan.
15. Risk ________ structure is a comprehensive way of ordering risks according to their source.
16. _______ scale is a numerical scale that assigns values from 0.0 to 1.0.
20. Expected Monetary Value (EMV) = Probability * _______.
22. A specific action that will be taken if opportunities or threats occur is called a _______ plan.
24. This tool is used to make decisions regarding individual risk using EMV.
25. Perform _______ Risk Analysis is the process of prioritizing risks for subsequent further analysis or action by assessing and combining their probability of occurrence and impact.

Down

1. Taking actions to reduce the probability and/or impact of an adverse risk event to an acceptable threshold.
3. Someone who does not want to take risks is risk ________.
4. Seeks to eliminate the uncertainty by making the opportunity definitely happen.
7. Risks that remain after execution of risk response planning are called ________ risks.
8. This is the type of analysis of the validity of assumptions, hypotheses, and scenarios.
10. Unplanned responses developed to deal with unanticipated risk events.
12. This scale assigns values as high, medium, or low.
13. This analysis helps to determine which risks have the most potential impact on a project.
14. A specific action that will be taken if the contingency plan is not effective is called a ______ plan.
17. Risk _______ is a group of potential causes for risk, such as technical, political, external, project, environmental, and others.
18. This diagram displays sensitivity analysis data by examining all the uncertain elements at their baseline values.
19. Perform ______ Risk Analysis is the process of numerically analyzing the effect of identified risks on overall project objectives.
21. A list of low-priority, non-critical risks is called a ______ list.
23. ________ acceptance requires no action.

Exercise 16: Answer the following:

1. Remove a work package or a person, extend the schedule, and change the strategy are examples of ________.
2. A company is ok with a financial risk of $40,000 but not more than that is an example of risk _______.
3. It is the product of the probability and consequences of an event or task.
4. The person is responsible for implementing the actions defined by mitigation and the contingency plan in risk management.
5. A new risk created due to the implementation of a selected risk response strategy.
6. Specific action or plan B that will be taken if the contingency plan or plan A is not effective.
7. This diagram can be used to display sensitivity analysis data by examining all the uncertain elements at their baseline values.
8. It is the analysis of the validity of assumptions, hypotheses, and scenarios developed in project initiation to identify risks from inaccuracies, incompleteness, and inconsistencies of assumptions.
9. This scale assigns values as high, medium, low, or a combination of these.
10. This numeric scale is expressed as values from 0.0 to 1.0 and can be stated in equal (linear) or unequal (nonlinear) increments.
11. This strategy seeks to eliminate the uncertainty by making the opportunity definitely happen.
12. Areas of risks where risks can be acceptable or unacceptable.
13. The specific action that will be taken if opportunities or threats occur.
14. It helps to determine which risks have the most potential impact on a project, or in other words, whether the occurrence of a particular threat would merely be an inconvenience or whether it would ruin the project.
15. Designing redundancy in the system, taking early action, adopting less complex processes, conducting more tests, and developing prototypes to reduce the impact and probability are example of ________.
16. The objectives of ________ are to increase the probability and impact of positive events and to decrease the probability and impact of adverse events.
17. These are symptoms or warning signs that a potential risk is about to occur in the project.
18. The process of prioritizing risks for subsequent further analysis or action by assessing and combining their probability of occurrence and impact.
19. A common way to organize identified risks into categories.
20. A cruise company might add tours to popular destinations during holidays in order to enhance traffic and profitability.
21. Risks that remain after execution of risk response planning and for which contingency and fallback plans can be created.
22. Unplanned responses developed to deal with the occurrence of unanticipated risk events.
23. The six processes of risk management are ________.
24. The key outputs of risk management processes are _______.
25. Risk data quality assurance, risk categorization, and risk urgency assessment are used as tools and techniques in ________ process.
26. Name some of the tools and techniques used in Identify Risks process.
27. Name some of the tools and techniques used in Control Risks process.
28. The acceptance that requires no action to avoid, transfer, or mitigate a threat, or to exploit, share, or enhance an opportunity.
29. A group of potential causes for risk, which can be grouped into categories, such as technical, political, external, project, environmental, and others.
30. Name some of the quantitative risk analysis and modeling techniques.
31. The reserves the project manager determines, manages, and controls to address the cost impact of the remaining risks during the Plan Risk Response process.
32. Contingency plans are associated with _________ acceptance.

Project Risk Management Summary

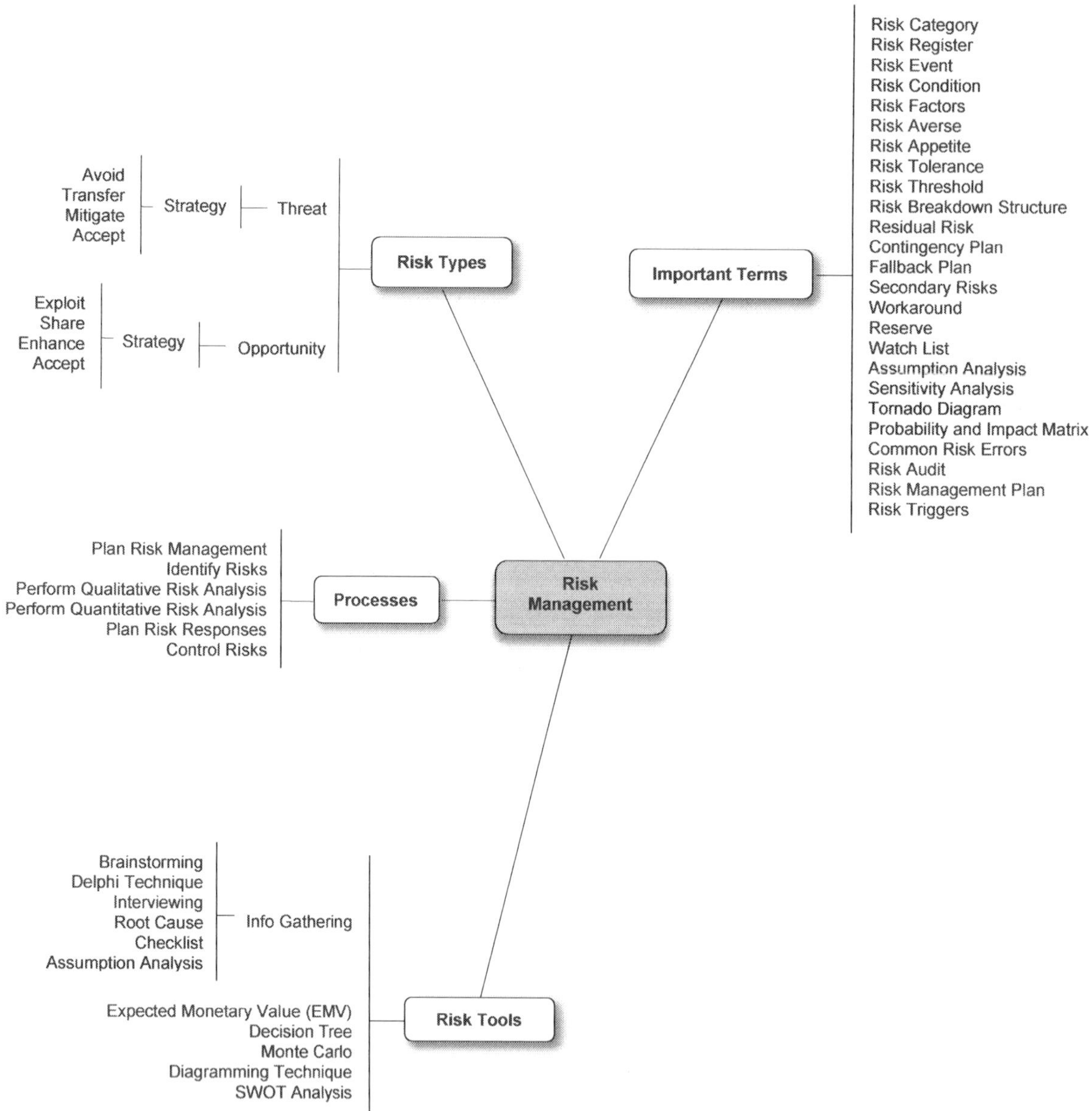

Figure 11-18: Project Risk Management Summary

Project Risk Management Key Terms

Risk Categories: A group of potential causes for risk, such as technical, political, external, project, and environmental
Risk Breakdown Structure (RBS): A comprehensive way of ordering risks according to their source
Probability and Impact Matrix: A matrix based on probability and impact of the risk
Risk Triggers: Symptoms or warning signs that a potential risk is about to occur
Risk Appetites: Acceptable level of risk in the project
Risk Tolerances: Areas where risks can be acceptable or unacceptable
Risk Threshold: Amount of risk that is acceptable
Residual Risks: Risks that remain after execution of risk response planning
Contingency Plan: Specific action that will be taken if opportunities or threats occur
Secondary Risk: A new risk created due to the implementation of the selected risk response strategy
Fallback Plan: Specific action that will be taken if contingency plan is not effective
Workarounds: Unplanned responses developed to deal with unanticipated risk events
Reserves: Contingency reserve for known unknown - residual risks, Management reserves for unknown unknown risks
Watch List: A list of low-priority, non-critical risks
Ordinal scale: Assigns values as high, medium, or low
Cardinal scale: Numerical scales that assign values from 0.0 to 1.0

Risk Tools

Information Gathering Techniques: Brainstorming, Delphi, interviewing, root cause, checklist analysis, assumptions analysis
Diagramming Techniques: Cause and effect diagrams, system or process flow chart, influence diagram
SWOT Analysis: Strengths, weaknesses, opportunities, and threats analysis
Expected Monetary Value (EMV): Probability * Impact
Decision Tree: Used to make decisions regarding individual risk using EMV
Sensitivity Analysis: Helps to determine which risks have the most potential impact on a project
Tornado Diagram: Displays sensitivity analysis data by examining all the uncertain elements at their baseline values

Risk Types and Strategies:

Threats (Negative Risks)	Opportunities (Positive Risks)
Avoid	Exploit
Transfer	Share
Mitigate	Enhance
Accept – Active, Passive	Accept

Project Risk Management Exercise Answers

Exercise 1: Refer to the "Figure 3-16: Process Groups Key Inputs and Outputs".

- **Project charter:** The project charter lists the initial, high-level risks. The charter also helps identify risks based on what is in and out of scope of the project. It will also be helpful in determining whether project objectives and constraints are risky or not.
- **Project scope statement:** The scope statement helps assess the complexity of the project and level of risk management effort.
- **Team information:** Knowing the availability, skills, knowledge, weaknesses, and other details of the team members will help identify team related risks.
- **Work breakdown structure:** The WBS is used to do all kinds of estimating in the project and will be very helpful in identifying risk items.
- **Past lessons learned:** Information such as what went wrong in similar projects, what mistakes were made helps identify several similar project risks.
- **Network diagram:** The network diagram helps determine the critical path and near critical paths where activities have the most schedule risks. It also identifies paths that converge into one activity.
- **Other organizational process assets:** Historical records from previous projects, risk items, including risk categories, templates, plus lessons learned will help identify risk items.
- **Time and cost estimates:** Time and cost estimates help identify the potential risks of the project not meeting the time and cost targets.
- **Schedule management plan:** The aggressive schedule objective from management stipulates an indication of the schedule risks.
- **Cost management plan:** Cost processes may help identify risks to accomplishing the project cost objectives and goals.
- **Communications management plan:** The communications management plan contains information such as effectiveness of the plan, adverse impact of communication errors, number of people to communicate with, and the impact of poor communication. Knowing this information will help identify risk items and structure communications around risks.
- **Staffing management plan:** The staffing management plan contains information such as type and number of resources needed, availability of resources, processes of releasing resources, and processes of acquiring and managing resources. Knowing this information will help identify risks related to resources.
- **Quality management plan:** The quality management plan contains information such as quality metrics, processes to enhance opportunities or minimize threats, and the process improvement plan. Knowing this information will help identify risks in the project.
- **Stakeholders' risk tolerance and thresholds:** Knowing in which areas stakeholders are willing to accept risks and the amount of risks they can take helps identify the impact, ranking, and response strategies to deal with risk items.
- **Stakeholder register:** The stakeholder register contains detailed information about the stakeholders who can help with identifying risk items. Knowing stakeholders' risk tolerance and threshold is also important in identifying the impact, ranking, and strategies to deal with risk items.
- **Assumption analysis:** Verifying which assumptions are still valid and which are not will help identify risk items. Assumptions that are not valid any more will be potential project risks.
- **Project background information:** Articles on similar projects, discussions from before the project was initiated, and other relevant information will help identify risks.
- **Other enterprise environmental factors:** Knowing in which areas the organization is willing to accept or not accept risks and the amount of risks they can take helps identify the impact, ranking, and response strategies to deal with risk items.

Exercise 2:

	Build on Strengths	Resolve Weaknesses
Internal	– Patent – Strong brand name – Favorable access to distribution network	– Limited patent protection – Limited working cash – A weak brand name
	Exploit Opportunities	**Avoid Threats**
External	– Arrival of new technology – Removal of international trade barrier – An unfulfilled customer need	– New regulation – Increased trade barrier – Emergence of substitute products

Exercise 3:

1. With the help of team members, review all existing documents and identify risk items in all areas. Refer to the "Figure 3-16" on page 60 and Exercise 1 on page 391.
2. Perform assumptions analysis and identify which assumptions are not valid any more. Invalid assumptions will be potential project risks.
3. Discuss and develop a Risk Breakdown Structure (RBS) to identify risk categories and sub categories in your project. Identify risk items in all these categories and sub categories with the help of team members and stakeholders.
4. Use a diagramming technique such as flow chart to figure out where in the project things can go wrong, where the bottleneck is, and what is out of your control to identify potential risk items.
5. Perform a Strength, Weakness, Opportunity, and Threat (SWOT) analysis to identify characteristics of your team and the organization. From these characteristics of your team and organization, you will find project risks.
6. Use a commercial risk checklist to identify risk items in your project.
7. Use information gathering techniques such as brain storming, Delphi technique, interview, and root cause analysis to identify risk items.
8. Seek help from experts with relevant experience and expertise in similar projects and business domains to identify risk items.

Exercise 4:

1. Enhance the impact
2. Transfer
3. Avoid
4. Mitigate the impact
5. Mitigate the probability
6. Mitigate the impact
7. Mitigate the impact
8. Avoid
9. Accept
10. Mitigate the probability
11. Avoid
12. Exploit
13. Share

Exercise 5:

(10 percent * – $9,000) + (25 percent * $6,000) + (35 percent * – $11,000) + (15 percent * $8,000) + (20 percent * – $4,000)
= – $900 + $1,500 – $3,850 + $1,200 – $800 = – $2,850
The project manager should have a contingency reserve of $2,850.

Exercise 6:

- Always prioritize the response that will save the project the most money.
- Choose the best mix of strategies for responding to each risk.
- Assign a risk owner to each risk and its planned response.
- Identify the one strategy that's most appropriate for responding to each risk.
- Plan a response for secondary risks.
- Ensure each planned response defines a specific action plan and fallback plan.
- Create a contingency plan and a fallback plan for residual risks.
- Involve the team, experts, and other stakeholders in risk response planning.

Exercise 7:
- Look for the occurrence of risk triggers or warning signs that a potential risk is about to occur in the project.
- Collect and communicate risk status to the appropriate stakeholders.
- If new risks are identified, perform qualitative and quantitative analysis and develop new responses.
- Monitor residual risks and come up with the contingency and fallback plans for them.
- Ensure proper execution of the risk management plan and procedures and identify any variance.
- Revisit the assumptions list and make sure all the assumptions are still valid.
- Revisit the watch list to see if additional risk responses need to be determined.
- Implement corrective actions to adjust to the severity of actual risk events.
- Look for any unexpected effects or consequences of risk events.
- Reevaluate risk identification and qualitative and quantitative risk analysis when the project deviates from the baseline.
- Update the risk management and response plan.
- Make changes to the project management plan and project documents when new risks are identified and new responses are developed.
- Perform variance and trend analysis on project performance data.
- Use contingency reserves and adjust for approved changes.

Exercise 8: Qualitative Risk Analysis is the process of prioritizing risks by assessing and combining their probability of occurrence and impact to the project if they occur.
Quantitative Risk Analysis is the process of numerically analyzing the effect of identified risks on overall project objectives. It is used to develop risk-related decisions using mathematical analysis and simulations that present possible outcomes of risk events.

Exercise 9:
Scenario 1
Best Case EMV= 25 percent * $185,000 = $46,250
Worst case EMV= 15 percent *(–$22,000) = –$3,300
Most likely case EMV= 60 percent * $80,000 = $48,000
Total EMV = $46,250 – $3,300 + $48,000 = $90,950

Scenario 2
Best case EMV = 25 percent * $210,000 = $52,500
Worst case EMV = 30 percent * $12,000 = $3,600
Most likely case EMV = 45 percent * $50,000 = $22,500
Total EMV = ($52,500 + $3,600 + $22,500) = $78,600
Since Scenario1 has the bigger EMV, it will provide the greater potential payoff.

Exercise 10:

Process Groups				
Initiating	**Planning**	**Executing**	**Monitoring & Controlling**	**Closing**
	– Plan Risk Management – Identify Risks – Perform Qualitative Risk Analysis – Perform Quantitative Risk Analysis – Plan Risk Responses		– Control Risks	

Exercise 11: There is a 100% - 35% = 65% probability that the project will be completed on time.
Also, there is a 100% - 40% = 60% probability that the project will be within budget.
Thus, there is a 65% * 60% = 39% probability that the project will be completed on time and within budget.

Exercise 12: 0.7 * 0.8 = 0.56

Exercise 13: Expected Monetary Value (EMV) for self-publishing = 65% * $500,000 + 35% * 40,000 = $339,000
Expected Monetary Value (EMV) for external publisher = 65% * $40,000 + 35% * 3,200 = $27,120
The cost of self-publishing should be subtracted from the revenue of $339,000. Thus, the income from self-publishing is 39,000 which is higher than $27,120. So, you should go for self-publishing.
In case of self-publishing, if the demand is low, the author will only be making $40,000 and will end up losing a considerable amount of money as the investment is $300,000.

Exercise 14:

1. D
2. A
3. G
4. B
5. C
6. E
7. F

Exercise 15:

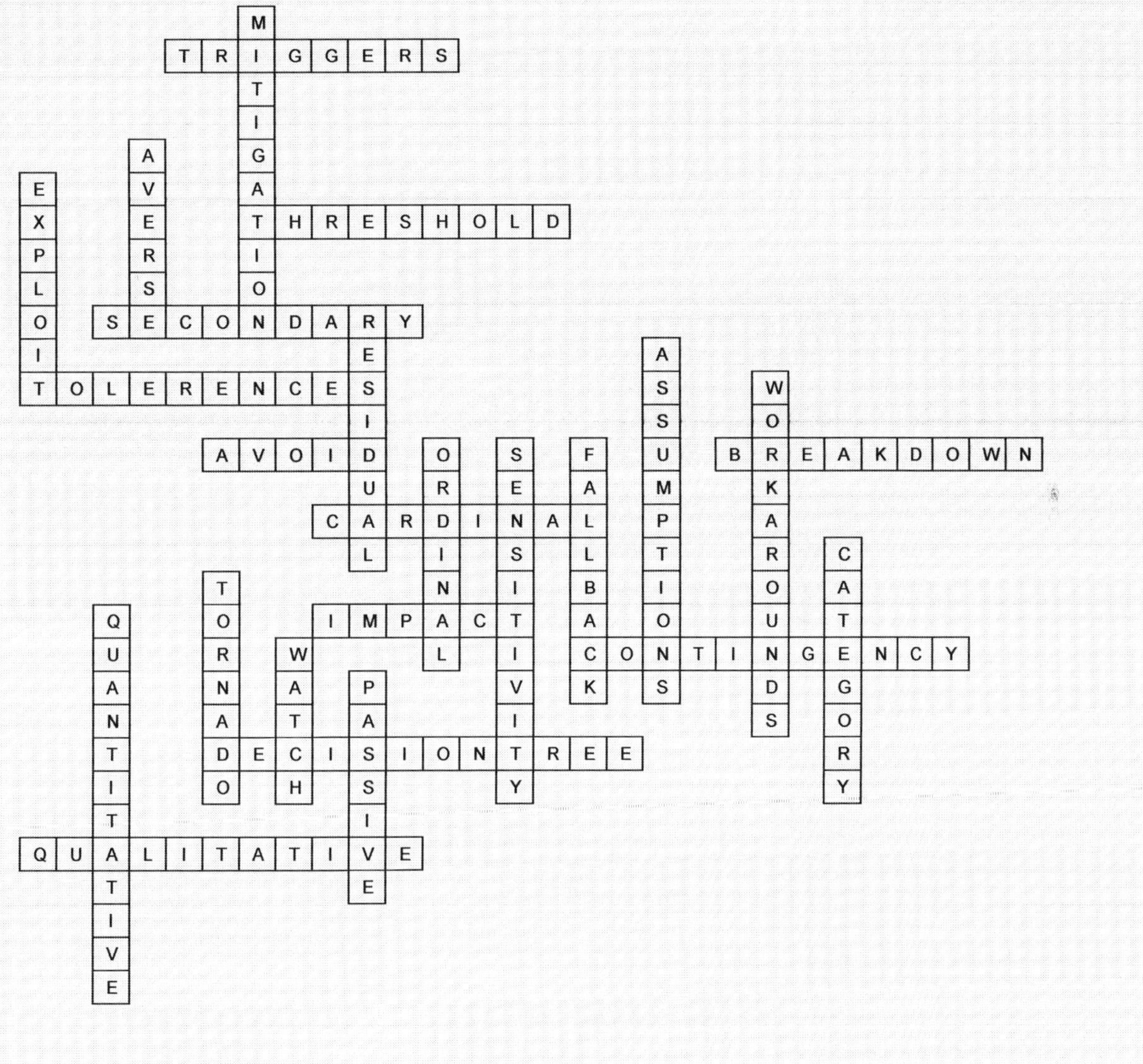

Exercise 16:

1. Avoid
2. Risk threshold
3. Expected monetary value
4. Risk owner
5. Secondary risk
6. Fallback plan
7. A tornado diagram
8. Assumptions analysis
9. Ordinal scale
10. Cardinal scale
11. Exploit
12. Risk tolerances
13. Contingency plan
14. Sensitivity analysis
15. Mitigation
16. Risk management
17. Risk triggers
18. Perform Qualitative Risk Analysis
19. Risk Breakdown Structure (RBS)
20. Enhance
21. Residual risks
22. Workarounds
23. Plan Risk Management, Identify Risks, Perform Qualitative Risk Analysis, Perform Quantitative Risk Analysis, Plan Risk Responses, and Control Risks
24. Plan Risk Management – Risk Management Plan
    Identify Risks – Risk Register
    Perform Qualitative Risk Analysis – Project Documents Updates
    Perform Quantitative Risk Analysis – Project Documents Updates
    Plan Risk Responses – Project Documents Updates
    Control Risks – Work Performance Information, Change Requests
25. Perform Qualitative Risk Analysis
26. Documentation reviews, information gathering techniques, checklist analysis, diagramming techniques, SWOT analysis, expert judgment
27. Risk reassessment, risk audits, variance and trend analysis, technical performance measurement, reserve analysis
28. Passive acceptance
29. Risk category
30. Sensitivity analysis - tornado diagram, expected monetary value analysis, decision tree analysis, modeling and simulation – Monte Carlo
31. Contingency reserves
32. Active

Project Risk Management Exam Tips

- Be able to name all six risk management processes and their key activities of risk management.
- Be able to answer questions where you will need to analyze a specific situation and determine what you should do next.
- Be able to define the risk register and its major elements.
- Be familiar with the concepts and terms in the project risk management summary table, Figure 11-18: Project Risk Management Summary.

Project Risk Management Questions

1. You are working on the Plan Risk Management process to decide how to approach, plan, and execute risk management activities. All of the following are inputs to the Plan Risk Management process EXCEPT:
   A. Stakeholder register
   B. Project charter
   C. Risk register
   D. Project management plan

2. You are delivering specialized medical equipment, which is worth $600,000. You have been delivering equipment for a while without much hassle or accidents in the past. This time you estimate that there is a 5 percent probability that the equipment could be damaged or lost. While exploring the possibility of transferring this risk to an insurance company, you found out the insurance premium is $15,000. What will be your BEST course of action?
   A. You do not have much information to make a decision.
   B. Do not buy the insurance premium.
   C. Develop a contingency plan.
   D. Buy the insurance premium.

3. Which one of the following is contained in the risk management plan and describes a risk category?
   A. Risk response plan
   B. Risk Breakdown Structure (RBS)
   C. Risk register
   D. Watch list

4. The team has identified several mitigation and contingency action plans to deal with potential risks within the project. Who is responsible for implementing the actions defined by mitigation and the contingency plan in risk management?
   A. Project expeditor
   B. Risk owner
   C. Project sponsor
   D. Project manager

5. You are working on a very critical and strategic project to develop a robust dynamic website, which will be available to approximately five million users your company has around the globe. You decided to survey the experts within your organization on any foreseeable risks with the design, structure, and intent of the website with an anonymous, simple form. You later sent out subsequent anonymous surveys to a group of experts with the collected information. This is an example of:
   A. A Delphi technique
   B. Identify Risks process
   C. Nominal group technique
   D. SWOT analysis

6. You are the project manager of a data center project. You have just completed an analysis of project risks and have prioritized them using a probability and impact matrix. The approach you used to prioritize the risks is:
   A. Qualitative analysis
   B. Quantitative analysis
   C. Sensitivity analysis
   D. Earned value analysis

7. Which one of the following is a comprehensive way of ordering risks according to their source?
   A. Product description
   B. Risk categories
   C. Assumptions
   D. Constraints

8. You are overseeing a project to implement an accounting application and are currently in the Identify Risks process of identifying and documenting the project risks. All of the following are tools & techniques for the Identify Risks process EXCEPT:

A. Information gathering techniques
B. Assumptions analysis
C. Diagramming techniques
D. Monte Carlo simulation

9. Your team is performing a quantitative risk analysis using the Monte Carlo simulator. Which one of the following statements is FALSE about this Monte Carlo analysis?

A. It translates the uncertainties specified at a detailed level into their potential impact on project objectives at the level of the whole project.
B. It is a modeling technique that computes project costs one time.
C. It involves determining the impact of the identified risks by running simulations to identify the range of possible outcomes for a number of scenarios.
D. It usually expresses its results as probability distributions of possible costs.

10. One of your hardware vendors sends you an e-mail stating that due to severe weather she may not be able to deliver the networking equipment on time. Which of the following statements is TRUE?

A. This is a residual risk.
B. This is a risk trigger.
C. This is a risk event.
D. This is a secondary risk.

11. You have identified several problems along with their causes in your web-based application development project. Which one of the following have you probably used to show the problem and its causes and effects?

A. Ishikawa diagram
B. System flow diagram
C. Process diagram
D. Histogram

12. Your team is performing a risk probability and impact assessment for each risk to investigate the likelihood and potential effect on the project objectives, such as time, cost, scope, and quality. The numeric impact scale is expressed as values from 0.0 to 1.0 and can be stated in equal (linear) or unequal (nonlinear) increments. Your team is using:

A. An ordinal scale
B. Monte Carlo analysis
C. Influence diagram
D. A cardinal scale

13. Expected Monetary Value (or simply expected value) is a statistical concept that calculates the average outcome of a decision. The two dimensions of risk used to determine this expected value are:

A. Probability and threshold
B. Probability and tolerance
C. Consequence and contingencies
D. Probability and consequence

14. While overseeing a complex software project to develop a sophisticated golf simulator for a local golf club, you realize that the team is lacking the required technical expertise and experience. You also do not have the required tools and development environment for this kind of complicated software development. After discussing with the sponsor, you decide to give the design and development work to a vendor who specializes in the specific technical area. This is an example of:

A. Passive acceptance
B. Active acceptance
C. Risk avoidance
D. Risk transfer

15. Steve, a project manager, has a robust risk response plan for his ERP implementation project. The team has utilized all of the appropriate tools & techniques and has executed the predefined preventive and contingency actions to respond to identified project risks. He finds out that some of the risks have been reduced in impact but still remain as potential threats. Steve decides to develop additional contingency and fallback plans for these risks as soon as possible. These risks are called:

A. Secondary risks
B. Residual risks
C. Primary risks
D. Workarounds

16. You are in the Control Risks process of identifying, analyzing, and planning for newly arising risks, keeping track of identified risks, reanalyzing existing risks, monitoring trigger conditions, monitoring residual risks, and reviewing the execution and effectiveness of risk responses. Outputs from the Control Risks process include all of the following EXCEPT:
   A. Variance and trend analysis
   B. Work performance information
   C. Change requests
   D. Project management plan updates

17. Project risk is an uncertain event or condition in the future; if it occurs, it will have a positive or negative impact on one or more project objectives including scope, schedule, cost, and quality. Project risk is typically characterized by three elements:
   A. Risk event, probability, and amount at stake
   B. Severity, duration, and cost of impact
   C. Source, probability, and frequency of risk
   D. Timing, frequency, and cost of risk

18. Designing redundancy in the system, taking early action, adopting less complex processes, conducting more tests, and developing prototypes are all examples of:
   A. Risk avoidance
   B. Risk transfer
   C. Risk mitigation
   D. Risk acceptance

19. You are the project manager assigned to a critical project that requires you to handle project risk intentionally and methodically, so you have assembled only the project team. The team has identified thirty-two potential project risks, determined what would trigger the risks, and have rated and ranked each risk using a risk rating matrix. You have also reviewed and verified all documented assumptions from the project team and verified the sources of data used in the process of identifying and rating the risks. You are continuing to move through the risk management process. Which one of the following important steps have you missed?
   A. Engage other stakeholders.
   B. Conduct a Monte Carlo simulation.
   C. Determine which risks are transferable.
   D. Determine the overall riskiness of the project.

20. You are managing the construction of a disaster center for a financial institute. After the preliminary survey, you found out that the location that was selected for the disaster center was highly prone to earthquakes. You raised your concern to management, but due to a specific strategic reason you were told that changing the location would not be an option. In order to deal with this situation, you have selected a specific architectural design that is technologically advanced and earthquake resistant. This is an example of which of the following?
   A. Accept risk
   B. Transfer risk
   C. Avoid risk
   D. Mitigate risk

21. During the initial stage of project planning, you made a guess that all the construction materials such as sand, cement, concrete, rods, and other items would be available within a reasonable price during building construction. While identifying the risk in your project, you found out that the price for cement significantly increased due to heavy demand and less supply. You decided to add this as a new risk in your project. This is an example of:
   A. Assumptions analysis
   B. Diagramming techniques
   C. SWOT analysis
   D. Expert judgment

22. Steve, an IT project manager, is overseeing a project to develop a new wireless media streaming device. He is using an influence diagram to figure out what could cause potential risks to his project. Which one of the following risk management processes is he in now?
   A. Plan Risk Management
   B. Identify Risks
   C. Perform Qualitative Risk Analysis
   D. Control Risks

23. You have been working on the Plan Risk Management process of establishing the basis to approach, plan, and execute risk management activities and have developed a risk management plan. Which one of the following will NOT be included in your risk management plan?
   A. Methodology: Defines approaches, tools, and data sources for risk management.
   B. Roles and Responsibilities: Defines the roles and responsibilities and sometimes includes non-team members who may have certain roles in risk management.
   C. Identified Risks: A list of identified risks in the project.
   D. Risk Categories: A group of potential causes for risk that can be grouped into categories, such as technical, political, external, project, environmental, and others.

24. Which one of the following will NOT be considered a valid way of reducing risks in your project?
   A. Plan to mitigate the risk.
   B. Develop a workaround.
   C. Select a specific contract type to distribute risk between the buyer and the seller.
   D. Purchase insurance against the risk.

25. You are in the Plan Risk Responses process of developing options and actions to reduce threats and enhance opportunities to your project objectives. The tools & techniques of the Plan Risk Responses process include:
   A. Risk audits
   B. Avoid, transfer, mitigate, and accept
   C. Technical performance measurement
   D. Variance and trend analysis

26. You planned a trip to a destination four hundred miles away from home. You found out that there is a long stretch of construction on one of the major highways that you are planning to use. You decide to use another highway for that stretch of driving so that you do not have to wait too long in traffic. This is an example of:
   A. Avoiding risk
   B. Creating contingency reserves
   C. Creating a workaround
   D. Creating a fallback plan

27. You will be overseeing a project to develop a smartphone application. While analyzing your project, you identify that there is a 55 percent probability of making $120,000 a 45 percent probability of losing $55,000. What does $41,250 represent in this case?
   A. Net Present Value (NPV)
   B. Return on Investment (ROI)
   C. Economic Value Added (EVA)
   D. Expected Monetary Value (EMV)

28. Your team has identified several risks in the project as well as their probability, impact, and priorities. The team is now exploring the response strategies to risks if they occur. The team identified that a couple of the programmers on the team might leave, which would significantly impact the project, but they decided to deal with it if and when it occurs. Which one of the following statements is true?
   A. This is passive acceptance.
   B. This is active acceptance.
   C. This is risk avoidance.
   D. This is risk mitigation.

29. You are overseeing a project to implement a smartphone application and are currently in the Identify Risks process of identifying and documenting the project risks. While exploring the elements of the enterprise environmental factors as inputs to the Identify Risks process, your team will be exploring all of the following elements EXCEPT:
   A. Organizational risk attitudes
   B. Commercial databases
   C. Assumptions analysis
   D. Published checklist

30. You have been working on the Plan Risk Management process of establishing the basis to approach, plan, and execute risk management activities and have developed a risk management plan. Each of the following statements is true regarding the Plan Risk Management process EXCEPT:
   A. The risk management plan, which is a part of the overall project management plan, is an input to all other risk processes.
   B. The risk management plan includes a description of the responses to risks and triggers.
   C. The risk management plan is an output of the Plan Risk Management process.
   D. The risk management plan includes methodology, roles and responsibilities, budget, risk categories, definition of risk probability and impact, revised stakeholder tolerances, reporting formats, and other items.

Project Risk Management Answers

1. C: The risk register is an output of the Identify Risks process.

2. D: The cost of probable loss or damage is $600,000 times 5 percent, which equals $30,000. The cost of the insurance premium is $15,000; therefore, you should purchase the insurance premium.

3. B: Risk categories are a group of potential causes for risk and can be grouped into categories, such as technical, political, external, project, and environmental. In order to systematically identify risks to a consistent level of detail, we can use the form of a simple list of categories or a Risk Breakdown Structure (RBS). It's a comprehensive way of ordering risks according to their source.

4. B: The risk owner for a particular risk is responsible for implementing the actions defined by mitigation and the contingency plan in risk management.

5. A: The Delphi technique is mainly focused on preventing group thinking and finding out the true opinions of the participants. This is done by sending a request for information to experts who are participating anonymously, compiling their responses, and sending the results back to them for further review until a consensus is reached.

6. A: Perform Qualitative Risk Analysis is the process of prioritizing risks by assessing and combining their probability of occurrence and impact to the project if they occur. This fast, relatively easy to perform, and cost effective process ensures that the right emphasis is on the right risk areas as per their ranking and priority and helps to allocate adequate time and resources for them. This process utilizes the experience of subject matter experts, functional managers, best practices, and previous project records. Even though numbers are used for the rating in Perform Qualitative Risk Analysis, it is a subjective evaluation and should be performed throughout the project.

7. B: Risk categories are a group of potential causes for risk that can be grouped into categories, such as technical, political, external, project, and environmental. In order to systematically identify risks to a consistent level of detail, we can use the form of a simple list of categories or a Risk Breakdown Structure (RBS). Assumptions are information not generally considered to be based on factual data items and should be verified. Constraints are limitations that should be considered when developing project plans. The product description provides details about the complexity of the product to be delivered.

8. D: Monte Carlo simulation is associated with the Perform Quantitative Risk Analysis process and determines the impact of identified risks by running simulations to identify the range of possible outcomes for a number of scenarios.

9. B: Monte Carlo simulation generates information through iterations. Project information at the activity level is chosen at random during the process and produces data that illustrates the likelihood of achieving specific cost or schedule targets.

10. B: Risk triggers are symptoms or warning signs that a potential risk is about to occur within the project. For instance, a key team member searching for a better job opportunity is a warning sign that the person may be leaving the team soon, causing schedule delay, increased cost, and other issues. Risk events are actual occurrences of an identified risk event. Residual risks are the remaining risks after the execution of risk response planning and for which contingency and fallback plans can be created. Secondary risks are new risks created by implementing the selected risk response strategies.

11. A: The Ishikawa diagram, also called a cause and effect flow chart or a fishbone diagram, shows the relationship between the causes and effects of problems.

12. D: Ordinal scales utilize a narrative description and assign values as high, medium, low, or a combination of these. This numeric scale, also called a cardinal scale, is expressed as values from 0.0 to 1.0 and can be stated in equal (linear) or unequal (nonlinear) increments.

13. D: Risk ratings are determined by the product of probability and impact or consequences when using qualitative analysis and to determine Expected Monetary Value (EMV) when utilizing a decision tree (quantitative analysis). EMV is the product of the probability and consequences of an event or task.

14. D: Transferring is shifting the negative impact of a threat, along with the ownership of the response, to a third party to make it their responsibility. It only gives another party responsibility for its management but does not eliminate the risk. It nearly always involves payment to the third party for taking on the risk. Risk mitigation simply means a reduction in the probability and/or impact of an adverse risk event to an acceptable threshold. Since it is seldom possible to eliminate all risks and also since the cost or impact of avoid, transfer, and mitigate is too high, acceptance can be the preferred strategy. It indicates that the project team is simply accepting the risk and will continue with the project. Passive acceptance requires no action. The active acceptance strategy aims to establish contingency reserves to handle threats. Avoid indicates that you are eliminating the threat by eliminating the root cause of the threat.

15. B: Residual risks are the risks that remain after the execution of risk response planning and for which contingency and fallback plans can be created. Their probability and impact have been reduced through mitigation. These risks are included in the outputs of the Plan Risk Responses process and are expected to remain as threats. Primary risks included in the initial risk identification process are generally most obvious. Secondary risks are new risks that are created due to the implementation of selected risk response strategies. Workarounds are unplanned responses developed to deal with the occurrence of unanticipated risk events.

16. A: Variance and trend analysis are tools & techniques used in the Control Risks process.

17. A: A risk event is the actual occurrence of the risk, such as an equipment failure. Risk probability is the likelihood that a risk event may occur. The amount at stake refers to the impact or consequence of the risk on one or more project objectives including scope, schedule, cost, and quality.

18. C: These are all examples of risk mitigation. Risk mitigation simply means a reduction in the probability and/or impact of an adverse risk event to an acceptable threshold. Transferring is shifting the negative impact of a threat, along with the ownership of the response, to a third party to make it their responsibility. An example of this would be insurance bonds, warranties, guarantees, and contracts. Avoidance is eliminating the threat by eliminating the cause or changing the project management plan. An example of this would be using a slower but reliable technology instead of a cutting-edge one to avoid associated risk. Since it is seldom possible to eliminate all risks and also since the cost or impact of avoid, transfer, and mitigate is too high, acceptance can be the preferred strategy. It indicates that the project team is simply accepting the risk and will continue with the project.

19. A: Stakeholders may be great contributors for identifying potential risks in the project. You should have involved other stakeholders instead of only working with the team members on risk management activities.

20. D: Since you are taking action to lower the probability and impact of the risk, you are mitigating the risk.

21. A: This is an example of assumptions analysis. This is an analysis of the validity of assumptions, hypotheses, and scenarios developed in project initiation to identify risks from inaccuracies, incompleteness, and inconsistencies of assumptions. The assumptions that turn out to be invalid should be evaluated, qualitatively and quantitatively analyzed, and planned for just like other risks.

22. B: The diagramming techniques such as Ishikawa diagrams, system or process flow charts, and influence diagrams, are used as tools & techniques in the Identify Risks process. An influence diagram shows how a set of influencers may influence others and affect outcomes. For instance, a delay in receiving equipment may influence other factors, such as triggering overtime work or a quality issue due to a lack of time to perform tasks.

23. C: A list of identified risks will be included in the risk register, not in your risk management plan.

24. B: Workarounds, unplanned responses developed to deal with the occurrence of unanticipated risk events, are not valid ways of reducing risks in a project.

25. B: Risk audits, technical performance measurement, and variance and trend analysis are tools & techniques used in the Control Risks process. Strategies for negative risks or threats such as avoid, transfer, mitigate, and avoid are used as tools & techniques in the Plan Risk Responses process.

26. A: Risk avoidance is the elimination of the threat by eliminating the cause or changing the project management plan. This is an example of avoidance since you are changing your travel plan to eliminate the threat of traffic delay.

27. D: The expected monetary value is calculated by multiplying the probability with the impact.

The EMV for the opportunity is 55 percent * $120,000 = $66,000 and for the threat is 45 percent * $55,000 = $24,750. The total EMV in this case is $66,000 – $24,750 = $41,250 profit.

28. A: Since it is seldom possible to eliminate all risks and also since the cost or impact of avoid, transfer, and mitigate is too high, acceptance can be the preferred strategy. It indicates that the project team is simply accepting the risk and will continue with the project. The team has decided to go for passive acceptance, which requires no action.

29. C: Assumptions analysis is a tool & technique in the Identify Risks process, not an input.

30. B: The Plan Risk Management process establishes the basis to approach, plan, and execute risk management activities throughout the life of the project and develops the risk management plan. The risk management plan does not include a description of the responses to risks or triggers. Responses to risks are documented in the risk register as part of the Plan Risk Responses process.

CHAPTER 12

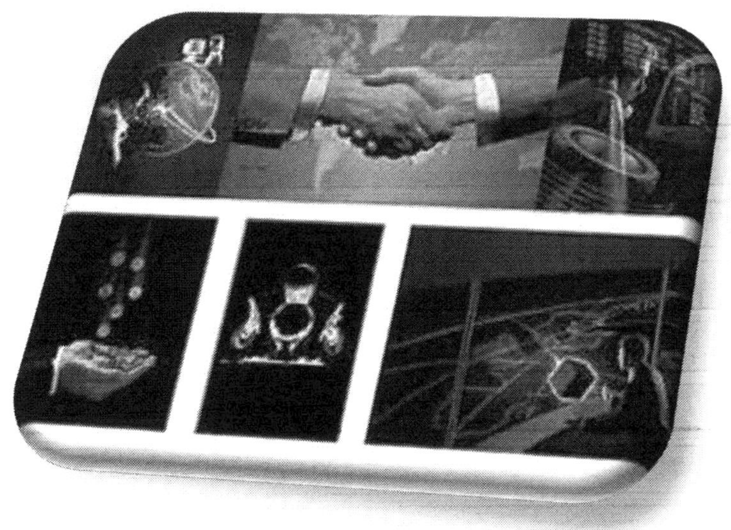

PROJECT PROCUREMENT MANAGEMENT

Project Procurement Management

In the context of a project, to procure something means to purchase or acquire goods, services, or results needed from outside the organization. Procurement involves the extensive use of contracts between a buyer and seller. The principle endeavor of procurement management is to arrange and manage contracts. Most large organizations have procurement departments that are ultimately responsible for soliciting, negotiating, administering, closing contracts, and monitoring contractual obligations placed on the project team.

Procurement management involves two important kinds of activities: managing contracts with suppliers and clients by developing and controlling any changes, and ensuring the project team fulfills its contractual obligations. Some examples of procurement activities include the following:

- Reviewing activity resource requirements to determine what goods and services are required
- Determining which goods and services need to be sourced externally
- Examining the schedule and ascertaining when goods and services are needed throughout the project
- Overseeing the creation of contracts with suppliers
- Ensuring all contractual obligations of suppliers are met

There are a number of names that are given to both buyers and sellers depending on the type of project, the work being done, or the kind of contract:

- A buyer can be known as a client, customer, contractor, prime contractor, acquiring organization, governmental agency, service requestor, or purchaser. Simply put, the buyer is the party who will receive the product or service and who provides monetary compensation for it.
- A seller can also be known as a contractor, subcontractor, vendor, service provider, or supplier. The basic definition is that the seller is the party providing a service or product in exchange for monetary compensation.

In procurement management, a project team is not limited to one of these roles. More than likely, the team will be engaged in a number of agreements, which means that the team can be a buyer for one agreement and a seller for another.

Project Manager's Role in Procurement Management

A project manager's role in procurement management depends on the corporation's methodology but should at least include the following:

- Be familiar with the procurement processes and policies.
- Understand contract terms and conditions and be involved during contract negotiation if possible.
- Act as a liaison between procurement and the project team.
- Identify project risks and incorporate mitigation and allocation of risks into the contract.
- Fit the schedule for completion of the procurement process into the schedule for the project.
- Work with the contract manager to manage changes to the contract.
- Make sure the contract contains all the project management requirements, such as meeting attendance, reports, actions, and needed communications.
- Help tailor the contract to the unique needs of the project.
- Verify that all the work in the contract is completed.

Project Contract

A project contract is a formal agreement between two parties and the principle endeavor of procurement management. It can include the following:

- An offer
- A proposal
- Acceptance: The criteria for accepting the project deliverables.
- Consideration: Something of value, not necessarily money.
- Legal capacity: Should be legally binding and backed by a court system in most countries.
- Legal purpose: Cannot have a contract for the sale of illegal goods. The contract should help reduce project risks.
- Legal language: Should be formal and in writing if possible. It is mandatory to complete all items specified in the contract, or a change order should be issued. Changes must be in writing; if it is not in the contract, it can only be implemented through the Perform Integrated Change Control process.
- Business terms regarding payments
- Reporting requirements
- Contract statement of work: All product and project management requirements should be stated in the contract.

Contracts: Terms and Conditions

Terms and conditions contained in a contract specify any or all aspects of an agreement that either side feels is important to stipulate. There are an infinite number of possibilities, but a list of the most common include the following:

Terms and Conditions	Details
Acceptance	Criteria for accepting the product, service, or result.
Agents	Authorized representatives for the buyer or seller.
Authority	The level of power to carry on certain activities.
Assignment	Circumstances under which parties can assign their rights and obligations to another party.
Arbitration	An alternative and cheaper method to the court system for dispute resolution. A neutral, private third party is assigned to resolve the dispute.
Bonds	Mostly refers to payment or performance bonds. For example, a performance bond would protect the buyer from nonperformance of the seller.
Breach/Default	Not meeting contractual obligation by the seller or the buyer.
Risk of Loss	The allocation of risk between the buyer and seller in the event of a loss or destruction of the goods and services.
Confidentiality	Information that must not be made public or given access to a third party.
Force Majeure	Allowable excuse for either party for not meeting a contractual obligation in the event of something considered to be an act of God, such as a fire, storm, flood, freak electrical storm, or other natural disaster. Since the event is considered to be neither party's fault, usually the seller receives a time extension. Risk of loss is borne by the seller, which is usually covered by insurance.
Incentives	Benefits that the seller will receive for aligning with the buyer's time, cost, quality, risk, and performance objectives.
Changes	The policy, procedure, time frame for notice and turnaround, and other items required for implementing changes in the project.
Indemnification	Parties liable for accidents, personal injury, or damages.
Intellectual Property	The ownership of the intellectual properties such as patents, trademarks, copyrights, source code, books, processes, data, and other items used in connection with or developed as part of the contract.
Material Breach	A breach so severe that it is not possible to continue work under the contract.
Warranties	Promises of sustaining the quality of the goods and services delivered under the contract for a certain time period.
Ownership	Ownership of the tangible items such as materials, equipment, buildings, and other things used in connection with or developed as part of the contract.
Termination	Cancellation of the project prior to completion due to specific reasons.
Waivers	Without the agreement of all parties, rights under the contract may not be waived or modified.
Time Is of the Essence	Any delay will be considered as a material breach as delivery dates are extremely important.
Retainage	In order to ensure full completion, an amount of money, usually 5 to 10 percent, is withheld from each payment and paid in full once the final work is completed.

Table 12-1: Contract Terms and Conditions

Supplier Contract Example for an Office Move Project

Due to ITPro Consultancy's dramatic growth in recent years, we have decided to relocate our administration and sales teams from our current office locations to a single office premise based in the Jamaica, Queens area. To ensure that this office move is undertaken smoothly and without affecting ITPro Consultancy's business, we have decided to outsource the design, fit-out, and relocation activities to an external supplier.

The preferred supplier of this project will be expected to meet the following objectives:

- Design the new premise to house a total of seventy-five staff, fifteen offices, three meeting rooms, a kitchen, and a staff entertainment area.
- Manage the entire fit-out of the new premise by installing cabling, fixed and moveable partitioning, plumbing, electrical fittings, and all interior decorating in accordance with the architectural design.
- Relocate all of ITPro Consultancy's administration and sales team members to the new premise within a single weekend to ensure that the business operation remains unaffected by the move.
- Clean up and rearrange our existing premise after the move to comply with the terms specified in our tenancy agreement.

MoveDoctor was selected as the preferred vendor. ITPro Consultancy and MoveDoctor agreed to the following contract:

Supplier Contract for ITPro Office Move Project

Introduction: This document serves as the formal contractual agreement between ITPro Consultancy and MoveDoctor for the design, fit-out, and relocation to a single office premise based in the Jamaica, Queens area. This contract lists the scope of work to be undertaken, responsibilities of both parties, and general terms for contract completion.

Purpose: The purpose of this supplier contract is to describe, in detail, the scope of work, responsibilities, terms, and conditions between ITPro Consultancy and MoveDoctor. Both parties agree to complete their assigned responsibilities and duties in accordance with the terms and conditions stated herein.

Recipients: The following parties have received this contract for authorization:

- John Johnson: President, ITPro Consultancy
- David Hall: Senior project manager, ITPro Consultancy
- Tom Crown: CEO, MoveDoctor
- Brad Goodman: Project manager, MoveDoctor

Definitions: The following table defines the common terminology used in this contractual agreement.

Term	Definition
The Project	The Office Move project undertaken by ITPro Consultancy.
We, the client, the project team	ITPro Consultancy, a duly incorporated company, with its head office based at 500 Lexington Avenue, Manhattan, NY.
You, the supplier	MoveDoctor, a duly incorporated company, with its head office based at 43 Central Ave, Meadow Ridge, NY.
Project plan	A document that lists the Work Breakdown Structure (WBS), time frames, and resources required to undertake the project.
Procurement items	The items that the supplier to the project is contractually obliged to provide.
Project life cycle	The phases undertaken to deliver the desired project outcome.
Resources	The labor, equipment, materials, and other items that are needed to undertake the project.
Supplier contract	The agreement between the client and the supplier for the completion of the defined scope of work.
General	Words used in singular shall include the plural definition and vice versa.

Scope of Work: The scope of work to be undertaken by the supplier is listed in the following sections.

Procurement Items: The following table lists each procurement item to be delivered by the supplier as well as respective quantity and price:

Procurement Item	Item Description	Item Price
Architectural design of the new premises	Design the layout of the new premises to meet the following criteria: – An open plan of facilities for seventy-five staff, fifteen offices, three meeting rooms, a kitchen, and a staff entertainment area. – Has practical partitioning, office, and meeting room layouts. – Uses natural lighting as much as possible. – Is structured to provide office views for managers. – Provides a boardroom suitable for fifteen people. – Has a friendly reception environment with seating for up to ten visitors. – Contains a network services room with space for three racks of equipment.	$5,000
Fit-out of the new premises	Construct the new office fit-out including installation of: – Office telecommunications links to desks. – Wi-Fi telecommunications links to the network room. – Power, lighting, and general services. – Partitioning of the new kitchen and offices. – The final interior fit-out (painting, partitioning, carpeting, lighting, and electrical fittings).	$18,000
Relocation to the new premises	Relocate all ITPro Consultancy staff to the new premises by: – Moving furniture, equipment, and personal belongings. – Documenting and communicating new seating locations. – Communicating the layout of the new premises to staff.	$4,000
Rearrangement of the existing premises	Completely rearrange the existing premises in accordance with the terms of our lease by: – Removing all surplus equipment, fittings, and partitioning. – Reinstating the original layout of the premises. – Cleaning the carpets, walls, and permanent fixtures and fittings.	$2,000

Delivery Schedule: This scope of work must be completed according to the following delivery schedule. To ensure that the supplier delivers the scope of work in accordance with the criteria listed above, the project will undertake four supplier reviews throughout the project life cycle.

Major Milestones	Start Date	End Date	Duration
Completion of architectural design	1/1/2013	1/30/2013	30
Completion of fit-out	2/1/2013	3/30/2013	60
Relocation to new premises	3/15/2013	4/29/2013	45
Rearrange existing premises	5/1/2013	5/30/2013	30
Reviews			
Review1	1/31/2013	1/31/2013	1
Review2	3/31/2013	3/31/2013	1

Responsibilities: To ensure that this scope of work is efficiently delivered by the supplier and accepted by the project team, we have listed each party's responsibilities below:

	Description
Supplier	The supplier will be responsible for the following: – Meeting the objectives stated in this supplier contract. – Delivering the specified procurement items within the time frames and costs agreed to in the supplier contract. – Informing the project team of any risks or issues occurring during the project. – Supplying the staff, equipment, subcontractors, and other resources required to deliver the scope of work.
Project Team	The project team will be responsible for the following: – Advising the supplier of the detailed requirements of the project. – Supporting the supplier throughout the project by resolving questions, issues, and risks promptly. – Approving any changes required to ensure that the supplier can meet the project objectives. – Communicating the status of this project within the ITPro Consultancy's business. – Identifying issues related to the supplier's performance.

Performance: This section describes how the performance of the supplier will be regularly reviewed throughout the project life cycle.
Review Criteria: The following criteria will be used to review the supplier's performance throughout the project life cycle.

Criteria	Description
Architectural design of the new premises	– Does the design layout of the new premise meet all required criteria? – Is the design well structured, and does it provide a user-friendly, high performance solution?
Fit-outs of the new premises	– Have all the features for the new office fit-out been installed? – Do the developed fit-outs match the specified design?
Relocation of the staff	– Have all ITPro Consultancy's staff been relocated to the new premises?
Reorganization of the existing premises	– Has the existing premises been reorganized as per expectation?

Review Process: The following process will be undertaken to review the supplier's performance in accordance with the review criteria listed above:

- Four supplier reviews will be undertaken as listed in the review schedule.
- The purpose of each review will be to determine whether the supplier has done the following:
  - Delivered the procurement items as described in the scope of work
  - Delivered the procurement items that meet the review criteria specified
  - Operated in accordance with the terms and conditions of this supplier contract
- The project procurement manager will be responsible for undertaking each supplier review.
- The supplier will be notified within ten working days of the completion of each review. He/she will be informed of any deviations as well as actions needed to correct them. The project manager will then provide the supplier with a time frame for resolving deviations before a dispute is raised.

Terms and Conditions: This section lists the terms and conditions required to administer the contract.

Terms and Conditions	Details
Agreement	This contract constitutes the entire agreement between both parties and supersedes all other contracts, agreements, or understandings previously or currently in existence. Only changes authorized in writing shall constitute a modification to this contract.
Law	This contract shall be governed by the legislation of the United States of America.
Acceptance	To be accepted by the project team, all procurement items must be – Reviewed and approved by the project manager – In accordance with the scope of work defined for this project – One hundred percent complete and ready for handover – Produced within the time frames and budget agreed on in the supplier contract, or there must be a satisfactory explanation given for the variance
Invoicing	All invoices should be dated the last day of the month to which the invoice applies. The project will raise any queries and/or issues to the supplier regarding the invoice within five days of receipt. Upon arrival, the invoice will be processed, and payment will be made by the fifteenth of the following month. If a dispute is raised regarding an invoice, the project team will pay the undisputed portion of the invoice, and the supplier will deal with the disputed amount separately.
Confidentiality	During the project, the supplier may acquire confidential information relating to our business, project, and/or customers. The supplier agrees to keep this information strictly confidential at all times.
Termination	Both parties have the right to dismiss this contract by providing the other party formal written notice within fifteen days. At that point in time, the supplier's invoices up to the date of termination will be paid and all intellectual property will be handed over unless the project team has formally raised a dispute with the supplier.
Disputes	A dispute may be raised at any point in the project life cycle. If an issue remains unsettled even after direct negotiation between the supplier and the project team, a formal dispute must be raised, and the other party should be notified in writing. The matter in dispute shall be referred to and settled by a mutually agreed-upon arbitrator and will be final and binding for both parties. After dispute's resolution, both parties shall continue to assume their responsibilities under this contract as if the dispute had not occurred.
Indemnity	The supplier guarantees that the procurement items delivered under this contract without failure for a period of twelve months from the completion date of the project life cycle.

Centralized/Decentralized Contracting

There are several ways a contract department can be organized.

- **Centralized:** In a centralized contracting environment, a procurement manager from the procurement department may handle procurements on several projects.
- **Decentralized:** In a decentralized contracting environment, a procurement manager is assigned to a project full time and reports directly to the project manager.

Advantages and Disadvantages of Contracting Organizations

	Advantages	Disadvantages
Centralized	Employees have a clearly defined career path in the procurement profession.	One procurement personnel may be assigned to several projects.
	Employees will have enhanced expertise in contracting and procurement.	Obtaining contracting help when needed may be challenging.
	There are continuous improvements, training, and shared lessons learned.	
	Standardized company practices increase efficiency and improve understanding.	
Decentralized	There is more loyalty to the project.	There is a tendency to have a lack of defined career path in the contracting profession.
	It is easier to access the contracting expert.	Once the project is completed, there is no home to return to.
	The procurement manager will be more involved and have a better understanding of the project and its procurement needs.	It is difficult to maintain a high-level of contracting expertise in the company.
		There is little standardization of contracting practices.
		There is inefficient use of contracting resources across projects.

Table 12-2: Advantages and Disadvantages of Contracting Organizations

Project Contract Types

There are several types of contracts to work with while acquiring goods and services needed for a project. The goal of contract type selection is to:

- Have reasonable distribution of risk between the buyer and the seller
- Provide the greatest incentive for the seller's efficient and economic performance

Secondary considerations include the following:

- How well defined the scope of work is
- Amount or frequency of changes expected once the project is initiated
- Level of effort and expertise the buyer can allocate for managing the seller
- Industry standards of all types of contracts used
- Amount of market competition
- Amount of risks in the project
- If the buyer wants to offer the seller any incentive, and if so how much

Types of Contracts

Three broad categories of contracts are:

- Cost Reimbursable (CR)
- Time and Material (T & M)
- Fixed Price (FP)

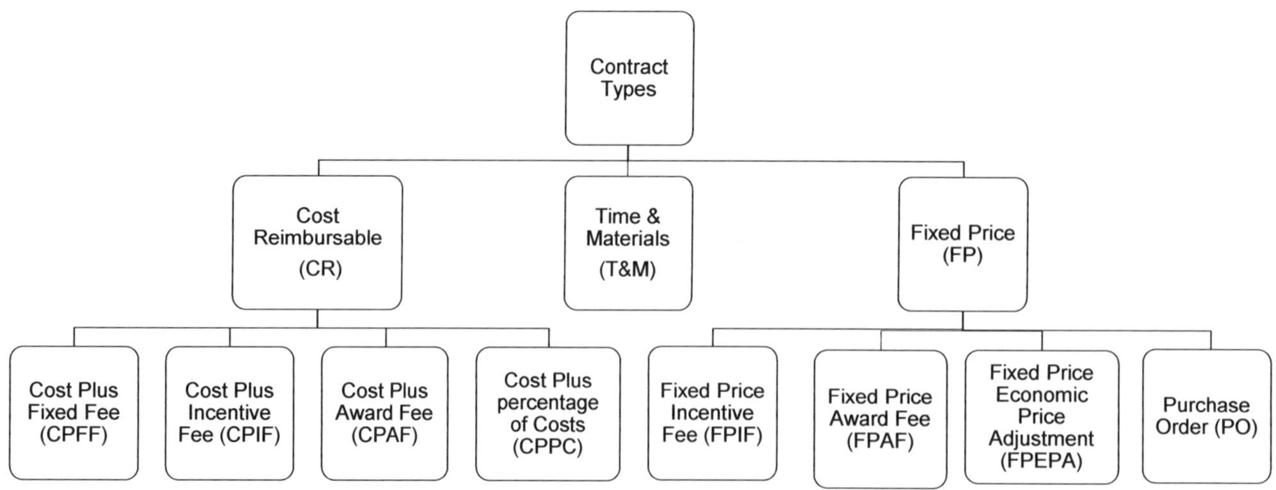

Figure 12-1: Contract Types

Cost Reimbursable (CR) Contract

A Cost Reimbursable (CR) contract is used when the exact scope of the work is uncertain and cost cannot be estimated accurately enough. In this type of contract the seller's allowable costs are reimbursed by the buyer; plus, an additional amount as fee or incentive.

- The buyer bears the most risk, as total cost is unknown until the project is finished.
- This is used when the buyer knows what is needed but not how to do it.
- Sellers usually write a detailed Statement of Work (SOW).

Example: Research and development or information technology projects use this type of contract when the scope is unknown.

There are four types of cost reimbursable contracts:

Cost Reimbursable (CR) Contract Types	Detail
Cost Plus Fixed Fee (CPFF)	This is the most common variety. The buyer pays the actual cost and a negotiated fee that is fixed prior to initiating the work. **Example:** Contract = Cost plus a fee of $100,000.
Cost Plus Incentive Fee (CPIF)	The buyer pays the actual cost and a set fee based on specific performance objectives. Usually the seller gets a percentage of savings, which is 80 percent to the buyer and 20 percent to the seller. **Example:** Contract = Cost and for every month early the project is finished, an additional $5,000 is paid to the seller.
Cost Plus Award Fee (CPAF)	The buyer pays the actual cost and an award amount (bonus) based on performance. **Example:** Contract = Cost, Maximum award = $50,000, every month performance is achieved an additional $5,000 will be awarded to the seller.
Cost Plus Percentage of Costs (CPPC)	The buyer pays the actual cost plus a percentage of the cost as a fee. This type of contract is illegal in the United States. **Example:** Contract = Cost plus 5 percent of costs as a fee.

Table 12-3: Types of Cost Reimbursable Contracts

Time and Material Contract

This time-based fee plus the cost of materials contract is used for smaller amounts and shorter time frames and requires little or no defined scope of work.

There is medium risk for the buyer but little incentive for the seller to complete the work as the profit is built into the rate. The buyer may put a "Not to exceed" clause to limit the cost.

Example: Contract = $30 per hour for tiles installation plus expenses or tiles and other supplies at a cost of $10 per square foot.

Fixed Price (FP, Lump Sum, or Firm Fixed Price) Contract

A fixed price or lump sum or firm fixed price is the most common form of a contract in the world and is used for acquiring goods and services with well-defined requirements or scope.

- There is one price for everything.
- There is the least risk for the buyer, and the risk of higher costs is borne by the seller, as sellers bear additional costs if the costs are more than the agreed-upon amount.
- Buyers usually write a detailed Statement of Work (SOW) document.

Example: Contract = $1.5 million.
There are four types of fixed price contracts:

Fixed Price (FP) Contract Types	Detail
Fixed Price Incentive Fee (FPIF)	The buyer pays a fixed price plus a set fee based on the seller meeting specific performance criteria, such as finishing the project early or reducing the cost. **Example:** Contract = $500,000 and for every month early the project is finished, an additional $5,000 is paid to the seller.
Fixed Price Award Fee(FPAF)	The buyer pays a fixed price plus an award amount (bonus) based on performance. **Example:** Contract = $500,000, Maximum award = $20,000, every month performance is achieved an additional $5,000 will be awarded to the seller.
Fixed Price Economic Price Adjustment (FPEPA)	This allows for price increases, especially for multi-year contracts, in cases where there are fluctuations in the exchange rate, interest rate, consumer price index, cost of living adjustments, or other factors that may impact the project. **Example:** Contract = $500,000 but a price increase will be allowed in year two based on consumer price increase or increase in specific materials cost.
Purchase Order (PO)	A purchase order is the simplest type of unilateral (signed by one party) instead of bilateral fixed price contract and is mostly used for simple commodity procurement. **Example:** Contract to purchase two thousand bags of cement at fifteen dollars per bag.

Table 12-4: Types of Fixed Priced Contracts

Advantages and Disadvantages of Each Type of Contract from the Buyer's Perspective

Contract Type	Advantages	Disadvantages
Cost Reimbursable (CR)	Simpler contract statement of work.	The total price is unknown.
	Usually requires less work to write the scope than the fixed price.	Compels auditing sellers' invoices.
	Seller does not have to add a huge amount as reserve to cover the risks; thus, the contract is usually cheaper than the fixed price.	More work for buyers to manage.
		Seller has only a moderate incentive to control cost.
Time and Material (T & M)	Quick to create.	Mostly applicable for small projects.
	Contract duration is short term.	Profits in every hour billed.
		Seller has no motivation to control cost.
		Requires the most day-to-day oversight from the buyer.
Fixed Price (FP)	Less work for buyers to manage.	Seller may underprice the work and try to make a profit on change orders.
	Seller has a strong motivation to control cost.	Seller may start cutting scope if they begin to lose money.
	Companies are more proficient with this type of contract.	More work for buyers to write the contract statement work.
	Buyers know the total price at project start.	The seller will need to add a huge reserve to the price for their increased risk.

Table 12-5: Advantages and Disadvantages of Each Type of Contract from the Buyer's Perspective

Risk in Contracting

Objective of Buyer: To place the maximum performance risk on the seller while maintaining a degree of incentive for efficient and economic performance.

Objective of Seller: To minimize the degree of risk while increasing profit potential.

In a fixed price contract, if the cost increases, the seller will pay for the additional cost and make less profit. On the other hand, if the cost increases in a cost reimbursable contract, the buyer will pay for the additional cost. The diagram below shows which contracts are risky for the buyer and which ones are risky for the seller.

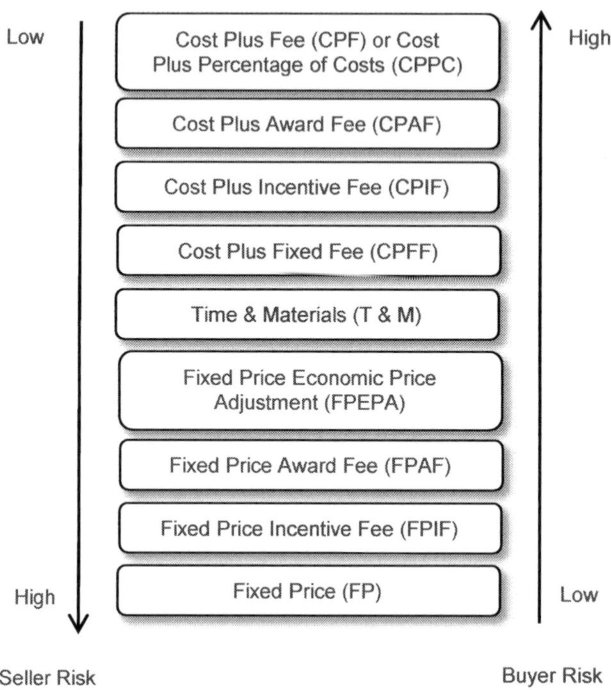

Figure 12-2: Contract Types and Associated Risk for Buyer and Seller

Contracts: Incentives Calculations

In order to calculate the incentives, we need to be familiar with the following terms:

Price: An amount the seller charges the buyer or the amount the buyer is willing to pay to the seller.

Incentive: A bonus on top of the agreed-upon price for exceeding time or cost objectives as specified in the contract.

For the seller, the focus is on profit. For buyers, the focus can be a combination of cost, time, and performance. Incentives help to bring the seller's objectives in line with those of the buyer.

With an incentive, both the buyer and the seller work toward the same objective (for instance, completing the project on time).

Target Price: From the buyer's point of view

Target Price = Target Cost + Target Fee

Sharing Ratio: This dictates how cost savings or cost overrun will be shared between the buyer and the seller. A sharing of 90/10 means the buyer will keep 90 percent and the seller will keep 10 percent of the cost savings or overrun.

Ceiling Price: The highest price the buyer is willing to pay.

Point of Total Assumption (PTA): The cost point in the contract where the seller assumes responsibility for all cost overruns as costs beyond that point are considered to be due to mismanagement.

PTA = Target Cost + [(Ceiling Price – Target Price)/Buyer's share of cost overrun]

PTA only applies to a Fixed Price Incentive Fee (FPIF) contract, and it helps identify the cost point in the contract where the seller has the most motivation to bring things to completion.

Exercise 1: Name the most appropriate contract type to use for the following situations. Your choices are: CR, CPFF, CPIF, CPAF, CPF or CPPC, FP, FPIF, FPAF, FPEPA, PO, or T & M contracts.

Situation	Type of Contract to use
1. You are buying standard commodities at a fifteen-dollar unit price.	
2. You are working on a multi-year project and just completed the scope of the work. Your team has come up with an independent estimate, but the economy is currently unpredictable.	
3. You are working on a hospital application project and know exactly what needs to be done and have also developed a procurement Statement of Work (SOW).	
4. You just signed a contract with the seller where you agreed to pay them a lump sum amount of $250,000; for every month performance exceeds the planned level by more than 10 percent, an additional $8,000 will be awarded to the seller with a maximum award of $40,000.	
5. You are working on a critical project for your organization and need work done, but you do not have time to audit invoices on this work or spend too much time with the vendors.	
6. You have three recently hired programmers on your team, and you plan to buy the services of a programmer to augment your new staff.	
7. You are working on a software development project that requires a high-level of expertise to complete, and you want to have the best performance possible for the finished product.	
8. You are assigned as a project manager for a research and development project and need to hire a contractor to perform research and development.	
9. You just signed a contract with your seller where you agreed to pay a lump sum amount of $250,000; also, every month early they finish the project you agreed to pay them an additional $6,000 as a fee.	
10. You are working on an IT project that is very challenging and was never done in your organization. You want to buy expertise in determining what needs to be done.	
11. Your manager has assigned you to a project and wants you to begin the work right away.	
12. You just signed a contract with your seller where you agreed to pay the total cost of the seller and 6 percent of the cost as an additional fee.	
13. The profit is included in the price but it is unknown to the buyer.	
14. You need to devote high-level of effort and expertise to manage the sellers.	

Exercise 2: Your management recently decided to split the procurement department and assign all procurement responsibilities to departments directly responsible for the projects. As a procurement professional, you understand that this change will only impact the procurement and will not really influence the organization's overall project management practices. Why would you still be against this kind of split considering what you would lose in a decentralized contracting environment?

Exercise 3: In a cost reimbursable contract, the cost is estimated at $300,000 and the fee at $35,000. If the seller beats that cost, they will share the savings at 80/20—buyer/seller. If the actual cost came in at $285,000, what are the final fee and final price?

Exercise 4: Company X is subcontracting a job to Company Y for an estimated $85,000. The contract type is a fixed price incentive fee. Company X imposed a cap (ceiling price: $94,000). Company Y's target cost is $78,000, and the target price is $85,000. Every dollar over target cost, the share ratio is 60:40 (X pays $0.60 and Y pays $0.40 of every dollar overrun). What is the PTA here?

Exercise 5: In a fixed price incentive fee contract, the target cost is estimated at $155,000 and the fee at $35,000. The buyer imposed a ceiling price of $200,000. The actual cost came to be $205,000. Since there was a cost overrun, the seller shares the added cost at a 70/30 ratio (70 percent to the buyer and 30 percent to the seller). What are the final fee, PTA, and final price?

Contracts: Negotiation

Negotiation is the process of clarifying and reaching mutual agreement on the structure and details of the contract prior to signing. In many cases, negotiation plays a vital role in procurement management; many projects fail due to poor negotiation. The project manager and other relevant members can help in negotiation and in clarifying project requirements.

Unlike a cost reimbursable contract, not much negotiation is needed in a fixed priced contract since, in this situation, the scope of work is mostly finalized and the contract is usually given to the lowest bidder based on price. In some cases, negotiation may be needed to cover parts of the proposed contract.

In the case of cost reimbursable and time & material contracts, there will likely be negotiation to finalize the price and other items. There will be more negotiations in all types of contracts if there are proposed changes to any part of the contract.

It is important to note that project managers, from both buyer and seller sides, should be involved in all kinds of negotiation to finalize the procurement Statement of Work (SOW), price, and other relevant terms and conditions if possible as they are responsible for facilitating project management and resolution of technical issues.

The goals of negotiation:

- To develop a good understanding and relationship with the seller.
- To obtain a fair and reasonable price for the product, service, and result.
- To discover and deal with disputes as much as possible prior to contract signing.

Negotiation Items: Subjects covered during the negotiation should include, but not be limited to, the following:

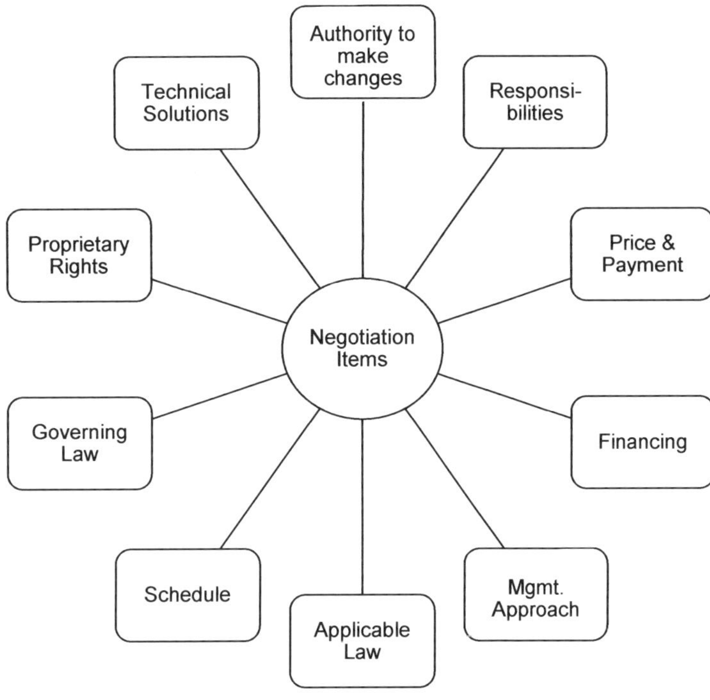

Figure 12-3: Negotiation Items

Effective negotiation helps you to resolve situations where what you want conflicts with what someone else wants. The aim of win-win negotiation is to find a solution that is acceptable to both parties, and leaves both parties feeling that they've won, in some way, after the event.

Negotiation Tactics: Tactics used to win during negotiation are as follows:

Tactic	Description
Attacks	Tactic of attacking the organization. "If your organization does not have a basic project management framework to manage a simple project, perhaps it should get out of the business."
Personal Insults	Tactic of attacking an individual. "We are not satisfied with your last year's performance, and if you do not show significant progress we will have to let you go."
Fair and Reasonable	Recommended tactic. Both parties try to be as fair and as reasonable as possible.
Delay	Tactic of delaying the negotiation as much as possible in order to impose a deadline. "I do not have any time to discuss the topic today, so let's revisit this issue the next time we get together."
Deadline	Tactic of imposing a deadline so that the other party does not have much time to explore the details while negotiating. "We have a flight to catch at 6:00 p.m. today and must finish negotiation on all the pending items by 4:00 p.m."
Lying	Tactic of not telling the truth directly (obvious) or indirectly (hidden).
Good Guy/Bad Guy	Tactic of making one person helpful to the other party while making another person very difficult to work with during negotiation.
Limited Authority	Tactic of using a lack of sufficient authority as an excuse during negotiation, which may or may not be true. "I am unable to give you a three-week extension as I am only authorized to offer one week."
Missing Man	Tactic of using a missing individual who has the power to authorize everything. "Only my boss can give you a three-week extension, but unfortunately he is not here. Why don't we agree to one week as discussed?"
Extreme Demands	Tactic of demanding something extreme in order to achieve something close to the expectation. "You must finish a seven hundred-page research paper within the next couple of days."
Withdrawal	Tactic of emotional and physical withdrawal as well as expressing lack of interest in the negotiation. "We do not want to proceed with this discussion anymore."
Fait Accompli	Tactic of using rules/laws, decisions already made, and other factors as mandatory to avoid any further discussion. "You must follow all the construction guidelines by the city council while managing the project."

Table 12-6: Negotiation Tactics

Project Procurement Management Processes

Procurement management is the set of processes related to obtaining goods and services from outside the organization. Part of the procurement planning process is to decide what needs to be procured. Once the decision of what needs to be procured and what should be done internally is made, the project manager can, often with the help of expert judgment, query the vendors for bids, quotes, or proposals based on the project's Statement of Work (SOW). Vendors may need to attend a bidder conference in order to get clarification on the SOW and a better understanding of what the project calls for. Vendors will then provide their quotes, bids, or proposals, according to what the project manager has requested. Once the project manager's organization selects the vendor for providing the goods and services, the contract is issued. Now, the project manager and the vendor should work together for the best interest of the project and both parties must live up to the terms and conditions of the contract. During contract closure, the buyer inspects the project work and other procurement items and confirms that the vendor delivered and performed according to the contract terms.

PMI identifies four key processes that are associated with the procurement management knowledge area.

Processes	Process Groups	Detail	Key Outputs
1. Plan Procurement Management	Planning	The processes of documenting what procurements are needed for the project, specifying the procurement approach, and also identifying potential sellers.	– Procurement Management Plan – Procurement Statement of Work (SOW) – Procurement Documents – Source Selection Criteria – Make-or-Buy Decisions
2. Conduct Procurements	Executing	The process of obtaining and evaluating seller responses, selecting a seller, and awarding a contract.	– Selected Sellers – Agreements
3. Control Procurements	Monitoring & Controlling	The process of managing procurement relationships, monitoring contract performance, and making changes and corrections to the contract as required.	– Work Performance Information – Change Requests – Project Management Plan Updates
4. Close Procurements	Closing	The process of completing each project procurement.	– Closed Procurements

Table 12-7: Four Project Procurement Management Processes and Key Outputs

The above four processes occur more or less sequentially in a project. Due to the nature of procurements and contracts, the processes of the project procurement management knowledge area are iterative by nature. As the project progresses, new needs may arise; therefore, new procurement relationships need to be developed. The Plan Procurement Management process can kick off at any stage of the project and even very late into a project.

Project Procurement Management Processes, Inputs, Tool & Techniques, and Outputs

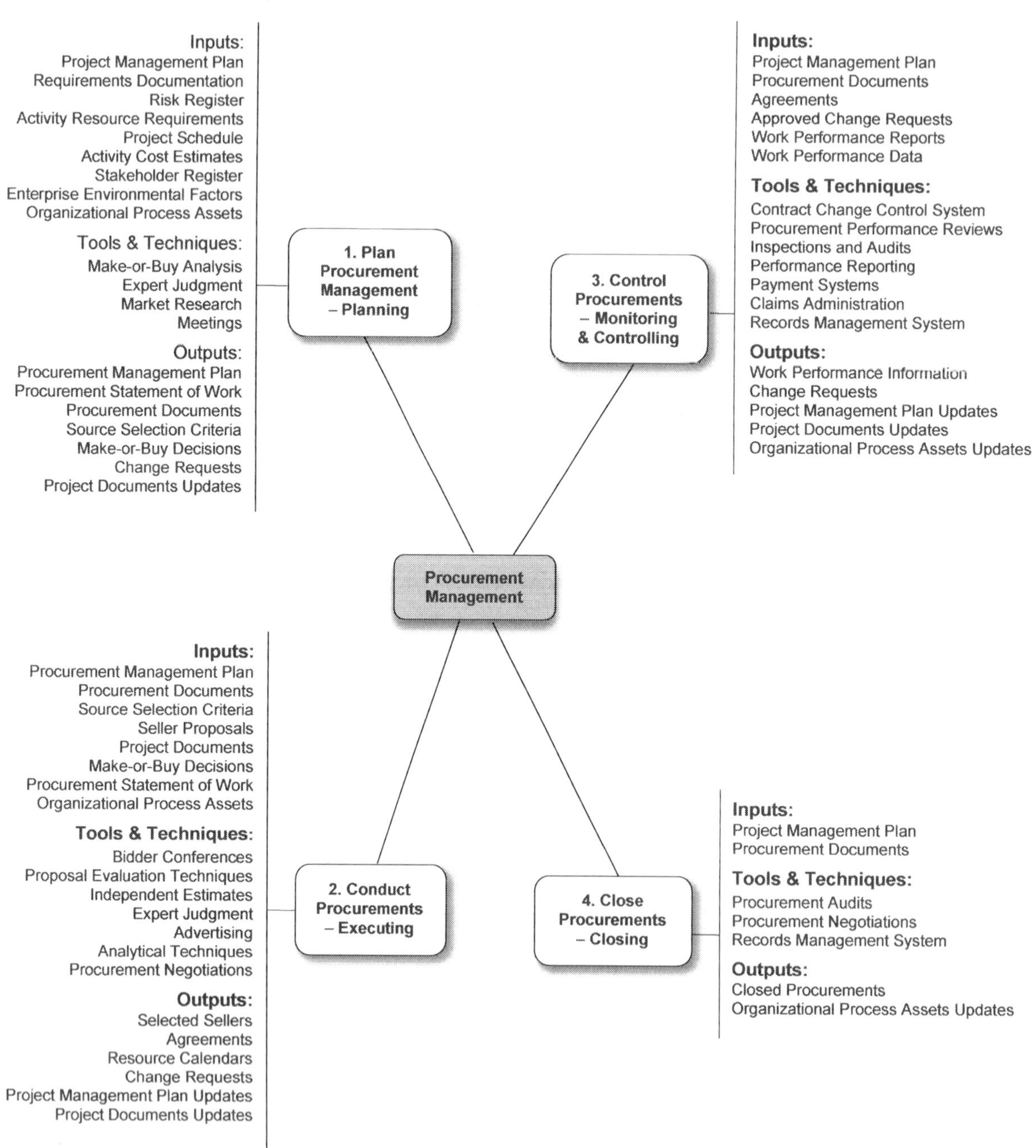

Figure 12-4: Project Procurement Management Processes, Inputs, Tool & Techniques, and Outputs

Plan Procurement Management

Plan Procurement Management is the process of documenting project purchasing decisions, specifying the approach, defining selection criteria to identify potential sellers, and putting together a procurement management plan. This process helps identify which components or services of the project will be performed internally and which of the needs can be best met by procuring products or services from outside the organization.

The following activities are usually carried out during the Plan Procurement Management process:

- Finalization of the Make-or-buy decision
- Creation of the Procurement Statement of Work (SOW)
- Selection of the appropriate contract type
- Creation of terms and conditions including standard and special conditions
- Creation of procurement documents
- Creation of source selection criteria
- Creation of a procurement management plan

As per the PMBOK®, the Plan Procurement Management process has the following inputs, tools & techniques, and outputs:

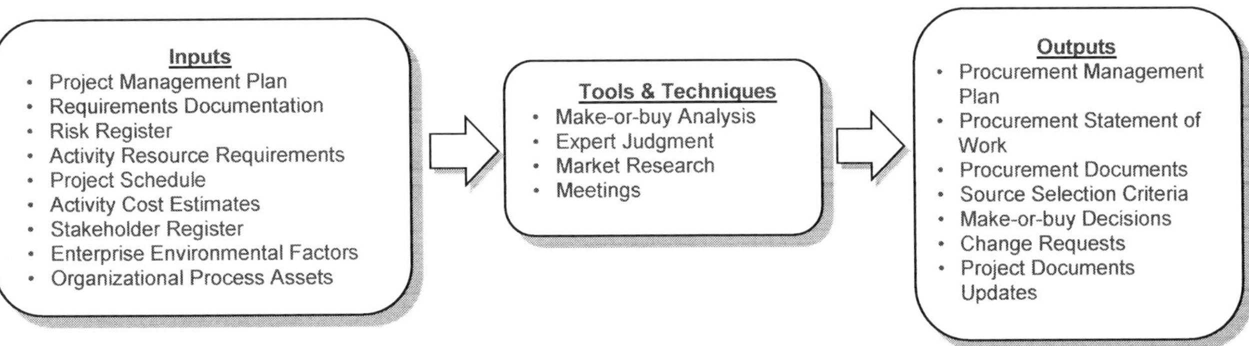

Figure 12-5: Plan Procurement Management: Inputs, Tools & Techniques, and Outputs

Plan Procurement Management: Inputs

- Project Management Plan
- Requirements Documentation
- Risk Register
- Activity Resource Requirements
- Project Schedule
- Activity Cost Estimates
- Stakeholder Register
- Enterprise Environmental Factors
- Organizational Process Assets

Project Management Plan: The project management plan includes the scope baseline, which is heavily used during the Plan Procurement Management process.

Project Scope Baseline: The project scope baseline whcih contains the project scope statement, the WBS, and the WBS dictionary defines the scope of the project and will be beneficial when considering what components of the scope will be procured.

The components of the project management plan, such as scope, cost, and schedule baselines help to identify any constraints on potential procurement efforts.

Requirements Documentation: All kinds of legal and contractual obligations that need to be considered in procurement can be found in the requirements document.

Requirements with risk-related contract decisions consist of agreements, including insurance, bonding, services, intellectual property rights, licenses, permits, and other items as appropriate. They are also prepared to distribute risks among the contracting parties and also specify each party's responsibility for specific risks.

Risk Register: The risk register can contain risk-related information, such as risk detail, categories, responses, and other factors in the procurement process.

Activity Resource Requirements: Activity resource requirements have details on particular needs, such as equipment, location, or manpower.

Project Schedule: The project schedule will have project road map information and/or mandatory delivery dates.

Activity Cost Estimates: Procurement items' cost estimates can assist to evaluate bids or proposals received from potential sellers.

Stakeholder Register: The stakeholder register contains details about project participants who are interested in the project and who can positively or negatively impact the project.

Enterprise Environmental Factors: Conditions of the marketplace; availability of products, services and results; sources; and terms and conditions can influence the procurement process.

Organizational Process Assets: Procurement-related policies, procedures, and guidelines, prequalified sellers based on past experiences, and management systems can play a vital role.

Plan Procurement Management: Tools & Techniques

- Make-or-buy Analysis
- Expert Judgment
- Market Research
- Meetings

Make-or-buy Analysis: This consists of determining whether a product can be cost effectively produced in-house or whether it should be purchased, leased, or rented. While performing this analysis, we must consider indirect as well as direct costs, contract types, core capabilities of the organization, and availability of resources in addition to related risk, schedule, and other factors.

Expert Judgment: Opinion provided by groups or individuals such as consultants, professional and technical organizations, and industry groups with specialized knowledge or training can be of tremendous value to develop seller proposal evaluation criteria and to deal with unique procurement issues, terms, and conditions. Planning procurements may rely on the following types of expertise:

- **Technical:** Technical experts can help the project team determine what procurements must be made.
- **Purchasing**: For the purposes of expanding or adjusting the decisive factor that is utilized to judge seller proposals, expert judgment is necessary.
- **Legal:** Expert legal judgment may be required to assist with the preparation and handling of procurement contracts. It can also help ensure that procurement processes are legally sound.

Market Research: The procurement team identifies the overall industry conditions and specific vendor and market capabilities by leveraging information gained from various sources, including online research, conferences, and other source types.

This kind of research is also beneficial for refining procurement objectives based on market conditions and technology trends as well as identifying risks associated with selecting a specific vendor who will be providing the required service or material.

Meetings: Meetings with team members, stakeholders, and especially potential bidders will be beneficial for the organization purchasing the material and service to formulate a procurement strategy.

Plan Procurement Management: Outputs

- Procurement Management Plan
- Procurement Statement of Work
- Procurement Documents
- Source Selection Criteria
- Make-or-buy Decisions
- Change Requests
- Project Documents Updates

Procurement Management Plan: It describes how project procurements will be carried out throughout the project including the following:

- What service, product, or result will be produced
- Types of contracts to be used
- Who will prepare independent estimates and when
- What procurements the project team may make on its own
- Which standard procurement documents will be used
- A list of pre-qualified sellers if there are any
- How the sellers will be selected
- How sellers' performance will be measured
- How procurement will be coordinated with other project aspects (scheduling and performance reporting)
- Assumptions and constraints related to procurements

Procurement Statement of Work: It describes the subject item in sufficient detail to allow prospective sellers to determine offerings (bids, proposals, and other types). It documents details of the work to be performed by the seller under a contract.

- May contain clear, complete, and concise descriptions of performance, design, functionality, reporting, format, and support requirements.
- May be revised frequently during procurement and prior to contract signing.
- Can be of several types depending on the nature of work and the type of industry.
- Can contain a section detailing risk management policies related to the required product or service.
- Can contain the performance data related to the required service.
- Can contain a description of the supply details, including the location and timing of supply and the type of contract to be used.
- Can contain a reference to the project's change integration management strategy.

Procurement Documents: These documents are used to solicit proposals from prospective sellers. Well-designed procurement documents help in easier comparisons of seller responses, more complete proposals, more accurate pricing, and a decrease in the amount of changes in the project.

- **Request for Proposal (RFP):** An RFP is the buyer's request to all potential sellers for the details of how work will be performed. It may include specific questions regarding performance of work and aspects of the seller's business (e.g., service capabilities, experience in this work, warranties, financing, and other things) as well as the following:
    - Background information about the project goal, objective, and other facts from the buyer's perspective
    - Procedure for applying
    - Guidelines for preparation of the response
    - Exact format of response required
    - Evaluation criteria that the buyer will use to evaluate the sellers
    - Pricing forms
    - Procurement statement of work
    - Terms and conditions
- **Invitation for Bid (IFB or Request for Bid, RFB):** A request from the buyer for all potential sellers to submit a total price bid for work to be performed.
- **Request for Quotation (RFQ):** A request from the buyer for a price quote per item, hour, foot, or other unit of measure.

Source Selection Criteria: Developed and used to provide sellers with an understanding of the buyer's need and also to help them decide whether to bid or make a proposal on the project. Later on it also helps to evaluate sellers by rating or scoring them.

Depending on the size and priority of the project, the selection criteria may just be the lowest price—for instance, purchasing a small amount of commodity—or it may be the price plus experience. In the case of construction service and for sophisticated services, source selection criteria may be more rigorous and extensive. Source selection criteria may include the following:

- **Buyer's need:** How well the sellers understand the needs of the buyers and address those needs in the Statement of Work (SOW) in their proposals.
- **Cost:** Proposed overall or life-cycle cost of the seller.
- **Capability:** Technical capability, methodologies, solutions, knowledge, skills, and approach of the seller.
- **Risk:** How good the seller can mitigate associated risks in the project.
- **Management approach:** Seller's capability to develop management procedures and processes to ensure project success.
- **Warranty:** Proposed type and duration of warranty for the final product from the seller.
- **Financial capacity:** Seller's capability to obtain required financial resources for the project.
- **Production capacity and interest:** Seller's capability and interest to meet potential future requirements.
- **Business size and type:** Does the seller meet a specific category of business, such as minority or woman-owned, disadvantaged small business, local business, and others as required by the project?
- **Past performance of sellers:** Any relevant past experience the buyers may have with the seller.
- **References:** Verification of seller's work and compliance with contractual requirements from prior customers of the seller.
- **Intellectual property rights:** Does the seller maintain intellectual property rights in the process and services in use or in the product they will produce?
- **Proprietary rights:** Does the seller maintain proprietary rights in the process and services in use or in the product they will produce?

Noncompetitive Forms of Procurement: Usually a seller is selected from a list of qualified sellers interested in and capable of doing the job. Even though competition can result in the selection of a better seller and decreased price, there is no reason for going through the entire procurement process unless law requires it.
A noncompetitive form of procurement can be considered in the following situations:

- A seller has unique qualifications that no other sellers have.
- There is no other seller except one who can provide the goods or services.
- A seller holds a patent for the item you need.
- The project is under intense time constraints and needs to be completed soon.
- There are means to verify and ensure that the seller's price is reasonable.

Two Types of Noncompetitive Forms of Procurement are described below:

- **Single Source (preferred seller):** In this case, the buyer has worked with the seller before and due to good experience and other convenience with the seller, the buyer does not want to look for another seller.
- **Sole Source (only seller):** In this case, the seller may be the only one in the market or may have a patent, thus limiting the option of selecting other sellers.

Privity: Contractual relationship that both the buyer and the seller have to realize and maintain.

Example: Company X subcontracted a project to Company Y. Company Y also subcontracted most of the project work to Company Z. Company X found out that Company Z is much more professional and easy to work with and started directly contacting them. The manager from Company X also asked the project manager of Company Z to follow up with her directly. As per the contractual relationship, this is not an ideal situation since Company X is only supposed to contact Company Y and Company Y should talk to Company Z.

Letter of Intent: A letter expressing the intention of the buyer to hire the seller. It is not a contract; thus, it does not have any legal binding. Usually the buyer gives a letter of intent to the seller in the following circumstances:

- The completion of contract negotiation and finalization will take a significant amount of time, but the project needs to be initiated as soon as possible.
- The seller has no option but to hire people and order equipment in order to meet contractual requirements before the contract is signed.

This letter gives the seller confidence and peace of mind that the contract will be signed soon and makes them comfortable making the investment for the project prior to signing the contract.

Make-or-buy Decisions: Make-or-buy decisions document the decisions and justification regarding what project products, services, or results will either be acquired or developed by the project team.

Change Requests: These are requests for changes to the project management plan and other subsidiary plans or to components resulting from the Plan Procurement Management process.

Project Documents Updates: Several documents such as the risk register, requirements document, requirements traceability matrix, and others may be updated.

Exercise 6: List all your major concerns with a noncompetitive procurement.

Exercise 7: You are trying to decide whether to lease or buy a specialized item for your project. The daily lease cost is $170/day. If you purchase the item, the purchase price will be $10,000 and the daily operational cost will be $30. You need the item for 80 days. Should you purchase the item or lease? How long it will take for the lease cost to be the same as purchase cost or what will be the break-even point in days?

Exercise 8: What is the difference between Project Statement of Work and Procurement Statement of Work?

Exercise 9: Identify which process group each process belongs to.

Process Groups				
Initiating	**Planning**	**Executing**	**Monitoring & Controlling**	**Closing**

Process Names:

- Conduct Procurements
- Control Procurements
- Close Procurements
- Plan Procurement Management

Conduct Procurements

Conduct Procurements is the process of obtaining seller responses, selecting a seller, and awarding the procurement, usually in the form of a contract. Throughout this process, the team will make sure the procurement document created earlier is available to the sellers, clarify sellers' queries, receive bids or proposals, and apply previously defined selection criteria to select one or more sellers.

The following activities are usually carried out during the Conduct Procurements process:

- Buyer finds potential sellers through advertising or the Internet.
- Buyer sends procurement documents to potential sellers.
- Buyer holds a bidder conference and answers sellers' questions.
- Seller makes a decision to bid/propose.
- Seller creates the proposals.
- Buyer receives the proposals.
- Buyer compares the proposals to source selection criteria using a weighting or screening system to pick/shortlist sellers.
- Buyer receives presentations from seller(s).
- Buyer compares seller's price proposal to independent estimates.
- Buyer holds negotiations with the seller.
- Buyer and seller sign a contract.

As per the PMBOK®, the Conduct Procurements process has the following inputs, tools & techniques, and outputs:

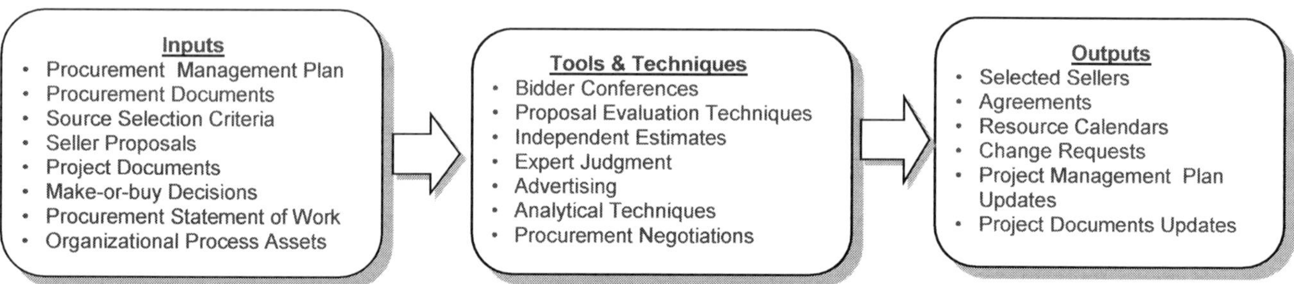

Figure 12-6: Conduct Procurements: Inputs, Tools & Techniques, and Outputs

Conduct Procurements: Inputs

- Procurement Management Plan
- Procurement Documents
- Source Selection Criteria
- Seller Proposals
- Project Documents
- Make-or-buy Decisions
- Procurement Statement of Work
- Organizational Process Assets

Procurement Management Plan: The procurement management plan portion of the project management plan document describes how procurement processes will be managed from developing the procurement document all the way to contract closure.

Procurement Documents: Will be used to solicit proposals from prospective sellers.

Source Selection Criteria: A list of criteria to evaluate and select qualified sellers.

Seller Proposals: An official response to a buyer's procurement document with the details the buyer is looking for in addition to how the work will be performed. It also includes pricing information.

Project Documents: The risk register and risk-related contract decisions are mainly used.

Make-or-buy Decisions: Document the decisions and justification regarding what project products, services, or results will either be acquired or developed by the project team.

Procurement Statement of Work: Describes the subject item in sufficient detail to allow prospective sellers to determine offerings (bids, proposals, and other types). It documents details of the work to be performed by the seller under a contract.

Organizational Process Assets: Organizational process assets like a listing of qualified sellers, sellers' relevant past experience, and other factors can be very useful.

Conduct Procurements: Tools & Techniques

- Bidder Conferences
- Proposal Evaluation Techniques
- Independent Estimates
- Expert Judgment
- Advertising
- Analytical Techniques
- Procurement Negotiations

Bidder Conferences: They are also called contractor conferences, vendor conferences, or pre-bid conferences. They are intended to assure that no seller receives preferential treatment and that all sellers have a clear, common understanding of the procurement (technical requirements, contractual requirements, and others). The key objective is to provide all potential contractors with the information they need to determine if they would like to continue with the contracting process. During a bidding conference, the project manager must be on alert so that:

- There is no collusion among sellers and/or buying agents.
- Sellers do not save questions for later private meetings in order to gain a competitive advantage.
- All questions are submitted in writing and issued to sellers as an addendum to the procurement document so that all sellers respond to the same scope of work.

Proposal Evaluation Techniques: Many different techniques are used to evaluate proposals; all will use some expert judgment and some form of evaluation criteria.

- An evaluation criterion includes objective and/or subjective components and usually includes assigned predefined weightings.
- An overall weighting system determines the total weighted score for each proposal.
- Evaluation techniques can also include a screening system and can utilize data from a seller rating system.

Weighting System: A method for quantifying qualitative data to minimize the effects of personal prejudice. It usually follows these steps:

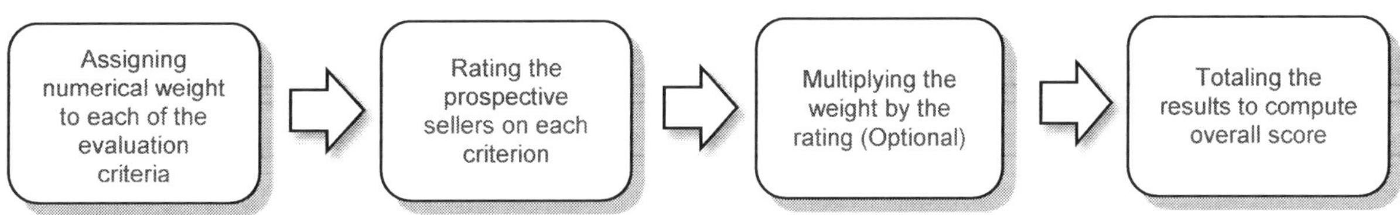

Figure 12-7: Weighting System

Seller		Overall Cost	Proposed Design	Past Performance	Technical Resources	Technical Capability	Overall Design	Total
	Weighting Factors (1–5)	**5**	**5**	**4**	**4**	**3**	**4**	
Seller 1	Score	4	3	2	3	2	2	
	Weighted Score	20	15	8	12	6	8	**69**
Seller 2	Score	5	4	3	4	2	3	
	Weighted Score	25	20	12	16	6	12	**91**
Seller 3	Score	3	2	1	2	2	2	
	Weighted Score	15	10	4	8	6	8	**51**

Table 12-8: Weighting System

Screening System: A set of minimum criteria the seller must meet to be considered, such as proficiency with certain products or techniques, safety record, number of years of relevant experience, and other factors.

Past Performance History: This is looking at the seller's history with the buyer.

Presentations: Some sellers will be asked to make presentations of their proposal so that the buyer can pick the most appropriate one. Giving a presentation provides the sellers with an opportunity to present their proposal, team, and approach to completing the work. The buyer also gets a chance to see the team that they may hire and can assess competency, knowledge, and ability.

Independent Estimates: They are sometimes known as in-house cost estimates.

- They are often provided by consulting services, or a procuring organization can prepare its own independent estimate.
- These estimates may help judge whether the statement of work was adequate in its description or if the seller fully understood or responded fully to the statement of work; these estimates also help check the reasonableness of the seller's response and proposed pricing.

Expert Judgment: Sellers' bids and proposals are evaluated by a multi-disciplined review team with expertise in each of the areas covered by the procurement documents and proposed contract.

Advertising: In order to expand sellers' lists and to improve the volume and quality of responses from a targeted audience, the procuring organization may place advertisements in general circulation publications, such as newspapers, online sources, or professional journals. Some government procurements require this kind of public advertising.

Analytical Techniques: Various analytical techniques are used by the procurement team to figure out the expected cost, to find ways to avoid cost overruns, and to identify the readiness of the vendor to provide the service, materials, or product. The objective of using these analytical techniques is to find ways that vendors can bring value to the organization. For example, by reviewing the past performance of vendors and cross-checking some of their customers, the procurement team can identify areas of high risks and can monitor them closely so that the project can be completed successfully.

Procurement Negotiations: The goal of procurement negotiation is to gain clarification and mutual agreement on structure, requirements, and other terms of the contract prior to signing. Topics such as responsibilities and authorities, applicable terms and law, technical and business management approaches, pricing, contract financing, proprietary rights, and authority to make changes may be negotiated.

The project manager may not always be the lead negotiator on procurement-related matters, but both the project manager and other team members can provide valuable input and clarification regarding procurement requirements.

Conduct Procurements: Outputs

- Selected Sellers
- Agreements
- Resource Calendars
- Change Requests
- Project Management Plan Updates
- Project Documents Updates

Selected Sellers: The selected sellers are those who are in a competitive range based on the outcome of the proposal or bid evaluation and who have been involved in the negotiation (all the procurement-related items, terms and conditions, and other factors) process.

Agreements: An agreement (which is also called an understanding, a contract, a subcontract, or a purchase order) is a legally binding, formal agreement between two parties that obligates the seller to provide the specified product, service, or result and obligates the buyer to compensate for it.

Resource Calendars: They are documents containing the quantity and availability of resources and the dates each specific resource can be available or idle.

Change Requests: Change requests include changes to the project management plan and subsidiary components.

Project Management Plan Updates: Cost, scope, and schedule baseline in addition to the procurement management plan can be updated.

Project Documents Updates: The requirements document, requirements traceability matrix, and risk register, along with other relevant documents, may need to be updated.

Control Procurements

Control Procurements is the process of ensuring the seller's performance meets contractual requirements, ensuring that both the seller and the buyer meet their contractual obligations, and making sure that both the seller's and the buyer's legal rights are protected. The focus here is to manage the relationship between the buyer and the seller, monitor contract performance, and make appropriate changes and corrections.

The following activities are usually carried out during the Control Procurements process:

- Both buyer and seller understand the legal implications of their actions.
- Buyer holds procurement performance reviews.
- Buyer requests changes and administers claims by the seller.
- Buyer manages interfaces among sellers.
- Seller reports performance and project status.
- Buyer monitors performance against the contract.
- Buyer reviews seller's cost submittals.
- Buyer makes payments to sellers.
- Buyer performs inspections and audits.
- Buyer maintains records of all procurement-related items.
- Seller completes project work.
- Buyer updates the project management plan and other project documents.

As per the PMBOK®, the Control Procurements process has the following inputs, tools & techniques, and outputs:

Figure 12-8: Control Procurements: Inputs, Tools & Techniques, and Outputs

The project management processes that are applicable to this process include the following:

- Direct and Manage Project Work process provides work performance information used to monitor the progress of contracted work or supplies to meet deliverables and dependencies.
- Manage Communications process uses performance reports ensuring that contracted work meets the agreed terms with regard to scope, cost, schedule, technical performance, and risk management.
- Control Quality process uses the results of quality tests to verify that procured goods or services meet the agreed-upon quality standards.
- Perform Integrated Change Control process generates approved change requests, which are used in the Control Procurements process to ensure that procurement- or contract-related changes are properly implemented, that the relevant parties are informed, and that the overall project plan is adjusted accordingly.
- Control Risks process uses its results to indicate whether procurements are effectively mitigating these risks.

Control Procurements: Inputs

- Project Management Plan
- Procurement Documents
- Agreements
- Approved Change Requests
- Work Performance Reports
- Work Performance Data

Project Management Plan: The procurement portion of the project management plan explains how procurement processes will be managed from creating the procurement document all the way to contract closure.

Procurement Documents: Contains procurement contract awards and a statement of work, which are useful to the Control Procurements process.

Agreements: An agreement (which is also called an understanding, a contract, a subcontract, or a purchase order) is a legally binding, formal agreement between two parties that obligates the seller to provide the specified product, service, or result and obligates the buyer to compensate for it.

Approved Change Requests: Modifications to terms of the contract, the statement of work, pricing, or the description of the product or service should be documented and approved before implementation.

Work Performance Reports: Work performance reports include work performance information and technical documentation. These reports demonstrate how effectively the seller is achieving the contractual objectives by reporting which deliverables have been completed and which have not. Sellers also provide technical documentation and relevant information on deliverables as per the terms of the contract.

Work Performance Data: Includes project execution performance information such as; at what level quality standards are being met, what costs have been incurred, which invoices have been paid, and the status of project activities being performed to accomplish the project work.

Control Procurements: Tools & Techniques

- Contract Change Control System
- Procurement Performance Review
- Inspections and Audits
- Performance Reporting
- Payment Systems
- Claims Administration
- Records Management System

Contract Change Control System: A part of the Integrated Change Control system, which defines the process by which procurements can be modified and includes change procedures, forms, dispute resolution processes, necessary paperwork, required authorizations, and tracking systems.

Procurement Performance Review: A structured review that consists of seller-prepared documentation, buyer inspection, and a quality audit of the seller's progress to deliver project scope and quality within cost and on schedule as compared to the contract. The objective is to identify performance progress or failures, noncompliance, and areas where performance is a problem.

Inspections and Audits: These activities are required by the buyer and supported by the seller as specified in the contract documentation and are mainly focused on the product itself and its conformance to specification. These activities can be conducted during the execution of the project to identify weaknesses in the seller's work processes or deliverables.

Performance Reporting: This reporting is an excellent tool that provides management with information about how effectively the seller is meeting contractual objectives. This report can produce earned values, schedule and cost performance index, trend analysis, and other items.

Payment Systems: They are usually handled by the accounts payable system of the buyer's organization and help avoid duplicate payments, ensure invoices and payments match up, and ensure that the right amount has been invoiced for the appropriate deliverables at the right time. The system must include appropriate reviews and approvals by the project management team.

Claims Administration: Claims handling is one of the most frequent activities in this process. Claims, disputes, or appeals are requested when the buyer and seller disagree on scope, the impact of changes, or the interpretation of some terms and conditions in the contract.

- All these claims should be documented, processed, monitored, and managed in accordance with the contract terms throughout the contract life cycle.
- It is desirable to resolve the disputes through negotiation, but unresolved claims may require escalation to dispute resolution procedures, such as arbitration or litigation, established in the contract.

Records Management System: This system can include indexing, archiving, and retrieval systems to capture and store all documents, correspondence, and communication relevant to the contract. For some projects, every record such as e-mails, payments, and written and verbal communication is recorded and stored.

Control Procurements: Outputs

- Work Performance Information
- Change Requests
- Project Management Plan Updates
- Project Documents Updates
- Organizational Process Assets Updates

Work Performance Information: Work performance information consists of reports on compliance from the vendors. It has the following advantages:

- Assists in tracking the expected and received deliverables from the vendors
- Assists in identifying and addressing potential issues to support later claims to the satisfaction of all parties
- Assists in procurement-related decision making, dispute resolution, forecasting, and risk management

Change Requests: Changes (approved and unapproved) are fed back through the appropriate project planning and project procurement processes so that the project plan or other relevant documentation is updated as appropriate.

Project Management Plan Updates:

Cost Baseline: Based on the current scenario, the cost baseline may be updated.

Schedule Baseline: The schedule may need to be updated to reflect current expectations if there are delays that impact overall project performance.

Procurement Management Plan: Any impact to cost or schedule due to approved changes should be updated in the procurement management portion of the project management plan document.

Project Documents Updates: This includes everything relevant to the contract, such as supporting details of the deliverables, work performance information, financial records, supporting schedules, requested unapproved contract changes, results from contract-related inspections, approved changes, invoices and payments records, and seller-developed technical documentation.

Organizational Process Assets Updates:

Correspondence: Contract terms and conditions often require written documentation of certain aspects of buyer/seller communications, such as warnings of unsatisfactory performance, contract changes, or clarifications.

Payment Schedules and Requests: Payments should be made as per the procurement contract terms and conditions.

Seller Performance Evaluation Documentation: This will be helpful for future projects to decide whether to use the seller in the future.

Exercise 10: List the specific things a project manager must watch out for during the Control Procurements process for the following contracts.

Cost Reimbursable	
Time & Material	
Fixed Price	

Close Procurements

The Close Procurements process is mainly concerned with completing each of the project's procurements. This process involves the following:

- Product verification as stipulated in the contract by making sure that all work and deliverables were acceptable and all the payments have been made.
- Administrative closeout of the contract such as making sure that all the open claims are finalized and all records are updated and archived for future reference.

Contract terms may prescribe specific procedures for closure, and procurements are closed when a contract is completed or terminated early prior to work completion.

The following activities are usually carried out during the Close Procurements process:

- Buyer performs a procurement audit.
- Buyer reaches a negotiated settlement with the seller on any open dispute.
- Buyer creates lessons learned.
- Buyer completes final contract performance reporting by analyzing and documenting the success and effectiveness of the procurement and seller.
- Buyer verifies the product.
- Buyer issues formal acceptance.
- Buyer updates all relevant procurement records.
- Buyer creates a procurement file to save all relevant e-mails, letters, conversation records, payment receipts, reports, and other items.
- Buyer performs financial closure.
- Buyer closes the procurement.

As per the PMBOK®, the Close Procurements process has the following inputs, tools & techniques, and outputs:

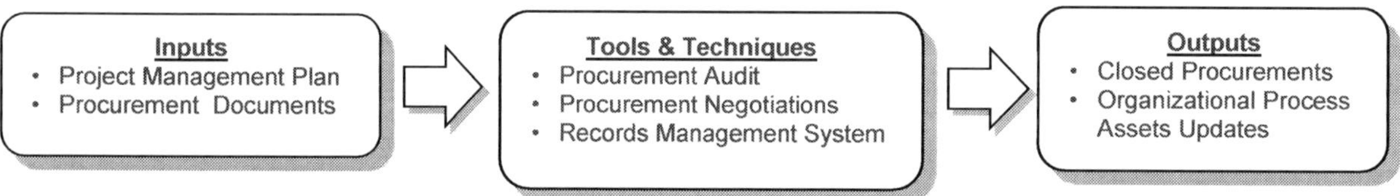

Figure 12-9: Close Procurements: Inputs, Tools & Techniques, and Outputs

It is important to understand the difference between the Close Project or Phase process and the Close Procurements process.

- Project closure happens at the end of the project or project phases, whereas there may be many procurement closures, as there may be several procurements in a project.
- All procurements must be closed prior to final project closure.
- Closure may happen at the end of each project phase and at the very end of the entire project. If a project has several phases such as the requirements phase, design phase, coding phase, testing phase, and others, closure will happen at the end of each of these phases. On the other hand, upon completion of the contract for each procurement, a procurement audit should be carried out to close the procurement.

Close Procurements: Inputs

- Project Management Plan
- Procurement Documents

Project Management Plan: The procurement management plan portion of the project management plan provides information and guidance on procurement closure.

Procurement Documents: All information and documents relevant to the contract such as contract schedule, scope, and quality, all implemented changes, schedule and cost performance information, inspection results, payment records, and other items should be collected, indexed, and archived for future reference.

Close Procurements: Tools & Techniques

- Procurement Audits
- Procurement Negotiations
- Records Management System

Procurement Audits: The objective of this structured review of the procurement process is to identify successes and failures as lessons learned. Basically, it is a verification of all the elements of the contract that were completed and stipulation and remedy of elements that were not.

Procurement Negotiations: The key objective of negotiated settlement is the settlement of all outstanding issues, claims, and disputes if possible. Some form of Alternative Dispute Resolution (ADR) technique such as mediation or arbitration may be explored if the settlement cannot be achieved through direct negotiation. Even though litigation in the courts is not the preferable option, it may be the only option when all other options fail.

Records Management System: This system can include indexing, archiving, and retrieval systems to capture and store all documents, correspondence, and communication relevant to the contract.

Close Procurements: Outputs

- Closed Procurements
- Organizational Process Assets Updates

Closed Procurements: The buyer's contract administration provides the seller with formal written notice that the contract has been completed as per the requirements for formal acceptance and closure defined in the contract.

Termination: The contract should have provisions for stopping the work before completion for a cause or convenience. The buyer may terminate a contract if a seller breaches the contract or if the buyer no longer wants the work done. It is rare for a seller to terminate a contract, but it can happen.

Organizational Process Assets Updates:

Procurement File: A complete set of indexed contract documentation including the closed contract.

Deliverable Acceptance: The buyer provides the seller formal written notice that the deliverables have been accepted or rejected as per the requirements for the formal acceptance and closure defined in the contract.

Lessons Learned: Things that went right or wrong, process improvement recommendations, what will be done differently next time, and other factors must be captured for future reference from all stakeholders, vendors, team members, and sponsors. These lessons are documented and disseminated throughout the organization.

Exercise 11: What is the difference between an inspection and an audit?

Exercise 12: List activities for procurements closure.

Exercise 13: Match the definitions to the contractual terms.

Terms and Conditions	Details
1. Incentives	A. Criteria for accepting the product, service, or result.
2. Waivers	B. Authorized representatives for the buyer or seller.
3. Retainage	C. The level of power to carry on certain activities.
4. Force Majeure	D. Circumstances under which parties can assign their rights and obligations to another party.
5. Risk of Loss	E. An alternative and cheaper method to the court system for dispute resolution. A neutral, private third party is assigned to resolve the dispute.
6. Ownership	F. Mostly refers to payment or performance bonds. For example, a performance bond would protect the buyer from nonperformance of the seller.
7. Intellectual Property	G. Not meeting contractual obligation by the seller or the buyer.
8. Arbitration	H. The allocation of risk between the buyer and seller in the event of loss or destruction of the goods and services.
9. Time Is of the Essence	I Information that must not be made public or given access to a third party.
10. Assignment	J. Allowable excuse for either party for not meeting contractual obligation in the event of something considered to be an act of God, such as a fire, storm, flood, freak electrical storm, or other natural disaster. Since the event is considered to be neither party's fault, usually the seller receives a time extension. Risk of loss is borne by the seller, which is usually covered by insurance.
11. Acceptance	K. Benefits that the seller will receive for aligning with the buyer's time, cost, quality, risk, and performance objectives.
12. Material Breach	L. The policy, procedure, time frame for notice and turnaround, and other items required for implementing changes in the project.
13. Warranties	M. Parties liable for accidents, personal injury, or damages.
14. Breach/Default	N. The ownership of the intellectual properties such as patents, trademarks, copyrights, source code, books, processes, data, and other items used in connection with or developed as part of the contract.
15. Changes	O. A breach so severe that it is not possible to continue work under the contract.
16. Indemnification	P. Promises of sustaining the quality of the goods and services delivered under the contract for a certain time period.
17. Bonds	Q. Ownership of the tangible items such as materials, equipment, buildings, and other things used in connection with or developed as part of the contract.
18. Termination	R. Cancellation of the project prior to completion due to specific reasons.
19. Agents	S. Without the agreement of all parties, rights under the contract may not be waived or modified.
20. Confidentiality	T. Delivery dates are extremely important, and any delay will be considered as a material breach.
21. Authority	U. In order to ensure full completion, an amount of money, usually 5 to 10 percent, is withheld from each payment and paid in full once the final work is completed.

Exercise 14: Crossword

Across

3. In this case, the seller may be the only one in the market or may have a patent.
9. A conference to provide all potential contractors with the information to determine if they would like to continue with contracting process.
11. A letter expressing the intention of the buyer to hire the seller.
13. Request for _______ is a request from the buyer for all potential sellers to submit a total price bid for work to be performed.
14. _______ Procurements is the process of obtaining and evaluating seller responses, selecting a seller, and awarding a contract.
15. Request for _______ is the buyer's request to all potential sellers for the details of how work will be performed.
16. Documents used to solicit proposals from prospective sellers and may include RFP, RFB, and RFQ.
18. A set of minimum criteria the seller must meet to be considered is called a ________ system.

Down

1. An audit to identify successes and failures in procurement as lessons learned and verify of all elements of a contract.
2. Point of Total __________ is a cost point where the seller assumes responsibility for all cost overruns.
4. An act of God.
5. An alternative and cheaper method to the court system for dispute resolution.
6. ________ estimates are sometimes known as in-house cost estimates.
7. ______ Selection Criteria is the criteria to evaluate sellers by rating or scoring them.
8. A ________ breach is so severe that it is not possible to continue work under the contract.
10. ________ Management System can include indexing, archiving, and retrieval systems to capture and store all documents, correspondence, and communication relevant to the contract.
12. Tactic of using rules/laws, decisions already made, and other factors as mandatory to avoid any further discussion.
17. Contractual relationship that both the buyer and the seller have to realize and maintain.

Exercise 15: Answer the following:

1. In this type of contract, buyers usually write a detailed statement of work (SOW) document.
2. The process is mainly concerned with managing procurement relationships, monitoring contract performance, and making changes and corrections to the contract as required.
3. A neutral, private third party is assigned to resolve the dispute.
4. In this contract, the buyer bears the most risk, as total cost is unknown until the project is finished.
5. It is the cost point in the contract where the seller assumes responsibility for all cost overruns as costs beyond that point are considered to be due to mismanagement.
6. Negotiation tactic of using rules/laws, decisions already made, and other factors as mandatory to avoid any further discussion.
7. Procurement documents, source selection criteria, and make-or-buy decisions are outputs of the ______ process.
8. A request from the buyer for a price quote per item, hour, foot, or other unit of measure.
9. In this contract, the buyer pays the actual cost plus a percentage of the cost as a fee.
10. The portion of the scope that the seller will be working on for the contract is defined in the procurement _____.
11. These estimates are sometimes known as in-house cost estimates.
12. A request from the buyer for all potential sellers to submit a total price bid for work to be performed.
13. Even if the contract has to be terminated early, a project manager should perform the _________ Procurements process.
14. A potential seller submits a seller _________ to explain how the terms and conditions in the contract will be fulfilled.
15. Some organizations have a _________ seller list of sellers to work with based on past experience with them.
16. A letter expressing the intention of the buyer to hire the seller.
17. Contractual relationship that both the buyer and the seller have to realize and maintain.
18. It is a set of minimum criteria the seller must meet to be considered.
19. These documents are used to solicit proposals from prospective sellers.
20. Two types of noncompetitive forms of procurement are single source (preferred seller) and _______.
21. A breach is so severe that it is not possible to continue work under the contract.
22. Conduct Procurements is a process in __________ process group.
23. Allowable excuse for either party for not meeting contractual obligation in the event of something considered to be an act of God, such as a fire, storm, flood, freak electrical storm, or other natural disaster.
24. It can include indexing, archiving, and retrieval systems to capture and store all documents, correspondence, and communication relevant to the contract.
25. This type of contract is used for smaller amounts and shorter times and requires little or no defined scope of work.
26. PTA = ___________+ [(Ceiling Price – Target Price)/Buyer's share of cost overrun]
27. The process of obtaining and evaluating seller responses, selecting a seller, and awarding a contract.
28. This is the only planning process that has change requests as an output.
29. This consists of determining whether a product can be cost effectively produced in-house or whether it should be purchased, leased, or rented.
30. The four processes of procurement management are _______.
31. The key outputs of procurement management processes are _______.
32. Make-or-Buy analysis is used as a tool & technique in the _______ process.

Project Procurement Management Summary

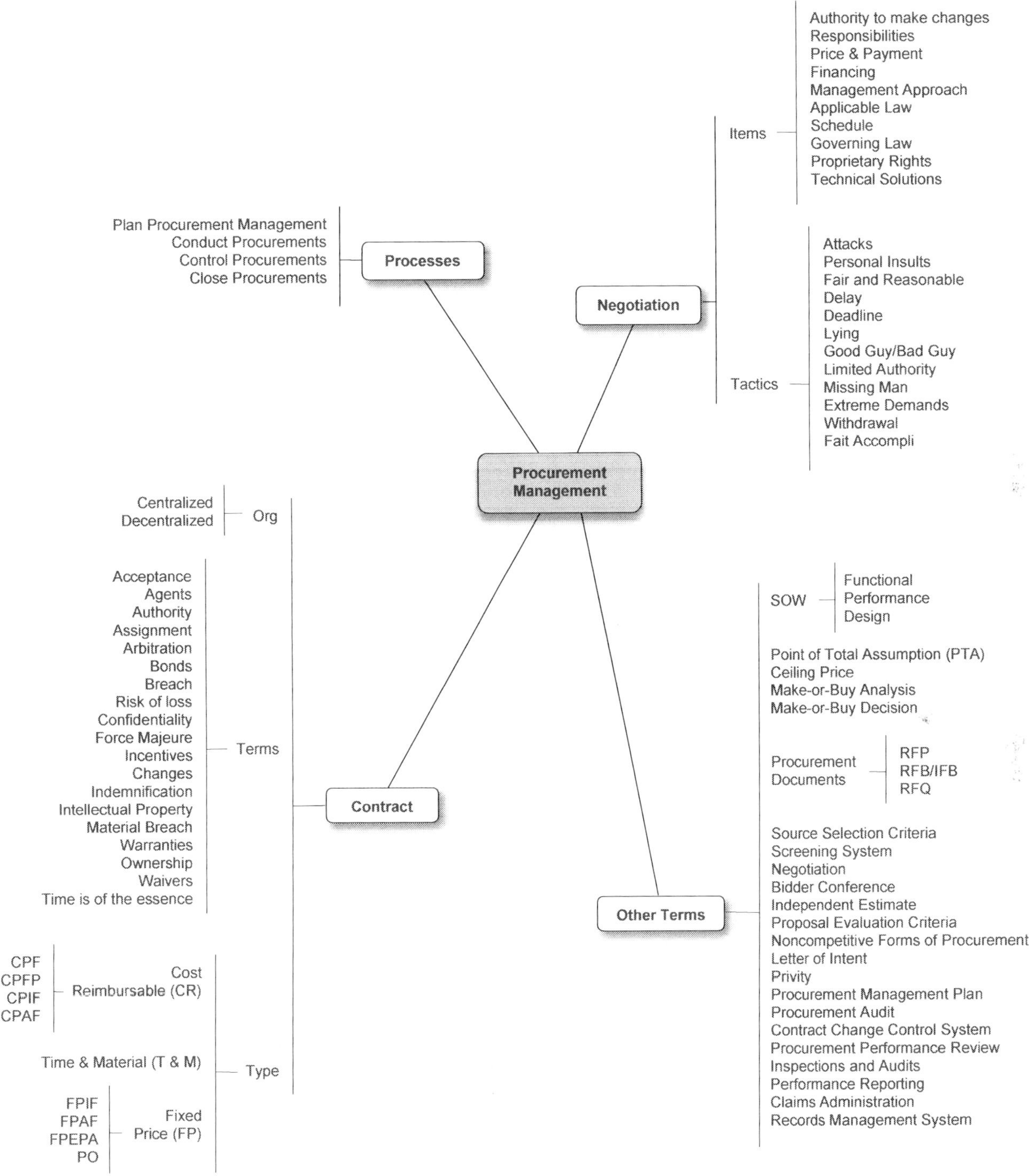

Figure 12-10: Project Procurement Management Summary

Project Procurement Management Key Terms

Point of Total Assumption (PTA): A cost point where the seller assumes responsibility for all cost overruns.
PTA = Target Cost + [(Ceiling Price – Target Price) / Buyer's share of cost overrun]
Target Price = Target Cost + Target Fee (profit)
Statement of Work (SOW): Describes subject item in sufficient detail to allow prospective sellers to determine offerings (bids, proposals, and other types). May contain functional, performance, and design specification
Ceiling Price: The highest price the buyer is willing to pay
Make-or-Buy Analysis: Determining whether a product can be cost effectively produced in-house or should be purchased, leased, or rented
Procurement Documents: Documents used to solicit proposals from prospective sellers: RFP, RFB/IFB, RFQ
Screening System: A set of minimum criteria the seller must meet to be considered
Bidder Conference: A conference to provide all potential contractors with the information to determine if they would like to continue with contracting process
Independent Estimate: In-house estimate
Source Selection Criteria: Criteria to evaluate sellers by rating or scoring them
Noncompetitive Forms of Procurement: Single source (preferred seller), sole source (only seller)
Letter of Intent: A letter expressing the intention of the buyer to hire the seller
Privity: Contractual relationship that both the buyer and the seller have to realize and maintain

Contract	Entity that Creates the SOW	Risk
Fixed Price	Buyer	Seller
Cost Reimbursable	Seller	Buyer
Contracts with incentives or award fees	Buyer / Seller	Shared
Time & Material	Usually does not require one. Brief	Buyer

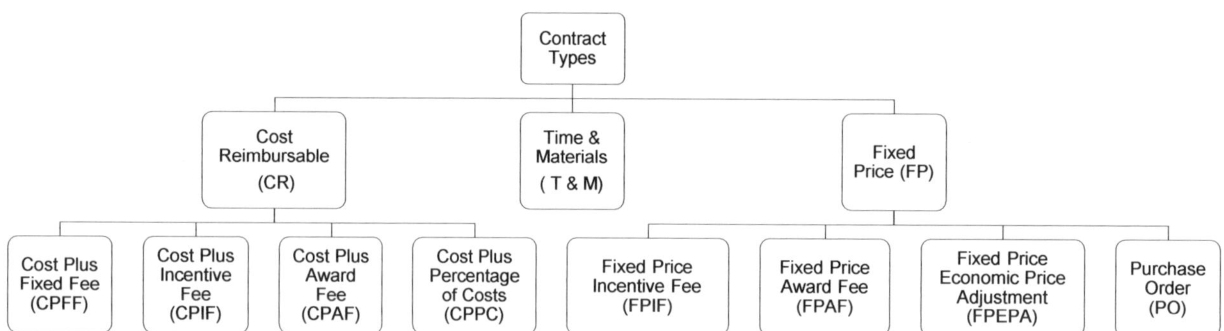

Figure: Contract Types

Procurement Audit: An audit to identify successes and failures in procurement as lessons learned and to verify all elements of a contract
Contract Change Control System: A part of the Integrated Change Control system, which defines the process by which procurements can be modified
Procurement Performance Review: A structured review to ensure that project scope and quality are within cost and on schedule as compared to the contract
Inspections and Audits: The buyer inspects deliverables (product or service) and audits processes
Performance Reporting: A report on how effectively the seller is meeting contractual objectives
Claims Administration: Is used when the buyer and seller disagree on scope, the impact of changes, or the interpretation of some terms and conditions in the contract
Records Management System: A system for indexing, archiving, and retrieval systems to capture and store all documents, correspondence, and communication

Project Procurement Management Exercise Answers

Exercise 1:

1. Purchase Order (PO)
2. Fixed Price Economic Price Adjustment (FPEPA)
3. Fixed Price (FP)
4. Fixed Price Award Fee (FPAF)
5. Fixed Price (FP)
6. Time & Material (T & M)
7. Cost Plus Incentive Fee (CPIF) or Cost Plus Award Fee (CPAF)
8. Cost Reimbursable (CR)
9. Fixed Price Incentive Fee (FPIF)
10. Cost Reimbursable (CR)
11. Time & Material (T & M)
12. Cost Plus Fee (CPF) or Cost Plus Percentage of Costs (CPPC)
13. Fixed Price (FP)
14. Cost Reimbursable (CR)

Exercise 2: In a decentralized procurement environment, there will not only be little standardization of contracting practices, but also less focus on maintaining the expertise or skill of the contracting function. Also, your access to other procurement professionals with comparable expertise would be reduced.

Exercise 3:

Target Cost	$300,000
Target Fee	$35,000
Target Price	$335,000
Actual Cost	$285,000
Sharing Ratio	80/20

Fee	Our target cost was $300,000, but the actual cost came to be $285,000; thus, there was a total savings of $300,000 – $285,000 = $15,000. The seller's portion of the savings will be $15,000 * 20 percent = $3,000 The final fee will be $35,000 + $3,000 = $38,000
Final Price	Final Price = Actual Cost + Final Fee = $285,000 + $38,000 = $323,000. **Note:** Both the buyer and the seller benefit since the buyer is now paying $323,000 instead of $335,000, and the seller is making $38,000 instead of $35,000.

Exercise 4: PTA = Target Cost + [(Ceiling Price – Target Price)/Buyer's share of cost overrun]
$78,000 + [($94,000 – $85,000)/0.60]
= $78,000 + $9,000/0.60 = $78,000 + $15,000 = $93,000
At the point the cost reaches $93,000, Company Y will assume total burden of cost overrun.

Exercise 5:

Target Cost	$155,000
Target Fee	$35,000
Target Price	$190,000
Actual Cost	$205,000
Sharing Ratio	70/30
Ceiling Price	$200,000

Final Fee	Our target cost was $155,000, but the actual cost came to be $205,000; thus, there was a total cost overrun of $155,000 – $205,000 = ($50,000). The seller's portion of the cost overrun will be $50,000 * 30 percent = $15,000. In this case, the seller will receive less of a fee; thus, the final fee will be $35,000 – 15,000 = $20,000.
Point of Total Assumption (PTA)	PTA = Target Cost + [(Ceiling Price – Target Price) /Buyer's share of cost overrun] = $155,000 + [($200,000 – $190,000)/0.70] = $155,000 + $10,000/0.70 = $155,000 + $14,286 = $169,286
Final Price	Final Price = Actual Cost + Final Fee = $205,000 + $20,000 = $225,000. Note that the final price is higher than the ceiling price of $200,000; thus, the final price will be $200,000. In this case, the seller will only be paid $200,000 even though the cost was $205,000; therefore, the seller will lose money in this case for not being able to control the project.

Exercise 6:

1. The seller may not spend adequate time defining requirements and completing a robust procurement statement of work document.
2. The seller may not be motivated to complete deliverables the first time at the desired quality level.
3. The seller may not have any incentive to control cost. The buyer may be forced to go for a multi-year agreement to prevent price increases in the future.
4. The seller may not be as committed to the buyer's schedule requirements.
5. The seller may not be as concerned to keep the buyer happy and satisfied all the time.
6. It will be a disaster if the seller owns a patent and goes out of business.

Exercise 7:

If we purchase the item, the total cost for 80 days will be: $10,000 + ($30 * 80) = $12,400
If you lease the item, the total cost for 80 days will be: $170 * 80 = $13,600
Since it will cost you less to purchase the item, you should purchase it.

Let x be the number of days when purchase and lease cost will be equal.
Therefore, 170 x = $10,000 + 30 x or 140 x = $10,000 or x = 71.42

The break-even point is 71.42 days.
Therefore, if you think that you will need the item for more than 71.42 days, you should consider purchasing it to reduce the total cost. If you use the item for less than 71.42 days, the correct decision will be to lease it.

Exercise 8: Project Statement of Work comes from our customers or sponsor describing the item they want to purchase (obtain) from us. On the other hand, Procurement Statement of Work is from us to our potential bidders describing the item we want to purchase (obtain) from them.

Exercise 9:

Process Groups				
Initiating	**Planning**	**Executing**	**Monitoring & Controlling**	**Closing**
	Plan Procurement Management	Conduct Procurements	Control Procurements	Close Procurements

Exercise 10:

Cost Reimbursable	– Watch for seller charges that were not part of the original plan. – Re-estimate and reevaluate the cost of the project as appropriate. – Watch for the seller adding excessive resources to the project that do not add value or perform real work. – Watch for experienced resources being shifted from the project and replaced with less experienced resources. – Make sure that the seller's work is progressing efficiently and smoothly. – Make sure all the costs charged by the seller are relevant to the project. – Make sure to audit the seller's invoices as appropriate.
Time & Material	– Make sure to provide day-to-day direction and guidance to the seller as appropriate. – Make sure the number of hours spent on the work is fair and reasonable. – Make every attempt to obtain tangible deliverables on time and within the budget. – Make sure the project is not delayed or the project length is not prolonged. – Make sure to switch to a different form of contract in situations when it makes more sense to do so.
Fixed Price	– Check for scope misunderstanding and take necessary steps. – Unless it is not stated in the contract, make sure that the seller is not charging the buyer for costs that have not yet incurred. – Make sure to minimize the number of change orders and watch for overpriced change orders. – Make sure that the seller is not cutting scope and is working on all the deliverables as per the contract. – Make sure that the seller is not cutting quality and is meeting the quality requirements as per the contract.

Exercise 11: We inspect deliverables (product or service) and audit processes.

Exercise 12:

- Perform a procurement audit.
- Reach a negotiated settlement on any open dispute.
- Create lessons learned.
- Complete final contract performance reports.
- Verify the product.
- Issue formal acceptance.
- Update all relevant procurement records.
- Create a procurement file.
- Perform financial closure.
- Close the procurement.

Exercise 13:

1. K	6. Q	11. A	16. M	21. C
2. S	7. N	12. O	17. F	
3. U	8. E	13. P	18. R	
4. J	9. T	14. G	19. B	
5. H	10. D	15. L	20. I	

Exercise 14:

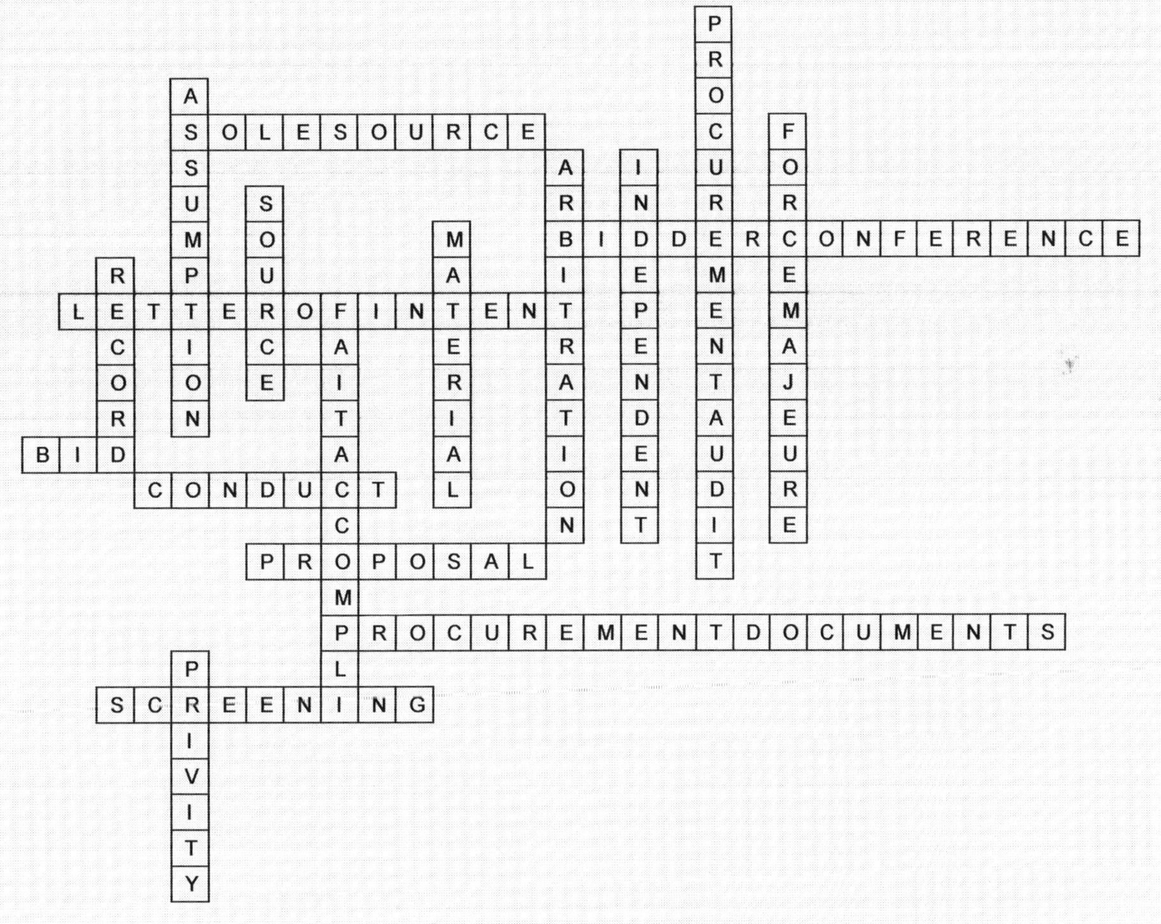

Exercise 15:

1. Fixed price
2. Control Procurements
3. Arbitration
4. Cost Reimbursable (CR)
5. Point of Total Assumption (PTA)
6. Fait accompli
7. Plan Procurement Management
8. Request for Quotation (RFQ)
9. Cost Plus Percentage of Costs (CPPC)
10. Statement of Work (SOW)
11. Independent estimates
12. Invitation for Bid (IFB or Request for Bid, RFB)
13. Close
14. Proposal
15. Qualified
16. Letter of intent
17. Privity
18. Screening system
19. Procurement documents
20. Sole source (only seller)
21. Material breach
22. Executing
23. Force majeure
24. Records management system
25. Time and materials
26. Target cost
27. Conduct Procurements
28. Plan Procurement Management
29. Make-or-buy analysis
30. Plan Procurement Management, Conduct Procurements, Control Procurements, and Close Procurements
31. Plan Procurement Management – Procurement Management Plan, Procurement Statement of Work (SOW), Procurement Documents, Source Selection Criteria, Make-or-Buy Decisions
    Conduct Procurements – Selected Sellers, Agreements
    Control Procurements – Work Performance Information, Change Requests, Project Management Plan Updates
    Close Procurements – Closed Procurements
32. Plan Procurement Management

Project Procurement Management Exam Tips

- Be able to describe the purpose of all four procurement management processes.
- Be able to name the inputs, tools & techniques, and outputs of all the procurement processes.
- Be able to identify the contract types and their usage.
- Be able to name the processes that integrate with the Control Procurements process.
- Be able to answer questions where you will need to analyze a specific situation and determine what you should do next.
- Be able to calculate final fee, final price, and Point of Total Assumption (PTA).
- Be familiar with the concepts and terms in the project procurement management summary table, Figure 12-10: Project Procurement Management Summary.

Project Procurement Management Questions

1. Your management asked you to finalize a contract for an online gaming portal with one of the vendors. You want to make sure that through negotiation you are clarifying and reaching mutual agreement on the structure and details of the contract prior to signing. You also want to make sure while negotiating that you cover major negotiation items, such as authority, responsibilities, price and payment, financing, management approach, and applicable laws. You estimate that it will take another ten days to complete the negotiation and finalize the contract, but the project manager needs to initiate work on several items right away in order to avoid drastic schedule problems in the future. What will be the BEST course of action in this situation?
   A. Verbally asked the vendor to start working while the negotiation is ongoing.
   B. Send the Statement of Work (SOW) to the vendor.
   C. Issue a letter of intent or letter contract.
   D. Inform the project manager that work cannot start prior to signing the final contract.

2. Which one of the following is NOT true about a cost reimbursable contract?
   A. The buyer bears the most risk as total cost is unknown until the project is finished.
   B. It requires auditing sellers' invoices.
   C. Buyers usually write a detailed Statement of Work (SOW).
   D. The seller has only a moderate incentive to control cost.

3. In a Cost Plus Incentive Fee (CPIF) contract, the target cost is estimated at $250,000 and the fee at $35,000. The actual cost came to be $210,000. Since there was a cost savings, the seller shares the savings at a 70/30 ratio (70 percent to the buyer and 30 percent to the seller). What are the final fee and final price?
   A. $47,000 and $257,000
   B. $47,000 and $210,000
   C. $35,000 and $257,000
   D. $35,000 and $210,000

4. You are working on a construction project and successfully completed all the work. Your stakeholders were very pleased and recently communicated their final acceptance of the project. You are now meeting with your team to update the organizational process assets with a record of knowledge gained about the project to help future project managers with their projects. Once the lessons learned are completed, what should you do NEXT?
   A. Release the team
   B. Close the contract
   C. Get formal acceptance
   D. Write lessons learned

5. You are in charge of the bidding process for a government railway project. You are trying to come up with a set of minimum criteria sellers must meet to be considered. Which of the following are you working on?
   A. Screening system
   B. Proposal evaluation technique
   C. A weighting system
   D. An independent or in-house estimate

6. Your company is working on a government railway infrastructure upgrade project. You have signed a Fixed Price (FP) contract and will be paid a fee of $380,000 to complete the work. It's now six months into the project, and your costs have just exceeded $340,000. As per the contract, your company is now responsible for any cost overrun from this point forward, and the buyer will not share any of it. This situation is BEST described as:
   A. The project manager spent too much money on the project.
   B. The project has reached the Point of Total Assumption (PTA).
   C. The buyer is cheating the seller.
   D. The project budget was miscalculated initially.

7. You are working on a software development project to automate an accounting process. You, your team, and your senior manager all feel that the work is complete. However, one of your important clients disagrees and feels that one of the deliverables is not acceptable, as it does not meet the requirements specification. What is the BEST way to handle this conflict?
   A. Issue a change order.
   B. Renegotiate the contract.
   C. File a lawsuit to force the stakeholder to accept the deliverable.
   D. Meet with the responsible team member to review the WBS dictionary.

8. While in the Control Procurements process, you are meeting with your seller to check on the product itself and its conformance to specification. Which one of the following are you performing?
   A. Performance reporting
   B. Procurement performance reviews
   C. Inspections and audits
   D. Claims administration

9. Which of the following is NOT true about the Close Project or Phase process and the Close Procurements process?
   A. Project closure happens at the end of the project or project phases, whereas there may be many procurement closures as there may be several procurements in a project.
   B. It is not required to close all procurements prior to final project closure.
   C. Project closure may happen at the end of each phase and at the very end of the entire project.
   D. Upon completion of the contract for each of the procurements, a procurement audit should be carried out to close the procurement.

10. You found your vendor's subcontractor to be much more professional and easy to work with and started directly contacting them for project updates and other concerns. You are informed by the vendor that, as per the contractual relationship, this is not an ideal situation since you are only supposed to contact the vendor and not the vendor's subcontractor. The legal contractual relationship that exists between a buyer and a seller after the contract is signed that the vendor is referring to is known as:
   A. Bilateral agreement
   B. Legally bonded relationship
   C. Obligation
   D. Privity

11. The risk associated with performance specifications is usually the responsibility of the:
   A. Project manager
   B. Buyer
   C. Project sponsor
   D. Seller

12. You requested your experts to prepare an independent estimate, or in-house estimate, for your contract to help judge whether the Statement of Work (SOW) was adequate in its description or that the seller understood or responded fully to it. You also want to check the reasonableness of the seller's response and proposed pricing. Which of the following BEST describes what you are doing?
   A. Plan Procurement Management
   B. Conduct Procurements
   C. Control Procurements
   D. Close Procurements

13. You are asked by management to select a contract type that will obligate the seller to accept all liability for poor workmanship, engineering errors, and consequential damages in the project. Which of the following contract types will you select?
   A. Fixed price
   B. Time & material
   C. Cost plus incentive fee
   D. Purchase order

14. You have tried to close most of the concerns and areas of disagreement with the vendor while negotiating prior to signing the final contract. You still do not rule out the possibility of misunderstanding and situations that may adversely affect your project. As an alternative, cheaper method to court for dispute resolution, you have assigned a neutral, private, third party to resolve the disputes. What is this referred to in contract terms and conditions?
   A. Force majeure
   B. Indemnification
   C. Arbitration
   D. Fait accompli

15. You were asked by your management to investigate the cause of severe cost overrun in one of the projects that was completed last year. You found out that a certain contract was used in the project that is considered to be very risky for the buyer, as it does not encourage the seller to control costs; rather, it incentivizes the seller to be inefficient. What sort of contract was used in the project?
   A. Cost Plus Percentage of Cost (CPPC)
   B. Cost Plus Award Fee (CPAF)
   C. Cost Plus Incentive Fee (CPIF)
   D. Fixed Price Economic Price Adjustment (FPEPA)

16. After reviewing your project schedule and resource calendars, you realize that your resources are 100 percent occupied and will have no time to work on a new component. So you decide to outsource the component and start negotiating with a couple of potential vendors. While outsourcing, which of the following should you be MOST concerned about?
   A. The technical background of the vendor
   B. The financial capability of the vendor
   C. The relevant experience of the vendor
   D. Proprietary data of your organization

17. Sabrina, a project manager for ITPro Consultancy, LLC, is overseeing the design and development of an indoor room temperature and humidity controlling device. While working on the procurement plan, she compared the cost of an off-the-shelf product to the cost of her programmers' design to develop the custom device. Sabrina is engaged in which of the following?
   A. Using expert judgment
   B. Coming up with source selection criteria
   C. Performing a Make-or-buy analysis
   D. Working on the procurement statement of work

18. While working on a data mining project, you realize that you need a data validation tool that was never thought of earlier. After reviewing your project schedule and resource calendars, you realize that your resources are 100 percent occupied and will have no time to work on this new component. So, you decide to outsource the component and start negotiating with a couple of potential vendors. You quickly realize that you do not have a clear definition of the scope, but the vendor agrees with you that the project will be relatively small and you have an urgent need. Which contract type is MOST appropriate in this kind of situation?
   A. Cost Plus Fixed Fee (CPFF)
   B. Cost Plus Award Fee (CPAF)
   C. Fixed Price Economic Price Adjustment (FPEPA)
   D. Time and Materials (T & M)

19. You are in the Control Procurements process and are ensuring that the seller's performance meets contractual requirements by monitoring contract performance and making appropriate changes and corrections. Which of the following will you most likely NOT use as an input in this process?
   A. Procurement documents
   B. Work performance information
   C. Contract
   D. Seller proposals

20. You are the project manager of a data center construction project. Your company made it mandatory to solicit quotes from three separate vendors before submitting the purchase request to the finance department for buying switches, routers, firewalls, PCs, servers, etc., for the data center. What type of input is this policy to the procurement process?
   A. Make-or-buy decision
   B. Procurement document
   C. Source selection criteria
   D. Organizational process assets

21. You are managing a software development project to automate an accounting process. In this Cost Plus Incentive Fee Contract, you have negotiated the following:
Target cost: $120,000 and target fee: $8,000
Max fee: $12,000 and min fee: $4,000
Sharing ratio: 80/20 (buyer/seller)
The actual cost was $145,000. What is the total price the buyer will pay?
   A. $148,000
   B. $149,000
   C. $144,000
   D. $153,000

22. Which of the following is the process of documenting project purchasing decisions, specifying the approach, defining selection criteria to identify potential sellers, and putting together a procurement management plan?
   A. Conduct Procurements process
   B. Plan Procurements process
   C. Close Procurements process
   D. Control Procurements process

23. Steve is a program manager overseeing an ERP implementation project where the team has already completed the finance, sales, and admin modules out of seven total modules. Steve was informed that the client has terminated the project as they found a cheaper and faster off-the-shelf solution for their need and no longer want the project to continue. Which of the following is TRUE?
   A. The team must keep working on the project to give senior management time to discuss with the client.
   B. Steve must stop all work and release the team immediately.
   C. Steve must work with the team to document the lessons learned.
   D. Steve must close the contract.

24. You are in the Close Procurements process and want to document the procurement lessons learned from everyone involved in your project to help improve how your organization will handle procurements in the future. Lessons learned are created as a result of the procurement audit and include all of the following EXCEPT:
   A. Things that went right or wrong
   B. Successes and failures that should be recognized
   C. Using the payment system to process considerations as per the terms of the contract
   D. Process improvement recommendations and what will be done differently next time

25. In which procurement management process will you ensure that the seller's performance meets contractual requirements, that both the buyer and seller meet their contractual obligations, and that the legal rights of both the buyer and seller are protected?
   A. Procurement performance reviews
   B. Inspections and audits
   C. Performance reporting
   D. Control Procurements

26. You are in charge of the bidding process for a government solar power plant project. You are trying to make sure that no seller receives preferential treatment and that all sellers have a clear, common understanding of the procurement (technical requirements, contractual requirements, etc.). Your key objective is to provide all potential contractors with the information they need to determine if they would like to continue with the contracting process. Which one of the following will assist you with your goal?
   A. Source selection criteria
   B. Bidder conference
   C. Independent estimate
   D. Procurement negotiation

27. Lars is a project manager overseeing an online age verification application for one of the very important clients for his organization. Three months in the project, Lars got a call from the client who informed him that they would end the contract due to a change in business direction. The client also discussed the compensation that the seller's organization is offering to Lars's organization for the work completed so far. This is an example of which one of the following?
   A. Letter of intent
   B. Breach of contract
   C. Material breach
   D. Termination for convenience

28. During the Plan Procurement Management process, your team developed the procurement document to solicit proposals from prospective sellers and to easily compare their responses. All of the following statements are true about the procurement document EXCEPT:
   A. It may include the procurement statement of work and evaluation criteria.
   B. It should not be too rigorous to allow any flexibility for the sellers to be innovative.
   C. It contains clear, complete, and concise descriptions of performance, design, functionality, reporting, format, and support requirements.
   D. It may contain a Request For Proposal (RFP), an invitation For Bid (IFB or Request For Bid, RFB), and a Request For Quotation (RFQ).

29. Sandi is working as a project manager in a drug manufacturing company, Ultra Medicine, LLC. Ultra Medicine is very excited to introduce a new drug in the market that will stop the human aging process and drastically improve the quality of health. Sandi initiated a conversation with one of the foreign vendors about outsourcing the production of this new drug. The vendor is also very enthusiastic about the potential of the new drug and has requested a copy of the Statement of Work (SOW) so that they can start learning about it. Which one of the following is FALSE about the SOW?

A. The SOW should contain the details of the new drug.
B. The SOW should have the details as required but not so much as to give out all the sensitive information and trade secrets of Ultra Medicine.
C. The SOW should have enough detail for the vendor to figure out if they are capable and qualified to manufacture the drug.
D. Ultra Medicine must write the SOW with the necessary detail.

30. While managing a nanotechnology project to build an elevator/tunnel from the ground to the space station, you need to procure a new material called carbon nanotube, which is extremely strong and resistant to heavy air pressure. Due to patent constraints, there is only one supplier in a different state who can provide you with this material. You checked the supplier's website and realized that the price listed for the material on the site would be within your approved limit. What should you do in this situation?

A. Consider purchasing the material from the source even though it is a sole source.
B. Keep exploring the option to use some other material to build the tunnel.
C. Notify management that there is only one source; thus, you cannot purchase the material from the single source.
D. Ask the procurement department to take care of this situation.

31. As a buyer's project manager, you always try to bring the seller's objectives in line with those of yours. You also understand that for the sellers, the focus is on the profit. Your project has an emergency and needs contracted work to be completed as soon as possible. Which one of the following would be most helpful to add to the contract under this crucial situation?

A. A Time is of the Essence clause
B. A robust procurement statement of work
C. A retainage clause
D. Incentives

32. Lars is a project manager overseeing an online age verification application for one of the very important clients for his organization. Three months into the project, Lars got a call from the client who informed him that they would not be able to make the partial payment for the design work due to a financial crisis. The client also mentioned that they were very unsatisfied with the quality of the requirement document that the seller submitted. The client's organization also thinks that the contract is no longer valid and needs to be terminated. Lars realizes that once signed, a contract is legally binding unless:

A. The contract is in violation of applicable laws.
B. The buyer's legal counsel considers the contract to be null and void.
C. The seller fails to perform.
D. The buyer fails to pay for the work.

33. As a buyer's project manager, what is the BEST way for you to ensure that the seller is not making extra profits in a Cost Plus Fixed Fee (CPFF) contract?

A. You only pay the fee when the project is completed.
B. You do not authorize any unexpected cost overrun.
C. You audit all invoices and make sure that you are not charged for items not chargeable to the project.
D. You ensure that the sellers are not cutting scope.

34. While working on a data mining project, you realize that negotiation is essential to develop a good understanding and relationship with the seller as well as to obtain a fair and reasonable price for the product, service, and result. During which procurement processes will procurement negotiation occur the MOST?

A. Conduct Procurements and Close Procurements
B. Plan Procurement Management and Close Procurements
C. Plan Procurement Management and Conduct Procurements
D. Control Procurements and Close Procurements

Project Procurement Management Answers

1. C: A letter of intent is a letter expressing the intention of the buyer to hire the seller. It is not a contract; thus, it does not have any legal binding. Usually, the buyer gives a letter of intent to the seller when completion of contract negotiation and finalization will take a significant amount of time but the project needs to be initiated as soon as possible.

2. C: In a cost reimbursable contract, sellers usually write a detailed statement of work. Buyers mostly use this sort of contract in research and development or in information technology projects where the scope is unknown.

3. A:

Target Cost	$250,000
Target Fee	$35,000
Target Price	$285,000
Actual Cost	$210,000
Sharing Ratio	70/30

Final Fee
Total savings is $250,000 – $210,000 = $40,000
Seller portion is $40,000 * 30 percent = $12,000
So the final fee will be $35,000 + $ 12,000 = $ 47,000
Final Price = $ 210,000 + $47,000 = $257,000

4. A: You should release the team once the lessons learned are documented and added to the organizational process assets. Most contracts have payment terms that allow for some period of time before full payment is required; thus, the last thing you do on the project is close the contract.
The order should be: get formal acceptance, write lessons learned, release the team, and close the contract.

5. A: A screening system is a set of minimum criteria a seller must meet to be considered, such as proficiency with certain products or techniques, safety record, number of years of relevant experience, etc. Prior to reviewing the detailed proposals, a buyer may review the qualifications of sellers who have indicated an interest to bid. A weighting system is generally utilized to score qualified sellers after proposals have been submitted. The procuring organization can prepare its own independent estimate to judge whether the statement of work was adequate in its description or that the seller fully understood or responded fully to the statement of work. This estimate also helps the organization check the reasonableness of the seller's response and proposed pricing.

6. B: The Point of Total Assumption (PTA) is the cost point in the contract where the seller assumes responsibility for all cost overruns as costs beyond this point are considered to be due to mismanagement.

7. D: The very first thing we should do is to find out the details of the issue by reviewing the requirements and meeting with the responsible team member to review the WBS dictionary. We need to find out if there is something wrong in the details of the work package or in how the team member completed the work. If needed, we can then issue a change order. When there's a dispute between a buyer and a seller, it's called a claim. Most contracts have some language that explains exactly how claims should be resolved—and since it's in the contract, it's legally binding, and both the buyer and seller need to follow it. Usually it's not an option to renegotiate a contract, especially at the end of the project after the work is completed. Lawsuits should only be filed if there are absolutely, positively no other options.

8. C: Inspections and audits are activities mainly focused on the product itself and its conformance to specification. Performance reporting is an excellent tool that provides management with information about how effectively the seller is meeting contractual objectives. This report can produce earned values, schedule and cost performance index, trend analysis, etc. Procurement performance review is a structured review that consists of seller-prepared documentation, buyer inspection, and a quality audit of the seller's progress to deliver project scope and quality within cost and on schedule as compared to the contract. The objective is to identify performance progress or failures, non-compliances, and areas where performance is a problem. Claims handling is one of the most frequent activities in the Control Procurements process. Claims, disputes, or appeals are requested when the buyer and seller disagree on scope, the impact of changes, or the interpretation of some terms and conditions in the contract.

9. B: Close Procurements occurs before Close Project or Phase. We should close all procurements prior to final project closure.

10. D: Privity is the contractual relationship that both buyer and seller have to realize and maintain. A bilateral agreement is a binding contract between the two parties that have agreed to mutually acceptable terms.

11. D: Function specifications and performance specifications are the responsibility of the seller, whereas design specifications are usually provided by the buyer; also, risks associated with design are the responsibility of the buyer.

12. B: We use independent estimate as a tool & technique in the Conduct Procurements process.

13. A: The fixed price or lump sum contract, which usually pays a lump sum amount for all the work, places the risk on the seller. The seller may include a contingency in the contract to assist in minimizing the risk of reduced profits.

14. C: Arbitration is an alternative, cheaper method to the court system for dispute resolution. A neutral, private, third party is assigned to resolve the dispute. Indemnification identifies parties liable for accidents, personal injury, or damages in a project. Fait accompli is a negotiation tactic of using rules/laws, decisions already made, etc., as mandatory to avoid any further discussion. Force majeure is the allowable excuse for either party for not meeting contractual obligations in the event that something is considered to be an act of God, such as fire, earthquake, flood, freak electrical storm, etc. Since the event is considered to be neither party's fault, usually the seller receives a time extension, and risk of loss is borne by the seller, which is usually covered by insurance.

15. A: In a Cost Plus Percentage of Cost (CPPC) contract, the buyer pays actual cost plus a percentage of cost as a fee. So the more cost the seller shows, the more money the seller makes. Sellers have no incentive to control cost; rather, they get awarded for being inefficient. This type of contract is illegal in the United States.

16. D: The technical background, financial capability, and relevant experience of the vendor are all very important factors while outsourcing, but we should be very concerned about the sensitive and confidential proprietary data of our organization that we may need to turn over to the vendor.

17. C: Make-or-buy analysis is concerned with determining whether a product can be cost effectively produced in-house or whether it should be purchased, leased, or rented. While performing this analysis, we must consider indirect as well as direct costs, availability in addition to related risk, schedule, etc. Source selection criteria is developed and used to provide sellers with an understanding of the buyer's need and also to help them in deciding whether to bid or make a proposal on the project. Later on, it also helps to evaluate sellers by rating or scoring them. The procurement Statement of Work (SOW) describes the subject item in sufficient detail to allow prospective sellers to determine offerings (bids, proposals, etc.). It documents details of the work to be performed by the seller under a contract.

18. D: This time-based fee plus cost of materials contract is used for smaller amounts and shorter times and requires little or no defined scope of work. In a T & M contract, the seller pays a rate for each of the people working on the team plus their material costs. The "time" part means that the buyer pays a fixed rate for labor, usually a certain number of dollars per hour. And the "materials" part means that the buyer also pays for materials, equipment, office space, administrative overhead costs, and anything else that has to be paid for.

19. D: Seller proposals are inputs to the Conduct Procurements process for obtaining seller responses, selecting a seller, and awarding the procurement, usually in the form of a contract. This is an official response to the buyer's procurement document, including the details the buyer is looking for, how the work will be performed, and pricing. Procurement documents, work performance information, and contracts all are used as inputs for administering procurements in the monitoring & controlling process group.

20. D: Any type of corporate policy or formal and official procurement procedure is an organizational process asset.

21. B: There is a cost overrun of $145,000 - $120,000 = $ 25,000.
Seller's fee will be decreased by $25,000 * 20% = $5,000. Thus, seller final fee will be $8,000 - $5,000 = $3,000.
The minimum fee was set to $4,000. So, in this case, the final fee will $4,000, not $3,000.
Buyer's total price will be $145,000 + $4,000 = $149,000.

22. B: Plan Procurement Management is the process of documenting project purchasing decisions, specifying the approach, defining selection criteria to identify potential sellers, and putting together a procurement management plan.

23. C: A project can be terminated any time for a certain cause or simply for convenience of the buyer. If a project is terminated before the work is completed, you still need to document the lessons learned and add them to the organizational process assets. There are always important lessons that you can learn when a project goes seriously wrong even when you did nothing to contribute to the disaster.

24. C: Unless there was a problem processing or making payment, the payment system will not be a part of the procurement audit. The other remaining choices will be included in the procurement audit and captured in the lessons learned.

25. D: Control Procurements is the process of ensuring the seller's performance meets contractual requirements, ensuring that both seller and buyer meet their contractual obligations, and ensuring that legal rights of both seller and buyer are protected. The focus here is to manage the relationship between buyer and seller, monitor contract performance, and make appropriate changes and corrections. Procurement performance reviews, inspections and audits, and performance reporting are tools & techniques used in the Control Procurements process.

26. B: A bidder conference is intended to assure that no seller receives preferential treatment and that all sellers have a clear, common understanding of the procurement (technical requirements, contractual requirements, etc.). The goal of the bidder conference is to make sure that all questions are submitted in writing and issued to sellers as an addendum

to the procurement document so that all sellers respond to the same scope of work, there is no collusion among sellers and/or buying agents, and sellers do not save questions for later private meetings in order to gain competitive advantage. Independent estimates are often prepared by the procuring organization to judge whether the statement of work was adequate in its description or that the seller fully understood or responded fully to the statement of work; these estimates also help the organization check the reasonableness of the seller's response or cost proposal and proposed pricing. The goal of procurement negotiation is to achieve clarification and agreement on the structure and requirements of the contract prior to signing.

27. D: Termination for convenience is a contract clause that permits the buyer to terminate a contract at any time for a cause or convenience. Usually, there will be specific conditions associated with the execution of this clause. A letter of intent is a letter expressing the intention of the buyer to hire the seller. It is not a contract; thus, it does not have any legal binding. Most of the time, the buyer gives a letter of intent to the seller in the following circumstances:

- Completion of contract negotiation and finalization will take significant amount of time, but the project needs to be initiated as soon as possible.
- The seller has no option but to hire people and order equipment in order to meet contractual requirements before the contract is signed.

A breach/default is not meeting contractual obligation by the seller or the buyer. A material breach is so severe that it is not possible to continue work under the contract.

28. C: Usually a Statement of Work (SOW) document contains a clear, complete, and concise description of performance, design, functional, reporting, format and support requirements, not a procurement document. Well-designed procurement documents help in easier comparison of seller responses, more complete proposals, more accurate pricing, and decrease in the amount of changes in the project. Procurement documents may contain all the work that is to be completed, as well as terms, conditions, and evaluation criteria. You want the seller to be as innovative as possible when they come up with the design and methods for completing your project. It may contain request for proposal (RFP), invitation for bid (IFB, or request for bid, RFB), and request for quotation (RFQ).

29. D: It is not mandatory for the buyer to come up with the SOW all the time. The seller can come up with the SOW through requirements collection tools & techniques. Also seller can update the buyer's SOW and get it reviewed and approved.

30. A: In noncompetitive forms of procurement, usually a seller is selected from a list of qualified sellers interested in and capable of doing the job. Even though competition can result in the selection of a better seller and decreased price, there is no reason for going through the entire procurement process unless law requires it. Two types of noncompetitive forms of procurement are described below:
Single source (preferred seller): In this case the buyer has worked with the seller before, and due to good experience and other convenience with the seller, the buyer does not want to look for another seller.
Sole source (only seller): In this case the seller may be the only one in the market or may have a patent, thus limiting the option of selecting other sellers.

31. D: Under normal circumstances, if you follow the proper project management processes, you should have good definition of scope. In this situation, you should have a quality procurement statement of work. You need good scope definition as well as incentives as you need the seller to share your need for speed. A quality procurement document alone will not ensure speed. Incentives will bring the seller's objectives in line with the buyer's and would be most useful in this case. The "Time is of the Essence" clause states that any delay will be considered as a material breach as delivery dates are extremely important. The "Retainage" clause states that in order to ensure full completion, an amount of money, usually 5 to 10 percent, is withheld from each payment and paid in full once the final work is completed. These two clauses may help but would not be as effective as incentives.

32. A: It is important to understand that once signed, a contract is legally binding unless it is in violation of any applicable law. The failure to perform or make payment usually does not alter the fact that the contract is binding. The contract will remain in binding if only one party considers that the contract is no longer valid. However, if both parties negotiate and agree to terminate the contract, the contract should move into the Close Procurements process.

33. C: In a Cost Plus Fixed Fee (CPFF) contract, the fee is usually paid on a continuous basis during the life of the project. It is unreasonable and unrealistic not to authorize any unexpected cost overrun. Cutting scope would not be a way for sellers to make additional profits as it decreases the profit for this type of contract. The best way is to audit all invoices and make sure that you are not charged for items not chargeable to the project.

34. A: During Conduct Procurements, negotiation occurs to finalize the terms and conditions of the contract. In this process, a contract or agreement is created that is approved by both parties through much negotiation. In order to settle any pending disputes or concerns, negotiation will also be used in the Close Procurements process.

CHAPTER 13

PROJECT STAKEHOLDER MANAGEMENT

Project Stakeholder Management

A stakeholder is a person or an organization that is actively involved with the work of the project or whose vested interests may be positively or negatively impacted by the execution or completion of the project.

Examples of stakeholders include project managers, customers, sponsors, functional managers, the project team, the board of directors, vendors, suppliers, department managers, PMO, operations management, and others.

Project stakeholder management consists of processes to identify the internal and external stakeholders, determine their expectations and influence over the project, develop strategies to manage them, and effectively engage them in project execution and decision.

Stakeholder management requires the following:

- Identifying both internal and external stakeholders
- Assessing stakeholders' skills, knowledge, and expertise
- Determining stakeholders' requirements
- Determining stakeholders' expectations
- Determining stakeholders' communication needs
- Addressing stakeholders' issues and concerns as they occur
- Maintaining a positive relationship and communicating with stakeholders throughout the project
- Identifying stakeholders' influence-controlling strategies
- Making sure that stakeholders are involved in the project at the required level throughout the project
- Confirming continuous interactions with the stakeholders

Exercise 1: What are the roles of a project manager in stakeholder management?

Project Stakeholder Management Processes

Project stakeholder management is made up of processes to identify internal and external stakeholders, determine their expectations and influence over the project, develop strategies to manage them, and effectively engage them in project execution and decision.

It is essential to identify stakeholders and classify them according to their level of interest, influence, importance, and expectations at the earliest stages of the project as much as possible. The project manager should define an approach to manage stakeholders throughout the entire project life cycle as per their interest, importance, impact, and influence over the project. This stakeholder management plan defines the strategies to build close relationships with stakeholders and increase the support of stakeholders who can impact the project positively and minimize the negative impacts or intentions of stakeholders who can negatively impact the project.

The project manager should always focus on meeting and exceeding stakeholders' expectations by continuously communicating with them, clarifying and resolving their issues, addressing their concerns, and improving the project performance by implementing their change requests. The project manager should also evaluate and monitor overall stakeholder relationships and ensure stakeholders' appropriate engagement in the project by adjusting plans and strategies as required.

PMI identifies four key processes that are associated with the stakeholder management knowledge area in the initiating, planning, executing, and monitoring & controlling process groups.

Processes	Process Groups	Detail	Key Outputs
1. Identify Stakeholders	Initiating	The process of identifying all people or organizations impacted by the project and documenting relevant information regarding their interests, expectations, involvement, and influence on the project success.	– Stakeholder Register
2. Plan Stakeholder Management	Planning	The process of defining an approach to managing stakeholders throughout the entire project life cycle as per their interest, importance, impact, and influence over the project.	– Stakeholder Management Plan
3. Manage Stakeholder Engagement	Executing	The process of meeting and exceeding the stakeholders' expectations by continuously communicating with them, clarifying and resolving their issues, addressing their concerns, and improving project performance by implementing their change requests.	– Issue Log – Change Requests
4. Control Stakeholder Engagement	Monitoring & Controlling	The process of evaluating and monitoring overall stakeholder relationships and ensuring stakeholders' appropriate engagement in the project by adjusting plans and strategies as required.	– Work Performance Information – Change Requests

Table 12-1: Four Project Stakeholder Management Processes and Key Outputs

Project Stakeholder Management Processes, Inputs, Tool & Techniques, and Outputs

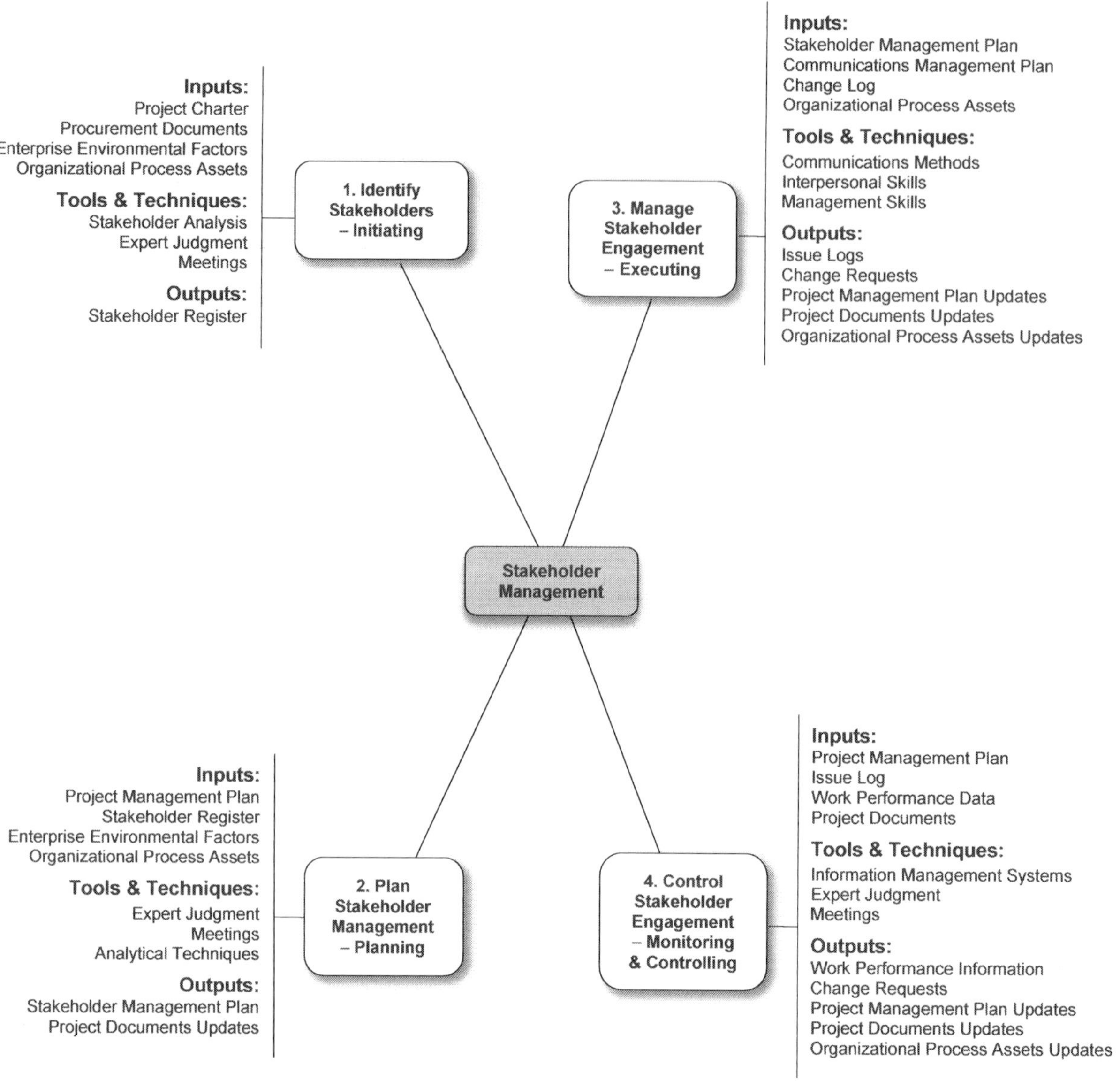

Figure 12-1: Project Stakeholder Management Processes, Inputs, Tool & Techniques, and Outputs

Identify Stakeholders

Identify Stakeholders is the process of identifying all people or organizations impacted by the project and documenting relevant information regarding their interests, expectations, involvement, and influence on project success. Examples of stakeholders include project managers, customers, sponsors, functional managers, the project team, the board of directors, vendors, suppliers, department managers, the PMO, operations management, and others.

Throughout the project we should do the following:

- Identify all the internal and external stakeholders.
- Determine stakeholders' interests, requirements, and expectations.
- Determine stakeholders' level of influence.
- Determine a communication plan for the stakeholders.
- Manage stakeholders' expectations and influence over the project.

Depending on the complexity, size, and type, most projects have a diverse number of internal and external stakeholders at different levels of the organization with different authority levels.

Stakeholder identification is a continuous and sometimes difficult process, and the influence of a stakeholder may not become evident until later stages of a project. It is essential to identify stakeholders and classify them according to their level of interest, influence, importance, and expectations at the earliest stages of the project as much as possible. Stakeholders who are missed during the identification process could potentially cause the project significant delay and additional cost by requesting changes to implement their requirements.

As per the PMBOK®, the Identify Stakeholders process has the following inputs, tools & techniques, and outputs:

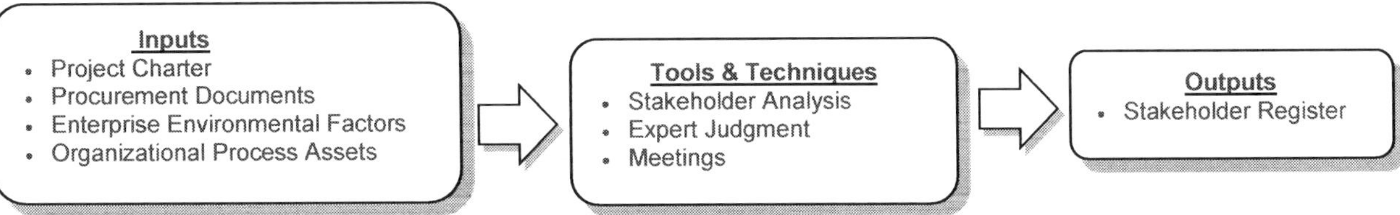

Figure 12-2: Identify Stakeholders: Inputs, Tools & Techniques, and Outputs

Identify Stakeholders: Inputs

- Project Charter
- Procurement Documents
- Enterprise Environmental Factors
- Organizational Process Assets

Project Charter: The project charter gives an overall picture of the project as well as describes some of the stakeholders and their interest in the project along with their requirements.

Procurement Documents: If a project is based on an established contract or the result of a procurement activity, the parties in that contract are key project stakeholders. Other relevant parties such as suppliers, legal parties, and people who will execute the contract should also be considered as part of the project stakeholders list.

Enterprise Environmental Factors: Organizational or company culture and structure, industry standards, and other factors may influence the Identify Stakeholders process.

Organizational Process Assets: The stakeholder register template, lessons learned, and the stakeholder registers from previous projects may influence the Identify Stakeholders process.

Identify Stakeholders: Tools & Techniques

- Stakeholder Analysis
- Expert Judgment
- Meetings

Stakeholder Analysis: It is not possible to treat all stakeholders equally in the project, and they are given different priorities as per their interests, expectations, and influence in the project. Stakeholder analysis is a process of systematically gathering and analyzing all relevant quantitative and qualitative information about the stakeholders in order to prioritize them and determine whose interests should be taken into consideration throughout the project.

As per PMI, stakeholder analysis is performed by the following steps:

Step 1: Identify all potential project stakeholders and their relevant information, such as their roles, departments, interests, knowledge levels, expectations, and influence levels.

Step 2: Identify the potential impact or support each stakeholder could generate and classify each stakeholder. As per the PMBOK®, there are several classification models below:

- **Power/Interest grid:** Based on the level of authority or power and the level of concern or interest a stakeholder has regarding the project outcome.
- **Power/Influence grid:** Based on the level of authority or power and active involvement or influence a stakeholder has.
- **Influence/Impact grid:** Groups the stakeholders based on their involvement or influence and their ability to affect changes to planning or execution (impact).
- **Salience model:** Addresses a stakeholder's power or ability to impose their will, urgency, or need for immediate attention from the team and legitimate involvement (their involvement is appropriate) in a project.

Step 3: In order to influence the stakeholders to enhance their support and to mitigate potential negative impacts, we should assess how key stakeholders are likely to react or respond in various situations.

Stakeholders who have high power or influence and high interest in our project should be managed closely and updated all the time. Stakeholders who have high power and low interest in our project should be kept satisfied. Stakeholders who have low power and low interest should be monitored, and stakeholders who have low power and high interest should be kept informed.

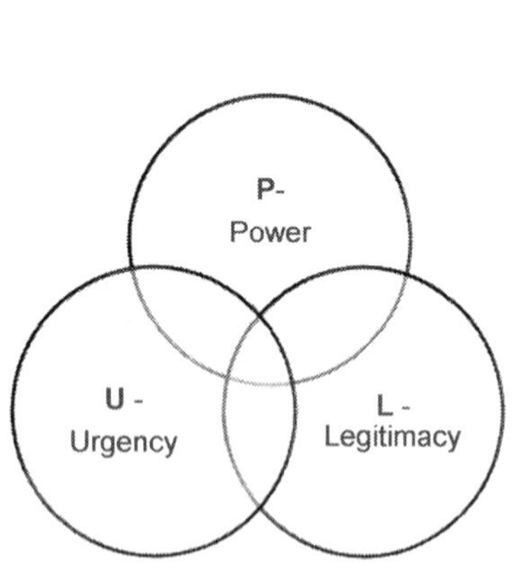

Figure 12-3: P U L - Salience Model

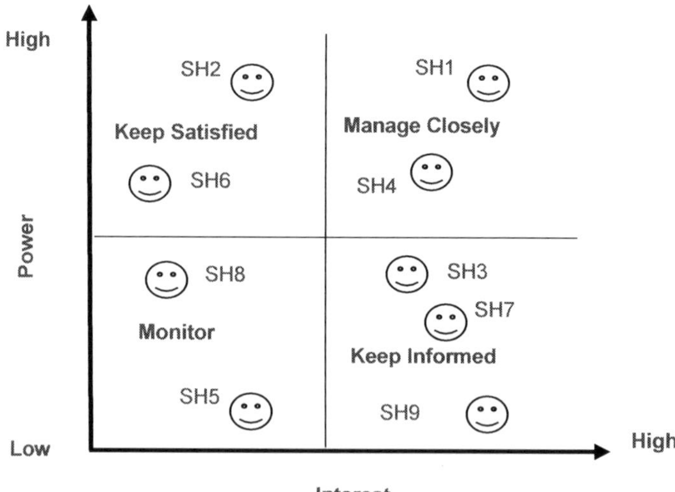

Figure 12-4: Power/Interest Grid for Stakeholders

Exercise 2: Answer the following questions:

1. Stakeholders who have low power and high interest should be __________.
2. Stakeholders who have high power and low interest should be __________.
3. Stakeholders who have high power and high interest should be __________.
4. Stakeholders who have low power and low interest should be __________.

Expert Judgment: Judgment and expert opinions can be gathered from senior management, project team members, project managers from similar projects, subject matter experts, industry groups and consultants, other units within the organization, and other people to identify stakeholders.

Meetings: Profile analysis meetings with team members and the sponsor will be beneficial to identify stakeholders and their knowledge, potential roles, importance, impact, interest, and expectations in the project.

Identify Stakeholders: Outputs

- Stakeholder Register

Stakeholder Register: This contains all details related to the identified stakeholders including but not limited to:

- **Stakeholder classification:** Internal/external, neutral/resistor/supporter, and others.
- **Identification information:** Name, title, location, organization, role in the project, position, and contact information.
- **Assessment information:** Key requirements and expectations, potential impact, importance, and influence on the project.

A project manager may publish the stakeholder register with other project documentation or keep it in reserve for personal use only.

Stakeholder Name	Title	Org	Contact Info	Influence Level (1–5)	Interest Level (1–5)	Classification	Key Expectations	Information Needs	Role(s) in Project
Mr. Seth Daniel	Budget Examiner	Finance	347-222-1111	4	5	Internal & Supporter	1.Functional module 2. Reporting tools	1.Status update 2.Issue logs	Verify proposed budget
Mrs. Diana Chang	Sales Executive	Sales, ITPro Consultancy	347-222-3333	5	4	Neutral	Sales modules	Weekly reports	Assist with sales plan

Table 12-2: A Stakeholder Register

Plan Stakeholder Management

The Plan Stakeholder Management process defines an approach to manage stakeholders throughout the entire project life cycle as per their interest, impact, importance, and influence over the project. It defines strategies to build close relationships with stakeholders, increase the support of stakeholders who can positively impact the project, and minimize the negative impacts or intentions of stakeholders who can negatively impact the project.

This is an iterative process and should be reviewed on a regular basis as the required level of engagement of the stakeholders changes in the project.

As per the PMBOK®, the Plan Stakeholder Management process has the following inputs, tools & techniques, and outputs:

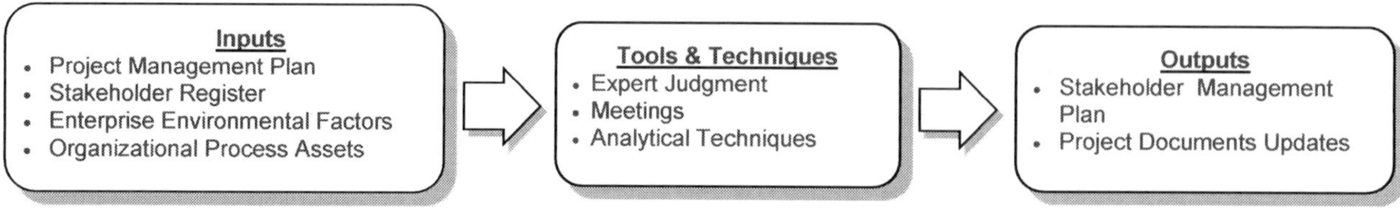

Figure 12-5: Plan Stakeholder Management: Inputs, Tools & Techniques, and Outputs

Plan Stakeholder Management: Inputs

- Project Management Plan
- Stakeholder Register
- Enterprise Environmental Factors
- Organizational Process Assets

Project Management Plan: Components of the project management plan such as the human resource management plan, staffing management plan, communications management plan, change management plan, and others are used in developing the stakeholder management plan.

Stakeholder Register: This contains all details related to the identified stakeholders, including identification information, assessment information, and classification.

Enterprise Environmental Factors: All environmental factors, such as the company's organizational structure, the organization's and stakeholder's appetite for risk, and the project management information system.

Organizational Process Assets: All organizational process assets, especially lessons learned and historical information are used.

Plan Stakeholder Management: Tools & Techniques

- Expert Judgment
- Meetings
- Analytical Techniques

Expert Judgment: Judgment and expert opinions can be gathered from senior management, project team members, identified stakeholders, project managers from similar projects, subject matter experts, industry groups and consultants, other units within the organization, and other people to identify the level of involvement required from each stakeholder at various stages of the project.

Meetings: Meetings with team members and the sponsor will be beneficial to identify the level of engagement required from each stakeholder.

Analytical Techniques: Various analytical techniques are used to identify the required level of engagement, such as unaware, resistant, neutral, supportive, leading, and others and to compare planned engagement to actual engagement.

Unaware: Stakeholders are ignorant about the project and apparent impacts.

Neutral: Stakeholders are aware of the project and apparent impacts, but neither accommodating nor resistant.

Resistant: Stakeholders are aware of the project and apparent impacts and opposed to changes.

Supportive: Stakeholders are aware of the project and apparent impacts and accommodating to changes.

Leading: Stakeholders are aware of the project and apparent impacts and enthusiastically involved in making certain the project is a success.

Stakeholder Engagement Assessment Matrix: The stakeholder engagement assessment matrix is used to assess the current and desired state of engagement of the stakeholders for the current phase of the project.

The following stakeholder engagement assessment matrix illustrates that only Stakeholder D is engaged in the project at the desired state. The project manager should consider additional communication and further actions to bring all other stakeholders to the supportive and leading states.

Stakeholder	Unaware	Neutral	Resistant	Supportive	Leading
Stakeholder A		Current			Desired
Stakeholder B	Current			Desired	
Stakeholder C		Current		Desired	
Stakeholder D				Current, Desired	
Stakeholder E				Current	Desired
Stakeholder F			Current	Desired	

Table 12-3: Stakeholder Engagement Assessment Matrix

Stakeholder engagement is critical to project success. Required actions and communication should be planned to minimize the gap between the desired level of engagement and the actual level of engagement.

Plan Stakeholder Management: Outputs

- Stakeholder Management Plan
- Project Documents Updates

Stakeholder Management Plan: The stakeholder management plan can be formal, informal, highly detailed, or broadly framed based on the needs of the project and is a subsidiary of the project management plan. The stakeholder management plan typically describes the following:

- Information needs of each stakeholder or stakeholder group
- Stakeholder communication requirements
- Format, method, time frame, and frequency for the distribution of required information to the stakeholders
- Person responsible for communicating the information with the stakeholders
- Methods of refining the stakeholder management plan
- Required engagement level of the stakeholders at various stages of the project
- Stakeholder management strategy that defines an approach to manage stakeholders throughout the entire project life cycle. It defines the strategies to increase the support of the stakeholders who can impact the project positively and minimize the negative impacts or intentions of the stakeholders who can negatively impact the project.

This portion of the plan contains sensitive information such as stakeholders' personalities, attitudes, and potential negative impacts that stakeholders may cause. These factors are not usually published and kept in reserve by the project manager for personal use only.

Stakeholder	Current Engagement	Desired Engagement	Expected Role	Potential Strategies for Gaining Support or Reducing Obstacles
John Smith	Resistor	Supportive	Will provide key team members and technical requirements.	– Find out the reason why the stakeholder is not supportive. – Notify the sponsor about the potential negative impact of the stakeholder. – Arrange a meeting with this stakeholder and also invite the sponsor to discuss project objectives. – Explain the benefits of the project to the stakeholder. – Try to gain commitment from the stakeholder on the resources and deliverables in the presence of the sponsor. – Engage the stakeholder on project steering committee.
Joe Don	Neutral	Leading	Will provide cost estimates and inputs in risk identification.	– Engage the stakeholder in planning session. – Ask the stakeholder to join the project management team and be an active member of the project.
John Doe	Unaware	Supportive	Will conduct user acceptance testing.	– Discuss project details and potential benefits with the stakeholder. – Engage the stakeholder in planning session.
Steve Ostin	Resistor	Supportive	Will provide key requirements for accounting and financial components.	– Find out from others who have experience with this stakeholder about how to work with this person. – Arrange a meeting with this stakeholder and also invite the sponsor to discuss project objectives. – Identify requirements clearly and get approval. – Send regular updates. – Engage the stakeholder in facilitated workshop.

Table 12-4: Stakeholder Management Plan

Project Documents Updates: Project documents such as the project schedule, stakeholder register, and others may be updated.

Manage Stakeholder Engagement

The Manage Stakeholder Engagement process is focused on meeting and exceeding the stakeholders' expectations by continuously communicating with them, clarifying and resolving their issues, addressing their concerns, and improving the project performance by implementing their change requests.

As per PMI, the project manager is responsible for managing the stakeholders' expectations. Meeting the stakeholders' expectations increases the probability of project success by enabling the stakeholders to be active supporters of the project, drastically reducing unresolved stakeholder issues, and limiting disruptions in the project.

As per the PMBOK®, the Manage Stakeholder Engagement process has the following inputs, tools & techniques, and outputs:

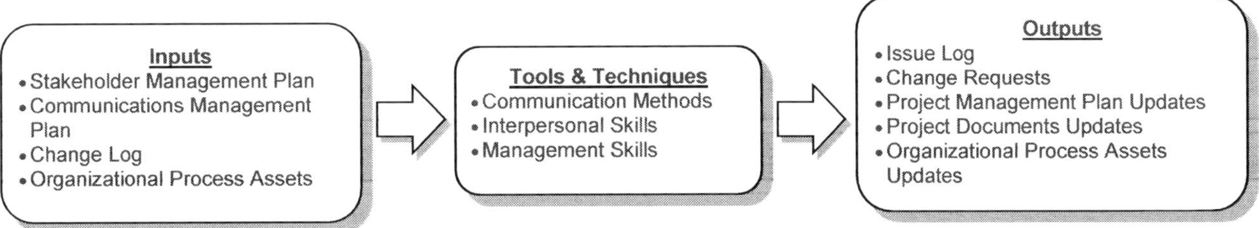

Figure 12-6: Manage Stakeholder Engagement: Inputs, Tools & Techniques, and Outputs

Manage Stakeholder Engagement: Inputs

- Stakeholder Management Plan
- Communications Management Plan
- Change Log
- Organizational Process Assets

Stakeholder Management Plan: The stakeholder management plan identifies the information needs, communication requirements, required engagement level at various stages of the project, stakeholder management strategy, and other factors to identify and manage stakeholders throughout the entire project life cycle.

Communications Management Plan: The communications management plan is a subsidiary of the project management plan. It can be formal, informal, highly detailed, or broadly framed based on the needs of the project. The communications management plan typically describes the following:

- Purpose for communication
- Information needs of each stakeholder or stakeholder group
- Stakeholder communication requirements
- Format, method, time frame, and frequency for the distribution of required information
- Person responsible for communicating the information
- Methods for updating the communications management plan
- Person or groups who will receive the information
- Glossary of common terms
- Issues/concerns escalation procedures

Change Log: A change log is used to document changes that occur during a project. Many of these changes can impact different stakeholder interests; thus, the change log is reviewed in this process.

Organizational Process Assets: Organization communication requirements, issue management procedures, change control procedures, and historical information are used.

Manage Stakeholder Engagement: Tools & Techniques

- Communication Methods
- Interpersonal Skills
- Management Skills

Communication Methods: According to the needs of the project, the methods of communication identified for each stakeholder in the communications management plan are utilized during the Manage Stakeholder Engagement process.

Interpersonal Skills: The project manager applies appropriate interpersonal skills or soft skills to manage stakeholder expectations by building trust and resolving conflict.

Management Skills: Management skills such as presentation skills, negotiation skills, writing skills, and public speaking skills used by the project manager can greatly influence how stakeholders feel about the project.

Manage Stakeholder Engagement: Outputs

- Issue Log
- Change Requests
- Project Management Plan Updates
- Project Documents Updates
- Organizational Process Assets Updates

Issue Log: An issue is an obstacle that threatens project progress and can block the team from achieving its goals. An issue log is a written log document to record issues that require a solution. It helps monitor who is responsible for resolving specific issues by a target date. There should be one owner assigned for each issue reported within the project.

ID	Issue Description	Date Added	Priority	Raised By	Owner	Due Date	Status	Date Resolved	Issue Resolution
01	Chris was moved to a higher priority project – need an urgent replacement.	3/3	High	Steve	Project manager	3/15	Closed	3/10	Miguel was assigned for next three months to replace Chris.
02	Equipment (PCs, servers, digital storages) were delivered late.	3/6	High	Rony	Project manager	3/20	Closed	3/15	Project duration was extended by three weeks.

Table 12-5: An Issue Log

Change Requests: Change requests can include a new change to the product or the project, corrective or preventive actions, and other items.

Project Management Plan Updates: The stakeholder management plan portion of the project management plan is updated as new stakeholders' requirements are identified, existing requirements are changed, or as a result of addressing concerns and resolving issues of the stakeholders.

Project Documents Updates: Project documents that may be updated include, but are not limited to, the following:

- **Issue Log:** This will be updated as resolutions to the current issues are implemented and new issues are identified.
- **Stakeholder Register:** This is updated as stakeholders' statuses change, new stakeholders are identified, registered stakeholders are no longer involved or impacted by the project, and other factors.

Organizational Process Assets Updates: Lessons learned from managing stakeholders, feedback from stakeholders, project records, causes of issues, and reasons for corrective actions chosen may be updated.

Control Stakeholder Engagement

Control Stakeholder Engagement is the process of evaluating and monitoring overall stakeholder relationships and ensuring stakeholders' appropriate engagement in the project by adjusting plans and strategies as required. As the project progresses and its environment changes, this process will maintain or increase the efficiency and effectiveness of stakeholder engagement activities.

As per the PMBOK®, the Control Stakeholder Engagement process has the following inputs, tools & techniques, and outputs:

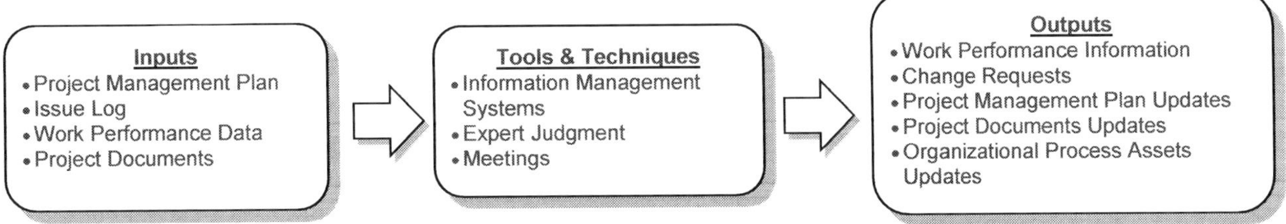

Figure 12-7: Control Stakeholder Engagement: Inputs, Tools & Techniques, and Outputs

Control Stakeholder Engagement: Inputs

- Project Management Plan
- Issue Log
- Work Performance Data
- Project Documents

Project Management Plan: Components of the project management plan such as the human resource management plan, staffing management plan, communications management plan, change management plan, and others are used in controlling stakeholder engagement.

Issue Log: An issue is an obstacle that threatens project progress. It can block the team from achieving its goals. An issue log is a written log document to record issues that require a solution. A modified issue log as a result of identifying new issues and resolving current issues will be used in this process.

Work Performance Data: Work performance data such as resource utilization, deliverables status, schedule progress, percentage of work completed, number of defects, number of change requests, technical performance measures, costs incurred, quality updates, and other factors are used in this process.

Project Documents: Project documents such as issue logs, the stakeholder register, the project schedule, the change log, and others are used in this process.

Control Stakeholder Engagement: Tools & Techniques

- Information Management Systems
- Expert Judgment
- Meetings

Information Management Systems: An information management system is an automated system that can serve as a repository for information, a tool to assist with communication, and a system for tracking documents and deliverables. An information management system also supports the project from beginning to end by collecting and distributing information about cost, schedule, and performance for the stakeholders. Several reporting techniques such as spreadsheet analysis, table reporting, presentations, graphics for visual representations, and others may be consolidated from various systems and communicated to the stakeholders.

Expert Judgment: Judgment and expert opinions can be gathered from senior management, project team members, identified stakeholders, project managers from similar projects, subject matter experts, industry groups and consultants, other units within the organization, and other people to identify new stakeholders, reassess the current stakeholders, and figure out the level of involvement required from each stakeholder at various stages of the project.

Meetings: Status review meetings with the team, sponsor, and other stakeholders will be beneficial to review information about stakeholder engagement.

Control Stakeholder Engagement: Outputs

- Work Performance Information
- Change Requests
- Project Management Plan Updates
- Project Documents Updates
- Organizational Process Assets Updates

Work Performance Information: Work performance information such as deliverables status, change request implementation status, and forecasted estimates to completion are distributed through communication processes.

Change Requests: Recommended corrective actions for bringing the imminent performance of the project as per the expectations in the project management plan and recommended preventive actions. This would reduce the probability and impact of future negative project performance.

Project Management Plan Updates: Most of the components of the project management plan may be updated to reflect changes in the stakeholder management strategy and the approach to effectively control stakeholder engagement in the project.

Project Documents Updates: Project documents such as the issue log, the stakeholder register, and others may be updated.

Organizational Process Assets Updates: Lessons learned from managing stakeholders, feedback from stakeholders, project records, causes of issues, reasons for corrective actions chosen, project reports, stakeholder notifications, and other items may be updated.

Exercise 3: Identify which process group each process belongs to:

Process Groups				
Initiating	**Planning**	**Executing**	**Monitoring & Controlling**	**Closing**

Process Names:

- Plan Stakeholder Management
- Control Stakeholder Engagement
- Manage Stakeholder Engagement
- Identify Stakeholders

Exercise 4: Crossword

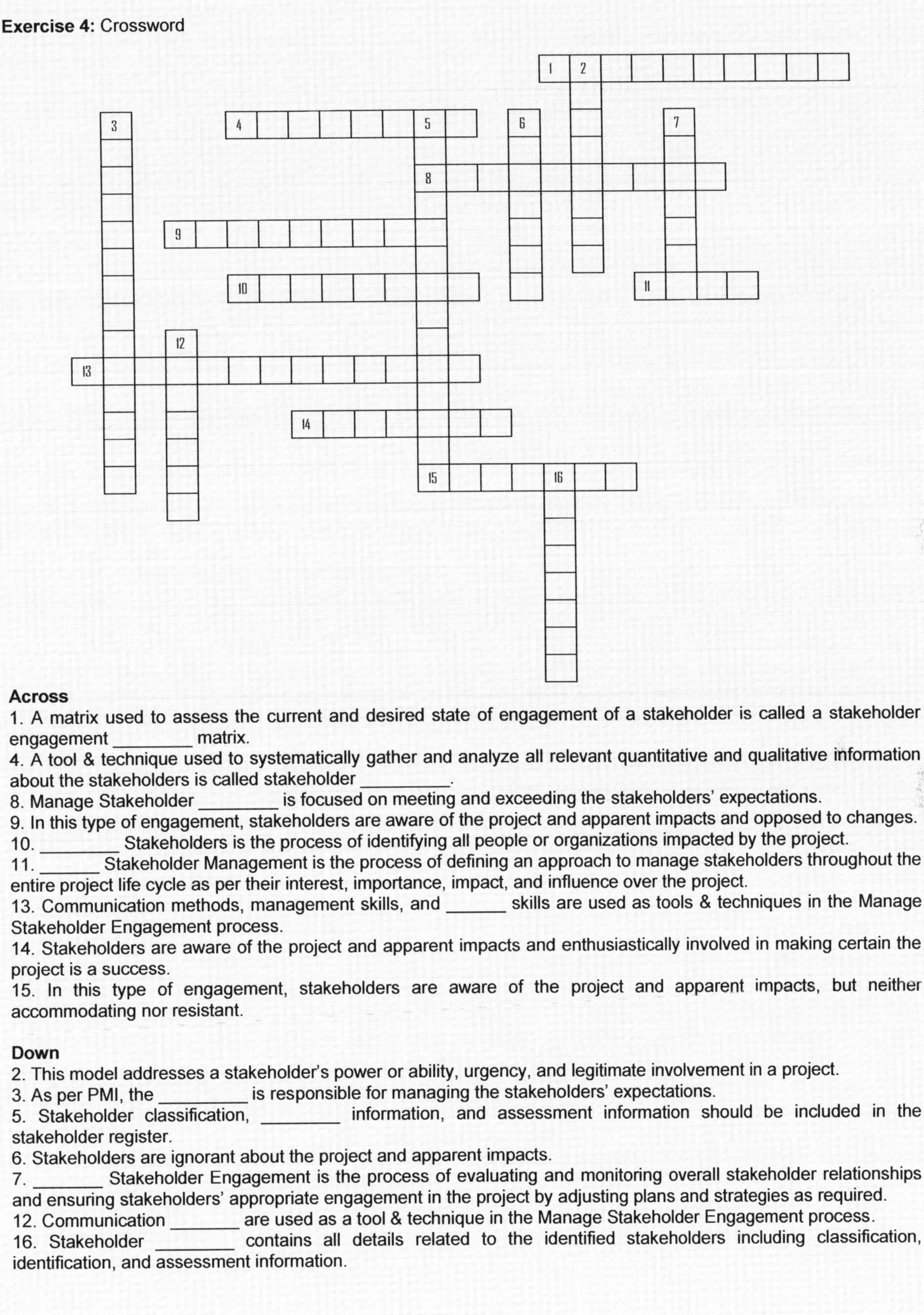

Across

1. A matrix used to assess the current and desired state of engagement of a stakeholder is called a stakeholder engagement ________ matrix.
4. A tool & technique used to systematically gather and analyze all relevant quantitative and qualitative information about the stakeholders is called stakeholder _________.
8. Manage Stakeholder ________ is focused on meeting and exceeding the stakeholders' expectations.
9. In this type of engagement, stakeholders are aware of the project and apparent impacts and opposed to changes.
10. ________ Stakeholders is the process of identifying all people or organizations impacted by the project.
11. ______ Stakeholder Management is the process of defining an approach to manage stakeholders throughout the entire project life cycle as per their interest, importance, impact, and influence over the project.
13. Communication methods, management skills, and ______ skills are used as tools & techniques in the Manage Stakeholder Engagement process.
14. Stakeholders are aware of the project and apparent impacts and enthusiastically involved in making certain the project is a success.
15. In this type of engagement, stakeholders are aware of the project and apparent impacts, but neither accommodating nor resistant.

Down

2. This model addresses a stakeholder's power or ability, urgency, and legitimate involvement in a project.
3. As per PMI, the _________ is responsible for managing the stakeholders' expectations.
5. Stakeholder classification, ________ information, and assessment information should be included in the stakeholder register.
6. Stakeholders are ignorant about the project and apparent impacts.
7. _______ Stakeholder Engagement is the process of evaluating and monitoring overall stakeholder relationships and ensuring stakeholders' appropriate engagement in the project by adjusting plans and strategies as required.
12. Communication _______ are used as a tool & technique in the Manage Stakeholder Engagement process.
16. Stakeholder ________ contains all details related to the identified stakeholders including classification, identification, and assessment information.

Exercise 5: Answer the following:

1. This is the process of meeting and exceeding the stakeholders' expectations by continuously communicating with them, clarifying and resolving their issues, addressing their concerns, and improving project performance by implementing their change requests.
2. This log is used to document changes that occur during a project.
3. It addresses a stakeholder's power or ability to impose their will, urgency, or need for immediate attention from the team and legitimate involvement (their involvement is appropriate) in a project.
4. This matrix is used to assess the current and desired state of engagement of a stakeholder for the current phase of the project.
5. There should be one _______ assigned for each issue reported within the project in an issue log.
6. A person or an organization that is actively involved with the work of the project or whose vested interests may be positively or negatively impacted by the execution or completion of the project.
7. It is a technique of systematically gathering and analyzing all relevant quantitative and qualitative information about the stakeholders in order to prioritize them and determine whose interests should be taken into consideration throughout the project.
8. This is the process of evaluating and monitoring overall stakeholder relationships and ensuring stakeholders' appropriate engagement in the project by adjusting plans and strategies as required.
9. Manage Stakeholder Engagement is a process in the _________ process group.
10. Stakeholder's level of engagement in a project may be unaware, resistant, neutral, supportive, or ______.
11. This is the process of identifying all people or organizations impacted by the project and documenting relevant information regarding their interests, expectations, involvement, and influence on project success.
12. Stakeholder ________ is a continuous and sometimes difficult process.
13. Stakeholder classification, identification information, and assessment information should be included in the stakeholder _________.
14. Purpose for communication, information needs of each stakeholder or stakeholder group, stakeholder communication requirements, format, method, time frame, and frequency for the distribution of required information can be found in the _________.
15. The four processes of stakeholder management are _________.
16. The key outputs of stakeholder management processes are _________.
17. _________ is responsible for managing stakeholder expectations.
18. Stakeholder analysis is used as a tool and technique in the _________ process.
19. Stakeholder engagement assessment matrix is an analytical technique used in the _________ process.
20. Name some of the tools and techniques used in Manage Stakeholder Engagement process.
21. In stakeholder management, issue log is an output in the _________ process.
22. A ________ is used to identify all key internal and external stakeholders who have interest in and influence over the project.
23. Stakeholders who have higher power or influence and high interest in our project should be ________.
24. Plans that are used as inputs in the Manage Stakeholder Engagement process.
25. Stakeholders who have higher power or influence and low interest in our project should be ________.
26. The legitimacy of a stakeholder is often defined as ________.
27. Stakeholders who have low power or influence and high interest in our project should be ________.
28. The change log, an output of the Perform Integrated Change Control process, is an input to the _______ process.
29. Stakeholders who have low power or influence and low interest in our project should be ________.

Project Stakeholder Management Summary

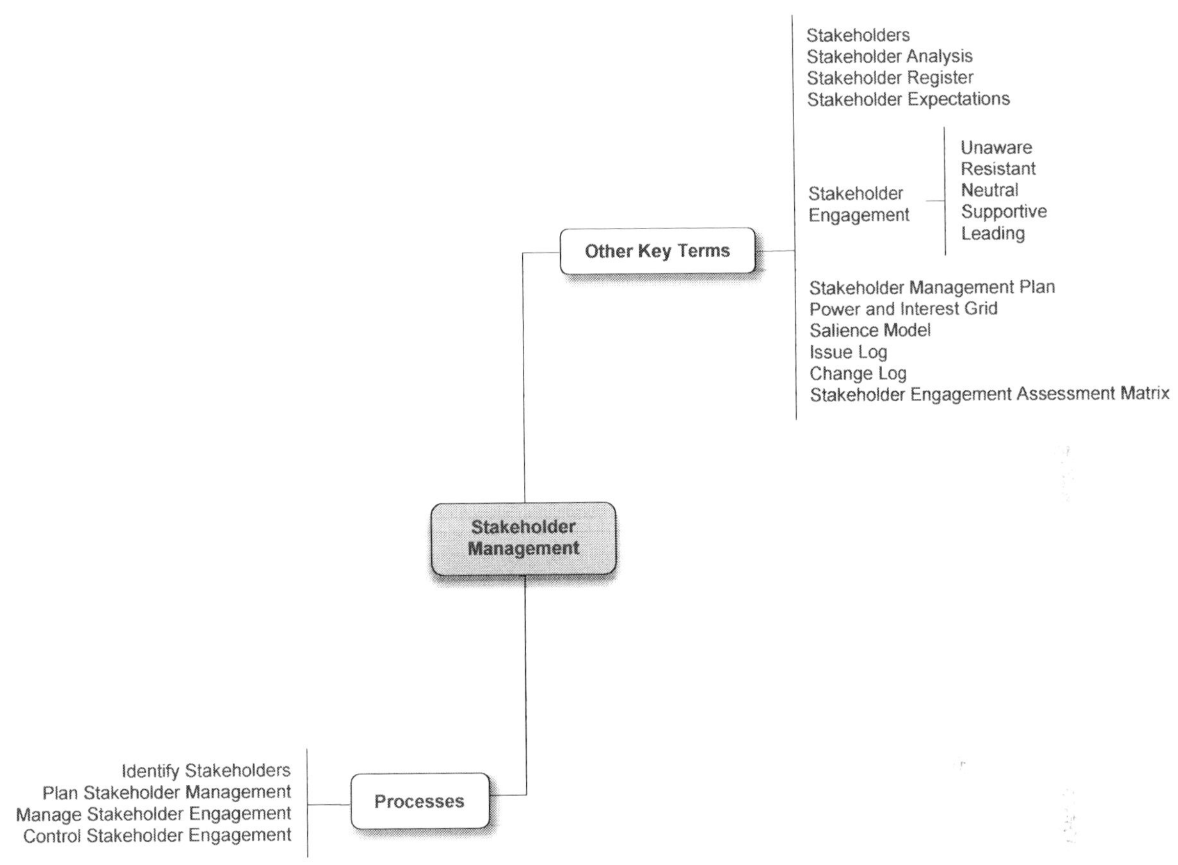

Figure 12-8: Project Stakeholder Management Summary

Project Stakeholder Management Key Terms

Stakeholder Analysis: A process of systematically gathering and analyzing all relevant quantitative and qualitative information about the stakeholders.
Stakeholder Register: A document that contains all details related to the identified stakeholders including classification, identification, and assessment information.

Other Terms

Stakeholder Engagement: Unaware, resistant, neutral, supportive, leading
Stakeholder Engagement Assessment Matrix: A matrix used to assess the current and desired state of engagement of a stakeholder.

Stakeholder	Unaware	Neutral	Resistant	Supportive	Leading
A	C			D	
B		C			D
C			C	D	
D				C, D	

Stakeholder Engagement Assessment Matrix C= Current, D = Desired

Salience Model: P U L – Power, Urgency, Legitimacy
Issue Log: A written log document to record issues that require a solution. One owner assigned for each issue reported
Change Log: A log used to document changes that occur during a project
Notes

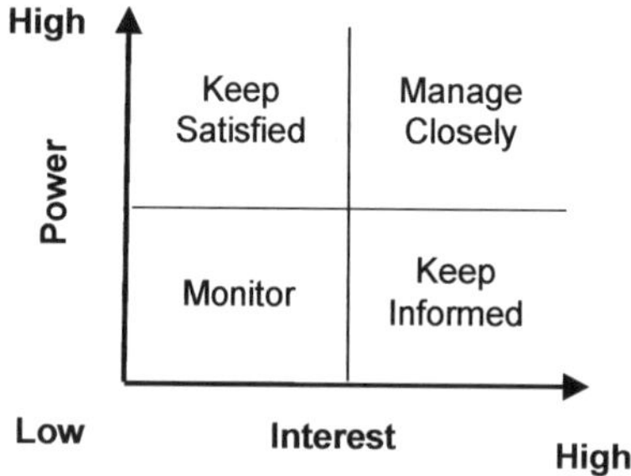

Power/Interest Grid for Stakeholders

- Stakeholders with high power and high interest should be managed closely
- Stakeholders with high power and low interest should be kept satisfied
- Stakeholders with low power and low interest should be monitored
- Stakeholders with low power and high interest should be kept informed

Project Stakeholder Management Exercise Answers

Exercise 1:

- Know the stakeholders by their names if possible.
- Identify stakeholders' expectations and requirements in the project.
- Determine stakeholders' level of interest in the project.
- Determine stakeholders' level of positive and negative influence over the project.
- Gain stakeholders' formal acceptance on the final requirement.
- Figure out how stakeholders' needs will be satisfied.
- Assess stakeholders' skill sets, expertise, and knowledge.
- Inform stakeholders what is in and out of scope in the project.
- Utilize the expertise and knowledge of the stakeholders.
- Try to fully involve stakeholders in the project and make sure to receive all supports from them as planned.
- Control stakeholders' influence over the project.
- Communicate project status to stakeholders on a regular basis.
- Find out stakeholders' issues and concerns.
- Keep stakeholders happy and satisfied all the time by addressing their concerns and implementing their approved change requests.
- Gain stakeholders' formal acceptance on the final product, service, or result.
- Obtain stakeholders' inputs in lessons learned.

Exercise 2:

1. Kept informed
2. Kept satisfied
3. Managed closely
4. Monitored

Exercise 3:

Process Groups				
Initiating	**Planning**	**Executing**	**Monitoring & Controlling**	**Closing**
Identify Stakeholders	Plan Stakeholder Management	Manage Stakeholder Engagement	Control Stakeholder Engagement	

Exercise 4:

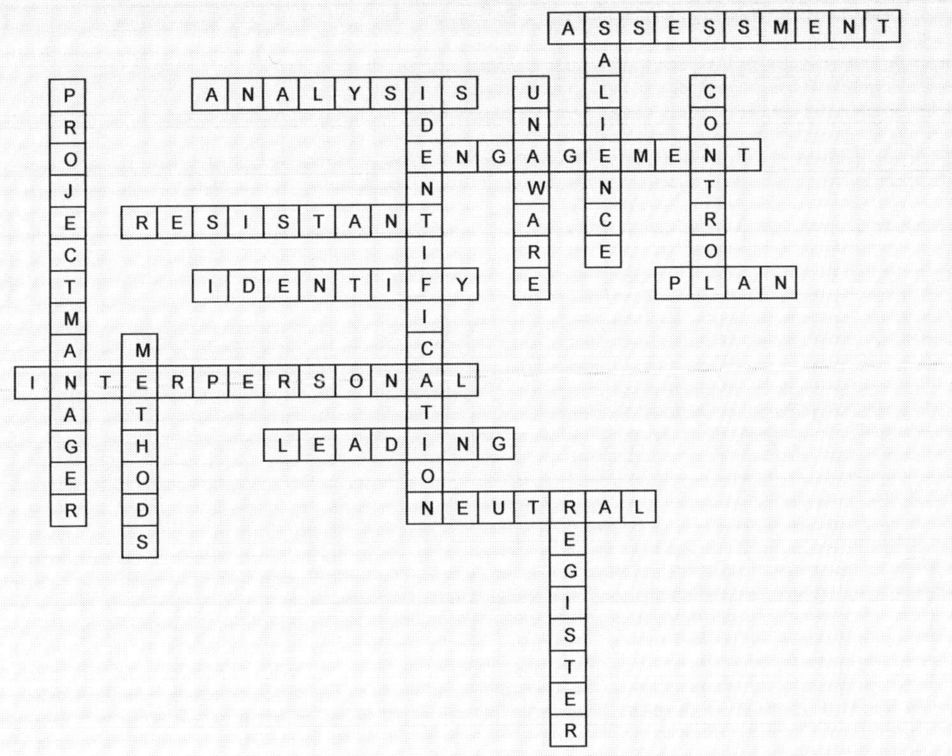

Exercise 5:

1. Manage Stakeholder Engagement
2. Change log
3. Salience model
4. Stakeholder engagement assessment matrix
5. Owner
6. Stakeholder
7. Stakeholder analysis
8. Control Stakeholder Engagement
9. Executing
10. Leading
11. Identify Stakeholders
12. Identification
13. Register
14. Communications management plan
15. Identify Stakeholders, Plan Stakeholder Management, Manage Stakeholder Engagement, and Control Stakeholder Engagement
16. Identify Stakeholders – Stakeholder Register
    Plan Stakeholder Management – Stakeholder Management Plan
    Manage Stakeholder Engagement – Issue Log, Change Requests
    Control Stakeholder Engagement – Work Performance Information, Change Requests
17. A project manager
18. Identify Stakeholders
19. Plan Stakeholder Management
20. Communication methods, interpersonal skills, management skills
21. Manage Stakeholder Engagement
22. Stakeholder register
23. Managed closely
24. Stakeholder management plan and communications management plan
25. Kept satisfied
26. Whether the involvement of the stakeholders is appropriate
27. Kept informed
28. Manage Stakeholder Engagement Process
29. Monitored

Project Stakeholder Management Exam Tips

- Be able to describe the purpose of the four stakeholder management processes.
- Be able to name the inputs, tools & techniques, and outputs of all the stakeholder management processes.
- Be able to answer questions where you will need to analyze a specific situation and determine what you should do next.
- Be familiar with all the terms in the stakeholder management summary table, Figure 12-8: Project Stakeholder Management Summary.

Project Stakeholder Management Questions

1. You are efficaciously managing a business automation project, and most of the deliverables were delivered on time by the team members. This project is extremely critical as it will drastically cut down the time and cost of regular business activities for several departments. Stakeholders and customers have articulated their satisfaction with the project, but you were also criticized for the number of changes made in the project. Which of the following is the MOST likely cause of the project problem?
   A. You failed to identify some of the key stakeholders in your project.
   B. You should have more project management training and experience.
   C. Change Control Board (CCB) members approved almost all of the change requests.
   D. The project should have had a better change control system.

2. You are in the Control Stakeholder Engagement process of evaluating and monitoring overall stakeholder relationships and ensuring stakeholders' appropriate engagement in the project by adjusting plans and strategies as required. Which one of the following is an important input to the Control Stakeholder Engagement process?
   A. Stakeholder register
   B. Project charter
   C. Change log
   D. Issue log

3. You are performing stakeholder analysis and utilizing different models to identify the interests, expectations, and influence of the stakeholders to classify them. The model that helps to analyze a stakeholder's power or ability to impose his or her will, urgency, or need for immediate attention from the project team along with the legitimacy of his or her involvement is the:
   A. Power/interest grid
   B. Salience model
   C. Power/influence grid
   D. Influence/impact grid

4. You are in the Plan Stakeholder Management process of defining an approach to manage stakeholders throughout the entire project life cycle as per their interest, impact, importance, and influence over the project. Which of the following is an input to this Plan Stakeholder Management process?
   A. Impact/power grid
   B. Stakeholder register
   C. Stakeholder engagement assessment matrix
   D. Issue log

5. You are in the Manage Stakeholder Engagement process and are focused on meeting and exceeding the stakeholders' expectations by continuously communicating with them, clarifying and resolving their issues, addressing their concerns, and improving project performance by implementing their change requests. Which of the following is a tool & technique used in this process?
   A. Interpersonal skills
   B. Change log
   C. Issue log
   D. Stakeholder management plan

6. You are assigned as a project manager for one of the most imperative and strategic projects in your organization. As the stakeholders will play a vital role in the success of your project, you are trying to identify all your internal and external stakeholders. In which project management process group will you identify stakeholders in your project?
   A. Initiating
   B. Initiating and planning
   C. All process groups
   D. Planning and monitoring & controlling

7. You have been managing a government railway project and dealing with several stakeholders. You have spent a considerable amount of time identifying all your internal and external stakeholders and their interest, influence level in your project, and their key expectations. Managing stakeholder expectations is the responsibility of which party?

A. Since the project manager alone cannot manage all the stakeholders on a complex, large project, the project manager and project team together are responsible for managing stakeholders' expectations.
B. Project sponsor, as this individual funds the project and has greater control over the stakeholders.
C. Stakeholders should make sure that their expectations are managed appropriately and that they receive the required information on the project as needed.
D. This is the responsibility of the project manager alone.

8. You have thirteen stakeholders in the construction project that you are overseeing. Your initial study about these stakeholders tells you that most of them will actively support your project to be successful, but you have a couple of stakeholders who may deleteriously impact your project. There is one specific stakeholder you are particularly concerned about as he is known to be exceptionally critical about the way the project managers in the organization manage projects. He also has the reputation for requesting many changes in projects and antagonistically pursuing his demands. You realized that you need to be meticulous in dealing with this stakeholder and plan to take which of the following approaches:

A. Carefully eradicate the need of this stakeholder and remove him from the stakeholder list.
B. Have a discussion with the stakeholder's boss and find a way to make the stakeholder support the project positively by not being too critical and aggressive.
C. Simply deal with the stakeholder and refuse his requests for changes.
D. Involve this stakeholder in the project as early as possible and work closely with him throughout the project.

9. A trustworthy, senior team member informs you that two of the stakeholders are very apprehensive about the ERP project you are overseeing. The first stakeholder is very panicky that once the ERP is implemented in his department a lot of people will lose their jobs. The second stakeholder is skeptical about the capability of the team to implement such large, multifaceted project. As the project manager, what should you do in this kind of situation?

A. Set up a meeting with these two stakeholders and discuss their concerns.
B. Report to the sponsor about these two stakeholders.
C. Set up a question-and-answer session about the project and invite all the stakeholders.
D. You should send an official e-mail to the stakeholders asking them to direct any queries about the project in writing to you.

10. You have several stakeholders in the shopping mall construction project that you are overseeing. You know that actively engaging the stakeholders throughout the project and getting their support is key for project success. In which of the following areas will the external stakeholders be able to assist you the MOST?

A. Project charter, assumptions, and project management plan
B. Activity resource constraints and needs
C. Requirements, deliverables, and schedule
D. Product deliverables and project constraints

11. You have thirteen stakeholders in the construction project that you are overseeing. Your initial study about these stakeholders tells you that most of them will actively support your project to be successful, but you have couple of stakeholders who may adversely impact your project. When do you think these stakeholders will have the MOST influence on your project?

A. Throughout the project life cycle
B. At the completion of the project
C. At the beginning of the project
D. During executing and monitoring & controlling process groups

12. What is the best way to manage stakeholders who are high on power but low on interest?

A. Monitor
B. Keep informed
C. Keep satisfied
D. Manage closely

13. While analyzing stakeholders in your project, you identified one stakeholder who is so formidable and influential that he forced the team to implement many of his last-minutes change requests in one of the previous projects. There is also a common understanding that he used his influence to dismiss a very important project during executing in the past. What will be your BEST course of action with such a persuasive stakeholder?

A. Involve this stakeholder as little as possible in the project.
B. Involve this stakeholder from the very beginning and closely manage him.
C. Give highest priority to his expectations, concerns, and issues.
D. Get approval from the sponsor to remove this stakeholder from the project.

14. You are assigned as a project manager to implement an ERP solution for one of the retailers in your area. Currently, you are working on identifying stakeholders and their level of involvement, roles, and responsibilities. Who will be able to help the team the MOST to identify what roles the stakeholders will play and how and what they will contribute to the project?

A. The sponsor
B. Senior management
C. Functional managers
D. Stakeholders

15. Due to time and budget constraints, senior management decided not to include the requirements of several stakeholders in a project. The project manager finalized the project management plan but encountered significant challenges in receiving formal acceptance. The stakeholders were extremely upset and tried every possible way to include their requirements in the project as it would take several years for the organization to initiate another project to implement their desired functionalities. After several attempts, the project was finally approved and initiated a couple of months ago. Which of the following preventive actions should the project manager NOT consider in this case?

A. Make sure that the stakeholders will not use the change control process as a mean to add their requirements.
B. Document what is out of scope and in scope in the project.
C. Review and confirm the requirements that will be out of scope in the project with the stakeholders.
D. Develop a stakeholder register and stakeholder management strategy.

16. Steve is trying to figure out whether a stakeholder is at an "unaware" state or not so that he can identify required actions and communication needed to minimize the gap between the desired and actual level of engagement of this stakeholder. Which of the following is a tool to assess the current and desired state of engagement of a stakeholder on the project?

A. Stakeholder engagement assessment matrix
B. Issue log
C. Stakeholder register
D. Stakeholder management plan

17. You are reviewing the stakeholder management plan and communications management plan and focusing on meeting and exceeding the stakeholders' expectations by continuously communicating with them, elucidating and resolving their issues, addressing their apprehensions, and improving project performance by implementing their change requests. Which stakeholder management process are you in at this time?

A. Control Stakeholder Engagement
B. Manage Stakeholder Engagement
C. Plan Stakeholder Management
D. Identify Stakeholders

18. You are overseeing a web-based application project to automate the business process of one of your clients. You are working on identifying all the internal and external stakeholders who have interest in your project and can positively or negatively impact your project. While identifying the stakeholders, you realize that stakeholder identification is:

A. To be focused only on stakeholders who will contribute positively to your project:
B. To be completed in the initial stage of the project life cycle
C. A responsibility of the project sponsor
D. To be carried out throughout the project life cycle

19. Stakeholder management necessitates all of the following EXCEPT:

A. Giving stakeholder extras if needed to meet and exceed their expectations
B. Identifying both internal and external stakeholders
C. Assessing stakeholders' skills, knowledge and expertise
D. Identifying stakeholders' influence-controlling strategies

20. You are overseeing a project to build a plant for a semiconductor company. You have completed your internal and external stakeholder identification and have come up with a list of thirteen stakeholders for the project. You expect that most of the stakeholders will play an affirmative role in the project and will contribute significantly. While working on your project management plan, you were notified by one of the team members that a stakeholder from the automation department is missing in the published stakeholder list. What will be your best course of action in this situation?

A. Add the stakeholder in your stakeholder list immediately and update everyone.
B. It is too late to add any more stakeholders and consider their requirements, so ignore the stakeholder.
C. Validate the information received from the team member.
D. Set up a meeting with the stakeholder and the team member.

21. You have been managing a government railway project and dealing with several stakeholders. You have spent a considerable amount of time identifying all your internal and external stakeholders and their interest, influence level in your project, and their key expectations. As part of your analysis of the level of engagement of stakeholders in your project you have classified them as:

Unaware: Stakeholders are ignorant about the project and apparent impacts.
Neutral: Stakeholders are aware of the project and apparent impacts but neither accommodating nor resistant.
Resistant: Stakeholders are aware of the project and apparent impacts and opposed to changes.
Supportive: Stakeholders are aware of the project and apparent impacts and accommodating to changes.
Leading: Stakeholders are aware of the project and apparent impacts and enthusiastically involved in making certain the project is a success.

What sort of techniques are you using in this case?

A. Information gathering techniques
B. Stakeholder Analysis
C. Delphi technique
D. Analytical Techniques

22. You identified all people who would be impacted by the project and documented relevant information regarding their interests, expectations, involvement, and influence on the project success in a stakeholder register. The stakeholder register will NOT be used as an input to which of the following processes?

A. Collect Requirements and Plan Scope Management
B. Plan Risk Management and Identify Risks
C. Plan Quality Management and Plan Communications Management
D. Develop Project Charter and Perform Integrated Change Control

23. Your company, ITPro Consultancy, has assigned you as the project manager to upgrade the call center in your organization. The number of calls the customer support agents have to answer each month has increased drastically in the last five months, and the phone system is approaching the maximum load limit. While identifying the stakeholders, you realize that there are more than 180 potential stakeholders, 19 team members, and 6 different vendors that you will need to deal with. What will be your BEST course of action?

A. Have an urgent meeting with the sponsor and request him not to include some of the stakeholders.
B. Identify an effective approach to determine the needs of all stakeholders.
C. Identify the key stakeholders and concentrate only on their needs.
D. Report to the management that the project is too large to manage by one person.

24. Project stakeholder management consists of processes to identify the internal and external stakeholders, determine their expectations and influence over the project, develop strategies to manage them, and effectively engage them in project execution and decision. Which one of the following is the key objective of the stakeholder management?

A. Keeping the stakeholders happy and satisfied
B. Maintaining a robust communication with all stakeholders
C. Keeping a positive relationship with all stakeholders
D. Establishing a good coordination among stakeholders

25. You are in the process of evaluating and monitoring overall stakeholder relationships and ensuring stakeholders' appropriate engagement in the project by adjusting plans and strategies as required. The work performance data that is an input to this Control Stakeholder Engagement process usually comes from:

A. Validate Scope
B. Perform Integrated Change Control
C. Monitor and Control Project Work
D. Direct and Manage Project Work

26. A stakeholder register includes all of the following items EXCEPT:

A. **Stakeholder classification:** Internal/external, neutral/resistor/supporter, and others.
B. **Identification information:** Name, title, location, organization, role in the project, position, and contact information.
C. **Assessment information:** Key requirements and expectations, potential impact, importance, and influence on the project.
D. **Strategies:** The strategies to interact with stakeholders, increase their positive influence, and control their negative influence.

Project Stakeholder Management Answers

1. A: The root cause of the significant number of changes in the project is that some of the key stakeholders were not identified and their requirements were not captured. These missing stakeholders have submitted several change requests to accommodate their needs. Nothing in this scenario advocates that the project manager does not have the required project management training and experience. A vigorous change control board will be efficiently evaluating the change requests to approve or reject them, but they cannot really help with the number of changes a project will have.

2. D: The issue log is an important input to the Control Stakeholder Management process. An issue is an obstacle that threatens project progress and can block the team from achieving its goals. An issue log is a written log document to record issues that require solution.

3. B: The salience model addresses stakeholder power or ability to impose their will, urgency, or need for immediate attention from the team and legitimize their involvement (their involvement is appropriate) in a project. Power/interest grid is based on the level of authority or power and level of concern or interest a stakeholder has regarding the project outcome. Power/influence grid is based on the level of authority or power and active involvement or influence a stakeholder has. Influence/impact grid groups stakeholders based on their involvement or influence and their ability to affect changes to planning or execution (impact).

4. B: The stakeholder register is an input to the Plan Stakeholder Management process.

5. A: An interpersonal skill is a crucial tool & technique used in the Manage Stakeholder Engagement process.

6. C: Stakeholders can be identified throughout the project management process groups of initiating, planning, executing, monitoring & controlling, and closing. In order to determine the requirements and expectations of the stakeholders, they should be identified and should be involved at the beginning of the project as much as possible. If all the stakeholders' needs and requirements are not taken into consideration prior to plan finalization, the results may be very expensive changes or dissatisfaction later in the project.

7. D: The project manager is responsible for managing stakeholder expectations.

8. D: The project manager simply cannot remove the stakeholder from the stakeholder list since he has a stake in the project. It will be best to involve this stakeholder in the project as early as possible and work closely with him throughout the project to understand his requirements and expectations and gain his constructive support.

9. A: An informal verbal communication by setting up a meeting with these two stakeholders and discussing their concerns should be the best approach here. Reporting to the sponsor without much detail about these two stakeholders will not solve any real problem. Since not all stakeholders have concerns, setting up a question-and-answer session about the project with all the stakeholders will not be appropriate. Sending an official e-mail to the stakeholders asking them to direct any query on the project in writing to the project manager will most probably estrange them.

10. D: The project manager creates the project management plan, schedule, and activity resource needs with input from the team members. The project sponsor will approve the project charter. External stakeholders may help the team in determining product deliverables and project constraints.

11. C: Stakeholder influence is highest at the start and diminishes as the project proceeds.

12. C: The strategy for stakeholders who are high on the power but low on the interest is "keep satisfied."

13. B: The project manager simply cannot remove the stakeholder from the stakeholder list since he has a stake in the project. It will be best to involve this stakeholder in the project as early as possible and work closely with him throughout the project to understand his requirements and gain his constructive support.

14. D: Stakeholders will be able to help the project manager and team members the most in identifying what roles they will play in the project. The project manager will decide how and what kind of contributions stakeholders will make in the project by discussing with team members, the sponsor, and stakeholders. The project manager should evaluate the knowledge and skill sets of stakeholders in order to identify stakeholders' roles and have a discussion with them to make sure that they approve the roles.

15. C: As the project was approved and work was begun, the issue should not be a concern anymore. Having further meetings with the stakeholders will be excessive and will not add any real value.

16. A: A stakeholder engagement assessment matrix is a tool to assess the engagement levels of the stakeholders on a project. The matrix can be utilized to compare the actual engagement levels to the planned levels. Any discrepancies can be examined, and communication to adjust the engagement levels can then be implemented.

17. B: All these activities typically belong to the Manage Stakeholder Engagement process.

18. D: Stakeholder identification will persist throughout the project life cycle. As the project proceeds through each phase, additional stakeholders may become involved while others will be released from the project. Some stakeholders will be identified during the initiating phase in the project charter, while other stakeholders may only be interested in the end product and will be involved only at the closing phase.

19. A: Giving stakeholder extras or gold plating should always be avoided. Gold plating is not the preferred way of meeting and exceeding stakeholder expectations.

20. C: Before you take any other step, you should validate the information received from the team member.

21. D: An analytical technique such as stakeholder engagement assessment matrix is used to classify stakeholders as per their level of engagement in the project during the Plan Stakeholder Management process.

22. D: The stakeholder register will be used as an input to the Collect Requirements, Plan Scope Management, Plan Risk Management, Identify Risks, Plan Quality Management, and Plan Communications Management processes. It is not an input to the Develop Project Charter, and Perform Integrated Change Control processes.

23. B: In order to minimize numerous changes later in the project, you need to identify all stakeholders and their needs as early as possible. Stakeholder analysis will be a more complicated task if there are numerous stakeholders and an effective way to determine their needs must be identified.

24. A: Keeping stakeholders happy and satisfied is the main objective of the stakeholder management. Maintaining a robust communication, keeping a positive relationship, and establishing a good coordination will collectively contribute to achieve stakeholder satisfaction.

25. D: All work performance data comes from executing process group. In this case, work performance data comes as an output of the Direct and Manage Project Work, an executing process.

26. D: The strategies to interact with the stakeholders are included in the stakeholder management plan, not in the stakeholder register.

CHAPTER 14

CODE OF ETHICS AND PROFESSIONAL CONDUCT

Code of Ethics and Professional Conduct

Code of ethics and professional conduct describes the expectations that we have of ourselves and our fellow practitioners in the global project management community. It conveys the ideals to which we aspire as well as the behaviors that are mandatory in our professional and volunteer roles.

A project manager should always adhere to the PMI code of ethics and professional conduct to avoid any kind of devastating impact on the project and the organization. It is expected that the project manager be a leader who will deal with issues and concerns in an honest and direct manner, who will be open and upfront, and who will act ethically and legally at all times. For this reason, concepts related to the code of ethics and professional conduct are tested in the PMP exam as a part of everything a project manager does from project initiating to closing. One single phrase that sums up this section of the exam is "stick to your principles and do the right thing" even if it is extremely painful and inconvenient or would be tempting to avoid.

Aspirational Standards: These standards describe the conduct that we strive to uphold as practitioners. Although adherence to the aspirational standards is not easily measured, conducting ourselves in accordance with these standards is an expectation that we have of ourselves as professionals—it is not optional.

Mandatory Standards: These standards establish firm requirements, and in some cases, limit or prohibit practitioner behavior. Practitioners who do not conduct themselves in accordance with these standards will be subject to disciplinary procedures before PMI's Ethics Review Committee.

Code of Ethics and Professional Conduct applies to the following:

- All PMI members
- Nonmembers who hold a PMI certification
- Nonmembers who apply to commence a PMI certification process
- Nonmembers who serve PMI in a volunteer capacity

The most important values of the project management community fall within the following four characteristics:

- Responsibility
- Respect
- Fairness
- Honesty

Responsibility

It is the act of making and taking ownership of our decisions, admitting our mistakes, and being responsible for our decisions and actions.

Aspirational Standards:

- Make decisions based on the best interests of society, public safety, and the environment.
- Accept only those assignments that are consistent with your background, experience, skills, and qualifications.
- Fulfill the commitments that you undertake – do what you promised to do.
- Accept accountability – when you make errors or omissions. Take ownership and make corrections promptly.
- Protect proprietary or confidential information.
- Uphold this Code and hold each other accountable to it.

Mandatory Standards:

- Stay Informed and uphold the policies, rules, regulations and laws that govern our work, professional activities, and volunteer activities.
- Report unethical or illegal conduct to appropriate management and, if necessary, to those affected by the conduct.
- Bring violations of this Code to the attention of the appropriate body for resolution.
- Only file ethics complaints when they are substantiated by facts.
- Pursue disciplinary action against an individual who retaliates against a person raising ethics concerns.

Respect

It involves the way we conduct ourselves in a professional manner, our ability to listen to other viewpoints, and how we treat resources entrusted to us, including people, money, reputation, safety of others, and natural or environmental resources.

Aspirational Standards:

- Respect personal, ethnic, and cultural differences.
- Avoid engaging in behaviors that might be considered disrespectful.
- Listen and understand others' points of view.
- Approach directly those persons with whom you have a conflict or disagreement.

Mandatory Standards:

- Do not exercise the power of our expertise or position to influence the decisions or actions of others in order to benefit personally at their expense.
- Do not act in an abusive manner toward others.
- Respect the property rights of others.

Fairness

It includes making decisions impartially and objectively, avoiding favoritism and discrimination against others, and reporting and avoiding conflict-of-interest situations.

Aspirational Standards:

- Practice with fairness and honesty.
- Strive for a fair solution.
- Ensure transparency in your decision-making process.
- Reexamine your impartiality and objectivity on a constant basis, and take corrective actions as appropriate.
- Provide equal access to information to those who are authorized to have that information.
- Make opportunities equally available to qualified candidates.

Mandatory Standards:

- When you realize that you have a real or potential conflict of interest, refrain from engaging in the decision-making process or otherwise attempting to influence outcomes, unless or until: you have made full disclosure to the affected stakeholders; you have an approved mitigation plan; and you have obtained the consent of the stakeholders to proceed.
- Do not hire or fire, reward or punish, or award or deny contracts based on personal considerations including but not limited to favoritism, nepotism, or bribery.
- Do not discriminate against others based on, but not limited to, gender, race, age, religion, disability, nationality, or sexual orientation.
- Apply the rules of the organization (employer, Project Management Institute, or other group) without favoritism or prejudice.
- Do not use your position for personal or business gain.

Honesty

It is the act of communicating and conducting ourselves in a truthful manner, reporting the truth regarding project status, not deceiving others, not making false or half-true statements, and being honest about our own experience and expertise.

Aspirational Standards:

- Be truthful in your communications and conduct.
- Provide accurate information in a timely manner.
- Provide accurate and truthful representation to the public.
- Negotiate in good faith.
- Make commitments and promises, implied or explicit, in good faith.
- Strive to create an environment in which others feel safe to tell the truth.
- Avoid conflict of interest or appearance of impropriety.

Mandatory Standards:

- Do not engage in dishonest behavior with the intention of personal gain or at the expense of others.
- Do not engage in or condone behavior that is designed to deceive others, including but not limited to, making misleading or false statements, stating half-truths, providing information out of context or withholding information that, if known, would render our statements as misleading or incomplete.

Professional and social responsibility terminology:

Term	Description
Patent	A government authority or license conferring a right or title for a set period, especially the sole right to exclude others from making, using, or selling an invention.
PMI Code of Ethics and Professional Conduct	A standard that describes the expectations that we have of ourselves and our fellow practitioners in the global project management community. It articulates the ideals to which we aspire as well as the behaviors that are mandatory in our professional and volunteer roles.
Professional and Social Responsibility	Ethics expected from project managers which includes reporting any violations and balancing stakeholder interests.
Non-disclosure Agreement (NDA)	A contract by which one or more parties agree not to disclose confidential information that they have shared with each other as a necessary part of doing business together.
Law	The system of rules that a particular country or community recognizes as regulating the actions of its members and may enforce by the imposition of penalties.
Intellectual Property	A work or invention that is the result of creativity, such as a manuscript or a design, to which one has rights and for which one may apply for a patent, copyright, trademark, etc.
Inappropriate Compensation	Money or other items of value that are gained via inappropriate actions.
Government	The system by which a state or community is governed.
Ethnocentrism	Evaluation of other cultures according to preconceptions originating in the standards and customs of one's own culture.
Ethics	Moral principles that govern a person's or group's behavior.
Copyright	The exclusive legal right, given to an originator or an assignee to print, publish, perform, film, or record literary, artistic, or musical material, and to authorize others to do the same.
Conflict of Interest	A situation occurring when an individual or organization is involved in multiple interests, one of which could possibly corrupt the motivation.
Confidentiality	A set of rules or a promise that limits access or places restrictions on certain types of information.
Company Policy	A plan of action adopted by a company.

Table 14 -1: Professional and Social Responsibility Terminology

Exercise 1: Answer the following:

1. Matching exercise

Term	Definition
1. Patent	a. A plan of action adopted by a company.
2. PMI Code of Ethics and Professional Conduct	b. Money or other items of value that are gained via inappropriate actions.
3. Professional and Social Responsibility	c. A contract by which one or more parties agree not to disclose confidential information that they have shared with each other as a necessary part of doing business together.
4. Non-disclosure Agreement (NDA)	d. Evaluation of other cultures according to preconceptions originating in the standards and customs of one's own culture.
5. Law	e. The exclusive legal right, given to an originator or an assignee to print, publish, perform, film, or record literary, artistic, or musical material, and to authorize others to do the same.
6. Intellectual Property	f. A government authority or license conferring a right or title for a set period, especially the sole right to exclude others from making, using, or selling an invention.
7. Inappropriate Compensation	g. Ethics expected from project managers which includes reporting any violations and balancing stakeholder interests.
8. Government	h. A standard that describes the expectations that we have of ourselves and our fellow practitioners in the global project management community. It articulates the ideals to which we aspire as well as the behaviors that are mandatory in our professional and volunteer roles.
9. Ethnocentrism	i. The system of rules that a particular country or community recognizes as regulating the actions of its members and may enforce by the imposition of penalties.
10. Ethics	j. The system by which a state or community is governed.
11. Copyright	k. A work or invention that is the result of creativity, such as a manuscript or a design, to which one has rights and for which one may apply for a patent, copyright, trademark, etc.
12. Conflict of Interest	l. A set of rules or a promise that limits access or places restrictions on certain types of information.
13. Confidentiality	m. A situation occurring when an individual or organization is involved in multiple interests, one of which could possibly corrupt the motivation.
14. Company Policy	n. Moral principles that govern a person's or group's behavior.

2. Code of Ethics and Professional Conduct applies to ______________.
3. The most important values to the project management community fall within the following four characteristics:
4. It is the act of communicating and conducting ourselves in a truthful manner, reporting the truth regarding project status, not deceiving others, not making false or half-true statements, and being honest about our own experience and expertise.
5. It includes making decisions impartially and objectively, avoiding favoritism and discrimination against others, and reporting and avoiding conflict-of-interest situations.
6. It involves the way we conduct ourselves in a professional manner, our ability to listen to other viewpoints, and how we treat resources entrusted to us, including people, money, reputation, safety of others, and natural or environmental resources.
7. It is the act of making and taking ownership of our decisions, admitting our mistakes, and being responsible for our decisions and actions.

Code of Ethics Exercise Answers

1.

1. **Patent:** f. A government authority or license conferring a right or title for a set period, especially the sole right to exclude others from making, using, or selling an invention.
2. **PMI Code of Ethics and Professional Conduct:** h. A standard that describes the expectations that we have of ourselves and our fellow practitioners in the global project management community. It articulates the ideals to which we aspire as well as the behaviors that are mandatory in our professional and volunteer roles.
3. **Professional and Social Responsibility:** g. Ethics expected from project managers which includes reporting any violations and balancing stakeholder interests.
4. **Non-disclosure Agreement (NDA):** c. A contract by which one or more parties agree not to disclose confidential information that they have shared with each other as a necessary part of doing business together.
5. **Law:** i. The system of rules that a particular country or community recognizes as regulating the actions of its members and may enforce by the imposition of penalties.
6. **Intellectual Property:** k. A work or invention that is the result of creativity, such as a manuscript or a design, to which one has rights and for which one may apply for a patent, copyright, trademark, etc.
7. **Inappropriate Compensation:** b. Money or other items of value that are gained via inappropriate actions.
8. **Government:** j. The system by which a state or community is governed.
9. **Ethnocentrism:** d. Evaluation of other cultures according to preconceptions originating in the standards and customs of one's own culture.
10. **Ethics:** n. Moral principles that govern a person's or group's behavior.
11. **Copyright:** e. The exclusive legal right, given to an originator or an assignee to print, publish, perform, film, or record literary, artistic, or musical material, and to authorize others to do the same.
12. **Conflict of Interest:** m. A situation occurring when an individual or organization is involved in multiple interests, one of which could possibly corrupt the motivation.
13. **Confidentiality:** l. A set of rules or a promise that limits access or places restrictions on certain types of information.
14. **Company Policy:** a. A plan of action adopted by a company.

2. All PMI members, nonmembers who hold a PMI certification, nonmembers who apply to commence a PMI certification process, nonmembers who serve PMI in a volunteer capacity.
3. Responsibility, respect, fairness, and honesty
4. Honesty
5. Fairness
6. Respect
7. Responsibility

Project Code of Ethics and Professional Conduct Exam Tips

- Be able to name the areas to which the code of ethics and professional conduct apply.
- Be able to define four key characteristics of the code of ethics and professional conduct.
- Be able to answer questions where you will need to analyze a specific situation and determine what you should do next.

Project Code of Ethics and Professional Conduct Questions

1. You are accountable for a large data center project and have requested proposals from several vendors. You will be purchasing $1.2 million worth of networking equipment, a software application, and an ERP solution for the project. Once informed about your upcoming family vacation on an island, one of the vendors offered you to stay in his summer cabin on forty acres land he happens to have on that island. What should you do in this situation?

   A. Decline the offer as it will be considered an integrity issue on the part of the vendor.
   B. Decline the offer as it is an integrity issue and will be considered as your personal gain.
   C. Accept the offer and also inform the project sponsor about it.
   D. Accept the offer as you do not see any integrity issue or conflict of interest.

2. While discussing the project schedule with the sponsor, both of you recognize that the project is behind schedule and that there is no way to meet the deadline that was committed. The sponsor asked you not to reveal this fact to the customer in the impending status meeting later on that day. What will be your BEST course of action?

   A. Have a quick chat with the customer and explain your situation.
   B. Request the sponsor to have a conversation with the customer.
   C. Postpone the status meeting.
   D. Explain to the sponsor that it is not ethical to knowingly report an incorrect project status to anyone in the project.

3. Your project to build a water park in one of the east side subdivisions has been going pretty well. Recently you noticed that two of the team members are unremittingly arguing about project priorities, work assignments, and technical options. This is having an adverse impact on the overall project, and other team members have also complained to you about this concern. What will be your BEST course of action?

   A. Have a discussion with the concerned functional manager.
   B. Remove those two team members from the team.
   C. Have a meeting with these two team members to discuss and understand their concerns and points of view.
   D. Issue a warning letter to both of the team members.

4. You are working for a consultancy firm that provides PMP training and consultancy. You notice that the firm is encouraging the candidates to be untruthful about their required project management experience and training hours to be eligible to take the test. What will be your MOST appropriate course of action?

   A. Since you are not involved in the registration process, simply ignore what is going on in the organization.
   B. Ask the manager responsible to stop any such unethical practice.
   C. Contact PMI and explain the situation.
   D. Quit your job.

5. You are a senior project manager, and recently you were asked to manage a project to build a brick manufacturing plant. While the team was conducting the feasibility study, you learned that the plant could severely contaminate the air and water in the neighborhood. You became apprehensive that this catastrophic impact could be long lasting. You discussed your concern with the sponsor and recommended to implement robust waste management procedures that will add cost to the project. The sponsor contended that the project should be completed as soon as possible with the defined scope and no extra cost. What will be your BEST course of action in this situation?

   A. Politely refuse to take charge of the project.
   B. Take charge of the project and inform the local residents about the potential negative impact of the manufacturing plant.
   C. Agree with the sponsor.
   D. Take charge of the project and do not disclose any information about the negative impact of the manufacturing plant to the local residents.

6. You have been assigned as a project manager for a project in a country where employees take long lunches and nap breaks, enjoy six weeks of paid vacation each year, and observe several supplementary holidays that are not offered in your home country. You have been asked by your local team members to authorize the same kind of vacation time and holidays to maintain team equality. What will be your BEST course of action?

   A. Inform the foreign team that they must follow the vacation and holiday guidelines of the head office.
   B. Be fair and allow the local team to enjoy the same kind of relaxed lifestyle.
   C. Treat all the extra vacation days and holidays as schedule constraints in your project.
   D. Explore the option of outsourcing this part of the project to some other geographic location.

7. The software project to build a new office application is in progress. While reviewing one of the components, you discover that it does not meet the quality standards of your company. Upon further investigation, you realize that the component does not necessarily need to meet the specified quality standards as it will function just fine as is. The team member responsible for the component also mentioned to you that meeting the specified quality standards will be time consuming and pricey. What should be your BEST course of action as a project manager?

A. Accept this particular component, but make sure that the remaining components meet the specified quality standards.
B. Report the concern about the level of quality and seek a solution.
C. Modify the specified quality standards to match the level achieved.
D. Report the component as satisfactory.

8. While managing a web-based application project to automate the accounting process, one of your valuable clients requested you to bypass developing a quality policy for the project to save time. There is no existing organizational or industrial quality policy that you can use in the project. You have expressed your strong disagreement with the customer, but they were pretty unwavering about their approach. What will be your BEST course of action?

A. Contact PMI immediately and report the situation.
B. Request the sponsor to have a discussion with the customer on the necessity of the quality policy.
C. Follow the customer's wishes as the customer is always right.
D. Ignore the customer's request and create the quality policy for your project.

9. There are several potential projects in your organization, but the organization needs to select the best project to work on due to limited resources, cash flow, and different strategic objectives and priorities. Higher management asked you to compare these potential projects and find out the best one with the most value based on the project triggers and benefit measurement methods. You are a project manager with several years of experience in implementing IT projects, but you are not conversant with project selection methods. What should you do in this situation?

A. Inform higher management that you are lacking experience and expertise in project selection methods.
B. Do your best and select the project that you think will bring the most value.
C. Politely inform management that you are unable to take the assignment at this time.
D. Seek expert opinion to select the best project.

10. You are substituting a project manager who just left the organization. While reviewing the deliverables and their status, you notice that several deliverables that were reported as completed are still in development. Additionally, management is under the impression that the project is on track when, in fact, it is behind schedule and over budget. What will be your BEST course of action?

A. Politely refuse the project assignment.
B. Revise the status and notify management.
C. Have an urgent meeting with the key stakeholders and ask for suggestions on what to do.
D. Explore crashing the project to bring it back on track.

11. While finalizing the biweekly project status and progress reports, you observe that a few deliverables that are reported as completed are not actually done and that the team members also did not report the days spent on the activities correctly. Your project statistics and updates become very unrealistic with these wrong estimates given by the team members. What should you do in this kind of situation?

A. Report the information as is.
B. Provide accurate and truthful project information in a timely manner.
C. Inform the functional managers about the actions of the team members.
D. Replace the team members who are providing wrong estimates

12. One of your best friends in charge of maintaining customers' finances and investments is working in the same financial institution with you. She shared a secret with you and asked you not to divulge the secret to anyone. She told you that she has been using clients' money to invest in the stock market and has made a substantial amount of money doing so. She also asked you to join with her so that both of you can make a fortune. What should you do in this kind of situation?

A. Report your friend to the appropriate authority.
B. Explore different stock options and find out the best way to make a large amount of money.
C. Find out if what your friend is doing is really illegal or not.
D. Ask your friend to stop the illegal activity, but do not mention it to anyone else.

13. You did not utilize all the tools & techniques of risk identification and disregarded a potential risk. The risk shows up during the project planning phase and surprises the team. What kind of response is expected from you as a project manager?

A. Have a discussion with the sponsor and seek guidance.
B. Develop the risk response plan and determine preventive and corrective actions.
C. Take responsibility and evaluate the impact of the risk item.
D. Immediately inform the customers about the risk event.

14. You recently found out that one of your best friends has been pretending to be a PMP. She thinks that the certification is helping her immensely, but she never thought of pursuing it in real life due to the difficulty of the exam. What will be your BEST course of action?

A. Report to your friend's boss.
B. Hand your friend over to the police immediately.
C. Encourage your friend to get the real certification.
D. Contact PMI and report the situation.

15. Higher management is exploring the option to open a branch office in a foreign county to outsource backup, storage, and support activities. While conducting the feasibility study, you found out that women are not allowed to work in several sectors, and the country's law also postulates that the salary of a woman should be 60 percent of that of a man's for the same job. The country is very welcoming to your business, and the process of opening a new business is simple and fast. Experts with required expertise are easily available, and your company will also save a substantial amount of money in labor, equipment, raw materials, and low taxes. What should be your recommendation?

A. Ignore the law and compensate the women you will be hiring equally.
B. Consider not hiring any women to avoid conflicts.
C. Negotiate with the official and ask to be excused from laws discriminating women.
D. Consider not opening the branch office in this country.

16. Your company has been working with numerous financial institutions for several years and has built spectacular relationships with them. Recently you submitted a proposal in response to a bid for a data and disaster center project for one of these financial institutions in which your company has no previous experience and lacks required expertise. Which of the following is TRUE regarding this situation?

A. It is a common practice to exaggerate expertise and experience when submitting a proposal for a bid.
B. You have not violated the PMI code of ethics and professional conduct, but you have violated the procurement code.
C. There is no violation in this situation.
D. You have violated the PMI code of ethics and professional conduct.

17. You are one of the members of the proposal evaluation team responsible for evaluating and awarding contracts to eligible vendors. While reviewing the list of potential vendors, you notice that one of your good friends is a participant in the bidding process. You know that your friend is an expert in his domain and the project will be greatly benefited if he is awarded the contract. What will be the BEST course of action in this situation?

A. Keep silent and continue with the procurement process.
B. Convince the proposal evaluation team to award your friend the contract.
C. Inform the sponsor and the evaluation team about your relationship.
D. Offer your friend some good tips to increase his chance of winning the bid.

18. As a project manager, you are assigned to oversee a network infrastructure project in a foreign country for six months. At the end of the first introductory meeting, all six participants from your team were given exclusive gifts. When you were reluctant to accept your gift, you were told that it is a custom in their country to give this kind of gift to business partners. What will be your BEST course of action?

A. Decline the gift as accepting it will be considered personal gain in your country.
B. Decline the gift as accepting it will be considered conflict of interest in your country.
C. Accept the gift and inform your management so that your integrity will not be questioned later on.
D. Accept the gift as you do not consider it to be a conflict of interest or integrity issue.

19. You are implementing a WIMAX network for one of your clients in a rural area. You recently implemented a similar network for another client and installed several towers and POPs for them throughout the same region. The current client can save a considerable amount of time and money if they can rent the existing infrastructure instead of setting up their own towers and POPs. You have a nondisclosure agreement with the previous client, and you are not supposed to disclose any information on their infrastructure or network architecture. What will be your BEST course of action?

A. Ignore the nondisclosure agreement as it is not legally enforceable and share the network architecture and infrastructure from the previous project.
B. Install new towers and POPs for the existing customer and ignore the fact that the existing infrastructure can be used for the benefit of both organizations.
C. Seek guidance from your Project Management Office (PMO).
D. Have a discussion with your previous client and seek permission to share the information on the existing infrastructure.

20. You are participating in a bid in a foreign country for a company that wants to procure several expensive pieces of hospital equipment. You are told by the procuring organization that you need to obtain a trade license from the local authority and that the entire process will take approximately four weeks. There is only one week left for the bidding, and you cannot really wait four weeks for the trade license. While discussing it with one of the local officials, you discover that you can fast-track the process and obtain the trade license in three days if you pay an "urgent fee" of $750. Which of the following should you consider if the fee is within the approved limit in the budget?

A. Wait four weeks if needed, but do not pay the additional fee under any circumstance.
B. Pay the urgent fee and obtain the license in three days.
C. Negotiate the urgent fee and try to lower it as much as possible.
D. Participate in the bidding without the local trade license.

21. Your company just assigned you as a project manager for a large data center project. You were asked by the sponsor to complete the project in six months and within $120,000. You soon realize that both the time and cost estimation from higher management is impractical. Your estimation shows that the project could take as long as ten months and that the cost will be at least 20 percent more than the initial estimation. The sponsor tells you that she is considering another project manager to take care of the project in case you do not agree with her time and cost estimations. What will be your BEST course of action?

A. Excuse yourself from the project.
B. Document the time and cost constraints and carry on with the project as instructed.
C. Submit your detailed time and cost estimations and justification to the sponsor.
D. Have an urgent meeting with the client and explain the situation.

22. You are in charge of a very important, big-budget video game project. You have thirteen identified stakeholders and ten team members in the project. You notice that one of the team members who has a major role in the project has been meeting with an anonymous stakeholder to discuss the project details. What should you do in this situation?

A. Have a discussion with the team member and express your concern.
B. Report it to the functional manager.
C. Have a meeting with the team member and the unidentified stakeholder.
D. Make sure you continue to keep an eye on the team member.

23. You are overseeing a software project to develop a challenging and innovative video game. One of your friends, who is a connoisseur in this field and has several of his very popular games in the market, has requested you to give him a copy of the game prior to its release so that he can check it out and provide his feedback. You know his feedback will be valuable to find any defects and improve the game. What should you do in this situation?

A. Ask your friend to sign a nondisclosure agreement prior to giving him a copy.
B. Give him a copy of the game since he is an expert and may provide valuable feedback about the game.
C. Make sure that your friend will provide you with the required feedback and suggestions prior to giving him a copy of the game.
D. Decline the request as the game is the intellectual property of your company.

24. Your company just initiated a project to install a Wi-Fi network in one of the Asian countries. One of the clients offers gifts to all your team members and requests you to give his office a dedicated connection with the max bandwidth possible. What should you do in this situation?

A. Reject the gifts and never communicate with that client again.
B. Accept the gifts but refuse to give the dedicated connection.
C. Reject the gifts as accepting gifts is a violation of the code of ethics and professional conduct.
D. Accept the gifts and agree to give the dedicated connection as it will not cost any extra to the project.

25. You are participating in a bid in a foreign country for a company that wants to procure several expensive pieces of hospital equipment. You have meticulously followed the bidding procedure and are expecting to be the most qualified and lowest bidder. One of the representatives of the procuring company contacted you and asked for 10 percent commission on the total price or they would award the deal to some other vendor. What will be your BEST course of action?

A. Contact PMI immediately and report the situation.
B. Negotiate the commission and try to bring it down as much as possible.
C. Deny the offer and notify your management.
D. Agree to give 10 percent to secure the deal.

Project Code of Ethics and Professional Conduct Answers

1. B: You should decline the offer based on the fact that it will be considered as personal gain on your part and your integrity will be questioned. Option A will not be the correct answer because you are not responsible for the integrity of others.

2. D: The best course of action will be to explain to the sponsor that under all circumstances you are obligated to conduct yourself in a truthful manner and report the truth regarding project status. You are also obligated not to deceive others and not to make false or half-true statements. It is not ethical to knowingly report an incorrect project status to anyone in the project.

3. C: One of the mandatory standards in the PMI code of ethics and professional conduct is respect. It involves the way we conduct ourselves in a professional manner and listen to other viewpoints. As a project manager, you should approach those two team members directly to understand their concerns. If this problem persists, you should have a discussion with the concerned functional manager, issue a warning letter, or remove them from the team (in an extreme situation).

4. C: You are obligated to report any violation of the PMI code of ethics and professional conduct to PMI.

5. A: One of the mandatory standards in the PMI code of ethics and professional conduct is responsibility. Responsibility is the act of making and taking ownership of our decisions, admitting our mistakes, and being responsible for our decisions and actions. As a project manager, you must make decisions based on the best interests of society, public safety, and the environment. It is not advisable to undertake a project that will work against the interests of the public.

6. C: One of the mandatory standards in the PMI code of ethics and professional conduct is respect. As a project manager, you should respect personal, ethnic, and cultural differences and avoid engaging in behaviors might be considered disrespectful. The only valid action will be to treat all extra vacation days and holidays as schedule constraints in your project.

7. B: You should report the concern with the level of quality so that the experts can find an appropriate resolution. It would be unethical to modify the specific quality standards and report the component as satisfactory. Making sure that the remaining components will meet the quality standards will not really solve the existing problem.

8. B: In a difficult situation that is beyond the control of the project manager, the sponsor may get involved and act as a liaison to the customer. When there is a dispute, we should always try to resolve it in favor of the customer, but as a project manager, you should also remember that the customer is not always right. You must create a quality policy for your project in case there is no existing organizational or industrial policy document that you can use.

9. A: One of the mandatory standards in the PMI code of ethics and professional conduct is honesty. Honesty is the act of communicating and conducting ourselves in a truthful manner, reporting the truth regarding project status, not deceiving others, not making false or half-true statements, and being honest about our own experience and expertise.. In this particular scenario, you should honestly report your lack of experience and expertise in project selection methods to higher management. Also, as per the PMI code of ethics, you should accept only those assignments that are consistent with your background, experience, skills, and qualifications. Higher management may help you in various ways, including suggesting you to seek expert opinion for selecting the project once they are informed about your lack of experience. So refusing the assignment will not be an appropriate action in this situation.

10. B: Since there are changes in project cost and schedule, you should revise the status and update management accordingly before you take any other action. Crashing the project usually adds cost to the project, so it will make things even worse. You cannot simply refuse to manage a project because it is behind schedule and over budget. As a project manager, you should be directing the project instead of asking the stakeholders to do so.

11. B: One of the mandatory standards in the PMI code of ethics and professional conduct is honesty. Honesty is the act of communicating and conducting ourselves in a truthful manner, reporting the truth regarding project status, not deceiving others, and not making false or half-true statements. As a project manager, you should always provide accurate and truthful information in a timely manner. It would be unethical to report the wrong project status to anyone in the project. You should have a discussion with the team members about the negative impact of their actions. If needed, you may need to inform functional managers about the actions of the team members.

12. A: You are obligated to report any illegal activity to the appropriate authority.

13. C: One of the mandatory standards in the PMI code of ethics and professional conduct is responsibility. Responsibility is the act of making and taking ownership of our decisions, admitting our mistakes, and being responsible for our decisions and actions. As a project manager, you must take responsibility for the failure in identifying the risk and evaluate the impact to develop the risk response plan. Once you have the detail on the risk item, you can have a discussion with the customer. Also, you may escalate the risk to the sponsor if the risk is beyond your control.

14. D: You are obligated to report any PMI code of ethics and professional conduct violation to PMI.

15. D: One of the mandatory standards in the PMI code of ethics and professional conduct is fairness. Fairness includes making decisions impartially and objectively and avoiding favoritism and discrimination against others. As a project manager you need to make sure that there will be no discrimination against others based on, but not limited to, gender, race, age, disability, nationality, or sexual orientation. You also need to make opportunities equally available to all qualified candidates. Your best course of action will be to recommend not opening the branch office in this country.

16. D: You have violated the PMI code of ethics and professional conduct. As a project manager, you should be honest about the experience and expertise of your organization.

17. C: Since there is a potential conflict of interest, you should discuss the relationship with the sponsor and evaluation team. It will be up to the evaluation team and sponsor to decide whether you should disassociate yourself from the bidding process or not.

18. C: You should accept the gift because if you decline and reciprocate the gesture, it can severely affect your relationship with the customer. You should also immediately inform your management so that your integrity will not be questioned later on.

19. D: You need to work in the best interest of your client and try to save money and time for them if possible by exploring the option of using the existing infrastructure rather than installing new towers and POPs. Even if the nondisclosure agreement is not legally enforceable, you are ethically bound to comply with it. The best course of action will be to have a discussion with the previous client and seek permission to share the information on the existing infrastructure. Seeking guidance from the PMO will not be essential since approval from the PMO to share the information will not make it acceptable.

20. B: In this case, the fee has a valid purpose and should not be considered a bribe. You should pay the urgent fee of $750 and obtain the trade license.

21. C: You cannot simply refuse to manage the project because you do not agree with the time and cost estimations of the sponsor. As a project manager, you are expected to present truthful and accurate information regarding time, cost, and other project objectives. So you should submit your detailed time and cost estimations and justification for the longer duration and additional budget. If your justification is reasonable, the sponsor should agree with your argument. Continuing with the project with unrealistic time and cost expectations will be a recipe for failure. Having an urgent meeting with the client will not be appropriate in this situation.

22. A: At first you should have a discussion with the team member to find out why she is meeting with the unidentified stakeholder. Reporting the incident to the functional manager will not be appropriate until you identify any problem.

23. D: You should decline the request as the video game is the intellectual property of your organization.

24. C: The client is making a request by offering gifts; thus, you should reject the gifts as it is a violation of the PMI code of ethics and professional conduct. A project manager is expected to be honest and should not engage in dishonest behavior with the intention of personal gain or at the expense of others. If it is customary in that country to offer gifts, you may accept the gift without agreeing to the client's request of dedicated connection. Not communicating with the specific client may impact the project.

25. C: You should never bribe even though it may help you win a project. Your best course of action will be to deny the offer and disclose the incident to higher management.

Formulas and Values

Acronym	Term	Formula	Interpretation
PV or BCWS	Planned Value or Budgeted Cost of Work Scheduled	BAC * (Time Passed / Total Scheduled Time) or BAC * Planned % Complete	What is the estimated value of the work planned to be done?
EV or BCWP	Earned Value or Budgeted Cost of Work Performed	BAC * (Work Completed / Total Work Required) or BAC * Actual % Complete	What is the estimated value of the work actually accomplished?
AC or ACWP	Actual Cost or Actual Cost of Work Performed	No Formula	What is the actual cost incurred for the work accomplished?
SV	Schedule Variance	SV = EV – PV	A comparison of amount of work performed during a given period of time to what was scheduled to be performed. Negative = behind schedule Neutral = on schedule Positive = ahead of schedule
CV	Cost Variance	CV = EV – AC	A comparison of the budgeted cost of work performed with actual cost. Negative = over budget Neutral = on budget Positive = under budget
CPI	Cost Performance Index	CPI = EV / AC	It measures the value of the work completed against actual cost. CPI < 1= over budget CPI > 1= under budget CPI = 1= on budget
CPI^c	Cumulative CPI	$CPI^c = EV^c / AC^c$	It represents the cumulative CPI of the project at the point the measurement is taken.
SPI	Schedule Performance Index	SPI = EV / PV	It measures the progress to date against the planned progress. SPI < 1 = behind schedule SPI > 1 = ahead of schedule SPI = 1 = on schedule
SPI^c	Cumulative SPI	$SPI^c = EV^c / PV^c$	It represents the cumulative SPI of the project at the point the measurement is taken.
BAC	Budget at Completion	No Formula	How much did we BUDGET for the TOTAL project effort?
EAC	Estimate at Completion	If CPI is expected to be the same, EAC = BAC / CPI If current variances are thought to be atypical of the future, EAC = AC + (BAC – EV) If both CPI and SPI influence the remaining work, EAC = AC+ [(BAC – EV) / (CPI * SPI)]	What do we currently expect the TOTAL project to cost?
ETC	Estimate to Complete	ETC = EAC – AC	From this point on, how much MORE do we expect it to cost to finish the project?
VAC	Variance at Completion	VAC = BAC – EAC	How much over or under budget do we expect to be at the end of the project?
TCPI	To Complete Performance Index	If targeting the current plan TCPI = (BAC – EV) / (BAC – AC) If targeting the current EAC TCPI = (BAC – EV) / (EAC – AC)	Performance that must be achieved in order to meet financial or schedule goals. TCPI >1 = harder to complete TCPI <1 = easier to complete

PERT	Program Evaluation and Review Technique	Triangular Distribution: Expected Activity Duration (EAD) = $\frac{(O + M + P)}{3}$ Beta Distribution: Expected Activity Duration (EAD) = $\frac{(O + 4M + P)}{6}$	Three-point estimate for the expected duration of a schedule activity using pessimistic, optimistic, and most likely durations. A probabilistic approach, using statistical estimates of durations.
SD	Standard Deviation	SD = $\frac{P - O}{6}$	
AV	Activity Variance	AV = $[\frac{P - O}{6}]^2$	
AR	Activity Range	Range = EAD – + SD	
PV	Present Value	PV = $\frac{FV}{(1+r)^n}$	Present Value is the value "today" of future cash flow due to a project or acquisition. The result is the amount of money you need to invest today (PV) for n years at r percent interest in order to end up with the target sum (FV). The higher the PV, the better.
NPV	Net Present Value	Net Present Value = Present Value – Cost	Positive NPV is good. Negative NPV is bad. The project with the higher NPV is the "better" project.
ROI	Return on Investment	ROI = (Benefit – Cost) / Cost	This is a percentage that shows what return you make by investing in something. The project with the higher ROI is better and should be selected.
ROIC	Return on Invested Capital	ROIC = Net Income (after tax) from the Project / Total Capital invested in the project	For every dollar of cash an organization invests in a project, how much should it expect in return.
EVA	Economic Value Added	EVA = After tax profit – (capital expenditures * cost of capital)	This concept is concerned with whether the project returns to the company more value than it costs.
IRR	Internal Rate of Return	Formula not required for exam.	Calculates the percentage of the project cost returned as interest over the years following project completion. The project with the higher IRR is better and should be selected.
	Payback Period	Add up the projected cash inflow minus expenses until you reach the initial investment.	This is the number of time periods it will take a project to recoup its costs. The project with the shorter payback period is better and should be selected.
BCR	Benefit Cost Ratio	Benefit / Cost	BCR < 1 is bad. BCR > 1 is good. The project with the bigger BCR is the "better" one.
	Opportunity Cost	Opportunity Cost = The value of the project not chosen.	Opportunity cost is the cost incurred by choosing one option over an alternative one. Thus, opportunity cost is the cost of pursuing one choice instead of another.
	Communication Channels	n * (n –1) / 2 or $(n^2 - n) / 2$	Total number of communication channels among n people of a group

EMV	Expected Monetary Value	EMV = Probability * Impact in currency	Expected Monetary Value (or simply Expected Value) is a statistical concept that calculates the average outcome of a decision. It is the product of the probability and consequences of an event or task.
PTA	Point of Total Assumption	PTA = Target Cost + [(Ceiling Price – Target Price) / Buyer's share of cost overrun]	It is the cost point in the contract where the seller assumes responsibility for all cost overruns as cost beyond this point is considered to be due to mismanagement.
	Average	The sum of all the members of the list divided by the number of items in the list. Average of 2, 4, 6 = (2 + 4 + 6) / 3 = 4	In mathematics, an average refers to a measure of the "middle" of a data set. The most common method is the arithmetic mean. That is why the "Average" is sometimes also and simply called the "Mean". The result is a number representing the arithmetic mean.
	Mean	See Average	
	Median	Arrange the values from lowest value to highest value and pick the middle one. Example: 4 is the median in 2, 4, 6 If there is an even number of values, calculate the mean of the two middle values. Example: 5 is the median in 2, 4, 6, 8 because 4 + 6 / 2 = 5	The middle value that separates the higher half from the lower half of the data set. The result is a number representing the median.
	Mode	Find the value in a data set that occurs most often. Example: 2 is the mode of 1, 2, 2, 3	The most frequent value in a given data set. The result is a number representing the mode.
	Working Capital	Working Capital = Current Assets – Current Liabilities	The amount of money the company has available to invest, including investment in projects.

Description	Value	Comment
1 sigma	68.26 percent	Also: 1 standard deviation
2 sigma	95.46 percent	Also: 2 standard deviations
3 sigma	99.73 percent	Also: 3 standard deviations
6 sigma	99.99985 percent	Also: 6 standard deviations
Control Limits	Usually 3 standard deviations above and below the mean	Control limits reflect the expected variation in the data.
Control Specifications	Not fixed. Defined by the customer	Must be looser than the control limits. Represents the customer's requirements.
Order of Magnitude Estimate	– 25 percent to + 75 percent	
Budget Estimate	– 10 percent to + 25 percent	
Definitive Estimate	– 5 percent to + 10 percent	
Final Estimate	0 percent	
Float on the Critical Path	0 days	
Pareto Diagram	80/20	For instance: 80 percent of your problems are due to 20 percent of the causes
Time a PM Spends Communicating	90 percent	According to Harold Kerzner
Crashing a Project	Crash the tasks with the least expensive crash cost first.	Only crash activities on the critical path.
Value of the Inventory in a Just in Time (JIT) Environment	0 percent (or very close to 0 percent.)	
Sunk Cost	A cost that has been incurred and cannot be reversed.	Sunk cost is never a factor when making project decisions.
In the USA the number –100 is the same as (100). Both indicate "minus one hundred".	(100) – 100	
Early Start or ES		The soonest a task can begin.
Early Finish or EF	Early Start + Duration – 1	The soonest a task can end.
Late Start or LS	Early Start + Float	The latest a task can begin without effecting the project duration.
Late Finish or LF	Late Start + Duration – 1	The latest a task can end without effecting the project duration.
Forward Pass		Is used to calculate Early Start and Early Finish.
Backward Pass		Is used to calculate Late Start and Late Finish.
Float or Slack	Float = LF – EF = LS – ES	

Formula Summary

Integration Management:

1. PV = FV / $(1+r)^n$ and FV = PV * $(1+r)^n$
2. NPV = PV – Cost
3. ROI = (Benefit – Cost) / Cost
4. ROIC = Net Income (after tax) From Project / Total Capital Invested in the Project
5. EVA = After Tax Profit – (Capital Expenditures * Cost of Capital)
6. BCR = Benefit / Cost
7. Opportunity Cost = Value of the Project Not Chosen
8. Working Capital = Current Assets – Current Liabilities

Time Management:

1. Expected Activity Duration (EAD) = (O + M + P) / 3 → Triangular or (O + 4M + P) / 6 → Beta
2. Standard Deviation (SD) = (P – O) / 6
3. Activity Variance (AV) = $[(P - O)/6]^2$
4. Activity Range (AR) = EAD – + SD
5. Early Start (ES) = No formula, WW01
6. Early Finish (EF) = Early Start + Duration – 1
7. Late Start (LS) = Early Start + Float
8. Late Finish (LF) = Late Start + Duration – 1
9. Float or Slack = LF – EF or LS – ES or Critical path duration – the longest path of the activity
10. Float on the critical path = 0
11. Critical Path: Longest path yet minimum time/Highest schedule risk

Cost Management:

1. PV = BAC * (Time Passed / Total Scheduled Time) or BAC * Planned % Complete
2. EV = BAC * (Work Completed / Total Work Required) or BAC * Actual % Complete
3. AC = No Formula
4. SV = EV – PV
5. CV = EV – AC
6. CPI = EV / AC
7. Cumulative CPI (CPI^c) = EV^c / AC^c
8. SPI = EV / PV
9. Cumulative SPI (SPI^c) = EV^c / PV^c
10. BAC = No Formula
11. EAC = BAC / CPI or AC + (BAC – EV)
12. ETC = EAC – AC
13. VAC = BAC – EAC
14. TCPI = (BAC– EV) / (BAC – AC) or (BAC – EV) / (EAC – AC)
15. Order of magnitude estimate = – 25 percent to + 75 percent
16. Budget estimate = – 10 percent to + 25 percent
17. Definitive estimate = – 5 percent to + 10 percent

Communication Management:

1. Communication Channels = n * (n – 1) / 2 or $(n^2 - n)$ / 2
2. Time a PM spends communicating = 90%
3. Nonverbal communication = 55%

Quality Management:

1. 1 sigma = 68.26 %
2. 2 sigma = 95.46 %
3. 3 sigma = 99.73 %
4. 6 sigma = 99.99985 %
5. Control Limits = Usually 3 standard deviations above and below the mean
6. Pareto Diagram = 80 / 20

Risk Management:

Expected Monetary Value (EMV) = Probability * Impact

Procurement Management:

1. Point of Total Assumption (PTA) = Target Cost + [(Ceiling Price – Target Price) / Buyer's Share of Cost Overrun]
2. Target Price = Target Cost + Target Fee

HOW TO PASS THE PMP® EXAM ON YOUR FIRST TRY

Passing the PMP® exam on your first try requires robust strategies and a lot of preparation. This entire topic is focused on the test strategies and techniques on how to pass the exam.

PMP® Exam Tips and important points

- Note that PMBOK® is a guide to the project management body of knowledge. This guide neither illustrates how to study for the PMP exam, nor how to manage a real life project. It cannot be a sole reference for test-takers as the exam does not cover materials only from the PMBOK® guide. The topic for each question may cover anything as long as it can be quoted in a contemporary project management resource.
- Study this book at least twice from beginning to end and go through all the questions to fully grasp the concepts. Make sure you understand the justification on why a certain answer is right or wrong.
- Make sure to study the "Quick Reference Guide" and "Flash Cards" of this book several times. These handy, easy to carry guides include hundreds of topics, processes, glossary items, general project management terms, test taking tips, and graphics to help jog the memory of students preparing for the exam. These materials are available at amazon. Please search the author's name at amazon.com to view the "Quick Reference Guide" and "Flash Cards".
- While taking the exam, try to go through the tutorial at the beginning as fast as you can and use the spare time to write down all your 47 processes and essential formulas on your scratch paper. You MUST be able create the summary or cheat sheet as discussed in chapter 18: Formulas and Value – Formula Summary and also in the "Quick Reference Guide" in less than 10 minutes.
- In order to pass, you must correctly answer a minimum of 114 to 121 (65 to 69 percent) of the 175 scored questions. Twenty-five pretest questions randomly placed throughout the examination will not be included in the pass/fail determination.
- Note that there will be approximately twenty-six questions from initiating, forty-eight from planning, sixty-two from executing, fifty from monitoring & controlling, and fourteen from closing in the exam. The exam can be thought of as divided into three categories:
  - Sixty easier questions = 30 percent of the exam
  - Eighty medium questions = 40 percent of the exam
  - Sixty harder questions = 30 percent of the exam
- All the questions have four choices and only one correct answer. Many of the answers will seem correct, but only ONE is the BEST answer. Be sure to read the question and all four answers carefully. You should never stop reading the answers as soon as you consider one to be the correct answer. Instead, go through all four answers before making your final selection.
- PMBOK® guide list over 500 inputs, tools & techniques, and outputs. It is simply not possible to remember all and you have to make your best guess at this one. It is essential to remember the most important and unique inputs, tools & techniques, and outputs in each process. Also pay attention to common inputs, tools & techniques, and outputs that we discussed in chapter 5: Project management framework.
- Always follow the processes. Be sure not to choose the answers that involve taking a shortcut or skipping steps in the process addressed by a question. There will be questions that give you a superficially innocent way to skip the formal process and save a substantial amount of time, or perhaps avoid conflicts by not following procedures. Do not give in to pressure from unsatisfied customers, stakeholders, or even your boss.
- Note that questions may jump from topic to topic, and a single question may integrate multiple concepts. The nature of the questions do not change based on the answers to the previous questions.
- The exam will test your knowledge of PMI's processes, your understanding of the terms used to describe the processes, and your ability to apply the processes to situations.
- The exam will test your ability to apply key formulas to scheduling, budgeting, estimating, and other areas. You can expect to have as many as ten to fifteen formula-related and ten to fifteen earned-value questions on the exam.
- The exam will test your understanding of professional responsibility as it applies to project management.
- The exam will not test your intelligence, common sense, knowledge of industry practices, knowledge on how to use software applications in project management, or any other location-/project-specific knowledge.
- Use your instincts and eliminate wrong answers. In most cases, you will easily be able to identify the two wrong choices out of four. Once you eliminate the two wrong answers, you have a 50/50 chance to select the right answer.
- Eliminate answers that involve terms that are unfamiliar (e.g., fake processes, inputs, tools & techniques, and outputs).

- Be wary of alternatives that include the words first, last, next, best, always, except, most likely, primary, initial, never, only, must, and completely.
- Most of the questions on the exam will be situational (e.g., What will be the best course of action? What will you do next? What have you done wrong? etc.). Such questions require you to integrate your real-life experience and your knowledge of the exam concepts.
- It is essential to understand that not all information included in a question will be relevant.
- There is no negative marking for wrong answers. If you are not sure about any particular question, make your best guess and select an answer since you have a 25% chance for your answer to be correct.
- Answer the questions as a prospective PMP.
- Keep in mind when answering questions that a good PM makes the decision, is proactive and professional, and does not pass responsibility of decision making to anyone else.
- Select the answers that suggest doing the following:
    - Determine the immediate problem to address.
    - Deal with the root cause first.
    - Deal with the problem with the greatest NEGATIVE impact first.
    - Solve the problem that occurred the earliest.
- Always follow the processes and be sure not to give in to the temptation to make decisions on the exam based on your own experience.
- Always be direct, honest, and proactive. If a choice seems to be devious, underhanded, or dishonest in any way, it is most probably not the right answer. Do the right thing even it is painful or would be appealing to avoid.
- Know the project roles and organization types.
- Mark questions for later review if you are unable to respond quickly. You will always find a few questions that you have no clue about. In such cases, do not panic. You may need to make an educated guess at some questions and should never get upset and undermine your confidence. If a question puzzles you, simply mark it for review and move on. You may find that questions later in the test will suggest you hints or jog your memory, helping you with those you originally found problematic.
- In most cases for long, wordy, situational questions, reading the last sentence first will help to find out what the question is all about.
- Take a two- to three-minute break after answering a set of fifty questions and utilize the entire exam time.
- When you make a review pass through the exam, do not be hesitant to change any answer that you feel you missed. You may miss few questions the first time but now they are obvious when you look at them again.
- Unless stated otherwise, assume that you are the project manager working in a matrix organization and that you belong to the buyer's organization.
- Unless stated otherwise, assume that proper project management procedures were followed in the given situation while answering the question. Even if it is not specifically mentioned, you need to assume that a project charter was created, WBS was developed, and the project management plan was completed.
- You may expect questions on international laws which can be very complicated and confusing. The best way to approach it is to figure out if it is illegal or unscrupulous in any way then it is wrong. Otherwise, the custom in the country where the work is being performed should prevail. For instance, if you are asked to make a payment to the bidding council to get a bidding permit, figure out whether or not the payment is a bribe, or it is customary, or even it is the law. Do not make the payment if it is a bribe and only consider to pay if it is customary or the law.
- Note that carrying out the right choice may involve standing up to your sponsor, denying an order from your boss, refusing the customers, and many other things that might have distasteful aftereffects.
- Anytime a project manager has the opportunity to share lessons learned, monitor, teach, coach, or lead to broaden the project management learning or training of someone else, there is a good possibility that it is the correct answer.
- Different cultures place distinctive values upon work, and it is not the obligation of the project manager to force them to the level of his or her own country.
- A project manager should factor in the interest of the community, the environment, and the society when making decisions. The project manager should avoid all circumstances and scenarios where the project would profit but society would deteriorate.

- Whenever you feel frustrated or alarmed over particular questions, take a deep breath, hold it for about five seconds, and repeat this breathing pattern to bring your brain chemistry back to steadiness. It will assist you to slow your heart rate and clear your mind for greater attentiveness on the remaining questions.
- Take as many practice exams as possible; this will eliminate any uncertainty or doubts.
- Common project management mistakes are often listed as choices on the PMP® exam. It is essential that you understand the following common mistakes even highly experienced project managers make so that you can answer the questions correctly:
    - Not understanding the business value of the project and how it is meeting the strategic goals and objectives of the organization
    - Considering a bar (Gantt) chart as a project management plan
    - Not obtaining finalized requirements
    - Not obtaining resource commitments
    - Not paying much attention to risk management
    - Not identifying all kinds of risk items
    - Not having a robust project management plan
    - Not having a robust change management system
    - Not having a recognition and reward system to encourage the team members
    - Concentrating mostly on percent complete
    - Demanding team members to cut their estimates by 10 to15 percent
    - Babysitting and spoon-feeding the team members
    - Putting the blame on management for unrealistic schedule and budget
    - Not paying much attention to quality
    - Not understanding that the project manager is fully responsible for the quality of the project
    - Not creating metrics to measure and evaluate performance
    - Not measuring performance against the plan
    - Not exploring and eliminating root causes of problems
    - Ignoring functional responsibilities of the team members
    - Not implementing corrective and preventive actions
    - Not updating the key documents to reflect project changes
    - Not understanding the human factors and organizational politics
    - Not understanding how others feel about the project
    - Not reevaluating the completeness or accuracy of schedule, scope, or cost
    - Not realizing that integrating different components of a project is the responsibility of the project manager
    - Not understanding that keeping the stakeholders happy and satisfied is the responsibility of the project manager
- While answering a situational question, you should recognize that there are different characteristics and components. If you can recognize noise, common terminology, superfluous information, and fake terms in the question, it will be lot easier to identify what the question is actually asking.

Common Terminology	PMI's terms and terminology are typically used in the exam. It is essential to get familiar with these terminologies. If a question has both the options of "Budget" and "Budget at Completion", you should select the latter since it is the common description used by PMI.
Superfluous Information	An exam question may contain a substantial amount of information in which several variables such as scope, time, cost, risk, and quality are discussed. It is important to realize that not all the information included in a question will be relevant. You need to review each variable and identify how it has any significance to what the question is asking about. You need to concentrate on the particular variable among all other variables that is facing issues, such as project duration is reduced, or you are behind schedule.
Noise	Noise or disinformation is content that has no value or bearing in a question and has been inserted to befuddle and confuse you. You need to identify noise and find out a way to disregard it.

Fake Terms	There are often fake or made-up terms in the exam and not all terms used in the choices should mean something. These fake terms are used to confuse you. So, if you see a term that you are not familiar with there is a good chance that it is not the correct answer. **Question:** Which of the following motivational theory proposes that average workers are incapable, avoid responsibility, have an inherent dislike of work, and are only interested in their own selfish goals? A. Theory X B. Theory Y C. Theory Z D. Theory M Correct answer is A. Note that D is certainly wrong since Theory M is a made-up term as there is no such theory in theories of motivation.

The exam may use several question formats. A single question may also use multiple formats. Understanding these formats assists you to dissect the question and the available answers. The formats that are commonly used:

Format	Description	Example
Situational	This is the most challenging and complicated format used in the exam. You should leverage your PM experience, understanding of the PMBOK® Guide, and the PMI way of thinking. You also need to understand processes, inputs, tools & techniques, outputs, and key roles and responsibilities.	You discovered a pattern of flaws in several projects you are working on as a senior project manager. You have the impression that some kind of deficiency in the process your organization is using may be contributing to these repetitive defects. You conducted a cause and effect analysis and formulated a few recommendations for process change to avoid this recurring problem in future projects. You are in which of the following processes? A. Perform Qualitative Risk Analysis B. Plan Quality C. Perform Quality Assurance D. Control Quality C is the correct answer.
Calculation	It is essential to know the formulas well to answer this type of question. Make sure you understand and remember the formulas discussed in chapter 18: Formulas and Value – Formula Summary on page 530.	Your project has a budget of $900,000 and is running well. In the latest earned value report, the team reported that the CPI = 1.1, the SPI = 0.9, and the PV= $600,000. You want to know, from this point on, how much more the project will cost but could not find it in the report. What will be the estimate to complete, or ETC, be in this case? A. $300,000 B. $327,272 C. $818,181 D. $490,909 B is the correct answer.
Best thing to do next	With this format, you need to understand the sequence or order of your activities. Evaluate the situation and determine the best answer based on the timeline given. Refer to the Figure 3-11: Process Groups Key Inputs and Outputs to understand the sequence of all processes and their key outputs.	The sponsor has just signed the project charter and assigned you as a project manager to oversee a project to implement a simulator for a local golf club. What should you do FIRST as the project manager? A. Focus on identifying the details of stakeholders in the project. B. Start working on the project management plan. C. Develop the project schedule. D. Create the WBS. A is the correct answer.

Select	The most straight-forward question format that will simply ask you to select the best answer. Note that it can be combined with other question formats as well.	Which one of the following will occur during the planning process group? A. Identify stakeholders B. Develop schedule C. Acquire project team D. Validate scope B is the correct answer.
Select NOT/ EXCEPT	For this type of question, you must select the answer that does not apply. The trick here is to identify the answer selection that is exceptional and does not have much in common with the other three options.	All of the following will occur during project initiating EXCEPT: A. Creation of a project scope statement. B. Identification of internal and external stakeholders. C. Development and review of the business case and a feasibility study. D. Assignment of the project manager to lead a project. A is the correct answer.
All (or a combination of)	For this type of question, all or a combination of the answers are acceptable. This is not too common in the PMP® exam.	As a project manager, you are required to report out project performance to all your stakeholders on a regular basis. Which one of the following can utilize earned value measurement (EVM) in its preparation for management? A. Status reports B. Trend reports C. Performance reports D. All of the above D is the correct answer.
None of the answers	With this format, every available answer except for "none of the above" fails to apply to the question. This is not too common in the PMP® exam.	What is considered to be a component of the triple constraint? A. Quality B. Risk C. Communications D. None of the above D is the correct answer.

- Most importantly, have a positive attitude and a strong confidence that you will pass the exam on your first try. If you have studied this textbook, understood the main concepts, memorized the 47 processes and essential formulas, and scored approximately 80% in multiple practice exams, you be in an excellent shape to take the real PMP® exam. I wish you all the best.

FINAL EXAM

Final Exam

This 4 hour, 200 question final exam is an excellent readiness indicator for anyone planning to sit for the PMP exam. You should repeatedly take this exam and review the answers until you secure a minimum score of 90 percent. You should write down your knowledge areas and processes chart and all formulas during the first 10 minutes and then complete the exam within 4 hours.

200 Questions Practice Test Answer Sheet

1.	41.	81.	121.	161.
2.	42.	82.	122.	162.
3.	43.	83.	123.	163.
4.	44.	84.	124.	164.
5.	45.	85.	125.	165.
6.	46.	86.	126.	166.
7.	47.	87.	127.	167.
8.	48.	88.	128.	168.
9.	49.	89.	129.	169.
10.	50.	90.	130.	170.
11.	51.	91.	131.	171.
12.	52.	92.	132.	172.
13.	53.	93.	133.	173.
14.	54.	94.	134.	174.
15.	55.	95.	135.	175.
16.	56.	96.	136.	176.
17.	57.	97.	137.	177.
18.	58.	98.	138.	178.
19.	59.	99.	139.	179.
20.	60.	100.	140.	180.
21.	61.	101.	141.	181.
22.	62.	102.	142.	182.
23.	63.	103.	143.	183.
24.	64.	104.	144.	184.
25.	65.	105.	145.	185.
26.	66.	106.	146.	186.
27.	67.	107.	147.	187.
28.	68.	108.	148.	188.
29.	69.	109.	149.	189.
30.	70.	110.	150.	190.
31.	71.	111.	151.	191.
32.	72.	112.	152.	192.
33.	73.	113.	153.	193.
34.	74.	114.	154.	194.
35.	75.	115.	155.	195.
36.	76.	116.	156.	196.
37.	77.	117.	157.	197.
38.	78.	118.	158.	198.
39.	79.	119.	159.	199.
40.	80.	120.	160.	200.

Final Exam Questions

1. A project manager managing a video simulator project was informed by one of the team members about a complex problem that can have a drastic negative impact on the project. The project manager immediately defined the cause of the problem by analyzing the problem using a fishbone diagram, identified a solution, and implemented the solution. The project manager recently received a call from the same team member and was informed that the same problem had resurfaced. What did the project manager most likely forget to do?
   A. Validate the solution with the sponsors.
   B. Confirm that the solution actually solved the problem.
   C. Use a Pareto chart.
   D. Identify why the problem occurred.

2. You are overseeing the implementation of a new computer structure at the local hospital. You are currently working on identifying all the internal and external stakeholders who have an interest in your project and can positively or negatively impact your project. While identifying the stakeholders, you realize that stakeholder identification is:
   A. The responsibility of the project sponsor.
   B. To be carried out throughout the project life cycle.
   C. To be completed in the initial stage of the project life cycle.
   D. To be focused only on stakeholders who will contribute positively to your project.

3. Company ABC invested $400,000 in a project with expected cash inflows of $40,000 per quarter for the first two years and $80,000 per quarter from third year. Another project has a payback period of 2.5 years for the same amount of investment. Which project should you select?
   A. The first project
   B. The second project
   C. Cannot be determined
   D. Both projects

4. Which of the following is NOT true about the fundamental functionality of the Control Quality process?
   A. Implement approved changes to the quality baseline.
   B. Recommend changes, corrective and preventive actions, and defect repairs to Integrated Change Control in order to eliminate noncompliance in the project deliverables.
   C. Ensure that the deliverables of the project comply with relevant quality standards.
   D. Ensure project work is directed toward the completion of the defined scope.

5. You are an IT project manager working on several networking and software development projects. It is becoming increasingly difficult for you to keep track of the latest trends in your field as technology is continuously changing. You would love to try out the latest technology and tools available, however your organization has advised you to play it safe. In the last three years, the organization has not invested in new technology and won't adapt to anything that is not well tested and used by others in the industry. In terms of risk attitude, your organization could best be described as:
   A. Risk Seeker
   B. Risk Neutral
   C. Risk Averse
   D. Risk Lover

6. You have been assigned as a project manager to implement a new office automation application. Management asks you to make sure that the new application will work on the existing infrastructure and can easily be integrated with other major applications currently running in the organization. This is an example of which one of the following?
   A. Assumptions
   B. Project scope
   C. Constraints
   D. Expectations

7. Which one of the following techniques translates project objectives into tangible deliverables and requirements by improving the project team's understanding of the product?
   A. Product analysis
   B. Alternative generation
   C. Inspection
   D. Decomposition

8. Negotiated settlement is used as a tool & technique in which of the following procurement management processes?
   A. Plan Procurement Management
   B. Conduct Procurements
   C. Control Procurements
   D. Close Procurements

9. You are working for a healthcare facility and are overseeing the implementation of a new computer infrastructure and office automation project at the local hospital. You made all the efforts to ensure that a rigorous test was done and scope was validated prior to any major release in the project. Recently, you made the final delivery to the customer and communicated the successful news to all the relevant members of the project. You were surprised when the customer called to inform you that he was not very happy with the release as it did not support one of his key functionalities and demanded that the feature be added as soon as possible. What should you do first in this kind of situation?

A. Estimate the time, cost, and resources required to add the feature as specified by the customer.
B. Have an urgent meeting with the sponsor to discuss the customer's concern.
C. Inform the customer that the project is delivered and closed and that any addition to the project must be handled as a new project.
D. Find out the lacks in scope validation and in-house testing procedures to identify the root cause.

10. A software company created a base package that must be implemented for each customer. Which one of the following will be used to ensure that the new base functionality does not break existing custom features and that these changes are evaluated across all relevant versions of the product?

A. Configuration management system
B. Process improvement plan
C. Perform Integrated Change Control
D. Work authorization system

11. Draw a network diagram based on the following criteria and answer the question below:

- Activity A can start immediately and has an estimated duration of 3 weeks.
- Activity B can also start immediately and has an estimated duration of 9 weeks.
- Activity C can start after activity A is completed and has an estimated duration of 5 weeks.
- Activity D can start after activity B is completed and has an estimated duration of 4 weeks.
- Activity E can start after both activities C and D are completed and has an estimated duration of 7 weeks.
- Activity F can start after activity D is completed and has an estimated duration of 4 weeks.

A new activity G is added to the project which will take 10 weeks to complete and must be completed before activity F and after activity D. You are worried that the addition of the new activity will add an additional 8 weeks to the project, so you calculate how much it will actually delay the project. What amount of time will be added to your project in this case?

A. 7 weeks
B. 6 weeks
C. 8 weeks
D. 28 weeks

12. Which of the following theories demonstrates that employees who believe their efforts will lead to effective performance and expect to be rewarded for their accomplishments remain productive as rewards meet their expectations?

A. Abraham Maslow's Hierarchy of Needs
B. Alderfer's Existence, Relatedness, Growth (ERG) needs
C. McClelland's Achievement Motivation theory
D. Victor Vroom's Expectancy theory

13. You have recently been assigned as a project manager for a new and highly complex project to send a satellite into space. There are several stakeholders in the project, and you are working on a communications plan to identify the information and communication needs of the people involved. You do this by determining what needs to be communicated, when, to whom, with what method, in which format, and how frequently. It is extremely important that you develop your communications plan:

A. Evenly throughout the project life cycle
B. At the earliest stages of the project
C. Upon completion of the project plan
D. During execution

14. Which one of the following statements is NOT true about a watchlist?

A. It consists of risks that do not have a high enough probability or impact to make it into the risk register, but that still need to be monitored.
B. It documents low probability and low impact risks for historical use only.
C. It is an output of the Perform Qualitative Risk Analysis process.
D. Noncritical risks on the watchlist need to be reviewed at intervals during the project to ensure they have not become critical.

15. Which of the following statements is FALSE concerning a Project Management Office (PMO)?
    A. It can be responsible for the direct management of projects and programs.
    B. It is an organizational body responsible for establishing and maintaining templates, policies, procedures, best practices, and standards for project management methodologies.
    C. In order to be managed together, the various projects supported by a PMO should be related.
    D. It conducts periodic project audits to monitor compliance with project management standards.

16. You are managing a large IT project when a severe cost overrun causes a major concern to the key stakeholders and the sponsor. You schedule an urgent meeting to discuss the root cause of the concern and illustrate the corrective and preventive actions you are planning to take. You are also planning to inform the audience in the meeting that the project is ahead of schedule and that most of the major deliverables are already completed and accepted by the stakeholders. What kind of communication does this meeting represent?
    A. Informal verbal
    B. Formal written
    C. Informal written
    D. Formal verbal

17. Which of the following is NOT true about Herzberg's Motivator-Hygiene theory?
    A. Hygiene factors are not sufficient to motivate people, and motivating agents provide the best positive reinforcement.
    B. Hygiene factors can destroy motivation, but improving them under most circumstances will not improve motivation.
    C. Motivating people is best done by rewarding people and letting them grow.
    D. Improving hygiene factors will certainly improve motivation.

18. Ashley, a senior project manager, recently took over a project to produce a safe and effective drug from another project manager who just left the company. Ashley was surprised to find out that there was no change control board or change control process established for the project. Why is it important to have a robust change control process for any project to be successful?
    A. It will ensure that only stakeholders with significant authority can submit the change requests.
    B. It will minimize the number of changes in the project.
    C. It will ensure that only necessary changes are considered and implemented.
    D. It will maintain the record of all changes for budget tracking purposes.

19. Your sponsor mentioned that the project must be completed within six months and should not exceed $50,000. You should consider this a:
    A. Project assumption
    B. Project constraint
    C. Stakeholder expectation
    D. Project boundary

20. You were given a budget of $3,000, and you spent $2,000. However you only completed $1,200 worth of work. What do you currently expect the TOTAL project to cost considering your situation?
    A. Not possible to estimate.
    B. $5,000
    C. $6,000
    D. $6,200

21. You are performing a quantitative risk analysis and modeling technique that helps to determine which risks have the most potential impact on a project. Your goal is to find whether the occurrence of a particular threat would be merely an inconvenience or would ruin the project. Which of the following tools will be most appropriate for your analysis?
    A. Tornado diagram
    B. SWOT analysis
    C. Expected Monetary value
    D. Reserve analysis

22. You have received many complaints from your customers indicating that the screens of laptops manufactured at your plant are getting black spots and marks after six months of use. Which of the following tools should your team members use to identify potential causes of this problem?
    A. Flowchart
    B. Statistical sampling
    C. Design of experiments
    D. Ishikawa diagram

23. While reviewing your project schedule, you realize that you have two pending activities that you need to complete as soon as possible. The plan would be for you to set up the development server in the lab and then start coding. But upon further investigation, you find out that you must run the server for 3 days, without failure, before the coding starts. This is an example of:
   A. Lead
   B. Crash
   C. Critical chain
   D. Lag

24. You are utilizing a technique of reconciling the expenditure of funds with the funding limits set for the project. As per the variance between the expenditure of funds and planned limit, you are trying to reschedule activities to level out the rates of expenditures. This technique is known as:
   A. Funding limit reconciliation
   B. Cost aggregation
   C. Reserve analysis
   D. Forecasting

25. You are overseeing a project to implement an online travel package reservation system that has 6 sponsors and 13 stakeholders. You want to make sure that your project stakeholders will receive the correct version of the product. Which of the following plans will you use to specify how versioning information will be tracked?
   A. Quality management plan
   B. Scope management plan
   C. Change management plan
   D. Configuration management plan

26. Senior management has asked you to shorten your project schedule by 2 months by any means. In order to achieve the target, you added a couple of additional resources to the team and also approved unlimited overtime for the team members. You realize that you are taking the risk of potential conflicts, additional management time, and cost to the project. The technique you are using is:
   A. Crashing
   B. Critical chain
   C. Critical path
   D. Fast tracking

27. You are overseeing a custom software development project to implement an accounting and financial system for one of your clients. Currently, you are in the process of obtaining the formal acceptance of the completed project scope and associated deliverables from the sponsor, customers, and other stakeholders. This process is closely related to which one of the following?
   A. Control Quality
   B. Manage Stakeholder Engagement
   C. Perform Quality Assurance
   D. Control Risks

28. During the executing stage of a project to develop a cashiering application for a retail customer, a senior stakeholder requested that you slightly modify the project scope to incorporate an additional feature. What will be your first course of action?
   A. Submit the change request to the change control board for their approval or rejection.
   B. Document the change request as per the project scope management plan.
   C. Perform an impact analysis on all project objectives such as scope, time, cost, quality, risk, resource, and others.
   D. Deny the request since it is too late in the project life cycle to incorporate any new change.

29. Which one of the following statements is NOT true about project life cycle?
   A. An iterative life cycle builds the concept in successive levels of details in order to create the end result.
   B. An incremental life cycle delivers a complete, usable portion of the product in each iteration.
   C. An adaptive life cycle defines the fixed scope, schedule, and cost with the clear understanding that it will be refined and adjusted as the project progresses.
   D. Iterative, incremental, and adaptive are different types of a plan-driven project life cycle.

30. You are trying to address the limitations associated with a network diagram and are utilizing a modified network diagram that will allow feedback loops and conditional branches. Which method are you using?
   A. PERT
   B. GERT
   C. Precedence diagram
   D. Arrow diagram

31. A project manager is in the Sequence Activities process of identifying and documenting relationships among defined activities and arranging them in the order they must be performed. While in this process, the project manager decides to utilize a Precedence Diagramming Method (PDM) for sequencing the activities. All of the following are true about a precedence diagramming method EXCEPT:
   A. This method creates a schematic display of the sequential and logical relationships of project activities.
   B. It usually shows dependencies and the order in which activities in a project must be performed.
   C. It uses four types of dependency relationships, including finish-to-start.
   D. This diagramming method uses Activity-on-Arrow (AOA) convention, as arrows are used to represent activities and circles show dependencies.

32. You are overseeing a project to build a robot, which will operate on electricity as well as solar power. The robot should have face and voice recognition capability. It should help the owner with daily household activities and keep him or her company. The robot should be able to learn from various experiences, develop its memory, and gradually make more complex decisions on its own. This information should be captured in which of the following documents?
   A. Project scope
   B. Scope baseline
   C. Product scope
   D. Requirements traceability matrix

33. One of your stakeholders is very disheartened about the fact that three of her key recommendations were not implemented in the project. She sends you an e-mail stating that she will not be able to review and approve the user test case document that you sent her as she thinks her feedback really does not matter much. What is your best course of action?
   A. Immediately implement her recommendations.
   B. Remove the stakeholder from the stakeholder register and avoid further communication.
   C. Explain to her that due to time and budget constraints her recommendations were not implemented, but the team will reassess them in the next release.
   D. Have an urgent meeting with the sponsor to discuss the next strategy.

34. You are managing a software application project to develop an online PMP exam simulator to assist students to practice exam questions in a similar real life environment. The team has completed design work, received approval from the technical review team, and initiated coding work. When your management asked what you currently expect the TOTAL project to cost, you assured that the current variances are atypical and similar variance will not occur in the future; thus, the rest of the job will be done as per budget. Which one of the following formulas will you use to get the most accurate Estimate at Completion (EAC)?
   A. EAC = AC+ (BAC – EV)
   B. EAC = AC + Bottom-up ETC
   C. EAC = (BAC – EV) / CPI * SPI
   D. EAC = BAC/CPI

35. A new stakeholder has recently been identified for your project. He will be helping team members with data validation and other testing. The stakeholder asks the project manager about the scheduling methodology and tools that will be used in the schedule development. He would also like to know about schedule change control procedures, reporting formats, and frequencies. Which one of the following documents may the project manager refer him to?

   A. Project charter
   B. Stakeholder register
   C. Schedule management plan
   D. Schedule baseline

36. Your team is working on the installation and configuration of a database server. A project manager from another project called to inform you that he is waiting for the completion of the server set up as his team will also be using the server for their testing. You were not aware of this and inform the project manager that the server installation and configuration will be delayed by a few days. What kind of dependency does the other project have on your project?
   A. Discretionary dependency
   B. Mandatory dependency
   C. Internal dependency
   D. External dependency

37. Vendor bid analysis is used as a tool & technique in which cost management process?
   A. Plan Cost Management
   B. Estimate Costs
   C. Determine Budget
   D. Control Costs

38. In multiphase projects, the projects are usually planned during developing phases that are performed sequentially to ensure proper control of the project and attain the desired product, service, or result. In some cases, it is necessary to accelerate the project life cycle by overlapping project phases. Which of the following is NOT true about this kind of overlapping relationship?

A. This technique can be applied as a schedule compression technique called "fast-tracking."
B. This kind of relationship may increase project risks and the potential for conflicts. A subsequent phase can progress before accurate information is available from the previous phase.
C. In this kind of relationship, a phase is planned at a given time; planning for a subsequent phase is carried out as work progresses on the current phase or deliverables.
D. This kind of relationship can reduce the ability to develop long-term planning, but it is suitable in an undefined, uncertain, and rapidly changing environment.

39. Your management asked you to negotiate with the vendor to implement an extremely important component as soon as possible in order to avoid losing a significant market share. What advice should you give to your management to include in the contract in this situation?

A. A force majeure clause
B. A time is of the essence clause
C. A retainage clause
D. Incentives

40. As a project manager, you and your team are mainly focused on finding a less costly way to do the same work and on achieving more out of the project in every possible way to increase the bottom line, decrease costs, improve quality, and optimize the schedule without reducing or impacting the scope. You are most likely using which of the following techniques?

A. Benchmarking
B. Value analysis
C. Life cycle costing
D. Reserve analysis

41. To calculate the project cost, the project manager utilizes the cost aggregation method by which activity costs are rolled up to the work packages costs; the work packages costs are then rolled up to the "control account" or "cost account" costs and finally to the project cost. At this moment the project manager is in the final stages of determining the cost baseline for the project and funding requirements. Which process is the project manager working on now?

A. Plan Cost Management
B. Estimate Costs
C. Determine Budget
D. Control Costs

42. A project manager working for an electric utility company has been assigned to create a new substation that will supply power to a newly developed subdivision. While performing the forecasting analysis, the project manager found that the EAC = $159,000 and became worried to discover that the SPI = 0.74 and the CPI = 0.86. What is the possible reason for this occurrence?

A. One of the subcontractors needed to be replaced due to poor performance.
B. An activity with no buffer unexpectedly took longer and required additional manpower to be completed.
C. The team had to purchase an expensive piece of safety equipment that was not originally planned.
D. The client made several scope changes.

43. You have been managing a top-secret government project, which has been progressing as planned up until last night. Suddenly, one of your team members called and informed you that an unexpected major problem occurred that was not included in the risk register. The problem will now cost the project an additional amount. What should be your first course of action?

A. Accept the risk.
B. Update the risk management plan.
C. Use the management reserves.
D. Have an urgent meeting with the stakeholders and find out the problem details.

44. A project manager working on implementing WIMAX connectivity in a rural area has to deploy several network devices and set up POPs to house those devices. She performed a cost-benefit analysis and was concerned about the high cost of nonconformance as a result of not following the proper quality procedures in the project. What should the project manager do?

A. Look for benchmarks.
B. Allocate additional budget to deal with the situation.
C. Utilize the existing reserve money to deal with the situation.
D. Perform a quality audit.

45. While supervising a construction project, a project manager noticed that for a construction process, standard deviation associated with the product variation was 0.7 inches and with the measurement variation was 0.5 inches. What is the total standard deviation here?
   A. 1.2
   B. 0.86
   C. 0.49
   D. 0.25

46. While working in quality management, you have identified the point where the benefits or revenue from improving quality equals the incremental cost to achieve that quality. You have performed which one of the following analyses?
   A. Marginal analysis
   B. Root cause analysis
   C. Benchmarking
   D. Quality control analysis

47. A project manager is trying to identify the specific training, coaching, mentoring, assistance, or changes required to improve the team's performance and effectiveness by making formal or informal assessments of the project team's effectiveness. Which of the following is the project manager performing?
   A. Team performance assessment
   B. Project performance appraisal
   C. Observations and conversations
   D. Team-building activities

48. A project manager overseeing a WIMAX deployment project just completed negotiation for three additional resources from different functional areas as well as extra reserve money for her project. During the negotiation, two of the functional managers were very skeptical about the request for additional resources and were reluctant to assign their resources to her project. She attempted to influence the functional managers by using her association with a high-level executive for leverage. Which of the following forms of power is she using in this situation?
   A. Referent
   B. Coercive
   C. Expert
   D. Reward

49. A project manager overseeing a construction project negotiated a deal with a tools and equipment rental company for ten different tools needed for his project. As part of the deal, the rental company will supply all ten pieces of equipment for a total price of $3,000/month for the duration of the project. This is an example of which of the following costs?
   A. Indirect cost
   B. Sunk cost
   C. Opportunity cost
   D. Fixed cost

50. A project manager is in the Acquire Project Team process and is trying to secure the best possible resources to build a project team for carrying out the project activities efficiently. What will be the output of this process?
   A. Human resource management plan
   B. Project staff assignments
   C. Team performance assessments
   D. Change requests

51. A contract is an entire formal agreement between two parties and it is the principle endeavor of procurement management. Which of the following is NOT true about contracts?
   A. Contracts are legally binding and backed by the court system in most countries.
   B. A contract cannot be terminated at any time by the buyer for a cause or convenience.
   C. A contract should help reduce project risks.
   D. A contract is legally binding unless it is in violation of applicable law.

52. Which one of the following is NOT true about issues in a project?
   A. An issue log is a document to record issues that require a solution.
   B. It helps monitor who is responsible for resolving specific problems by a target date.
   C. There should be one owner assigned for each issue reported in the project.
   D. Issues and risks refer to the same thing.

53. In Abraham Maslow's Hierarchy of Needs, accomplishment, respect, attention, and appreciation are categorized as:

A. Physiological
B. Self-actualization
C. Esteem
D. Social

54. You presented your project cost estimates to the sponsor, and she is upset about the inaccuracy of the estimates and demands that the estimates be as accurate as possible. Which of the following techniques will help you most in this situation?

A. An order of magnitude estimate
B. A heuristic estimate
C. A bottom-up estimate
D. A top-down estimate

55. Steve is a systems engineer who is extremely dedicated and hardworking. His deliverables are always on time, accurate, and of desired quality. He also has a reputation of being a "nice guy" and being liked by everyone in the organization. Considering all these factors, senior management has decided to assign Steve as a project manager in a new critical engineering project. This is an example of which of the following?

A. Rewarding good behavior
B. The Halo effect
C. Victor Vroom's Expectancy theory
D. Perquisites

56. A project manager utilizes different conflict resolution techniques to resolve conflicts in his project. He created an open environment so that his team members feel free to discuss their concerns and issues. He is also focused on resolving issues rather than fixing the personalities of his team members, and he pays more attention to the present than the past. Which of the following conflict resolution techniques will lead to the LEAST sustaining positive result?

A. Withdrawing or avoiding
B. Forcing
C. Confronting or problem solving
D. Compromising

57. This tool & technique is a graphical representation of a process to help analyze how problems occur and also identifies potential process improvement opportunities:

A. Benchmarking
B. Root cause analysis
C. Flow chart
D. Design of Experiments (DOE)

58. A communications management plan is a subsidiary of the project management plan that can be formal or informal, highly detailed or broadly framed, and is based on the needs of the project. It should include all of the following EXCEPT:

A. Project communications
B. Stakeholder communication requirements
C. Method, time frame, and frequency for the distribution of required information
D. Glossary of common terms

59. You are responsible for making all kinds of arrangements for your company's annual picnic. You have taken all the necessary actions and have reserved an outdoor park on a particular day. You are now only three days away from the big event, and the weather forecast suggests a light rain shower on the day of the picnic. You bought umbrellas and rented tents just in case you need them. Which of the following risk response strategies are you using in this case?

A. Passive acceptance
B. Contingency planning
C. Avoidance
D. Transference

60. In the communication process, a basic model of communication that exhibits how information is sent from the sender and how it is received by the receiver has all of the following components EXCEPT:

A. Sender
B. Message and feedback message
C. Urgency
D. Noise

61. Steve is a project manager for a power company and is currently supervising a solar panel installation project for a local real estate builder. The project has around fifteen team members and eighteen internal and external stakeholders. One of the team leads sent Steve a status report on his team's deliverables where he indicated that a major component was completed. Steve is convinced that the team lead was not fully honest in his communication, and the major component is far from being completed. Steve is about to have a meeting with the key stakeholders on the project status. What is the best course of action for Steve in this kind of situation?

A. Ask the team under the team lead to explain the cause of the discrepancy.
B. Challenge the team lead about the validity of the report.
C. Attend the status meeting with the stakeholders and do not mention anything about the major component.
D. Inform the stakeholder that you need a little more time to verify the information about the major component and will follow up with him/her shortly.

62. While overseeing a software engineering project, you find that one of the subcontractors failed to deliver on the last three projects. Upon further investigation, you learn that there are several complaints filed against this subcontractor, and that they have a very bad reputation in the market. Realizing that it is too big of a risk, you terminate the contract with the subcontractor and instead hire a couple of individuals to work on the components. Which risk response strategy did you use in this situation?

A. Accept
B. Transfer
C. Mitigate
D. Avoid

63. Your management asked you to study the work method to determine a faster, less costly, and more efficient method to complete the project. This is an example of which one of the following?

A. Value engineering
B. Resource leveling
C. Schedule compression
D. Learning curve

64. You are in the Control Risks process of identifying, analyzing, and planning for newly arising risks, taking corrective actions, and overall reviewing the execution and effectiveness of risk responses. All of the following are tools & techniques for Control Risks EXCEPT:

A. Risk reassessment
B. Variance and trend analysis
C. Enhance
D. Risk audits

65. Why is it essential to document assumptions from the point of initiation in your project?

A. Failure to validate assumptions may result in significant risk events.
B. Assumptions are absolute and nonnegotiable.
C. Assumptions allow for baseline adjustments in case of project crisis.
D. Assumptions limit the project team's options for decision making.

66. Which of the following is NOT a tool & technique of the Perform Qualitative Risk Analysis process?

A. Risk probability and impact assessment
B. Probability and impact matrix
C. Expected monetary value analysis
D. Risk data quality assessment

67. You are overseeing a large construction project to build a power plant. Your company has purchased a big piece of land close to a mountain and far away from the city for the plant. One of your team members reported to you that while digging the ground they found some artifacts. Upon initial assessment, you realize that these artifacts have some archaeological significance. What should you do in this situation?

A. Ask the team members to keep it a secret and collect all the artifacts for the benefit of the project.
B. This kind of finding is a norm in construction projects; thus, ignore the finding and proceed with the project as per the plan.
C. Proceed with the project as planned, but inform higher management about the finding.
D. Stop digging and call the archaeological department to quickly research the findings.

68. An important stakeholder identified a problem with one of the features of a software application your team is working on and submitted a change request. Even though it was out of the project's scope, the change control board has approved the change. What is the BEST action to take next?

A. Add the risk to the risk register and gather information about its probability and impact.
B. Disregard any risk at this stage of the project life cycle.
C. Have a meeting with the stakeholder to discuss the risk.
D. Identify what went wrong in the Identify Risks process.

69. Your team is trying to determine which risks have the most potential impact on the project, in other words, whether the occurrence of a particular threat would merely be an inconvenience or whether it would ruin the project. The team is using a diagram to display this sensitivity analysis data by examining all the uncertain elements at their baseline values. Which one of the following diagrams is the team using in this case?

A. Influence diagram
B. Cause and effect diagram
C. Scatter diagram
D. Tornado diagram

70. While working on a construction project, you need to find out if any of your team members are available to work during the upcoming weekend. Which one of the following documents will help you the MOST in this situation?

A. Project team directory
B. Responsibility Assignment Matrix (RAM) chart
C. Resource Breakdown Structure (RBS)
D. Resource calendar

71. You will be making $10,000 in a two year project. The cost of capital is 10 percent and the initial investment is $6,000. You have another project that has a net present value of $9500. If you compare the net present values, which project should you select?

A. The first project
B. The second project
C. Neither one
D. Cannot be determined

72. Company ABC invested $210,000 in a project, and that project returned a net profit of $14,000 in the first year of operation. The organization could have invested that same $210,000 and earned a 4 percent return. What is the Economic Value Added (EVA) in this case?

A. $5,600
B. $196,000
C. $224,000
D. –$5,600

73. While reviewing the status of your project you found out the following EV, AC, and PV. Find out the cumulative CPI and cumulative SPI for month 4.

Month	PV	EV	AC
Month 1	$30,000	$27,000	$25,000
Month 2	$35,000	$40,000	$45,000
Month 3	$90,000	$80,000	$70,000
Month 4	$150,000	$125,000	$89,000

A. 1.18 and 0.891
B. 0.891 and 1.18
C. 1.40 and 0.833
D. 0.833 and 1.40

74. Your team members have created a requirement document, a project scope statement, and a work breakdown structure. They have identified twenty work packages and completed the WBS dictionary. Some of these team members were also involved in creating the business case and conducting the feasibility study at the early stage of this project. Which one of the following items will the team members work on now?

A. Help the project manager to develop the schedule.
B. Create the detailed activity list.
C. Create the network diagram.
D. Identify the sequence of the activities.

75. Your twenty mile railway construction project is not going well. You were supposed to complete the project today, exactly forty weeks from the start of the project. You found out that only 75 percent of the work is completed. Based on this status, approximately when would you expect the project to be completed?

A. 13.3 weeks
B. 10 weeks
C. 15 weeks
D. 5 weeks

76. You created a Change Control Board (CCB) for your project since there is no centralized one in your organization. You also want to follow a robust Integrated Change Control process in your project. Which of the following is not a primary goal for performing the Integrated Change Control process?

A. Prevent unnecessary changes in your project.
B. Denying changes whenever possible.
C. Evaluate the possible impacts of the changes in your project.
D. Managing changes as they occur.

77. One of your hardware vendors sends you an e-mail stating that due to severe weather she will not be able to deliver the networking equipment on time. You decide to respond to this risk by leasing the required equipment from a local company until yours arrives. Which of the following statements is TRUE?

A. This is risk avoidance.
B. This is risk mitigation.
C. This is risk acceptance.
D. This is risk exploitation.

78. You are trying to measure how diverse the population is in your data set. First you find the mean by taking the average of all data points, and then calculate the average of how far each individual point is from that mean. You are using:

A. Standard deviation
B. Statistical sampling
C. Mutual exclusivity
D. Normal distribution

79. You are overseeing a twenty mile railway construction project. You were supposed to spend $10,000 per mile of railway construction and complete the project today, exactly forty weeks from the start of the project. You found out that only 75 percent of the work has been completed. What is your Budget at Completion (BAC)?

A. $200,000
B. $150,000
C. $300,000
D. $400,000

80. Your organization is having a severe cash flow problem and you were asked to minimize the cost in your small project as much as possible. Which of the following processes may you consider eliminating in such a scenario?

A. Perform Quantitative Risk Analysis
B. Control Risks
C. Identify Risks
D. Plan Risk Management

81. Which of the following is TRUE about Request for Bid (RFB) or Invitation for Bid (IFB)?

A. Buyer's request to all potential sellers for the details of how work will be performed.
B. Buyer's request to all potential sellers to submit a total price bid for work to be performed.
C. Buyer's request to all potential sellers to submit a price quote per item, hour, foot, or other unit of measure.
D. Buyer's request to all potential sellers to submit a detailed statement of work from the buyer.

82. According to Herzberg's Motivator-Hygiene theory, which of the following is NOT a hygiene factor?

A. Variety of work
B. Compensation
C. Personal life
D. Working conditions

83. You decide to use a combination of tools and techniques to identify risks in your data center project. Which one of the following tools is NOT used for risk identification?

A. SWOT analysis
B. Assumptions analysis
C. Brainstorming
D. RACI chart

84. Which one of the following processes documents configuration management activities in a project?

A. Collect Requirements
B. Define Scope
C. Plan Scope Management
D. Validate Scope

85. While overseeing a construction project, you are informed by the site supervisor that the painting team showed up even though the dry wall team is not even half done. The painting team lead is not sure when his team is supposed to start the work. Which one of the following is contributing MOST to this issue?
    A. This is due to poor team cohesiveness.
    B. Lack of communication management plan.
    C. A proper work authorization system was not established in the project.
    D. The site supervisor is lacking experience.

86. You remind your manager about your great contribution in a couple of projects and ask him to recommend you for a 10 percent salary increase. The manager mentions that management decided to give all the employees performing above average a 5 percent salary increase; thus, there is no need to discuss this topic any further. This is an example of which of the following?
    A. Good guy/bad guy
    B. Personal insult
    C. Fait accompli
    D. Missing man

87. You are managing a software application project to develop an online PMP exam simulator budgeted for $90,000 to assist students to practice exam questions in similar real life environment. The team has completed design work, received approval from technical review team, and initiated coding work. When asked by management what you currently expect the project to cost, you think that the costs you have incurred till now are typical for the rest of the project. While reviewing at the current status of the project, you found that AC = $30,000 and EV = $ 35,000. What is your Estimate at Completion (EAC)?
    A. $85,000
    B. $77,586
    C. $90,000
    D. $60,000

88. While in the Control Procurements process, you are meeting with your seller to inspect the seller's progress to deliver project scope and quality within cost and schedule as compared to the contract. Your objective is to identify performance progress or failures, non-compliances, and areas where performance is a problem. Which one of the following are you performing?
    A. Performance reporting
    B. Procurement performance reviews
    C. Inspections and audits
    D. Payment systems

89. You are working for a cruise company as a project manager. Your company offers luxury tours to couples at a reasonable price. Currently, the company is considering adding more tours to a few other popular destinations during the holiday season in order to increase traffic and profitability. Which risk response strategy is in use?
    A. Share
    B. Exploit
    C. Accept
    D. Enhance

90. Your organization has outsourced a large portion of the activities of an ERP implementation project to a vendor. According to the contract, the vendor is supposed to review the design and code of any major component with the Technical Review Group (TRG) of your organization. So far, the vendor has completed and deployed three major components without the approval of the TRG team. As a project manager, what should you do in this situation?
    A. Terminate the contract immediately as the vendor has breached the contract.
    B. Stop payment for the components that were deployed without approval.
    C. Do not worry too much as the approval of the TRG is not that important.
    D. Issue a default letter to the vendor.

91. Which of the following are the outputs of the Plan Scope Management process?
    A. Scope management plan and requirements management plan
    B. Requirements document and requirements traceability matrix
    C. Project scope statement and scope baseline
    D. WBS and WBS dictionary

92. Which of the following analyses integrates scope, cost, and schedule measures to assess project performance?
    A. Trend analysis
    B. Project presentations and review
    C. Earned value analysis
    D. Variance analysis

93. You are having an issue with one of the manufacturing processes used to create the required parts for routers and switches that your company produces. Due to this major quality problem, only 15 percent of the parts manufactured have been within the control limits set by the Quality Assurance team. Higher management asks you to review the process activities to determine where the process went wrong. Which type of diagram should you use to gather this information?
   A. Control chart
   B. Pareto chart
   C. Scatter diagram
   D. Flow chart

94. As an employee, working conditions, salary, status, and job security matter a lot to you, just like your other coworkers. However, you always feel that you will be more motivated and will contribute more if you are rewarded for your contribution to a project and given the opportunity to grow professionally. Which motivational theory are you referring to?
   A. McGregor's Theory X and Theory Y
   B. Maslow's Hierarchy of Need
   C. Herzberg's Motivation-Hygiene Theory
   D. Dr. William Ouchi's Theory Z

95. While determining the funds needed for your project, you obtained historical information from previous projects as the basis to determine the price per square foot of carpeting. You used this information to calculate the cost of 20,000 square feet of carpeting that is required for the project. Which technique did you use to create the estimate?
   A. Analogous estimating
   B. Three-point estimating
   C. Heuristic estimating
   D. Parametric estimating

96. The flexibility or total float in a schedule is measured by subtracting the early dates from the late dates. Which one of the following will help you to identify the flexibility in your schedule?
   A. Precedence diagramming method
   B. Resource leveling
   C. Critical Path Method (CPM)
   D. Fast tracking

97. You recently completed the SOW detailing the specifications and other requirements for an expensive item you would like to purchase for one of your projects. While working on the SOW, you identified some of the source selection criteria, terms and conditions, and the contract type that you want to use. Also, you put together some documents to solicit proposals from your potential vendors. What tools and techniques will you use in the next process?
   A. Market research, make-or-buy analysis, and expert judgment.
   B. Bidder conference, proposal evaluation techniques, and independent estimates.
   C. Procurement audits, procurement negotiations, and records management system.
   D. Contract change control system, procurement performance reviews, and claim administration.

98. An independent team from your organization has identified wasted steps that are not necessary for creating the product for your project. They have recommended a few actions for process improvement and have requested that some of the process documents be updated. Which of the following best describes what is being performed?
   A. They are performing quality assurance activity.
   B. They arc performing quality control activity.
   C. They are monitoring and controlling activities.
   D. They are directing and managing project work.

99. A project manager is in the Plan Communications Management process of identifying the information and communication needs of the people involved in a project by determining what needs to be communicated, when, to whom, with what method, in which format, and how frequently. Which of the following is NOT a tool & technique in this process?
   A. Performance reporting
   B. Communication requirements analysis
   C. Communication methods
   D. Communication technology

100. Which of the following is NOT an output for the Conduct Procurements process?
   A. Procurement contract award
   B. Selected sellers
   C. Source selection criteria
   D. Resource calendars

101. While overseeing a new wireless media streaming device development project, you notice that your team members are having significant difficulties resolving an issue that they have discovered during unit testing. After working on the issue for a week, the team members identify a number of possible causes for the issue and narrowed it down to two main causes. You asked the team members to determine if there is any interdependency between these two causes that would necessitate further action. Which one of the following tools would be the BEST to use in this situation?

A. Histogram
B. Flow chart
C. Scatter diagram
D. SWOT analysis

102. ITPro Consultancy, LLC, an Internet Service Provider (ISP), is planning to establish its own network infrastructure. It figured out that it would cost around $180,000 to establish its own network by in-house resources. Once the network is established, there will be a recursive cost of $4,000/month for operational and maintenance activities. An experienced vendor has offered ITPro to set up the infrastructure based on a license fee of ten dollars per user per month. ITPro will have two thousand users using the network per month. It will also need to pay a junior accountant $2,000/month to manage the billing. How many more months will ITPro have to use the infrastructure after establishing the network by the in-house resources rather than hiring the vendor?

A. Ten months
B. Nine months
C. Twenty months
D. Fifteen months

103. You are overseeing a construction project to build twenty identical custom houses. Your initial estimate suggests that each of the houses will take approximately two months to complete at a cost of $50,000. The sponsor strongly disagrees with your estimate due to which of the following?

A. You have not considered the law of diminishing return.
B. You have not considered the learning curve.
C. You cannot estimate the time and cost until you complete one house.
D. The estimates are way too high.

104. You have been managing a software application project to automate the accounting system for your client. Your team has completed work as specified in the contract statement of work. You get a call from the buyer and are told that he is disappointed with the result, even though he admits that the project team has met the terms and conditions of the contract. In this situation the contract is considered to be:

A. Complete
B. Waived
C. Closed
D. Null and Void

105. You have just finished negotiation on all terms and conditions of the contract with a selected vendor. As both parties are fully satisfied with the outcome of the negotiation, you started working on a draft official letter of notification of the contract award. Which one of the following processes are you in at this time?

A. Plan Procurements
B. Procurement Negotiations
C. Close Procurements
D. Conduct Procurements

106. Steve, the project manager for an ERP implementation project, was asked by the client via a change request to delay the implementation of one of the modules by one week. What should Steve do first in this situation?

A. Instruct the team member responsible for the module to delay the implementation as per the client's request.
B. Deny the request as it will delay the entire project.
C. Inform the sponsor about the change request.
D. Evaluate the impact of the requested change.

107. The cost baseline is displayed as an S-curve because of the way project spending occurs. This S-curve indicates that:

A. The bulk of the project cost is spent during the initiating and the closing phases.
B. The cost starts off low, accelerates throughout the later phases of the project, and gradually slows down during the closing.
C. The project cost is directly proportional to the size of the project.
D. Projects run in a cycle.

108. Your company worked on a new video console game for several months and invested a large amount of money in the development of the game. Unfortunately, the game was a flop, as one of the competitors also launched a similar but more sophisticated and higher quality game at the same time your company launched its game. The cost for research and development, patents, manpower, equipment, and intellectual property that your company spent in the development of the game is referred to as:

A. Sunk costs
B. Opportunity cost
C. Depreciation
D. Law of diminishing returns

109. Which of the following can be used to manage and store all documents, correspondence, and communication relevant to a contract?

A. Lessons learned
B. Records management system
C. Audit reports
D. Procurement documents

110. You are conducting a procurement performance review of the seller's progress to deliver the project. It is a structured review consisting of seller-prepared documentation, buyer inspection, and a quality audit of the seller's progress to deliver project scope and quality within cost and on schedule as compared to the contract. Your objective is to identify performance progress or failure, noncompliance, and areas where performance is a problem. You are working on which of the following processes at this time?

A. Plan Procurements
B. Conduct Procurements
C. Control Procurements
D. Close Procurements

111. You strongly disagree with the customer's interpretation of a clause in the contract. The customer submitted a change request and demanded that two new deliverables be implemented as per the contract immediately. You think that the customer is just being unreasonable and that her demand is simply unrealistic. What will be the best course of action to resolve the situation?

A. Have an urgent meeting with the customer and explain the implications of accepting such a request on schedule and cost.
B. Ignore the customer's request and continue with your project work as planned.
C. Document the dispute and refer to claims administration.
D. Accept the customer's demand as the customer is always right.

112. You have a signed contract in place with one of your major vendors. The vendor recently informed you that they can no longer deliver equipment on the agreed due date. This will cause a major disaster in your project since the vendor will have to wait at least three months before they can deliver the equipment. You know that there is another vendor who can deliver the equipment for a small increase in costs. What will be your best course of action?

A. Sue the vendor.
B. Terminate the contract stating that it is for convenience.
C. Terminate the contract with the vendor for defaulting.
D. Give the vendor a time extension.

113. According to McClelland's Achievement Motivation theory, individuals who work best when cooperating with others and working in a team, seek to maintain good relationships and approval rather than recognition, and perform well in a customer-facing team position have which of the following needs?

A. Need for power
B. Need for affiliation or association
C. Need for achievement
D. Need for nothing

114. A stakeholder register contains stakeholder classification, identification, and assessment information. It also points out challenges related to working with the stakeholders as well as the project manager's impression of their knowledge, skills, capabilities, and attitude. Which of the following is TRUE regarding the stakeholder register?

A. It should be accessible to all the team members and stakeholders.
B. It should be accessible only to the sponsor.
C. A project manager may publish it with other project documentation or keep it in reserve for personal use only.
D. It should be accessible only by the PMO.

115. While reviewing the stakeholder engagement assessment matrix, you notice that one of the important stakeholders is at an "unaware" state at the moment and has no clue about what is happening in your project. As this stakeholder can contribute significantly to your project success, you decide to bring him to a "supportive" or "leading" state. Which of the following will help you to achieve your goal with this stakeholder?
   A. Send him regular reports on the project and its benefits.
   B. Offer him a paid vacation in Hawaii in exchange for his support.
   C. Assign top priorities to his expectations, concerns, and issues.
   D. Involve him in some project activities.

116. The higher management in your organization is very averse to risk. While planning the procurement strategy, you would like to make sure that you select the contract type that will have the least risk for the organization. Which of the following contract options will be best in this scenario?
   A. Cost reimbursable
   B. Fixed price economic price adjustment
   C. Fixed price
   D. Time & material

117. You are responsible for delivering a couple of very expensive pieces of equipment to a hospital in a foreign country. As per the agreement, your company is responsible for coordinating moving the equipment all the way to the nineteenth floor of the client's premises. Your local contact informs you that you need to pay a certain fee to the liftman for coordinating the movement of the equipment through the elevator to the specific floor at nighttime. What should you do in this situation?
   A. Pay the fee.
   B. Have a discussion with the customer and express your concern about the bribe.
   C. Consider the fee a bribe and refuse to pay it.
   D. Hire a local subcontractor to arrange the delivery.

118. You are currently working in the Direct and Manage Project Work process to complete the work defined in the project management plan to satisfy the project specifications and objectives. All of the following are outputs from the Direct and Manage Project Work process EXCEPT?
   A. Deliverables
   B. Final products, service, or result transition
   C. Change requests
   D. Work performance data

119. Your management has asked you to lead a team to negotiate and finalize a deal with one of the vendors. While negotiating you will mainly be focused on all of the following EXCEPT:
   A. Developing a good understanding and relationship with the seller
   B. Obtaining a fair and reasonable price for the product, service, or result
   C. Obtaining the lowest possible price and commitment for the shortest project duration from the vendor
   D. Discovering and dealing with disputes as much as possible prior to contract signing

120. You are overseeing a large data center project and have requested bids from several vendors to procure numerous networking devices such as routers, switches, firewalls, PCs, and servers. You decide to go for the lowest bidder since all the bidders are offering the devices from the same manufacturer. Senior management suggests that you conduct a bidder conference prior to selecting a specific seller. A bidder conference will satisfy which of the following mandatory standards in the PMI code of ethics and professional conduct?
   A. Respect
   B. Honesty
   C. Fairness
   D. Responsibility

121. While reviewing a deliverable due today to the customer, you noticed a technical defect in the deliverable. Upon further inspection, you realize that even though the deliverable fails to meet the project quality standards, it fully satisfies the contractual requirements. You are aware that the customer does not have the domain knowledge and technical expertise to notice the defect. The team member responsible for this deliverable tells you that fixing the defect will be time consuming and superfluous. What is your best course of action?
   A. Contact the customer immediately and inform them that the deliverable will be late due to some unavoidable consequences.
   B. Make sure that the issue is captured in the lessons learned so that future projects can benefit.
   C. Have a discussion with the customer about the issue with the deliverable.
   D. Do not mention anything and get formal acceptance from the customer.

122. You are overseeing a project to implement a new computer infrastructure at the local hospital. While evaluating the exact cost impact of some risks identified in the project, you found it extremely incomprehensible to estimate the value of the impact. In this kind of situation, you should consider evaluating on a:

A. Numerical basis
B. Quantitative basis
C. Qualitative basis
D. Forecast basis

123. You have been managing a top-secret government project, which has been progressing as planned up until last night. Suddenly, one of your team members called and informed you that an unexpected major problem occurred that was not included in the risk register. What should be your first course of action?

A. Take corrective and preventive actions.
B. Update the risk management plan.
C. Create a workaround.
D. Create a fallback plan.

124. While overseeing a web-based application project, you notice that one of the team members is extremely dedicated to the project and a consistent overachiever. In order to appreciate her spectacular work and great contribution to the project, you offer her a nice corner office where she can concentrate on her work without much interruption. This kind of reward is regarded as:

A. Perquisite
B. Fringe benefit
C. Special achievement award
D. Bribe

125. It is important to realize that stakeholders play a major role in project success. In order to ensure that stakeholders' expectations are managed properly throughout the life of a project, the project manager needs to do all of the following EXCEPT:

A. Build trust with the stakeholders.
B. Resolve conflicts among the stakeholders.
C. Actively listen to the stakeholders' concerns.
D. Convey ground rules to the stakeholders.

126. One of the team members informed you that she had identified a design defect that will delay the project by two weeks. You check the risk register and realize that no response plan for this situation has been documented. What action should you take FIRST?

A. Replace the team member who made the mistake in design.
B. Call the customer immediately and inform them about the situation.
C. Contact the sponsor for advice.
D. Evaluate the impact and brainstorm options with the team members.

127. Which one of the following would most likely result in a change request?

A. An overall SV of 230.
B. An overall CV of 50.
C. A short delay of a critical path activity.
D. A major delay of a non-critical path activity.

128. You recently awarded a contract to one of the vendors after rigorous negotiations. You realize that you have missed out on a couple of very important clauses that you wanted to include in the contract. You decide to modify the contract and include 'time is of the essence' and "retainage" clauses. How should you proceed in this case?

A. You should proceed with a contract change control system at your end.
B. You should inform the seller about the change through a formal written communication.
C. You should have an urgent meeting with the seller to discuss the change.
D. It is too late to make any changes in the contract as it is legally binding and cannot be modified once signed.

129. You are managing a project to build a new plant for a semiconductor company. You just found out that the entire site was badly affected by a severe tornado and your newly developed structures were destroyed. Your client demands that you continue work despite the disaster and refuses to take any responsibility for the damage or allow you a time extension. You reviewed the contract and found a clause that states that you are not responsible for any more work. This is referred to as:

A. An indemnification clause
B. A mitigation clause
C. An arbitration clause
D. A force majeure clause

130. You are approaching the end of your project and were asked to release the resources so that they can be assigned to other projects. Before releasing the resources you want to make sure that you have completed the necessary actions. Which of the following is the correct order of actions that you take during the Closing processes?

A. Get formal acceptances, write lessons learned, release the team, and close the contract.
B. Get formal acceptances, release the team, write lessons learned, and close the contract.
C. Write lessons learned, release the team, get formal acceptances, and close the contract.
D. Release the team, get formal acceptances, close the contract, and write lessons learned.

131. Your team members have sent you their weekly updates on the deliverables they are working on. While reviewing and scrutinizing updates from the team members, you find out that the CPI = 1.1 and SPI = 1. What should you do next with the results of your analysis?

A. Distribute the results to project stakeholders as per your communications management plan.
B. Since the project is on track, you do not have to do anything at this time.
C. Find out where you can spend the money that was saved.
D. Instruct the team members to improve their timing.

132. A project manager overseeing an age verification online tool is in the Control Procurements process of ensuring the seller's performance meets contractual requirements, ensuring that both seller and buyer meet their contractual obligations, and ensuring that the legal rights of both the buyer and seller are protected. Which of the following tools & techniques is NOT used in this process?

A. Claims administration
B. Procurement performance review
C. Inspections and audits
D. Procurement negotiations

133. Which one of the following integration management processes is responsible for implementing process improvement activities?

A. Direct and Manage Project Work
B. Monitor and Control Project Work
C. Develop Project Charter
D. Perform Integrated Change Control

134. You have been assigned to create a diagram that will demonstrate the logical relationships that exist between activities. You are also asked to display how long the project activities will take. Which of the following methods will you utilize to achieve this goal?

A. Pareto chart
B. CPM
C. Checksheet
D. PDM

135. You recently took over a project from a senior project manager who just left the company. You found out that several of your team members are lacking critical skills to carry out the project activities. The previous project manager also mentioned that many of the team members will need specialized training. Which of the following actions should you take next to identify the appropriate training for the team members?

A. Refer to the PMBOK® guide.
B. Review the WBS and WBS dictionary
C. Analyze the responsibility assignment matrix
D. Refer to the staffing management plan

136. During which specific process does the project manager prevent scope changes from overwhelming the project?

A. Define Scope
B. Validate Scope
C. Control Scope
D. Perform Integrated Change Control

137. A Cost Plus Incentive Fee (CPIF) contract has an estimated cost of $250,000 with a predetermined fee of $15,000. If the seller can save the buyer any money, the sharing ratio will be 75/25 (buyer/seller). The maximum fee is $24,000, and the minimum fee is $8,000. The actual cost of the project is $225,000. What will be the final fee for the seller and the total savings for the buyer?

A. $21,250, $18,750
B. $15,000, $25,000
C. $25,000, $20,000
D. None of the above

138. As a project manager, you have managed several projects in your organization. You notice that not all the projects are given the proper support and importance from higher management. You also notice that projects get terminated while in progress due to other higher-priority projects in the organization. You will be managing an IT project soon and want to make sure that your project will get the required support from the performing organization. What will be your best course of action?

A. Make sure that the project meets the personal objectives of the sponsor.
B. Communicate the project details and benefits with higher management on a regular basis.
C. Correlate the need for the project to the organizational strategic objective and goal.
D. Justify that your project should be the highest-priority project in the organization.

139. While managing an ERP project, you realize the targeted project end date will be delayed by several days. Upon further investigation you identify some activities that can be performed in parallel. You also realize that you have not fully utilized some of your resources in the project. What will be the BEST course of action in this situation?

A. Apply leads and lags.
B. Apply resource leveling.
C. Apply fast tracking and crashing.
D. Develop a new project schedule.

140. Which one of the following is NOT true about the goal and objective of a bidding conference?

A. All questions are submitted in writing and issued to sellers as an addendum to the procurement document so that all sellers respond to the same scope of work.
B. There is no collusion among sellers and/or buying agents.
C. Sellers do not save questions for later private meetings in order to gain a competitive advantage.
D. Select the seller who is best capable of performing the project work.

141. In a negotiated Cost Plus Incentive Fee (CPIF) contract, the following figures were finalized:
a target cost of $355,000, a target fee of $45,000, and a sharing ratio of 75/25. If the actual cost of the project is $390,000, what will be the final fee to the seller?

A. $36,250
B. $8,750
C. $35,000
D. $45,000

142. In the data center project that you are managing, you identified several internal and external restrictions or limitations that will affect the performance of a process within the project. Which of the following BEST identifies these issues?

A. Project assumptions
B. Project scope
C. Project requirements
D. Project constraints

143. You have been assigned to identify the key stakeholders for an internal project that has recently been formally approved. Which of the following is your starting point?

A. Project charter
B. Business case
C. Statement of work
D. Procurement document

144. You are currently in the Monitoring and Controlling Project Work process of a networking project that you are overseeing to implement a WIFI network in a rural community. Which of the following tasks will you perform as a part of this process?

A. Manage the project's vendors closely.
B. Compare the plan to the actual performance.
C. Collect requirements from the stakeholders.
D. Produce the deliverables of the project.

145. Your team has estimated that there is a 40 percent probability of a delay in the receipt of required parts with an additional cost of $15,000 to the project. This delay will cost the company $20,000 in lost business. Upon further investigation, you identified that if an existing component could be adapted it would save the project $10,500 in engineering costs. There is a 30 percent probability that the team can take advantage of that opportunity. What is the total Expected Monetary Value (EMV) of these two events?

A. $10,950
B. –$10,850
C. $14,000
D. $3,150

146. You are overseeing a project to implement a payroll application and are currently in the Identify Risks process of identifying and documenting the project risks. All of the following information gathering techniques are used in the Identify Risks process EXCEPT:
   A. Checklist analysis
   B. The Delphi technique
   C. Interviewing
   D. Brainstorming

147. Which of the following is TRUE about stakeholders?
   A. Only the stakeholders who can positively impact the project should be listed in the stakeholder register.
   B. Stakeholder identification is a continuous and sometimes strenuous process.
   C. Change requests from the stakeholder with the most influence should be given the highest priority.
   D. Stakeholders should be given extras in order to meet and exceed their expectations.

148. Which process is MOST closely associated with continuous process improvement?
   A. Perform Qualitative Risk Analysis
   B. Perform Quality Assurance
   C. Control Quality
   D. Plan Quality Management

149. You are trying to identify and categorize as many potential risks as possible in the mission critical project that you are overseeing. Which of the following will NOT help you with your effort of identifying risks?
   A. Delphi technique
   B. Brainstorming
   C. SWOT analysis
   D. Risk register

150. The cost of developing a product fix is related to which costs of quality category?
   A. A prevention cost
   B. An internal failure cost
   C. An appraisal cost
   D. An external failure cost

151. Which of the following statements is FALSE about qualified sellers in a project?
   A. It is a list of preapproved or prequalified prospective sellers interested in and capable of doing contract services for the organization.
   B. It is a part of the project management plan.
   C. It is a list of pre-screened sellers.
   D. It is a tool in the Conduct Procurement process.

152. The change control board just approved a change request to modify one of the major deliverables. In which process will this change be implemented?
   A. Perform Integrated Change Control
   B. Monitor and Control Project Work
   C. Close Project or Phase
   D. Direct and Manage Project Work

153. You have been assigned as a project manager for a project expected to last five months. The project has a budget of $450,000 and should be implemented in three different departments in your organization. While reviewing the status of the project after two months, you find that the project is 35 percent complete. Which of the following statements is TRUE about your project?
   A. Your project is on schedule.
   B. Your project is behind schedule.
   C. Your project is ahead of schedule.
   D. You cannot determine if your project is behind or ahead of schedule from the information given.

154. Your organization has enough resources only to work on one of two potential projects and decides to use the Net Present Value (NPV) to assess and select the best project for the organization. Project Alpha has an NPV of $45,000 and Project Beta has an NPV of $60,000. Project Alpha will take 3 years to complete and Project Beta will take 4 years. What will be the opportunity cost of the project chosen?
   A. $60,000
   B. $45,000
   C. $25,000
   D. $105,000

155. Which one of the following is NOT an input in the Conduct Procurements process?
   A. Qualified seller list
   B. Make-or-buy analysis
   C. Teaming agreements
   D. Seller proposals

156. You have been appointed as a project manager in a well-reputed hospital. While working on a project, you find that your employer is violating several codes issued by the local health department. What should be your first action in this situation?
   A. Have a discussion with your employer to find out if they are aware of the violations.
   B. Immediately resign from the company.
   C. Immediately inform the local health department about the violations.
   D. Do not worry about it since it is none of your business.

157. You are a project manager working for the healthcare system and have been tasked with overseeing the implementation of a new network infrastructure at the local hospital. A month into the project, you just finished creating the project charter and identifying the key stakeholders. You are about to move to the planning process group when the hospital authority requests that you provide them with the budget and cost baseline. Your best response should be:
   A. Inform them that cost is a project secret and cannot be shared.
   B. Hand over the project charter to them for the details about the budget and cost baseline.
   C. Inform them that the budget and cost baseline will be finalized during the planning process group.
   D. Inform them that there is no need to worry about the budget and cost baseline for this kind of small project.

158. Higher management has assigned you as the project manager very early in the project life cycle for a very critical project. You were asked to start working on the project charter immediately. You will be performing all of the following activities EXCEPT:
   A. Develop the project scope statement document.
   B. Identify and document high level risks.
   C. Identify project constraints and assumptions.
   D. Perform order of magnitude estimating.

159. You are a shy project manager struggling with your communication skills. You like to keep to yourself unless you are prompted for your input. On the other hand, Steve is highly regarded by everyone and very well liked. You consider Steve to be your role model as he is capable of getting others to see his way on many issues. What type of power does Steve possess?
   A. Expert power
   B. Reward power
   C. Referent power
   D. Legitimate power

160. While managing an ERP solution implementation project, you realize that you are not utilizing your resources evenly in the project. You found out that you are using almost all of your resources in some of the work weeks and hardly using any in some other work weeks. You consider moving around some of the activities and resources so that you can utilize your resources evenly throughout the project life cycle. Which of the following techniques are you using?
   A. Fast tracking
   B. Crashing
   C. Resource leveling
   D. Critical chain

161. Ashley, a senior project manager, recently took over a project to produce a safe and effective drug from another project manager who just left the company. Ashley was surprised to find out that there is no change control board to review, approve, or deny a change request for the project. Upon further investigation, she finds that there is no organizational change control board to manage changes for the entire organization. What should Ashley do in this situation?
   A. Carry on with the change request without a change control board.
   B. Establish a Change Control Board (CCB) for her project.
   C. Make all the decisions about the requested changes herself with the help of the team members.
   D. Ask the sponsor to approve or deny the change requests.

162. As a project manager you have collected information about Sabrina, a team member, from multiple sources including other team members and management staff. You have identified several areas for improvement for Sabrina that you want to discuss with her. You are particularly concerned that Sabrina is having many conflicts with other team members. During the one-on-one meeting, both of you agree on a training program to address the concern of conflicts with other team members. You also make sure that Sabrina understands she needs to submit her status and progress reports at the beginning of every week. Which action are you currently engaged in with Sabrina?

A. Observation and conversation
B. Project performance appraisals
C. Team performance assessment
D. Conflict management

163. You are having an issue with one of the manufacturing processes being used to create the required parts for routers and switches that your company produces. What should you use to identify the cause of this issue, and the effect it may have on your project?

A. Continuous improvement
B. Histogram
C. Ishikawa diagram
D. Flow chart

164. While working with clients on the final acceptance of the application, you were delighted to find out that the application exceeded the performance criteria specified in the requirement specification approved by the clients. You implemented several features that were not in the project scope to meet and exceed client's expectations. What can you conclude about the project performance?

A. The project was a success as it provided the features beyond the customers' expectation without any cost and schedule impact.
B. The project was a success as it exceeded the customers' specified performance criteria.
C. The project was unsuccessful as it has been gold plated.
D. The project was a success as it made the clients really happy.

165. You are the project manager overseeing the development of a new console video game. It has 10 components, and 5 team members are working on it. There are 15 stakeholders for this project, and one of the stakeholders is the previous owner of this company. One of the components is of major concern because it is a difficult one to implement. You found out that the soonest you can start working on that component will be early next week, and it will take 10 days to complete. You also found out that as of now the CPI=.81, and the SPI=1.2. What should be your main concern in this project at this time?

A. The stakeholder who was the previous owner
B. Schedule
C. Number of stakeholders in this project
D. Cost

166. While managing a WIFI project, you discovered that a few of your team members are not getting along. You also realized that three team members are not sure how to complete their deliverables. All of your team members are working together in the same building. You also set up regular weekly meetings with all the team members in a single meeting room. Which technique will NOT be helpful in this situation?

A. War room
B. Training
C. Reward and recognition
D. Negotiation

167. While creating the stakeholder register, you realize that some of the stakeholders can negatively impact your project. Which of the following elements should you NOT include in your stakeholder register?

A. List of key expectations identified for each stakeholder.
B. Contact information of the stakeholders.
C. A rating of the stakeholder's impact and influence on the project.
D. A plan to increase support and minimize obstruction for each stakeholder.

168. The trustworthiness of a message to its receivers may be prejudiced by their level of trust in the communicator. This is an example of which of the following?

A. Encoding
B. Decoding
C. Noise
D. Medium

169. Your sponsor is not very happy about the cost estimate you submitted for a construction project. The sponsor suggested that you come up with an exceptionally accurate cost estimate at your earliest convenience. What will be your best course of action in this situation?

A. Use the historical information from a similar project and make adjustments for known differences.
B. Use a rule of thumb estimate.
C. Perform a cost aggregation for raw materials and labor for each activity in the WBS.
D. Use the three-point estimates technique.

170. You are overseeing an ERP implementation project that will cost the company $1 million and will take three years to complete. Six months into the project, higher management decided to terminate your project as they found an off-the-shelf solution that can be implemented in three months at a fraction of the planned cost. What is the first thing you should do in this situation when your project no longer seems commercially viable for the company?

A. Conduct scope verification.
B. Release the team immediately.
C. Document the lessons learned.
D. Have an urgent meeting with the sponsor to discuss the situation.

171. You are overseeing a software project to develop a new video console game. Which of the following statements is TRUE about your project?

A. A phase will never start until the deliverables for the previous phase have been reviewed and approved.
B. Your internal and external stakeholders will have the same level of influence throughout your project.
C. Any scope change during the initial phase of the project will be very time consuming and expensive.
D. You will be acquiring several of your team members during the executing phase.

172. While overseeing a new smartphone application development project, you notice your team members are measuring the quality of an item on a pass/fail basis. Which of the following methods are the team members using?

A. Mutual exclusivity
B. Statistical independence
C. Normal distribution
D. Attribute sampling

173. You decided to use a technique called rolling wave planning in your web-based insurance and tax payment application project. Which one of the following may be your key reason for selecting this technique?

A. To prioritize project activities.
B. To achieve the appropriate level of detail in each work package at the right time.
C. To sequence project activities.
D. To estimate the duration of project activities.

174. Your PMO stipulates that plurality support is the minimum level of support for any major decision in a project. You disagree with a block of supporters on a plan to purchase a piece of expensive equipment for your project. This block is larger than any other in your team even though it is only 45 percent of the total team. What should you do in this kind of situation?

A. Have an urgent meeting with the sponsor.
B. Insist that any major decision should be supported by more than 50 percent of the team.
C. Do nothing as PMO permits decisions to be made by a plurality, rather than a majority.
D. Ask PMO to reevaluate their policy.

175. You have been assigned as a project manager for an ongoing project and asked to provide activity duration estimates as soon as possible. You were surprised to find out that there was no detailed information available on the project. You explored your organizational process assets and identified a few similar projects that had been completed in the past. Which one of the following will be the correct tool to utilize in this kind of situation?

A. Analogous estimate
B. Three-point estimate
C. Heuristic estimate
D. One point estimate

176. A control chart measures the results of processes over time, displays them in a graphical format, and measures variances to determine whether process variances are in control or out of control. The upper and lower control limits are usually set as:

A. + –1 Sigma – 68.26 percent of the occurrences will fall within 1 sigma from the mean.
B. + –2 Sigma – 95.46 percent of the occurrences will fall within 2 sigma from the mean.
C. + –3 Sigma – 99.73 percent of the occurrences will fall within 3 sigma from the mean.
D. + –6 Sigma – 99.99985 percent of the occurrences will fall within 6 sigma from the mean.

177. Five process groups are by no means completely linear, and they interact and overlap with each other. Which two process groups do not usually overlap unless a project is canceled or terminated?

A. Planning and closing
B. Planning and executing
C. Initiating and closing
D. Executing and monitoring and controlling

178. Referring to the following table, determine the cost to crash the project schedule by seven days.

Task	Duration	Predecessor	Normal Cost	Crash Cost (per day)	Max Crash Days
M	8	–	$3,000	$300	0
N	10	M	$4,000	$300	2
O	9	N	$3,000	$400	2
P	10	O	$5,000	$400	1
Q	6	O	$4,000	$600	2
R	5	P, Q	$2,000	$500	3

A. $5,000
B. $3,500
C. $2,800
D. $3,000

179. Workarounds, or unplanned responses to emerging risks that were previously unidentified or accepted, are determined during which risk management process?

A. Plan Risk Management process
B. Control Risks process
C. Plan Risk Responses process
D. Perform Quantitative Risk Analysis process

180. You identify that there are 36 communication channels in your project. How many members do you have in your team?

A. 9
B. 10
C. 36
D. 18

181. While identifying risks in your project, your team cannot find any efficient ways to reduce the impact and probability or to insure against one of the risks. The relevant work is integral to the project; thus, you cannot simply remove the work package, and there is no suitable company to outsource the work to either. What is the best course of action in this situation?

A. Identify ways to transfer the risk.
B. Accept the risk and have contingency reserves.
C. Identify ways to avoid the risk.
D. Keep looking for ways to mitigate the probability and impact of the risk.

182. You notice that you are not utilizing your resources evenly in the project. You want to apply resource leveling by moving some of your activities from the week when you are using many resources to a week when you are hardly using any. Which of the following tools and techniques would be a good choice in this situation?

A. Network diagram
B. Responsibility assignment matrix
C. Organizational breakdown structure
D. Resource histogram

183. A project manager is using a chart that cross-references team members with the activities or work packages they are to accomplish. Which one of the following is an example of this kind of chart?

A. Gantt chart
B. RACI chart
C. Milestone chart
D. Flowchart

184. Steve, a project manager, is overseeing a web-based accounting automation project that needs rigorous testing prior to implementation. The project is behind schedule and customers are strongly opposed to an extension of the duration since it was delayed twice in the past. Steve's manager asks Steve to skip most of the volume and stress testing and, if asked, instructs him to tell the customers that the testing was completed according to the approved specifications. What is Steve's best course of action in this situation?

A. Skip the volume and stress testing as suggested by his manager.
B. Only do a limited amount of volume and stress testing to make sure that the system will function correctly.
C. Discuss the situation with the sponsor and seek advice.
D. Politely refuse to skip the volume and stress testing.

185. What are the end results of the Plan Quality Management process?

A. Quality control measurements, validated changes, and change request
B. Quality management plan, quality metrics, and process improvement plan
C. Quality management plan, quality checklist, and quality control measurements
D. Work performance information, quality management plan, and process improvement plan

186. A project manager is interested to know the approximate cost of her project so that she can identify the rationality of the vendors' offered price. The best tool to use in this scenario is:

A. Inspection and audits
B. Independent estimate
C. Screening system
D. Weighting system

187. During a brainstorming session your team members came up with several ideas and later ranked and prioritized them using the nominal group technique. Which of the following techniques will you use to sort these ideas into groups by similarities for review and analysis?

A. Delphi technique
B. Mind mapping
C. Group decision making techniques
D. Affinity diagram

188. While planning human resources for a data center project you are overseeing, you used a graphical and hierarchical structure of the identified resources arranged by resource category (such as labor, material, equipment, and supplies) and type (such as expertise level, grade, and experience). This hierarchical chart is also helpful in tracking project costs and can be aligned with the organization's accounting system. You are using a:

A. Work Breakdown Structure (WBS)
B. Resource Breakdown Structure (RBS)
C. Cost breakdown structure
D. Human resource cost chart

189. While overseeing a new wireless media streaming device development project, you notice that your team members are having significant difficulties resolving an issue that they discovered during unit testing. Upon further investigation, you realize that the approach team members are using to resolve the issue is arbitrary and disorganized. What is the correct approach for the team members to take in this kind of situation?

A. Use the cause and effect diagram to identify the root cause of the issue.
B. Use the Pareto chart to identify the causes causing 80 percent of the problem.
C. Use the control chart to determine where the process is going out of control.
D. Use the Monte Carlo analysis to do a detailed what if analysis.

190. You may have two activities to design a software component and test it. Depending on the result of the testing, you may or may not redesign the component. Which of the following network diagram techniques will you use that permits loops to represent non-sequential activities?

A. Graphical Evaluation and Review Technique (GERT)
B. Activity on Node (AON)
C. Activity on Arrow (AOA)
D. Precedence Diagramming Method (PDM)

191. A bidder conference is:

A. An output of the Conduct Procurements process.
B. A method for selecting the best vendor for the project.
C. A technique to review the proposals from the vendors.
D. A tool and technique to provide all competing vendors with the same information about the project and bidding process.

192. While working in a foreign country, you are asked to pay the security guard for private protection service every time there is a need to transfer expensive equipment from one warehouse to another. You know this would not be a common practice in the US as it may be considered a bribe, but it is customary in the country you are now working. What is your best course of action?

A. Pay for the service, as it is customary in the country you are now working.
B. Never pay for the private protection service.
C. Ask for guidance from PMO.
D. Ask for guidance from the sponsor.

193. You have been working with a few vendors to procure the services and goods you need for one of the critical projects you are overseeing. You sent out your RFP template to these vendors so that they can submit their proposals to you. The RFP contains a narrative description of the products and services that you need for the project. Which part of the RFP document does this BEST describe?

A. Statement of Work (SOW)
B. Business case
C. Resource management plan
D. Project charter

194. Your organization is working on several critical projects and none of them are going well. Higher management has decided to adopt the Kaizen approach to improve the performance of all the projects. You have been assigned as a project manager to apply this approach throughout the organization. What kind of service are you involved in?

A. Quality plan
B. Quality control
C. Quality assurance
D. Quality inspection

195. You are working for a healthcare facility and overseeing the implementation of a new computer infrastructure and office automation project at the local hospital. The project is progressing well, and not many change requests have been submitted so far. Recently, you made a major release in the project and communicated the successful news to all the relevant members of the project. You were surprised when the customer called to inform you that he was not very happy with the deliverable and would be asking for a major modification soon. What should you do first in this kind of situation?

A. Do a scope verification of this deliverable to check if it satisfies project objectives.
B. Have an urgent meeting with the sponsor to discuss the situation.
C. Ignore the customer's concern and concentrate on the next deliverable to complete the project on time.
D. Assure the customer that the next deliverable will have additional features to meet and exceed his expectations.

196. One of your clients did not approve a major component that your team has just completed and requested several changes. You consider the component to be fully completed as per the specifications. It also meets all the required quality criteria. You were unable to come up with an agreement on the appropriate compensation for the changes the client was asking for. Both of you have been handling the disputes in accordance with the resolution procedures outlined in the contract. You are currently involved in:

A. Procurement negotiations
B. Procurement audits
C. Claims administration
D. Procurement performance review

197. One of the projects that you are currently managing has recently been canceled due to a change in marketplace conditions. What is your best course of action in this situation?

A. Renegotiate with the higher management to continue the project.
B. Gather lesson learned.
C. Complete the project deliverables.
D. No action is needed since the project is canceled.

198. Your organization has recently been awarded a fixed price contract and also received an SOW. As a project manager for the project, you will expect to see all of the following components in the SOW EXCEPT:

A. Business need
B. Product scope description or what is to be done
C. How the project supports the strategic plan
D. Market conditions

199. While reviewing the status of your project, you found that for a given time period your AC is $390,000 and PV is $380,000. You have a budget of $900,000 and so far have completed 40 percent of the work. What should you report to the management about your project?

A. The project is behind schedule and over budget.
B. The project is behind schedule but under budget.
C. The project is progressing according to the plan.
D. The project is ahead of schedule and under budget.

200. A noncompetitive form of procurement can be considered in all the following situations EXCEPT:

A. The project is under extreme time constraints and needs to be completed soon.
B. The law requires at least three quotations or proposals.
C. A seller has unique qualifications that no other sellers have.
D. There is no other seller except one who can provide the goods or services.

Final Exam Answers

1. B: Even though the project manager spends a great deal of energy and time preventing problems, there are still problems that need to be resolved. Below is the problem-solving technique:
   - Define the cause of the problem (not just the symptoms)
   - Analyze the problem (cause and effect diagram)
   - Identify solutions
   - Implement the selected solution
   - Review the solution
   - Confirm that the solution solved the problem

Here the project manager probably forgot to confirm that the solution actually solved the problem.

2. B: Stakeholder identification will continue throughout the project life cycle. As the project proceeds through each phase, additional stakeholders may become involved while others will be released. Stakeholder identification is conducted primarily by the project management team, but some stakeholders may be identified in the project charter. Stakeholders may include people and organizations that may be affected either negatively or positively by the project outcome.

3. A: The initial investment is $400,000. There are 4 quarters (3 months in each) in a year thus
Cash inflows for the first year is 4 * $40,000 = $160,000
So in two years the cash inflow will be $160,000 * 2 = $320,000
In the first quarter of the third year the cash inflow will be $80,000, thus total cash inflow by that time will be $320,000 + $80,000 = $400,000 which is equivalent to the initial investment.
The payback is 2 years and 3 months since it will take this amount of time to get the initial investment back. The second project has a longer payback period so we should go for the first project.

4. D: The Control Quality process is about monitoring specific project results to determine if they comply with relevant quality standards and identifying ways to eliminate causes of unsatisfactory results. Monitoring adherence to the project scope is addressed in the Control Scope process, not in the Control Quality process.

5. C: Risk averse is someone who does not want to take risks, and the project manager seems to be part of such an organization. Risk neutral describes a person or an organization indifferent to risk. Risk seeker suggests an aptitude to take risks with an opportunity for higher returns. Risk lover is a made-up term.

6. C: This is an example of constraints. Constraints are limitations that limit the available options for a project.

7. A: Product analysis techniques such as product breakdown, systems analysis, system engineering, value engineering, value analysis, functional analysis, and others, may be used to perform a detailed analysis of the product, service, or result. This technique translates project objectives into tangible deliverables and requirements by improving the project team's understanding of the product.

8. D: Negotiated settlement is used as a tool & technique in the Close Procurements process. The key objective of negotiated settlement is the settlement of all outstanding issues, claims, and disputes if possible.

9. C: Once the project scope has been completed, validated and final delivery has been made, the project is considered to be completed. Any kind of disputes should be resolved in favor of the customers as much as possible, but the project manager should also be aware that customers are not always right and should resist in this sort of situation. Once the project is completed, any addition to the project should be considered as a new project, and detailed impact analysis should be carried out.

10. A: A configuration management system is the subset of the Project Management Information System (PMIS) that describes the different versions and characteristics of the product, service, or result of the project and ensures accuracy and completeness of the description. It is all about managing different configurations of a product. At some point in time, a product will be base lined, and different configurations, versions, and branches are managed from that point. The process improvement plan looks at processes and outlines the activities and steps that will enhance their value. Perform Integrated Change Control is the process necessary for reviewing change requests and, approving or disapproving, and managing changes to the deliverables, project management plan and documents, and the organizational process assets. A work authorization system is a formal, documented procedure to describe how to authorize and initiate work in the correct sequence at the appropriate time.

11. A:

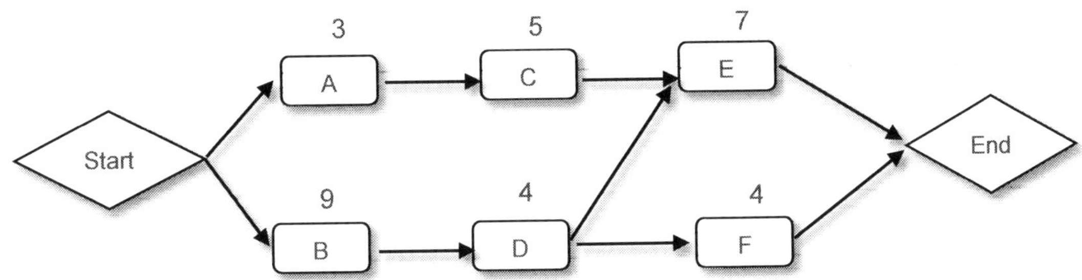

We have three paths in the network diagram as below:
Start, A, C, E, End = 15 wks.
Start, B, D, F, End = 17 wks.
Start, B, D, E, End = 20 wks.
The duration of the critical path is 20 wks.

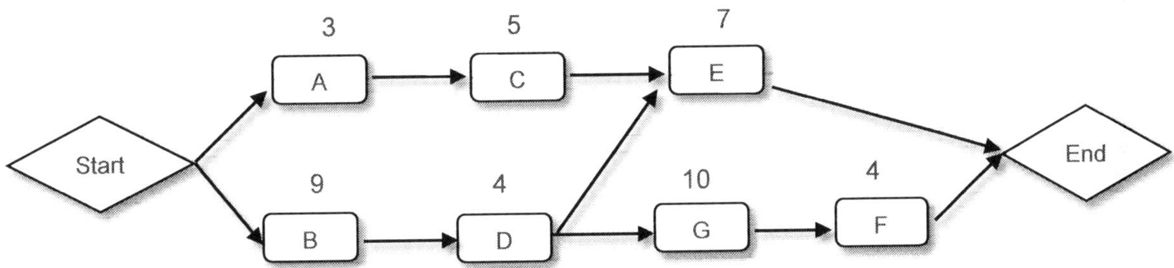

After adding the new activity G we have a new critical path – Start, B, D, G, F, End = 27 wks. The old duration of the project was 20 weeks thus additional 27 – 20 = 7 wks will be added to the project to complete the new activity G.

12. D: Victor Vroom's Expectancy theory demonstrates that employees who believe their efforts will lead to effective performance and who expect to be rewarded for their accomplishments remain productive as rewards meet their expectations.

13. B: Plan Communications is included in the planning process, which is generally completed prior to executing. Updates to the project plan, including the communications management plan, will occur during the entire project life cycle.

14. B: Noncritical risks on the watchlist are not only for historical use, but also need to be monitored at intervals during the project to ensure they have not become critical.

15. C: The nature and structure of a PMO depends on the needs of the organization it supports. The projects supported by a PMO may not be related other than being managed together.

16. A: The subject matter and topics discussed in the meeting may be important, but meetings are considered as informal verbal.

17. D: As per Herzberg's Motivator-Hygiene theory, hygiene factors are not sufficient to motivate people, and motivating agents provide the best positive reinforcement. Hygiene factors can destroy motivation, but improving them under most circumstances will not improve motivation.

18. C: A robust change control process will ensure that only the necessary changes are considered and implemented. A change control process cannot really help with the number of changes that will be requested in the project as the number of changes depend on how well defined the scope of the project is. Again, all stakeholders, regardless of their authority, should be able to submit change requests.

19. B: Constraints are restrictions, such as limitations on time, budget, scope, quality, schedule, resource, and technology a project faces. An imposed deadline and budget are examples of constraints.

20. B: Estimate at Completion (EAC) = BAC / CPI
Here we have BAC = $3,000, AC = $2,000 and EV = $1,200
CPI = EV / AC = 1200 / 2000 =.6
So EAC = 3000 / .6 = 5,000

21. A: A tornado diagram is a diagramming method to display sensitivity analysis data by examining all the uncertain elements at their baseline values. It gives a quick overview of how much the project will be impacted by various elements. The element with the greatest impact on the project appears at the top. This diagram can be used to determine sensitivity in cost, time, and quality objectives and is helpful in determining detailed response plans for elements with greater impacts.

22. D: Ishikawa diagram is a tool used for systematically identifying and presenting all the possible causes and sub causes of a particular problem in a graphical format. It can help in quality control by identifying the causes which contributed to a quality problem.

23. D: Lag is an inserted waiting time between activities. In this case, there is a 3 day delay before we can start coding.

24. A: Funding limit reconciliation is a technique of reconciling the expenditure of funds with the funding limits set for the project. As per the variance between the expenditure of funds and planned limit, the activities can be rescheduled to level out the rates of expenditures.

25. D: Configuration management plan is a subset of the project management information system (PMIS) that describes the different versions and characteristics of the product, service, or result of the project and ensures accuracy and completeness of the description.

26. A: Crashing is a technique of adding additional resources to a project activity to complete it in less time. Examples of crashing could include approving overtime, bringing in additional resources, or paying to expedite delivery to activities on the critical path. Crashing does not always produce a viable alternative and may result in increased risk, more management time, and/or cost. Increasing the number of resources may decrease time, but not in a linear amount as activities will often encounter the law of diminishing returns.

27. A: You are in the Validate Scope process, which is closely related to the Control Quality process. Both the Control Quality and Validate Scope processes can be performed simultaneously, but Control Quality is usually performed prior to Validate Scope. Control Quality verifies correctness of the work, whereas Validate Scope confirms completeness. Control Quality is focused on measuring specific project results against quality specifications and standards, whereas Validate Scope is mainly focused on obtaining acceptance of the product from the sponsor, customers, and others.

28. B: The project manager should document the change request as per the project scope management plan and then submit the change request to the change control board once the impact analysis is completed. The change control board will either approve or deny the request.

29. D: Iterative, incremental, and adaptive are different types of change-driven project life cycles.

30. B: GERT is a modified network diagram drawing method that allows conditional branches and loops between activities. For example, you may have two activities to design a software component and test it. Depending on the result of the testing, you may or may not redesign the component.

31. D: The Precedence Diagramming Method (PDM) usually uses the Activity-on-Node (AON) convention where boxes/nodes are used to represent activities and arrows show dependencies.

32. C: Product scope describes the features, functions, and physical characteristics that characterize a product, service, or result. On the other hand, project scope describes the work needed to deliver a product, service, or result with the specified features and functions. Product scope may include subsidiary components, and project scope results in a single product, service, or result. Product scope completion, measured against the product requirements to determine successful fulfillment and project scope completion, is measured against the project plan, project scope statement, Work Breakdown Structure (WBS), WBS dictionary, and other elements.

33. C: You should proactively work with stakeholders to manage their expectations, address their concerns, and resolve issues.

34. A: You are assuming that the current variances are atypical and similar variance will not occur in the future; thus, the rest of the job will be done as per budget; all you need to do is take the remaining work (BAC – EV) and add funds spent, AC.

35. C: The schedule management plan defines how the project schedule will be planned, developed, managed, executed, and controlled throughout the project life cycle. It serves as guidance for the scheduling process and defines the roles and responsibilities for stakeholders, along with scheduling methodologies, tools, schedule change control procedures, reporting formats, and frequencies.

36. D: An external dependency is related to a non-project activity and is considered outside the control of the project team. This is an example of external dependency since the other project manager does not have control over the completion of the server setup but the project has a dependency on it.

37. B: Vendor bids, especially the winning ones from qualified vendors, are analyzed during the Estimate Costs process.

Cost baseline is a time-phased budget used to monitor, measure, and control cost performance during the project. It is developed by summarizing costs over time and is usually displayed in the form of an S-curve. This suggests that the cost starts off low and then accelerates throughout the later phases of the project gradually slowing down during the closing.

38. C: In iterative relationships, a phase is planned at a given time; planning for a subsequent phase is carried out as work progresses on the current phase or deliverables. In overlapping relationships, the successor phase can start prior to the completion of the predecessor phase. This approach can be applied as a schedule compression technique called "fast-tracking." This kind of relationship may increase project risk and the potential for conflicts as a subsequent phase progresses before the accurate information is available from the previous phase. This kind of relationship can reduce the ability to develop long-term planning, but it is very suitable in an undefined, uncertain, and rapidly changing environment.

39 D: Incentive is a bonus in addition to the agreed-upon price for exceeding time or cost objectives as specified in the contract. For the seller, the focus is on profit, and for buyers, the focus can be a combination of cost, time, and performance. Incentives help bring the seller's objectives in line with those of the buyer. With an incentive, both the buyer and seller work toward the same objective—for instance, completing the project on time. In this specific situation, an incentive will be most effective. Force majeure is an allowable excuse for either party for not meeting contractual obligations in the event of something considered to be an act of God, such as fire, storm, flood, and freak electrical storm. Since the event is considered to be neither party's fault, usually the seller receives a time extension, and risk of loss is borne by the seller, which is usually covered by insurance. Time is of the essence indicates that delivery dates are extremely important and that any delay will be considered as a material breach. With a retainage clause, in order to ensure full completion, an amount of money, usually 5 to 10 percent is withheld from each payment and paid in full once the final work is completed.

40. B: Value analysis is also referred to as "value engineering" or "value methodology." It is the technique of finding a less costly way to do the same work and of achieving more out of the project in every possible way to increase the bottom line, decrease costs, improve quality, and optimize the schedule without reducing or impacting the scope.

41. C: The project manager is in the process of determining the project budget. The cost baseline and the project funding requirements are outputs of the Determine Budget process.

42. B: Both the SPI and CPI are less than one, which suggests that the project is behind schedule and over budget. An activity with no buffer suggests that it is on the critical path. If a critical path activity takes longer and needs more manpower to complete, then it will obviously negatively impact both time and cost. The subcontractor who was replaced may not be working on a critical path activity. Purchasing an expensive piece of equipment will definitely add additional cost, but it will not necessarily add time. The client may add or reduce the scope, so there is a possibility that it will reduce the cost and time.

43. D: Your first course of action should be to find out more information about what happened so that you can chose the correct course of action. Meeting with the stakeholders and finding out the details will assist you to address the crisis. Since the problem has occurred, the next thing you should do as a project manager is address the risk. You accept the risk when you have no other option. As a project manager, you would use your available reserves in this kind of situation. The contingency reserves are for "known unknowns;" thus, you use them to pay for risks that you've planned for. You may need to use the management reserves as they are for "unknown unknowns," or problems that you did not plan for but they showed up anyway. Once the issue is addressed, you may need to reevaluate your risk identification process, look for unexpected effects of the problem, inform management, update the risk management plan, create a fallback plan, and take corrective and preventive actions.

44. D: A quality audit is a scheduled or random structured review performed by internal or third-party auditors to determine whether quality management activities comply with organizational and project processes, policies, and procedures. It ascertains inefficient and ineffective activities and processes used in the project as well as lessons learned, such as gaps and best practices, that can improve the performance of the current project or future ones. A quality audit to correct any deficiencies in the quality processes should result in a reduced cost of quality and an increase in stakeholders' acceptance of the product.

45. B: In chapter 6, project time management, we learned the following two formulas:

Standard Deviation (SD) = $\frac{P-O}{6}$

Variance = $[\frac{P-O}{6}]^2$

We can see that variance is the square of standard deviation, so if we take the square root of variance, we will also get the standard deviation. We also know that total SD cannot be calculated by adding up the SD of two processes. We need to add the variances and then take the square root of the sum to get the SD. In this case, the SD for product variation is 0.7 inches and the measurement variation is 0.5 inches.

0.7 * 0.7 = 0.49 and 0.5 * 0.5 = 0.25. So, total SD is the square root of (0.49 + 0.25) = 0.86.

46. A: A marginal analysis refers the point where the benefits or revenue from improving quality equals the incremental cost to achieve that quality.

47. A: The goal of team performance assessments is to identify the specific training, coaching, mentoring, assistance, or changes required to improve the team's performance and effectiveness. The project management team makes formal or informal assessments of the project team's effectiveness while team development efforts, such as training, team building, and colocation are implemented. A team's performance is measured against the agreed-upon success criteria, schedule, and budget target.
The evaluation of a team's effectiveness may include indicators such as:

- How well the team is performing, communicating, and dealing with conflicts
- Areas of improvement in skills that will help individuals perform assignments more efficiently and areas of improvement in competencies that will help the team perform better as a team
- Increased cohesiveness where team members work together to improve the overall project performance by sharing information and experiences openly and helping each other more frequently
- Reduced staff turnover rate

48. A: Referent power is based on referring to someone in a higher position to leverage some of the superior's power. Penalty (coercive/punishment) is predicated on fear and gives the project manager the ability to penalize a team member for not meeting the project goals and objectives. Expert power is based on the knowledge or skill of a project manager on a specific domain. Being the subject matter expert or project management expert will give the project manager substantial power to influence and control team members. Reward power imposes positive reinforcement, and it is the ability of giving rewards and recognition.

49. D: This is an example of fixed cost since regardless of how many times the team will use the tools they will pay $3,000/month.

50. B: Project staff assignments are the output in the Acquire Project Team process. The human resource management plan is an output of the Plan Human Resource Management process, team performance assessments is an output of the Develop Project Team process, and change requests is an output in the Manage Project Team process.

51. B: Termination for convenience is a contract clause that permits the buyer to terminate a contract at any time for a cause or convenience. Usually there will be specific conditions associated with the execution of this clause.

52. D: Issues and risks are not the same thing. An issue is an obstacle that threatens project progress and can block the team from achieving its goals. Risk is an uncertain event or condition that may have a positive or negative effect on the project's objective if it occurs.

53. C: In Abraham Maslow's Hierarchy of Needs, accomplishment, respect, attention, and appreciation are represented as esteem.

54. C: A bottom-up estimate is the most time-consuming and generally the most accurate estimate. In this technique, one estimate per activity is received from the team members. This estimate can be based on expert judgment, historical information, or an educated guess. A rough order of magnitude is an approximate estimate (–25 percent to 75 percent) made without detailed data. It is used during the formative stages for initial evaluation of a project's feasibility. A heuristic estimate is based on rule of thumb, such as the 80/20 rule. A top-down estimate is usually given to the project manager from management or the sponsor. This type of estimate measures the project parameters, such as budget, size, complexity, and duration based on the parameters of a previous similar project and historical information. It is usually done during an early phase of the project when not much information is available; thus, it is less accurate even though it is less costly and less time consuming.

55. B: The tendency to rate high or low on all factors due to the impression of a high or low rating on a specific factor is known as the Halo effect. This kind of action has negative impacts on the project and the performing organization.

56. A: Withdrawing or avoiding is the technique of retreating from conflict and avoiding or postponing resolution. This technique leads to the least sustaining positive results.

57. C: A flow chart helps the project team anticipate and identify where quality problems might occur in a project, which in turn, helps the team develop alternatives when dealing with quality problems.

58. A: Project communications is an output of the Manage Communications process. All other items listed are included in the communications management plan.

59. B: The contingency plan is the specific action that will be taken if opportunities or threats occur.

60. C: Urgency is not included in the basic communications model but should be considered when determining the method of communication to be used.

61. D: A project manager should always be truthful in his/her communications and should provide accurate information in a timely manner. A project manager should not deceive others or make misleading half-truths or false statements. None of the options listed in 'A,' 'B,' or 'C' will resolve this issue immediately, and Steve should inform the stakeholder that he needs a little more time to verify the information about the major component and will follow up with him/her shortly when he has an accurate update.

62. D: Avoid is the elimination of the threat by eliminating the cause or changing the project management plan. Here you utilized the avoid strategy by terminating the contract with the subcontractor to eliminate the threat to your project.

63. A. Value engineering is mainly focused on finding a less costly way to do the same work and on achieving more out of the project in every possible way to increase the bottom line, decrease costs, improve quality, and optimize the schedule without reducing or impacting the scope.

64. C: Enhance is a strategy to deal with an opportunity. By influencing the underlying risk triggers, this strategy increases the size, probability, likelihood, and positive impact of an opportunity.

65. A: Assumptions are not based on factual information, and failure to validate an assumption may result in significant risk events. Assumptions are usually documented during the project initiating and planning processes. These assumptions are not absolute and can be negotiable. Assumptions do not limit the project team's options for decision making, however constraints do. Assumptions also do not allow for baseline adjustments in case of project crisis as it's not the correct process for adjusting project baselines.

66. C: Perform Qualitative Risk Analysis is the process of prioritizing risks by assessing and combining their probability of occurrence and impact to the project if they occur. This fast, relatively easy to perform, and cost effective process ensures that the right emphasis is on the right risk areas as per their ranking and priority and helps to allocate adequate time and resources for them. Even though numbers are used for the rating in Perform Qualitative Risk Analysis, it is a subjective evaluation and should be performed throughout the project. Perform Quantitative Risk Analysis is the process of numerically analyzing the effect of overall project objectives of identified risks. It mostly performs numerical analysis using a modeling technique such as Expected Monetary Value (EMV) of the probability and impact of risks moved forward from the Perform Qualitative Risk Analysis process.

67. D: A project manager should understand the significance of this sort of findings and must consult the experts before proceeding further.

68. A: Any time you come across a new risk, the first thing you should do is document it in the risk register and then analyze the impact as well as the probability of that risk. You should not take any further action until you've analyzed the risk.

69. D: Sensitivity analysis helps to determine which risks have the most potential impact on a project, or in other words, whether the occurrence of a particular threat would merely be an inconvenience or whether it would ruin the project. A tornado diagram can be used to display the sensitivity analysis data by examining all the uncertain elements at their baseline values. It gives a quick overview of how much the project will be impacted by various elements, and the element with the greatest impact on the project appears at the top. This diagram can be used to determine sensitivity in cost, time, and quality objectives and will be helpful to determine a detailed response plan for the elements with greater impacts.

70. D: A resource calendar shows who is and who is not available to work during any given time period. The resource calendar may consider attributes such as experience, skill level, expertise, capabilities, and geographical locations for human resources to identify the best resources and their availability.
A project team directory includes information about the team members, such as name, contact details, role, and functional area. A Responsibility Assignment Matrix (RAM) is a chart that cross-references team members with the activities or work packages they are to accomplish. One example of a RAM is a RACI (Responsible, Accountable, Consult, and Inform) chart, which can be used to ensure clear divisions of roles and responsibilities. A Resource Breakdown Structure (RBS) is a graphical and hierarchical structure of the identified resources arranged by resource category (such as labor, material, equipment, and supplies) and type (such as expertise level, grade, and experience).

71. B: We know PV = $\frac{FV}{(1+r)^n}$
Initial cost = $6,000 and interest rate= 10 percent
So present value for the first project is $10,000 / $(1+.1)^2$ = $9,009
The other project has a bigger NPV of $9,500. So we should select the second project.

72. A: EVA = After Tax Profit – (Capital expenditures * Cost of Capital)
= 14,000 – (210,000 * .04) = $5600
ABC gained $5600 as determined by EVA.

73. A:

Month	PV	EV	AC
Month1	$30,000	$27,000	$25,000
Month2	$35,000	$40,000	$45,000
Month3	$90,000	$80,000	$70,000
Month4	$150,000	$125,000	$89,000

The cumulative AC for all four months was $25,000 + $45,000 + $ 70,000 + $89,000 = $229,000
The cumulative PV for all four months was $30,000 + $35,000 + $90,000 + $150,000 = $305,000
The cumulative EV for all four months was $ 27,000 + $ 40,000 + $ 80,000 + $125,000 = $272,000
We know $CPI^c = EV^c/AC^c$, so CPI^c = $ 272,000 / $229,000 = 1.18
And $SPI^c = EV^c/PV^c$, so SPI^c = $ 272,000 / $305,000 = .891

74. B: Once the WBS is created with all the work packages, the team members should work on decomposing the work packages to create the detailed activity list. Network diagram and activity sequencing can be performed only after the activity list is created.

75. A: You have completed only 20 * 75 percent = 15 miles of the railway so far. 20 miles of railway project was supposed to be finished in 40 weeks so, every mile is to be completed in 2 weeks. In this case only 75% or 15 miles of railway is completed in 40 weeks, thus, every mile is completed in 40 / 15 = 2.66 weeks. At this rate, remaining 20 – 15 = 5 miles of railway will take another 5 * 2.66 = 13.3 weeks.

76. B: Some changes in the project are inevitable. A project manager should make sure that the change requests are evaluated and presented to the CCB for review. The project manager should not have the attitude to deny changes whenever possible. The focus of the project manager should be to prevent unnecessary changes, evaluate the impacts, and manage changes as necessary.

77. B: Risk mitigation simply means a reduction in the probability and/or impact of an adverse risk event to an acceptable threshold. Leasing the equipment reduces the consequence of the threat in this specific situation.

78. A: The standard deviation measures how diverse the population is in the data set. It is calculated by finding out the mean, then calculating the average of the distance of each data point from the mean.

79. A: You have 20 miles to complete at a rate of $10,000/mile. Your budget at completion is 20*10,000 = $200,000.

80. A: Perform Quantitative Risk Analysis is the process of numerically analyzing the effect of overall project objectives of identified risks. It mostly performs a numerical analysis of the probability and impact of risks moved forward from the Perform Qualitative Risk Analysis process. A small project with limited budget may consider skipping this process if management decides that quantitative statements about risk and impact are not needed.

81. B: Invitation for Bid (IFB/request for Bid (RFB): Request from a buyer for all potential sellers to submit a total price bid for work to be performed. Request for Proposal (RFP): Buyer's request to all potential sellers for the details of how work will be performed. Request for Quotation (RFQ): Buyer's request to all potential sellers for a price quote per item, hour, foot or other unit of measure.

82. A: Variety of work is a motivational agent, not a hygiene factor.

83. D: RACI is a type of responsibility assignment matrix chart which can be used to ensure clear divisions of roles and responsibilities (RACI stands for responsible, accountable, consult, and inform). SWOT analysis, assumption analysis, brainstorming – an information gathering technique are used to identify risks in the project.

84. C: How changes to the requirements will be handled and configuration management activities are documented as a part of the requirements management plan which is an output of the Plan Scope Management process.

85. C: Work authorization system is a formal, documented procedure to describe how to authorize and initiate work in the correct sequence at the appropriate time. The other options listed here could be contributory factors, but most likely a work authorization procedure was either not properly established or not properly followed.

86. C: Fait accompli is a negotiation tactic of using rules/laws, decisions already made, etc., as mandatory to avoid any further discussion. Personal insults are a negotiation tactic of attacking an individual. Good guy/bad guy is a negotiation tactic of making one person helpful to the other party while making another person very difficult to work with during negotiation. Missing man is a negotiation tactic of using a missing individual who has the power to everything.

87. B: If CPI or past results are typical or expected to continue, the correct EAC formula is EAC = BAC/CPI.
In this case, BAC = $90,000
CPI = EV / AC = $ 35,000 / $30,000 = 1.16
EAC = $90,000 / 1.16 = $77,586

88. B: Procurement performance review is a structured review that consists of seller-prepared documentation, buyer inspection, and a quality audit of the seller's progress to deliver project scope and quality within cost and on schedule

as compared to the contract. The objective is to identify performance progress or failures, noncompliances, and areas where performance is a problem. Inspections and audits are activities mainly focused on the product itself and its conformance to specification. Performance reporting is an excellent tool that provides management with information about how effectively the seller is meeting contractual objectives. This report can produce earned values, schedule and cost performance index, and trend analysis. The payment system is usually handled by the accounts payable system of the buyer organization and helps avoid duplicate payments, ensures invoices and payments match up, and ensures that the right amount has been invoiced for the appropriate deliverables at the right time.

89. D: The cruise company is using the enhance strategy to increase the traffic and profitability. By influencing the underlying risk triggers, this strategy increases the size, probability, likelihood, and positive impact of an opportunity.

90. D: Anytime the vendor is not following the instructions stated in the contract, the project manager should inform the vendor that they are in default. Without informing the vendor about the concern and what they are doing wrong, you cannot terminate the contract. You also cannot simply stop any payment.

91. A. The scope management plan and requirements management plan are the outputs of the Plan Scope Management process.

92. C: Earned value analysis is used to integrate scope, cost, and schedule measures to assess project performance. Trend analysis and variance analysis are included in earned value analysis. Variance analysis may include only a comparison of actual performance with one specific baseline. Presentations may be used to deliver information obtained during earned value analysis.

93. D: A Flowchart is a graphical representation of a process to help analyze how problems occur and to identify potential process improvement opportunities. There are many styles, but all flowcharts show activities, decision points, the order of processing, points of complexity, and interrelationships between elements in the process.

94. C: According to Herzberg, destroying hygiene factors such as working conditions, salary, status, and security can destroy motivation, but improving them under most circumstances will not improve motivation. The hygiene factors are not sufficient to motivate people, and motivating agents provide the best positive reinforcement. Motivating people is best done by rewarding and letting people grow.

95. D: Parametric estimating is a technique that reviews historical data for statistical correlations. Variables are then used to estimate the costs in the current project. For example, if historical information identifies that the flooring installed in a similar project cost $1.50 per square foot, then the 20,000 square feet of flooring required for the new project would cost $30,000. Typically, this technique has been known to produce a high level of accuracy, but it will be costly due to the level of sophistication that is required to implement it. In most cases, the technique is performed when the performing organization conducts many similar projects, historical information is accurate, and the model used for the estimate is scalable.

96. C: Critical Path Method (CPM) is a technique of schedule analysis that considers activity durations, logical relationships, dependencies, leads, lags, assumptions, and constraints to determine the float of each activity and the overall schedule. This method identifies the critical path with the least flexibility and the highest risk so that it can be managed appropriately.

97. B: You just finished the Plan Procurement Management process and should be moving to the next process of Conduct Procurements. In Conduct Procurement process you should be obtaining and evaluating seller responses, selecting a seller, and awarding a contract. The tools and techniques you will be using in Conduct Procurement process are bidder conference, proposal evaluation techniques, and independent estimates.

98. A: Perform Quality Assurance is a process to determine if the project activities are complying with organizational and project policies, standards, processes, and procedures. This process is primarily concerned with overall process improvement and does not deal with inspecting the product for quality or measuring defects. The primary focus is on steadily improving the processes and activities undertaken to achieve quality.

99. A: Performance reporting is a tool & technique in the Manage Communications process, not in the Plan Communications Management process. Communication requirement analysis, communication methods, and communication technology are tools & techniques in Plan Communications Management process.

100. C: Source selection criteria is not an output of the Conduct Procurements process; it is an output of the Plan Procurement Management process. It is developed and used to provide sellers with an understanding of the buyer's need and also to help them in deciding whether to bid or make a proposal on the project. Later on, it also helps to evaluate sellers by rating or scoring them.

101. C: A scatter diagram is a tool and technique used in quality management processes to analyze two characteristics of a process and see if there is any interdependency between them. Based on the outcome of the scatter diagram, appropriate actions can be taken to improve quality.

102. A: Let n equal the number of months when both options' cost will be the same
((2000 * 10) + 2000) n = 180,000 + 4000 n or (20,000 + 2,000) n = 180,000 + 4000 n
or 22,000 n = 180,000 + 4000 n or 18,000 n = 180,000 or n = 180,000/18,000 or n = 10

103. B: According to the learning curve theory, when a large number of items are produced repetitively, productivity will increase but at a diminishing rate. Learning curve data indicates that as work is repeated, the time required to complete the work is reduced, but the rate of improvement decreases. For instance, installing carpet in the fiftieth room in a construction project will take less time than it did in the first room due to increased efficiency as workers become more efficient with the installation procedure.

104. A: If there are no complaints or claims filed earlier, no term or condition in the contract is breached, and work is completed as per the SOW, then we will consider the contract to be complete. Note that it does not necessarily mean the contract is closed when we say that a contract is complete. The Close Procurements process must be carried on in order to close the contract.

105. D: Conduct Procurements is the process of obtaining seller responses, selecting a seller, and awarding the procurement, usually in the form of a contract. Plan Procurements is the process of documenting project purchasing decisions, specifying the approach, defining selection criteria to identify potential sellers, and putting together a procurement management plan. Procurement negotiation is not a process but is a tool & technique used in the Conduct Procurements process. The Close Procurements process is mainly concerned with completing each project procurement.

106. D: The very first thing the project manager should do upon receiving a change request is to evaluate the impact to the project objectives, such as scope, time, cost, quality, risk, resources, and others. The change request then should be submitted to the change control board for approval or rejection. Instructing the team member and informing the sponsor of the requested change would not be done prior to evaluating the impact of the requested change. Also, the project manager should make every effort to prevent unnecessary changes in the project as much as possible.

107. B: The cost baseline is a time-phased budget used to monitor, measure, and control cost performance during the project. It is developed by summarizing costs over time and is usually displayed in the form of an S-curve. This suggests that the cost starts off low, then accelerates throughout the later phases of the project, and gradually slows down during the closing.

108. A: The sunk cost is a retrospective cost that is already paid for a project and often used to describe what is written off from a canceled project as unrecoverable.

109. B: A records management system can include indexing, archiving, and retrieval systems to capture and store all documents, correspondence, and communication relevant to a contract. For some projects, every record such as e-mails, payments, and written and verbal communication, is recorded and stored.

110. C: You are performing a procurement performance review as part of the Control Procurements process. It is a structured review of the seller's progress to deliver project scope and quality within cost and on schedule, as compared to the contract.

111. C: Claims administration or handling of claims is one of the most frequent activities in the Control Procurements process. Claims, disputes, or appeals are requested when the buyer and seller disagree on the scope, the impact of changes, or the interpretation of some terms and conditions in the contract. All these claims should be documented, processed, monitored, and managed in accordance with the contract terms throughout the contract life cycle. It is desirable to resolve the disputes through negotiation, but unresolved claims may require escalation to dispute resolution procedures, such as arbitration or litigation, established in the contract.

112. C: In this case, the seller's failure to deliver the equipment on time will drastically impact the project. So the contract can be terminated with the vendor for defaulting. But in other instances, a contract can also be terminated for a convenience by the buyer.

113. B: According to McClelland's Achievement Motivation theory, individuals who work best when cooperating with others and working in a team, seek to maintain good relationships and approval rather than recognition, and perform well in customer-facing team positions have a need for affiliation or association. People with a need for achievements should be given projects that are challenging but reachable. These people may prefer to work alone and also like recognition. People who like to organize and influence others have a need for power.

114. C: Since a stakeholder register contains sensitive information, a project manager may publish it with other project documentation or keep it in reserve for personal use only.

115. D: Involving the stakeholders in some project activities is a good way to bring them to a supportive or a leading state.

116. C: Fixed price contract will be the best option in this case as this type of contract will have less risk for the buyer and most risk for the seller.

117. A: You should pay the fee since the fee has a valid purpose and should not be considered a bribe.

118. B: Final product, service, or result transition is an output in the Close Project or Phase process, not in the Direct and Manage Project Work process.

119. C: You should always try to have a win-win situation. The lowest possible price and shortest possible duration will put the vendor in an extremely difficult situation and increase the potential for failure. Your main objective of negotiation will be to build trust, obtain a fair and reasonable price that both parties are comfortable with, and uncover the points of conflict and dispute prior to final contract signing.

120. C: The bidder conference is also called the contractor conference, vendor conference, or pre-bid conference. It is intended to assure that no seller receives preferential treatment and that all sellers have a clear, common understanding of the procurement (technical requirements, contractual requirements, etc.). The key objective is to provide all potential contractors with the information they need to determine if they would like to continue with the contracting process. The bidder conference will ensure the mandatory standard of fairness in the PMI code of ethics and professional conduct by making the opportunity equally available to all qualified vendors.

121. C: You should have a discussion with the customer about any issue with the deliverable so that a mutual solution can be identified. Capturing the issue in the lessons learned will not solve the current problem. Issuing the deliverable as is and getting the formal acceptance will not serve the best interest of the customer.

122. C: If you cannot estimate the value of the impact, you can utilize qualitative estimates such as low, medium, high, and others. Qualitative Risk Analysis is the process of prioritizing risks by assessing and combining their probability of occurrence and impact to the project if they occur. This fast, relatively easy to perform, and cost effective process ensures that the right emphasis is on the right risk areas as per their ranking and priority and helps to allocate adequate time and resources for them. Even though numbers are used for the rating in the Perform Qualitative Risk Analysis process, it is a subjective evaluation and should be performed throughout the project.

123. C: Since the problem has occurred, the first thing you should do as a project manager is address the risk by creating a workaround. Once the issue is addressed, you may need to reevaluate your risk identification process, look for unexpected effects of the problem, inform management, update the risk management plan, create a fallback plan, and take corrective and preventive actions.

124. A: Giving special rewards to some employees, such as assigned parking spaces, corner offices, and executive dining, are considered perquisites. Fringe benefits are the standard benefits formally given to all employees, such as education benefits, health insurance, and profit sharing.

125. D: A project manager should actively listen to the stakeholders' concerns, resolve conflicts among the stakeholders, and build trust. The project manager should convey the ground rules to the team members, not to the stakeholders.

126. D: In this kind of situation you should always find out details of the design defect before you have a discussion about it with the sponsor or the customers. The very first thing you should do is to evaluate the impact of the design defect and have a brainstorming session with the team members on possible solutions.

127. C: A short delay of a critical path activity will result in an overall delay of the project duration so a change request should be created. A major delay of a non-critical path activity may not have any impact on the overall project duration. A project manager can use the contingency reserve to deal with the cost and schedule variances. Fast tracking and crashing methods can also be used to deal with schedule variance.

128. A: The only way to modify a contract is through a formal, written change request. This change request then follows the formal contract change control process. Contract change control system is a tool & technique in the Control Procurements process that defines the process by which procurements can be modified and includes change procedures, forms, dispute resolution processes, necessary paperwork, required authorizations, tracking systems, and other items.

129. D: Force majeure is a kind of clause that states that if a natural disaster such as fire, hurricane, freak electrical storm, tornado, etc., happens, the event will be an allowable cause for either party for not meeting contractual obligations, as the event is neither party's fault. These are considered to be acts of God, and in most cases, you should receive a time extension and the damage should be covered by insurance.

130. A: You should not release the team until the lessons learned are documented and added to the organizational process assets as you need their help with the lessons learned. Most contracts have payment terms that allow for some period of time before full payment is required thus the last thing you do on the project is close the contract.

131. A: When the project manager ascertains the current project status, it should be communicated to the project stakeholders as per the communications management plan.

132. D: Procurement negotiation is a tool & technique in the Conduct Procurements process, not in the Control Procurements process.

133. A: Process improvement activities including corrective actions, preventive actions, and defect repairs, are implemented in the Direct and Manage Project Work process.

134. B: Critical Path Method (CPM) is a technique of schedule analysis that evaluates the activities considering activity duration, logical relationship, dependency, leads, lags, assumptions, and constraints to determine the float of each activity and the overall schedule. This method identifies the critical path with the least flexibility and the highest risk so that it can be managed appropriately. The critical path duration is the longest path in the network diagram and the shortest amount of time the project will take to complete.

135. D: To identify the appropriate training for the team members, we should refer to the staffing management plan as it identifies the training needs and certification requirements of the team members.

136. C: Control Scope is the process of monitoring the status of the project and product scope, maintaining control over the project by preventing overwhelming scope change requests, and managing changes to the scope baseline. It also assures that underlying causes of all requested changes and recommended corrective actions are understood and processed through the Integrated Change Control Process.

137. A:

Target Cost	$250,000
Target Fee	$15,000
Actual Cost	$225,000
Sharing Ratio	75/25

Here target cost = $250,000, and actual cost = $225,000; thus, savings = $250,000 – $225,000 = $25,000.
Seller portion of savings is 25 percent of $25,000 = $6,250.
Buyer portion of savings is 75 percent of $25,000 = $18,750.
Final fee for seller is $15,000 + $6,250 = $21,250.
Thus, total cost for the buyer is $225,000 + 21,250 = $246,250. Again, initial cost was $250,000 + $15,000 = $265,000. Now the total cost is $246,250; thus, the buyer is saving $18,750.

138. C: Correlating the need for the project to the organizational strategic objective and goal is the best approach to gain support for the project from the performing organization. Organizational planning can establish the funding and support for the component projects on the basis of specific lines of business, risk categories, and other factors. An organization's strategic goals and objectives are the primary factor guiding investments. Projects, programs, or other related works that contribute the least to the portfolio's strategic objectives may lose the support of the performing organization as soon as there is a higher-priority project that is more oriented toward the strategic objective. It is a good idea to meet the personal objectives of the sponsor, but it will not confirm the support from the performing organization. Communicating the project details and benefits will not be sufficient enough to gain support from the performing organization.

139. C: Fast tracking is a schedule compression technique of performing critical path activities in parallel when they were originally planned in series. Crashing is another schedule compression technique of adding additional resources to project critical path activities to complete them more quickly. This technique looks at cost and schedule trade-offs and resources are added either from inside or outside the organization. Since some of the activities in the project can be performed in parallel and resources have not been fully utilized, we can use fast tracking and crashing in this project.

140. D: A bidder conference is intended to assure that no seller receives preferential treatment and that all sellers have a clear, common understanding of the procurement (technical requirements, contractual requirements, etc.). The bidder conference should help sellers determine if they should participate in the bidding process and submit their proposals.

141. A:

Target Cost	$355,000
Target Fee	$45,000
Actual Cost	$390,000
Sharing Ratio	75/25

There is a cost overrun of $390,000 – $355,000 = $35,000.
Seller portion of the cost overrun is 35,000 * 25 percent = $8,750.
So the final fee will be $45,000 – $8,750 = $36,250
The cost plus incentive fee contract shares the cost savings but could also result in reduced fees to the seller if there is a cost overrun.

142. D: Project constraints specify the limitations and restrictions, such as limitations on time, budget, scope, quality, schedule, resource, and technology a project faces.

143. A: The internal project has been formally approved recently so it should have an approved project charter. The project charter has the list of key stakeholders and their major expectations along with other project related information, thus it should be a good starting point for identifying key stakeholders.

144. B: The Monitoring and Controlling Project Work process usually measures the work results against the plan.

145. B: The cost of the risk is $15,000 + $20,000 = $35,000, so its EMV is 40 percent * – $35,000 = –$14,000. The value of the opportunity is $10,500 and its probability is 30 percent, so the EMV is 30 percent * $10,500 = $3,150. The total EMV for the two is –$14,000 + $3,150 = – $10,850.

146. A: A Checklist analysis is not an information gathering technique.

147. B: Stakeholder identification is a continuous and sometimes grueling process as not all stakeholders will be identified during the initiating process. Some of the stakeholders will only be interested in the end product and will get involved in the project at its closing. Stakeholders with both positive and negative influence should be listed in the stakeholder register. All of the stakeholders should be treated equally, and change requests should be prioritized according to project need. Giving stakeholders extras or gold plating is not a preferred way to meet and exceed stakeholder expectations.

148. B: Perform Quality Assurance is the process to determine if the project activities are complying with organizational and project policies, standards, processes, and procedures. This process is primarily concerned with overall process improvement and does not deal with inspecting the product for quality or measuring defects. The primary focus is on steadily improving the processes and activities undertaken to achieve quality. Below are the key functionalities in this process:

- Identify ineffective and inefficient activities or processes used in the project.
- Perform continuous improvement as appropriate.
- Perform quality audit to determine if project activities comply with organization and project policies, processes, and procedures.
- Identify required improvements, gaps, and shortcomings in the processes.
- Identify and correct deficiencies.
- Recommend changes and corrective actions to integrated change control.

149. D: Risk register is an output of the Identify Risks process. SWOT analysis and information gather techniques such as brainstorming and Delphi techniques are used in the Identify Risks process in order to identify and categorize potential risks in the project.

150. B: A product fix will require rework and the cost associated with it will fall under the cost of nonconformance internal failure cost category.

151. D: A qualified sellers list is a list of preapproved or prequalified prospective sellers interested and capable of doing the contract services for the organization. Prequalified sellers for a project are entered into the procurement management plan, which is part of the project management plan, as an output of the Plan Procurement process. The qualified seller list is used as an input in the Conduct Procurement process, and not as a tool and technique.

152. D: An approved change request for corrective actions, preventive actions, and defect repairs will be implemented in the Direct and Manage Project Work process.

153. B: The project is 5 months long so every month you are scheduled to complete 20 percent of the work.

We know PV = BAC * planned % complete
After two months the Planned Value (PV) should be $450,000 * 40 percent = $ 180,000
We know EV = BAC * actual % complete
After two months you completed 35 percent of the work so the Earned Value (EV) is $450,000 * 35 percent = $157,500

We know SPI = EV/PV = 157,000 / 180,000 = .872. SPI less than 1 indicates that the project is behind schedule.

154. B: We will select Project Beta since it has a larger NPV. The number of years is irrelevant here since it is already factored into the NPV. We are not selecting Project Alpha which has a NPV of $45,000. The opportunity cost for the Project Beta will be the value of the project that we did not select or the opportunity that we missed out, in this case Project Alpha.

155. B: Make-or-buy decision is the input in the Conduct Procurements process, not make-or-buy analysis. Make-or-buy analysis is determining whether a product can be cost effectively produced in-house or whether it should be purchased, leased, or rented. While performing this analysis, we must consider indirect as well as direct costs, availability in addition to related risk, and schedule. Make-or-buy decisions document the decisions and justification regarding what project products, services, or results will either be acquired or developed by the project team.

156. A: The best option is to verify your observation by having a discussion with your employer about the violations and learn about the employer's perspective.

157. C: The project charter may contain the high-level budget but not the detailed cost estimates. You should inform the hospital authority that they have to wait as the project budget and the cost baseline will be finalized and accepted in the planning process group.

158. A: A project charter identifies the high level business objectives and needs, current understanding of the stakeholders' expectations, and the new product, service, or result that the project is intended to satisfy. The project charter is developed in the initiating phase, but project scope statement document is developed in the Define Scope process in planning phase.

159. C: Referent power is based on referring to someone in a higher position to leverage some of the superior's power. This power is also based on the respect or the charismatic personality of the project manager.

160. C: Resource leveling is used to produce a resource-limited schedule by letting the schedule slip and cost increase in order to deal with a limited amount of resources, resource availability, and other resource constraints. It can be used when shared or critically required resources are only available at certain times, in limited quantities, or when resources have been over-allocated. We may have several peaks and valleys in our resource histogram. In order to level the resources, evenly utilize them as much as possible, or to keep resource usage at a constant level, we can move some of our activities from the week when we are using many resources to a week when we are hardly using any.

161. B: A Change Control Board (CCB) consists of members including stakeholders, managers, project team members, senior management, and other people, and it is responsible for reviewing, approving, or denying change requests. Some organizations have permanent CCB staffed by full-time employees to manage changes for the entire organization, not only for the projects. The project manager should consider establishing a CCB for the project if the organization does not have one.

162. B: While performing the project performance appraisals, the project management team meets with the team members and provides feedback about team members' performance and how effectively they are performing their tasks. A 360 degree feedback is used to receive feedback from all directions including peers, superiors and subordinates, and sometimes includes vendors and external contractors.

163. C: Ishikawa diagram, or cause and effect diagram, is a tool used to systematically identify and present all the possible causes and sub causes of a particular problem in a graphical format. It can help in quality control by identifying the causes that contributed to a specific quality problem. Cause and effect diagrams are particularly useful for identifying the causes of risks.

164. C: The project was unsuccessful as it has been gold plated. We should always focus to meet and exceed customer expectations by delivering the features and functionalities as per the requirement specification approved by the clients. Gold plating or giving extras to the clients should be avoided by all means.

165. D: Your SPI is more than 1, which indicates that you are ahead of schedule, but your CPI is less than 1, which suggests that you are over budget. Cost should be the main concern in this project at this time.

166. A: Colocation/war room is a technique of placing many or all of the most active project team members in the same physical location to enhance their ability to perform as a team. Since all the team members are in the same building and having meetings in the same meeting room most of the time already, colocation is not a technique we should be considering in this case. Other techniques listed here will be beneficial to resolve conflict and concern about deliverables.

167. D: The stakeholder register contains all details related to the identified stakeholders including, but not limited to:

- Stakeholder classification: Internal/external, neutral/resistor/ supporter, and others.
- Identification information: Name, title, location, organization, role in the project, position, and contact information.
- Assessment information: Key requirements and expectations, potential impact, importance, and influence on the project.

Stakeholder management plan, an output of the Plan Stakeholder Management process contains stakeholder management strategy. The stakeholder management strategy defines an approach to manage stakeholders throughout the entire project life cycle. It defines the strategies to increase the support of the stakeholders who can impact the project positively and minimize the negative impacts or intentions of the stakeholders who can negatively impact the project.

168. C: Anything that interferes with the meaning of a message is considered noise or a communication blocker. Source credibility, or the credibility of a message to its receivers, may be influenced by receivers' level of trust in the communicator. This may act as a distraction in effective communication.

169. C: Cost aggregation describes the bottom-up estimate, which will provide the most accurate estimate in this case. Other estimates such as heuristic and analogous specified in other choices are very quick, but will not produce the most accurate estimate. Three-point estimate is also not the best option in this scenario.

170. A: A project can be terminated at any time due to a specific reason or convenience. The project manager should conduct a scope verification to measure the amount of completed work up to the cancellation. All other options can be done once the scope verification is completed and the project manager has the details about the current situation.

171. D: Your project can move into a subsequent phase even if the deliverables of the prior phase are not completely

approved. Any scope change in the initial stage will be the least expensive and consume the least amount of time. Stakeholder influence is highest at the start and diminishes as the project proceeds. You will mostly acquire your team members during the project executing phase.

172. D: Attribute sampling is a method of measuring quality that consists of observing the presence (or absence) of some characteristics (attributes) in each of the units under consideration to determine whether to accept a lot, reject it, or inspect another lot.

173. B: Rolling wave planning takes the progressive elaboration approach and plans in great detail current/near term work while future work is planned in a more abstract and less detailed way. During the early strategic planning phase, work packages may be decomposed into less defined milestone levels as all details are not available. At a later date, they will be decomposed into detailed activities. This kind of planning is frequently used in IT and research projects where unknowns tend to be intangibles but less so in construction projects where unknowns are generally extremely expensive and destructive.

174. C: Plurality is a group decision making technique where a decision is based on the largest block in a group even if a majority is not achieved. Since PMO permits plurality you have no option but to agree with the largest block in the group. Asking PMO to reevaluate their policy will not resolve the problem immediately.

175. A: An analogous estimate measures the project parameters, such as budget, size, complexity and duration based on the parameters of a previous, similar project and historical information. It is usually done during an early phase of the project when not much information is available.

176. C: Upper and lower control limits are usually set as + –3 Sigma – 99.73 percent occurrences will fall within 3 sigma from the mean.

177. C: As a project is refined, iterative process groups might be revisited and revised several times throughout the project life cycle as more information becomes available. Some planning must take place, then some executing, then some monitoring controlling processes, followed by further planning, further executing, and so on. Initiating and closing process groups are separated by the other three groups and the only time they will overlap when a project is canceled or terminated.

178. C:

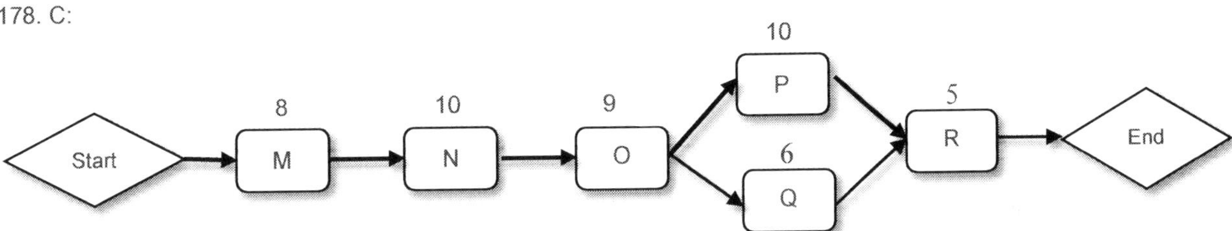

Here the critical path is Start, M, N, O, P, R, End = 42 days. So crashing the schedule by 7 days can be achieved by crashing activities N,O,P,R (2 + 2 + 1 + 2) for a cost of ((300 x 2) + (400 x 2) + (400 x 1) + (500 x 2)) = $2800.

179. B: The project must be in the Control Risks process if risks have occurred. Workarounds are unplanned responses developed to deal with the occurrence of unanticipated risk events that were not included in the risk register.

180. A: We know # of communication channels = n (n –1) / 2, where n = number of members in the team

So 9 (9 – 1) / 2 = 72/ 2 = 36. We have 9 members in the team to have 36 communication channels.

181. B: Since the relevant work is integral to the project, you simply cannot remove the work package nor can you transfer it to a third party. The best approach will be to accept the risk and have a contingency plan to deal with it in case it happens.

182. D: A resource histogram is a graphic display that can be used to track resources through time when shared or critically required resources are only available at certain times, in limited quantities, or when resources have been over-allocated. We may have several peaks and valleys in our resource histogram in the stated situation. In order to level the resources, evenly utilize them as much as possible, or to keep resource usage at a constant level, we can move some of our activities from the week when we are using many resources to a week when we are hardly using any.

183. B: A Responsibility Assignment Matrix (RAM) chart cross-references team members with the activities or work packages they are to accomplish. One example of a RAM is a Responsible, Accountable, Consult, and Inform (RACI) chart, which can be used to ensure clear divisions of roles and responsibilities.

184. D: It is important to complete all aspects of the project, as agreed by the specification, even if it means the project will be delayed. The project managers should maintain their integrity and make the appropriate decision even in a situation where they have to deny their manager's request.

185. B: Plan Quality Management is the process of identifying all the relevant quality requirements, specification and standards for the project and product, and specifying how the specification will be met. Quality management plan, quality metrics, and process improvement plan are the outputs in this process.

186. B: Independent estimates or in-house cost estimates are often provided by consulting services, or a procuring organization can prepare its own independent estimate. These estimates may help judge whether the statement of work was adequate in its description, or the seller fully understood or responded fully to the statement of work as well as check reasonableness of the seller's response and proposed pricing.

187. D: Affinity diagram is a technique in which the ideas generated from other requirements gathering techniques are sorted into groups by similarities. Each group of requirements is then given a title. This sorting makes it easier to see additional scope (or risks) that have not been identified.

188. B: A Resource Breakdown Structure (RBS) looks like a typical organizational chart, but this one is organized by types of resources. RBS can help track project cost as it ties to the organization's accounting system. For instance, you may have junior, mid-level, and senior QA testers working on your project. These testers have an average salary recorded in the organization's accounting system, which can be used to calculate the cost of these resources.

189. A: The first step to resolve an issue is to identify the root cause of the issue. Cause and Effect (Ishikawa/Fishbone) diagram is a tool used for systematically identifying and presenting all the possible causes and sub causes of a particular problem in a graphical format. It can help in quality control by identifying causes contributed to quality problems.

190. A: Graphical Evaluation and Review Technique (GERT) is a modified network diagram drawing method that allows conditional branches and loops between activities.

191. D: It is intended to assure that no seller receives preferential treatment and all sellers have a clear, common understanding of the procurement (technical requirements, contractual requirements, etc.). The key objective is to provide all potential contractors with the information they need to determine if they would like to continue with the contracting process. The bidder conference is also called a contractor conference, vendor conference, or pre-bid conference.

192. A: If it is customary in the country, you are working in to pay for the private protection service, then it will not be a bribe. As long as it is acceptable, reasonable, and legal in that country you should pay the security guard the protection fee.

193. A: In the case of an external project, the client will send out the statement of work as a part of the bidding document, such as a Request for Proposal (RFP). The SOW is a narrative description of products, results or services to be supplied by the project including the business need, product scope description or what is to be done, and how the project supports the strategic plan.

194. C: Perform Quality Assurance is a process to determine if the project activities are complying with organizational and project policies, standards, processes, and procedures. This process is primarily concerned with overall process improvement and does not deal with inspecting the product for quality or measuring defects. The primary focus is on steadily improving the processes and activities undertaken to achieve quality.

195. A: In this specific situation, the project manager should do a scope verification of the deliverables to ensure that they satisfy project objectives and were completed satisfactorily. A project manager should always get all the details first before taking any other action, such as discussing the concern with the sponsor. Gold plating or offering customers extra or additional features will not solve any real problem and should be avoided.

196. C: Claims administration is a technique in the Control Procurements process that documents, monitors, and manages disputed changes when the buyer and seller disagree on scope, the impact of changes, or the interpretation of some terms and conditions in the contract. You would attempt to resolve the claim in this case, but if agreement cannot be reached, it should be handled in accordance with the resolution procedures outlined in the contract.

197. B: You should make sure to gather lessons learned so that future projects can benefit. There is no reason to renegotiate with the higher management at this time. The project manager should document the number of completed and pending deliverables when the project was canceled.

198. D: SOW is a narrative description of products, results or services to be supplied by the project including the business need, product scope description or what is to be done, and how the project supports the strategic plan.

199. A: We know EV = BAC * actual % complete. So EV = $900,000 * 40 percent = $360,000.
SV = EV – PV. So SV = $360,000 – $380,000 = – $20,000.
CV = EV – AC. So CV = $360,000 – $390,000 = –$30,000.
Since both CV and SV are negative, you are over budget and behind the schedule.

200. B: In noncompetitive forms of procurement, usually a seller is selected from a list of qualified sellers interested in and capable of doing the job. Even though competition can result in the selection of a better seller and decreased price, there is no reason for going through the entire procurement process unless the law requires it. If the law requires at least three proposals or quotations, then we cannot go for a single source or sole source.

GLOSSARY OF TERMS

Common Acronyms

AC	Actual Cost	**PDM**	Precedence Diagramming Method
ACWP	Actual Cost of Work Performed	**PERT**	Program Evaluation and Review Technique
BAC	Budget at Completion	**PMBOK**	Project Management Body of Knowledge
AON	Activity on Node	**PMIS**	Project Management Information System
AOA	Activity on Arrow	**PMO**	Project Management Office
BCWP	Budgeted Cost of Work Performed	**PMP**	Project Management Professional
BCWS	Budgeted Cost of Work Scheduled	**PV**	Planned Value
CAPM	Certified Associate in Project Management	**QA**	Quality Assurance
CCB	Change Control Board	**QC**	Quality Control
CAP	Control Account Plan	**RACI**	Responsible, Accountable, Consult, and Inform
COQ	Cost of Quality	**RAM**	Responsibility Assignment Matrix
CPAF	Cost Plus Award Fee	**RBS**	Risk Breakdown Structure
CPFF	Cost Plus Fixed Fee	**RFI**	Request For Information
CPI	Cost Performance Index	**RFP**	Request For Proposal
CPIF	Cost Plus Incentive Fee	**RFQ**	Request For Quotation
CPI^c	Cumulative Cost Performance Index	**SF**	Start to Finish
CPPC	Cost plus Percentage of Cost	**SOW**	Statement of Work
CPM	Critical Path Method	**SPI**	Schedule Performance Index
CV	Cost Variance	**SPI^c**	Cumulative Schedule Performance Index
DOE	Design of Experiment	**SS**	Start to Start
EAC	Estimate at Completion	**SV**	Schedule Variance
EEF	Enterprise Environmental Factor	**SWOT**	Strengths, Weaknesses, Opportunities, and Threats
EF	Early Finish	**T&M**	Time & Material
EMV	Expected Monetary Value	**TQM**	Total Quality Management
ES	Early Start	**WBS**	Work Breakdown Structure
ETC	Estimate to Complete	**VAC**	Variance at Completion
EV	Earned Value		
EVM	Earned Value Management		
FF	Finish to Finish		
FP	Fixed Price Contract		
FMEA	Failure Mode and Effect Analysis		
FPEPA	Fixed Price Economic Price Adjustment		
FPIF	Fixed Price Incentive Fee		
FS	Finish to Start		
IFB	Invitation for Bid		
LF	Late Finish		
IRR	Internal Rate of Return		
LOE	Level of Effort		
LS	Late Start		
OBS	Organizational Breakdown Structure		
OPA	Organizational Process Assets		

A

Acceptance: An act of signing off on all project deliverables as complete. Acceptance is also a strategy to deal with threats or opportunities.

Acceptance Criteria: Requirements a project must meet before stakeholders accept the final product or service.

Achievement Theory: A motivational theory that suggests people are most motivated by one of the following three needs: need for achievement, need for affiliation/association, or need for power.

Acquire Project Team: An executing process of carrying out the Develop Human Resource Plan. Primary goal is to secure the best possible resources to build the project team, so they can carry out the project activities efficiently.

Activity: A scheduled task that must be performed in order to complete project work.

Activity Attributes: Additional information such as Activity ID, WBS ID, activity name, completion date, description, predecessor and successor activities, resources assigned, constraints and assumptions, level of effort, etc. are called attributes. Attributes may be stored with the activity list or in a separate document.

Activity List: A detailed list of the discrete tasks needed to complete the project.

Activity on Arrow (AOA): A project network diagram in which arrows represent activities and circles show dependencies. This diagram has been replaced by Activity on Node (AON).

Activity on Node (AON): A project network diagram in which boxes/nodes represent activities and arrows show dependencies.

Actual Cost (AC): The cost incurred for work completed. It is also called Actual Cost of Work Performed.

Actual Cost of Work Performed (ACWP): See **Actual Cost**

Activity Duration Estimates: Estimates of the likely number of work periods required for each activity. Frequently represented by a range of optimistic, pessimistic, and most likely estimates, known as the three-point estimate.

Adaptive Life Cycle: Also referred to as an agile life cycle, an adaptive life cycle broadly defines the fixed scope, schedule, and cost with the clear understanding that it will be refined and adjusted as the project progresses. In this life cycle, requirements from customers are documented and prioritized in a backlog, work is planned in brief, quick increments so the customers may modify and reprioritize requirements within time and cost constraints.

Advertising: In order to expand sellers' lists and to improve the volume and quality of responses from a targeted audience, the procuring organization may place advertisements in general circulation publications, such as newspapers, online sources, or professional journals. It is a tool and technique in the Conduct Procurement process, used for informing potential vendors that an RFP, RFQ, or RFB is available. Some government procurements require this kind of public advertising.

Affinity Diagram: A technique where ideas generated from all other requirements gathering techniques are sorted into similar groups. Each group of requirements is then given a title. An affinity diagram makes it easier to see additional scope (or risks) that have not been identified.

Alternative Generation: A tool and technique of the Define Scope process that is used to discover different methods or ways of accomplishing a project.

Analogous Estimating: An estimating technique in which the overall project estimate is given to the project manager from management or the sponsor. This type of estimate measures project parameters such as budget, size, complexity, and duration based on previous, similar projects and historical information. It is usually done during an early phase of a project when not much information is available. Although it is less costly and time consuming, it is also less accurate.

Appraisal Costs: Costs expended to examine a product or process and ensure requirements are being met. These costs include costs associated with inspections and testing.

Arbitration: An alternative, cheaper method to the court system for dispute resolution. A neutral, private, third party is assigned to resolve the disputes.

Assumption: The elements of a project that are assumed and believed to be true. Assumptions are often considered alongside constraints.

Assumptions Analysis: An analysis of the validity of assumptions, hypotheses, and scenarios developed in project initiation to identify risks from inaccuracies, incompleteness, and inconsistencies of assumptions. The assumptions that turn out to be invalid should be evaluated, qualitatively and quantitatively analyzed, and planned just like other risks.

Attributes: Additional information such as activity ID, WBS ID, activity name, completion date, description, predecessor and successor activities, resource assignment, constraints and assumptions, and level of effort are called attributes and may be stored with the activity list or in a separate document.

Attribute Sampling: A method of measuring quality that consists of observing the presence (or absence) of some characteristics (attributes) in each of the units under consideration to determine whether to accept a lot, reject it, or inspect another lot.

Avoid: A strategy to eliminate a threat by eliminating the cause or changing the project management plan.

B

Backlog: A listing of product requirements and deliverables to be prioritized, written as stories, and completed by the business to manage and organize the project work.

Backward Pass: A technique used in Critical Path Method (CPM) to calculate late start and late finish dates for activities.

Balanced Matrix: An organizational structure in which power is shared evenly between a project manager and a functional manager.

Bar Chart: A time-phased graphical display of activity including start dates, end dates, and durations. It is also referred to as a Gantt chart.

Baseline: The representation of the original, approved scope, cost, or schedule, plus all approved changes. It is usually compared with the actual results to identify variances.

Benchmarking: A technique of comparing actual or planned practices to those of other projects both in and beyond the performing organization to provide a basis for performance measurement, generate improvement ideas, and identify best practices.

Benefit Measurement Methods: Methods for establishing value to analyze and prioritize projects.

Bottom-up Estimating: A technique used to estimate overall project duration, effort, or cost. This is done by estimating the lowest levels of the schedule or Work Breakdown Structure (WBS) and aggregating those numbers up to the summary nodes on the WBS.

Bidder Conference: This is also called contractor conference, vendor conference, or pre-bid conference. It is intended to assure that no seller receives preferential treatment and all sellers have a clear and common understanding of the procurement (technical requirements, contractual requirements, etc.). The key objective is to provide all potential contractors with the information they need to determine if they would like to continue with the contracting process.

Brainstorming: An information gathering technique focused on group thinking as opposed to individual ideas. It involves individual idea generation, but ideas are shared, discussed, synthesized, and improved upon by the entire group. This technique does not assure that all participants' ideas are captured; rather, it encourages a collaborative process of idea formation based upon sharing and building ideas as a group.

Budget: The allotted money a project or project phase has available.

Budget at Completion (BAC): The amount budgeted for the TOTAL project effort.

Budgeted Cost of Work Performed (BCWP): See **Earned Value**

Budgeted Cost of Work Scheduled (BCWS): See **Planned Value**

Buffer: The maximum amount of time an activity can be delayed without delaying the entire project. It may be included in the overall project schedule to accommodate scheduled uncertainty. This additional time can be calculated using quantitative methods or by taking a percentage of the estimated duration or fixed number of work periods. It should be modified, reduced, or eliminated based on actual information as it becomes available.

C

Cardinal Scale: A numeric scale that is expressed as values from 0.0 to 1.0 and can be stated in equal (linear) or unequal (nonlinear) increments.

Cause and Effect Diagrams: A tool used to systematically identify and present all the possible causes and sub causes of a particular problem in a graphical format. It can help in quality control by identifying the causes that contributed to a specific quality problem. Cause and effect diagrams are particularly useful for identifying the causes of risks.

Certified Associate in Project Management (CAPM): A project management certification for an individual who has experience working in projects, has the required education, and an adequate understanding of the PMBOK® guide. This certification is created and managed by Project Management Institute (PMI).

Change Control: A process necessary for reviewing change requests, approving or disapproving and managing changes to the deliverables, project management plan and documents, and the organizational process assets.

Change Control Board (CCB): A group of members, including stakeholders, managers, project team members, and senior management, responsible for reviewing and approving or denying change requests. Some organizations have a permanent CCB staffed by full time employees to manage changes for the entire organization, not only a project. The project manager should consider establishing a CCB for the project if the organization does not have one.

Change Control System: A subset of the configuration management system. These are the documented procedures that describe how the deliverables of a project and associated project documentation are controlled, changed, and approved. A Change Control System also describes how to submit and manage change requests including emergency changes. This system also tracks the status of the change requests, including their approval status. Approved changes are filed in the change control log for future reference.

Change Request: Any changes impacting the project are communicated and appropriate actions are put into place to realign the objectives. These change requests, which may be direct or indirect, externally or internally initiated, and optional or contractually mandated, may modify the project's policies and procedures, scope, cost, schedule, or quality. Other change requests may cover required corrective and preventive actions to reduce the probability of negative impact in the future.

Charter: A document to formally authorize a project or a phase. The charter identifies the business objectives and needs, current understanding of the stakeholders' expectations, and the new product, service, or result that the project is intended to satisfy.

Chart of Accounts: The organization's accounting system. Control accounts or cost accounts associated with the WBS are linked to the chart of accounts.

Checklist: A component specific, structured tool used to verify that a set of required steps have all been performed and that they were performed in the proper sequence. It is often available from professional organizations or commercial service providers of the application area. Also, many organizations have their own checklists to ensure consistency in frequently performed tasks.

Claim: A dispute between a buyer and a seller.

Claim Administration: A technique in the Control Procurements process that documents, monitors, and manages disputed changes when the buyer and seller disagree on scope, the impact of changes, or the interpretation of some terms and conditions in the contract.

Close Procurements: A process that is mainly concerned with completing each project procurement. This process involves:

- Product verification as stipulated in the contract by making sure all work and deliverables were acceptable and all the payments have been made.
- Administrative closeouts of the contract such as making sure all open claims are finalized and all records are updated and archived for future reference.

Close Project or Phase: A process of finalizing all activities across all project management process groups to formally complete the project or phase.

Closing Process Group: A process that finalizes activities across all project management process groups to formally complete the project, phase, or contractual obligations. This group consists of two important processes – Close Project or Phase and Close Procurements.

Collect Requirements: A process of defining and documenting the quantifiable needs and expectations of the sponsor, customer, and other stakeholders for meeting the project's objectives.

Co-location: A technique of placing many or all of the most active project team members in the same physical location to enhance their ability to perform as a team.

Code of Accounts: A unique code or account number assigned to the control account that links directly to the performing organization's accounting system.

Collaborating: A conflict resolution technique, also known as problem solving, is focused to combine multiple differing perspectives into one shared perspective for resolving the real problem so the problem goes away.

Compromise: A conflict resolution technique of bargaining to some level of mutual (dis)satisfaction to both parties. Parties are asked to give up something on order to gain something.

Common Cause: A factor which is always present, unavoidable, inherent, and to be expected in a process. It is also called an unassignable cause.

Communication: The process of exchanging information. Communication between a sender and a receiver is the act of appropriately encoding, sending, receiving, decoding, and verifying a message.

Communication Channels: The number of possible formal or informal communication paths that exist in a project. Communication channels are represented by nodes with lines connecting the nodes that indicate the number of communication paths. Communications are complex and need to be managed properly as adding additional people to team communication channels makes the channels grow exponentially.

# of channels = n * (n –1) / 2 or $(n^2 - n) / 2$, n = # of team members

Communications Management Plan: A subsidiary of the project management plan which can be formal or informal, highly detailed or broadly framed, based on stakeholder information need, when and how frequently information should be distributed, and the method of communication.

Conduct Procurements: An executing process of obtaining seller responses, selecting a seller, and awarding the procurement, usually in the form of a contract.

Conflict: The incompatibility of goals, which often leads to one party opposing or obstructing the other party from accomplishing their goals. Conflict is inevitable, and managing it in a constructive way can be beneficial for the project as it may actually present opportunities for improvement and help improve team morale and performance.

Conflict of Interest: A conflict that occurs due to giving more priority to personal interests than to the interests of the project.

Configuration Management System: A subset of the Project Management Information System (PMIS) that describes the different versions and characteristics of the product, service or result of the project and ensures accuracy and completeness of the description.

Consensus: Management decides via group agreement.

Constraints: The limitations and restrictions such as limitations on time, budget, scope, quality, schedule, resource, and technology that a project faces.

Contingency Plan: The specific action taken if opportunities or threats occur.

Contingency Reserves: The reserves the project manager determines, manages, and controls to address the cost impact of the remaining risks during the Plan Risk Response process. This kind of reserve for known unknown risks is also taken into consideration during the Determining Budget process.

Contract: A formal and legally binding agreement between two parties and the principle endeavor of procurement management.

Contract Statement of Work (SOW): A narrative description of products, results or services to be supplied by the project including the business need, product scope description or what is to be done, and how the project supports the strategic plan.

Control: See **Monitoring & Controlling**

Control Account: A Control Account (CA) in the WBS is used to measure, monitor, and control project cost, schedule, and scope by using earned value performance measures.

Control Chart: A tool and technique in the Control Quality process used to determine whether or not a process is stable or in control. It measures the results of processes over time, displays them in graph format, and measures variances to determine whether process variances are in or out of control.

Control Costs: An essential process for ensuring that costs are carefully monitored and controlled. It ensures that costs stay on track and that change is detected whenever it occurs.

Control Limits: An acceptable range of variation of a process that is set by the project manager and stakeholders based on the expected quality standard.

Control Procurements: A monitoring and controlling process that is mainly concerned with managing procurement relationships, monitoring contract performance, and making changes and corrections as required.

Control Quality: A process of monitoring specific project results to determine if they comply with relevant quality standards and identifying ways to eliminate causes of unsatisfactory results.

Control Risks: A process of identifying, analyzing, and planning for newly arising risks, keeping track of and re-analyzing the identified and existing risks, monitoring trigger conditions, monitoring residual risks, choosing alternative strategies, executing a contingency or fallback plan, taking corrective actions, and reviewing the overall execution and effectiveness of risk responses.

Control Schedule: A process of monitoring the status of the project by comparing the result to the plan, updating project progress, and managing changes to the project schedule baseline.

Control Scope: A process of monitoring the status of the project and product scope, maintaining control over the project by preventing overwhelming scope change requests, and managing changes to the scope baseline.

Corrective Actions: Any change to bring the expected future results in line with the project management plan.

Cost Account: See **Control Accounts**

Cost Baseline: A time-phased budget used to monitor, measure, and control cost performance during the project. It is developed by summarizing costs over time and is usually displayed in the form of an S-curve, suggesting that the cost starts off low, accelerates throughout the later phases of the project and gradually slows down during closing.

Cost Management Plan: A component of the project management plan that describes how cost and changes to cost will be managed and controlled throughout the life of the project.

Cost of Quality (COQ): Costs that will be needed to ensure quality in the product or service of the project according to standards. It includes a complete analysis of cost of conformance and cost of nonconformance to quality.

Cost Performance Index (CPI): Measure of cost efficiency on a project expressed as a ratio of earned value to actual cost. CPI = EV/AC.

Cost plus Fixed Fee (CPFF): A type of cost reimbursement contract in which the buyer pays actual cost and a negotiated fee fixed prior to work initiation.

Cost plus Incentive Fee (CPIF): A type of cost reimbursement contract in which the buyer pays actual cost and a set fee based on specific performance objectives.

Cost plus Percentage of Cost (CPPC): A type of cost reimbursement contract in which the buyer pays actual cost plus a percentage of cost as a fee.

Cost Reimbursable Contract: A type of contract where seller's allowable costs are reimbursed by the buyer for producing the goods or services of the project. This is used when the exact scope of the work is uncertain and cost cannot be estimated accurately.

Cost Variance: A comparison of the budgeted cost of work performed with actual cost. It provides cost performance of the project and helps determine if the project is proceeding as planned.

Cost Benefit Analysis: A comparison between the cost of the effort needed to implement the project and the benefit of the project.

Crashing: A schedule compression technique of adding additional resources to a project's critical path activities to complete them more quickly. This technique looks at cost and schedule trade-offs and resources are added either from inside or outside the organization.

Create WBS: A planning process of developing a deliverable-oriented decomposition of the work specified in the current approved project scope statement. It defines the total scope of the project and subdivides the project work into smaller, more manageable pieces.

Critical Activity: An activity that is considered to be of great importance in a project. Critical path activities are not necessarily the most critical activities in the project.

Critical Chain Method: A way to develop an approved, realistic, resource-limited, and formal schedule. It provides a way to view and manage uncertainty when building the project schedule.

Critical Path: The longest path through a network diagram that determines the shortest time to complete the project. This path has the least flexibility and the highest risk as any delay in the critical path activities will result in a delay in the project.

Critical Path Method (CPM): A technique of schedule analysis that considers activity durations, logical relationships, dependencies, leads, lags, assumptions, and constraints to determine the float of each activity and the overall schedule. This method identifies the critical path with the least flexibility and the highest risk so that it can be managed appropriately.

Critical Success Factors: The elements that must be completed in order for the project to be considered complete and successful.

Culture Shock: The disorienting experience that occurs while working in an unfamiliar foreign culture or surrounding.

Cumulative Cost Performance Index (CCPI): The cumulative CPI of the project at the point the measurement is taken. $CPI^c = EV^c/AC^c$

Customer: Individuals or organization(s) who will receive the projects' product, service, or result.

D

Decision Tree: A type of visual display of information primarily used in risk management to make decisions regarding individual risks by taking into account risk probabilities and impacts.

Decomposition: A technique of subdividing project deliverables into progressively smaller, more manageable components. The goal with decomposition is breaking down the deliverables to a point that planning, executing, monitoring & controlling, and closing become much easier.

Defect: An identified issue that is caused when the project's product, result, or service does not match the documented scope.

Defect Repair: Actions taken to repair defects or entirely replace the affected components.

Define Activities: A planning process of creating a detailed list of the discrete tasks needed to accomplish the project.

Define Scope: A planning process of developing a comprehensive, detailed description of the project (the project management work) and product (the features and characteristics of the product, service, or result of the project).

Deliverables: A unique and verifiable product, result, capability or service that must be produced in order to complete a process, phase, or project.

Delphi Technique: A form of expert judgment that is mainly focused on preventing group thinking and discovering the true opinions of participants by sending a request for information to experts who participate anonymously. The responses are compiled and results are sent back for further review until a consensus is reached.

Dependency: A relationship between two or more activities. See **Logical Relationships**

Design of Experiments (DOE): A statistical method, usually applied to the product of a project, that provides a "what if" analysis of alternatives to identify which factors may improve quality. It provides statistical analysis for changing key product or process elements all at once to optimize the process.

Determine Budget: A planning process of determining a budget, also known as the cost baseline, that takes the estimated project expenditures and maps them back to dates on the calendar to help organizations plan for cash flow and likely expenditures.

Develop Human Resource Plan: A planning process of identifying and documenting project roles, responsibilities, required skills, competencies, and reporting structure.

Develop Project Charter: A planning process of developing a document to formally authorize a project or a phase and identifying the business objectives and needs, current understanding of the stakeholders' expectations, and the new product, service, or result that it is intended to satisfy.

Develop Project Management Plan: An iterative and ongoing process to establish the total scope of effort, define the objectives, and identify the course of action required to attain those objectives.

Develop Project Team: A process that is performed throughout the project with the focus to enhance the project performance by building a sense of team, improving the competencies, team interaction, and overall team environment.

Develop Schedule: A relatively complex iterative process of analyzing activity sequence, dependencies, durations, logical relationship, resource (materials, manpower, equipment, supplies, etc.), requirements, constraints, and assumptions to develop the project schedule with planned dates for project activity completion.

Dictatorship: A group decision making technique where decisions are made for the group by one individual.

Direct and Manage Project Work: A process of performing the work defined in the project management plan to achieve the project's objectives.

Direct Cost: A type of cost directly attributable to project work. For example, wages and materials used in the project.

Discretionary Dependencies: A dependency that is determined as per the preference of the project planner and team members. These dependencies may be determined by best practices or local methodology and may vary from project to project. These are also called preferred logic, preferential logic, or soft logic.

Disputes: An instance when an issue is identified and remains unresolved even after direct negotiation between the supplier and the buyer. A formal dispute must be raised and the other party notified of that dispute in writing. The matter in dispute shall be referred to and settled by a mutually agreed-upon arbitrator, whose decision will be final and binding for both parties.

Distribute Information: An executing process of making relevant information available to project stakeholders in a timely manner as planned.

Dummy Activity: A fake schedule activity mostly used in an Activity on Arrow (AOA) diagram to create logical relationships. The dummy activity is represented as a dashed line in the AOA and has a duration of 0.

Duration: The time span involved in any phase of the project. It can also be viewed as the amount of time needed to complete a schedule activity or work package.

E

Early Finish (EF): The soonest a task can end.

Early Start (ES): The soonest a task can begin.

Earned Value (EV): The estimated value of the work actually accomplished.

Earned Value Management (EVM): A commonly used method of project performance and progress measurement that involves integrating project scope, cost, and schedule measures.

Effort: The amount of work required to complete an activity in the project.

Efficiency Indicators: Schedule variance and cost variance together are known as efficiency indicators.

Enhance: A Risk Response plan strategy that increases the size, probability, likelihood, and positive impact of an opportunity by influencing the underlying risk triggers.

Enterprise Environmental Factors (EEF): Any factors that impact the project but are not part of the project itself.

Estimate: A numerical representation of cost and time that is usually originated from project team members most familiar with the activity and then progressively elaborated. It is important that all estimates use common work units/periods.

Estimate Activity Durations: A planning process that utilizes scope and resource information such as who will be doing the work, resource availability, and number of resources assigned to estimate durations for the activities of the project.

Estimate Activity Resources: A planning process of estimating the resources (such as material, equipment, manpower, and supplies) required to perform activities in the project.

Estimate at Completion (EAC): A type of budget forecast, EAC is the projected total cost of a project at its completion.

Estimate Cost: A planning process of developing an approximation of the costs of all resources, such as labor, materials, equipment, services, facilities, and any other special items associated with each schedule activity.

Estimate to Complete (ETC): The forecasted amount that is determined by figuring out what funds will be needed to complete a project from a specific point.

Evaluation Criteria: A method of rating and scoring proposals from vendors.

Executing Process Group: A group of processes to complete the work defined in the project management plan and ultimately satisfies the project specifications and objectives.

Exit Gate: A review of the deliverables and related work that is conducted upon the conclusion of each project phase. This could also be called a stage gate or a kill point.

Expectancy Theory: A theory demonstrating that employees who believe their efforts will lead to effective performance and who expect to be rewarded for their accomplishments remain productive as rewards meet their expectations.

Expected Monetary Value (EMV): A statistical concept that calculates the anticipated outcome of a decision. It is the product of the probability and consequences of an event or task.

Exploit: A strategy for opportunities under the tools and techniques of the Plan Risk Responses process. It is associated with managing opportunity or risks that may have a positive impact on a project. It seeks to eliminate the uncertainty by making the opportunity definitely happen.

External Dependencies: Dependencies driven by circumstances or authority outside the project and must be considered during the process of sequencing the activities.

Expert Judgment: A technique of relying upon or consulting with an individual, or group of people, who have specialized skills, knowledge, and training in a particular area for project decisions.

F

Fait Accompli: A negotiation tactic of using established rules, laws, and decisions as mandates to avoid any further discussion.

Fast Tracking: A schedule compression technique of performing critical path activities in parallel when they were originally planned in series.

Feasibility Study: A study conducted by some organizations prior to making a final decision about initiating a project. A feasibility study helps to determine if the project is viable and also to figure out the probability of the project's success.

Finish Date: A predetermined date that an activity is supposed to finish, based on the schedule plan.

Finish to Finish (FF): A relationship where a predecessor activity must be completed before the successor activity is completed.

Finish to Start (FS): A relationship where a predecessor activity must be completed before the successor activity can be initiated.

Fitness for Use: A quality theory by Joseph Juran which specifies that a product or service must satisfy a real need.

Fishbone Diagram: See **Cause and Effect Diagram**

Fixed Priced Incentive Fee (FPIF): A type of fixed contract where the buyer pays a fixed price plus a set fee based on the seller meeting specific performance criteria, such as finishing the project early or reducing total cost.

Fixed Price Contract: A fixed price contract (sometimes called a Lump Sum or Firm Fixed Price contract) is the most common form of contract in the world and is used for acquiring goods and services with well-defined requirements or scope.

Float: The maximum amount of time an activity can be delayed without delaying the entire project.

Flowchart: A graphical representation of a process showing the relationships among process steps. A flowchart can be used to predict where quality problems may occur.

Forecasting: Making estimates or predictions of conditions in the project's future including Estimate to Complete (ETC) and Estimate at Completion (EAC).

Force Majeure: An allowable excuse for either party not meeting its contractual obligation in the event of something considered to be an act of God, such as fires, storms, floods, freak electrical storms, and hurricanes.

Forcing: A conflict resolution technique of exerting one opinion over another. It destroys team morale, does not help resolve the problem, and almost never provides a long term solution.

Formal Acceptance: A formal approval by the stakeholders on project deliverables.

Forward Pass: A part of the critical path method that is used to calculate early start and early finish.

Free Float: Amount of time an activity can be delayed without affecting the early start of its successor.

Functional Manager: Also called a department manager, the functional manager holds the majority (or all) of the authority and resource control in a functional organization, holds very little authority and resource control in a projectized organization, and shares authority and resource control with a project manager(s) in a matrix organization.

Funding Limit Reconciliation: A technique of reconciling the expenditure of funds with the funding limits set for the project. As per the variance between the expenditure of funds and planned limit, the activities can be rescheduled to level out the rates of expenditures.

Functional Organization: An organizational structure grouped by areas of specialization within different functional areas (e.g., accounting, marketing, engineering).

G

Gantt Chart: See **Bar Chart**

Gatekeeper: An impartial person from senior management who draws others in or judges whether the project should continue at different stages.

Grade: A term used in quality management which refers to the number of features a product has. A low grade means a low number of features and high grade means a high number of features.

Ground Rules: Rules of conduct that identify acceptable and unacceptable behavior on the project in order to minimize negative impacts of bad behavior.

H

Hammock Activity: The aggregate activities or summary-level activities on a project schedule network diagram.

Handoff: The process of completing one project life cycle phase and initiating the next.

Hard Logic: The mandatory and unavoidable dependencies that are inherent in the nature of the work or contractually required. They are like the laws of nature and also called mandatory dependencies.

Histogram: A graph that shows the distribution of data. It is designed to show the centering, dispersion (spread), and shape (relative frequency) of the data; therefore, it displays a count of the data points falling in various ranges. Histograms can provide a visual display of large amounts of data that are difficult to understand in a tabular or spreadsheet form.

Historical Information: Any information such as activity duration estimation, resource estimation, etc. from previous and similar projects that has been archived by the performing organization. Historical information is used to evaluate future project decisions and can drastically improve estimates.

Human Resource Management Plan: A subsidiary of the project management plan that documents roles and responsibilities, the project organization charts, and the staffing management plan.

Hygiene Theory: See **Motivation-Hygiene Theory**

I

Identify Risks: An iterative planning process of identifying all the risks that may impact the project, documenting them, and identifying their characteristics.

Identify Stakeholders: An initiating process of identifying all people or organizations impacted by the project, and documenting relevant information regarding their interests, expectations, involvement, and influence on project success.

Impact: The amount of opportunity or damage a risk event can have to a project.

Impact Scale: A scale that assigns a cardinal value or actual numeric value to illustrate the severity of a potential risk impact.

Independent Estimates: In-house cost estimates that are often provided by consulting services, but can be prepared by a procuring organization. These estimates may help judge whether the statement of work was adequate in its description, or if the seller fully understood or responded to the statement of work, and the fair value of the seller's response and proposed pricing.

Influence Diagram: A chart that shows how one set of influencers may influence another and affect outcomes.

Influencer: People or groups not related to the product or use of the product, but who, due to position, can influence the course of a project positively or negatively.

Information Distribution Tools: Tools that are used to distribute project information.

Imposed Date: A date that is provided by the senior management or other external sources to the project and may not be moved. It is considered a constraint in the project.

Indirect Cost: An overhead cost or cost that is incurred for the benefit of more than one project, such as cafeteria services, facilities, and fringe benefits.

Initiating Process Group: A process group that defines a new project or phase and is made up of only two processes: Develop Project Charter in integration management and Identify Stakeholders in stakeholder management.

Input: Any item, whether internal or external to the project, required by a process before that process can proceed. It may be an output from a predecessor process.

Inspection: A tool in the Validate Scope and Control Quality processes that includes activities such as measuring, examining, and verifying to determine whether work and deliverables meet requirements and product acceptance criteria.

Internal Rate of Return (IRR): The percentage of the project cost returned as interest over the years following project completion.

Interrelationship Digraphs: A graphical display that maps out the cause and effect links among complicated, multivariable problems or desired outcomes. It can be utilized to assess particular issues or general organizational concerns when it is difficult to identify the interrelationships between the concepts and is ambiguous as to whether the issue is the problem or the solution.

Invitation for Bid (IFB): See **Request for Proposal**

Ishikawa Diagram: See **Cause and Effect Diagram**

Iterative: A descriptive term for processes that are repeated.

J

Just-in-Time (JIT): An inventory management method whereby materials, goods, and labor are scheduled to arrive or be replenished exactly when needed in the production process, thereby bringing inventory down to zero or almost near to a zero level.

K

Kaizen: A quality methodology based on the Plan-Do-Check-Act. It is also called continuous improvement as it is an ongoing effort to improve organizational quality and performance. Its aim is to improve customer satisfaction through continuous improvements to products, services, or processes. Kaizen is a philosophy that stresses constant process improvement, in the form of small changes in products or services.

Kill Point: See **Exit Gate**

Knowledge Area: One of the competency domains within project management. The PMBOK® organizes the project processes according to ten knowledge areas.

L

Lag: An inserted waiting time between activities.

Late Finish (LF): The latest a task can end without affecting the project duration.

Late Start (LS): The latest a task can begin without affecting the project duration.

Lead: An acceleration or jump-start of a successor activity. A lead may be added in order to start an activity before the predecessor activity is completed.

Lessons Learned: Formally documented information that the team has acquired during the execution of the project. Lessons Learned includes information about variances in the project, what went right, what went wrong, and what the team would plan or execute differently.

Lessons Learned Knowledge Base: A repository of historical information and lessons learned from previous projects.

Level of Effort (LOE): A supporting activity that does not produce definitive end products, such as support or follow-up activities. Level of effort is measured by the passage of time and is tracked and reported at a high level.

Life Cycle: See **Project Life Cycle**

Line of Communications: The number of communication channels among a group of project team participants.

Logical Relationship: The dependencies between two activities in a project. The four types of logical relationships are finish-to-start, finish-to-finish, start-to-start, and start-to-finish.

Lump-sum Contract: Also called a fixed price contract, a lump-sum contract usually pays a lump-sum amount for all the work and places the risk on the seller.

M

Majority: A group decision making technique where a decision is based on support from more than 50 percent of group members.

Make-or-Buy Analysis: A procurement analysis to determine whether a product can be cost effectively produced in-house or should be purchased, leased, or rented. While performing this analysis, it is important to consider indirect as well as direct costs, availability, related risk, and schedule.

Manage Project Team: A process of managing the team through observation, using issue logs, keeping in touch, providing feedback, completing performance appraisals, and resolving issues and conflicts.

Manage Stakeholder Engagement: A process of meeting and exceeding the stakeholders' expectation by continuously communicating with them, clarifying and resolving their issues, addressing their concerns, and improving project performance by implementing change requests.

Mandatory Dependencies: See **Hard Logic**

Maslow's Hierarchy of Needs: A motivation theory that groups human needs into five basic categories and insists that one proponent need must be relatively satisfied before an individual can move on to the next level. At some point, people no longer work for security or money. Rather, they work to contribute and to use their skills. Maslow calls this self-actualization.

Master Schedule: See **Milestone Schedule**

Matrix Diagrams: A graphical tool that shows the matrix's tabular format of connections or correlations between ideas or issues. A present or absent relationship exists at each intersection of rows and columns.

Matrix Organization: An organizational structure where both the project manager and the functional manager direct resources, but resource reporting goes directly to the functional manager. Performance issues are also handled by the functional manager.

Methodology: A set of steps used to manage a project. It is an organization's specific implementation of project processes.

Milestones: A major significant event or point of interest in the project.

Milestone Chart: A chart that shows major events in a project. The milestone chart is a good tool for reporting to management and customers.

Mitigation: A reduction in the probability and or impact of an adverse risk event to an acceptable threshold.

Monitor and Control Project Work: A process of tracking, reviewing, and regulating work progress to meet the performance objectives defined in the project management plan.

Monitoring and Controlling Process Group: A process group that usually measures the work results against the project management plan.

Monte Carlo Analysis: A risk management technique to determine the impact of the identified risks by running simulations to identify the range of possible outcomes for a number of scenarios.

Motivational Theories: The theories that examine recognition and reward in team management.

Motivation-Hygiene Theory: A motivational theory that suggests hygiene factors can destroy motivation, but under most circumstances, improving hygiene factors will not improve motivation. This theory stipulates that motivating people is best done by rewarding employees and letting them grow.

N

Net Present Value (NPV): The present value of the benefits (income or revenue) minus the costs over many time periods. NPV is useful as it allows for a comparison of many projects to select the best to initiate.

- If NPV is positive we can consider the investment is a good choice unless a better one exists.
- The project with the highest NPV is selected.
- The number of years and cost are not relevant, as they are accounted for in the NPV calculation.

Network Diagram: A diagram that shows logical relationships, dependencies, and order of activities.

Networking: The process of formal and informal interaction with others in an organization, industry, or professional environment. A project manager can identify the political and organizational forces that will influence the project by networking within the organization.

Node: A box that is used to represent activities in a network diagram.

Nominal Group Technique: A technique usually performed during the same session as brainstorming where the meeting participants vote, rank, and prioritize the most useful ideas generated during the brainstorming session.

O

Objective: The envisioned result from the product and/or service of the project.

Operations: Ongoing activities needed to continue business in an organization.

Opportunity: Risks with positive effects. Opportunity creates a favorable situation in the organization's environment.

Opportunity Cost: The value of a project that is not done so that another project can be executed. It is the cost of a lost opportunity, or missing the benefit of an unselected project.

Ordinal Scale: A scale that utilizes a narrative description when rating or ranking items that require attention.

Organizational Breakdown Structure (OBS): A chart that is similar to a company's standard organizational chart but only includes the positions and relationships in a top-down, graphic format. It is arranged according to an organization's existing departments, units, or teams and their respective work packages.

Organizational Process Assets (OPA): Any and all process-related assets, including information, tools, documents or knowledge that an organization possesses that can help plan for a project.

Outputs: Documents or items that are produced by a process. Outputs may become an input to successor processes.

P

Parametric Estimate: An estimate that uses mathematical models based on historical records from other projects. It utilizes the statistical relationship that exists between a series of historical data and a particular delineated list of other variables. Depending upon the quality of the underlying data, this estimate can produce higher levels of accuracy and can be used in conjunction with other estimates to provide estimates for the entire project or specific segments of a project. Measurements such as time per line of code, time per installation, and time per linear meter are considered in this type of estimate.

Pareto Chart: A chart used in quality management to illustrate causes of error that are the most serious. The Pareto Chart has the same format as a histogram and shows the frequency of error according to cause. The concept is based on the 80/20 Rule: "80 percent of the problems come from 20 percent of the causes." Thus, it is important to pay close attention to the 20 percent of critical causes in order to resolve 80 percent of the problems.

Passive Acceptance: The acceptance that requires no action to avoid, transfer, or mitigate a threat, or to exploit, share, or enhance an opportunity.

Path Convergence: A relationship in which multiple paths converge into one or more activities in the network diagram and add risk to the project. This is a relationship in which a schedule activity has more than one predecessor.

Path Divergence: A relationship in which a schedule activity has more than one successor.

Payback Period: The number of time periods it will take a company to recoup its initial costs of producing the product, service, or result of the project. This method compares the initial investment with the expected cash inflows over the life of the product, service, or result of the project.

Perform Integrated Change Control: A process of reviewing all change requests, approving changes, and managing changes to the deliverables, organizational process assets, project documents, and the project management plan.

Perform Quality Assurance: A process to determine if the project activities are complying with organizational and project policies, standards, processes, and procedures. This process is primarily concerned with overall process improvement and does not deal with inspecting the product for quality or measuring defects. The primary focus is on steadily improving the processes and activities undertaken to achieve quality.

Perform Qualitative Risk Analysis: A process of prioritizing risks for subsequent further analysis or action by assessing and combining their probability of occurrence and impact.

Perform Quantitative Risk Analysis: The process of numerically analyzing the effect of identified risks prioritized in the previous process as having substantial impact. Generally, this process follows Qualitative Risk Analysis and prioritizes risks by assigning a numerical rating to them. This process is not required for all projects and sometimes may be skipped to jumpstart the Plan Risk Responses process.

Performance Measurement Baselines: The project plan baseline, schedule baseline, and cost baseline are collectively known as performance measurement baselines.

Performance Report: A report that organizes and summarizes the information gathered and shows how the project is progressing against the various baselines, such as scope, time, cost, quality, and other elements. Various common formats for performance reports include bar charts, S-curves, histograms, and tables. Variance analysis, earned value analysis, and forecast data is often included as part of performance reporting.

Performing Organization: The enterprise whose employees are involved in doing the project work.

Plan Communications Management: A planning process of identifying the information and communication needs of the people involved in a project by determining what needs to be communicated, when, to whom, with what method, in which format, and how frequently.

Plan Procurement Management: A process of documenting project purchasing decisions, specifying the approach, defining selection criteria to identify potential sellers, and putting together a procurement management plan. This process helps identify which components or services of the project will be performed internally and what needs are best met by procuring products or services from outside the organization.

Plan Quality Management: The planning process of identifying all the relevant quality requirements, specifications and standards for a project/product, and stipulating how the specifications will be met.

Plan Risk Management: A planning process of deciding how to approach, plan, and execute risk management activities.

Plan Risk Responses: A planning process of developing options and actions to enhance opportunities and reduce threats to project objectives.

Planned Finish Date: A planned date when an activity is supposed to be completed.

Planned Start Date: A planned date when an activity is supposed to be started.

Planned Value (PV): The estimated value of the work planned to be done.

Planning Processes: A group of processes associated with planning or creating a project plan.

Plurality: A group decision making technique where a decision is based on the largest block in a group even if a majority is not achieved.

PMBOK: An acronym for the Project Management Body of Knowledge.

PMI Code of Ethics and Professional Conduct: The ethical code inaugurated by PMI to ensure personal and professional conduct on the part of PMPs.

Portfolio: A group of projects or programs and other works to achieve a specific strategic business goal.

Portfolio Management: A management strategy of identifying, prioritizing, authorizing, managing, and controlling the collection of projects, programs, other work, and sometimes other portfolios to achieve strategic business objectives.

Position Description: A text-oriented position description or role-responsibility-authority form that is particularly important in recruiting and used to describe team member position titles, responsibilities, authority-levels, competencies, and qualifications in detail.

Pre-Assignment: Under most circumstances a role is defined first, and then the resource is assigned to perform the role and fulfill the responsibilities; however, some of the team members will be selected in advance and considered as pre-assigned to fill roles before the Human Resource Plan has been created or the project has been formally initiated.

Precedence Diagramming Method (PDM): A method of creating a schematic display of the sequential and logical relationships of the activities which comprise a project.

Predecessor Activity: An activity that must be completed prior to starting successor activities.

Preferential Logic: See **Discretionary Dependencies** or **Soft Logic**

Preferred Logic: See **Discretionary Dependencies** or **Soft Logic**

Prevention: Prevention is the current approach to quality management. Quality should be planned, designed, and built into processes, not looked at as an afterthought to be achieved through inspection after completion. It costs much less to prevent mistakes earlier in the process than to correct them when they are found by inspection.

Preventive Action: Actions to be taken to prevent a risk from occurring.

Probability: The likelihood that something will occur, usually expressed as a decimal or a fraction on a scale of zero to one.

Prioritization Matrices: A matrix that provides a way of sorting a diverse set of items into an order of importance. It also enables their relative importance to be identified by deriving a numerical value of the importance of each item. In Perform Quality Assurance, this tool is expended to prioritize both issues and appropriate solutions for implementation.

Probability and Impact Matrix: A tool used to determine whether a risk is considered low, moderate, or high by combining the two dimensions of risk: its probability of occurring and its impact on objectives.

Procedure: A sequence of steps used to execute a process in order to accomplish a consistent performance or result.

Process: A systematic series of activities directed toward producing an end result.

Process Analysis: A part of continuous improvement effort that looks at process improvement from an organizational and technical point of view. It identifies the needed improvements by following the steps outlined in the process improvement plan, examining the problems and constraints experienced, and identifying non-value-added activities during process operations.

Process Decision Program Charts (PDPC): A technique designed to help formulate contingency plans. The emphasis of the PDPC is to identify the consequential impact of failure on activity plans, and create appropriate contingency plans to limit risks.

Process Group: Project management is performed by applying and integrating the 47 project management processes, which are logically grouped into five process groups: initiating, planning, executing, monitoring & controlling, and closing.

Process Improvement Plan: An improvement plan that looks at processes to find inefficiencies and outlines the activities and steps that will enhance their value.

Procurement Audits: This is a structured review of the Procurement process to identify successes and failures as lessons learned. Basically, it is a verification of all the elements of the contract that were completed and a stipulation and remedy of those elements that were not. This tool and technique of the Close Procurements process scrutinizes the procurement processes to verify their effectiveness.

Procurement Documents: Documents that are used to solicit proposals from prospective sellers. Well-designed procurement documents help in easier comparison of seller responses, more complete proposals, more accurate pricing, and a decrease in the amount of changes in the project.

Procurement File: A complete set of indexed contract documentation including the closed contract.

Procurement Management Plan: A subsidiary of the project management plan that describes how project procurements will be carried out throughout the project including:

- What service, product, or result will be produced
- Types of contracts to be used
- Who will prepare independent estimates and when
- What procurements the project team may make on its own
- What standard procurement documents will be used
- Listing of prequalified sellers if there are any
- How the sellers will be selected
- How sellers' performance will be measured
- How procurement will be coordinated with other project aspects (scheduling and performance reporting)
- Assumptions and constraints related to procurements.

Procurement Negotiations: A tool and technique of the Conduct Procurement Process that is focused on gaining clarification and mutual agreement on structure, requirements, and other terms of the contract prior to signing. Topics may include responsibilities and authorities, applicable terms and law, technical and business management approaches, pricing, contract financing, proprietary rights, and authority to make changes.

Product Life Cycle: A series of phases that represent the development of a product, from concept through delivery, growth, maturity, and to retirement.

Product Scope: The description of the features and functions that characterize a product, service, or result.

Product Scope Description: A product related scope description found in the project scope statement that consists of detailed information on product characteristics to determine activity sequencing.

Product Verification: A technique of making sure that all work and deliverables are acceptable and all payments have been made.

Program: A group of related projects managed in a coordinated way to capitalize benefits and control what is not achievable by managing those projects individually.

Program Evaluation and Review Technique (PERT): An estimate that takes optimistic, pessimistic, and most likely estimates from the estimator and provides a risk-based expected duration estimate by taking a weighted average of the three estimates using the following formula:

- Optimistic estimate: O
- Most likely estimate: M
- Pessimistic estimate: P

Depending on the assumed distribution of values, we use the following two formulas:

- Triangular Distribution: Expected Activity Duration (EAD) = $\frac{(O + M + P)}{3}$
- Beta Distribution: Expected Activity Duration (EAD) = $\frac{(O + 4M + P)}{6}$

Program Management: The centralized and coordinated management of a program to obtain the strategic objectives and benefits sought through the inception of the program.

Progressive Elaboration: A process of taking incremental steps to examine and refine the product characteristics of the project. It indicates that everything is not known up front, and that processes, assumptions, requirements, and decisions are continually reviewed and adjusted throughout the project's life cycle as it progresses.

Project: A temporary endeavor that produces a unique product, service, or result.

Project Boundaries: An outline of what is and is not incorporated in the work of the project.

Project Charter: A document that formally authorizes a project or a phase and documents the business objectives and needs, current understanding of the stakeholders' expectations, and the new product, service, or result that it is intended to satisfy.

Project Coordinator: A supporting project manager role that is weaker than the project manager in terms of authority. This role is similar to an expeditor, except the project coordinator has some power to make decisions and reports to higher management.

Project Expeditor: A staff assistant and communication coordinator in the project who cannot personally make or enforce decisions.

Project Life Cycle: A representation of the generally sequential and sometimes overlapping project phases that a project typically goes through.

Project Management Information System (PMIS): A part of the enterprise environmental factors that consists of the data sources and tools & techniques used to gather, integrate, analyze, and disseminate the results of the combined outputs of the project management processes. It is an automated system that can serve as a repository for information and a tool to assist with communication and tracking documents and deliverables. PMIS also supports the project from beginning to end by optimizing the schedule and helping to collect and distribute information.

Project Management Knowledge Area: A knowledge area that represents a complete set of activities, concepts, and terms that make up an area of specialization, project management field, or a professional field. The project manager must master the areas of knowledge specifically developed for project management. The PMBOK® organizes the project processes according to ten knowledge areas.

Project Management Office (PMO): A centralized organizational unit to oversee and coordinate the management of projects and programs under its domain throughout the organization.

Project Management Plan: The single approved document that defines how the project is executed, monitored & controlled, and closed.

Project Management Professional (PMP): One of the most important, prestigious, well reputed, and industry-recognized certifications for project managers.

Project Management Process Groups: See **Process Groups**

Project Management Team: Members directly involved in PM activities.

Project Manager: The individual ultimately responsible for managing the project.

Project Organization Chart: A graphical display of project team members and their reporting relationship.

Project Schedule: The result of schedule network analysis that includes a planned start date and a planned end date for each activity. It can be presented in a summary form or in detail that is typically represented graphically.

Project Schedule Network Diagram: A diagram that can be produced manually or by using project management software to display project activities, their relationships, and dependencies among them.

Project Scope: The work needed to deliver a product, service, or result with specified features and functions.

Project Scope Statement: An output of the Define Scope process which contains deliverables, product description, acceptance criteria, constraints, and assumptions about the project.

Project Statement of Work (PSOW): A document that describes project deliverables and the work required to create them in detail, enables the project team to perform more detailed planning, guides the project team's work during execution, and provides the baseline for evaluating changes.

Project Records: All relevant information of the project, including project reports, memos, schedule, plan, and other documents.

Projectized Organization: An organizational structure that is most commonly found in consulting environments and structured by projects. In such organizations, project managers run projects and have official authority over the project team.

Q

Qualified Sellers Lists: A list of preapproved or prequalified prospective sellers interested in and capable of doing the contract services for an organization.

Quality: The degree to which the project fulfills requirements.

Quality Audit: A scheduled or randomly structured review performed by internal or third party auditors to determine whether quality management activities are complying with organizational and project processes, policies, and procedures. The objective of the quality audit is to identify inefficient and ineffective activities or processes used on the project.

Quality Baseline: The quality objective of the project used to measure and report quality against throughout the project.

Quality Metrics: The operational definition that specifically defines how quality will be measured.

Quality Management Plan: A formal, approved document which includes quality control, quality assurance, and continuous process improvement approaches. The quality management plan also describes how the project team will implement its quality policies.

R

RACI Chart: A type of responsibility assignment matrix chart that can be used to ensure clear divisions of roles and responsibilities (RACI stands for Responsible, Accountable, Consult, and Inform).

Recognition and Rewards: A technique of Develop Project Team process that plays a vital role in improving a team's performance and keeping team members motivated to work more efficiently and produce better results for the project.

Record Management System: A system that includes indexing, archiving, and retrieval systems to capture and store all documents, correspondence, and communication relevant to a contract. For some projects, every record such as e-mails, payments, and written and verbal communications is recorded and stored.

Regulation: Requirements imposed by a governmental body to establish product, process, or service characteristics, including applicable administrative provisions that have government mandated compliance.

Report Performance: A process of collecting and distributing performance information, specially focused on reporting against the performance baseline.

Request for Information (RFI): A buyer's request to all potential sellers for various pieces of information related to product, service, or seller capability.

Request for Proposal (RFP): A buyer's request to all potential sellers for the details of how work will be performed.

Request for Quotation (RFQ): A buyer's request for a price quote per item, hour, foot, or other unit of measure.

Requirement: A capability or condition that is required to be present in a product, service, or result to meet the contractual or other formally imposed specification.

Requirement Document: A document that describes how individual requirement meets the business need and the expectations of the project sponsor and stakeholders.

Requirement Traceability Matrix: A mapping for requirements that links them to their origin and traces them throughout the project life cycle.

Reserve: An additional time and fund to address the impact of the risks remaining and to cover unforeseen risks or changes to the project.

Reserve Analysis: A technique that accommodates the costs and time risk associated with the project estimate through the use of contingency and management reserves.

Residual Risk: Risks that remain after risk response planning and for which contingency and fallback plans can be created.

Resource: The labor, material, equipment, and supplies needed to complete a project phase.

Resource Breakdown Structure (RBS): A graphical and hierarchical structure of the identified resources arranged by resource category (such as labor, material, equipment, and supplies) and type (such as expertise level, grade, and experience).

Resource Calendar: A calendar showing when and how long resources (such as material, equipment, manpower, and supplies) will potentially be available during the project life cycle. Resource calendars may consider attributes such as experience, skill level, expertise, capabilities, and geographical locations for human resources to identify the best resources and their availability.

Resource Histogram: A graphic display that can be used to track resources through time when shared or critically required resources are only available at certain times, come in limited quantities, or have been over-allocated.

Resource Leveling: A technique used to produce a resource-limited schedule by letting the schedule slip and the cost increase in order to deal with a limited amount of resources, resource availability, and resource constraints.

Responsibility Assignment Matrix (RAM): A chart that cross-references team members with the activities or work packages they are assigned to accomplish. One example of a RAM is a RACI (Responsible, Accountable, Consult, and Inform) chart, which can be used to ensure clear divisions of roles and responsibilities.

Rework: Actions taken to bring a nonconforming or flawed component into compliance with respect to requirements or specifications.

Risk: An uncertain event or condition in the future, and if it occurs it will have a positive or negative impact on one or more project objectives including scope, schedule, cost, and quality.

Risk Acceptance: See **Acceptance**

Risk Avoidance: See **Avoid**

Risk Breakdown Structure (RBS): A comprehensive way of ordering risks according to their source.

Risk Category: A group of potential causes for risk, which can be grouped into categories such as technical, political, external, project, environmental, and others. In order to systematically identify risks to a consistent level of detail, we can use the form of a simple list of categories or a Risk Breakdown Structure (RBS). It's a comprehensive way of ordering risks according to their source.

Risk Enhancement: See **Enhance**

Risk Exploitation: See **Exploit**

Risk Management Plan: A roadmap to all other risk processes that describes how risk management will be structured and performed during the project.

Risk Mitigation: See **Mitigation**

Risk Register: A register that summarizes the details of each risk and should be analyzed during cost estimation to consider risk prevention and mitigation costs.

Risk Tolerance: Areas of risk in which risk-taking can be acceptable or unacceptable. A risk that will affect the reputation of a company will not be tolerated, but a financial risk can be acceptable, thus reputation is not an area of risk tolerance but finance can be.

Risk Threshold: The amount of risk that is acceptable.

Risk Transference: A threat response strategy of shifting the negative impact of a threat, along with the ownership of the response, to a third party to make it their responsibility.

Role: This defines the position of each individual involved in a project and specifies a title, authority, level of responsibility, and skill level or competency needed to be able to perform a specific role.

Rolling Wave Planning: A technique that takes the progressive elaboration approach and plans in great detail current/near term work while future work is planned in a more abstract and less detailed way. During the early strategic planning phase, work packages may be decomposed into less defined milestone levels as all details are not available. Later, the work packages will be decomposed into detailed activities.

Root Cause Analysis: A technique in process analysis that identifies a problem, discovers the underlying causes and develops preventive actions.

Run Chart: A line graph that displays process performance over time. A Run Chart is ideal for charting progress and looking for trends.

S

Scatter Diagram: A tool and technique used in quality management processes to analyze two characteristics of a process and determine if there is any interdependency between them.

Schedule Activity: A scheduled task that must be performed in order to complete the work on the project.

Schedule Baseline: An approved project schedule that is an essential component in schedule management for determining necessary changes and corrective or preventative actions.

Schedule Compression: A process of shortening the project schedule without changing the project scope or sacrificing desired quality.

Schedule Data: This refers to information such as schedule templates, activities and their attributes, estimated duration, constraints and assumptions, resource requirements, and alternative schedules – best case or worst case, resource leveled or not leveled, with or without imposed dates, and schedule reserve are among the items that are used to model and create the project schedule. All these schedule data will be reviewed and updated in the Control Schedule process.

Schedule Management Plan: An essential component in the project management plan specifying how the schedule will be managed and controlled.

Schedule Network Analysis: A method of using a schedule model and other analytical techniques of the critical path method, the critical chain method, what-if analysis, and resource leveling to generate the project schedule.

Schedule Performance Index (SPI): A measure of schedule efficiency on a project. It is the ratio of earned value to planned value and is used to determine if a project is behind, on, or ahead of schedule.

Schedule Variance (SV): A comparison of the amount of work performed during a given period of time to what was scheduled to be performed.

Scope: A description of the work needed to deliver a product, service, or result with specified features and functions.

Scope Creep: Unapproved and undocumented changes that occur when changes to the scope are not detected early enough or managed. These minor changes slowly accumulate and may have a drastic impact on budget, schedule, and quality.

Scoring Model: A project selection method used to score and rank project proposals.

S-Curve: See **"Cost Baseline"**

Screening System: A set of minimum criteria a seller must meet to be considered, such as proficiency with certain products or techniques, safety record, number of years of relevant experience, etc.

Secondary Risk: A new risk created by implementing the selected risk response strategies.

Seller Invoices: Sellers' requests for the payments for the goods, services, or materials that were delivered.

Seller Rating System: A component of the proposal evaluation technique of the Conduct Procurement process to determine seller qualification and performance.

Sensitivity Analysis: A quantitative risk analysis and modeling technique that helps determine which risks have the most potential impact on a project. In other words, whether the occurrence of a particular threat would be merely an inconvenience or would ruin the project.

Sequence Activities: A planning process of identifying and documenting relationships among defined activities, and arranging them in the order they must be performed.

Share: A Plan Risk Response strategy of working with another party or allocating ownership to a third party who is best able to capture the opportunity for the benefit of the project.

Six Sigma: A disciplined quality process that strives to develop and deliver near-perfect products and services. The aim of Six Sigma is to measure how many defects are in a process and then systematically figure out how to eliminate them.

Slack: The maximum amount of time an activity can be delayed without delaying the entire project. It is also called float and buffer.

Smoothing: A conflict resolution technique that emphasizes areas of agreement and downplays differences of opinions.

Soft Logic: See **Discretionary Dependencies**

Specification: A relevant quality requirement.

Specification Limits: The customer's expectations or contractual requirements for performance and quality in the project and can appear either inside or outside of the control limits.

Special Cause: A cause that is not normal to a process and which can be avoided and should be investigated. It is also sometimes called an assignable cause.

Sponsor: A person or entity that provides financial resources for the project.

Staffing Management Plan: A component of the human resource plan that describes how to develop team members as well as when and how human resource requirements will be met.

Stage Gate: See **Exit Gate**

Stakeholder: A person or an organization that is actively involved with the work of the project or whose vested interests may be positively or negatively impacted by the execution or completion of the project.

Stakeholder Register: A register to identify all key internal and external stakeholders who have interest in and influence over the project. A stakeholder register contains all the details related to the identified stakeholders including classification, identification, and assessment information.

Start-to-Finish: A logical relationship in which a predecessor activity must be started before the successor activity is completed.

Start-to-Start: A logical relationship in which a predecessor activity must be started before the successor activity is started.

Statistical Sampling: A tool and technique of the quality management process that involves choosing part of a population of interest for inspection instead of measuring the entire population.

Status Review Meeting: A review meeting to analyze and report project progress and performance.

Steering Committee: A committee that consists of high level managers and executives who are involved in project prioritization and decision making processes.

Strength, Weakness, Opportunities, and Threats (SWOT) Analysis: A brainstorming technique and a key component of strategic development. It is the analysis of strengths, weaknesses, opportunities, and threats of an organization or project to identify potential risks in the project and prompt actions and responses.

Successor Activity: A dependent activity that logically comes after another activity in a project schedule.

T

Tailoring: The determination of which processes and process groups should be performed for the project by taking into consideration the size, complexity, and various inputs and outputs of each of the processes.

Task: A scheduled activity in the project. A task and an activity should be treated as equivalent terms.

Team: Members directly involved in planning, executing, and monitoring and controlling of the project activities.

Team Building: A technique of forming the project team into a cohesive group working for the best interest of the project in the most effective and efficient manner possible.

Theory X: A motivational theory that proposes average workers are incapable, avoid responsibility, have an inherent dislike of work, and are only interested in their own selfish goals. Theory X managers believe that constant supervision or micro management is essential to achieve expected results in a project. These managers are like dictators and impose very rigid and rigorous controls over their subordinates.

Theory Y: A motivational theory that proposes workers are creative and committed to the project objective and goals. They are willing to work without supervision, need very little external motivation, can direct their own efforts, and have a desire to achieve.

Threat: The external elements in the environment which arise from political, economic, social, and technological (PEST) forces that could cause trouble for the business. Examples include new regulations, increased trade barriers, and the emergence of substitute products.

Three-Point Estimate: A tool and technique for the Estimate Activity Duration process that takes optimistic, pessimistic, and most likely estimates from the estimator and provides a risk-based expected duration estimate by taking a weighted average of the three estimates using the following formula:

- Optimistic estimate: O
- Most likely estimate: M
- Pessimistic estimate: P

Depending on the assumed distribution of values, we use the following two formulas:

- Triangular Distribution: Expected Activity Duration (EAD) = $\frac{(O + M + P)}{3}$
- Beta Distribution: Expected Activity Duration (EAD) = $\frac{(O + 4M + P)}{6}$

Time-Phased Budget: The authorized budget for the project as it disburses funds at different periods throughout the life of the project.

Time and Material Contract (T & M): A time-based fee plus cost of materials contract, used for smaller amounts and shorter times and requires little or no defined scope of work. Preset units are agreed at contract signing, but costs are charged to the buyers as they are incurred.

To Complete Performance Index (TCPI): The calculated projection of cost performance that must be achieved on the remaining work to meet a specified management goal or earned value targets such as the Budget at Completion (BAC) or the Estimate at Completion (EAC).

Top-Down Estimate: See **Analogous Estimate**

Tornado Diagram: A diagramming method to display sensitivity analysis data by examining all the uncertain elements at their baseline values. It gives a quick overview of how much the project will be impacted by various elements. The element with the greatest impact on the project appears at the top. This diagram can be used to determine sensitivity in cost, time, and quality objectives and is helpful in determining a detailed response plan for elements with greater impacts.

Total Float: Amount of time an activity can be delayed without effecting the project completion date.

Total Quality Management (TQM): A management strategy that focuses on finding ways to improve quality and embed quality awareness in all organization processes, business practices, and products. Everyone in the organization is responsible for quality and is capable of making a difference in the ultimate quality of the product.

Transfer: A threat response strategy of shifting the negative impact of a threat, along with the ownership of the response, to a third party to make it their responsibility. It gives another party responsibility for threat management but does not eliminate the risk. Transferring nearly always involves payment to the third party for taking on the risk.

Trend Analysis: A type of analysis that examines project performance over time to determine if performance is improving or deteriorating. This statistical forecasting technique predicts results related to scope, time, or cost by plotting a trend line based on previous performance.

Tree Diagram: A representation of a tree structure, this is a way of representing the hierarchical nature of a structure in a graphical form. This diagram can be used for decision analysis and to represent decomposition hierarchy, such as Work Breakdown Structure (WBS), Risk Breakdown Structure (RBS), and Organizational Breakdown Structure (OBS). It can also be utilized for structuring data, plotting relationships, decomposing processes to ascertain a solution to a problem, and developing preventive and corrective procedures.

Trigger: The symptoms or warning signs that a potential risk is about to occur in the project. For instance, a key team member searching for a better job opportunity is a warning sign that the person may be leaving the team, thereby causing schedule delays, and increased costs.

Triple Constraint: A framework for understanding trade-offs in managing competing project requirements. Originally, project constraints were referred to as the triple constraint and included cost, time, and scope. When one of the components of the triple constraint is changed, the other two are affected.

U

Unanimity: A group decision making technique where decisions are based on a single course of action decided by everyone in the group.

V

Validate Scope: A process of obtaining the stakeholders' formal acceptance of the completed project scope and associated deliverables.

Value Engineering: A method of finding a less costly way to do the same work, and to achieve more out of the project in every possible way to increase bottom line, decrease costs, improve quality, and optimize the schedule without reducing or impacting the scope.

Variance: A difference between the original plan and the actual results.

Variance Analysis: An analysis to compare actual project performance to the planned or expected performance. Cost and schedule variances are most frequently analyzed.

Variance at Completion (VAC): An estimate of how much over or under budget we expect to be at the end of the project. VAC = BAC – EAC

Verification: A process of inspecting the product, service, or result to ensure the scope is implemented completely as per specification.

Virtual Teams: A group of people who never or rarely meet but have the shared goal of successful completion of the project. The use of virtual teams makes it possible to achieve the following items:

- Carry on with projects that would have never been initiated due to heavy travel expenses.
- Include members of the team who live in widespread geographic areas, employees who work from home or have different shifts/hours, and people with mobility limitations or disabilities.
- Add special expertise and competency to a project team from outside of the project's geographic area.

W

War Room: A technique of placing many or all of the most active project team members in the same physical location to enhance their ability to perform as a team.

Weighted Scoring Model: See **Weighting System**

Weighting System: A method of ranking and scoring vendor proposals or project proposals. It assigns numerical weights to evaluation criteria and then multiplies this by the weight of each criteria factor resulting in a total score for each vendor and project. It can be best described as a method for quantifying qualitative data to minimize the effects of personal prejudice.

Withdrawal: A negotiation tactic of emotional and physical withdrawal as well as expressing lack of interest.

Work Authorization System: A formal, documented procedure that describes how to authorize and initiate work in the correct sequence at the appropriate time.

Work Breakdown Structure (WBS): A Work Breakdown Structure (WBS) is the foundational block to the initiating, planning, executing, monitoring & controlling, and closing phases. Normally presented in chart form, it is a deliverable-oriented hierarchical decomposition of the work to be executed by the project team to accomplish project objectives and create required deliverables. It organizes and defines the total scope of the project. Deliverables not in the WBS are beyond the scope of the project. The WBS is the foundation of a project and forces team members to think through all aspects of the project.

Work Breakdown Structure Dictionary: A document that consists of the detailed description of the work to be done for each work package. The WBS dictionary contains:

- A number identifier
- Related control accounts (for cost)
- A statement of the work to be done
- The person/group responsible for the work
- Any schedule milestones.

Work Package: The lowest hierarchical level of the WBS and represents deliverables in the project. Work packages are decomposed into activities for duration and cost estimation.

Work Performance Information: The work performance data collected in the executing processes is analyzed in context, aggregated, and transformed, becoming information used during the monitoring and controlling processes. This can include, for example, the status of deliverables, the implementation status of change requests, and forecasted estimates to complete, among other things.

Workaround: Unplanned responses developed to deal with unanticipated risk events.

Z

Zero Defects: The concept of performing the task correctly the first time to avoid rework, additional cost, and loss of productivity. Philip B. Crosby popularized the concept of the cost of poor quality, advocated prevention over inspection and "zero defects" and defined quality as conformance to specification (that the project produces what it was created to produce).

Index

A

B

C

D

E

F

G

H

I

J

K

L

M

N

O

P

Q

R

S

T

U

V

W

Z

Made in the USA
Lexington, KY
02 November 2015